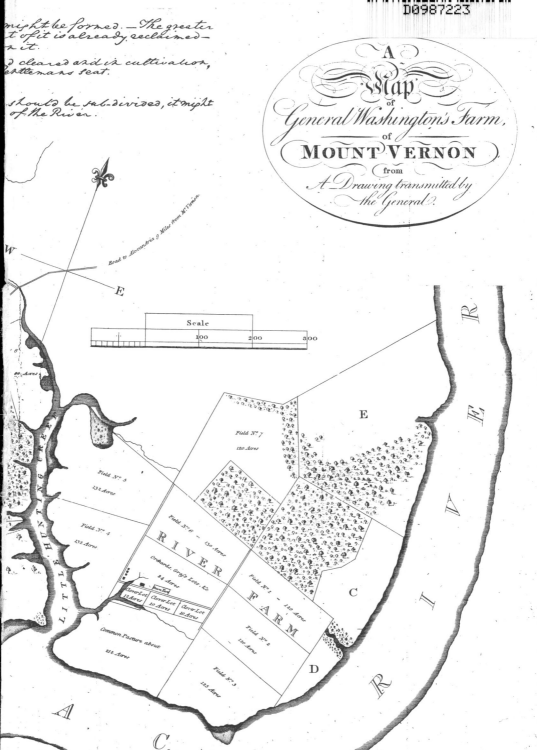

might be formed. — The greater
t of it is already reclaimed —
n it.

d cleared and in cultivation,
entlemans seat.

should be sub-divided, it might
of the River.

A
Map
of
General Washington's Farm,
of
MOUNT VERNON
from
A Drawing transmitted by
the General.

W

E

Road to Alexandria 9 Miles from Mt Vernon.

Scale

100   200   300

Field N.º 7
120 Acres

E

Field N.º 5
132 Acres

Field N.º 6 — 130 Acres

Field N.º 4
132 Acres

R I V E R

Orchards, Grass Lots, &c.
84 Acres

Field N.º 1 — 120 Acres

C

Clover Lot
12 Acres

Clover Lot
10 Acres

Clover Lot
10 Acres

F A R M

Field N.º 2
120 Acres

Common Pasture about
212 Acres

D

Field N.º 3
125 Acres

LITTLE HUNTING CREEK

R I V E R

A

C

The Papers of
George Washington

Frontispiece: Portrait of George Washington by Edward Savage, 1793.
(National Portrait Gallery, Smithsonian Institution.)

The Papers of
George Washington

Theodore J. Crackel, *Editor in Chief*

Philander D. Chase, *Senior Editor*

David R. Hoth, Edward G. Lengel, Christine Sternberg Patrick,

and Beverly H. Runge

Associate Editors

William M. Ferraro and Jennifer E. Stertzer
Assistant Editors

Presidential Series
14

1 September–31 December 1793

David R. Hoth, *Editor*

UNIVERSITY OF VIRGINIA PRESS

CHARLOTTESVILLE AND LONDON

This edition has been prepared by the staff of
The Papers of George Washington sponsored by The Mount Vernon Ladies'
Association of the Union and the University of Virginia with the support of
the National Endowment for the Humanities and the National Historical
Publications and Records Commission.

The preparation of this volume has been made possible by
gifts from the Elis Olsson Memorial Foundation of West Point, Va.,
Stephen and Ann West of Bernardsville, N.J., and
Alison Ward Burdick of Wilmington, Delaware.

The publication of this volume has been supported by a grant from the
National Historical Publications and Records Commission.

UNIVERSITY OF VIRGINIA PRESS

First published 2008

The paper used in this publication meets the minimum requirements of
ANSI/NISO Z39.48–1992 (R 1997) (Permanence of Paper).

Library of Congress Cataloging-in-Publication Data
Washington, George, 1732–1799.
    The papers of George Washington, Theodore J. Crackel, ed.
    Presidential series vol. 14 edited by David R. Hoth.
    Includes bibliographical references and indexes.
    Contents: v. 1. September 1788–March 1789—
[etc.]—v. 14. 1 September 1793–31 December 1793
        1. United States—Politics and government—1789–1797.
    2. Washington, George, 1732-1799—Correspondence.
    3. Presidents—United States—Correspondence. I. Crackel,
    Theodore J.; Hoth, David R. II. Presidential series. III. Title.
    E312.72 1987b   973.4'1'092   87-410017
    ISBN 0-8139-1103-6 (v. 1)
    ISBN 978-0-8139-2759-6 (v. 14)

Front endpapers: "A map of General Washington's farm of Mount Vernon from
a drawing transmitted by the General," in *Letters from His Excellency General
Washington, to Arthur Young, Esq. F.R.S., containing An Account of His Husbandry,
with a Map of His Farm; His Opinions on Various Questions in Agriculture; and
Many Particulars of the Rural Economy of the United States* (London, 1801). [This
illustration was based on a sketch enclosed in GW to Young, 12 Dec. 1793.]
Library of Congress, Geography and Map Division.

Back endpapers: [L'Enfant] Plan of the City of Washington in the Territory of
Columbia . . . [as drawn by Andrew Ellicott and engraved by Samuel Hill of
Boston in 1792]. Library of Congress, Geography and Map Division.

Frontispiece: Portrait of George Washington, by Edward Savage. Mezzotint,
1793. National Portrait Gallery, Smithsonian Institution.

This volume is dedicated
to Beverly H. Runge, 1929–2008

Contents

NOTE: Volume numbers refer to the *Presidential Series*.

Contents

Contents

Contents

Contents   xvii

Contents   xix

Illustrations

Maps

Introduction

During the last four months of 1793, as in the summer preceding, GW and his administration were chiefly involved with maintaining the neutrality of the United States during the war that pitted France against Great Britain and her allied powers. The main problem for the administration was the operations of French privateers. Letters to GW from New York governor George Clinton, Maryland governor Thomas Sim Lee, and North Carolina governor Richard Dobbs Spaight reported their attempts to implement the government's neutrality policy at the ports of New York City, Baltimore, and Wilmington, N.C., and asked for guidance. British minister George Hammond and various British consuls, in letters to Secretary of State Thomas Jefferson, continued to press for restoration of prizes seized by the privateers, which required an additional decision on that issue as well as a definition of U.S. territorial waters. French consuls were warned not to hold admiralty courts on the prizes seized by their privateers, and the exequatur of the consul at Boston was revoked for his interference with American officials attempting to take possession of a prize ship.

With Spain allied to Great Britain, reports of French-sponsored expeditions from Kentucky into Louisiana (Jefferson to GW, 6 and 16 Nov.), and from South Carolina and Georgia into Florida (William Moultrie to GW, 7 Dec.), raised another threat to American neutrality.

None of this was made easier by bad relations with French minister Edmond Genet. The cabinet agreed in early September to inform Genet of their request (made in August) for his recall, but his replacements would not arrive until February 1794. In the meantime, Genet continued to be involved in public controversy: denying that he had said that he would appeal GW's decisions to the people, while publishing his instructions from France and some of his correspondence with the U.S. government in an apparent attempt to do just that.

Numerous resolutions of county meetings, mostly supportive of GW's policies, registered something about public opinion on these issues. GW returned polite answers to those addressed specifically to him, and both the resolutions and his answers were generally published. A memorandum from Thomas Jefferson of 22 Sept. suggests that GW took particular care with his reply to the resolutions from Caroline County, Va., which incorporated a draft designed by James Madison and James Monroe to stress solidarity with France (GW to Edmund Pendleton, 23 Sept.).

The arrival in July of refugees from the civil conflict on the French island of Saint Domingue also created problems for GW. The British minister Hammond complained about the continued presence of the French fleet at New York Harbor, and the French minister Genet requested U.S. assistance in apprehending deserters from the fleet, and later in preventing certain refugees from returning to the island. Moreover, GW received numerous letters from refugees asking for various types of assistance.

Nonetheless, the signature event of these four months was the epidemic of yellow fever at Philadelphia. Diagnosed in mid- to late August, the growing epidemic soon depopulated the city, as those who were able fled. The deaths and departures greatly reduced the operations of government. Thomas Jefferson justified his return to Virginia by noting that the State Department had but one clerk left and business could not be carried on. Secretary of War Henry Knox moved his office to a house outside the city before he departed for New England. Treasury Secretary Alexander Hamilton left for New York not long after recovering from a bout with the fever, and Comptroller of the Treasury Oliver Wolcott, Jr., moved with Knox outside the city.

GW himself left the city on 10 Sept., making a previously planned trip to Mount Vernon that was perhaps speeded by the progress of the disease (he wrote to Tobias Lear on 25 Sept., "It was my wish to have stayed there longer; but as Mrs Washington was unwilling to leave me amidst the malignant fever which prevailed, I could not think of hazarding her & the Children any longer by my remaining in the City"). Moreover, the epidemic delayed his return to Philadelphia well beyond his planned 15- to 18-day absence, leaving him without public papers necessary for decisions requested from him (GW to Lee, 13 Oct.). Letters sent to GW from correspondents such as Knox, Wolcott, and Timothy Pickering document the severity of the epidemic at Philadelphia and the fear that the disease aroused in the country.

In late September GW determined that, epidemic or not, it would be necessary that he and his cabinet meet at Philadelphia or in the vicinity on 1 Nov., the date offered by Knox as "the earliest period at which it would be safe for you to return" (Knox to GW, 18 Sept.). Lodgings were found in Germantown, where GW stayed on his return in November. Some, however, hearing reports of the devastation in Philadelphia, questioned whether Congress should meet there as scheduled. GW sought advice from the cabinet and others about his proper course of action, which involved both the constitutional question of whether he had the power to alter the location at which Congress would convene and the question, touching on sectional concerns, of where the government should move if forced temporarily from the capital. Ultimately, the waning strength of the disease made action unnecessary, and Congress convened without incident in December, but the correspondence reveals much about GW's understanding of his responsibilities as president.

This volume also records the preparation of GW's annual message, delivered 3 Dec., in which he discussed his neutrality policies, military preparedness, commerce with Indian tribes and frontier defense, financial accounts of the United States, and repeal of the charge for mailing newspapers. The numerous drafts and outlines show that preparation of the address was an extended process that involved input from each member of the cabinet.

While overshadowed by the issue of neutrality, the problem of frontier defense continued. On the northwest frontier, military preparations for an expedition against hostile Indians, slowed during unsuccessful treaty negotiations with the tribes, moved forward with more urgency. With Indian hostility blamed in part on British influence, the administration continued to press for a response to their request that Great Britain evacuate northwestern forts in accordance with the 1783 Treaty of Paris. The southwest frontier, too, saw conflicts between settlers and Indians.

America's diplomats and others living abroad wrote to GW as well as to the secretary of state. Several letters warned that a truce between Portugal and Algiers would unleash the Barbary power as a threat to American commerce. Letters from Gouverneur Morris, the American minister to France, gave GW gloomy assessments of events and people in that country.

The ubiquitous applications for appointments to federal office also swelled GW's correspondence—the contest for district attorney for Rhode Island revealing political differences in that state.

The proceedings of the commissioners for the District of Columbia added to GW's responsibilities: during these months, he appointed auditors, issued authorizations for a sale of lots, and advised on various topics. GW's interest in the District was personal as well as official: he purchased a number of lots at the September sale (Certificate for Lots Purchased, 18 Sept.).

Among other personal matters, the management of Mount Vernon claimed much attention from GW at this time. He signed a contract, dated 23 Sept., with a new farm manager, William Pearce, and between that time and Pearce's arrival at the estate in January 1794, GW wrote several letters conveying information and advice to Pearce and to interim manager Howell Lewis. Moreover, in a letter of 12 Dec. to the English agriculturalist Arthur Young, GW broached a proposal to rent out four of the five farms at Mount Vernon to immigrant farmers, describing his estate in considerable detail.

Editorial Apparatus

Transcription of the documents in the volumes of *The Papers of George Washington* has remained as close to a literal reproduction of the manuscript as possible. Punctuation, capitalization, and spelling of all words are retained as they appear in the original document, except as noted below; only for documents printed in annotations is paragraphing ever modified. Dashes used as punctuation have been retained, except when a dash and another mark of punctuation appear together. The appropriate marks of punctuation have always been added at the end of a paragraph. When a tilde (~) is used in the manuscript to indicate a double letter, the letter has been doubled. Washington and some of his correspondents occasionally used a tilde above an incorrectly spelled word to indicate an error in orthography. When this device is used the editors have corrected the word.

In cases where a tilde has been inserted above an abbreviation or contraction, usually in letter-book copies, the word has been expanded. Otherwise, contractions and abbreviations have been retained as written, except that a period has been inserted after an abbreviation when needed. If the meaning of an abbreviation or contraction is not obvious, it has been expanded in square brackets: "H[is] M[ajest]y." Editorial insertions or corrections in the text also appear in square brackets. Angle brackets ⟨ ⟩ are used to indicate illegible or mutilated material. When there is a basis for doing so, conjectural text is supplied within the brackets. Footnotes or source note will indicate if the text is taken from another version of the document. A space left blank in a manuscript by the writer is indicated by a square-bracketed gap in the text [ ].

Material deleted by the author of a manuscript is ignored unless it contains substantive material, and then it appears in a footnote. If the intended location of marginal notations is clear from the text, they are inserted without comment; otherwise, they are recorded in the notes. The ampersand has been retained, and the thorn(Þ in Old English, but by Washington's day essentially indistinguishable from the letter Y) is transcribed as "th." Superscripts have been lowered. The symbol for per (⅌) is used when it appears in the manuscript. The dateline has been placed at the head of a document, regardless of where it occurs in the manuscript.

Where multiple versions of a document are available, the document closest to the one actually received by the addressee is printed. The other versions have been collated with the selected text, and significant variations are presented in the annotation.

Since GW read no language other than English, incoming letters written to him in foreign languages were generally translated for his information. Where this contemporary translation has survived, it has been used as the text of the document. If there is no contemporary translation, the document in its original language has been used as the text.

All of the documents printed in this volume, any documents omitted or not printed in full, the original foreign language documents (where otherwise not provided), and a number of ancillary materials ultimately will be available in a digital edition of the Washington Papers. The reports of Washington's farm managers at Mount Vernon, some of which have been printed in previous volumes of the *Presidential Series,* from now on will appear only in the electronic edition. To learn more about the electronic edition, visit the website of the Papers of George Washington (www.gwpapers.virginia.edu) or of Rotunda, the digital imprint of the University of Virginia Press (http://rotunda .upress.virginia.edu).

During both of Washington's administrations, he was besieged with applications for public office. Many of the applicants continued to seek appointment or promotion. The editors usually have printed only one of these letters in full and cited other letters, both from the applicant and in support of his application, in notes to the initial letter. When Washington replied to these requests at all, the replies were generally pro forma reiterations of his policy of noncommitment until the appointment to a post was made. In such cases, his replies have been included in the notes to the original application and do not appear in their chronological sequence. These and other letters to or from Washington that, in whole or in part, are printed out of their chronological sequence are listed in the table of contents, with an indication of where they may be found in the volumes.

Individuals mentioned in the text usually are identified at their first substantive mention in each series. The index to each volume indicates where identifications appear in earlier volumes of the *Presidential Series.*

For his secretarial services in late 1793, Washington depended primarily on Bartholomew Dandridge, Jr., and Howell Lewis. Dandridge had entered the president's employment in 1791, and Lewis began in 1792. Most drafts not written by Washington were written by Dandridge, and for the most part only he communicated in writing directly with cabinet members or others in the name of the president. In some instances, the drafts contain emendations by Washington.

For most of the correspondence found in Record Group 59, State Department Miscellaneous Letters, in the National Archives, there are also letter-book copies in the Washington Papers at the Library of Congress. Some of the letters for this period probably were copied into the letter books close to the time they were written, but others obviously were entered much later. When the receiver's copy of a letter from Washington has not been found, the editors generally have assumed that the copy in Miscellaneous Letters was made from the receiver's copy or the draft and have used it as the text rather than the letter-book copy, and they have described the document either as a copy or a draft, depending on the appearance of the manuscript.

Washington never used the term *cabinet* when referring as a group to the attorney general and the heads of the State, War, and Treasury Departments. However, for the sake of clarity, the editors have used this term to indicate corporate meetings by these individuals, both with and without Washington, and to describe documents issued as a result of these meetings.

Symbols Designating Documents

AD   Autograph Document: a document in the handwriting of the author

ADS   Autograph Document Signed: a document in the handwriting of, and signed by, the author

ADf   Autograph Draft: a draft in the handwriting of the author

ADfS   Autograph Draft Signed: a draft in the handwriting of, and signed by, the author

AL   Autograph Letter: a letter in the handwriting of the author

ALS   Autograph Letter Signed: a letter in the handwriting of, and signed by, the author

D   Document: a document (not a letter) neither signed by, nor in the handwriting of, the author

DS   Document Signed: a document (not a letter) signed by the author, but not in the author's handwriting

Df   Draft: a draft in the handwriting of someone other than the author

DfS   Draft Signed: a draft of a letter or document signed by the author, but not in the author's handwriting

L   Letter: a letter neither signed by, nor in the handwriting of, the author

LS   Letter Signed: a letter signed by the author, but not in the author's handwriting

LB   Letters copied into a bound letter-book
[S]   Replaces S when author's signature has been cut from the
            original manuscript
Copy   A contemporaneous handwritten representation made of
            any version of a letter or document
Tran-   A non-contemporaneous, handwritten representation
script   made of a letter or other document (generally not used
            or cited unless no other version is available, except in
            the case of a Sprague transcript)
Sprague   Handwritten transcripts made in the 1820s by
tran-   William B. Sprague to replace documents that he
scripts   removed from GW's papers

Repository Symbols and Abbreviations

CSmH   Huntington Library, Art Collections and Botanical
            Gardens, San Marino, Calif.
CStbK   Karpeles Manuscript Library, Santa Barbara, Calif.
CtHi   Connecticut Historical Society, Hartford, Conn.
CtNhHi   New Haven Colony Historical Society, New Haven,
            Conn.
De-Ar   Delaware Department of State, Division of Historical
            and Cultural Affairs, Hall of Records, Dover, Del.
DeHi   Historical Society of Delaware, Wilmington, Del.
DLC   United States, Library of Congress,
            Washington, D.C.
DLC:GW   United States, Library of Congress, George
            Washington Papers, Washington, D.C.
DNA   United States, National Archives and Records
            Administration, Washington, D.C.
DNA:PCC   United States, National Archives and Records
            Administration, Papers of the Continental
            Congress, Washington, D.C.
FrPMAE   France, Ministère des affaires étrangères, Archives,
            Paris, France
ICU   University of Chicago, Chicago, Ill.
MdAA   Maryland, Hall of Records Commission, Annapolis,
            Md.
MdAN   United States, Naval Academy, Annapolis, Md.
MHi   Massachusetts Historical Society, Boston, Mass.
MiU-C   University of Michigan, William L. Clements Library,
            Ann Arbor, Mich.

N-Ar	New York State Archives, New York State Department of Education, Albany, N.Y.
Nc-Ar	North Carolina, Office of Archives and History, Raleigh, N.C.
NHi	New-York Historical Society, New York, N.Y.
NjMoHP	Morristown National Historical Park, Morristown, N.J.
NjP	Princeton University, Princeton, N.J.
NN	New York Public Library, New York, N.Y.
NNGL	Gilder Lehrman Collection, on deposit at the New-York Historical Society, New York, N.Y.
NNYSL	New York Society Library, New York, N.Y.
OHi	Ohio Historical Society, Columbus, Ohio
PHarH	Pennsylvania Historical and Museum Commission, Harrisburg, Pa.
PHi	Historical Society of Pennsylvania, Philadelphia, Pa.
PPAmP	American Philosophical Society, Philadelphia, Pa.
PPRF	Rosenbach Museum and Library, Philadelphia, Pa.
P.R.O.	Public Record Office, Kew, Surrey, England
PWacD	David Library of the American Revolution, Washington Crossing, Pa.
R-Ar	Rhode Island State Archives, Providence, R.I.
RHi	Rhode Island Historical Society, Providence, R.I.
RPJCB	John Carter Brown Library, Providence, R.I.
SwSR	Riksarkivet (National Archives), Stockholm, Sweden
UkLBM	British Museum, London, England
UkNcU	University of Newcastle upon Tyne, Newcastle upon Tyne, United Kingdom
Vi	Library of Virginia, Richmond, Va.
ViHi	Virginia Historical Society, Richmond, Va.
ViMtvL	Mount Vernon Ladies' Association of the Union, Mount Vernon, Va.
ViU	University of Virginia, Charlottesville, Va.
ViW	College of William and Mary, Williamsburg, Va.
ViWnFreCh	Frederick County Courthouse, Winchester, Va.

Short Title List

ABPC.   *American Book-Prices Current.* New York, 1895—.

Adam Library.   Adam, Robert Borthwick. *The R. B. Adam Library Relating to Dr. Samuel Johnson and His Era.* 3 vols. Buffalo, N.Y., 1929.

Annals of Congress.   Joseph Gales, Sr., comp. *The Debates and Proceedings in the Congress of the United States; with an Appendix, Containing*

Important State Papers and Public Documents, and All the Laws of a Public Nature. 42 vols. Washington, D.C., 1834–56.

Archives parlementaires.   Jérôme Mavidal et al., eds. *Archives parlementaires de 1787 à 1860.* 1st ser., 101 vols. to date. Paris, 1868—.

ASP.   Walter Lowrie et al., eds. *American State Papers: Documents, Legislative and Executive, of the Congress of the United States.* 38 vols. Washington, D.C., 1832–61.

Baynard, *History of the Supreme Council.*   Samuel Harrison Baynard, Jr. *History of the Supreme Council, 33°, Ancient Accepted Scottish Rite of Freemasonry, Northern Masonic Jurisdiction of the United States of America, and Its Antecedents* 2 vols. Boston, 1938.

Bee, *Reports of Cases.*   Thomas Bee. *Reports of Cases Adjudged in the District Court of South Carolina.* Philadelphia, 1810.

Bodinier, *Dictionnaire des officiers de l'armée royale.*   Gilbert Bodinier. *Dictionnaire des officiers de l'armée royale qui ont combattu aux Etats-Unis pendant la guerre d'indépendance, 1776–1783.* Vincennes, France, 1982.

Buell, *Putnam Memoirs.*   Rowena Buell, ed. *The Memoirs of Rufus Putnam and Certain Official Papers and Correspondence.* Boston and New York, 1903.

Butterfield, *Rush Letters.*   Lyman H. Butterfield, ed. *Letters of Benjamin Rush.* 2 vols. Princeton, N.J., 1951.

Calendar of Virginia State Papers.   William P. Palmer et al., eds. *Calendar of Virginia State Papers and Other Manuscripts.* 11 vols. Richmond, Va., 1875–93.

Carey, *Short Account of the Malignant Fever.*   Mathew Carey. *A Short Account of the Malignant Fever, Lately Prevalent in Philadelphia.* 1794. Reprint. New York, 1970.

Carter, *Territorial Papers.*   Clarence Edwin Carter et al., eds. *The Territorial Papers of the United States.* 27 vols. Washington, D.C., 1934–69.

Chassin, *Vendée Patriote.*   Charles-Louis Chassin, *La Vendée Patriote, 1793–1800.* 4 vols. 1893–95. Reprint, Mayenne, France, 1973.

Counter Case.   *The Counter Case of Great Britain as Laid before the Tribunal of Arbitration, Convened at Geneva under the Provisions of the Treaty between the United States of America and Her Majesty the Queen of Great Britain, Concluded at Washington, May 8, 1871.* 42d Cong., 2d sess., 1872. H. Exec. Doc. 324.

Crozier, *Virginia County Records.*   William Armstrong Crozier, ed. *Virginia County Records.* Vol. 1, *Spotsylvania County, 1721–1800.* New York, 1905.

Curzon, "Mythe de 'Monsieur de Gaston.'"   Alfred de Curzon. "Le Mythe de 'Monsieur de Gaston' Généralissime des Armées Royales. Contribution a l'Histoire des Émigrés." *Revue Historique* 221 (1959):49–55.

"Denny Journal." "Military Journal of Major Ebenezer Denny, an Officer in the Revolutionary and Indian Wars. With an Introductory Memoir. By William H. Denny." *Memoirs of the Historical Society of Pennsylvania* 7 (1860): 204–498.

Diaries. Donald Jackson and Dorothy Twohig, eds. *The Diaries of George Washington.* 6 vols. Charlottesville, Va., 1976-79.

Documentary History of the Supreme Court. Maeva Marcus et al., eds. *The Documentary History of the Supreme Court of the United States, 1789–1800.* 8 vols. New York, 1985–2007.

Evans, *Journal of William Savery.* Jonathan Evans, comp. *A Journal of the Life, Travels, and Religious Labors of William Savery, a Minister of the Gospel of Christ, of the Society of Friends, Late of Philadelphia.* Philadelphia, 1873.

Federal Cases. *The Federal Cases; Comprising Cases Argued and Determined in the Circuit and District Courts of the United States. . . .* 30 vols. St. Paul, Minn., 1894–97.

Ford, *Noah Webster.* Emily Ellsworth Fowler Ford, comp., and Emily Ellsworth Ford Skeel, ed. *Notes on the Life of Noah Webster.* 2 vols. New York, 1912.

"Gaston." "Du Nouveau sur le chef vendéen Gaston." *Annales Historiques de la Révolution Française* 30, no. 1 (1958):67–69.

Griffin, *Catalogue of the Washington Collection.* Appleton P.C. Griffin, comp. *A Catalogue of the Washington Collection in the Boston Athenæum.* Cambridge, Mass., 1897.

Hamilton Papers. Harold C. Syrett et al., eds. *The Papers of Alexander Hamilton.* 27 vols. New York, 1961–87.

Hening. William Waller Hening, ed. *The Statutes at Large;Being a Collection of All the Laws of Virginia from the First Session of the Legislature, in the Year 1619.* 13 vols. 1819–23. Reprint. Charlottesville, Va., 1969.

Household Accounts. Presidential Household Accounts, 4 March 1793–25 March 1797. Manuscript ledger on deposit at Historical Society of Pennsylvania, Philadelphia.

Humphreys, *Life and Times of David Humphreys.* Francis Landon Humphreys. *Life and Times of David Humphreys, soldier—statesman—poet, "belov'd of Washington".* 2 vols. New York and London, 1917.

JCC. Worthington C. Ford et al., eds. *Journals of the Continental Congress.* 34 vols. Washington, D.C., 1904-37.

Jefferson, *Notes on the State of Virginia.* Thomas Jefferson. *Notes on the State of Virginia.* Philadelphia, 1788.

Jefferson Papers. Julian P. Boyd et al., eds. *The Papers of Thomas Jefferson.* 33 vols. to date. Princeton, N.J., 1950—.

Journal of the House.   Martin P. Claussen, ed. *The Journal of the House of Representatives: George Washington Administration, 1789–1797.* 9 vols. Wilmington, Del., 1977.

Journal of the Senate.   Martin P. Claussen, ed. *The Journal of the Senate: George Washington Administration, 1789–1797.* 9 vols. Wilmington, Del., 1977.

JPP.   Dorothy Twohig, ed. *Journal of the Proceedings of the President, 1793–1797.* Charlottesville, Va., 1981.

Kappler, *Indian Treaties.*   Charles Joseph Kappler, ed. *Indian Affairs: Laws and Treaties.* 7 vols. Washington, D.C., 1903–41.

Knopf, *Wayne.*   Richard C. Knopf, ed. *Anthony Wayne, a Name in Arms: Soldier, Diplomat, Defender of Expansion Westward of a Nation: The Wayne-Knox-Pickering-McHenry Correspondence.* Pittsburgh, Pa., 1960.

Md. Laws 1790.   *Laws of Maryland, Made and Passed at a Session of Assembly, Begun and held at the city of Annapolis on Monday the first of November, in the year of our Lord one thousand seven hundred and ninety.* Annapolis, Md., [1791].

Md. Laws 1791.   *Laws of Maryland, Made and Passed at a Session of Assembly, Begun and held at the city of Annapolis on Monday the seventh of November, in the year of our Lord one thousand seven hundred and ninety-one.* Annapolis, Md., [1792].

Md. Laws 1792.   *Laws of Maryland, Made and Passed at a Session of Assembly, Begun and held at the city of Annapolis on Monday the fifth of November, in the year of our Lord one thousand seven hundred and ninety-two.* Annapolis, Md., [1793].

Md. Laws 1793.   *Laws of Maryland, Made and Passed at a Session of Assembly, Begun and held at the city of Annapolis on Monday the fourth of November, in the year of our Lord one thousand seven hundred and nine-ty-three.* Annapolis, [1794].

Ledger B.   Manuscript Ledger in George Washington Papers, Library of Congress.

Ledger C.   Manuscript Ledger in Morristown National Historical Park, Morristown, N.J.

Lindley, "Expedition to Detroit."   Jacob Lindley, Joseph Moore, and Oliver Paxson. "Expedition to Detroit, 1793: The Quakers, the United States Commissioners, and the Proposed Treaty of Peace with Northwestern Indian Tribes." Michigan Pioneer Historical Society, *Historical Collections* 17 (1890): 565–668.

Maclure, *To the People.*   William Maclure. *To the People of the United States.* Philadelphia, 1807.

Madison Papers.   William T. Hutchinson et al., eds. *The Papers of James Madison, Congressional Series.* 17 vols. Chicago and Charlottesville, Va., 1962–91.

"Mangourit Correspondence." Frederick Jackson Turner, ed. "The Mangourit Correspondence in Respect to Genet's Projected Attack upon the Floridas, 1793–94." pp. 569–679 in *Annual Report of the American Historical Association for the Year 1897.* Washington, 1898.

Microfilm Collection of Early State Records. Microfilm Collection of Early State Records prepared by the Library of Congress in association with the University of North Carolina, 1949.

Miller, *Artisans and Merchants of Alexandria.* T. Michael Miller, comp. *Artisans and Merchants of Alexandria, 1784–1820.* 2 vols. Bowie, Md., 1991–92.

Miller, *Treaties.* Hunter Miller, ed. *Treaties and Other International Acts of the United States of America.* Vol. 2. Washington, D.C., 1931.

Pa. Acts, 1792–93 session. *Acts of the General Assembly of the Commonwealth of Pennsylvania, Passed at a Session, Which Was Begun and Held at the City of Philadelphia on Tuesday, the Fourth Day of December, in the Year One Thousand Seven Hundred and Ninety-Two, and of the Independence of the United States of America, the Seventeenth.* Philadelphia, 1793.

Papers, Colonial Series. W. W. Abbot et al., eds. *The Papers of George Washington, Colonial Series.* 10 vols. Charlottesville, Va., 1983–95.

Papers, Confederation Series. W. W. Abbot et al., eds. *The Papers of George Washington, Confederation Series.* 6 vols. Charlottesville, Va., 1992–97.

Papers of James Monroe. Daniel Preston and Marlena C. DeLong, eds. *The Papers of James Monroe.* 2 vols. to date. Westport, Conn., and London, 2003—.

Papers of John Adams. Robert J. Taylor et al., eds. *Papers of John Adams.* 13 vols. to date. Cambridge, Mass., and London, 1977—.

Papers, Retirement Series. W. W. Abbot et al., eds. *The Papers of George Washington, Retirement Series.* 4 vols. Charlottesville, Va., 1998-99.

Payments of Awards. *Statement Showing the Payments of Awards of the Commissioners Appointed under the Conventions between the United States and France, Concluded April 30, 1803, and July 4, 1831, and between the United States and Spain, Concluded February 22, 1819 . . .,* Sen. Ex. Doc. 74, 49th Cong., 1st sess., 1886.

Pernick, "Politics, Parties, and Pestilence." Martin S. Pernick, "Politics, Parties, and Pestilence: Epidemic Yellow Fever in Philadelphia and the Rise of the First Party System." pp. 119–46 in J. Worth Estes and Billy G. Smith, eds. *A Melancholy Scene of Devastation: The Public Response to the Philadelphia Yellow Fever Epidemic.* Canton, Mass., 1997.

Read, *Life of George Read.* William Thompson Read. *Life and Correspondence of George Read, a Signer of the Declaration of Independence; with Notices of Some of His Contemporaries.* Philadelphia, 1870.

Recueil des actes du Comité de salut public.   *Recueil des actes du Comité de salut public, avec la correspondance officielle des représentants en mission et le registre du Conseil exécutif provisoire.* 27 vols. Paris, 1889–1923.

Senate Executive Journal.   *Journal of the Executive Proceedings of the Senate of the United States of America.* Vol. 1. Washington, D.C., 1828.

1 *Stat.*   Richard Peters, ed. *The Public Statutes at Large of the United States of America.* Vol. 1. Boston, 1845.

6 *Stat.*   Richard Peters, ed. *The Public Statutes at Large of the United States of America.* Vol. 6. Boston, 1848.

Turner, *Correspondence of the French Ministers.*   Frederick J. Turner, ed. *Correspondence of the French Ministers to the United States, 1791–1797.* 2 vols. Annual Report of the American Historical Association for the Year 1903. Washington, D.C., 1904.

Wolf and Whiteman, *Jews of Philadelphia.*   Edwin Wolf II and Maxwell Whiteman. *The History of the Jews of Philadelphia from Colonial Times to the Age of Jackson.* Philadelphia, 1957.

The Papers of George Washington
Presidential Series
Volume 14
1 September–31 December 1793

To Gouverneur Morris

Dear sir,   Philadelphia Septr 1st 1793

This letter will be presented to you by Mr Lear, whom I beg leave (if he should go to France) to recommend to your civilities.[1] He is a person who possesses my entire friendship & confidence; and will not be found unworthy of your acquaintance, as he will have it in his power to give you an acct, which you may rely on, of the true Situation of things in this Country.

Mercantile pursuits have induced him to leave my family; by these he is carried to Europe for a short stay, only.[2] I shall not repeat to you the sincere esteem & regard with which I am Dear Sir Your sincere friend and affecte Servt

Go: Washington

ALS, NNGL; ALS (letterpress copy), DLC:GW; LB, DLC:GW.

1. Tobias Lear sailed for Europe on 10 Nov. 1793 and returned to the United States in August 1794. While in Europe, he visited Scotland, England, and Holland (see Lear to GW, 9 Nov. 1793, 25 Dec. 1793, 22 Aug. 1794).

2. Although Lear continued to function as GW's secretary until the end of August 1793, he had joined, around June 1793, with Tristram Dalton, former U.S. senator from Massachusetts, and James Greenleaf, appointed as U.S. consul at Amsterdam, to form T. Lear & Co., a mercantile establishment to be located at the new Federal City. The European trip was to make commercial contacts and arrange suppliers for the new company.

To Thomas Pinckney

Dear Sir,   Philadelphia Septr 1st 1793

Notwithstanding Mr Lear is already known to you, I cannot suffer him to depart without this letter of introduction to your civilities, whilst he may remain in London.

He is a person whose conduct has entitled him to my warmest friendship & regard—and one from whom you may obtain the best oral information of the real state of matters in this Country.

Mercantile pursuits with draws him from my family, and carries him to Europe for the purpose of facilitating the measure he has adopted, for his future walk.

Present, if you please, my respects to Mrs Pinckney; and be assured of the sincere esteem & regard with which I am ⟨Dear Sir Your Obedt & Hble Ser.

Go: Washington⟩[1]

AL[S] (photocopy), NjP: Edward Ambler Armstrong Photostats; ALS (letterpress copy), DLC:GW; LB, DLC:GW.

1. Where text has been clipped from the AL[S], the words in angle brackets are supplied from the letterpress copy.

To William Short

Sir,   Philadelphia Septr 1st 1793.

If this letter should reach your hands, it will be presented by Mr Lear, a Gentleman who has lived with me more than Seven years—The last four of which as my Secretary.

He is now withdrawing himself from this Office; having engaged in a mercantile scheme; which, for a short stay, takes him to Europe—His conduct during the period he has resided in my family, has been so uniformly good as to entitle him to my affectionate regard, and is my apology for recommending him to your civilities, in case he should fall in your way, during his absence from this Country. From none wd you be able to obtain oral information more to be relied on, of the situation of affairs in this Country. With esteem & regard I am—Sir Your Obedt Hble Servt

Go: Washington

ALS (letterpress copy), ViMtvL; LB, DLC:GW.

To Nicholas Van Staphorst

Sir,   Philadelphia Sept. 1st 1793

I have the pleasure to acknowledge the receipt of your letter of the 2d of may, giving me information of the steps you had taken respecting the bill of Exchange which I remitted to you in January last[1]. Your attention to this business merits and receives my best thanks.

This letter will be put into your hands by Mr Tobias Lear, a Gentleman who has been my Secretary, and[2] a member of my family for seven years last past[3]—He has been making arrangements for forming an extensive commercial establishment at the Federal City on the River Potomak, and now goes to Europe for the purpose of taking measures th⟨ere⟩ to carry his plan into effect[4]—His uniform good conduct having entitled him to my highest esteem & regard must be my apology for taking the liberty of introducing him to your civilities while he shall remain in Holland. I have the honor to be Sir Your Most Obedt Hble Ser.

Go: Washington

DfS, partially in the writing of GW, PHi: Society Collection; LB, DLC:GW. Nicholas Van Staphorst (c.1742–1801), of the firm of Willink, Van Staphorst & Hubbard, had acted as a financial agent for the United States in Holland since 1782.

1. GW enclosed the bill of exchange, which was intended to provide funds to the Marquise de Lafayette, in his letter to Van Staphorst of 30 January.

2. GW added "my Secretary, and" above the line.

3. A caret appears on the draft at this point, but no words are inserted.

4. The remainder of the draft is in GW's handwriting.

To Arthur Young

Sir,   Philadelphia Septr 1st 1793.

Instead of commencing this letter with an apology for suffering your favor of the 17th of last Jany to remain so long unacknowledged, I will refer you to the bearer, who is perfectly acquainted with my situation, for the reason why it has done so.

The bearer Sir, is Mr Lear, a gentleman who has been a member of my family seven years; and, until the present moment, my Secretary—consequently cannot, as I have observed before, be unknowing to the nature, & pressure of the business in which I am continually involved.

As a proof, however, that I have not been altogether inattentive to your commands, I enclose the result of Mr Peters's answer to some enquiries of yours; and the copy also of a letter from Mr Jefferson to whom I had propounded, for solution, other queries contained in your letter of the above date[1]. The documents I send, have the signature of these gentlemen annexed to them, but for your satisfaction only. Mr Peters is, as you will perceive by a vein in his letter, a man of humour. He is a theorist, and admitted one of the best practical farmers in *this* part of the State of Pennsylvania.

But, as it is not so much what the soil of this Country actually produces, as what it is capable of producing by skilful management that I conceive to be the object of your enquiry, & to know whether this produce would meet a ready Market & good prices. What the nature of the Climate in general, is. The temperature thereof in the different States. The quality & prices of the lands, with the improvements thereon, in various parts of the Union. The prospects which are unfolding in each &ca &ca. I can do no better than refer you to the Oral information of the bearer, who is a person of intelligence; & pretty well acquainted with the States from New Hampshire (inclusive) to Virginia; and one in whom you may, as I do, place entire confidence in all he shall relate of his own knowledge, & believe what is given from information, as it will be handed with caution.

Mr Lear has been making arrangements for forming an extensive commercial establishment at the Federal City on the River Potomac; and now goes to Europe for the purpose of taking measures, there, to carry his plan into effect. I persuade myself that any information you can give him, respecting the Manufactures of Great Britain, will be gratefully received;[2] and as I have a particular friendship for him, I shall consider any civilities shewn him by you, as a mark of your politeness to Sir Your Most Obedient & Very Hble Servt

Go: Washington

ALS, PPRF; ALS(letterpress copy), ViMtvL; LB, DLC:GW.

1. See Richard Peters to GW, 20 June, and n.1, and Thomas Jefferson to GW, 28 June 1793. Peters responded to Young's questions about the inattention of American farmers to the calculation of return on capital and about cattle and sheep production. Jefferson touted the productivity of Virginia land.

2. Tobias Lear discussed his meetings with Young in a letter to GW of 26[–30] Jan. 1794.

From George Clinton

Sir   NewYork 2 September 1793.

I transmit for your information, the enclosed papers respecting an event of national concern which lately took place on board the Ship of War Jupiter belonging to the French Squadron in this harbor, and the measures which were adopted in consequence thereof.[1] The application of the Consul General of the French Republic on this occasion, you will readily perceive, placed me in a very delicate situation, as a refusal to interfere might under the peculiar circumstances of this case not only have been construed into a denial of the aid stipulated by the Convention with his Nation but in that view, considering the constitutional obligation of treaties on the State Officers, have been considered an omission of duty.[2] Thus circumstanced I conceived it most adviseable to issue the enclosed requisition to the Officers of the State, in which opinion the Attorney of the District for the United States, with whom I consulted, concurred.[3] I am sensible that by the Act of Congress passed in April 1792 concerning Consuls & Vice Consuls, doubts may be entertained whether cases of this kind are not exclusively committed to the District Judges and Marshals, but should this construction prevail in its full extent, that article of the Convention, in most instances and especially in the present, from the remote residence of the District Judge, must become a dead letter.[4] It may be proper to mention that the persons charged with desertion were pursued and overtaken in the County of WestChester, from whence they have escaped and I have reason to believe have gone out of this State.[5]

I have neglected to mention in my former communications, that it was not in my power to detain the Republican a Prize to the English Frigate Boston agreeably to your request, as she had sailed from this harbor previous to my receipt of the Secretary of War's Letter.[6]

Yesterday the French Privateers Carmagnole and Petit Democrat arrived in this Port—and measures shall be immediately taken, in the mode pointed out on such occasions, to cause their departure.[7] I have the honor to be, with the greatest respect Your most Obedient servant

Geo: Clinton

LS, DNA: RG 59, Letters from Governors of States, 1790–1812; LB, N-Ar: Papers of George Clinton.

This letter was considered in a cabinet meeting of 4 Sept., and Thomas Jefferson replied to Clinton in a letter of 10 Sept. (see *JPP*, 237–38; *Jefferson Papers*, 27:32–34, 75–76).

1. Gen. François Thomas Galbaud du Fort, governor general of Saint Domingue, was technically under arrest aboard the French naval vessel *Jupiter* as a result of his destructive conflict with the civil commissioners of that colony. However, many of the seamen aboard the *Jupiter* supported Galbaud and resisted French minister Edmond Charles Genet's efforts to re-

move Galbaud from the vessel and reorganize the fleet (for their explanation of their actions, see *Diary; or, Loudon's Register* [New York], 20 Aug.).

On 28 Aug. Genet issued a proclamation "to re-establish order and discipline on board the JUPITER," directing the crew to leave the vessel, assigning an officer to take charge of the vessel and of Galbaud, directing that provisions be issued only to a small guard on the vessel, and declaring as "Traitors to their Country, incapable of serving her, and unworthy the name of French Republicans all those who shall refuse to obey this Proclamation" (*Diary; or, Loudon's Register* [New York], 3 Sept.). That night, Galbaud, with the apparent connivance of the *Jupiter*'s crew, escaped from his confinement (see the report of the officer of the guard, Lelois, 29 Aug., DLC: Genet Papers). The crew then left the ship, as ordered by Genet's proclamation, but many took arms with them. A second order, dated 30 Aug., directed them to give up their arms and threatened with arrest any crew members found carrying them (*Diary; or, Loudon's Register,* 31 Aug.).

2. For the application, see enclosure I. Clinton was referring to article 9 of the "Convention Defining and Establishing the Functions and Privileges of Consuls and Vice Consuls," 14 Nov. 1788 (see enclosure II and n.1 to that document).

3. Clinton's proclamation of 1 Sept. "To all Judges, and other Officers of the Said State whome it may concern" required them "to give all due aid and assistance for the Search Seizure and arrest of the Said deserters and for their detention in prison until an Oportunity shall be found to send them back to the said Ship, but such detention is nevertheless not to exceed the term of three Months from the Day of the said arrest" (DNA: RG 59, Letters from Governors of States, 1790–1812). The United States district attorney for New York was Richard Harison (c.1747–1829).

4. Section 1 of "An Act concerning Consuls and Vice-Consuls," 14 April 1792, stated that district judges shall "be the competent judges, for the purposes expressed in the ninth article of the said convention, and it shall be incumbent on them to give aid . . . in arresting and securing deserters from vessels of the French nation according to the tenor of the said article." The same section specified that "where by any article of the said convention, the consuls and vice-consuls of the King of the French, are entitled to the aid of the competent executive officers of the country . . . the marshals of the United States and their deputies shall . . . be the competent officers" (1 *Stat.,* 254). When this letter was read in the cabinet meeting of 4 Sept., the "remote residence" of New York District Judge James Duane drew the secretaries' attention, and it was proposed to write him "that the place of his residence was not adapted to his duties," but Jefferson's letter to Duane of 10 Sept. merely referred the enclosed papers to him for action (*Jefferson Papers,* 27:32–33, 76–78).

5. For an account of the effort to arrest Galbaud at Chester, see Arnaud Prêtes to Edmond Genet, 30 August. Prêtes believed that Galbaud had remained in the area, as he reported to Genet in subsequent letters of 1, 2, 6, and 7 Sept. (all documents, DLC: Genet Papers).

6. The *Republican,* a French privateer of eight guns out of Cap-Français, was taken by the *Boston* off Sandy Hook on the morning of 29 July and sent as a

prize to New York City (*New-York Journal, & Patriotic Register,* 31 July). Clinton wrote GW on 30 July describing his response to the incident and seeking "the sense of the executive of the United States" on the subject. For Secretary of War Henry Knox's reply of 2 Aug., see n.4 to Clinton's letter. Meanwhile, French minister Edmond Genet protested to Secretary of State Thomas Jefferson that the vessel had been improperly taken within U.S. waters, and Jefferson wrote British minister George Hammond on 4 Aug. to request that the British consul at New York "retain the vessel in his custody until the Executive of the US. shall consider and decide finally on the subject" (*Jefferson Papers,* 26:612–13). Knox wrote Clinton on 3 Aug. that he had been "directed" by GW to inform him "of this circumstance and to request your conforming thereto" (N-Ar: Papers of George Clinton). Clinton's "former communications" included a letter of 18 Aug. from his secretary DeWitt Clinton to Knox, which was referred to GW on 21 Aug. (see Knox to Tobias Lear, 21 Aug., and *JPP,* 228).

7. GW's directions that any "armed vessel which has been or shall be originally fitted in any port of the United States, as a Cruiser, or Privateer, by either of the Parties at War . . . be ordered to depart immediately" were transmitted in a circular letter to the governors of 16 Aug., signed by Knox (see Knox to Tobias Lear, 17 Aug., n.1). Knox's circular specifically listed the *Petite Démocrate* and *Carmagnole* among those ships to which the order applied.

Enclosure I
Edmond Genet to George Clinton

New York le 30 Aout 1793

Monsicur   l'an 2e de la Republique

Le General Galbaud, l'aude de Camp Concience, et le Caporal Bonne, se sont evader cette nuit a m am[1] armée âu bord du Jupiter. ces hommes sont tous deserteurs et à ce titre nous avons le droit de les reclamer⟨.⟩ Je vous prie enconsequence Monsieur de vouloir bien faire deliverer des Warrants au Consul de la republique pour qu'il soient arretés et condutés a bord d'un des Vaissaus de l'Escadre.

Voici le Signalement de *Galbaud.* agés de 50 ans, taille de 5 pied, tête petite figure bléme, visage alongé, l'œuil vif, Sourcils blond nei long, bouche grande, front élevé, menton pointu, portant perruque, maigre de Corps, marchant trés droit.

Signalement de l'aude de Camp Concience agé de 20 ans, taille de 5 pieds trois pouce, mince de corps, bienfait, petite figure, l'œuil petit et enfoncé, le tient basané, le fron⟨t⟩ elevé, le nez ordinaire, bouche moyenne, mento⟨n⟩ ordinaire, cheveux chatains noirs.[2]

Signalement du Caporal Bonne agé de 30 ans environs taille 5 pieds 4 pouce figure ronde, nes pointu, yeux petits, cheveux chatains, front court et large, bouche petite, le corps gros.[3] Agréés mes respectueux sentiments

Genet

P. S. Je crois que ces trois personnes ne parlent pas l'anglais. le Consul de la Republique, Monsieur, presentera au Maire de cette Ville le rolle du Jupiter que constateront que les personnes que Je reclame faisoient partie de l'equipage de ce Vaissau.[4]

G.

Copy, DNA: RG 59, Letters from Governors of States, 1790–1812; copy (signed by Genet), DLC: Genet Papers; LB (translation), N-Ar: Papers of George Clinton.

1. Clinton's copyist should have written "main," which is the word that appears on Genet's retained copy.

2. André Conscience reportedly was an officer in the 8th regiment as well as Galbaud's aide. His later testimony before the French national convention was published as *André Conscience à La Convention Nationale sur les derniers événements de Saint-Domingue* (Paris, 1794).

3. Genet's papers also contain copies of a circular letter of this date to the state governors. This document describes Bonne somewhat differently: "Bonne, Sa taille est de 5. Pieds Cinq Pouces agé de 28. ans, Phisionomie interessante, visage Rond, yeux Mobilles Nez Pointû, Cheveux Blond chatains, taille bien Prète ayant un peu l'accent allemand" (DLC: Genet Papers). In a letter to the French consul at Baltimore, Genet characterized Bonne as a corporal "of the former regiment of the Queen . . . who was imprisoned 8 months at C. Francois, by the determination of his fellow soldiers" (*Diary; or, Loudon's Register* [New York], 19 Sept.). On 20 Aug., Bonne had been active in encouraging resistance to Genet's efforts to reorganize the fleet at New York (see the statement of Sarazin, 20 Aug., DLC: Genet Papers).

4. An "Extrait du Roll d'Equipage du Vaisseau de la Republique française le Jupiter," among Clinton's papers, asserts that Galbaud and his aide-de-camp, Conscience, who were in a state of arrest on board the *Jupiter,* deserted the vessel on 31 Aug., and that "Bonnet," a grenadier of the 41st regiment who had taken refuge on the vessel, deserted the same day. (N-Ar: Papers of George Clinton).

Enclosure II
George Clinton to Edmond Genet

Sir　　　　　　　　　　　　　　　New York 30th August 1793

In consequence of the Request contained in your Letter of equal Date, I have issued my Requisition to the Judges & other

Officers of this State to give all due Aid and Assistance (pursuant to the 9th Article of the Consular Convention between our two Nations) for the Search Seizure and Arrest of the Deserters (mentioned in your Letter) from the Ship Jupiter belonging to your Republic[1]—It may not be improper however to mention that altho I conceive the Exhibition of the Ships Roll as proof sufficient to Justify this Measure in the first Instance, yet by the same Article it would appear that a Right is reserved to the Party proceeded against to disprove the Fact; should this therefore be done to the Satisfaction of the Judge before whom those Persons when apprehended are brought, it may then become a Question whether instead of causing them to be confined it will not in such Case be his Duty to liberate them.[2] I am &c.

G. C.

Copy, DNA: RG 59, Letters from Governors of States, 1790–1812.

1. For the requisition, see Clinton to GW, 2 Sept., note 3. Article 9 of the "Convention Defining and Establishing the Functions and Privileges of Consuls and Vice Consuls," 14 Nov. 1788, gave the consuls authority to "cause to be arrested" deserters from ships and defined their ability to obtain aid from "courts, judges, and officers competent" (see Miller, *Treaties,* 237–38).

2. In Secretary of State Thomas Jefferson's letter to Clinton of 10 Sept. acknowledging these documents, he warned that "the power of arresting, derived from the 9th: article of the consular convention with France, is capable of great abuse. . . . the facility which is afforded by that instrument, for obtaining the interposition of the Magistracy, merely by exhibiting the register of a vessel, or a ship's roll, may often expose to a temporary imprisonment those, who never constituted a part of any crew whatsoever. The President therefore feels an assurance, that by the cautions which Your Excellency will prescribe to yourself on such occasions, you will save the United States from every possible embarrassment" (*Jefferson Papers,* 27:75).

Enclosure III
George Clinton to François Thomas Galbaud du Fort

Sir   New York 31st August—1793.

In Issuing my directions which I presume from your Letter of this day have been shewn to you[1] I have proceded only in pursuance of the Ninth article of the consular Convention between France and the United States—in requiring the Judges and other Officers of the State to perform that duty which by law is required of them.

Whether you & the other persons named in my directions do or do not belong to the Crew of the Jupiter is a question I can only decide from an Inspection of the Roll of that Ship which has been exhibited[2]—If any deception has been practised the persons who are guilty of it are alone answerable.

It is true there is the mistake you notice in the date of my directions—but this will be immaterial as they will take Effect from the time they were Issued—especially as the law without the formality of an order enjoins this duty on the Majistrate.[3]

You may be assured that your claim of protection & every duty of Hospitality from this State would be allowed in any case except where an interference between the Government of your Cuntry and its Citizens would as in the present instance be improper. Yours

Geo. Clinton

Copy, DNA: RG 59, Letters from Governors of States, 1790–1812.

1. For Clinton's directions, see Clinton to GW, 2 Sept., n.3. Galbaud's letter to Clinton of 31 Aug. protested the order for his arrest, as he had committed no crime in America and had not deserted the fleet, having never belonged to it. Galbaud agreed, however, to obey the order if promised protection until he could return to France to defend his conduct: "⟨*Mutilated*⟩ avec Surprise l'ordre que vous avez donnez de m'arreter ainsi ⟨que les⟩ Cîtoyens Conscience et Boune n'ayant commis aucune de lit ⟨con⟩tre le territoire americain Je croyois que nul homme n'avoit droit ⟨*mutilated*⟩ur ma personne: mais comme Je n'ai Jamais en d'autre desir que celui d'aller en france Je suis pres à obtemperer a tout vos ordres si, comme tout Citoyen a droit de l'esperer, vous me promettez sureté a protection jusqu au moment ou je pourrai sans crainte passer en france pour y justifier sa conduite. . . . vous m'accusez dans votre ordre d'etre déserté de la flotte, ou vous a trempè, Je ne fait pas partie de la flotte, les Citoyens Conscience et Boune n'en sont pas d'avantage" (N-Ar: Papers of George Clinton).

2. On the *Jupiter*'s roll, see enclosure I, n.4.

3. Galbaud's letter complained that although Clinton's order was dated 1 Sept., it was being enforced on 31 August. The French officer who was sent after Galbaud complained that his effort to make an arrest failed in part because local citizens would not acknowledge the orders as valid before 1 Sept. (Arnaud Prêtes to Edmond Genet, 30 Aug. and 1 Sept., DLC: Genet Papers).

To Alexander Hamilton

Dear Sir,   Monday Morning 2d Sepr [1793]

Interwoven in the enclosed Address, are Sentiments as difficult to answer, as it would seem odd to pass by unnoticed—believing, as I do, that they are the sentiments of a large part of the people of this Country.[1]

I would thank you for making such alterations in the expression of the draft of an answer (enclosed) as in your judgment will make it palatable on all sides, or unexceptionable. The bearer will wait, as I wish to return the answer by the Mail of to day.[2] Yours always

Go: Washington

No matter how rough the answer comes to me, so it can be read.

ALS, DLC: Hamilton Papers.

1. GW is referring to the address in support of his Neutrality Proclamation from the citizens of New London, Conn., 22 Aug. 1793. The "difficult to answer" sentiments in that address were probably those related to the citizens' statement of "partiality for the French."

2. GW sent his reply to the citizens of New London, Conn., on this date. Neither the draft of that response nor any reply by Hamilton to this letter has been found.

From Thomas Jefferson

[2–4 September 1793]

Th: Jefferson has the honor to inclose to the President his letter of Aug. 7. to mister Hammond, which was confined to the special cases of three vessels therein named. the object of mister Hammond's letter of Aug. 30. is to obtain from the government a declaration that the principle of those special cases shall be extended to all captures made within our waters or by the proscribed vessels, whether *before* or *after* the 7th of Aug. & to establish, as a general rule, *restitution*, or *compensation*.[1] the forming a general rule requires great caution. Th: J. in preparing the draught of an answer to mister Hammond, has endeavored to establish what he thinks the true grounds on which a general rule should be formed. but, if the President approves of it, he would wish to send the draught to the Secretaries of the Trea-

sury & war, & Attorney Genl for their consideration & amendments, or to meet on the subject, when an answer to the latter
part of the letter might also be agreed on.[2]

AL, DNA: RG 59, Miscellaneous Letters; AL (letterpress copy), DLC: Jefferson Papers; LB, DNA: RG 59, George Washington's Correspondence with His
Secretaries of State.

The docket on the back of the AL reads, "From the Secy of State begining of Septr 1793." The letter-book copy contains a similar phrase. Jefferson
probably wrote this letter between 2 and 4 Sept. (see notes).

1. Jefferson's letter to George Hammond of 7 Aug. promised restoration
of, or compensation for, the *Lovely Lass, Prince William Henry,* and *Jane* (of
Dublin), taken as prizes by French privateers armed within U.S. ports (*Jefferson Papers,* 26:634–35). For Hammond's letter to Jefferson of 30 Aug., see
Jefferson Papers, 26:789–90. Jefferson submitted Hammond's letter to GW on
2 Sept. (see *JPP,* 236).

2. Jefferson proposed distinguishing cases where the U.S. had "used all
the means in our power" to obtain restitution of the vessel from those in
which the U.S. had failed to make such an effort, and offering compensation only when a full effort had not been made. On 4 Sept. a divided cabinet
approved Jefferson's reply to Hammond of 5 Sept., which made that distinction (see *Jefferson Papers,* 27:32–34). The latter part of Hammond's letter of
30 Aug. claimed "reparation for any loss, which the vessels captured or their
cargoes may sustain, from detention, waste, or spoliation" and asked Jefferson to "prescribe the mode" whereby such damages could be ascertained
(*Jefferson Papers,* 26:790). In the 5 Sept. reply, Jefferson proposed that, "as a
provisional measure," the collectors of customs and British consuls should
appoint persons for that purpose (*Jefferson Papers,* 27:35–38).

From James Lloyd

Chester Town—Kent County Maryland

Sir,   2d Septr 1793.

I have the honor of transmitting to you the inclosed resolutions, entered into by the Citizens of Kent County, at a very respectable meeting at Chester Town on the 31st of August last.

It gives me the highest satisfaction to believe that the spirit
which dictated those resolutions pervades every part of the State
of Maryland.

Whilst I am performing the pleasing duty, of communicating
the sentiments of my fellow Citizens of this County, permit me
to add my most fervent wishes for the happiness of a Life on
which the public safety so much depends. I have the honor to

be, with the most respectful regard, Sir, Your most humble & Obedt Servt

James Lloyd

ALS, DLC:GW; LB, DLC:GW. This letter was published in the *Maryland Herald, and Eastern Shore Intelligencer* (Easton), 17 Sept., and other Maryland newspapers.

Enclosure
Resolutions from Kent County, Md., Citizens

[31 August 1793]

At a meeting of the Citizens of Kent County in the State of Maryland, convened at the Court-House in Chester Town, on the 31st day of August 1793, for the purpose of declaring their sentiments relative to the proclamation of neutrality issued by the President of the United States, the following unanimous resolutions were entered into.[1]

James Lloyd in the Chair.

1st   Resolved that the Citizens of Kent County are deeply impressed with a sense of the excellence of the Government under which they have the happiness to live, and that they will use their best endeavours to support and maintain the said Government.

2d   That they consider the preservation of the public peace as essentially necessary to the welfare and prosperity of the United States of America.

3d   That the proclamation of neutrality, issued by the President of the United States, was dictated by *wisdom and moderation*— that it is perfectly consistent with our treaties with foreign Nations, and promotive of the best interests of America.[2]

4th   That we will exert our best endeavours to discountenance and prevent all infringements of the said neutrality.

5th   That we consider our fellow Citizen George Washington, President of the United States of America, as deserving of the highest veneration and love of his Country—equally great and useful in his present situation as formerly in the field, and that whilst the whole tenor of his conduct proves him to have no views, no wishes, but for the public good, we think him justly entitled to the *confidence* of United America.

6. That we will ever oppose all attempts of foreign nations or their *agents,* to deprive our beloved fellow Citizen the said

President of the United States, of the love and esteem of his Country.[3]

7. That the United States of America, being by the blessing of GOD, free and independent, it is our duty as good Citizens, both with our lives and fortunes, to defend the freedom and independence against all internal intrigue and cabal, as well as against all attacks from without.

8. That the Chairman be requested to transmit a copy of these resoluti⟨ons⟩ to the President of the United States.[4]

James Lloyd Chairman

DS, DLC:GW; LB:DLC:GW.

These resolutions were published in the *General Advertiser* (Philadelphia), 10 Sept., and *Maryland Herald, and Eastern Shore Intelligencer* (Easton), 17 September.

1. GW's Neutrality Proclamation of 22 April declared the United States to be neutral in regard to the European war and warned citizens that violations of neutrality would leave them liable to punishment.

2. The treaties in question were the Treaty of Amity and Commerce and the Treaty of Alliance between France and the United States, both of 6 Feb. 1778 (see Miller, *Treaties*, 3–44).

3. This resolution refers to French minister Edmond Charles Genet, whose differences with GW's administration had become public (see Genet to GW, 13 Aug., and n.4 to that document).

4. GW responded to the resolutions in his letter to Lloyd of 10 September.

From Thomas Mifflin

Sir   Philade. 2d Sept. 1793

I have the honor to lay before you, copies of several letters, which I have recd from the French Consul, respecting the approach of a very considerable body of armed Deserters, from the French Ships of War, now lying at New York and expressing his solicitude to obtain the aid of the Militia, in executing a Warrant, which the Chief Justice has issued, for apprehending them.[1] With that view, as well as to preserve the public peace (obviously at this moment endangered) I have given orders (a copy of which is enclosed) for making a draft from the Militia;[2] but being apprehensive, that this arrangement cannot be seasonably effected, I request your sanction for calling in the assistance of Capt. Sedan's Company, to act, upon the request of the Civil authority, until the Militia are prepared to discharge the duty which the occasion requires.[3] I am, with perfect respect Sir Your most obedt Hble Servt

Thos Mifflin

Df, PHarH: Executive Correspondence, 1790–99; LB, PHarH: Executive Letterbooks.

1. The enclosed letters from François Dupont, the French consul at Philadelphia, have not been identified, but Dupont discussed two of them in his letter to Genet of 2 Sept. (DLC: Genet Papers). One enclosed a letter from Genet to Dupont warning that thirty or forty of the sailors who had left the *Jupiter* were en route to Philadelphia, and requested Mifflin's assistance in apprehending them. A second revised the estimate of the number of "deserters" upward to between 150 and 200 men.

2. Mifflin wrote Pennsylvania Adjt. Gen. Josiah Harmar on this date directing him to "immediately make a draft from the City Brigade of the Light Infantry Companies, the Company of Light Horse, and a Company of Artillery, with four field pieces; and direct the whole detachment to parade on the height above Phillips's old rope walk, between Second & First street, at 9 o'Clock tomorrow" (PHarH: Executive Correspondence, 1790–99).

3. Cornelius Ryer Sedam (Suydam; 1759–1823), who served as an ensign in the 1st New Jersey regiment during the latter stages of the Revolutionary War, was appointed an ensign of U.S. infantry in 1786 and a lieutenant in 1790. His promotion to captain in March 1793 was backdated to April 1792. After leaving the army in November 1796, he settled in Ohio, where he became a farmer. No reply to this request has been identified.

To the New London, Conn., Citizens

Fellow Citizens,   [2 September 1793][1]

The motives which have induced a public expression of your sentiments at the present juncture, are such as naturally operate upon good Citizens, when points which materially concern the happiness of their Country are the subjects of discussion.

Your approbation of my conduct on the occasion, to which it relates, could not fail to give me particular pleasure, and to serve as a support to my confidence in pursuing measures which, dictated by official duty, have for object the peace & happiness of our common Country.[2]

Sentiments sincerely friendly to the French Nation, & the most cordial wishes for their welfare, unite, I doubt not, all the Citizens of the United States; but it cannot be incompatible with these dispositions to give full weight to the great & commanding considerations which respect the immediate welfare of our own Country.

Experienced as we have lately been in the calamities of war, it must be the prayer of every good Citizen that it may long be averted from our land, and that the blessings which a kind providence has bestow'd upon us, may continue uninterrupted.

Go: Washington

LB, DLC:GW. This letter was published in the *Connecticut Gazette* (New London), 12 Sept. 1793.

1. This document is undated, but GW enclosed it in a letter to Richard Law of 2 Sept., which reads: "I enclose to you an answer to the Address, transmitted by you to me, of the Inhabitants of the City of New London; & beg leave thro' you, to communicate it to them" (LB, DLC:GW).

2. The address of 22 Aug. from the citizens of New London expressed approval of GW's Neutrality Proclamation of 22 April.

Resolutions from Petersburg, Va., Citizens

[2 September 1793]

At a Meeting of a number of respectable Inhabitants of the Town of Petersburg and its Vicinity held at Mr Edwards's Coffeehouse in the said Town, on Saturday the 31st of August 1793 pursuant to public Notice, for that purpose given, to take into Consideration the late proclamation of the President of the United States.[1]

The President's proclamation being read on Motion made & seconded, Resolved, that a Committee be appointed to draw up & propose to the next meeting for their Consideration, Certain Resolutions expressive of the sentiments of the Inhabitants of this Town, and its Vicinity, respecting the president's said proclamation declaring the neutrality of the States in the present European War, and respecting the Conduct of Administration with regard to the powers at War; and The following Gentlemen, viz. Joseph Weisiger, Docter Hall, Thomas G. Peachy, Docter Shore, Burrel Starke, James Campbell and George K. Taylor, were appointed a Committee for that purpose—The Meeting was then adjourned till Monday morning next at 10, OClock, to be then held at the Town Court house.[2]

At a general Meeting of the Inhabitants of the Town of Petersburg and its Vicinity at the Court house of the said Town on Monday the 2nd Sept. 1793.

The Committee appointed by the Town Meeting held on saturday last, to draw up & propose to the present Meeting, for their Consideration, certain resolutions; this day proposed to the Meeting the Resolutions following Vizt.

Resolved that it is Consistent with the true Interests of the United States as well as their good faith, to preserve the strictest Neutrality in the present situation of Europe.

That we highly approve, and are firmly resolved strictly to observe the Presidents late proclamation, because we believe it was dictated by a profound knowledge of the interests of these States and by a sincere & honest desire of promoting their real happiness & prosperity.

That we will use every exertion to discountenance and suppress all such designs & proceedings as in any manner tend to interrupt that harmony & tranquility which we enjoy under a just & pacific Administration of the happiest of Governments.

That the interference of any foreign power or Minister in the internal Administration of our Government, is an infringement of the Sovereignty of the people, tends to destroy public Confidence, to introduce Confusion & Anarchy, and therefore should excite the indignation & reprehension of every Independent American.[3]

That any Attempts to diminish that Confidence which our Citizens repose in the Wisdom Justice & disinterestedness of the present Chief Magistrate of the United States are equally ungrateful, illiberal and unjust.

Resolved, That the Chairman transmit the foregoing Resolutions to Thomas Jefferson Esqr. & request him to Communicate the same to the President of the United States.[4]

And the said Resolutions being severally & distinctly read were unanimously adopted.

And the Meeting Continuing, the following resolution was proposed & agreed to.

Resolved, That We Consider the Combination of the despots of Europe against the Liberties of France as having a direct tendency to destroy the political happiness of Mankind and though we feel an Interest in preserving our Neutrality, yet it is our sincere wish that Liberty & the Rights of Man may be the prevailing principle's throughout the Universe.

T. G: Peachy Chairman.

DS, DLC:GW; LB, DLC:GW. The resolutions from this document were published in *Gazette of the United States* (Philadelphia), 18 September.

1. The meeting was to consider GW's Neutrality Proclamation of 22 April.

2. Thomas Griffin Peachy (1734–1810) served as clerk of Amelia County, Va., 1757–91. George Keith Taylor (1769–1815), a brother-in-law of John Marshall, represented Prince George County in the Virginia house of delegates, 1795–96, 1798–99, and was appointed judge of the U.S. Court of Appeals for the Fourth Circuit in 1801. Doctors Isaac Hall (1747–c.1806) and John Shore, Jr. (1756–1811), both medical graduates of the University of Edinburgh, entered into a partnership at Petersburg in 1779. Hall served as sheriff for Prince George County in 1791. Shore, who served as mayor of Petersburg in 1783, was appointed collector of the port of Petersburg in 1802 and retained that post until his death. Joseph Weisiger (c.1760–1796) was a captain in the Prince George County light infantry and, at the time of his death, a partner in the firm of Baird and Weisiger, which operated a store at Blandford, Virginia.

3. This paragraph responds to the activities of French minister Edmond Charles Genet, whose differences with GW's administration had become public (see Genet to GW, 13 Aug., and n.4 to that document).

4. Peachy enclosed this document in a letter to Thomas Jefferson of 3 Sept. (*Jefferson Papers*, 27:28–29). Jefferson enclosed the resolutions in his letter to GW of 15[–16] September, and GW responded to the resolutions in a letter to Peachy of 24 September.

From William Augustine Washington

[Haywood, Va., 3 September 1793]

I have been making enquiries respecting the hire of carpenters as you desired. I have at length met with a per[s]on who is a regular bred Carpenter and has four Negro Carpenters that work with him; he says if you will contract with him for twelve months, he will agree to move up to Mount Vernon—his terms are £10 per month for himself and four Negro Carpenters. . . . he will expect himself and hands to be found in provision and a house to be furnished him[1] . . . my love to my aunt, . . .

Extract, George H. Richmond, *Autograph Letters . . .* , 1904, item 329.

1. GW drew up and signed a contract, witnessed by Bartholomew Dandridge, Jr., for the employment of this carpenter: "Articles of Agreement entered into between George Washington of Mount Vernon in Virginia, at present President of the United States & residing in Philadelphia of the one

part, and [   ] of the County of Westmoreland & State aforesaid House Carpenter & Joiner of the other part, Witness that the said [   ] for the wages and other considerations hereafter mentioned, doth oblige himself and four Negro Carpenters belonging to him, who he engages to be good workmen, to wit, [   ] to serve the said George Washington one year from the time they shall enter upon the execution of their duties at Mount Vernon (which he promises shall be on or before the [   ] day of [   ] next ensuing. During which time he, & they, will conduct themselves soberly, honestly and diligently in whatever business (in the line of their profession) they shall be employed in. That he will besides attending to his own, superintend all such Negro Carpenters belonging to the said George Washington as shall be placed under his care & direction; and to the utmost of his skill & industry, so order & contrive the work for the whole, or any part thereof, as to carry it on to the best advantage & with the greatest facility. That he will be particularly attentive as well to the conduct of his own as to such other Carpenters as may be entrusted to him, suffering no idleness when they are in health, nor no neglect of them when sick. That he will cause proper care to be taken of the Tools, & see them forthcoming whenever called for; or a satisfactory account rendered of them if they are not. That he will enter in a book to be kept for that purpose an acct of all the work which has been done by himself and the Carpenters over whom he is placed, and report the same weekly. That he will never be away from his people when they are at work and he is in health; nor be absent from his duty without permission from the said George Washington or his Manager; but on the contrary, by close attention, & an industrious conduct, will set an example to them worthy of imitation. And Whereas it too often happens that men (regardless of their engagements & of course their reputation) when working on standing wages are apt to be idle, careless & indifferent to the interest of their Employers, thereby setting the reverse of good examples, it is hereby clearly understood and expressly agreed to by the said [   ] that he will be at his business as soon as it is light, and remain thereat until dark, when he is in health; & when not employed in laying out, or marking off work for others, that he will labour as faithfully, & as effectually as any hand under him; as well for the purpose of fulfilling this agreement as for the good example he would set by so doing to those who are under his care, and who are not so ignorant (knowing this is required of him) as not to relax as he relaxes, and be idle in proportion as he is idle; because all of them have discernment enough to know that no man can, with propriety, or a good conscience, correct others for a fault he is guilty of himself; the consequence of which is, that indolence & sloth take possession of the whole. Lastly, the said [   ] doth hereby oblige himself, during the term aforesaid, to conform to all orders & directions in the line of his business, or in any other that is reasonable (his time being paid for by the said George Washington) which he the said George Washington, or person having the general Superintendency of his business, shall require⟨.⟩ In consideration of these Services well & truly performed on the part of the said [   ] and his four Negro Carpenters before named, the said George Washington doth hereby oblige himself to pay the said [   ] the sum of ten pounds pr

Kalender month—estimating dollars at Six shillings & other gold & silver at that rate, for the hire of the said [   ] and the four Negro Carpenters beforementioned; and in that proportion in case any of them should be unable to come, or die in the service after they have entered upon it. The said George Washington doth moreover agree to furnish the said [   ] and his four Negro Carpenters with provisions; himself with [   ] lbs. of Porke or Beef, and [   ] bushels of Indian Meal or midling flour equivalent in value thereto; and his Negros with the same provisions in quantity & quality as his own Negro Carpenters are allowed—And will provide the whole with Tools, & pay their taxes. He also agrees to furnish the said [   ] with a house to live in, or if this cannot be done in time, conveniently, then, & in that case, a room seperate & distinct from any other person or persons. But the said [   ] is to provide his own bed and necessaries; as also such kind of bedding as he chuses to allow his own Negros. For the true & faithful performance of this agreement, the parties do bind themselves each to the other in the sum of [   ] pounds this [   ] day of [   ] 1793" (ViMtvL).

The carpenter probably was Mr. Stone, mentioned in GW's letter to William A. Washington of 21 Oct., in which case the proposed agreement was not completed, because the four assistants were not as initially represented.

From William Willcocks

Sir,   Cork [Ireland] 3d Septemr 1793

Having had the honour of being introduced to Your Excellency by Mr Purvyance at Baltimore last March, and being Elected Mayor of this City Since my return, but do not come into Office till the 30th of the present Month; In that Situation it occurs to me that I may be useful, particularly to Your new City, which I hinted to Col: Deakins, who I had the pleasure to see at George Town, I therefore take the liberty to make a tender of my best Services, As I will be happy to serve America in every matter that does no injury to Great Britain, Ireland, or their dependencies.[1]

Inclosed I send You Two Cork, & One Waterford, Newspapers, there is from London this day a Gazette Extraordinary arrived dated the 28th Ult: which gives an Accot of a battle between the Ally'd Army, & French, near Lefferinks Hook, in which the former were Victorious, but Suffered very Considerably. The Austrian Genl Dalton was Killed, likewise Col: Eld of the Coldstream Regt, with many other Officers, The Duke of Yorks head Quarters was about a League from Dunkirk.[2] With the Utmost respect, I have the honor to be, Your Excellency's Most Obedient, Humble Servant,

Will: Willcocks

ALS, DLC:GW.

1. GW stopped at Baltimore on 30 March, en route from Philadelphia to Mount Vernon, but other than this letter, no written evidence has been identified pertaining to Willcocks's meeting with GW. Willcocks's contacts probably were Robert Purviance, who served as naval officer of Baltimore, 1789–94, and William Deakins, Jr., treasurer for the District of Columbia. Willcocks served one year as mayor of Cork. During that term he twice wrote GW. In his letter of 23 Oct., he confirmed the "tender of my best Services for the good of the United States, & particularly of Your New City," and added, "for Your Amusement I send a few Newspapers by this opportunity" (DLC: GW). His letter of 29 April 1794 again enclosed newspapers (DLC:GW). No reply to any of the letters from Willcocks has been found.

2. The enclosed newspapers have not been identified. Lt. Col. George Eld of the Coldstream Guards and Austrian Lt. Gen. Edward D'Alton were killed on 24 Aug. in an action near the canal of Furnes (*Times* [London], 2 Sept.). Furnes (Veurne) is in West Flanders province, West Belgium, six miles west-southwest of Nieuport. The British commander, Frederick Augustus, Duke of York, sent his report of the action to George III on 26 Aug. from Leffrinckoucke, a village four miles east of Dunkirk (Arthur Aspinall, ed., *The Later Correspondence of George III* [5 vols., Cambridge, England, 1962–70], 2:79–80).

To James B. M. Adair

Sir, Philadelphia Sepr 4. 1793

I have recd your letter of the 31st ulto from New York enclosing one from Sr Edwd Newinham—also the magazines, the Packet from Sr John Sinclair &c. for your care And attention in forwarding them I beg you to accept my thanks.[1]

Any civilities which it may be in my power to shew you while you remain in this Country, will give me Pleasure. I am Sir your Mot obt Sert

Go: Washington

LB, DLC:GW; copy, DNA: RG 59, Miscellaneous Letters.

1. For the enclosures in Adair's letter of 31 Aug., see Edward Newenham to GW, 7 June, and John Sinclair to GW, 15 June, and n.2.

To John Eccleston

Sir,   Philada 4 Septr 1793.

The address, to which the enclosed is an Answer, was sent to me by Mr Murray.[1] I take the liberty of enclosing it to you, as Chairman of the Meeting, with a request that you will communicate it to the Landholders & other citizens of Dorchester County, being, Sir &c.

Go. Washington.

LB, DLC:GW.

1. GW enclosed his undated reply to the 19 Aug. address of the citizens of Dorchester County, Md., approving of his Neutrality Proclamation. The reply read: "Fellow Citizens, No one can more sincerely deprecate the horrors of war, or more ardently wish to continue to our Country the blessings uniformly attending peace, than I do.

"To meet your approbation of a measure resulting from these motives, & from the fullest conviction that it was the duty & interest of this Country to remain neuter in a contest which has engaged most of the powers of Europe, at the expense of much blood & treasure, cannot but be extremely pleasing to me.[2]

"The miseries attending war are recently within our own experience; and though the issue of our struggle was glorious, and the prosperity & happiness we have derived from it unequalled perhaps in any other Country, yet, I trust the good sense of the people of these United States will never (if peace can be preserved consistently with our dignity & honor) suffer themselves to be drawn into another.

"As far as my endeavours can contribute towards the preservation of this desirable object, my most active exertions shall not be wanting" (LB, DLC:GW).

2. For the Dorchester County approbation of GW's Neutrality Proclamation, see the Citizens of Dorchester County, Maryland, to GW, 19 Aug.

From John Eager Howard

Sir   Belvidere [Md.] 4th Septr 1793

Immediately upon the receipt of your Excellencys letter of the 25th ult. I wrote by the post to Capt. Kilty at Annapolis, to know whether the appointment of Collector of Annapolis would be agreeable to him, and I delayed answering your letter in hopes of being able to communicate his determination; but have not yet heard from him.[1]

I very much doubt his acceptance of that office, as the Salary,

I am informed is only two hundred dollars, and the fees very trifling, so that it would not be equal to his Salary as a member of the Council.

I have also had conversation with Capt. Plunkett respecting Mr Purviance; Capt. Plunkett thinks that office would not suit him, as his great object is a situation that would enable him to take a house and support his Sisters who at present are dispersed among their friends.[2]

Mr Delozier is well acquainted with the duties of the office to which he is appointed, and I am persuaded he will execute the trust with reputation to himself, and to the satisfaction of the publick.

Permit me to express my ardent wishes that you may not be exposed to the malignant fever which at this time rages in Philadelphia, and the great respect with which I have the honor to be Your Excellencys Obedt Servt

J. E. Howard

P.S. Since writing the above I have received Capt. Kilty' answer to my letter, which I take the liberty of enclosing to your Excellency, though I ought to make an apoligy for giving you the trouble of reading so long a letter[3]—With the highest respect—I have the honor to be Yr Obedt Servt

J. E. Howard

ALS, DNA: RG 59, Miscellaneous Letters.

1. After choosing to nominate Daniel Delozier as surveyor for the port of Baltimore, rather than John Kilty, whom Howard had suggested, GW asked Howard if Kilty would accept the post of collector at Annapolis (Howard to GW, 13 Aug., and GW to Howard, 25 Aug.).

2. David Plunket had recommended John H. Purviance for the surveyor position (Plunket to GW, 7 Aug.). GW's second choice for the collector's office at Annapolis was Purviance, but he eventually appointed John Randall to the post (GW to John Eager Howard, 25 Aug., and to U.S. Senate, 27 Dec.).

3. The enclosure has not been identified, but in addition to declining the Annapolis post Kilty apparently complained about the process by which the decision about the Baltimore surveyor was made (see Kilty to GW, 23 July 1794, DLC: GW). GW replied to Howard from Mount Vernon on 16 Sept.: "⟨On my way home, I met at the Post Office in Alexandria, your favor of the 4th instant, enclosing Mr Kilty's letter to you; the latter I return without any comment upon it.⟩

"My compliments if you please to Mrs Howard; and praying you to accept my thanks for the expression of your kind wishes for my health, I remain with very great esteem & regard Dear Sir Your most Obedt Servant" (ALS [frag-

ment], owned 1991 by The Gallery of History; ADfS, PPRF; LB, DLC:GW.
The text in angle brackets is taken from the ADfS).

From "A true Friend to virtuous
Liberty and Equality"

SIR,   *Wyoming, Sept.* 4. 1793.
   A Short time ago having a few leisure weeks, curiosity led me
to take a tour on horse back from this place through the central
parts of the eastern states to Portsmouth in New-Hampshire,
from thence along the post road to Savanna in Georgia, and
from there back to this place, passing through the central parts
of the southern and middle states on my return. A report having
prevailed previous to my commencing my journey, as scandalous
to the United States as it was to humanity, induced me to pay a
short visit to every gaol in all the cities and towns through which
I passed, when, to my great surprise and astonishment, I found
the report true; there were no less than 547 of the old continental army, who continued in the service during the whole war, confined in those dreary prisons; 327 of which had families while
they were in service; 187 have married since the establishment
of peace, and among the unhappy number, there were 63 commissioned officers, viz. 1 lieutenant-colonel, 3 majors, 11 captains, 21 lieutenants, 22 ensigns, 2 adjutants, 1 quarter-master
and 2 surgeons. Upon a strict investigation of the causes of their
detention, I found every one was for debt, having received no
pay of any value during the war. When they returned from the
victorious field of glory and honor, to the shade of private life,
with nothing to shew for the laurels they had justly acquired but
scars, infirmities and wounds, they expected to have shared at
least an equal advantage with their fellow-citizens of those blessings which their gallantry had insured to their country—but
what was their treatment? What did they receive in return for all
their services? Final settlement notes, as substitutes for their real
pay, which they kept until dire necessity, their calamities, sufferings and distressed families compelled them to part with them
from 2s.9 down to 1s.3 on the pound, which was not half equal
to the interest then due.[1] Good heavens! is this the case? Will
future posterity be made to believe that their ancestors received

such usage as this, after sealing the independence of the United States with their blood. Many stupid ignorant people say, if the army had kept their final settlements till now, they might receive their full pay; or in other words, their nominal value. Such language is an insult to common understanding. As well might the ravisher of his mistress plead innocence, as for people to make use of such foolish sordid language. It is well known that most of these brave men, in returning triumphant from the field of glory, were but in indigent circumstances, their business of every kind having lain dead for seven years, those in particular who had families, being obliged to run more in debt for their maintenance, while in service, than their whole pay would sell for at the close of the war. Is there no way to extricate these brave men from cruel confinement, and worse than Babylonian captivity? Shall the very men who were covered with scars in securing the liberty of America, loose their own liberty through the cruel, the infamous, the scandalous and perfidious injustice of that very country their swords have rescued from worse than Algerine slavery? Does justice already wear so sickly a countenance in these infant republics, that the distemper has become mortal? Shall the miserly speculator, the dark designing infamous tory, and other paracides in America, whose councils, aid, and arms during the late war, assassinated the virtuous patriot and deluged their country with the blood of its inhabitants, reap all the advantages which is due to the brave indefatigable worn out soldier? It is unnecessary for me to point out a mode for their relief; the able pens and the eloquent speeches of a Madison, a Jackson and a Wadsworth, whose names and memory will shine with unfading lustre and brilliancy, many hundreds of years after which we shall be no more (while their opposers in this most just of all causes will lay buried in obscure silence) have pointed a mode of redress for those grievances complained of, as obvious as the .sun in its meridian height.[2] It is not only this part of the army, but eight tenths of all the rest are equal sufferers, except confinement. The old army are much surprised to find that never since your circular letter to the governors of the union, and your farewel orders to them (both wrote ten years ago) that not a single public speech, nor a single address to any public body has made its appearance from you, favorable towards mitigating their sufferings.[3] Their dependence in the time of the war was not on any energy in congress, nor on any friendly disposition a great many of the community bore towards them. It was your repeated general orders to them, your positive promises, your solemn engagements to them for seven years together, and your having spontaneously assumed yourself their advocate; it was this that kept them in the field half naked, half starved, bare-foot in the middle of winter, and the cold frozen ground to lay on without a blanket, when a month's pay would not purchase a gill of whiskey. It was the almost immortal light in which they viewed you, the incomparable love they had for you, the veneration, respect and adoration they paid you, that made them encounter more distress and difficulties than any other army ever did for the rights and liberties of the human race; therefore to you General Washington, while they are experiencing worse than Gothic barbarity, they now look for relief, they have a just right so to do; of you, sir, they surely have a right to claim your influence towards the accomplishment of that justice which you so often and so solemnly pledged your word and honor as commander in chief, that they should receive; and if the ensuing congress neglects or denies doing them justice, there will be something more to fear than a breach of neutrality or western savages. The wound too often irritated may at last become incurable; and how truly awful and melancholy does it appear, to see the legislature of a nation, with impunity, look on such injustice, and wantonly make sport of the most humble entreaties and tears for justice of the bewailing widow, the distressed orphan, and the ruined, heart broken patriot. It is not only the army, but every true republican's breast in America, that pants for an end to these iniquitous, cruel and unjust sufferings. I am, sir, and hope ever shall have reason to be, with the most exalted sentiments of respect, your sincere well wisher, and obedient humble servant,

A true Friend to virtuous LIBERTY and EQUALITY.

Printed, *New-Jersey Journal* (Elizabeth), 23 Oct. 1793. This letter was reprinted in newspapers such as the *Boston Gazette*, 4 Nov.; *Norwich Packet*, 14 Nov.; and *State Gazette of South-Carolina* (Charleston), 5 Dec. 1793.

1. By an act of 4 July 1783, the Continental Congress authorized the paymaster general "to settle and finally adjust all accounts whatsoever, between the United States and the officers and soldiers of the American army. . . . And . . . give certificates of the sums which may appear due on such settlements" (*JCC*, 24:426). The certificates issued in accordance with this law by Paymaster General John Pierce bore 6 percent interest annually until the principal was paid.

2. The "mode of redress" may have been the proposal that, in the settlement of the national debt, discrimination should be made in favor of the original holders of certificates, as opposed to speculators who had acquired such certificates later. James Madison, in speeches to the House of Representatives in February 1790, appealed to "the sufferings of the military part of the creditors" to support the justice of such discrimination (*Madison Papers*, 13:36–37, 57). Congressman James Jackson of Georgia, in a speech of 28 Jan. 1790, supported such discrimination specifically in the case of final settlement certificates (*Annals of Congress*, 1st Cong., 2d sess., 1137–38). Jeremiah Wadsworth, however, opposed discrimination and contended that "the American soldiery has been well paid" and had no right to special consideration (*Annals of Congress*, 1st Cong., 2d sess., 1281–83).

3. GW's circular letter to the state governors, sent at various dates in June 1783, had endorsed the necessity of paying the debts incurred during the war, and in particular "the half pay & commutation granted by Congress to the Officers of the Army" (Df, dated 8 June 1783, DLC:GW). In GW's farewell orders to the army, delivered 2 Nov. 1783, he had written: "Nor is it possible to conceive that any one of the United States will prefer a National Bankrupcy and a dissolution of the Union, to a compliance with the requisitions of Congress and the payment of its just debts—so that the Officers and Soldiers may expect considerable assistance in recommencing their civil occupations from the sums due to them from the Public, which must and will most inevitably be paid" (Df, DLC:GW).

To the Commissioners for the District of Columbia

Gentlemen,   Philadelphia Sep: 5th 1793
    Mr Winstanley, a celebrated Landskip Painter, is disposed to take a view of the Federal City, or of the grounds in the vicinity of it. As you will be there about the time he may arrive, I take the liberty of giving him this letter of introduction to you.[1]

    His designs are more extensive—and I have suggested the Great & little Falls; the passage of the River Potomac through the Blew Mountains—the Natural bridge; &ca as grand objects. I am always Your Most Obedt Sert

                                                    Go: Washington

ALS (facsimile), UkNcU.
    1. William Winstanley (1775–1806) was an English painter of landscapes and portraits who worked in the United States from the early 1790s until around 1801. On 6 April 1793 GW paid Winstanley "for two painting of Views on the North River," which are now in the collections at Mount Vernon, and in April 1794 he purchased from Winstanley "2 large paintings" (Household Accounts, 1793–1797, PHi).

From the Commissioners for the
District of Columbia

sir,   Washington 5th Sepr 1793
   we have now before us your Letters of the 13th & 29th of last
month, the surveyor will be informed of your direction, in consequence of our Letter of the first of august and of the result of
our views with him of the two short avenues on the spot which
we intend this morning[1]—we have so good an opinion of the
probity and disinterestedness of Capn Conway and Mr David
Ross of Bladensburgh, whose christian name we suppose you
have mistaken, that we could cheerfully submit to their examination of the Accounts, but suspect Capn Conway's close attention to his own business, for which he is remarkable and his
general disinclination which has been strongly marked, to enter
into any publick affairs might totally hinder or very much delay
the proposed investigation[2]—We have no wish for any particular man Mr Hartshorn, Colo. Hooe—Colo. Gilpin or any other
Gentleman of Alexandria has not that we hear of been mixed in
the business of the City nor is interested[.][3] We have always been
of opinion that the donation or Loans from Virginia and Maryland and the other means make but one aggregate all equally
liable to be disposed of for the necessary purposes of surveying
and other expences of the City, as well as errecting the public
buildings[4] and have acted under that idea and the accounts are
so kept—We propose to shew on this investigation, that all the
money which has come to the hands of our treasurer,[5] for we
have never handled any of it ourselves, hath been expended, except what now remains that it has not been wantonly spent, and
the Vouchers will shew we have had no Favourites—These things
evinced, we shall rest easy for even if we are mistaken as to the
state money being applicable to the expences of surveying and
the like, we have only done what any others must have done, bor-
row of that money to be replaced by the sales or stop the work[.]
It would be inconvenient to the Gent. to go into this business at
our next meeting, frequent interruptions would prove very disagreeable, we would propose they should be attended by one or
more of us, and confine attention to the single object—and thus
we believe it might be finished in a few days for which we imag-

ine they ought to receive some, at least as much compensation as the Commissioners for the like time. We are &ca

Th. Johnson
Dd Stuart
Danl Carroll

LB, DNA: RG 42, Records of the Commissioners for the District of Columbia, Letters Sent, 1791–1802.

1. The commissioners' letter of 1 Aug. had conveyed a request by surveyors Benjamin Ellicott and Isaac Briggs to make alterations to the printed plan of the Federal City. GW's letter of 13 Aug. approved two of the changes but expressed doubts about the third: "to strike out two short Avenues leading from the Intersection of Massachusetts & North Carolina."

2. The D.C. commissioners had suggested an audit of their accounts in their letter to GW of 11–12 March. GW's letter of 29 Aug. suggested Alexandria merchant Richard Conway and "Major John Ross, of Bladensburg" as auditors.

3. GW appointed Robert Townsend Hooe and David Ross to examine the D.C. commissioners' accounts (GW to the D.C. Commissioners, and GW to Ross and Hooe, both 9 Sept.).

4. In 1790 the legislatures of Virginia and Maryland had agreed to advance $120,000 and $72,000, respectively, for the erection of public buildings in the federal district, the sums to be paid in three annual installments (*Va. Statutes,* 13:125; *Md. Laws 1790,* Resolutions).

5. The treasurer was William Deakins, Jr.

From Abraham Freeman

Western territory September 5th 1793

The petition of Abraham Freeman a citizen of the United States, late of the State of [N]ew[1] Jersey now of the territory of the United States North West of the river Ohio most humbly sheweth

That Whereas Doctor Clarkson Freeman late of the State of New Jersey, a son of your unfortunate petitioner in the year of our Lord one thousand seven hundred and ninety one, was impeached for aiding and assisting, in counterfeiting the public securities of the United States. And Whereas the same Doctor Clarkson Freeman, did render himself up to the hands of justice; upon which Abraham Ogden Esquire attorney general for the New Jersey district of the supreme federal court of the United States took the Examination of the said Doctor Clarkson Freeman in writing; before a magistrate, respecting the aiding and assisting in the counterfieting of the public securities and of the several accomplices therein concerned And whereas the said attorney general for the said district, did promise to secure to the said Doctor Clarkson Freeman your Excellency's most gracious pardon, if the said Doctor Clarkson Freeman would approve the said several accomplices; whereupon the different accomplices were apprehended, and bills of indictment prefered against them, by the Grand inquest of the district federal court at Trenton. And whereas the several accomplices were confined in different prisons to receive their respective trials when the honorable court should order them on And whereas afterwards the said Doctor Clarkson Freeman, was remanded back to the prison at Newark in New Jersey, to give testimony when the trials of the said accomplices should be ordered on. And whereas in the vacation of the sitting of the district federal court of New Jersey, the several accomplices, who were confined in prison, in manner aforementioned, effected their several escapes from the different prisons; and fled from justice to parts unknown, nevertheless the said Doctor Clarkson Freeman, was still held in confinement for upwards of six months as an approver, to give testimony against the several accomplices, who had already fled and was not to be found And the Attorney general for the New Jersey district federal court, still continued to withhold your excellencie's pardon by the said attorney general so promised, to the said Doctor Clarkson Freeman, until he the said Doctor Clarkson Freeman, grew weary and languid, for a long time, in prison, without receiving the benefit of the said attorney general's promised pardon. And then the said Doctor Clarkson Freeman also left his confinement, and went to canada, out of the jurisdiction of the United States; yet the said Doctor Clarkson Freeman being very desirous to return to his native home, without being in jeopardy of his life, on account of his said impeachment and become a free citizen; and subject himself to the good and wholsome laws of the United States.[2] And your petitioner begs leave further to represent, to your excellency, that in the month of April, in the year of our Lord, one thousand seven hundred and ninety two Isaac Freeman another of your petitioner's sons, was commissioned and left fort Washington, on the banks of the Ohio, by the special request and direction of brigadier General James Wilkinson, and a flag of truce in the service of the United

States, for the purpose of effecting a treaty of peace with the hostile tribes; and that the said Isaac Freeman, together with others, in pursuance of their directions, were murdered by the merciless savages, in attempting to bring about the said treaty.[3] For the truth of this representation I beg leave to refer your excellency to the Honorable Winthrop Sargent Esquire, secretary for the territory north west of the river Ohio, who will verefy the same. Therefore the promises being considered, your petitioner doth implore your excellency, in whose breast is lodged a store of, both grace and mercy to commiserate his unfortunate situation and the loss of his two sons—he being deprived of the assistance, comfort and affection of the principal branch of his family, to grant unto the said Doctor Clarkson Freeman, the benefit of your excellencies most gracious pardon that the said Doctor Clarkson Freeman, once more, may become, a citizen and free subject of the United States, should it seem meet to your excellency: and your petitioner will ever pray &ca

Abraham Freeman

Copy, DNA: RG 59, Petitions for Pardon. A note beneath the docket reads, "inclosed in Mr Ogdon's letter of 18 nov. 1795" (see Abraham Ogden to Timothy Pickering, 18 Nov. 1795, DNA: RG 59, Miscellaneous Letters).

The original petition was sent to Thomas Jefferson by Ezra Fitz Freeman (*JPP*, 245–46), and Jefferson transmitted it to GW with his letter of 5 November. Abraham Freeman (1743–1828) and his son Ezra Fitz Freeman (1771–1819) resided at this time in Hamilton County, Northwest Territory, where Ezra had been appointed in July to act as an attorney for the United States. Ezra Freeman served in that post until November 1794. By 1806 the two men apparently had moved to Butler County, Ohio.

1. The copyist wrote "Wew."

2. For Clarkson Freeman's (1764–1843) counterfeiting case, jailbreak, and attempt to receive a pardon, as well as for the role of N.J. district attorney Abraham Ogden, see John Jay to GW, 11 March 1791, and notes. GW asked Thomas Jefferson to submit this petition to N.J. district judge Robert Morris. Morris opposed a pardon but nonetheless wrote Ogden and, after receiving his reply, reported back to Jefferson that "a pardon to him is already filled up, and resting in Mr Ogdens hands. The opperation of it, under all the circumstances, will necessarily become a question before the Court, if he should ever be apprehended." Morris's letter and enclosed materials were submitted to GW, who returned them to Jefferson on 14 Dec. (*JPP*, 252, 268–69; Jefferson to Morris, 13 Nov., and Morris to Jefferson, 25 Nov. and 8 Dec., *Jefferson Papers*, 27:355, 439–43, 495).

The petition was still unanswered in April 1794 when Winthrop Sargent wrote then Secretary of State Edmund Randolph to request a reply. At that time, Randolph reported that GW "does not think proper, under the circumstances of the case, to give any further order concerning the pardon of Freeman" (Sargent to Randolph, 19 April 1794, and Randolph to Sargent, 30 April 1794, in Carter, *Territorial Papers*, 2:478–79). Ogden's letter to Pickering of 18 Nov. 1795 recommended delivery of the pardon to Freeman. Whether or not the pardon was delivered, Freeman did return: first to the Northwest Territory and then, in 1802, to Lancaster, Pa., where, with the exception of a period in Ohio from 1811 to 1815, he resided until his death.

3. Wilkinson had sent Isaac Freeman (1768–1792), an early settler at Cincinnati, with a message to the Miami Indians in April 1792. The manner of his death was later recounted to a survivor of another failed embassy headed by Maj. Alexander Trueman: "The Indian said they came across them about four days after they left Fort Washington; that they travelled with them about two days and a half, when they killed them in the following manner: First they tomahawked Mr. Joseph Gerrard, then shot the Frenchman, who was spreading out some things to dry; on which Mr. Freeman ran—that he himself shot at him and broke his arm—that he then came up with him and tomahawked him" (*Gazette of the United States* [Philadelphia], 30 March 1793).

Letter not found: to Alexander Hamilton, 5 Sept. 1793. GW wrote Hamilton on 6 Sept.: "The inclosed was written & sent to your office yesterday."

From Thomas Mifflin

Sir—   Phil: 5 Sep. 1793

I received your Excellency's communication, respecting the unfavorable issue of the negotiations for peace with the hostile Indians, in a letter from the Secretary at War, of the 3d instant;[1] and I have the honor to transmit, for your information, a copy of the orders, which I have given to the Adjutant General, for providing effectually for the protection of the Frontier of this State.[2] As I do not concieve, that the three Riffle Companies will be adequate to that object, should an actual attack be made within our territory, I have thought it proper in cases of emergency to authorize competent drafts from the Militia. I am, with perfect respect, Sir, Yr most obed. Ser.

Df, PHarH: Executive Correspondence, 1790–99; LB, PHarH: Executive Letterbooks.

1. Secretary of War Henry Knox wrote Mifflin on 3 Sept.: "I am instructed by the President of the United States to state to your Excellency, that information has this day been received by express, that notwithstanding the utmost efforts of the Commissioners, the pacific overtures to the hostile Indians north of the Ohio have been rendered abortive by their insisting upon the

Ohio as the boundary." After briefly describing the course of negotiations, including that "the tribes most determined for war, are the Wyandots, Delaware, Shawnees, and Miamis, although it is said a considerable proportion of these were for peace," and that the Six Nations had urged peace, Knox continued: "Affairs being thus circumstanced it is probable that the sword only can afford ample protection to the frontiers.

"It is understood that the militia embodied on the frontiers of Pennsylvania under your orders together with the patroles called scouts, are deemed sufficient for their defence. But it may be proper to caution the people immediately that every measure necessary to guard against surprize should be adopted" (PHarH: Executive Correspondence, 1790–99).

2. The enclosed copy of Mifflin's letter to Pennsylvania Adjt. Gen. Josiah Harmar of 4 Sept. has not been identified, although GW sent it to Knox for filing at the War Department (*JPP*, 238). Mifflin directed Harmar to "immediately transmit to the Commanding Officers of the respective Brigades of Washington, Westmoreland, Fayette and Allegheny Counties, orders for paying the strictest attention to my letters of the 18 of March & 29 May 1791; and authorising them in case of an actual invasion of the Savages, or of a well grounded apprehension of their approach, to call, either in concert, or separately, a competent draft of the Militia of their Brigades into service. You will, at the same time, instruct the Brigadiers of Washington, Allegheny and Westmoreland, to place the Riffle Companies of their respective Counties, upon the best possible footing" (PHarH: Executive Correspondence, 1790–99; see also PHarH: Executive Letterbooks).

To Robert Morris

Dear Sir,   Thursday Morning 5th Septr 1793
    The enclosed is, at Mr Powells request, returned to you; with my thanks for the perusal.[1]
    I take the liberty (and for the reason therein mentioned) to lay before you General Spotswoods letter to me respecting his Son—assuring you at the sametime that it is for the *sole* purpose of complying with his request it is done—& not that I wish, in the smallest degree to urge the request further than it may coincide entirely with your own convenience & Plans.[2] Yours always and Affectionately

                                                Go: Washington

ALS, MdAN.
    1. The enclosure has not been identified.
    2. GW was referring to Alexander Spotswood's letter of 27 Aug. 1793. Spotswood's attempt to have his son John Augustine Spotswood appointed to a berth on one of Morris's merchant ships was unsuccessful (GW to Spotswood, 3 Oct.).

George Taylor, Jr., to Bartholomew Dandridge, Jr.

Thursday 5 Septr 1793

G. Taylor Jr presents his respectful Compliments to Mr Dandridge—and informs him that Mr Jefferson desired the Commissions to be filled up agreeably to the Presidents desire on the day the present ones should determine, which will be on the 26 of the present month. This has accordingly been done having all been commissioned on that day in 1789.[1]

Will Mr Dandridge be so obliging as to send 100 Blank Sea letters? We want that number to make up the 500 per month with which we furnish the Treasury.[2]

AL, DNA: RG 59, Miscellaneous Letters; LB, DNA: RG 59, George Washington's Correspondence with His Secretaries of State.

1. This paragraph concerns new commissions for federal marshals whom the Senate had confirmed on 26 Sept. 1789 for four-year terms (see GW to U.S. Senate, 24 Sept. 1789; *JPP*, 236). Secretary of State Thomas Jefferson had written a circular letter to several of those marshals on 4 Sept. 1793 indicating GW's desire that they continue in office (DNA: RG 59, Domestic Letters).

2. GW signed and sent 102 sea letters to Jefferson on this date and an additional 715 sea letters by 9 Sept. (*JPP*, 238–39).

From William Nelson, Jr.

sir   York town Virginia Sepr 5. 1793.

As Chairman of a meeting of the Inhabitants of the County & town of York I have the honor of enclosing to you a copy of several resolutions agr⟨e⟩ed to by them. I am sir with every sentiment of Respect yr ob. servt

Wm Nelson Jr

ALS, DLC:GW; LB, DLC:GW.

Enclosure
Resolutions from the York County, Va., Citizens

[2 September 1793]

At a Meeting of the Inhabitants of the County & Borough of York, on Tuesday the 2nd day of September 1793, the following Resolutions, were enter'd into, Vizt.

1st   Resolved, That peace to a Nation is a blessing too, Valuable to be Wantonly interrupted.

2nd   Resolved, That it is peculiarly the Interest of the infant Republick of America to Cultivate peace, Agriculture & Commerce.

3rd   Resolved, That the faith of Treaties, which have for their Object, the Establishment, & continuance of peace, Ought to be held Inviolate.

4th   Resolved, That the conduct of the American Government in their Exertions to preserve peace & Neutrality in the present War of Nations, is strictly conformable to her Treaties, & ought to be Supported with firmness.[1]

5th   Resolved, That any Interference in the politicks of our country by Foreigners, more especially a public Minister, is an unprecedented indignity Offer'd to the people, and Government, derogatory to the Independency of the Nation, & shou'd Speedily recieve, its Merited disapprobation.

6th   Resolved That any attempt of any Foreign Minister to excite the people of the United States, against the Establish'd Government, because his construction of a Treaty, has been denied by that Government, is a Violation of his Mission and a daring insult to the people of America.[2]

7th   Resolved, That those Citizens of America (if any there be) who have advocated the pretensions of any Ministor, in exciting the United States of America to an unjust War, Ought to be consider'd by all good Citizens, as the lawless advocates for plunder, and disturbers of the peace of the Nation.

8th   Resolved, That we sensibly feel the Glorious cause in which France has been Engaged to establish the Liberty of the Nation. Yet, while we most ardently wish a free, equal & orderly Government to that people, we cannot but reprobate any designs to Introduce anarchy and disorder into these happy States.

9th   Resolved, That the thanks of this Meeting be presented to the President of the United States, for his patriotic exertions and commendable firmness, in promoting the happiness and Maintaining the Independency of his Country.[3]

Thos Gibbons Secty   Wm Nelson jr chairman

DS, DLC:GW; LB, DLC:GW. The DS is in the writing of Thomas Gibbons. These resolutions were printed in the *Virginia Gazette, and General Advertiser* (Richmond), 11 September.

1. GW issued a proclamation on 22 April declaring the United States neutral in the war between France and a coalition of European nations led by Great Britain. For the applicable treaties between France and the United States, see Miller, *Treaties,* 3–44.

2. For the reports that Edmond Genet, the French minister to the United States, intended to excite the American people against the government, see Genet to GW, 13 Aug., and n.4 to that document.

3. GW responded to these resolutions in a letter to William Nelson, Jr., of 23 September.

To John Eccleston

Sir,   Philada 6th Septr 1793.

By the post of Wednesday last, I enclosed you an answer to an address of the Landholders & other citizens of the county of Dorchester.[1]

An answer to this address had been before transmitted to you; and the address having, without my knowledge, been put into the hands of Mr Murray, on it's being returned, received a second answer, without my adverting to the circumstance of it's being already answered.[2] This explanation will be sufficient to show you, why two answers were given to the same Address. I am Sir &c.

Go. Washington

LB, DLC:GW.

1. See GW to Eccleston, 4 Sept., and n.1.

2. Neither the transmittal of the address to Maryland Congressman William Vans Murray nor Murray's return of the address to GW has been identified. GW's earlier answer to the address was published in the *Gazette of the United States* (Philadelphia), 4 Sept.: "YOUR approbation of the measure which I have taken to declare to the world the Neutrality of the United States, towards the belligerent powers of Europe, gives me sincere pleasure. And it is no less pleasing to me to observe the disposition which you manifest to preserve our country in a state of peace, as the only means of promoting our national prosperity, and ensuring a continuance of those blessings which our country enjoys in an eminent degree."

To Alexander Hamilton

My dear Sir,   Philadelphia Septr 6th 1793

With extreme concern I receive the expression of your apprehensions, that you are in the first Stages of the prevailing fever.

I hope they are groundless, notwithstanding the malignancy of the disorder is so much abated, as with proper & timely applications, not much is to be dreaded.[1]

The enclosed was written & sent to your Office yesterday, with direction if you were not there, to be brought back. And it would be a very pleasing circumstance if a change so entirely favourable as to justify it, would permit your attendance, & to bring Mrs Hamilton with you, to dine with us at three Oclock.[2] I am always & Affectly Yours

Go: Washington

ALS (photocopy), Kenneth W. Rendell, Inc., catalog 106 (c.1975), item 71; copy, DLC: Alexander Hamilton Papers.

1. No written communication by Hamilton informing GW that he had contracted yellow fever has been identified. By 11 Sept., when Hamilton wrote a public letter extolling his physician, he considered himself "compleatly out of danger" (*Hamilton Papers*, 15:331–32).

2. The enclosed letter from GW to Hamilton of 5 Sept. has not been found, but it probably was a form of the dinner invitation mentioned in this letter. Elizabeth Schuyler Hamilton (1757–1854), a daughter of Gen. Philip Schuyler, had married Hamilton in 1780.

Letter not found: from Thomas Jefferson, 6 Sept. 1793. GW wrote Jefferson on 7 Sept.: "I have received your letter of yesterday's date."

Henry Knox's Report on Military Preparations, with Cabinet Opinion

War Department September 6. 1793.

The Secretary of War humbly reports to the President of the United States

That the following measures appear necessary to be taken in order in some degree to place the United States in a situation to guard themselves from injury by any of the belligerent powers of Europe.

1st To have all the small arms of the United States put in order for immediate use.

2dly To have all the cannon in possession of the United States whether for the field or for batteries, either new mounted or repaired as the case may require.

3d To purchase one hundred tons of Lead.

4th   To purchase one hundred tons of Saltpetre or the equivalent in Gun powder.

5th   To have the useless brass cannon in the arsenal at Springfield cast into field pieces, and to have the same mounted.

6th   To engage one thousand rifles to be made.[1]

7th   To remove the surplus arms and stores from Philadelphia to Trenton.[2]

8th   To remove the surplus stores from West point to Albany.[3]

9th   To make certain repairs at Forts Putnam, and Clinton at West point on Hudson's river, so as to prevent its being surprized or insulted.[4]

Most of these measures have been put in train in pursuance of certain verbal directions from the President of the United States, but the subscriber humbly conceives it proper to submit a connected view thereof for his approbation, as it will be necessary to prepare estimates of the expences attendant thereon, in order to be laid before the next session of Congress.[5] All which is respectfully submitted.

H. Knox secy of War

We are of opinion that the preceding measures should be carried into effect.[6]

Th: Jefferson
Edm: Randolph

DS, DLC:GW.

1. This suggestion may have been related to a proposed expedition to "punish" the Creek Indians and secure the southwestern frontier. In a meeting with Knox on 24 July, Gen. Andrew Pickens of South Carolina suggested that the army for that purpose should include "One thousand good riflemen," although he thought that the rifles "might with difficulty be collected upon the frontiers" (see the enclosure in Knox to GW, 25 July).

2. Knox's return of ordnance, arms, and military stores, submitted to GW on 14 Dec. and to the Senate on 16 Dec., included ordnance and stores at Philadelphia (*ASP, Military Affairs,* 1:50–52).

3. Knox's letter to GW, 14 Dec., states that the surplus stores had been "removed temporarily."

4. In Knox's "Estimate of the Expenses of the War Department, for the Year One thousand, Seven hundred and Ninety four," 10 Dec. 1793, he suggested an appropriation of $10,000 for "Repairs of Fortifications at West-Point" (DNA: RG 233, Reports of the Treasury Department, 2nd Congress, 2nd Session–4th Congress, 1st Session, 4:104–15). By the summer of 1794,

repairs had begun on Fort Putnam and were in contemplation for Fort Clinton (see *ASP: Military Affairs,* 1:104).

5. In December, when Knox made the "Estimate of the Expenses" for 1794, he included appropriations for most of these items among "the following enumerated buildings, repairs, and articles, directed to be made and purchased by the President of the United States." In the War Department appropriation approved on 21 March 1794, Congress included $202,783.34 "For repairs and articles directed to be made and purchased by the President of the United States" (1 *Stat.* 346–47).

6. The preceding sentence is in Thomas Jefferson's writing. Alexander Hamilton probably was absent because of illness (see GW to Hamilton, this date).

From Jeremiah Banning

sir,   Easton, Maryland, Septr 7th 1793.

I am injoined by such of the Citizens of Talbot County as were present at a Meeting held this day at Easton, to communicate to you the inclosed Resolutions; and at the same time to express to you their Esteem and Attachment to your person, and their heartfelt Wishes for your constant Health and Happiness. I accordingly comply with their Injunction; and in the Execution of this Office I feel the most distinguished pleasure. I have the Honor to be, Sir, Your most obedient servant,

Jeremiah Banning chairman

ALS, DLC:GW; LB, DLC:GW. The cover for this letter, which was sent "Free" by "mail," is marked "Easton, Sept. 8." The letter was published in the *Maryland Herald, and Eastern Shore Intelligencer* (Easton), 15 October.

Jeremiah Banning (1733–1798), a merchant, served as a colonel in the Talbot County militia during the Revolutionary War and as a justice for Talbot County from 1778 to 1789. Banning also represented Talbot County at Maryland's convention to ratify the U.S. Constitution in 1788. He was at this time collector of the customs and inspector of the port at Oxford, Md., having been appointed to those posts by GW in 1789 and 1791 (the latter submitted and confirmed in 1792).

Enclosure
Resolutions from the Talbot County, Md., Citizens

[7 September 1793]

At a Meeting of the Citizens of Talbot County held at Easton on Saturday the 7th day of September instant, in consequence of a previous Notification in "the Maryland Herald," for the purpose of expressing their Sense of the Duty & Interest of their Country in observing a strict Neutrality with the powers at war, & their Opinion of such measures as have been taken upon that subject—Jeremiah Banning Esqr. was chosen Chairman.[1]

Whereupon a Committee of five Citizens was appointed to draught a set of suitable resolutions expressive of the Sentiments of the Meeting. The Committee accordingly retired, and after some time return'd, and reported the following resolutions; which were proposed to the Citizens assembled, duly considered by them, and unanimously adopted.

Resolved that the Citizens assembled are deeply impressed with the Excellence of their General Government, and are fully persuaded that the happiness & prosperity enjoyed by the United States proceed from the administration thereof.

Resolved that in the Opinion of the Citizens assembled it is unquestionably the Duty and Interest of the people of the United States to observe a friendly and impartial Conduct, and a strict Neutrality, with all the powers now at War in Europe.

Resolved that the Proclamation of Neutrality issued by the President of the United States was, in the Opinion of the Citizens assembled, a measure flowing from Wisdom and sound Policy, and a constitutional Act; and that the great and good George Washington, the said President, hath proved himself upon that Occasion, as he hath upon all others of a public Nature, the FRIEND of the People.[2]

Resolved that the Governor and Council of Maryland, by their prompt and timely promulgation of the said proclamation, injoining it upon the Citizens of this State to observe a friendly and impartial Conduct, & a strict Neutrality, with the powers at war, have entitled themselves to the thanks and approbation of the people.[3]

Resolved that, in the Opinion of the Citizens assembled, every person whatsoever, who censures the Conduct of the President in issuing the said proclamation, or who, directly or indirectly, endeavors to involve the United States into a participation of the War, is inimical to the Interests and happiness of this Country; and that all lawful means ought to be exerted to bring to his merited punishment every Citizen who shall in any manner infringe the Neutrality of the United States.

Resolved that the people of the United States, in the Opinion of the Citizens assembled, are fully competent to the management of their own Affairs, and that they detest the Idea of all foreign Influence upon the Government thereof: Wherefore the Citizens assembled consider the Interference of Foreigners, whatever Character they may bear, in the measures of the administration, either by joining with ill-disposed Societies, or by intriguing with Individuals, for the purpose of thwarting such measures, or otherwise, except in a course established by the Usage of Nations, as injurious and insulting to the Government and people of the United States, and as meriting their most public Contempt.[4]

Resolved that the Citizens assembled are ready and willing, with their Lives and Fortunes, to support the Government of the United States as established by the people, and every wise and constitutional Act of the Administration, and to defend their common Country against all secret and traitorous Conspiracies, and against all external Hostilities: But while they are thus disposed to support the just and lawful measures of their Government, they at the same time declare, that they will not tamely suffer a Departure from those principles, which promoted the freedom & Independence of the people.

Resolved that the foregoing Resolutions be communicated by the Chairman to the President of the United States, accompanied by Expressions of our Esteem and Attachment to his person, and of our heartfelt Wishes for his constant Health and happiness.[5] By Order of the Meeting,

Jeremiah Banning Chairman.

DS, DLC:GW; LB, DLC:GW. These resolutions were printed in the *Maryland Herald, and Eastern Shore Intelligencer* (Easton), 10 September.

1. The notification, dated 1 Sept., was printed in the *Maryland Herald, and Eastern Shore Intelligencer,* 3 September.

2. GW issued the Neutrality Proclamation on 22 April.

3. Thomas Jefferson enclosed a copy of GW's Neutrality Proclamation in his circular letter to the state governors of 26 April (*Jefferson Papers,* 25:588– 89), and the proclamation was published in Maryland newspapers by 2 May. On 4 May, Maryland governor Thomas Sim Lee issued a proclamation "with the advice and consent of the council . . . earnestly exhorting the good people of this state to observe the peaceable and impartial conduct recommended as aforesaid by the President of the United States, and I do further enjoin all the officers of this state to be zealous and active in discouraging all proceedings

that may be inconsistent with the pacific disposition announced as aforesaid, and endanger the happy state of tranquillity which this country at present enjoys" (*Maryland Gazette* [Annapolis], 9 May).

4. In the spring and summer of 1793, a number of societies were formed in support of the French cause. The most influential of these societies, the Democratic Society of Pennsylvania, issued a circular letter on 4 July setting out their view of the national interest and asking their fellow citizens to join them in a "constant correspondence" on the subject: "Every mind capable of reflection, must perceive, that the present crisis in the politics of nations is peculiarly interesting to America. The European confederacy, transcendent in power, and unparalleled in iniquity, menaces the very existence of freedom. Already its baneful operation may be traced in the tyrannical destruction of the constitution, and the rapacious partition of the territory of Poland: and should the glorious efforts of France be eventually defeated, we have reason to presume, that for the consummation of monarchial ambition, and the security of its establishments, this country, the only remaining depository of liberty, will not long be permitted to enjoy in peace the honors of an independent, and the happiness of a republican government.

"Nor are the dangers arising from a foreign source the only causes, at this time, of apprehension and solicitude. The seeds of luxury appear to have taken root in our domestic soil; and the jealous eye of patriotism already regards the spirit of freedom and equality, as eclipsed by the pride of wealth, and the arrogance of power.

"This general view of our situation has led to the institution of the Democratic Society. A constant circulation of useful information, and a liberal communication of republican sentiments, were thought to be the best antidotes to any political poison, with which the vital principles of civil liberty might be attacked: For, by such means a fraternal confidence will be established among the citizens; every symptom of innovation will be studiously marked; and a standard will be erected, to which, in danger and distress, the friends of liberty may successfully resort.

"To obtain these objects, then, and to cultivate on all occasions the love of peace, order and harmony, an attachment to the constitution, and a respect to the laws of our country, will be the aim of the Democratic Society. Party and personal considerations are excluded from a system of this nature; for in the language of the articles under which we are united, men and measures will only be estimated according to their intrinsic merits, and their influence in promoting the prosperity of the state" (*Pennsylvania Gazette* [Philadelphia], 17 July).

The Talbot County resolution was aimed at those Democratic Societies and what opponents saw as the related activities of Edmond Genet, the French minister to the United States.

5. GW responded to these resolutions in his letter to Banning of 16 Sept.: "The approbation which the administration of the general Government has met from my fellow Citizens throughout these States cannot fail to excite in me the liveliest satisfaction; & the assurances given by them of their firm

intentions to unite in keeping our Country in a state of peace at this important moment, is an additional & pleasing testimony of the unanimity & good sense of the Citizens of the U. States.

"While I beg you to assure the Citizens of Talbot, of the reliance I place on their disposition towards the general Government, manifested in the resolutions, I also request you to make known to them the pleasure I receive from their expressions of esteem & attachment for my person; & to you, Sir, for your polite manner of transmitting these resolutions, my best thanks are offered" (LB, DLC:GW).

Cabinet Opinion on Relations with France and Great Britain

At a meeting at the Presidents   Sep. 7. 1793.

A circular letter from the Secretary of state to the Consuls & Vice Consuls of France, informing them that their Exequaturs will be revoked if they repeat certain proceedings, also one to mister Genet covering a copy of the letter of the Secretary of state to mister Gouverneur Morris desiring the recall of mister Genet, were recd & approved.[1]

A letter from the Governr of Georgia to the Secy of state dated Aug. 21. 1793 was read, communicating the demand by the Vice Consul of France in Georgia of certain individuels under prosecution in a court of justice. it is the opinion that he be answered that the law must take it's course.[2]

A Memorial from mister Hammond dated Sep. 6. complaining of the capture of the British brig the William Tell by the French brig le Cerf, within the limits of the protection of the U.S. and the refusal of the French minister & Consul to have the prize delivered into the hands of a marshal charged with process from a court to arrest her, was recd. it is the opinion that a letter be written to mr Genet calling for evidence in the cases of the vessels heretofore reclaimed & not yet finally decided on, & which were permitted to remain in the hands of the French Consuls in the meantime, informing him that the letter of June 25. was not intended to authorize opposition to the officers, or orders, of courts respecting vessels taken within the limits of our protection. that therefore the brig William Tell ought to be delivered into the hands of the officer charged to arrest her, and that in the event of the court's deciding that it has no jurisdiction of the case, as in that of the ship William whereon the letter of June 25. was written, she may again be replaced in the Consul's hands till the Executive shall have decided thereon.[3]

A letter from Lt Govr Wood dated Aug. 29. stating that the French vessel the Orion was arrived in Norfolk & had brought in the Sans Culottes as a prize, and doubting whether from the particular circumstances of this prize she came within the generel orders heretofore given. it is the opinion that the situation of the Sans culottes is the same in respect to England & France as any other French vessel not fitted in our ports, and therefore that the Orion is within the 17th article of our treaty & the rules heretofore given on the subject.[4]

A Memorial from mister Hammond dated Sep. 4 was recd complaining of the long stay of a French fleet in New-York, that a regular succession of them appears to be appointed for cruizing on the coasts, that a jurisdiction over prizes is exercised by the French Consuls, and desiring to be informed whether it be the intention of the Executive to permit this indefinitely. it is the opinion that mister Hammond be informed that effectual measures are taken to put an end to the exercise of admiralty jurisdiction by the French Consuls, that the French have by treaty a right to come into our ports with their prizes, exclusively, that they have also a right by treaty to enter our ports for any urgent necessity, that this right is exclusive as to privateers but not so as to public vessels of war and has therefore not been denied to British ships of war nor has the Executive as yet prescribed to either any limits to the time they may remain in their ports.[5]

A letter from mister Bordman at Boston dated Sep. 4 was recd complaining of the capture of the schooner Flora an American vessel by the Roland, one of the illicit privateers. it is the opinion he must seek redress in the courts of law.[6]

The draught of a letter to mister Pinckney on the Additional instructions of the court of St James's dated June 8. 93 was read and approved.[7]

A Question was proposed by the President Whether we ought not to enquire from mister Hammond if he is prepared to give an answer on the subject of the inexecution of the treaty? it is the opinion that it will be better to await the arrival of the next packet, then to make the application to mister Hammond, and if he be not prepared to answer, that mister Pinckney be instructed to remonstrate on the subject to the British court.[8]

Th: Jefferson
H. Knox.
Edm: Randolph

DS, in Thomas Jefferson's writing, DLC:GW; Df (partial), in Jefferson's writing, DLC: Jefferson Papers. The Df is a slightly different version of the last sentence of the fifth paragraph.

1. Jefferson's circular of this date to the consuls and vice-consuls noticed that "they claim, and are exercising, within the United States a general admiralty jurisdiction, and in particular assume to try the validity of prizes, and to give sentence thereon as Judges of Admiralty; and moreover that they are undertaking to give Commissions within the United States, and to enlist, or encourage the enlistment of men, natives or inhabitants of these States, to commit hostilities on nations with whom the United States are at peace." He then gave notice, "in charge from the President of the United States . . . that if any of them shall commit any of the acts beforementioned, or assume any jurisdiction not expressly given by the Convention between France and the United States, the Exequater of the Consul so transgressing, will be immediately revoked, and his person be submitted to such prosecutions and punishments as the laws may prescribe for the case" (*Jefferson Papers,* 27:51).

Jefferson's letter to Genet of this date complained of Genet's failure to restrain the consuls, but its primary purpose was to inform Genet that "the acts which you have thought proper to do, and to countenance, in opposition to the laws of the land, have rendered it necessary in the opinion of the President to lay a faithful statement of them before the government of France, to explain to them the reasons and the necessity which have dictated our measures," which "has accordingly been directed to be done" in Jefferson's letter to Gouverneur Morris of 16 August. Jefferson added that the executive would "admit the continuance of your functions so long as they shall be restrained within the limits of the law" (*Jefferson Papers,* 27:52–53).

For the letter to Morris, which detailed the administration's dissatisfaction with Genet and directed Morris to "Lay the case then immediately before his government," see *Jefferson Papers,* 26:697–715. For the approval of that document, see Cabinet Opinion, 23 Aug., and notes.

2. For Gov. Edward Telfair's letter to Jefferson concerning the case of Capt. Joseph Riviere and his lieutenants of the French privateer *Anti-George,* and Jefferson's reply of 9 Sept., see *Jefferson Papers,* 26:736–37, 27:73–74. John Brickell had requested their release as the vice-consul of France at Savannah, but Jefferson's reply denied that Brickell had any such standing. Brickell was probably John Brickell (1749–1809), a physician and amateur botanist. For a report of the men's trial in November, at which they were found not guilty, see the *Georgia Gazette* (Savannah), 5 December.

3. British minister George Hammond's memorial is printed in *Jefferson Papers,* 27:44–46. The *William Tell,* out of Dominica, was taken on 29 Aug. and

sent to New York. Jefferson's letter to Genet of 25 June, which said that "vessels suggested to be taken within the limits of the protection of the united States" by French privateers "should be detained under the orders of yourself or of the Consuls of France in the several ports, until the Government of the united States shall be able to inquire into and decide on the fact" (*Jefferson Papers*, 26:358), was Genet's authority for his refusal to deliver the *William Tell* to the marshal. For the 21 June decision of the U.S. District Court of Pennsylvania that it lacked jurisdiction in the similar case of the British ship *William*, seized by the French privateer *Citoyen Genet* and brought to Philadelphia, see *Federal Cases*, 9:57–62. Jefferson wrote to Genet, as indicated, on 9 Sept. (*Jefferson Papers*, 27:67–69).

4. For the letter from Virginia lieutenant governor James Wood to Jefferson, see *Jefferson Papers*, 26:787. Jefferson here mistakenly calls the *Orion* a "French vessel," but it was a British warship. Article 17 of the Treaty of Amity and Commerce between France and the United States (1778) forbade American ports from offering refuge to foreign ships that had captured French vessels, confiscated their cargoes, or detained French citizens (Miller, *Treaties*, 16–17). The French privateer *Sans Culotte*, however, had been ordered to depart American ports (see the cabinet opinions on French privateers of 1 and 17 June). On the "rules" to which Jefferson is referring, transmitted to the state governors by a circular letter from Henry Knox of 7 Aug., see Cabinet Opinion on the Rules of Neutrality, 3 August.

5. For Hammond's memorial of 4 Sept., see *Jefferson Papers*, 27:30–32. The exclusive rights of French privateers derived from articles 17 and 22 of the 1778 Treaty of Amity and Commerce, while article 19 gave French ships the right to enter for any urgent necessity (Miller, *Treaties*, 16–20). Jefferson addressed these issues in his letter to Hammond of 9 Sept., which also pointed out that the French fleet docked at New York since early August had brought refugees from Saint Domingue and was no threat to British commerce (*Jefferson Papers*, 27:70–72).

6. The letter from William Bordman, probably Capt. William Bordman, Jr., who chartered ships and sold goods from an office at No. 10 Butler's Row in Boston, has not been identified. Jefferson's summary journal of letters indicates that the letter was actually dated 29 Aug. and received on 4 Sept. (DLC: Jefferson Papers; see also *Jefferson Papers*, 27:50). For discussion of the *Roland*, see Cabinet Opinion, 31 Aug., and n.2 to that document. The *Flora*, a schooner from Nova Scotia, was advertised for condemnation at Boston on 23 Aug. (*Independent Chronicle: and the Universal Advertiser* [Boston], 26 Aug). The *Columbian Centinel* (Boston), 18 Sept., reported that the ship would be returned to her owners "by order of the Supreme Executive of the United States."

7. Jefferson's letter to Thomas Pinckney, the U.S. minister to Great Britain, 7 Sept., protested new British rules governing the treatment of neutral merchant vessels sailing to nations unfriendly to Great Britain. The protest was "provisionally written only," as the copy of the rules of 8 June discussed in the cabinet meeting of 31 Aug. had not been authenticated (*Jefferson Papers*, 27:55–59).

8. Jefferson had written Hammond on 19 June 1793, requesting a reply to his letter of 29 May 1792 regarding the nonexecution of the 1783 Treaty of Paris (*Jefferson Papers*, 26:322, 23:551–613). With GW's approval, Jefferson again wrote Hammond on 13 Nov. to request a reply (see Record of Cabinet Opinions, 22 Nov., and *Jefferson Papers*, 27:353).

To Thomas Jefferson

Sir,   Philadelphia 7 Septr 1793
    I have received your letter of yesterday's date,[1] and approving the measures sugg[e]sted therein, desire you will make arrangements for carrying them into effect with as little loss of time as may be.

                                                Go: Washington

LB, DNA: RG 59, George Washington's Correspondence with His Secretaries of State.
    1. Jefferson's letter to GW of 6 Sept. has not been found.

From D'Acary

                                    philadelphie le 8—7bre 1793.
    d'Acary ler Lieutenant Colonel du 15e Regiment d'infanterie française demende a Son exellence le General Washington la permission de lui aller offrir ces respectueux homages et prendre ces ordres pour france ou il va Se rendre et come le Navire Sur lequel il S'embarque part demain il desire que Son exelence veuilt bien lui accorder un moment d'audience aujourdhuit.

AL, DLC:GW. This document is docketed in part, "Complimentary"; no reply has been found.

From George Clinton

Sir   New York 8th September 1793.
    I have now the honor of transmitting to you, a Copy of a corespondence with the Minister of the Republic of France, relative to the two french Privateers, mentioned in your last as having arrived in this Port, and also respecting a British Brigantine lately sent in here as a Prize alledged to have been captured

within the territoria⟨l⟩ Jurisdiction of the United States, by the
Cerf a French Corvette.[1] In ⟨the⟩ latter case I presume nothing
more is expected of me, than to give notice to the French Consul of the allegations made respecting the circumstances of the
capture. But as the measures proposed with respect to the privateers by the Minister cannot be considered as a direct compliance with your ⟨re⟩quisition in such cases, and yet as it may probably be deemed satisfactory I conceive it proper to suspend any
further proceedings respecting them until I shall receive your
advice on this Subject.[2] I am &c.

G: C.

LB, N-Ar, Papers of George Clinton.

1. It was Clinton's last letter to GW (of 2 Sept.), not GW's last letter to him,
that mentioned the two French privateers.

Clinton's letter to Edmond Genet of 3 Sept. stated GW's determination
that "the fitting out of Privateers or Cruisers by any of the Parties now at
War in any of the Ports of the United States" was "incompatible with our
present state of Neutrality," and that the commanding officers of the *Petite
Democrat* and *Carmagnole* "will receive your directions immediately to depart
with their said vessels from this Port." Clinton added, "it has been alledged to
me that a British Brigantine called the William Tell lately sent into this Port
as a Prize to the French Corvet the Cerf was captured within the Territorial
Jurisdiction of the United States—It is therefore expected that the said Prize
will remain in the Possession of the Consul of your Republic conformably to
your Agreement with the General Government of the United States until the
President shall have decided thereon" (DLC: Genet Papers).

Genet's reply, the letter-book copy and draft of which are dated 6 Sept.,
informed Clinton that the *Petite Démocrat,* "taken by the Ambuscade, entered
Philadelphia already armed," while the *Carmagnole* "was indeed fitted out in
the Ports of the United States ⟨in⟩ virtue of our treaties." Genet claimed that
he had already conformed "as much as was in my power" to GW's decision
"by advising the captains of those vessels, to deliver to me their commissions,
for cruising against the enemies of my coun⟨try *mutilated*⟩ they have complied
with my council, and henceforth the Petit Democrat and the Carmagnole,
shall be employed as advice Boats. I have defended as long as I was able, the
incontestible right of the Fren⟨ch⟩ Republic, to fit out armed vessels in the
Ports of the United States, by virtue of the treaties of commerce and Alliance subsisting betwee⟨n⟩ the two Nations. It now belongs to my country to
direct me what course I am finally to pursue. it belongs to the French nation
⟨to⟩ determine whether, to the sacrifices they have already made to you⟨r⟩
country, they ought to add that of renouncing a right, the Exerc⟨ise⟩ of which
alarms the Politics of your government, and makes it a⟨ppre⟩hensive of being
suspected of acting an underhand part, in ⟨*the war*⟩ of Liberty. I heartily wish,
Sir, that this mark of weakness may not draw on your Country those verry
Calamities which it design⟨ed⟩ to ward off, and it is my further wish that this

may be the only answer of my fellow Citizens, to the proceedings which have so long ⟨excited⟩ my complaints." As for the *William Tell,* it would "remain in the possession of the consul of France in this Port until the President of the United States explains what he means by a line of protection by that territorial Jurisdiction so often apealed to by the agents of our Enemies, to cause our Prizes to be taken from us, even by our freinds," but, Genet protested, "I think one ought not speak of protection and Jurisdiction until one is able to protect a⟨nd⟩ render effectual Justice to all" (LB, N-Ar: Papers of George Clinton; where that document is mutilated, text is supplied by translation from the draft, in French, in DLC: Genet Papers).

2. This letter was received by GW on 14 Sept., and GW wrote Secretary of War Henry Knox on 16 Sept. to give directions about a proper answer. However, no reply was sent until 15 Nov., when Knox wrote Clinton that the "malady which lately raged in the city of Philadelphia" had "hitherto prevented an answer being given to your Excellencys letter of the 8th of September last to the President of the United States which with its enclosures were duly received". Knox informed Clinton that withdrawal of the privateering commissions of the *Petite Democrate* and *Carmagnole* "was not the only measure which our neutrality requires of us," and directed, "If therefore those vessels should again come into our ports, it is conceived to be our duty, that La petite Democrate should be reduced to her force at the time she was sent in as a prize to the Ambuscade, and the La Carmagnole should be entirely divested of her warlike equipments" (PHi: Conarroe Collection).

To the Commissioners for the District of Columbia

Gentlemen, Philda Sepr 9th 1793.

I have duly received your Letter of Septm. 5th and in consequence thereof have Authorised Mr David Ross of Bladensburg & Colo. Robert Townsend Hooe of Alexandria to examine the accounts and Vouchers of the expenditure of the monies appropriated to your trust as Commissioners of the publick buildings of the Federal Territory & to certify to me the result.[1] With esteem, I am Gent. your most Obt Hon. Servt,

Go. Washington

LB, DNA: RG 42, Records of the Commissioners for the District of Columbia, Letters Sent, 1791–1802; Df, in Thomas Jefferson's writing, DLC:GW; LB, DLC:GW.

1. See GW to Ross and Hooe, 9 September. For the results of the audit, see Hooe and Ross to GW, 31 Oct. (see also D.C. Commissioners to GW, 3 Nov.).

From Alexander Contee Hanson

Sir,   Annapolis Septr 9, 1793

Having been informed, that the place of collector for the port of Annapolis will shortly be vacant, by the resignation of Mr Davidson, I take the liberty of recommending Mr Burton Whetcroft, as his successor.[1] The very high opinion I entertain of this gentlemans merit has prompted me to advise him to become a candidate for an office, which will be compatible with his present employment of assistant, a principal clerk to the register of the court of chancery in Maryland, which he has held for more than eight years. During a great part of that time, he has conducted the whole business of the office, with perfect ability, with an attention and assiduity, which I have never known to be excelled, and with the approbation of all, with whom he has been concerned. Permit me, Sir, to assure you, that, in my opinion, his qualifications, behaviour, and reputation, are such, as might amply justify his appointment to a much higher office, than the one he sollicits; and that many of the most respectable citizens of Annapolis would be gratified by his success.

I cannot, Sir, forbear to add a circumstance, which, I am persuaded, will plead in his behalf. Altho' his income might be supposed hardly adequate for himself, an amiable wife, and an infant family,[2] he has, for a considerable time past, entirely maintained both his aged parents, who have been reduced, solely by misfortune, from a comfortable and decent situation, to rely on his filial gratitude and affection. I have the honour to be, Sir, with the most profound veneration Your obedient Servant,

                                                    A.C. Hanson

ALS, DLC:GW. Hanson was chancellor of Maryland.

1. Burton Whetcroft (c.1753–1822) was clerk of the Maryland Court of Appeals, 1795–1805, and mayor of Annapolis, 1807–8, 1809–10. On 23 Nov., GW wrote a commission for Robert Denny as collector of Annapolis, but Denny declined the appointment. GW then filled the post with John Randall (*JPP,* 257; GW to U.S. Senate, 27 Dec.).

2. Elizabeth Knapp (c.1759–1809) married Whetcroft in 1789; their only daughter, Frances E. Whetcroft, married Satterlee Clark in 1810.

From Moses Hazen

Dear Sir, New York September 9th 1793

I am encouraged by politeness to address Your Excellency on the present occasion—As I cannot be heard by the Legislature of America by memorials I must seek some other method—The secretary of the Treasury may possibly be able to account for his conduct towards me, to his superiors.[1]

I am sorry to find that those words in Your Excellency's speach at the oppening of the last Session works so great an evil to me and some Officers of my late Regiment, vizt "certain foreign Officers"—I do not find them to be approved of by any Act of the Senate, or Law of the Union.[2] I have the honour to be, Dr Sir Your most obedt humble servant

Moses Hazen

ALS, DLC:GW.

1. In 1789 Hazen sent a memorial to GW requesting compensation for his service as an officer in the Continental Army. GW forwarded Hazen's memorial to Alexander Hamilton, but the issue remained unresolved (Tobias Lear to Hamilton, 18 Dec. 1789). Hazen then submitted a petition on behalf of himself and Andrew Lee to the U.S. House of Representatives, which on 29 March 1790 considered Hazen's appeal for "a settlement of certain claims against the United States, as officers in the late army." The House requested a report from Hamilton, whose response, read in the House on 9 Aug. 1790, has not been identified. Hazen's 1791 memorial to the House also met with failure, and Hazen died in 1803 without seeing the resolution of his claims (*Journal of the House,* 2:67, 69, 207; 4:28, 61). Although the U.S. Congress granted a pension of $200 per year to his widow, Charlotte Hazen, in 1805, Hazen's heirs and legal representatives continued to submit claims to Congress as late as 1830 asking indemnification for Hazen's loss of British half-pay (as promised in a resolution of 22 Jan. 1776) and for Hazen's disbursements for the army in Canada. Bills to indemnify for half-pay were passed on 26 May 1828 and 3 March 1832 (6 *Stat.* 56, 392, 466; S. Doc. 4, 21st Cong., 2d sess., Serial 203).

2. In GW's address to the U.S. Senate and House, 6 Nov. 1792, he stated that "Among the Objects to which" funds obtained through three new loans "have been directed to be applied, the payment of the debts due to certain foreign Officers, according to the provision made during the last Session, has been embraced." For that provision, see 1 *Stat.* 281–83. For discussion of the payment of the U.S. debt to foreign officers who fought in the Revolutionary War, see Hamilton to GW, 27 Aug. 1792, and notes 1 and 2, and 22 Sept. 1792, and note 7. Hazen had commanded the 2d Canadian Regiment.

From Thomas Jefferson

Sep. 9. 1793.

Th: Jefferson with his respects to the President has the honor to inclose him draughts of letters to mister Genet & mister Hammond, as agreed on Saturday. if Genl Knox & the Attorney Genl should wait on the President to-day, it would be well they should see them.[1] Th: J. will have that honour before he leaves town.

AL, DNA: RG 59, Miscellaneous Letters; LB, DNA: RG 59, George Washington's Correspondence with His Secretaries of State.

1. The drafts of Jefferson's letters to Edmond Genet and George Hammond, both of this date, are now signed "Approved H. Knox" (DLC: Jefferson Papers; see also *Jefferson Papers,* 27:67–72). For the agreement on their content, see Cabinet Opinion, 7 Sept., and notes 3 and 5.

To Henry Knox

(Private)
Dr Sir,   Philadelphia Sepr 9th 1793.

It was the opinion of the Gentlemen at their meeting on Saturday last if I mistake not, that Mr Wolcott should be desired to request Mr Webster to substantiate the language of the Minister of the French Republic as related by him in the enclosed letter.[1]

Colo. Hamilton's situation—for which I feel extreme regret—does not permit his having any agency in the matter at present;[2] I therefore send the letter which he forwarded to me from Mr Webster to Mr Wolcott to your care, being persuaded that whatever measure shall be deemed right & proper[3] will be put in train by you.

I think it would not be prudent either for you or the Clerks in your Office, or the Office itself to be too much exposed to the malignant fever, which by well authenticated report, is spreading through over the City; The means to avoid your own judgment under existing circumstances must dictate.

As the spreading & continuance of the disorder may render it unadvisable for me to return to this City as soon I at first intended, I wd thank you, in case you should remain in the vicinity of it to write me a line by every Monday's Post informing me concisely of the then state of Matters—with other occurrences which may be essential for me to be made acquainted with.[4]

And I would thank you also for your advice to Mr Fraunces or Mrs Emmerson (the House keeper) if, by means of the Disorder my Household Affairs in this City should be involved in any delicacy.[5]

I sincerely wish, & pray, that you & yours, may escape untouched and when we meet again that it may be under circumstances more pleasing than the present—I am always and very sincerely Yr Affecte

Go: Washington

ADfS, DLC:GW; LB, DLC:GW.

1. GW presumably was referring to the cabinet meeting on 7 September. The enclosed letter has not been identified. However, Comptroller of the Treasury Oliver Wolcott, Jr., wrote Noah Webster on 19 Sept., "I recd your Letter containing an account of Genets conversation & gave it to one of the heads of departments—it has been considered and the subject is considered as one which will warrant Notice.... I wish therefore ... that you would ... make out & transmit your affidavit, of the purport of the Conversation alluded to."

Webster responded with an affidavit, dated 25 Sept. and sworn on 26 Sept., "that on or about the twenty sixth day of August last past, the deponent with Mr Timothy Phelps of New Haven, & a Mr Haxhall of Petersburgh in Virginia, dined in company with Mr Genet, the French Minister, Capt Bompard, & Mr Genet's Secretaries, at the house of Mr Bradley, in Maiden Lane, New York. After dinner, but before the Gentlemen rose from table, the deponent related the report from Boston, which had that day been circulated 'that the Governor of Massachusets had taken measures to secure a prize or two which had been sent into that port by a proscribed privateer, (so-called) for the purpose of restoring the said prizes to the owners; that in consequence of this the Commander of the Concord, frigate, had taken the prize or prizes under his protection, & determined to resist by force any attempt to take possession of the said prize or prizes for the benefit of the owners.' When the deponent had related this story, Mr Pascal, one of Mr Genet's Secretaries, immediately replied in French 'Mon. Washington fait la guerre a la nation Francaise,' or in words to that effect; to which Mr Genet & Capt Bompard both assented by saying *Yes*. Mr Genet proceeded & said that the Executive of the United States was under the influence of British Gold—the deponent asked him if he meant the President of the United States; he replied No—Mr Genet further said that the officers of our government were in the British interest, or words to that effect. & further that a plan was formed to subject us to Great Britain, & that we should soon be the slaves of that Kingdom. Mr Genet declared he had very good letters which gave him this information. The deponent representing to Mr Genet that it would be impossible to subject the independent freemen of America to British or any other foreign power, & that the Executive officers of our national government knew the people too well to harbor a thought of effecting any such purpose, asked Mr Genet whether he believed our Executive Officers, the President, Mr Jefferson, Mr Hamilton, & Gen. Knox to be fools; to which Mr Genet replied, Mr Jefferson is no fool.

"The Deponent says further that in another conversation, Mr Genet railed agt some of the measures of Congress & particularly agt the funding system, in very severe language" (Ford, *Noah Webster,* 1:368–71).

2. GW was referring to Alexander Hamilton's illness.

3. At this point of the draft, GW wrote and struck out "the latter may be requested to have done."

4. Knox wrote GW twice, on 15 and 18 Sept., before leaving Philadelphia for Boston on 19 September.

5. Samuel Fraunces (c.1722–1795), former proprietor of Fraunces' Tavern in New York City, was GW's steward. He left GW's household in June 1794, and in July of that year he opened "an Ordinary at his house in Second Street, next door to the British Ministers No. 166" (entries of 9 June 1794, Household Accounts; *Dunlap and Claypoole's American Daily Advertiser* [Philadelphia], 19 July 1794). In 1795 Fraunces moved the tavern to South Water Street, but he died in October (*Gazette of the United States and Daily Evening Advertiser* [Philadelphia], 17 June 1795; *Gazette United States* [Philadelphia], 13 and 29 Oct. 1795).

From Elizabeth Willing Powel

Monday

My dear Friend & very dear Madam   [Sept.][1] 9th 1793

Your affectionate & friendly Attention to me, at this awful Moment,[2] filled my Heart with so much Sensibility as rendered me incapable of expressing my Feelings on the Subject of our Conversation, and when my amiable Friend, the President, renewed his Invitation to me to accompany you to Virginia, I could only say that I would let you know, this Evening, the Result of a Conference I meant to have with Mr Powel. After a long Conversation with him, I collected that he saw no Propriety in the Citizens flying from the only Spot where Physicians conversant in the Disorder that now prevails could be consulted;[3] nor does he appear to be impressed with the degree of Apprehension that generally pervades the Minds of our Friends—however, he wished me to follow my own Inclination and the Dictates of my own Judgement in a Matter that may eventually affect my Life and his Happiness—this has thrown me into a Dilemma the most painful. The Conflict between Duty and Inclination is a severe Trial of my Feelings; but as I believe it is always best to adhere to the line of Duty, I beg to decline the Pleasure I proposed to myself in accompanying you to Virginia at this Time. The Possibility of his being ill during my Absence, & thereby deprived of the Consolation and Aid, he might derive from my Attention to him woud be to me a lasting Source of Affliction;[4] and, God knows, I need not voluntarily add to the List of Sorrows. My Life has been sufficiently embittered to make me now very little anxious about protracting or preserving it. Death has robbed me of many Friends, and Time has abated the Ardor of others, so that Life in my latter Years has been little more than a Sieve to let thro some Joy or some Blessing. Mr Powel, who is highly sensible of your Friendship to me, desires to unite in every good Wish for you & yours. That God may preserve and bless you both, and that you may safely return in a short Time, is the unfeigned Prayer of your sincere affectionate

Eliza. Powel

Mr Powel would have done himself the Pleasure of waiting upon you before your Departure, had he not apprehended that a Visit in the Moment of Preparation for a Journey would have been illtimed.

ALS, DLC:GW. The internal address reads "The President and Mrs. Washington."

1. Powel wrote "August," but GW's docket reads "Mrs. Eliza. Powell 9th Sep: 1793." In 1793, 9 Aug. fell on a Friday and 9 Sept. on a Monday. Powel correctly wrote "September 9th 1793" on GW's undated reply. The Washingtons left Philadelphia for Mount Vernon on 10 Sept. and arrived there on 14 September.

2. The "awful moment" is a reference to the yellow fever epidemic that began in Philadelphia in July 1793 and killed an estimated 10 percent of the city's population before the epidemic ended in November. For a contemporary description, which includes necrology lists, see Carey, *Short Account of the Malignant Fever.*

3. Dr. Benjamin Rush identified the disease on 19 August. On the subsequent medical and political debates over the treatment and causes of yellow fever, see Pernick, "Politics, Parties, and Pestilence." For a contemporary account of conflicting medical practices, see Timothy Pickering to GW, 21 October.

4. Samuel Powel died from yellow fever on 29 September.

To Elizabeth Willing Powel

Dear Madam.   Monday Evening [9 September 1793][1]
    Persuaded as Mrs Washington and myself are, that your own good sense will always dictate what under existing circum-

stances shall appear best, we have only to regret that in the present instance it will deprive us of the pleasure of your company to Virginia.[2]

We unite in every good wish for you & Mr Powell, and I have the honor to be with the most Affectionate regard, Your most obedt Servt

Go: Washington

ALS, ViMtvL.

1. Powel wrote "September 9th 1793" at the bottom of the manuscript.

2. Powel had declined the Washingtons' invitation in her letter to GW of this date.

To David Ross and Robert Townsend Hooe

Sir,[1]   Philadelphia Sep. 9. 1793.

The Commissioners of the public buildings in the federal territory having expressed to me their desire to have their accounts settled, I have to ask and to authorize you in conjunction with mister David ross of Bladensburg (& vice versa), as I hereby do, to undertake to examine their accounts and vouchers relative to the expenditure of the monies appropriated to their trust, & to certify to me the result thereof.[2]

Df, in Thomas Jefferson's writing, DLC:GW; LB, DLC:GW. Changes on the draft that do not appear on the letter-book copy suggest that a decision was made to address Ross and Hooe separately after this document was entered into the letter book (see notes 1 and 2).

1. On the draft, Bartholomew Dandridge, Jr., struck "Gentlemen" and inserted "Sir," whereas the letter-book copy reads "Gentlemen."

2. For the commissioners' request, see D.C. Commissioners to GW, 5 Sept., and GW to D.C. Commissioners, 9 Sept. For the results of the audit, see Hooe and Ross to GW, 31 Oct. (see also D.C. Commissioners to GW, 3 Nov.). The phrase "in conjunction with mr David Ross of Bladensburg (& vice versa)" was inserted on the draft and does not appear in the letter-book copy.

To Dennis Whelen

Sir,   Philada 9 Sept: 1793.

I feel much satisfaction in receiving thro' you, at this critical period when it becomes the duty of every good Citizen to preserve peace to his Country, assurances from the late Grand Jury of Chester County, of their intention to pursue every means to ensure to the United States that inestimable blessing.[1]

The motive which led to a declaration of the neutrality of these States, was a conviction of it's being for their interest & happiness; and it affords me singular pleasure to find that measure so generally approved by my Fellow Citizens, whose prosperity & ease it will always be my first care to promote.

Go. Washington

LB, DLC:GW.

1. See the Grand Inquest of Chester County, Pennsylvania, to GW, c.26 Aug. 1793, which was forwarded with a cover letter by Whelen on 26 August.

From Joseph Harper

Sir   Philada 10th Septr 1793

We have that Honor of inclosing to you a Memorial which most deeply interests us, we presumed that cases of a Similar kind had been laid before you, but upon enquiry we are led to believe that there is something so Special in our Situation, as not to suffer any decision which has yet been made in any case to be applicable to ours—Permit us therefore to intreat you Sir to consider the embarrassment into which we have been thrown and to extend to us such relief as your attention to the Wellfair of your fellow Citizens justifies us in expecting. We are with due Respect Sir Your Most Humble Servts

Joseph Harper
for Self &C.

ALS, DNA: RG 76, International Claims: France.

Joseph Harper had been a Philadelphia merchant at least since 1776. GW received this letter and enclosure on 26 Sept. while at Mount Vernon, and he replied to Harper the next day.

Enclosure
Memorial on the Andrew

Philada 9th Septr 1793.

The Memorial of James King, Henry Pratt, Joseph Harper, & Isaac Snowden Citizens of these United States and Owners of the Ship Andrew and of a Considerable part of her Cargo & of William Bell in his own right and Henry Pratt & Geo. C. Schroeppel as administrators to the Estate of the late William Starman deceased as Owners of the remaining part of the said Ships

Cargo Beg leave to represent in the first place that all the Claimants interested in the said Ship and Cargo are, & were at the time of Sailing of the said Ship from Charlestown Citizens of the United States of America, and as Such entitled to a full protection from the Government of the same;[1] and which they now Claim having been divested of a very Considerable property—as by the following Narrative will more fully appear—Vizt.

The Ship Andrew. Samuel Makins Master Sailed from Charlestown in the State of So. Carolina bound for Amsterdam on or about the 28th of February last, at which time no declaration of War was Known to have been Made by the Government of France against any foreign power,[2] that her Cargo Consisted of Eight hundred & Seventy five Whole Casks & Two hundred & two half Tierces of Rice, and of fifty seven bags of Pimento—Was Consigned to our respective Correspondents in the said Port of Amsterdam—there to have been disposed of for our Accounts—& the proceeds to be Applied agreeable to our Orders, that in the prosecution of the said Voyage to Wit on the 10th day of April last the said Ship was boarded by a French Privateer called L'ambitieux Capt. John Pontevin Who put a Prize Master and a number of hands on board the said Ship Andrew—Ordering them to Conduct her to some Port in France—at the same time taking the said Capt. Saml Makins & Six of his Seamen from on board of the said Ship and keeping them Prisoners on board the said Privateer untill after her Arrival in the Port of Brest in France; which was on the 19th of April, where he was detained on board untill the 22nd—when he was Orderd on Shore & informed of the Arrival of his Ship at Port LOrient. that being furnished with a Pass, himself and Men went to LOrient, and on the 25th of the same were there Examined by the Chamber of Commerce Who after a full hearing declared both Vessel and Cargo free & the Capturing illegal being American Property, that on the 26th of same Month in Consequence of a decree of the General Council of the said place at which were present two Commissaries deputed by the Convention of the department of Finistere and Morbihan, and by the National Assembly—the said Capt. Makins was Orderd to deliver up his Cargo for the use of the Republic (they being in great Want) at same time it was Order'd that the Ordonnature of the Marine of said Port shou'd pay the Freight; against the whole of which proceedings Capt. Makins regularly Protested but was obliged to Comply—and on the 14th of May Officers appointed by the Magistrates Came on board and proceeded to discharge the said Cargo which was Continued from day to day untill the 24th when the last of the Cargo was discharged—That Capt. Makins applied to the different Officers of Governmen⟨t⟩ in the Said Port to Endeavour to procure satisfacti⟨on⟩ for his detention as well as payment for his Cargo & Freight, but all without effect untill the 17th day of June—when he received from the deputy Paymaster of the Marine the Sum of Fifty One Thousand three hundred & twenty Eight Livres Nine Sols and one denier in Assignats—being according to a Statement by them made the Amount of the Freight—they having previously deducted from the Gross amount thereof the sum of One Thousand two hundred & Ninety Livres—being for five Casks of Rice difficient in the Cargo and which in the said Account (reference being thereunto made) appears to have been Calculated at the rate of Sixty Livres ⅌ hundred—that the said Capt. Makin after using every other Means in his power to Procure Satisfaction & Payment found himself at last under the Necessity of abandoning any further proceedings in that Port & having received from the Mayor & Municipal Officers of L'Orient a Certificate of his having deliverd into the Stores of that Port in Consequence of a decree of the 26th April, the quantity of One Thousand & seventy hogsheads or half hogshead⟨s⟩ of Rice, weighing together Five hundred & Eighty Ni⟨ne⟩ thousand & thirty pounds Gross—for the Use of the⟨ir⟩ Marine & War departments, as also Fifty seven ba⟨gs⟩ of Pimento weighing together Eight thousand Nin⟨e⟩ hundred & Eighty Seven pounds—he then Ballast⟨ed⟩ his Vessel and on the 3d day of July left L'Orient and proceeded for this Port, where he arrived the 29th Ult. On the whole of this Narrative your Memorialists beg leave to Observe that they are in possession of authentic documents to Prove every thing herein set forth—and by which it will plainly appear that in direct Violation of the Treaty existing between the Two Nations of America & France, the Property of your Memorialists hath been forcibly, illegally, and without any Colour of Right whatever taken from them[3]—that a Ship Sailing under the American Flag hath been in Open defiance of Said Treaty taken upon the high Seas—Carried in to Port & there detained at very Considerable Expence—the Captain and a part of the Crew taken out, and Confined as Prisoners—and after the utmost exertions on the part of the said Captain to Obtain Payment and satisfaction, he hath not been able to Obtain Any[.] They beg leave also to represent that in addition to the actual loss sustained, had the Ship been sufferd to proceed on her said Voyage without molestation in Consequence of the previous Arrangements that had been taken at Amsterdam, she woud have made a return Freight from at least One thousand pounds Sterling—& for which the Owners of said Ship do think themselves intitled to have full Satisfaction and for which the Owners of sd Ship as Citizens of the United States of America they Conceive they are not bound to prosecute their Claims at any Foreign Government—but Pray that the Government under which they live, and to which they very largely Contribute, will indemnify them for all losses they have sustained which they believe can be more readily done, as it has it at this time in its Power to do it, by an appropriation to which with submission we Concieve there Can be no reasonable Objection either by our Own Government or that of France.[4]

James King	Henry Pratt
Harper & Snowden	Geo. C. Schroeppel
	William Bell

DS, DNA: RG 76, International Claims: France.

1. James King (1751–1832), Henry Pratt (1761–1838), and William Bell (c.1739–1816) were merchants living in Philadelphia in 1793, and Isaac Snowden, Jr. (1764–1835), was Harper's partner in the firm of Harper & Snowden, which dissolved in 1794. George Casper von Schroeppel (1747–1825), originally from Germany, was naturalized at Philadelphia in 1784. By 1795 he was a merchant at New York City, and he later founded the town of Schroeppel in Oswego County, New York. Frederick William Starman (d. 1793), another Philadelphia merchant, was a victim of the yellow fever epidemic.

2. France declared war on Great Britain and the Netherlands on 1 Feb. and on Spain on 7 March 1793. News of the former declaration reached Philadelphia around the first of April. Samuel Makins (d. 1802) lived at 15 Lombard Street in Philadelphia. In 1794 he obtained an invalid pension based on naval service in Massachusetts in 1779.

3. The petitioners were referring to the Treaty of Amity and Commerce between France and the United States (1778), which is printed in Miller, *Treaties*, 3–34.

4. The ship *Andrew* is number 79 on "A statement of the claims of citizens of the United States upon the French Republic, presented by Mr. Skipwith,

Consul general of the United States at Paris..." 20 Nov. 1795. At that time the claims "for the value of the cargo, and for an indemnity for the detention of the vessel" were "not determined" (*ASP: Foreign Relations,* 1:753–57). The claim evidently was settled under the French treaty of 30 April 1803 (Maclure, *To the People,* 104; *Payments of Awards,* 10, 12, 135, 138).

To Thomas Jefferson

Dear Sir, Chester [Pa.] Septr 10th 1793

I return, from this place, the Papers which you put into my hands on the Road, to day.[1]

The unpromising state of the Negotiation at Madrid, and the opinion of the Commissioners that their Commission should be withdrawn, and matters at that Court placed in Statu quo, deser⟨ves⟩ very serious consideration. I pray you to give it; & if it rests altogether with the Executive (after the Agency th⟨e⟩ Senate has had in the business) let me know the result.[2]

Mr Carmichael must not be the person left there; for, from him we should never hear a tittle of wha⟨t⟩ is going forward at the Court of Madrid.[3] I am Your Affecte

Go: Washington

ALS, DLC: Jefferson Papers; Df, in Bartholomew Dandridge, Jr.'s, writing, DNA: RG 59, Miscellaneous Letters; LB, DNA: RG 59, George Washington's Correspondence with His Secretaries of State. The letters in angle brackets are supplied from the draft. Jefferson docketed the ALS as received 12 September.

1. The only identified enclosure was a letter from William Carmichael and William Short, the U.S. commissioners charged with negotiating a variety of issues with Spain, to Jefferson of 6 June (*Jefferson Papers,* 26:206–12). In that letter, the commissioners reported that, because of Spain's recent alliance with England against France, they had delayed pressing negotiations involving the navigation of the Mississippi River and territorial limits, and they requested new instructions.

2. Jefferson responded to Carmichael and Short on 11 Sept., telling them, "the President approves of your proceedings and views. Proceed in the plan your letter of June 6. expresses; we make no other alterations in our instructions" (*Jefferson Papers,* 27:88–89).

3. Carmichael failed to write regularly to his diplomatic superiors (David Humphreys to GW, 4 April 1793, and n.3).

To James Lloyd

Sir,   Philada Septr [10][1] 1793.

The spirit which breathes throughout the resolutions of the Inhabitants of Kent County in the State of Maryland, lately convened at Chester town, does honor to their character as citizens.[2] 'Tis by such a spirit, seconding the endeavours of the Government, that we shall have the fairest prospect of preserving our peace. 'Tis by such a spirit that in any event we shall secure the internal tranquility of our Country—its respectability, and shall be enabled to encounter with firmness any attempt, hostile to its safety, its honor, or its welfare.

The expressions of confidence & attachment towards myself contained in the same resolutions, impress me with sensations analagous to their fervour & earnestness, and to the true esteem & regard which I always feel for the respectable Citizens from whom they come.

Go. Washington

LB, DLC:GW.

This letter was published in the *Maryland Herald, and Eastern Shore Intelligencer* (Easton), 17 Sept., and other Maryland newspapers.

1. The letter-book copy and newspaper publications give no exact date, but the preceding document in the letter book is dated 9 September. GW left Philadelphia on 10 Sept., which is also the date that the referenced resolutions were printed in a Philadelphia newspaper, so the letter presumably was written on 9 or 10 September.

2. The resolutions of the residents of Kent County, Md., dated 31 Aug., were enclosed with Lloyd's letter to GW of 2 September.

From Harriot Washington

Frederickburg [Va.] Septber 10 1793

I now embrace this opportunity of writeing to my honour'd Uncle, to thank him for the money he was so good as to send me beleive me my dear Uncle, that my heart most greatfully acknowledge's, your's, and Aunt Washingtons kindness to me, you may rely on my word that I will not get any thing that I can possibly, do without, but there is a great many little thing's, that I could get at Mt Vernon by applying to Aunt Washington that

I am obleiged to purchase now. Aunt Lewis has a very large fa-
maly at present and a great deal of company, which makes my
cloath's ware out much faster than if I was in the country, where
any thing would do to ware, but I will take a great deal of care
of them.[1] Aunt Lewis desired me to inform you, that she sent
the letter's to Cousin Rob, but whether he received them or not
she dose not no.[2] Cousin Laurence left this, with an intention of
going to Bath, we have never heard from him since.[3] Aunt Lewis
and Cousin Carter[4] join me in love to you and Aunt Washington,
I am Honor'd Uncle Your affectionate Neice

Harriot Washington

ALS, ViMtvL.

1. On Harriot Washington's request for financial help, see Betty Washington Lewis to GW, 29 Jan., and n.1.

2. Betty Washington Lewis evidently was referring to GW's letter to Robert
Lewis of 6 January.

3. Lawrence Lewis was Betty Washington Lewis's son. Bath is now Berkeley
Springs, West Virginia.

4. Betty Lewis Carter, wife of Charles Carter, was Betty Washington Lewis's
daughter.

To Thomas Jefferson

Sir,   Elkton [Md.] 11 Septr 1793.

I will thank you to have made out and forwarded to me a Commission for the Collector of Annapolis, in place of [   ] Davidson, leaving the name of the person blank to be filled up by me.[1]

You will please to have the U: States seal affixed thereto, and
countersigned by you, so that it may be sent directly from me to
the person who shall be appointed. With much esteem, I am Sir,
Your mo: humble Servt

Go: Washington

LS, in Bartholomew Dandridge, Jr.'s, writing, DLC: Jefferson Papers; Df, in
Dandridge's writing, DNA: RG 59, Miscellaneous Letters; LB, DNA: RG 59,
George Washington's Correspondence with His Secretaries of State. Jeffer-
son docketed the LS as received on 12 September.

1. On 23 Nov. GW signed a commission for Robert Denny to replace Annapolis collector John Davidson. Denny, however, declined the appointment,
and GW appointed John Randall to the post (*JPP*, 257; Denny to GW, 6 Dec.;
GW to U.S. Senate, 27 Dec.).

From Edmund Pendleton

Sir   Caroline County Virga Sepr 11. 1793

I am Hond with the Commands of a very respectable body of Citizens, my County men, to transmit to Yr Excellency the inclosed Copy of certain Resolutions which they yesterday judged it wise & necessary to enter into, declaratory of their Sentiments on certain Political Subjects.

I can truly say that the Numbers, their information as to the Subjects discussed, but above all their pure Patriotism, untainted by the baneful influence of Attachment to Party, rendered the meeting very respectable. Their resolutions must speak for themselves, And I can only say that if they shall contribute in any degree towards the Smothering the seeds of dissention in Embrio, and preserving the peace & happiness of America, our wishes will be gratified.

The meeting judged that this mode of transmitting the genuine Effusions of their sincere respect for, confidence in, & lasting gratitude to you, Sir, would be at least as acceptable, as if accompanied by a formal address; and for that reason only, forbore to give you that trouble. I have the Honr to be with sentiments of the most profound respect & Esteem Your Excellys mo. humble & Obt Servt

Edmd Pendleton

ALS, DLC:GW; LB, DLC:GW.

Enclosure
Resolutions of Caroline County, Va., Citizens

[10 September 1793]

At a very Numerous Meeting of the Substantial Planters, Farmers & other Yeomanry of the County of Caroline in Virginia, at the Court House on the 10th day of September 1793; being the day of holding the County Court, on which they had been previously requested to Assemble for the purpose of taking into consideration the present political State of American Affairs.[1]

It being considered that it is at all times the right, and at certain periods the duty of the People to declare their principles and Opinions on Subjects which concern the National Interest; and that in the present juncture, the exercise of that duty is rendered indispensible, By the prevailing practice of Declaratory Resolutions in places where the Inhabitants can more easily Assemble & Consult than in the Countrey at large; but where Interests, Views & Political Opinions different from those of the great body of the people, may happen to predominate; whence there may be danger of unfair & delusive inferences concerning the true and General sense of the People. In declaring Ours, however, since from our remote situation from the great Scene of Public transactions, we cannot possess a timely & correct knowledge of political incidents, & the Conduct of persons concerned therein; it is judged most prudent to wait with a decent reserve, for clear & full information relative thereto: and in Public Declarations to abide by those great principles, just sentiments and established truths, which can be little affected by transitory or Personal Occurrences.

Therefore, as the Unanimous sence of this Meeting,

Resolved That the Constitution of the United States, Ought to be firmly and vigilantly supported against all direct or indirect attempts that may be made to subvert or violate the same.

Resolved That, as it is the true Interest of the United States to cultivate the preservation of Peace by all just & Honorable Means, the Executive Authority ought to be supported in the exercise of it's Constitutional Powers & functions for inforcing the laws existing for that purpose.

Resolved That the eminent Virtues & Services of our Illustrious fellow-Citizen George Washington, President of the United States, entitle him to the highest respect, confidence, and lasting Gratitude of his Countrey; Whose peace, Liberty & Safety must ever remind It of his distinguished Agency in the Attainment of those inestimable blessings.

Resolved That the eminent and generous Aids rendered to the United States in their Arduous strugle for liberty, by the French Nation, ought ever to be remembered and acknowledged with gratitude and kind affection; And that the Spectable exhibited by the glorious & severe contest It is now engaged in for it's own liberty, ought & must be peculiarly interesting to the Wishes, the friendship & the Sympathy of the people of America.

Resolved—That all Attempts which may be made, in whatever form or disguise, to alienate the good Will of the people of America from the cause of Liberty & republican Government in France, have an evident tendency to weaken their Affection for the free principles of their own Governments, and manifest designs which ought to be narrowly watched & seasonably counteracted.

Resolved That such Attempts to disunite Nations mutually attached to the cause of Liberty, and viewed with unfriendly Eyes by all who hate it; ought to be more particularly reprobated at the present crisis, when such Vast Efforts are making by a combination of Princes—& Nobles to crush an example, which they fear may open the Eyes of all Mankind to their Natural & political rights.

Resolved That a dissolution of the Honorable & beneficial connection between the United States and France, must Obviously be Attempted with a view to forward a plan of a more intimate Union & connection of the former with Great Britain; as a leading step towards Assimilating the American Government to the form and Spirit of the British Monarchy: And these Apprehensions will be greatly strengthened, if it shall appear that the Active Zeal displayed in propogating prejudices against the French Nation & Revolution, hath proceeded from persons either disaffected to the American Revolution, Or of known Monarchical Principles.[2]

Resolved That all foreign Ministers to the United States ought to Negotiate the purposes of their Mission with the President. If at any time a difference in Opinion should happen, on the exposition of Treaties, or other subjects, the same ought to be stated by the Minister to the Governing powers of his Nation; that on a discussion between the two Governments, an Amicable Adjustment may be effected, & peace & friendship preserved: And all Applications of a Minister, in such a Case, to the people, who Act with foreign Nations, only by their representatives, in the different departments of Government, are highly improper, & tend to create parties & dissentions amongst Us. Nevertheless if a Minister shall adopt such improper Conduct on any Occasion, altho' the Application ought to be treated with Contempt by the people, yet it should not affect his Nation, Unless It shall Avow & justify his conduct therein. We therefore declare our disapprobation of certain Attempts in late News-paper publications, to make some alledged behaviour of that kind in the Minister of the French Nation, if any such really existed, the means of withdrawing our affection, either from the beloved President, or our Respectable Allies.[3]

Ordered That the foregoing Resolutions be forthwith printed in the Several News-papers in the State; and that a fair Copy of them be transmitted to the President of the United States by the Chairman.

By Order of the Meeting

Attest Wm Nelson Secretary[4]   Edmd Pendleton Chairman

DS, in Edmund Pendleton's writing, DLC:GW; LB, DLC:GW.

The resolutions were printed in the *Virginia Gazette, and General Advertiser* (Richmond), 25 Sept.; *Virginia Herald, and Fredericksburg Advertiser,* 26 Sept.; and other newspapers. For GW's response, see GW to Pendleton, 23 Sept. (first letter).

1. The notifications for this meeting had been distributed by John Taylor at the suggestion of James Madison (see Taylor to Madison, 25 Sept., *Madison Papers,* 15:123).

2. The preamble and preceding resolutions closely follow a draft produced by Madison in late August. For that text and discussion of efforts by Madison and James Monroe to have such resolutions passed at meetings in Virginia, see Resolutions on Franco-American Relations, c.27 Aug., and Madison to Thomas Jefferson, 2 Sept., *Madison Papers,* 15:76–80, 92–95 (see also *Jefferson Papers,* 27:16–20).

3. In a public letter of 12 Aug., John Jay and Rufus King had asserted that French minister Edmond Genet "had said he would Appeal to the People from certain decisions of the President" (*Diary; or Loudon's Register* [New York], 12 Aug. 1793), a charge denied by Genet in a letter to GW of 13 Aug. that was made public by late August.

4. William Nelson was the Caroline County clerk.

From Edmund Pendleton

Dear Sir   Edmundsbury[1] [Va.] Sepr 11. 1793

Being called to a public communication with you, I feel an Indispensible duty & inclination to pay you my personal respects at the same time, if it were only to reiterate, which I hope is unnecessary, sincere Assurances that neither time, or the dirty scriblings with which the public has been lately pestered, have produced the smallest abatement in my private Affection for you, or my unlimited confidence in yr Public Administration, both which are so rivited as not to be shaken by attacks much more weighty than those "Trifles light as Air." such I hope and beleive is their estimation with you, so as to give you no uneasiness.[2]

Sequestered as I am in a manner from the Public world, I know little of what is doing in it, further than is retailed in the papers; and those appear to me in most instances a source of Partial, false or delusive Information. I find however that the Officer at the head of the fiscal department stands charged by some Members from hence, with misapplication of the public money, a charge & enquiry which will probably be revived & pursued with spirit at next Session—my wish is that it may be probed to the bottom, Impartial Justice done and the Public guarded agt all deviations from the laws of appropriation, (before the mischief is become considerable, or the practice acquires the strength of Custom,) except in extraordinary cases, by order of the Executive, and to be communicated to Congress for their approbation.[3]

I am an Utter stranger to the Gentn at the head of that department, & pretty much so to the detail of his Conduct, but I will confess to you Sir, that all his reports on Ways & means, from that on the funding System to the present day, have impressed me with an Idea of his having made the System of the British Minestry, the model of his conduct as assumed American Primate—chusing rather to trust to a monied Interest he has created, for the Support of his measures, than to their *rectitude*—I don't say these were his motives, but such they appear to me, & I fear we shall long feel the effects of the System even if it were now to be changed, wch it is supposed would be improper, at least as to the funding System.

The Nondiscrimination he so much laboured, appeared to me a Sacrifice of the substance of Justice to it's shadow; its effects do throw unearned wealth into a few unmeriting hands, instead of diffusing it (after repaying them their purchase money) to those who entitled themselves to it by the most Meritorious consideration.[4]

The assumption of the State debts in a lump before it was ascertained that they were created for common benefit (which would make them an equitable charge on the Union) seemed to me unaccountable, unless derived from the Secretary's position that increase of public debt is beneficial; A maxim adopted by the British Cabinet, but unsupported by reason or other example, & it's National effects there strangely misrepresented.[5]

The various kinds & Value of the new Certificates, I see inconveniencies in, but can discover no other reason for than to give the rich Speculators at or near the Seat of Government an advantage over the distant, uninformed, unwary or distressed Citizens and the recommended irredeemable quality, as a means of increasing their Credit in circulation, is a paradox of which no Solution has yet Occurred to my mind.[6]

A moderate Impost on all imported articles ad valorem, for the sole purpose of Revenue, laid equally through the States, altho' it would have fallen more heavily on some than others, would yet have been unexceptionable, since the inequality would have been the effect of the chosen System of each. But to point out particular Articles as the subjects of high taxation, either as a Sumptuary regulation, or as a bounty, premium, or protecting duty to encourage American Manufactures, appears to Me an improper intermedling of Governmt with the labour of the Citizens[7]—peculiarly inconvenient, & producing effects partial & unjust in an Union of confederated States, dissimilar in their Systems of employing their labour; And rendring the amount of the estimated revenue precarious, which must be dim[in]ished in proportion, as the end proposed of prohibiting the importation, is answered, or the smugling of it increased by that of the temptation.

To the Sinking fund & Bank Systems have been attributed the Character of Handmaids in the hands of the Secretary, to aid his money'd Interest in accumulating still more Wealth to their unbounded Mass, by Speculations:[8] but as I don't throughly understand them, & they seem to be the Subjects of principle charge agt him & remain to be Agitated before the proper Tribunal, I will forbear any Observations as to them, and proceed to beg pardon for the Liberty I have taken in the free expressions of my sentiments on the others: I seldom wish to obtrude my Opinions where I am not called by duty, or request to give them—To you, Sir, I can do it freely, because I know you will make no improper use of what I say—if there be any hint which may be useful & has not occur'd, you will improve it to Public benefit; if none such, you will throw by the whole as the well meant reveries of a fireside Politician, who never had much Pretensions to the Character of a Statesman, but cordially hates all Intrigues, finesse & Stratagems in Government, as well as in Private transactions.

It may be thought that I owe a particular Appology for my freedom in the cases which have been sanctioned by Laws, to you who approved them but I can truly say I neither meant, nor do I think you involved in the mistaken Policy, if it was such; and as this may seem as great a paradox as that I have imputed to the Secretary, I will at Least attempt it's Solution, as thus—I ever considered Your modified Negative upon the Laws, tho' useful, as the most delicate part of the Presidential duty, (until the preservation of Neutrality in the present situation of things Occur'd.) For one man to set up his Opinion agt that of a Majority of two numerous bodies, representing the people to be governed by a law, & on that ground only to disapprove a law so Passed, would be very disagreable & no doubt much complained of: I always considered the Power as intended to be exercised on great Occasions, either when A law violates the Constitution (& so it has been once exercised, I believe wth general Approbation)[9] or is produced by sudden heat of Parties. I therefore do not consider your suffering an Act to pass, as a proof that you would as a Member have voted for it, but to evince that you do not judge it a case in wch the Constitution meant you should interpose yr Negative. If this Solution don't furnish my Appology, I know I shall find one in yr Candor, & on that I rest.

I am sorry to hear that Philadelphia is visited by a Pestilential fever, & cordially wish you may escape it, for your own Sake & that of mankind. After strugling for 8 years through various complaints apparently of a Chronic kind, I find myself tolerably easy, except as to lameness & the effects of 72, an old age for a man who has spent upwards of 50 of them in a Stretch of his mental powers, tho' not equal to Mansfield or Franklin.[10]

That you may Long Continue here & happy, & when removed from this, experience increased & never ending Felicity in a better Countrey; & that the good Mrs Washington may participate in both, is the Cordial wish of Millions, but of none more so, than of My Dr Sir Yr ever Affectionate & mo. Obt Servt

Edmd Pendleton

ALS, DLC:GW.

1. Edmundsbury was the name of Pendleton's plantation on Maracossic Creek, about nine miles southeast of Bowling Green in Caroline County.

2. In his public letter to GW of this date, Pendleton enclosed resolutions from a meeting of Caroline County, Va., citizens. "Trifles light as Air" is a reference to Iago's lines in Act 3, Scene 3 of William Shakespeare's "Othello": "Trifles light as air / Are to the jealous confirmations strong / As proofs of holy writ."

3. For the congressional investigation into Alexander Hamilton's actions as secretary of the treasury, see U.S. House of Representatives to GW, 23 Jan.,

n.1. Representative William Branch Giles of Virginia set out the case against Hamilton in a speech on 23 Jan. (*Annals of Congress,* 2d Cong., 835–40).

4. Pendleton is alluding to Hamilton's argument in his Report on Public Credit of 9 Jan. 1790 that in the funding of the public debt no discrimination should be made "between original holders of the public securities, and present possessors, by purchase" (*Hamilton Papers,* 6:73–78). In urging the contrary view, which was rejected in a House vote on 22 Feb. 1790, James Madison had argued that non-discriminatory funding would result in "exhorbitant accumulation of gain...made at the expence of the most meritorious part of the community" (Discrimination between Present and Original Holders of the Public Debt, 18 Feb. 1790, *Madison Papers,* 13:47–58, quotation at 57).

5. Hamilton's Report on Public Credit also argued for the assumption of state debts by the United States, which, along with funding, was made part of "An Act making provision for the [payment of the] Debt of the United States," 4 Aug. 1790 (*Hamilton Papers,* 6:78–83; 1 *Stat.* 138–44).

6. The "Act making provision for the [payment of the] Debt of the United States" provided for subscriptions to "a loan to the full amount of the... domestic debt...payable in certificates issued for the said debt" of six different types therein listed (1 *Stat.,* 139–40).

7. Here Pendleton is evidently taking issue with Hamilton's Report on Manufactures of 5 Dec. 1791, which recommended the protection of a range of American manufactures by bounties or protective duties (*Hamilton Papers,* 10:230–340). Hamilton had also used a sumptuary argument in partial justification of the increases in duties on wine, spirits, tea, and coffee recommended in his Report on Public Credit (*Hamilton Papers,* 6:99–104).

8. In Hamilton's Report on Public Credit, he recommended applying the post office revenue to a sinking fund for the payment of the national debt. He also briefly recommended the establishment of a national bank, although he saved the detailed exposition of his bank proposal for his "Second Report on the Further Provision Necessary for Establishing Public Credit," 13 Dec. 1790, which was communicated to the House on 14 Dec. 1790 (*Hamilton Papers,* 6:106–8, 7:305–42).

9. See GW to the United States House of Representatives, 5 April 1792, which stated two constitutional objections to "An Act for an apportionment of Representatives among the several States according to the first enumeration."

10. Pendleton was referring to Benjamin Franklin and, probably, the noted judge William Murray (1705–1793), first earl of Mansfield.

From John Sinclair

Whitehall [London], September 11th 1793.

Sir John Sinclair presents his respects to General Washington, with Copies of the additional Papers printed by the Board of Agriculture, since he last had the Honor of writing to His

Excellency, which he begs may also be communicated to Mr Adams & Mr Jefferson[1]—He is just setting out for Scotland, but he hopes to have the pleasure of hearing from his friends in America when he returns to London, which will probably be in November.

L, DLC:GW.

  1. In his letter to GW of 15 June, Sinclair informed GW of the creation of the Board of Agriculture, an institution aimed at promoting scientific farming and internal improvements in Great Britain, and he sent the board's first publications to GW on 15 August. The items enclosed with this letter have not been identified, but for a list of the agricultural surveys and essays produced by the Board of Agriculture that were in GW's library, see Griffin, *Catalogue of the Washington Collection,* 89–95. Although no transmission of the enclosures to John Adams or Thomas Jefferson has been identified, when GW acknowledged this letter on 20 July 1794, he assured Sinclair, "Both Mr Adams and Mr Jefferson had the perusal of the papers which accompanied your note of the 11th of Sept." (ALS, UkLBM).

From John Doughty

Sir   Morris Town [N.J.] 12th Septr 1793
  I have the Honor to enclose you the Resolutions of the County of Morris, passed the 10th inst: They contain the free & unbiassed sentiments of a respectable Body of free Men, who haveing dearly earned, know well how to estimate the Blessings, we all enjoy under the federal Constitution—May those Blessings be long continued to us, & may you Sir be continued the happy Instrument of administering them, in the sincere prayer of sir, your most devoted Humble servt

                                        Jno. Doughty

ALS, DLC:GW; LB, DLC:GW.

Enclosure
Resolutions from the Morris County, N.J., Citizens

                                        [10 September 1793]
  At a meeting of the Inhabitants of the County of Morris, held at the Courthouse in Morris Town agreeably to public notice on Tuesday the 10th of September 1793.
  Brigadier Genl Jno. Doughty was chosen Chairman & William Campfield Secretary.[1]

The following resolutions were agreed to
Resolved

1. It is the unanimous opinion of this meeting that the prosperous circumstances of our Country are owing under Divine Providence in a great measure to the wise, prudent & discreet management of its affairs by the Legislative & Executive departments of Government agreeably to the directions of our invaluable constitution.

2. That the late Proclamation issued by the President of the United States, reminding his fellow citizens of the obligations they are under by Treaties, as well as interest, to avoid every act of hostility against any of the European powers now at War & requiring all magistrates to exert themselves to prosecute & punish offenders, together with his instructions to the revenue officers of the union, are additional proofs as well of his zeal & affection to his fellow Citizens, as of that political foresight & wisdom in the management of our public affairs by which he has so often benefited his Country.[2]

3. That this meeting highly disapprove of the interference of any foreign power or influence, if any have or shall be made with the internal police of our Government & that we do view every such interference as an insolent affront & derogatory to the Dignity and Independancy of our Country.[3]

4. That this meeting will at all times chearfully support the Executive authority of the United States with their lives & fortunes, while it continues to manifest so strict an attention to the best interests of the union.

5. That the Chairman transmit the foregoing resolutions to the President of the United States & that the same be published in the Newark & Elizabeth town papers.[4]

a True Copy
attest   Jno. Doughty
William Campfield Secretary   Chairman

DS, DLC:GW; LB, DLC:GW.

1. William Campfield (Canfield; 1766–1812), a 1784 graduate of Princeton, was a Morris County physician. He served as Morris County sheriff, 1797–99, acted as a captain in the Morris County unit of the state cavalry, 1798–1807, and represented Morris County in the New Jersey general assembly, 1799.

2. This resolution is referring to GW's Neutrality Proclamation of 22 April.

3. This resolution is aimed at the activities of French minister Edmond Genet.

4. The resolutions were printed in the *New-Jersey Journal* (Elizabeth) of 18 Sept. and in *Woods's Newark Gazette and Paterson Advertiser* of the same date.

From Edward Newenham

Dear Sir—   Dublin [Ireland] 12 Sept. 1793

To the mind of a most Sincere & unalterable Friend, it must appear a Length of years Since I was favoured with a Line from the Man, whom I have & ever shall revere, as the Greatest ornament of this Century—The Freind of the real & Constitutonal rights of Man, who, in his Glorious Career of Victory, united the Soldier, the Citizen, & Legislator—who, Equaly disdaining Popular applause, when unmerited, or Monarchial offers of Titles & Employments, Served the Cause of *true* Liberty, & in the Conclusion of the Noble Contest, became the Chosen favourite of the Conquerors & Conquered—whose departing hours will not be disturbed by the Remembrance of murders without the Common Tryals of the most Savage Nations—who Supported the Impartial Tryal of the accused, & though possessed of Power, & which power might in many Cases have been justly exercised by inflicting the pains of Death on *Convicted* Criminals, yet, my Dear & Ever respected George Washington, proved himself Superior to the modern mode of Domination, & of raising himself above his fellow-Citizens, Except where merit so justly placed him—no rewards were offered for Assasinations of Commanders of Armies or the Despots of Tyranny—your Great Soul revolted at Such Deeds—you was, you are & Ever will be the real Example of Patriotism—the Name of Patriot is disgraced in Europe—the Late King of France (with all his Faults) gave way to our most Virtuous & respectable freind the Marquiss of La Fayett's advice—& Surrendring all the Pomp & Splender of the Crown of France, agreed to a New Constitution; that he Endeavoured to Escape from France—I admit—but it was at a Period, when his Life was in *dayly* danger—In my humble opinion Fayette was a true Friend to a proper & Free Constitution his Confidential Letters to me in 1790 prove it—they are a record of his most Virtuous Principles—had ill-fated France adopted his measures & Plan, she would have reigned the *Arbitrer* of Europe, & her People been the best Governed—he wished to Adopt the British Constitution, with a few Alterations; these Alterations would have made a Perfect System of Happiness for the Governer & Governed;[1] I cannot presume to Dive into the Secrets of Courts—but *I will say,* that the Prussians Keeping La Fayette in Prison, is contrary to the rules of War—Justice—Generosity or Policy—I have not heard of or from him, Since Six days before he declared a Prisoner—I Know not whether he is alive or Not—for the Reports are so Various & Contradictory—I have addressed a few *open* Lines to him, but never receivd an Answer—I have a thought, to apply to the Austrian Embassader, to Know where he is, & whether he is alive—& whether a Letter open for the Embassadors Inspection, could be forwarded to him—that Letter containing nothing but family affairs.

This Kingdom has been for some Time convulsed with the most dangerous Kind of Democratical Principles—Viz. an Entire Equality of Property—one house of Representatives—no Second House—or Council, Except 21 to be Chosen out of the Representatives & Changed Every Six years; Vacansies to be filled up by Election from the Representatives, who are to be Chosen annualy; a President to be Chosen Every Month—a Total repeal of all the Acts of forfeiture—all the Nobility to be laid aside—all the military to be nominated by the 21—In short, the plan was for those Men who had no landed Property, to rize into power by the aid of the People, & then become their Tyrants—not 10 Men of Farming or Landed Property of £300 a year approved of Such a System.

I feel alarmed at the reports circulated in the English & foreign news papers, Stating, that the united States & Great Brittain are likely to break the bonds of Peace—God! forbid it, as it would be ruin of Both Countries—their Natural Interest ought to unite them (for Ever) as the most warm Allies—Should any disagreable occurence happen, I trust it will be done away by an amicable Conference—& that the Sword will never be drawn between them.

Under Pretence of Reform, a set of Men instigated the very lowest of the People, to Rob, Murder & Pillage the Protestants. In many Counties the[y] disarmed the Protestants & then another party Robbed them—The papers attached to this party is using Every Endeavour to insinuate to the Public at Large, that there will be an Immediate Declaration of War between America & England.

This day orders were issued for 3 Regiments of Cavalry & 8 of foot to Embark immediatly to Join the Duke of Yorke—the foot were under orders for some Service in the West Indies, but that plan is Suddenly Changed, as it seems, that the Duke of Yorke is thought to be in Danger; Should all the Able of Men in France rize at once, they would soon overpower their opponents, but I imagine that their internal Divisions will prevent Such unanimity; it reminds me of Arnolds proclamation, before the Convention at Saratoga; I was & am an advocate for the first glorious Revolution in 1789—but am an Enemy to the Present System of Government in France.

My fourth Son who was settled at Marsaills & a Captain in the National Guards, left them, as soon, as the King was executed; he lost all his property; he has some thoughts of going to Philadelphia—⟨he⟩ is a most accomplishd young Man, but we do not wish to ⟨*mutilated*⟩ with him; my Family is Encreasing in Grand Children, two of my Sons having had Sons, last week[2]—our Harvest here is most abundant & good; & if we have good weather to save it, we shall be able to Export some to Germany; the Host of Combatants on the Continent will require great Quantities of Corn, of which I Suppose America will Supply one Quarter.

Lady Newenham joins me in most respectfull Compliments to Mrs Washington & you. I have the Honor, to be, Dear Sir with unalterable Esteem & respect—your most Obt & Very Hble Sert

Edward Newenham

P.S. want of money obliged me to sell my beautyfull Estate of Bell Chaupe for £6000, though it Cost me above £10,000.[3]

ALS, DLC:GW. The cover was addressed to GW at Mount Vernon and marked "(post paid)"; later, "Philadelphia" was added, "post paid" was struck out, and the cover was postmarked "N. YORK Jan 11" and stamped "FREE."

1. Lafayette's letters to Newenham have not been identified.

2. Newenham's fourth surviving son was Robert O'Callaghan Newenham (b. 1770), who belonged to the Marseilles trading firm of Folsch and Hornbostel. A son of Edward Worth Newenham (b. 1762), who married Elizabeth Persse (1768–1831) in 1787, was born on 6 September. The other grandson was probably a child of William Thomas Newenham (b. 1766), who married a Miss Lynam in September 1792.

3. Newenham's estate, Belcamp (or Bellechamp), was about five miles north of Dublin. Newenham had acquired property in the area by the mid-1760s and spent some £7,000 on the construction of a new house there in

the 1780s. Plagued by debts, however, he agreed in January 1793 with Henry Otiwell, collector of the Dublin excise, to sell the house and lands in exchange for payment of debts of £5,500 (James Kelly, *Sir Edward Newenham, MP, 1734–1814: Defender of the Protestant Constitution* [Portland, Ore., 2004], 40, 190–92, 261).

From Arthur St. Clair

Sir,   Fort Washington September 12th 1793

General Wayne has informed me that Ensign Morgan, who has been tried upon the charges exhibited against him by me, is found guilty, and sentenced to be dismissed from the Army; but that the Court Martial having been held by Orders from th⟨e⟩ W⟨ar⟩ Office to him, he does not think himself at Liberty ⟨mutilated⟩ Sentence into execution, but refers it back to you ⟨mutilated⟩ approbation or disaproval; otherwise, the Application I am about to trouble you with, would have been made to him.[1]

I should despise myself Sir, were I capable of prostituting a public prosecution to the gratification of private resentment. And although there can be no doubt that Mr Morgan intended an Injury to me, at the same time that he was committing a public Offence, he failed in effecting it; and I have not, nor have had any resentment, but that of contempt. My sole Object in arresting him was, to vindicate the military Laws and the discipline of the Army, which I considered as a Duty incumbent on me; and that Object is, perhaps, as much effected by the condemnation as it would be by inflicting the punishment: If then, Sir, it should appear to you, in the same light, and there be no impropriety in it, I would request that the punishment may be remitted.

Mr Morgan is a young Man, Sir, who, in this case has, I suppose, been misled by others, without much considering what he was about. (Why others should have either engaged in calumniating me, or inducing him to do it, I know not: And the Business has led me to a very serious retrospection; and I declare that I cannot find the instance, in my whole life, where I have given any person an unprovoked cause of offence) ⟨mutilated⟩ has no other profession, and, if the risque he has now run ⟨mutilated⟩r Effect, he may yet be of Service to his Country ⟨mutilated h⟩ave another reason for interceding for him, which is the great Affection I bore to his Grand father Mr John Baynton, a Man who was truly amiable, and respectable in every sense of the Word.[2] With the greatest Respect and regard I have the honor to be Sir, Your most obedient Servant

Ar. St Clair

ALS (retained copy), OHi: Arthur St. Clair Papers.

1. For discussion of the court-martial of John Morgan, see Henry Knox to GW, 28 July 1792, and n.8, and Knox to GW, 15 Sept. 1792, and n.10. The charges were based on St. Clair's letter to Knox of 29 March 1792 (see copy in Anthony Wayne's general orders of 30 Dec. 1793, PHi: Wayne Papers). For an account of the trial sympathetic to Morgan and critical of St. Clair, see *Federal Gazette and Philadelphia Daily Advertiser,* 17 Oct. 1793. For the final disposition of the case, see Edmund Randolph to GW, 24 Nov. 1793, and source note to that document.

2. John Baynton (1726–1773) was a partner in the Philadelphia mercantile firm of Baynton and Wharton (after 1763, Baynton, Wharton and Morgan), which was active in western trade and land speculation. A Quaker, Baynton represented Philadelphia County in the Pennsylvania legislature from 1756 through 1761.

From David Humphreys

My dear Sir.   Lisbon [Portugal] Septr 13th 1793.

The consolation I derive from your good & friendly letter of the 23d of March compensates a great deal for the cruel chagrine I feel for so long an absence from every thing my heart holds most dear. It is particularly a cordial for many uneasy sensations I feel at the present moment, respecting the interesting affair in which I am engaging.

It was somewhat of a curious circumstance that I should have been writing to you almost at the instant you was writing to me, and in part upon the same subject, viz., your re-election to & re-acceptance of the office of President. My sentiments are so clearly expressed in that letter, that I need not repeat them in this.[1]

You will have the goodness to recollect, that, long ago, I told my friend Mr Lear, I was afraid of writing to you, lest you should give yourself more trouble than you really ought to do in answering my letters. Be persuaded, my dear & most beloved General, it is only under condition of your absolutely suffering no inconvenience on the account, that I shall continue at times to use the permission of giving you such remarkable & interesting articles of information as may come to my knowledge, so as to be communicated earlier than through other channels.

We have at this moment one article of News of very great importance, which you can hardly receive from any other quarter so soon as from this. On the 28th of last month the Loyalists of Toulon gave up the Town & fleet to co-operate with the English & Spanish fleets before it, commanded by Lord Hood & Admiral Langara, in the establishment (as they term it) of Louis the 17th King of France. The Toulon fleet consisted of upwards of 30 Sail, of which 17 were manned & fit for Sea, and seven more in great forwardness. This intelligence came in so short a space of time as to render it suspicious, if it were not official to the Spanish Ambassador & the Portuguese Secretary of State for foreign Affairs, from whom I have it myself. Deputies from Merseilles were likewise said to be on board the combined fleet for the purpose of making the same cession of that City.[2] An article which is more certain, is, that the advanced Corps of the French Army on the frontiers of Spain has been defeated by General Ricardos with the loss of 15 Cannon & a considerable number of men.[3]

Other reports of events of sufficient magnitude are rife in circulation, but by no means of equal authenticity—such as the capture of Cambray, Lisle & some other strongly garrisoned Towns, the approach of the Prince of Coburg on the one hand & Gaston (at the Head of the Loyalists) on the other, to some position within nine leagues of Paris, and that these two forces had opened a friendly intercourse with each other—this I do not greatly rely upon.[4] We have no Packet since my last letter to the Secretary of State, but by an English Gazette accidentally received, it appears from an Official Account, the Duke of York had gained a splendid success over a superior force near Dunkirk.[5] From other channels of intelligence, it seems that the French fleet from Brest, & Lord Howe's channel fleet are both at Sea.

The Troops destined by this Court to serve in Spain are certainly ordered to embark on Monday next—I learn this from the Secretary of State, who was so exceedingly polite as to offer me a passage to Gibralter on board one of the Men of War. This was when I called upon him yesterday to introduce Mr Church, as remaining in charge with the affairs of the U.S. during my absence. I had only to thank him for his politeness, for I could not have carried my effects by that conveyance without exciting improper conjectures, even if I had not already engaged another conveyance. I was glad to find he had no suspicions of the real object.[6]

It is impossible to be more sensible of the good policy of our preserving in all events an unshaken resolution of neutrality, than I am. I rejoiced therefore most sincerely in the measures you had taken for that purpose. And I have endeavoured to co-operate in the same system, as far as lay in my power, by making every body believe it was not less our inclination than interest to avoid being involved in a war of such a complicated nature & at such a distance. In the name of every thing sacred & dear, let us persevere firmly in the same inoffensive line of conduct, and let us improve diligently the natural & political advantages with which Heaven has favoured us. By those means we shall acquire the resources & power to redress hereafter any partial & temporary inconveniences & wrongs we may suffer at present, on account of our pertinacious adherence to the pacific system. Yes—my dear General, I do verily believe we can finally preserve Peace for ourselves, if we seriously determine upon it. The Atlantic is our best friend. Notwithstanding the unfavorable dispositions of Spain (which I have communicated to the Secretary of State in two letters,[7] & which I have reason to believe exist in as great a degree as ever) England, as a Maritime Power, is the only nation that can force us into a war. And whatever the dispositions of that Government may be, rest assured, if we use all the reasonable & just means in our power to prevent our being dragged into hostility, the People of England will either prevent the Government from causing that deplorable event; or, after a short time, they will take part (I mean with a powerful & effectual opposition) against the Government, with us. In the last resort, a dignified, spirited & calm address to the People of England might not be without its effect. I am, therefore, well assured, you will continue to make the World believe, we are unalterably determined, by words & actions of the clearest demonstration, to follow as a nation the paths of justice & peace alone. In the event of a war, this must render our Cause popular. This cannot fail to make an opposite conduct on the part of others, with respect to us, odious in the eyes of the World in general. In my judgment, we had better even make temporary & inconsiderable sacrifices, than be forced into measures, which, however they may ultimately terminate to our national glory, must, in the mean time, be attended with great misfortunes & losses. particularly, as they will serve to check our actual, progressive improvements. Let us remember that Switzerland, Genoa & some other little States are able to preserve their neutrality; and if it were not for the too intimate connection of Portugal with England & Spain, She would be able to do the same—The hostile preparations on her part, are unpopular here in a high degree.

And now, my dear & respected General, to make a transition from the unpropitious affairs of war to the more desirable ones of peace, I cannot help expressing the strong sensations of joy, which your pleasing account of the prosperous state of our Country afforded me—It is from the plough, not the sword, the greatness & happiness of a nation must be ultimately derived. Apropos—of the plough—Mr Close (an English Clergyman & a great farmer, now here for his health) has ordered one of the newest & best construction to be shipped from England for you, in my name. This you will perceive by the enclosed extract of a letter from his Correspondent to him. I offered & insisted to pay the Bill for the plough, but Mr Close would not in any manner permit it: so it is a present from him to you. And I have no doubt will prove an acceptable & useful one.[8]

I intended fully to have written to my friend Mr Lear by this opportunity, but in my hurry of departure, I have not in truth time to do it. Pray, in apologising to him, have the goodness to offer my best compliments & sincerest regards to Mrs Washington and all my *friends* around you (the loss of one you know I sincerely lament)—and ever remain possessed of the sure & certain knowledge, that you have no *one* more cordially attached to you, or who more ardently wishes for the long & uninterrupted continuance of your health & happiness than your most affe. friend & grateful Servant

D. Humphreys.

ALS, DLC:GW.

1. See Humphreys to GW, 24 March 1793.

2. Samuel Hood, viscount Hood (1724–1816), a career naval officer ranking at this time as vice admiral, was appointed in February 1793 to be British commander in the Mediterranean. He arrived off Toulon, France, on 16 July and instituted a naval blockade. Commissioners from Marseilles came

aboard Hood's flagship on 23 Aug. to sue for peace by declaring for a monarchy and the constitution of 1789. It was agreed that the fleet and forts should be held by Hood for the French king until peace was declared. Hood's fleet, joined by the Spanish fleet under Don Juan de Langára, occupied Toulon over minimal resistance on 27 Aug. and held the town until December, when investing French troops forced the fleets to withdraw.

Juan de Lángara y Huarte (1736–1806) was a career naval officer who ranked at this time as a *capitán general* in the Spanish navy. Louis-Charles (1785–1795), who had become dauphin upon the death of his elder brother in 1789, was proclaimed by French Royalists as King Louis XVII but remained imprisoned until his death. Luís Pinto de Sousa Coutinho, viscount of Balsemão (c.1735–1804), was appointed Portugal's secretary of state for foreign affairs and war in 1788 and acted as Portugal's prime minister from December 1788 to 1801 and again in 1803. The Spanish ambassador to Portugal from 1792 to 1798 was Vicente Maria Imperiale, marqués de Oyra et de Latiano.

3. Antonio Ricardos y Carrillo de Albornoz (1727–1794) was the Spanish commander for Catalonia.

4. Friedrich Josias (1737–1815), prince of Saxe-Coburg-Saalfeld, commanded the Austrian army in the Netherlands. Gaston was reputedly one of the leaders of the Vendée insurrection. A declaration of 25 May issued in his name was widely published, as were biographies claiming a considerable military background, but later it was stated that he was a former wigmaker who had been soon killed (see, for example, *Providence Gazette and Country Journal,* 21 Sept.; *Mercury* [Boston], 3 Sept.; *Columbian Gazetteer* [New York], 12 Dec.). The wigmaker insurgent was evidently a Jean François Gaston (c. 1770–1793), who was killed at an engagement near Saint-Gervais in April (Chassin, *Vendée Patriote,* 1:191–94; "Gaston," 67–69). The report of a Gaston as the commander of a major force appears to have been largely a myth (Curzon, "Mythe de 'Monsieur de Gaston,' " 49–55).

5. Humphreys was referring to his letter to Thomas Jefferson of 3 Sept. (*Jefferson Papers,* 27:24–25). For discussion of the action near Dunkirk, see William Willcocks to GW, 3 Sept., and n.2 to that document.

6. Humphreys had been appointed minister plenipotentiary to negotiate a treaty with Algiers (GW to the Dey of Algiers, 21 March; Jefferson to Humphreys, 21 March, *Jefferson Papers,* 25:420–22).

7. See Humphreys to Jefferson, 29 May and 3 Sept. (*Jefferson Papers,* 26:140–41, 27:24–25).

8. Humphreys may have been referring to Henry Jackson Close (c.1753–1806), a distinguished agriculturalist and rector of Hitcham Suffolk.

Enclosure
Extract of a letter to Mr. Close

Dear Sir   [c. 1 August 1793]
I have this day shipped the above on Board the William Penn, James Josiah, Comr for Philadelphia,[1] by this post I have en-

closed in a letter to Clement Biddle Esqr. the Bill of Loading, and have said to him that through the direction of Col. Humphrey's, I have consigned it to his Care, and from whom I apprehended that his Excellency or himself woud hear farther on the Business—I have done this thinking that the Vessell might arrive at the port of Philadelphia, before the Bill of Loading cou'd reach Mr Biddle, if sent Via Lisbon.

Copy, DLC:GW. An additional line of text at the bottom of the manuscript is illegible because of the way the manuscript was torn.

1. James Josiah (1751–1820), of Philadelphia, saw service in the Revolutionary War as an officer in the Continental navy and as a commander of privateer and armed merchant vessels. The *William Penn*, under Josiah's command, made frequent runs between London and Philadelphia during the 1790s. The ship arrived at Philadelphia on 27 Sept. carrying news dating from 31 July (see *Carlisle Gazette, and the Western Repository of Knowledge,* 2 Oct.).

From Tobias Lear

My dear honored Sir,   Portsmouth [N.H.] Septr 13th 1793

The desire which Mrs Washington had the goodness to express to know how my little boy got through his journey, has given her the trouble of the inclosed letter, which You will be so kind as to do me the favor to give to her.[1]

I arrived here this morning with my young companion in good health, we met with no accident of any kind on the road. Of rain we had only a sprinkling one day, and such appeard to be the gratitude of the inhabitants in that part of the Country where it fell (near Boston) for a blessing so long wished for, that it gave me pleasure even to ride in it. The drough, particularly about Boston, has been so severe as leave the ground at this season without the appearance of verdure—and I was informed that in many places the farmers had been obliged to begin already to feed out their very scanty store of winter food to the half starved Cattle. Happily, however, the severity of the drough is not general, the Country about Boston has suffered most.

I am happy to inform you that whenever I have, in the course of my journey, heard a sentiment expressed respecting the late measures of Government in regard to privateers, prizes &c.—it has been that of high approbation—and such seems to be the abhorrence in which the act of any Citizens of the U.S. engaging in that piratical species of warfare is viewed, that whoever may engage in it must expect, even if he should escape the punishement due by the laws to such crime, to be execrated by his fellow Citizens, at least in this quarter. I find however, that there is a very general & serious complaint of the capture of American Vessels by the West Indian Privateers. The trade of this part of the Country has suffered much thereby—and more evil is apprehended from the same source: But I presume proper & regular representations of this greeivance will be made to the Government.[2]

I shall leave this place for New York about the 25 of the present month.

Among the Millions who pray for your health & happiness there is no one does it with more truth & sincerity than my dear honored Sir, Your grateful, affectionate & Obediant Servant

Tobias Lear.

ALS, DLC:GW.

1. The enclosure has not been identified.

2. On the injury to U.S. commerce by West Indian privateers, see Edmund Randolph to GW, 2 March 1794, which quotes extensively from the complaint of a Philadelphia committee. GW transmitted that letter to Congress on 5 March 1794 (*ASP, Foreign Relations,* 1:423–24).

From Mr. Meifren

Mon General   de Richemont Le 13. 7bre 1793
    une victime des Malheurs de st domingue S'adresse A vous Avec Confiance je suis un de ceux qui ont perdu dans un jour le fruit de plusieurs Années de travaux, et qui ont fui pour Se Soustraire Aux feu et aux flammes. j'etois bien eloigné de Croire que me Souvant en rade j'aurais été enlevé de mes foyers, et d'aupres d'une epouse vertueuse, que je n'ay Cessé de cherir. de ma fortune j'en Suis en quelque façon Consolé; mais le Sort de mon Epouse me donne des Cruelles, et justes inquietudes.

    j'ay été forcé Ainsy que tant dautres de la quitter. j'ay après etant à baltimore quelle existoit, mais me trouvant aujourdhuy A Richemont Aupres d'un Amy qui m'a apellé,[1] je ne suis point Aportée d'avoir de ses Nouvelles.

    Ma position est donc des plus tristes. vous etez le Seul mon General qui puissiez porter Remede A Mes Maux; Votre vertu, votre Merite, et votre humanité A Secourir les Malheureux; me

Sont un Sur garant, que prennant part A mon Sort vous voudrez bien charger un Capitaine partant pour le Cap de me mener Mon epouse. je joint Sous ce ply une lettre pour elle dont le Capitaine pourra Se charger.[2]

vous devez Mon General la preference que je vous donne quoique françois A votre Cœur bienfaisant. heureux sont ceux qui Sont Sous vos Loix. Croyez que je ne Cesse d'etre Avec le plus profond Respect Mon General Votre tres humble et tres obeissant serviteur

Meifren

ALS, DNA: RG 59, Miscellaneous Letters.

1. At the bottom of the letter, Meifren wrote: "Mon adresse Meifren habitant proprietaire de st domingue chez Mr trouin fils A Richemont." Meifren remained in Richmond, apparently without his wife, as late as mid-January 1794. By then he had moved to "a French Lady's, who lives close by Gab. Wood," and he was "supported altogether by charity" (John Barret to Henry Lee, 17 Jan. 1794, Vi: Executive Department, Letters Received, Governor Henry Lee, 1791–1794, RG 3; see also *Calendar of Virginia State Papers*, 7:14–15). He may be the Joseph Meyfren (born c.1751) who was a member of a Masonic lodge at Portsmouth, Va., in 1798 (*Tableau des F.F. qui composent la Loge Provinciale Française, Sous le Titre Distinctif de la Sagesse: a L'Orient de Portsmouth, en Virginie, Etat de l'Amerique Septentrionale. A l'Epoque de la St. Jean, 5798* [Norfolk, 1798], 4). The friend may have been Francis Trouin (d. 1804).

2. The enclosed letter to Meifren's wife has not been identified.

From John Butler

SIR,   *New-York, Sept.* 14, 1793.

NOTHING can be more gratifying to me, than the pleasure of dedicating a portion of my labors to a character of your eminence, distinguished as you are in the political world by an uniformity of your patriotic rectitude, and a faithful discharge of those important duties to which you have been called by the voice of a free people—the impartial system of the American government, and the equitable frame of her legislation, are such as puts censure to defiance, and the most insidious despot to silence.

I am neither addicted to adulation or fulsom flattery, yet I cannot but exult, with a joy of unaffected purity, on the numerous blessings resulting to the American States, under the smiles of your auspices.

Being early initiated into those principles, in which you have so eminently signalized the valor and virtue of a true republican, I rejoice at the priviledge of laying this essay at your feet, as an oblation offered upon the altar of liberty and equality.

Posterity will look back with veneration on the name of *Washington,* as the secondary source from which republican liberty derived its energy. We know of few nations which have not experienced their revolutions, and changes of government, by the fate of war. May the wisdom of your counsel stimulate the united Americans to preserve, inviolate, that freedom they now enjoy; and may they long continue to participate in the blessings of mutual laws, reciprocal government, and impartial legislation, which are the dazling symbols of liberty and freedom.

Convinced that liberty is no exemption from labor or industry, but is a powerful incentive to both–so in all free nations there must be hewers of wood and drawers of water; and it appears the essential duty of the whole community of republicans, to unite their efforts in erecting the plain, but magnificent edifice of equality, as a monument sacred to *liberty and the freedom of conscience.*

These are the sentiments of a fugitive who has emigrated from the severe rigor of political persecution, to avoid the crushing power of haughty rulers, under whose despotism the thunder of anarchy roars from pole to pole. Storms and tempests shock the affrighted villager. The rapacity of kings and courtiers shed alike their sedition and their desolation: They plunge their sabres into the blood of innocence. Contending for power, they transform liberty into slavery; and, by their intrigue and subtlety, inveigle their subjects into vassalage.

To see Europe tranquilized by a speedy adoption of those principles which inspire men with the sacred love of liberty—to see the sabre of despotism arrested from the hands of tyrants—to see thrones leveled with the earth's smooth surface—and to see liberty reign paramount, is the fervent prayer of A devoted Advocate for the Cause of Liberty,

JOHN BUTLER.

Printed, John Butler, *The Political Fugitive: Being a Brief Disquisition into the Modern System of British Politics; and the Unparalleled Rigor of Political Persecution: Together with Several Miscellaneous Observations on the Abuses and Corruptions of the English Government* (New York, 1794), iii–v. This document serves as the dedication for Butler's book, which was advertised beginning in September 1793 but not published until March 1794 (*Diary; or, Loudon's Register* [New York], 4 Sept. 1793; *Greenleaf's New York Journal, & Patriotic Register,* 19 March 1794).

From Charles Fierer

Sir   Dumfries [Va.] Sept. 14th 1793

I received your Excellency's answer to my letter, of the 7th of July last,[1] which induces me to hope that (as this favourable opportunity offers) your Excellency will be kindly pleased to indulge me with a copy of the letter, which was the object of my former application; The letter was dated (I think) sometime in August 1778—Head quarters, at the White plains, and directed to Henry Laurens Esqr. then President of Congress.[2] I have the Honour to remain with profound respect, Your Excellency's most humble & most obedient Servant

Charles Fierer
Late Capt. of the Virginia State Cavalry

ALS, DLC:GW.

1. Fierer apparently intended a reference to Tobias Lear's letter to him of 17 July, which replied to Fierer's letter to GW of 10 July.

2. See GW to Laurens, 9 Aug. 1778. Fierer wanted a copy of this letter to support his petition to the Virginia legislature for compensation for Revolutionary War services.

From Alexander Contee Hanson

Sir,   Annapolis Septr 14, 1793

The inclosed address was last week sent to Mr Henry Hill at Philadelphia, to be by him presented, in behalf of the citizens of Annapolis;[1] but, as they have heard of your departure from Philadelphia, and are apprehensive, that you have not received it, I take the liberty of transmitting it by post, and have the honour to be, Sir, with every sentiment of profound veneration. Your most obedient and devoted servant

A. C. Hanson

ALS, DLC:GW.
   1. Hanson is referring to Philadelphia wine merchant Henry Hill.

Enclosure
Address from Annapolis, Md., Citizens

Sir   [Annapolis, 5 September 1793]

    The citizens of Annapolis conceive it their duty, at this time, to unite their voices with those of their fellow citizens in various parts of the United States; and they beg leave to assure you, that they are deeply and indelibly impressed with a sense of the paternal vigilance exalted wisdom and dignified firmness manifested by your proclamation on the subject of neutrality.[1] It is their fixed determination to conduct themselves, agreeably to the principles, therein expressed; and they will exert their best endeavours, to prevent any infringement of them by others.

    They are, at the same time, persuaded, that on the faithful observance of subsisting treaties, according to their true intent and obvious construction, the prosperity and honour of our country greatly depend. They cannot be unmindful of the important advantages, derived from our generous allies, the citizens of France; and they doubt not, that, throughout the United States, there prevails a disposition, on all proper occasions, to testify their gratitude and affection. But they never can consent to the adoption of a conduct, which would violate the rules of universal justice, exceed greatly the extent of our national engagements, and hazard the blessings, we have acquired, without serving materially the cause of our friends.[2]

    They cannot but lament that any diversity of sentiment, relative to the construction of a treaty has taken place in America; but they do not believe, that a real difference of opinion will elsewhere prevail. They reprobate the idea of the intervention of any foreign minister to correct supposed abuses in our government. Every communication of such a minister, to them, or any of their fellow citizens, unless thro' the regular constituted authorty, and every interference by such a minister with the administration of our internal affairs, they hold not only repugnant to the usage of nations, but derogatory to the dignity of a free, and enlightened people.[3]

    Permit them further to declare, that they feel a sublime gratification in avowing their steady attachment to the man, whom Providence seems to have raised up for the salvation of their country, and to have preserved, as the favoured instrument, for securing to millions the inestimable blessings of liberty independence and peace.

That the people of America may always duly prize these blessings; that they may always possess discernment to detect the varying arts of delusion and that you, Sir, may for ever be happy, is the sincere and ardent wish of the citizens of Annapolis.

By order of the citizens of Annapolis at a meeting, held at the Stadt-house, on Thursday September 5, 1793

A. C. Hanson Chairman

ADS, DLC:GW; ADS, DLC:GW; LB, DLC:GW. The second ADS was presumably sent by Henry Hill. This address was printed in the *Maryland Gazette* (Annapolis), 26 September.

1. On 22 April GW proclaimed the United States neutral in the war between France and an alliance of European nations.

2. For the Treaty of Alliance and the Treaty of Amity and Commerce between the United States and France (1778), see Miller, *Treaties*, 3–44.

3. In a public letter of 12 Aug., John Jay and Rufus King had asserted that French minister Edmond Genet "had said he would Appeal to the People from certain decisions of the President" (*Diary; or Loudon's Register* [New York], 12 Aug. 1793). Genet's letter to GW of 13 Aug., which demanded that GW deny Genet had made such a threat, had been made public by late August. While disavowing the rumored threat, Genet's letter nonetheless intimated that GW's policies were indeed contrary to American public opinion.

From Joseph Prentis

Sir: Wmsburg Septr 14. 1793.

It is with peculiar pleasure that I obey the request of the Citizens of Williamsburg, in transmitting to your Excellency, sundry resolutions expressing their Sentiments, respecting the neutrality recommended by your late proclamation. I have the Honour to be with much deference, Yr Mo. Ob. Sr.

Jos: Prentis

ALS, DLC:GW; LB, DLC:GW.

Joseph Prentis (1754–1809) represented York County in the Virginia House of Delegates, 1778–88, and was speaker from 1786 until January 1788, when he was elected a judge of the General Court, a position he held until his death.

Enclosure
Resolutions from Williamsburg, Va., Citizens

[11 September 1793]

At a Meeting of the Citizens of Williamsburg convened at the Courthouse of the said City on Wednesday the Eleventh day of September 1793.

Resolved that William Russell be appointed Clerk to the meeting.[1]

Resolved that the Honorable Joseph Prentis be appointed President of the meeting.

Resolved that a Committee be appointed to take into consideration the Proclamation of the President of the United States recommending a strict Neutrality towards the several European powers now at War. And a Committee was appointed consisting of The Reverend John Bracken John C. Byrd, Benjamin C. Waller, Samuel Griffin, Robert H. Waller, James Southall, Robert Greenhow, and Charles Hunt esquires, who retired and after some time Mr Bracken from the said Committee Reported that they had come to several Resolutions which being read were agreed to and are as follows to wit,[2]

Resolved that the conduct of the President of the United States hath been uniformly marked with that disinterested and unwearied attention to the duties of his Office and that prudent and persevering zeal for the welfare and liberties of his Country which give additional dignity and lustre to his former merits, and justly demands the approbation and gratitude of his fellow Citizens.

Resolved that the late Proclamation of the President recommending the observance of a strict Neutrality by the Citizens of the United States towards the several European powers now at War was a prudent and wise measure, and furnishes a further proof of his vigilant attention to the interests of our Country.[3]

Resolved that we consider the original Arming and fitting out Privateers within any of the Ports of the United States as inconsistent with that Neutrality which we are bound to observe, and that we particularly consider it as a violation of duty in any Citizen to be concerned in or enter on board such Privateers.

Resolved that the Executive is the Organ or medium through which Foreign Ministers ought to hold any communication of a publick nature with these United States; and that every attempt of any such Foreign Minister by himself or his Agents directly or indirectly to interfere in the concerns of the said States, or to prosecute the business on which he may be appointed to negotiate through any other medium, would be a daring insult on the sovereignty of the Union and call forth the warmest resentment and indignation of every good Citizen.[4]

Resolved that the several late publications which were intended to censure the conduct, or to asperse the reputation of our worthy fellow Citizen the President of thee United States, we consider as illiberal, and deserving our utmost contempt and detestation.[5]

Resolved that it is the duty of the constituted authorities of these United States, to observe with the most punctual fidelity, all their public engagements to foreign Powers, and particularly towards France, their generous Ally, whose real and disinterested friendship they have so often, and so effectually experienced.

Resolved that the President of this meeting be requested to transmit to the President of the United States, a Copy of the foregoing Resolutions.[6] Signed by Order of the Meeting

Joseph Prentis Pr.
Will: Russell Clerk

D, DLC:GW; LB, DLC:GW. These resolutions were printed in the *Virginia Gazette, and General Advertiser* (Richmond), 25 September.

1. William Russell (d. 1812) served as clerk of the James City County Court and as clerk of the Williamsburg General Court.

2. John Bracken (c.1747–1818), rector of Bruton Parish in Williamsburg from 1773 to 1818, served on the faculty of the grammar school at William and Mary College from 1775 to 1779 and was again appointed to the faculty when the grammar school was revived in 1792. He became president of the college in 1812 and served in that position until 1814. He also served during the 1790s as a mayor of Williamsburg. Williamsburg lawyer Samuel Griffin (1746–1810) served as a Virginia representative to Congress, 1789–95. Charles Hunt (c.1753–1794) was a Williamsburg merchant. Benjamin Carter Waller (1757–1820) and Robert Hall Waller (b. 1764) were sons of Judge Benjamin Waller (1716–1786). Benjamin Carter Waller represented York County in the 1792 session of the Virginia House and later represented Williamsburg for two sessions, 1799–1801. Robert Hall Waller was county clerk for York and James City counties. James Southall was probably James Barrett Southall (1726–1801), proprietor of the Raleigh Tavern at Williamsburg. Robert Greenhow (1761–1840) was a Williamsburg merchant who represented James City County in two sessions of the Virginia House, 1806–8. He later

moved to Richmond, where he served for a time as mayor during the War of 1812. John C. Byrd was probably John Carter Byrd (b. 1751), son of William Byrd III of Westover.

3. GW's Neutrality Proclamation was dated 22 April.

4. For the charge that French minister Edmond Genet had threatened to appeal some of GW's decisions to the American people, see Genet to GW, 13 Aug., and n.4.

5. While GW received criticism in a number of publications, the most well-known and damning critique of the president and his neutrality policy appeared under the pseudonym "Veritas" in the *National Gazette* (Philadelphia) on 1, 5, 8, and 12 June (three letters to GW, dated 30 May, 3 June, and 6 June, and an essay complaining of the "idolatry" of those "sycophants" who would attempt to silence criticism). Throughout the summer, the *National Gazette,* in particular, published other letters criticizing GW or defending Genet and denouncing his accusers (see, for example, "A CITIZEN" to GW, 4 July, and "AN AMERICAN" to GW, 14 Aug.).

6. GW replied to these resolutions in a letter to Prentis of 23 September.

From David Ross

Sir   George Town Septr 14th 1793
    Yours of the 9th has been just handed me—Being sensible of the honor—I shall endeavour to justify your choice by an exertion to a faithful discharge of the Trust thereby reposed in Your respectful & obedt Servant

                                                    David Ross

ALS, DNA: RG 59, Miscellaneous Letters. The cover was addressed, "the President present."

From Charles Carter of Ludlow

My Dr Sr   Fredbg [Va.] Septr 15th 1793
    Nothing but a very particular, and critical circumstance, shoud imbolden me to address you on a private affair. but tis of such a tender nature to a Parent, that Im certain of your Pardon. I have two Sons, in Philadelphia, in a most critical situation exposed to the raging Fever, that by accts sweeps, all before it. during the month of August I made them a remittance, of 150 Dollars. this accepted Bill was put into the hands of a Gentleman to receive the money, but by a letter from my Son Charles of the 1st of this month, he had not, nor did not expect, to get the money. Chs is

a Pupil of Doctr Hutchisons, who is carried off by this malignant Fever & must be in great danger, as he has constantly attendd the Doctor. I coud remit another Bill, but all negotiations, are now stopd, during I hope but a short period. Youl add to the many favors already conferrd, if youl direct 100 Dollars to be paid to Walker Randolph Carter, at Mr Hunters the Coachmakers, or to Charles Landon Carter living, at the late Doctor James Hutchison.[1] this is the only method I can devise, for their relief. as soon as business returns into its regular channel the money shall certainly replaced. after wishing you health & Happiness give me leave to assure you I am Yr Affectionate Friend & very Humble Servant

Chs Carter

ALS, DLC:GW.

1. Philadelphia coach maker William Hunter (1756–1814) resided at 319 High Street, while Dr. James Hutchinson resided at 155 South Second Street.

From Thomas Jefferson

Dear Sir   Schuylkill [Pa.] Sep. 15[–16]. 1793.

I have duly received your two favors from Chester and Elkton, and have now the honour to inclose you an address from the town & vicinity of Petersburg, which in a letter from mister Peachey I was desired to deliver you.[1]

I also inclose you a letter from mister Genet on the subject of Galbaud, and his conspiracies, with my answer sent to him. my hurry of business has prevented my translating the former, but if it cannot be done in your family, I shall be in time to do it myself.[2]

I inclose also mister Hammond's reply to my letter of the 9th[3] Mr Pinckney's letter of July 5. Mr Hammond's letter of Sep. 12. communicating the English instructions for the seizure of corn, and the answer I propose to send to him if approved by you.[4] I expect also to recieve from the office the blank commission for the collector of Annapolis in time to inclose it herein.[5]

Having found on my going to town, the day you left it, that I had but one clerk left, & that business could not be carried on, I determined to set out for Virginia as soon I could clear my own letter files. I have now got through it so as to leave not a single letter unanswered, or thing undone, which is in a state to be done, and expect to set out tomorrow or next day. I shall hope to be at Mount Vernon on the 5th day to take your orders. the fever here, is still diffusing itself. it is not quite as fatal. Colo. Hamilton & mistress Hamilton are recovered. the Consul Dupont is dead of it. so is Wright.[6] the Consul Hauterive has sent me an answer to my circular letter, as proud as could have been expected, and not very like a desisting from the acts forbidden.[7] As I shall probably be with you as soon as this letter, I shall add nothing further than assurances of the high respect & esteem with which I have the honor to be sincerely Dear Sir Your most obedt & most humble sert

Th: Jefferson

P.S. Sep. 16. I find I shall not be able to get away to-day. since writing the above I have more certain accounts from the city. the deaths are probably about 30. a day, and it continues to spread. Saturday was a very mortal day. Dr Rush is taken with the fever last night.

ALS, DNA: RG 59, Miscellaneous Letters; ALS (letterpress copy), DLC: Jefferson Papers; LB, DNA: RG 59, George Washington's Correspondence with His Secretaries of State. The letterpress copy lacks the postscript.

1. GW wrote Jefferson from Chester, Pa., on 10 Sept., and from Elkton, Md., on 11 September. For the enclosed address to GW, see Resolutions from Petersburg, Va., Citizens, 2 September. For the letter from Thomas Griffin Peachy to Jefferson of 3 Sept., see *Jefferson Papers*, 27:28–29.

2. Edmond Genet's letter to Jefferson of 6 Sept. announced his discovery of "la plus affreuse conspiration" against French vessels and colonies involving François Thomas Galbaud and Claude Corentin Tanguy de la Boissière (d. 1799). He noted that he had obtained warrants against Galbaud and the other conspirators in New York, but when the conspirators had escaped, he requested federal warrants, since the effect of the New York warrants was limited to that state. Genet also requested that the government exercise "la Surveillance la plus active" against these plots (*Jefferson Papers*, 27:41–43).

Jefferson's response of 12 Sept. stated that no federal warrant could be issued. Since "The laws of this Country take no notice of crimes committed out of their jurisdiction," the men could be arrested only if they were part of a ship's crew and covered by the consular convention with France, and in that case Congress had left the remedy to the district judges of each state, with no authority "to any one officer to send his process through all the States of the Union." However, for preventing future hostile acts, if Genet would provide "such information as to persons and places as may indicate to what points the vigilance of the officers is to be directed, proper measures will be immediately taken for preventing every attempt to make any hostile expedition from these States against any of the dominions of France." Jefferson added that he would immediately communicate the matter to GW, and "if he shall direct any thing in addition or alteration, it shall be the subject of another letter" (*Jefferson Papers,* 27:97–99).

For discussion of the New York warrants against three of the accused conspirators, see Clinton to GW, 2 Sept., and enclosures. Tanguy de la Boissière was a journalist refugee from Saint Domingue who was in the process of establishing a newspaper (*Journal des Révolutions de la Partie Française de Saint-Domingue*) at New York. Publication of the paper, which was highly critical of Genet, had shifted to Philadelphia by 27 September. Tanguy went on to edit other short-lived papers before he returned to France in 1798.

3. For discussion of Jefferson's letter to British minister George Hammond of 9 Sept., see Cabinet Opinion, 7 Sept., and n.5 to that document. Hammond's first letter to Jefferson of 12 Sept. took issue with Jefferson's assertion that the French squadron at New York had merely brought refugees from Saint Domingue and was not involved in cruising against the British. Hammond claimed "the *establishment of a regular succession of cruizers*" and cited the *Favorite, Cerf, Concorde,* and *La Normande* as vessels so employed (*Jefferson Papers,* 27:100).

4. Thomas Pinckney's letter to Jefferson of 5 July enclosed a copy of "additional Instructions to the Commanders of British men of War and Privateers," dated 8 June and issued by the British admiralty on 28 June, which authorized the commanders to stop all vessels carrying corn, flour, or meal to any port controlled by the French and send them into British ports, where they would be required to sell those provisions to the British government or to give security that the provisions would be delivered to countries at peace with Britain. In addition, the commanders were authorized to seize for condemnation all ships, regardless of cargo, attempting to enter a blockaded port.

Hammond's second letter to Jefferson of 12 Sept. transmitted a copy of those same instructions with the British justification for their policy. Jefferson's reply to that letter, dated 22 Sept., informed Hammond that "The paper had been before communicated to the President, and instructions immediately sent to our Minister at London to make proper representations on the subject, in the effect of which we have all that confidence which the justice of the British Government is calculated to inspire" (*Jefferson Papers,* 26:439–42, 27:100–102, 143–44). An ADfS of Jefferson's reply is in DLC: Jefferson Papers. The dateline, "Mount Vernon Sep. 22 93," may have been added later.

5. GW had requested this in his letter to Jefferson of 11 September.

6. Joseph Wright (1756–1793) went to London in the early 1770s, studying with Benjamin West and establishing a reputation as a portrait painter. He returned to America in 1782 and thereafter worked in New York and Philadelphia, completing a portrait of GW in 1784 (see GW to Wright, 10 Jan. 1784, *Papers, Confederation Series,* 1:32–33).

7. For Jefferson's circular letter to French consuls and vice-consuls, 7 Sept., see Cabinet Opinion, 7 Sept., and n.1 to that document. Alexandre Maurice Hauterive, the French consul at New York, replied on 10 Sept. that his

activities, including enlistments, were to maintain his nation's rights. It was impossible for him to respond to Jefferson's threats because they "attentent à L'honneur d'une puissante République qui m'a imposé une Loi que je trouvé bien facile à Suivre": to fear nothing in the world but compromising their rights or his duties. On this subject, he would, he told Jefferson, receive the orders of the French minister and obey them. (*Jefferson Papers*, 27:83–84).

From Henry Knox

sir   Near Philadelphia 15 Septr 1793

On the 13th I received a letter from General Wayne dated the 8th ultimo. He acknowledges to have received mine of the 20th of July, written in consequence of an express from the Commissioners forbidding him from encreasing his force at the head of the line. He complains of these orders and says that "our greatest difficulty will result from the want of timely supplies of provisions at *the head of the line.*" [1]

One of the contractors is here and says they have an abundance of provisions at Fort Washington, and means, to carry on at once a large Supply equal to 200000 rations. I have directed him to make specific and official returns of the quantity on hand, the quantity he can move with the Army, and the supply he can keep up with the Army while operating towards the Miami villages and the rapids of the Omee river. [2]

Brigr General Posey has been into Kentucky and reports to Genl Wayne that the voluntiers are all or nearly all engaged so as to march at a moments warning.

The express from the Commissioners arrived at Pittsburg the 1st instant and was sent off the same day, the three copies, also arrived before the 3d, and were also all sent off to head quarters. [3] General Wayne would probably receive the first on the 8th, his voluntiers would I should imagine all arrive by the 1⟨9⟩ [4] or 20th instant, so that he would then be able then to move forward at the rate of 15 miles a day—I should hope that he would move with his whole force from Fort Jefferson—the 1st of October at furthest. he states his regular troops for action to be about 2800, officers included. to these will be added of the detachments not arrived, at least 200—If he obtains his whole number of 1500 mounted voluntiers, his force will be equal to every savage combined, to the south of the lakes, and north of the Ohio. God grant him success!

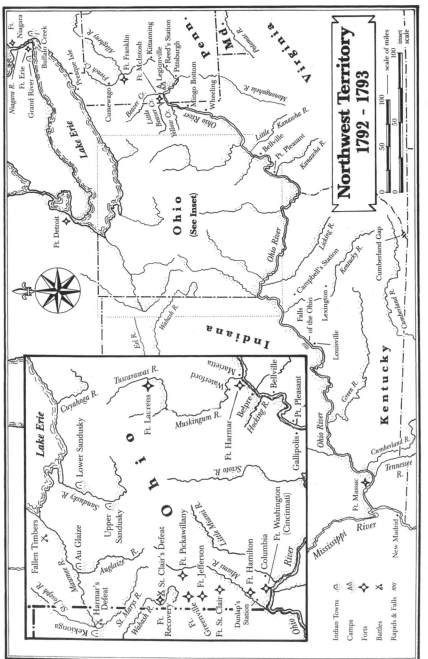

Map 1. Northwest Territory, 1792–1793. (Illustrated by Rick Britton. Copyright Rick Britton 2003.)

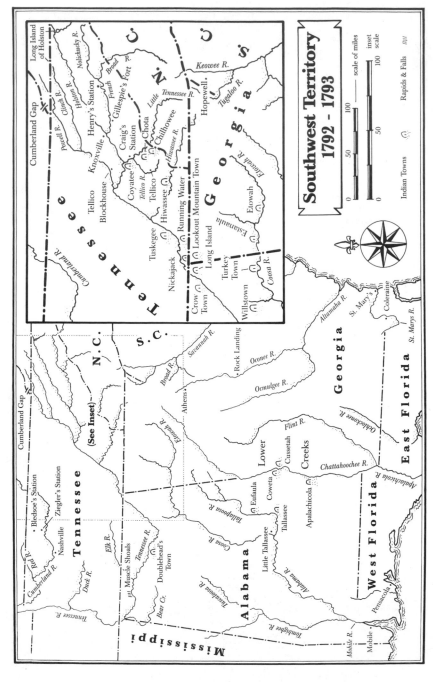

Map 2. Southwest Territory, 1792–1793. (Illustrated by Rick Britton. Copyright Rick Britton 2003.)

I have received a letter from Genl Smith secretary of the southern territory dated the 23 August giving an account of another lawless expedition against the cherokees, in which were killed ten indian men, two Women, and sixteen women taken prisoners this expedition consisted of 180 mounted voluntiers under Colo. Dohorty.[5] The consequence of this and such other expeditions is, that the cherokees are preparing to attack the territory with their whole Force. Apprehensions are great, and a considerable force is called out for the defence of the Country. An expence of one hundred thousand Dollars will probably be thus incurred by the said expeditions before the meeting of Congress!

I have received a letter from Mr Seagrove of the 22 ultimo dated at Savannah in which he says that all continues quiet and that he was preparing to set off to the Rock Landing with the intention of going into the Indian Country provided the party should meet him at the Oakmulgee as he had requested to escort him into the nation.[6]

Colonel Pickering and Mr Randolph have arrived. The former found the yellow fever in his family having a son and servant sick with it but both likely to do well. Mr Randolph is with the attorney General. I have not seen either of them but Colonel Pickering has sent me their journal.[7]

The fever made great havoc the last week. among others Doctr Warner Washington. Doctor Rush's success however is great indeed. I understand that he has given his medicine to upwards of 500 patients. He does not pretend to say they have all had the yellow fever but many undoubtedly had, and he lost only one since he adopted his new mode. He has acquired great honor in visiting every body to the utmost of his power. but his applications have been so general that it was utterly impossible to attend to all of them. But he directs the medicine and the Apothecaries prepares it.[8]

Mr Dupont the french Consul is dead with it. Mr Willing and Mr Barclay are well.

Colonel and Mrs Hamilton have both recovered by a mode quite different from Rushes, and which is published under the signature of A.K.[9]—Doctor Kuhn—They set off on saturday last for New York.

The different opinions of treatment excite great inquietude—But Rush bears down all before him—so that I think if the weather should be cold, together with some rains that the fever will hardly be known on the 1st of Novr. from the opinions collected from a variety of quarters I do not think it encreases. the great seat of it at present seems to be from 2d to 3d street, and thence to Walnut streets. Water street however continues sickly. But the alarm is inexpressible. Every body who could, has removed into the Country.

I hope to be able to set off hence eastward on the 19th or 20th—All the public offices of the State and of the U.S., are shut I beleive, or at least that very litle is done in them, exepting the war office—But as all my efficient clerks have left me from apprehension, mine will be as the others. According to my view however nothing will suffer during my absence as I shall put into train of execution, all the preparations directed.

I beleive the french ships did not sail until the 15th from NewYork. Not a word has transpired of the communications to Mr Genet.[10] The July packet has arrived. No news from Europe.

Since writing the above I have seen Colonel Pickering, and also I have read the Journal. The verbal information, added to the written, remove every doubt of the source of the opposition, covered however in the most plausible manner. From his information it would appear impracticable to collect of the hostile Indians *more than one thousand.* He says that the most sensible of the quakers are of opinion that the United states have offered all that they ought to offer.[11] He is of opinion that Brant has acted faithfully, and that the English do not much like him. I am Sir With the most perfect respect and attachment Your humble Servt

H. Knox

ALS, DLC:GW; LB, DLC:GW.

1. Treaty commissioners Benjamin Lincoln, Beverley Randolph, and Timothy Pickering wrote Knox on 10 July reporting that they had promised the Indians they would request orders to Anthony Wayne, "not only to abstain from hostilities, but to remain quietly at his posts" (*ASP, Indian Affairs,* 1:351). In response, Knox wrote Wayne on 20 July instructing him to withdraw any troops "exceeding the usual Garrisons" from his forward posts and to keep the army "in the vicinity of Fort Washington until the event of the Treaty be known" (Knopf, *Wayne,* 256–57).

Wayne's reply to Knox of 8 Aug. argued that the intelligence that the Indians had given to the commissioners to elicit the order was unfounded—that very few new troops had been stationed at the advanced posts and that there was no buildup of provisions—and he complained, "I had presumed that as Commander in Chief of the Legion of the United States, some *confidence* ought to have been placed in my *honor,* as well as *conduct;* when I promised not to advance into the Indian Country or to establish any new Posts in front of those we then possessed, until the result of the pending treaty was known." He had, however, "obeyed with promptitude, by ordering Genl Wilkinson to withdraw the one hundred and eighty seven officers & men from the advanced Posts." Wayne enclosed intelligence "of the depredations and murders committed by the savages" and noted, "that there is a general confederacy forming against us I have not a doubt." He then summarized his preparations for the possible Indian campaign, ending with the sentence quoted here by Knox (although Knox's quotation differs slightly from the surviving letterbook copies by adding the words "of provision" and removing the underline from "timely supplies") (MiU-C: Wayne Papers, see also Knopf, *Wayne,* 260–66).

2. The Omee River now is called the Maumee River.

3. The expresses carried a letter of 23 Aug. in which the treaty commissioners informed Wayne that the Indians had "finally determined not to treat at all" (*ASP, Indian Affairs,* 1:359).

4. The letter-book copy has "16th," but "19th" seems to be the best reading of the over-written character on the ALS.

5. Daniel Smith's letter to Knox of 23 Aug. has not been found. The *Knoxville Gazette* of 27 Aug. reported on this expedition: "On Sunday the 4th inst. a volunteer company consisting of one hundred and eighty men, from the counties of Knox and Jefferson, under the command of Col. George Doherty assembled at Gambles Station, on Little River, for the purpose of marching into the Cherokee towns, and on the same day crossed the Tennessee. The next day they marched to Big Tellico, where they killed two fellows and a squaw, and took one squaw prisoner. On Tuesday they crossed the mountain to Tyno⟨tla⟩, a town on the Highwassee river, wounded one fellow and a squaw, took nine prisoners, burnt the town, and destroyed a large quantity of growing corn. After liberating 9 prisoners, the company proceeded to the Big Valley Town, passing several small villages on their march, which they burnt, and destroyed the growing corn. On Wednesday morning the Indians fired on a party of white men in view of their camp, and wounded Archibald Lackey. The same day a party of Indians posted themselves in the gap of a mountain, where the white men had to pass, and on their approach fired on them; the white men returned the fire, killed three Indians, wounded several, and put them to flight. The next day the Indians fired on their rear, and wounded one man. The same day the company took six prisoners at a village gathering provisions; and towards the close of the day they killed four fellows and a squaw, and wounded several others. On Saturday morning, the 10th, (before day) a party of Indians fired on the white men in their encampment, and wounded James Henderson, Nicholas Davis, and John Frame. On Mon-

day the 12th inst. the volunteers returned to the settlements, by way of Big Pigeon, in Jefferson county—The prisoners they brought in (who were examined separately) say, that the Indians had received notice of the intended visit of the white people from Swannanoe, a frontier settlement in North Carolina; and that all their young men and warriors had gone to John Watts, at Eufenaula where they were to hold a council and war dance.

"The party killed in the whole of their rout nine Indian men, and, by mistake, two squaws, and brought home seven women and children prisoners."

George Doherty (1749–1833), a veteran of the battle of King's Mountain, rose to serve as a brigadier general of East Tennessee militia in the Creek War of 1813–14. He represented Jefferson County in the Tennessee Senate, 1797–98, and House, 1799–1801.

6. Knox may have been referring to James Seagrove's letter of 21 Aug. (*ASP, Indian Affairs*, 1:407). Rock Landing is located on the Oconee River in Baldwin County, a few miles southeast of Milledgeville.

7. For the journal of the treaty commissioners, see *ASP, Indian Affairs,* 1:342–60.

8. Dr. Benjamin Rush directed that "as soon as" one was "affected" by symptoms, he should take a powder "consisting of ten grains of Calomel, and fifteen grains of Jalap, for an adult," in sugar and water "every six hours, until they produce four or five large evacuations from the bowels." By 18 Sept., William Delany, chemist and druggist, was advertising for sale "Doctor Rush's Mercurial Sweating Purge for the Yellow Fever, with the Doctor's Directions," and a similar advertisement was placed by the druggists Goldthwait and Baldwin the next day (*General Advertiser* [Philadelphia], 14, 18, and 19 Sept.).

9. The letter-book copy reads "H.K." The letter from A.K. was printed in the *Federal Gazette* (Philadelphia), 11 September. It recommended against the use of emetics or laxatives unless the patient had a specific problem. A.K. instead administered twenty drops of "elixir of vitriol" every two hours, along with bark and laudanum. However, he placed "the greatest dependance for the cure of the disease, on throwing cool water twice a day over the naked body." He also recommended a diet using ripe fruit and wine, keeping the patient in a spacious chamber with good circulation and frequent changes of bedclothes, and vinegar and olive fumes to sweeten the air. A postscript to the letter, printed in the *Federal Gazette* of 12 Sept., credited Edward Stevens, Alexander Hamilton's physician, for many of the observations on which the cure was based.

Dr. Adam Kuhn (1741–1817), who received an M.D. degree from Edinburgh University in 1767, had been employed as a professor at the College of Philadelphia, now Pennsylvania University, since 1768, serving at this time as professor of the theory and practice of medicine. He was also on the staff of the Pennsylvania Hospital and a member of the American Philosophical Society.

Edward Stevens (c.1755–1834), who had known Hamilton since boyhood in the West Indies, graduated from King's College (now Columbia University) in 1774 and took an M.D. from the University of Edinburgh in 1777. In

1794 he joined the medical faculty of Columbia College for one year, and in 1799 he was appointed U.S. consul general for Santo Domingo.

10. Knox may be referring to the letters from Thomas Jefferson to Edmond Charles Genet of 7 and 9 Sept. (*Jefferson Papers,* 27:52–53, 67–69).

11. A delegation of six Quakers had attended the treaty conference (see GW to Henry Knox, 5 April, and n.2 to that document). For some of their accounts of the treaty, see Lindley, "Expedition to Detroit," and Evans, *Journal of William Savery,* 28–75.

From Alexander Spotswood

Dear Sir   Virga Nottingham Septr 15th 1793

I did myself the honr to write you sometime past; that my Eldest Daughter had married a Mr Francis Brooke a gentleman in the profession of the law—and requested that if ever the naval officers place was Vacant at Hobs Hole where he lives, that you would be so good as to give him the appointment.[1]

I now have Some reason to Suppose it will be soon Vacant; (this post to my Son in law, in addition to his practice, would enable him better to provide for a riseing family; and I will Venture to assure you Sir, that the Bussiness will be conducted by him, with the greatest rigidness & punctuality—and I would not on any Acct recommend him to you, if I had not have had, many years proof, of his Strickt honour & Integrity—yr freindship in this Instance will lay me under Additional Obligations. with the Sincerest regard & Esteem an Attachment I remn yr obedt st

A. Spotswood

ALS, DLC:GW. A note on the cover reads: "To be returned to the President."

1. Spotswood's previous letter on this subject has not been found. His daughter Mary Randolph Spotswood (d. 1803) married Francis Taliaferro Brooke (1763–1851), a Revolutionary War veteran, in October 1791. Brooke represented Essex County in the Virginia House of Delegates, 1794–95, and served in the Virginia Senate, 1800–1804, acting for thirteen months as speaker. In January 1804 Brooke was appointed a judge of the General Court, and in 1811 he was appointed a judge of the Virginia Court of Appeals, where he served until his death. Hobs Hole is Tappahannock, Virginia. As no naval officer had been appointed to that port, presumably Spotswood was referring to the post of collector and inspector of the revenue, held by Hudson Muse, who was replaced in March 1794 by Laurence Muse.

From the Commissioners for the District of Columbia

Sir,   Sepr 16th 1793

We forgot the other day to apply to you for your permission to make sales of the publick property in the City of Washington[1]— We therefore transmit to you a Couple of Instruments for your signature similar to those given at former times[2]—Considering it as a mere matter of form, we shall commence tomorrow, agreeable to advertizement, and expect you will favour us with the return of them by the Post of Wednesday.[3] Your Hum. Servts

Dd Stuart ⎫
          ⎬ Com.
Danl Carroll ⎭

LB, DNA: RG 42, Records of the Commissioners for the District of Columbia, Letters Sent, 1791–1802.

1. The commissioners, who met at Georgetown from 13 to 19 Sept., presumably talked with GW when he passed through that town on 14 Sept. en route to Mount Vernon.

2. These instruments are dated 16 Sept. and were received by the commissioners prior to the sale on 17 September. The first, which varies from GW's proclamations for the sales of 17 Oct. 1791 and 8 Oct. 1792 only in the date, reads: "The President of the United States doth hereby order and direct that the sale of Lots in the City of Washington, to commence on the 17th Instant be of such Lots as the Commissioners or any two of them shall think proper: That the same sale shall be under their direction and on the Terms they shall publish" (Copy, DNA: RG 42, Records of the Commissioners for the District of Columbia, Proceedings [13–19 Sept. 1793], 1791–1802; Df, DLC:GW; LB, DLC:GW).

The second, which is similar to an order issued on 29 Sept. 1792, reads: "The President of the United States doth hereby order and direct that any Lot or Lots in the City of Washington, may after the public sale to commence on the 17th Inst. be sold and agreed for by the Commissioners or any two of them at private sale for such price and on such Terms as they may think proper" (Copy, DNA: RG 42, Records of the Commissioners for the District of Columbia, Proceedings [13–19 Sept. 1793], 1791–1802; Df, DLC:GW; LB, DLC:GW).

3. The commissioners' advertisement of the sale of a number of lots in Washington on 17 Sept. had been issued over the signature of John M. Gantt, clerk, and dated 7 Jan. 1793 (*Gazette of the United States* [Philadelphia], 19 Jan.). GW purchased lots in the Federal City during this sale (see Certificate for Lots Purchased in the District of Columbia, 18 Sept.).

To Henry Knox

Sir,   Mount Vernon Sepr 16th 1793

The Packet herewith sent, I fd at the Post Office in Alexandria, as I passed through that Town on Saturday after noon.[1]

The letter from the Minister of the French Republic, dated the 7th instt, in answr to one he had received from Govr Clinton of the 3d preceeding, breathes (as far as I can understand it from Mr Dandridge's translation) the same language as all others do which have been received from that Gentlemen lately.[2]

The points in it to be decided on are two, first the proposition or *rather information* of Mr Genet respecting the Privateers Little Democrat & Carmagnole—and 2d the William Tell, Prize to the Cerf. If the latter should have got into the Court of Admiralty, it will not, (at least in the first instance) require the interference of the Executive; But if this should not have been the case, any opinion which you, the Secretary of State & Attorney General of the U. States, shall agree in (I take for granted that Colo. Hamilton is not in a situation to attend) may be forwarded to the Governor of New York as my decision in both, or either case; without refering it to me.[3] With best wishes for your continuance in health. I remain Yours &ca

                           Go: Washington

ADfS, DLC:GW; LB, DLC:GW.

1. The packet evidently contained George Clinton's letter to GW of 8 Sept. and its enclosures. The previous Saturday was 14 September.

2. For these letters, see Clinton to GW, 8 Sept., n.1. The surviving letter-book copy and draft of Edmond Genet's reply to Clinton are dated 6 September. The translation by Bartholomew Dandridge, Jr., has not been identified.

3. It appears that Knox had left the city before this letter was received. It was probably the "letter from the President" forwarded to Knox on 24 Sept. by War Department clerk Philip Audebert (NNGL). Knox did not reply to Clinton until 15 Nov.; for that reply, see Clinton to GW, 8 Sept., n.2.

From the Rev. James Madison

Sir   Williamsburg Sep. 16th 1793.

The Inhabitants of the County of James City, who formed the Resolves, which I have now the Honour of transmitting to you, had at their Meeting two objects principally in View; the one was, to bestow upon you, the greatest Reward which the patriotic Benefactor of his Country can receive, Viz. the Approbation of his Fellow-Citizens; the other, to express their Solicitude for the sacred Preservation of the Sovereignty of the United States, & the Continuance of the Blessings of Peace.

In the Integrity of your Views, & unwearied Attention to the general Weal, they have that firm Confidence, which the Tenor of your Life so justly warrants; nor have they a Doubt, but it will continue glorious to yourself, & prosperous to them, so long as it shall please the great Disposer of Events to protract it. I am, Sir, with the greatest Respect, Your most obedt Servt

Js Madison

ALS, DLC:GW; LB, DLC:GW.

James Madison (1749–1812) was ordained to the priesthood while in England in 1775 and later became the first bishop of the Virginia Protestant Episcopal Church. A professor of natural philosophy at the College of William and Mary, he served as that school's president from 1777 to 1812.

Enclosure
Resolutions from James City County, Va., Citizens

[12 September 1793]

At a meeting of several Freeholders and Freemen of James City County convened by public advertizements at the Courthouse in Williamsburg the twelfth day of September 1793. for the purpose of taking into consideration the proclamation of the President of the United States, and other Subjects of a political nature.[1]

The Right Revd Doctr Madison, elected Chairman.

Robert H: Waller appointed Clerk to the meeting.

The meeting appointed a Committee of Mr Pierce, Mr Saml Griffin, Mr Lee, The Revd Mr Bracken, Mr William Walker, and Mr Coleman, to prepare Resolutions on the subject of the President's Proclamation, who retired, and after some short time, returned and reported sundry resolutions thereon, which were severally read, approved and adopted as follows.[2]

1st Resolved—As common sense points out to us, it is essential to the welfare of America, that the strictest neutrality be preserved towards all the belligerent powers of Europe; so we conceive, that nothing but the madness of Party, or the Folly of Individuals can suggest any measures, which may tend to the violation of such neutrality; or, in any way, involve the United States of America, seperated as they are by nature from Europe, in her sanguinary, ambitious and destructive contests.

2d   Resolved, that the late Proclamation of the President of the United States was founded in wisdom, and such as the Citizens of America, not only had a right to expect, both from his invariable patriotism and uniform attention to the Duties of his Office; but also such, as they are bound strictly to observe and enforce.

3d   Resolved, that it is the sacred Duty of the governing Powers to cause all existing Treaties to be observed with that exactitude, which the Laws of nations require.[3]

4th   Resolved That as the People of America are fully competent to the conduct and management of their own political concerns; all foreign Interference of whatever nature, ought to be considered as a most presumptuous and dangerous attack upon their Sovereignty; and therefore, should such Interference, in the smallest degree, be discovered, it ought to be instantly repelled with that indignation, which becomes Freemen who know how to value and to preserve their political Liberty.[4]

5th   Resolved, that this Meeting is conscious of the obligations which the People of America owe to the French nation for their generous assistance during the late War, and will at all times be ready to testify towards them the most cordial Friendship.

. 6th   Resolved that the Chairman be requested to transmit a Copy of the foregoing resolutions to the President of the United States.[5]

Signed, James Madison
Chairman of the Meeting

D, DLC:GW; LB, DLC:GW. These resolutions were printed in the *Virginia Gazette, and General Advertiser* (Richmond), 25 September.

1. This refers to GW's Neutrality Proclamation of 22 April.

2. Robert H. Waller, Samuel Griffin, and John Bracken helped formulate similar resolutions at an earlier meeting of GW supporters in Williamsburg, Va. (see enclosure to Joseph Prentis to GW, 14 Sept.). John Pierce represented James City County in the Virginia general assembly for eleven terms, 1777–78, 1789–98. Mr. Lee probably was William Lee (1739–1795), a brother of Richard Henry Lee and U.S. commissioner to the courts of Vienna and Berlin, 1777–79. He had retired to Green Springs in James City

County after his return from Europe in 1783. William Walker represented James City County in the Virginia general assembly for three terms, 1784–87. Mr. Coleman probably was William Coleman (c.1740–1819), who operated a grist and sawmill complex on Mill Creek in James City County and served in 1807 as mayor of Williamsburg.

3. This resolution had reference to the 1778 treaties of Alliance and of Amity and Commerce between the United States and France (Miller, *Treaties*, 3–44).

4. This resolution was aimed at the activities of French minister Edmond Genet (see Cabinet Opinion, 7 Sept., and n.3 of the enclosure to Edmund Pendleton's first letter to GW of 11 Sept.).

5. GW responded to these resolutions in a letter to Madison of 23 September.

From Henry Lee

My dear sir   Richmond sepr 17th 93

The letter which you did me the honor to write to me dated 21st July got to hand just as I was departing for Winchester, from which place I am late returned.

To this cause is to be attributed cheifly the lateness of my reply, tho my wish to have known with accuracy the mind of my country men relative to those matters which were beginning to agitate the community, would of itself have induced some delay.

I ever attributed the mad conduct of a certain foreigner to the insidious & malignant councils of some perverse ambitious americans—I had grounded my opinion on this point from a variety of circumstances which progressively took place shortly after the arrival of the foreign gentleman & I concluded long before the publication signed by Mr J. & Mr K. made its appearance that a party was formed under the auspices of this foreigner to draw america into the veiws of France however unjust & disastrous such conduct might be—among the many symptoms of this wicked combination no one affected me more than the establishment of a society in Philada called the democratic society. This was intended as a standard for the people to rally under, & menaced from its very nature the destruction of the constitution & government under which we live[1]—The gratitude & just affection felt by the americans towards france, it was supposed would bury in the public mind a regard even for their own country for a while, which space of time would be sufficient to produce the contemplated embroilment—The part you had taken on the subject of neutrality opposed their views—you became of course an object of their hatred, as well as an obstruction, to be removed—Encouraged by the silly & impudent declamations published in some of the public prints they were hardy enough to beleive that could they impress a conviction of your enmity to France & its cause, that you too would be prostrated.

Little did they know the american people—Elated with this hope their partizans circulated every where reports calculated to foster the temper they had given birth to, & to fan the fire they had kindled—To complete their well fabricated plan they introduced the administration as favoring G.B., for which nation they well knew the deep rooted hatred possessed by the people of the U.S.

At first success seem to hover over their efforts, then it was that the unparallelled exhibition of the agent of a foreign nation publicly inviting the people to unite with him agst their own government was presented to the world—an epoch memorable indeed, whether we regard the atrocity of the act, or the moderation of the power against whom it was directed.

The transaction soon flew into every part of the continent, it became the subject of constant enquiry & conversation—Finally it was understood, & consequently detested.

the people began to speak out, & their utterance stopped the farther efforts of the conspirators.

However sir the matter is not over, the first plan may be in part relinquished, but its main object will never be abandoned until those among ourselves who engender these nefarious plans be dismissed from Nation & confidence—It is suspected by many that such characters are to be found in high employments; that many may be readily met with in state & congressional offices no one doubts—to detect the designs of these men & to expose them to the public eye is the work of true patriotism, & I hope will be soon commenced by those who have leisure & ability. In this country, much will depend on the assembly—If they act on the business, & act with becoming energy, a deadly blow will be struck to the malignant combination, & great good result to our country—they meet next month. On their patriotism & good sense I rely with confidence.

I am very sorry to hear of the loss of your manager & I hear you cannot soon replace him.[2]

An Englishman well recommended arrived last summer in this state & has engaged to live with me at the little falls.

He is said to be a thorough farmer—His name is Workman & he is now at the little falls—If you will send for him & find that he answers your purposes, I will chearfully permit him to obey your orders—the man brought with him letters of credit from merchants of respectability in London.[3]

While I was in the upper Countys I called at Col. L. Talia-ferros to examine his threshing mill—It appeared to me perfectly calculated to answer to various purposes for which it was constructed—It is on a small scale & has little water—I saw it thresh Wheat, nothing could be done more satisfactorily I think—It can in its present situation & (it has been in use four years without repair) get out 100 bushels pr day—one old negro only attended it.[4]

Besides threshing wheat it shells corn, beats Saw yard bark, breaks hemp flax & grinds into a homony the corn husks—persuaded of the vast utility of the machine where convenient water seats were possessed, I engaged a Mr Payne the builder of the mill to visit my plantation in Fairfax, from whence he proceeds to Stratford—presuming you might wish such a mill at Mt Vernon I directed him to call there, & examine your water courses, that I might communicate to you his report, & gave him a letr to your manager—He tells me that he can improve very much on Mr Taliaferro's mill & I credit the man, because I have seen what he has done & am informed that he is a man of good character—Should you think proper to precede me in the attempt you may so do—or I will after my mill is done put it in your power to employ him.[5] I learn with great pleasure that you have left Phida. where the pestilential disease there raging seems to render the life of man very precarious indeed.

I hope Mrs W. & your family have got back in good health & free from the seeds of that terrible disorder—so then please to present my best respects & be assured of the constant affection of your friend & h. ser.

Henry Lee

ALS, DLC:GW.

1. The "certain foreigner" was French minister Edmond Genet. For the publication of 12 Aug. signed by John Jay and Rufus King and stating that Genet "had said he would Appeal to the People from certain decisions of the

President," see Genet to GW, 13 Aug., n.4. For discussion of the Democratic Society of Pennsylvania, see n.4 of the enclosure with Jeremiah Banning to GW, 7 September.

2. Anthony Whitting died on 21 June. Howell Lewis was temporarily acting as manager at Mount Vernon until William Pearce, whom GW hired on 23 Sept., arrived to take up the position in January 1794.

3. The Little Falls of the Potomac River were located near the current boundary between Arlington and Fairfax counties. Lee's first wife, Matilda, had inherited property there from her father, Philip Ludlow Lee (Fairfax County Deed Book U, 18–19).

4. Lawrence Taliaferro (1734–1798), of Rose Hill in Orange County, served in 1775 as colonel of a battalion of minutemen recruited from Culpeper, Orange, and Fauquier counties, and in 1778 he was appointed a lieutenant colonel of Orange County militia. An undated sketch and plan of Taliaferro's mill, signed by Taliaferro, is to be found in DLC:GW (at the end of 1757). According to Taliaferro's description on the sketch: "with the Stream small as it is, I have got out 40 Bushells of Wheat a Day. & not Imploy'd one hand Half his time to Attend her, She will Shell 20 Barrels of Corn, in 15 Minutes, fit for Market & Scarcely leave a Grain on the Coars or Cobs. She will Break 500Wt of Hemp or Flax in a Day. And Mill 400Wt of Hemp fine enough for the Finest Linnen."

5. The letter has not been identified. Lee's residence was at Stratford Hall plantation, about six miles northwest of Montross, Va., in Westmoreland County, which his first wife, Matilda Lee, had inherited from her father.

To Alexander Contee Hanson

Sir,   Mount Vernon 18. Septr 1793.

Your favor of the 14 instant, enclosing an Address from the Citizens of Annapolis, I had the honor to receive in the afternoon of yesterday.[1] The answer to it, I give you the trouble, as Chairman of the meeting, to receive under cover of this letter; praying you at the same time to be assured of the very great esteem & regard with which I am &c.

Go. Washington

LB, DLC:GW.

1. GW's executive journal recorded his reply to the Annapolis address in the entry for Monday, 16 Sept. (*JPP*, 239). It is possible that by that date GW had received the copy of the address sent via Henry Hill of Philadelphia and had written the undated reply enclosed below. It is also possible that the letter-book copyist misdated this cover letter, or that GW miswrote at this point.

Enclosure
To Annapolis, Md., Citizens

Fellow Citizens,   [c.16 September 1793]

Conscious of having had in view the Interest & Happiness of the people of the United States, in the discharge of my public duties; and fully persuaded that remaining in a state of neutrality during the present contest between the powers of Europe, if not absolutely necessary to these objects, would tend in a very considerable degree to promote them, I receive with infinite satisfaction, testimonies from my Countrymen, from various parts of the Union, expressive of their approbation of a measure intended to advance the welfare of my fellow Citizens;[1] & none have given me more pleasure, than receiving that of the Citizens of Annapolis.

The present flourishing situation of our affairs, & the prosperity we enjoy, must be obvious to the good Citizens of the United States; it remains therefore for them to pursue such a line of conduct as will ensure these blessings, by averting the calamities of a War.

The manner, Gentlemen, in which you are pleased to express yourselves towards me personally, merits & receives my warmest gratitude; and it will always be my greatest pride & happiness to receive the approving voice of my fellow Citizens.

                                        Go. Washington

LB, DLC:GW. This letter was printed in the *Maryland Gazette* (Annapolis), 26 September.

1. The measure was GW's Neutrality Proclamation of 22 April.

From Henry Knox

(Private)

sir   near Philadelphia 18th September 1793

I had the honor of writing to you on the 15th instant since which nothing further of a public nature has occurred excepting a report that Admiral Gardiners fleet has been seen off Sandy Hook. But considering the shattered condition of that fleet, and the near approach to the equinox the report may be doubted.[1] It is said this is the cause the french ships have not sailed from New York, which they have not yet done.

Mr Randolph has arrived and will set off in two or three days for Virginia.

The mortality in the city where I was yesterday is excessive One has not nor can they obtain precise information but the best accounts of the 14th 15th and 16th which were warm days the numbers buried were not short of an hundred each day—some aver much more, and some much less. The streets are lonely to a melancholy degree—the merchants generally have fled—Ships are arriving and no consignees to be found. Notes at the banks are suffered to be unpaid. In fine the stroke is as heavy as if an army of enemies had possessed the city without plundering it.

Mr Wolcot the Comptroller of the treasury and myself have taken Doctor Smiths house at the falls for temporary offices so that the public business should not be entirely at a stand.[2]

I shall set out for Boston tomorrow. Mrs Knox and all my children but the Youngest will to go Newark for a fortnight or three weeks. I understand Mr Jefferson set out yesterday. Mrs Randolph is urgent for Mr Randolph to go to Winchester, but he refuses, although he is impressed with the propriety of the measure, had you been previously informed of it. But he thinks some person ought to remain here to whom You may address your letters.

Colonel and Mrs Hamilton it is said have excessively alarmed Mr Morris Family at Trenton having lodged there The people of Trenton refused to let them pass, and compelled them to return again to Mr Morris's.[3]

I do not understand that the fever is much west of 4th Street— below that particularly in Water front 2d and 3 streets it is pretty general. The Weather yesterday and today is quite cool and favorable to checking the disorder. Everybody whose head aches takes Rush. Mr Meredith took upon an alarm 20 grams of calomel and as many of Jallap. although it cured him of his apprehensions of the yellow fever it has nearly killed him with the gout in his stomach.

From the present view of the subject the earliest period at which it would be safe for you to return would be the first of November. I sent to inquire at your house yesterday and found them all well. I am sir With perfect respect and attachment Your obedient Servant.

H. Knox

ALS, DLC:GW.

1. This report of the movements of British Rear Admiral Alan Gardner's West Indies fleet was evidently false.

2. William Smith (1727–1803), a former rector of the College of Philadelphia and an Episcopalian divine, had retired to his country house above the Falls of the Schuylkill after the merger that created the University of Pennsylvania in 1791.

3. Knox may be referring to the family of Anthony Morris (1766–1860), a Philadelphia merchant and member of the Pennsylvania senate. During the yellow fever epidemic, the family retreated to their summer residence on the Schuylkill River (*Hamilton Papers*, 15:356).

Certificate for Lots Purchased in the District of Columbia

Territory of Columbia, 18th September 1793

(Duplicate)

At a Public Sale of Lots in the City of Washington, George Washington, President of the United States of America became purchaser of Lots No. twelve, No. thirteen & No. fourteen in Square No. six hundred & sixty seven for the consideration of one thousand and sixty six dollars & two thirds of a Dollar, subject to the Terms and Conditions concerning the manner of improvement published, and on the further terms of paying down one fourth part of the purchase money, and also paying the residue in three equal annual payments, with yearly interest on the whole principal unpaid, under forfeiture of the said fourth to be paid down: and he hath accordingly paid the said one fourth, to wit, two hundred and sixty six Dollars and two thirds of a Dollar, and he or his Assigns, on making the said other Payments, will be entitled to a conveyance of the said lot in Fee.[1]

Lots No. 12. 13. & 14   Dd Stuart,
Square No. 667.   Danl Carroll
                                                          COMMISSIONERS.

DS (duplicate), NN. A similar document recording GW's purchase on this date of lot 5 in square 667 was offered for sale by Parke-Bernet Galleries, *Autograph Letters & Documents. Property of the Late Forest G. Sweet. Part I*, sale 1756 (1957), item 376.

1. A description of these three lots and lot 5 is to be found at NjMoHP: "Lot No. 14 on Square No. 667.—Beginning at the end of 147. Feet 5¼ I[nches] from the South East corner of the said square, measured on the West side

of Water Street, running thence west 100. F. 4. I. then north 32. F. then East 107. F. 3. I. to water Street and with water Street South 12°. 18' West 32. F. 8¼ I. to the beginning—With a privilege of improving, in front of the Lot, into the Eastern branch.

"Lot No. 13. in same Square—Beging at the end of the third line of Lot No. 14. run[nin]g thence with said line reversed 107. F. 3. I. then North 32. F. then East 114. F. 1½ I. to water street & with water Street South 12°. 18' West 32. F. 8¼ I. to the beging with the privilege of improving, in front of the lot, into the eastern branch.

"Lot No. 12. in same Square—Beging at the end of the third line of Lot No. 13. running thence with said line reversed 114. F. 1½. I. then north 48. F. then East 124. F. 7½ I. to water Street, & with it South 12°. 18' West 49. F. 1¾. I. to the beging with the same privilege of improvement.

"Lot No. 5 in same Square—Beging at the end of 165. F. 9. I. north from the South west corner of the Square then running north with 1st Street west 68. F. 6. I. then East 173. F. 7. I. then South 68. F. 6. I. then west 173. F. 7 I. to the Beging."

For the location of square 667, on the waterfront south of the Capitol, see Fig. 1.

Letter not found: from William Wootton Brewer, 20 Sept. 1793. GW wrote Brewer on 29 Sept.: "A Letter from you of the 20th inst: has been received."

From Oliver Wolcott, Jr.

Sir,   Philadelphia Sept. 20th 1793

At the request of Colo. Hamilton I have the honour to enclose a copy of a memorandum describing the mode of treatment which was adopted in his case, when attacked with the prevailing fever.[1]

I am happy to announce, that the malady has within two days considerably abated, and I have no doubt that each successive day will present still more favourable aspects. I have the honour to be with the most perfect respect Sir, your most obedt servant

Oliver Wolcott Jr

ALS, DLC:GW.

1. The enclosed memorandum has not been identified. However, Hamilton's physician, Edward Stevens, described his mode of treatment in a letter to Dr. John Redman, published in the *Federal Gazette* (Philadelphia), 16 Sept. (see Timothy Pickering to GW, 21 Oct., n.5).

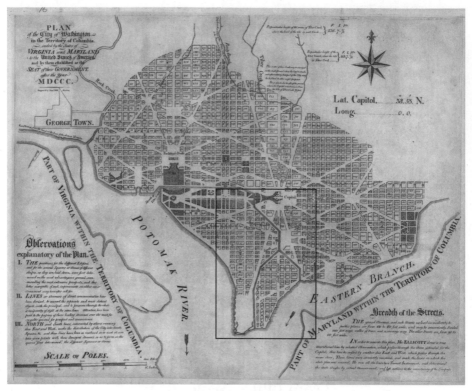

Fig. 1. (above): *"Plan of the City of Washington in the Territory of Columbia,"* as drawn by Andrew Ellicott and engraved by Samuel Hill of Boston in 1792. *(Library of Congress, Geography and Map Division.)*

Fig. 1a. (opposite): *Detail from the above plan showing numbered lots on the south end of the District of Columbia.*

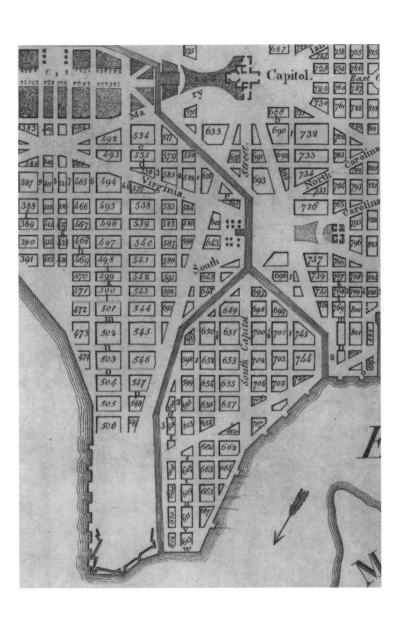

Memorandum from Thomas Jefferson

Sep. 22. 1793.

Heads of answer to the Caroline resolutions.[1]

Taking them up in their order, they appear susceptible of answer in the following way.

The 1st & 2d by a concurrence of sentiment for the maintenance of the constitution, & preservation of peace, & the pleasure with which the President recieves their assurances of support in these objects.

3. Notice of the expressions of their personal respect.

4. Approbation of their expressions of gratitude to the French nation for aids extended in a time of need, and the honorable trait evidenced in the National character by a strong remembrance of it, even in the moment when the justice due to others imposes laws on the manifestation of it. that being firmly persuaded that the interest & happiness of all the parties engaged in the present contests of Europe will be most promoted by their obtaining every one what is right, & no more, we may innocently & justly pray to heaven that such may be the result of these afflicting contests.

5. 6. 7. to express a firm attachment to the free principles of our government, & a confidence that the virtue & good sense of our citizens will counteract & defeat all measures which might tend to weaken their affection to these principles to alienate them from the republican government they have established for themselves, or to innovate on it's character.

8. it would seem more delicate & dignified to pass over this altogether.[2]

AD, DLC: Jefferson Papers.

1. The resolutions of Caroline County citizens, 10 Sept., were enclosed with Edmund Pendleton's first letter to GW of 11 September.

2. For GW's reply to the Caroline County resolutions, which indeed ignored their resolution about the alleged misconduct of French minister Edmond Genet, see GW to Pendleton, 23 Sept. (first letter).

To John Doughty

Sir,   Mount Vernon 23d Septr '93.

Your Letter, conveying to me the resolutions, agreed to by the Inhabitants of Morris County, the 10 inst: has reached my hands.[1]

Their firm & manly sentiments, declared in the resolutions, & united determination to protect & defend the honor & dignity of our Country, are such as become the freemen & citizens of the United States; & evince their firm & commendable resolution to preserve their liberty & independence inviolate. With such aid & support, under direction of Divine providence, I trust the flourishing condition & inestimable blessings now enjoyed, will be long continued to our Country.

Go. Washington

LB, DLC:GW.

   1. These resolutions in support of GW's policy of neutrality came enclosed in Doughty's letter to GW of 12 September.

To the Rev. James Madison

Sir,   Mount Vernon 23d Sep: 1793.

Every well-wisher of the U. States must derive pleasure from the disposition which has been shewn generally, by the citizens thereof, to repel with firmness any attempts tending to disturb their present repose. It was with much satisfaction therefore that I received the Resolutions of the Inhabitants of James City County, enclosed in your Letter of the 16th instant—containing sentiments which accord with those which have been expressed by so many respectable Citizens in every part of the Union.

While such a disposition & such sentiments are retained by my Fellow Citizens, on whose aid & support, in the discharge of the trust which they have confided to me, I place entire confidence, we may expect, under the protection of a Kind providence, a continuation of those blessings which these States enjoy in a superior degree.

Go. Washington

LB, DLC:GW.

To William Nelson, Jr.

sir,   Mount Vernon 23d Sept. '93.

Your Letter of the 5. instant, enclosing a copy of several resolutions entered into by the Inhabitants of the County & borough of York, I have had the pleasure to receive.

That the well-being of our Country rests upon the cultivation of peace (consistently with public faith & our own rights) agriculture & commerce, I am well convinced; & I beg you to express to my fellow Citizens of York County & Borough, the satisfaction I derive from the declaration of their intentions to join in preserving these blessings to the United States, and to present them my best thanks for their favorable expressions towards me personally.

Go: Washington

LB, DLC:GW. Printed in the *Virginia Gazette, and General Advertiser* (Richmond), 9 Oct., and other newspapers.

Agreement with William Pearce

[Mount Vernon, 23 September 1793]

Articles of Agreement made and entered into this twenty third day of September in the year of our Lord one thousand seven hundred & ninety three, by & between George Washington, President of the United States, on one part; and William Pearce of Kent County in the State of Maryland, on the other part—Witness, that for and in consideration of the wages and allowances herein after mentioned, the said William Pearce doth promise and agree to superintend, and manage to the best of his skill and judgment, the interest of the said George Washington at Mount Vernon and it's Dependencies, comprehending the several farms, Mill, Fishery, Tradesmen of different kinds, Ditchers, Spinners, the person who has charge of the Jacks, Stud horse, mules &ca; and will enter upon the duties thereof on or before the first day of January next ensuing, and remain therein until the first day of January in the year one thousand seven hundred and ninety five; during which period he will, in all things, to the utmost of his abilities, discharge the trust reposed in him with diligence and integrity, following the plans that are, or shall be adopted, and such directions as he shall receive; & where these are not clear and definite, then to pursue the dictates of his own judgment in the premises; and even in cases where they may happen to be explicit, if repugnant to the ideas of the said William Pearce, the said George Washington will always, & with pleasure listen to any suggested alterations which may be offered by him with a view to the advancement of the Crops, increase of the Stocks, and for the general improvement of the Estate: the great objects of the said George Washington being to crop the Land in such a manner (by judicious rotations) as to keep it in an improving instead of a declining state;[1] to make permanent meadows of wet or sunken lands capable of being reclaimed; to introduce Clover & other Grasses as far, and as fast as it can be done in tillable fields that are in condition to bear it, but avoiding at the same time too great an expense in the purchase of Seed; to substitute live in place of dead fences where it is practicable; and this with as much facility as the seasons and the nature of the case will admit, as the Inclosures are numerous, timber becoming scarce, & the common materials for fencing, in most instances, far to remove. These with regular weekly reports from each Farm & class of people—due attention to the Stocks on the several farms—to the tools & implements of husbandry thereon, taking an exact list thereof, & making the overseers accountable, not only for their forthcoming, but for the preservation of them from the weather; and in a word, to keep as regular accounts with each Farm, & with every seperate branch of business—debiting and crediting the same with every thing that goes to, or comes from them, as if they were the property of another person, thereby ascertaining the profit and loss—correcting, by a strict & close inspection into matters, the many abuses which there is too much reason to fear has crept into every branch of my business, from the little personal attention I have been able to bestow on it for many years last past; and lastly keeping all the Overseers and subordinate characters who are or may be placed under your management, strictly to their respective duties, will (together with clothing the people, providing for, & disposing of things belonging to the Estate on the best terms, & rendering regular accounts thereof) constitute the great out-lines of the trust which I have reposed in you. To go more into detail would be as tedious as it is unnecessary to a person competent to the superintendence of such a Concern as mine. for to tell a farmer that his fences ought to be in good order; his fields secured against trespassers of every kind; his grounds well ploughed; his Crop kept clear of grass & weeds; his seeds put in in good order & in due season; his Grain & hay cut at a proper time, & well stacked, & the former got out of the straw as soon after harvest as circumstances will permit, & that without Waste or loss of grain or straw; making butter & selling all that can be spared, as also such stock of different kinds as will by being culled out, render the remainder healthy & thriving; that his Cattle &ca ought to be regularly penned in summer & secured from bad weather in winter; and the utmost attention paid to the making of manure for the improvement of his fields at both seasons; that his work horses & oxen should be well attended to and kept in good & fit condition, thereby enabling them to perform the labour which they must undergo: to remind him of those things would, I say, be only observing what every Farmer must be thoroughly sensible his duty enjoins—but it may not be amiss to repeat that one of the most effectual steps to accomplish all these ends, is to see that the Overseers of the Farms & the Superintendants of other business are constantly at their posts; for it may be received as a maxim that if they are away or entertaining company at home, that the concerns entrusted to them will be neglected, & certainly go wrong: and it is not less certain that relaxation on his part will serve only to beget liberties on their's; therefore strictness with justice is the sure means of having the business well conducted.

In consideration of these Services well & truly performed on the part of the said William Pearce, the said George Washington doth hereby promise to pay him the said Pearce, the Sum of one hundred Guineas per annum, and in that proportion for a greater or lesser time actually employed in the said Washington's service; and will allow him over and above, twelve hundred pounds of Pork; about five hundred pounds of beef, to be received at different times as it may happen to be killed for the use of the Mansion House or for market, and some fresh meat from what may be occasionally killed for like purposes, together with bread sufficient for his family; he is also to be allowed the use of Three Cows for the purpose of affording milk & butter therefor, and to raise poultry for the same, but not for sale. And if he brings Horses (not exceeding two) he is to be allowed Grain, & fodder or hay, for them; in which case he is not to use any horse or horses belonging to the Estate. The said George Washington doth moreover agree to allow the said William Pearce the use of a negro woman to wash & cook for his family—and a boy & girl to aid & attend in the House & garden; the first not to exceed fourteen or fifteen years of age, & the other twelve; and will put the House now occupied by Mr Hyland Crow, with the Kitchen adjoining, in decent repair and fitness for the purpose intended. And lastly, in order that the said William Pearce may have the entire controul over the Overseers of the different Farms, & others, hired as overlookers of any other business, he is hereby vested with full power and authority to engage such as he may have confidence in, & discharge those who do not conduct themselves well. Witness our hands & Seals the day & year first above written.

Go: Washington
William Pearce

Teste Bw Dandridge.

DS, DLC:GW.

1. For some of GW's ideas about crop rotation at this time, see the crop rotations for Mount Vernon farms enclosed with GW to Pearce, 18 Dec., and Rotations of Crops for Dogue Run, 1793.

To Edmund Pendleton

Sir,   Mount Vernon 23d September 1793.

The Resolutions of the Inhabitants of the County of Caroline, transmitted to me by you, were received with peculiar pleasure; because no Citizen of the United States can have a more sincere desire than I have to see all attempts at subverting or violating the Constitution or Laws of the Land, frustrated; and it gives me much satisfaction to be assured of the firm support of my Fellow Citizens in preserving the peace & Safety of our Country.[1]

The expressions of gratitude and affection, by the Citizens of Caroline, towards the French Nation for their generous aid and assistance extended to us in a time of need, are truly laudable, & must meet the approbation of every grateful mind.

I beg you, Sir, to assure the Citizens of Caroline of my fixed attachment to the free principles of our Government, and of the confidence I have in the virtue & good sense of my Fellow Citizens which I trust will always counteract any measures which might tend to weaken their affection to these principles, or to alienate them from the republican Government they have established for themselves, & under which they have hitherto enjoyed unequalled prosperity and happiness.

The marks of respect and affection for my person, manifested in the Resolutions, demand & receive my unfeigned acknowledgments & gratitude, which I request you to communicate to the Citizens of Caroline, and to assure them of my unremitted endeavours to advance their welfare, as far as my powers & abilities extend.

Go: Washington

LS (photocopy), ViMtvL; LB, DLC:GW. This letter was printed in the *Virginia Gazette, and General Advertiser* (Richmond), 2 Oct., and other newspapers.

1. The resolutions from the Caroline County, Va., citizens of 10 Sept. came enclosed with Pendleton's first letter to GW of 11 September.

To Edmund Pendleton

My dear Sir,   Mount Vernon Sep: 23d 1793

With very sincere pleasure I received your private letter of the 11th instant.[1] This pleasure was not a little enhanced by your reiterated assurance of my still holding that place in your estimation which, on more occasions than one, you have given me the most flattering testimony—highly gratifying to my mind. This assurance came opportunely, as I had begun to conceive (though unable to assign a cause) that some part of my public conduct—how ever well meant my endeavors—had appeared unfavorable in your eyes, for you will please to recollect that, formerly you promised me, and I always expected, an annual letter from you. It is now (if my memory has not failed me) at least four years since I have had that pleasure.[2]

Sequestered you say you are, from the World, and know little of what is transacting in it but from Newspapers. I regret this exceedingly. I wish you had more to do on the great theatre; and that your means of information were co-equal to your abilities, and the disposition I know you possess to judge properly of public measures. It would be better perhaps for that public it should be so; for be assured we have some infamous Papers—calculated for disturbing if not absolutely intended to disturb, the peace of the community.[3]

With respect to the fiscal conduct of the S—t—y of the Tr—s—y I will say nothing; because an enquiry, more than probable, will be instituted next Session of Congress into some of the Alligations against him, which, eventually, may involve the whole; and because, if I mistake not, he will seek, rather than shrink from, an investigation. A fair opportunity will then be given to the impartial world to form a just estimate of his Acts, and probably of his motives. No one, I will venture to say, wishes more devoutly than I do that they may be probed to the bottom—be the result what it will.[4]

With the most scrupulous truth I can assure you, that your free & unreserved opinion upon any public measure of importance will always be acceptable to me, whether it respects men, or measures—and on no man do I wish it to be expressed more fully than on myself; for as I can conscientiously declare that I have no object in view incompatible with the Constitution, and the obvious interests of this Country—nor no earthly desire *half* as strong as that of returning to the walks of private life, so, of consequence I only wish whilst I am a Servant of the public, to know the will of my masters, that I may govern myself accordingly.

You do me no more than justice when you suppose that from motives of respect to the Legislature (and I might add from my interpretation of the Constitution) I give my Signature to many Bills with which my judgment is at varience. In declaring this, however, I allude to no particular Act. From the nature of the Constitution, I must approve all the parts of a Bill, or reject it in toto. To do the latter can only be justified upon the clear and obvious ground of propriety; and I never had such confidence in my own faculty of judging as to be over tenacious of the opinions I may have embibed in doubtful cases.

Mrs Washington who enjoys tolerable good health joins me most cordially in best wishes for you and Mrs Pendleton.[5] I wish you may live long—continue in good health—and end your days as you have been wearing them away, happily and respected. Always, and most affectionately, I am Your Obedt Servt

Go: Washington

ALS, MHi: Washburn Papers; ADfS, DNA: RG 59, Miscellaneous Letters; LB, DLC:GW. The draft and letter-book copy differ slightly in wording from the ALS at several points, the most significant of which is reported in n.3.

1. GW was referring to Pendleton's second letter of 11 September.

2. Pendleton's most recent extant letter to GW, of 9 April 1791, was a recommendation of George Flowerdew Norton for office (see GW to Hannah

Fairfax Washington, 1 April 1791, n.1). GW evidently had in mind Pendleton's letter of 13 Oct. 1789 explaining his rejection of a federal judgeship, the last extant letter with significant personal content (see GW to Pendleton, 28 Sept. 1789, n.3). Pendleton's promise of an annual letter has not been identified, but in Pendleon's letter to GW of 16 Feb. 1781 he begged "Pardon for having so long delayed to pay you my Annual Acknowledgment of regard & Esteem" (PHi: Gratz Collection).

3. On the draft, GW initially wrote "we have some very infamous papers," before crossing out "very" and adding "calculated to disturb the public mind if not absolutely intended to do mischief." The letter-book copy follows the final phrasing of the draft.

4. Alexander Hamilton's actions as secretary of the treasury had been investigated by Congress in early 1793 (see U.S. House of Representatives to GW, 23 Jan., n.1). However, criticism of that investigation led Hamilton to request in December "that a new Inquiry may be without delay instituted, in some mode most effectual for an accurate and thorough investigation" (Hamilton to Frederick A. C. Muhlenberg, 16 Dec., *Hamilton Papers*, 15:460–67). That investigation culminated with a report on the "Condition of the Treasury Department" submitted to the House on 22 May 1794. The committee found that Hamilton had not "either directly or indirectly . . . procured any discount or credit" from the banks "upon the basis of any public moneys which . . . have been deposited therein under his direction," and that "no moneys of the United States . . . have ever been . . . used for, or applied to any purposes, but those of the Government, *except*, so far as all moneys deposited in a bank are concerned in the general operations thereof" (*ASP: Finance*, 1:281–301).

5. Sarah Pollard (1725/26–c.1814) married Pendleton in 1743.

To Joseph Prentis

Sir,   Mount Vernon 23d Sep: 1793.

With no less pleasure than you transmitted them, I received, enclosed in your Letter of the 14th instant, sundry resolutions expressing the sentiments of the Citizens of Williamsburg, on the late declaration of the neutrality of these States.[1]

Sentiments like these, evidencing the good dispositions of my Fellow Citizens, to retain the advantages we at present enjoy from a state of peace, must be pleasing to every friend of the United States, and add to the testimonies already given of the good sense of the people thereof.

I request you, Sir, to offer my sincere acknowledgments to the Citizens of Williamsburg, for their pointed approbation of my personal endeavours to promote their interests, & the assur-

ances of my best endeavours to guard their interests in whatsoever shall depend upon the Executive powers.

Go. Washington

LB, DLC:GW. This letter was printed in the *Virginia Gazette, and General Advertiser* (Richmond), 9 Oct., and subsequently in the *Federal Gazette and Philadelphia Daily Advertiser,* 16 October.

1. GW's Neutrality Proclamation was dated 22 April.

From Jonathan Shaw

Sir, [New York][1] September, 23rd 1793.

when I think of Intruding upon your Excellency it puts me
to the blush and almost determins me not to be thus troublesome but Necessity that Frequently puts us upon what we have
not a mind to, and often forces us against our Inclinations is
now the motive that Induces me to be thus trouebsome. At the
Commencement of the War between America and Britan, I was
deprived of a Parent, one who took up Arms in the cause of Liberty, only a private soldier, but soon fell a Victim in the Cause
in which he was engaged, and left a Wife, and Eight Children,
to lament his Death in poverty the Eldest sixteen, Immediately
joind the Army, and soon met the same fate his Father had done,
the next two, as soon as their Age admited, joind the Army, and
were preserved till it hapily dccided in favor of America: ⟨an⟩d
Myself the youngest have been exposed to Hardships ⟨mutilated⟩
my earliest Infancy till now; being under a pertic⟨ular⟩ disadvantage of having much sickness, and am now not able to Labour
for a support, and have not any Friend to apply to for assistance,
that is able to assist me in setting up in business: Therefore, Sir
I have taken the Liberty of letting your Excellency, kno my Circumstances, and most humbly to ask your Excellencys' kind assistance in affording me some help in seting up a small Grocery
in N. york, to set me a bove the reach of want, for which I believe I shall soon have it in my power to repay tho not to make
a full satisfaction such an Act of Generosity would lay me under. When I first thought of making known my Circumstances,
and Petitioning to your Excellency, for assistance; the great and
Immortal Charracter, and Name your Excellency has so justly
merited, struck me with an Awe that for some time past has kept

me in silence, for fear of Offending; but upon maturely considering that the Welfare of Mankind has been your Excellencys'
greatest Delight, and that it is by your Excellencys' wise Administration America now enjoys Peace, I say these Considerations
have encouraged me to make known my Circumstances: And I
most humby Pray that your Excellency will excuse the Liberty I
have taken. I am with great respect Sir, your Excellencys' most
humble and most Obedient Servant,

Jonathan Shaw

P.S. Sir the sickness in Philidelphia, has been the Cause of my
not coming personally. The enclosed are from Gentlemen of Veracity. If your Excellency is disposed to assist the unfortunate
and unhappy, If the trouble would not be to great, A line to me
at N. york soon, with those two papers inclosed, will be gratefully received by your Excellencys' humble, servant[2]

Jonathan Shaw

ALS, DNA: RG 59, Miscellaneous Letters.
    1. The cover of this letter, which was addressed to GW at Philadelphia, is
stamped "N-York Sep. 23" and "Free."
    2. Neither the enclosures nor the gentlemen have been identified. The two
certificates were returned to Shaw with Bartholomew Dandridge, Jr.'s, reply
to him of 29 September.

From David Austin, Jr.

Eliza[beth] Town [N.J.]
May it please yr Excellency   Sepr 24th 1793
    Having this day receivd the enclosed from my Hond father
at New Haven, to forward[1]—beg leave to say, so far as may be
decent for a son to say of a father; that the application made,
in the issue, will be found to be founded on reason, equity &
Justice; & if granted will give universal satisfaction, unless it be
to individuals who might have interest in wishing to be remembered themselves. Praying an excuse for this imperfect Scrawl,
the Mail just closing, have the honor to subscribe yr Excellency's
Most Obedt & Humble servt

David Austin

ALS, DLC:GW. GW's endorsement with this letter indicates that it was "Recommending his father—to be Collector—New havn."

David Austin (1759–1831), son of David Austin (1732–1801), graduated from Yale College in 1779 and was licensed to preach by the New Haven Association of Ministers in May 1780. He was pastor of the Presbyterian church at Elizabethtown, N.J., from 1788 to 1797. GW appointed David Austin, Sr., who was also endorsed by Samuel Huntington in a letter to GW of 14 Oct., to be collector at New Haven in November 1793, and the appointment was confirmed by the Senate in December (*JPP,* 251; *Senate Executive Journal,* 143–44).

1. The enclosure has not been identified.

From Henry Knox

Private

Sir   Elizabeth Town New Jersey 24th Septr 1793

I arrived here on the 19th after much delay and difficulty on the road. The alarm of the people in all the Towns and villages on the road, and at New York, on account of the prevailing fever is really inexpressible. The militia are posted at Trenton Brunswick and Newark and New York. This place seems to possess less fear and more reason. At New York reason appears to been entirely lost. Among many serious evils such as frightning some Philadelphians to death by placing them on Governors island without proper accommodations the following laughable incident is said to have occured a day or two past. A Boat arrived at NewYork from Jersey with passengers. the Mob collected and insisted upon it they were infected, and after they had landed the Mob forced them on board again, and with them a Mr Mercier of New York, who plead in vain, that he had not been out of New York for along time. the Mob however swore otherwise and the poor man was forced into the boat with persons whom he believed to be infected with *the plague* and did not return to his family for a day afterwards.

Poor Courtney the Taylor with his family were at a tavern on 2d river at which place he felt the symptoms of an intermittent or yellow fever—He took rushs medecines so frequently that he really became ill—The people ordered his coffin in his presence, and his wife sent to Newark for a Physician who pronouncd it a common intermittent But to mark the monstrous absurdity which prevails the people came into the sick mans room in shoals to see *the curious fever,* and he has been so worried that his life is in great danger—There are innumerable instances of the like unreasonable conduct.[1]

I sent to NewYork to endeavo⟨ur⟩ to get a passage to Rhode Island—But the Masters of the packets said that it was as much as their lives were worth, as it was reported at Newport that the yellow fever, *or plague* killed in NewYork 40 people ℞ day. If a person has been from Philadelphia 14 days and continued in perfect health during that time he may be admitted into New-York. I have yet six days *quarantine* to perform, which of the choice of evils is the least. This circumstance will retard my return as soon as I intended, for it is of the highest personal importance to me that I should go to Boston, and I am too bulky *to be smuggled* through the Country.

The french fleet is still in New-York, in a wretched state of disorganisation which prevents its sailing. Mr Genet has been low spirited for ten days past. The fleet have been told by him that the executive of the United States prevents their selling their prizes, and Citizen Bompard who belongs to a club in france as well as all his sailors, say that they shall represent the matter upon their return in its proper colours—some of the sailors lately attacked the Marquis de Rouvrays house with an intention it is said of Massacring him and his son. They have fled to this Town.[2] I do not find Mr Genet has promulgated the last letter of the secretary of state, excepting as to the effect of the measures with the Consuls, which prevent their selling their prizes—Would to God it had been thought proper to publish the letter to Mr Morris.[3] The minds of our own people would have been convinced of the propriety of the measures which have been adopted, and all cavil at the meeting of Congress prevented!

Colonel Hamilton experienced inconveni⟨ences⟩ on the road. Not being ad⟨mit⟩ted into NewYork he has gone to Albany. ⟨*mutilated*⟩ respectful compliments to Mrs Washington, I am Sir with perfect respect Your humble Servt

H. Knox

ALS, DLC:GW.

1. Richard Courtney (d. 1793) was a merchant tailor at 27 N. Second Street in Philadelphia. GW's household account book indicates that he paid Courtney $311.88 on 30 Aug. for "his Taylor's bill in full to this date," and that Courtenay's widow, Sarah, was paid $75.50 on 23 Dec. "for taylor's work done by her late husband" (PHi; see also Account Book, 2 Sept. 1793–4 April 1794,

DLC:GW). Second River, now Belleville, N.J., lay on the west bank of the Passaic River about three miles north of Newark. For discussion of Dr. Benjamin Rush's medicine, see Knox to GW, 15 Sept., n.8.

2. Jean-Baptiste François Bompard (1757–1841) commanded the French frigate *Embuscade*. Serving in the French navy by 1778, he participated in engagements at Grenada and Savannah during the Revolutionary War. He was promoted to captain in 1793. Laurent François Le Noir, Marquis de Rouvray (1743–1798), began serving in the French army as an ensign in 1756. Sent to Saint Domingue in 1761, he made his military career there, rising to the rank of maréchal de camp. Deported from Santo Domingo in late 1792, by January 1793 he had arrived at New York City, where he resided at 27 Great George Street.

3. Knox was referring to Thomas Jefferson's letter to Gouverneur Morris of 16 Aug., laying out for presentation to the French government the case for Edmond Genet's recall (*Jefferson Papers*, 26:697–715), and Jefferson's letter to Genet of 7 Sept. informing him of that action (see Cabinet Opinion, 7 Sept., and n.1 to that document).

From Betty Washington Lewis

[Fredericksburg, Va.]

my Dear Brother   September 24th 1793.

the Sickness in my family has Prevented my Writing Sooner my Daughter Carter has been Extreamly ill but is at this time better and my self owing to great fatigue am Scarcely able to attend them, Harriot wishes to know what time it will be Convenient for you to send for her, was it Convenient for me to keep her I know of none that I would sooner have to live with me but my Income is so small and few Servants that I Cannot Afford it I am Oblig'd to Buy Every thing that I Eat with the addishon of sope Candles &c. in short the most trifling things made Use of in the House, and my Income so small that I find it a hard matter to live and keep out of debt it is a Confinement to me as I have only two Horses to my Carriage that I Cannot go to Visit at any distance as I have two Grand Children liveing with me that I am Oblige to Carry with me.[1]

I shall be glad to hear from you by the first Stage as I intend as soon as my Daughter Carter leaves this to go up the Country if this Place Continues So Sickly—the family all Join me in love to you and My Sister Washington I am Dear Brother your Affct. Sister

Betty Lewis

ALS, owned (1973) by Mr. William Claiborne Buckner, Kansas City, Missouri.

1. Betty Washington Lewis was at this time helping to care for the younger children of her son Fielding Lewis, Jr., and may be referring to his daughters Ann ("Nancy") Alexander Lewis (1787–1835) and Catherine Dade Lewis (b. 1790).

To Thomas Griffin Peachy

Sir,   Mount Vernon 24. Sep: 1793.

The resolutions of the Inhabitants of the Town of Petersburg and its vicinity, were transmitted to me from Philada by the Secretary of State.[1]

The zealous & firm declaration of my Fellow Citizens of Petersburg & its vicinity, of their conviction of the necessity of peace in order to the preservation of our present state of tranquillity and prosperity, while the people of Europe are distressed by a calamitous war. and their determined resolution to support every measure of Government, adopted with a view to the true interests of our Country, affords me much pleasure.

That the principles of Liberty and the rights of man may be universally disseminated, is my ardent wish; and, as far as in my power, my constant endeavours will be to advance them.

Go. Washington

LB, DLC:GW.

1. See Resolutions from Petersburg, Va., Citizens, 2 Sept. 1793; and Thomas Jefferson to GW, 15–16 September.

From Hezekiah Rogers

Sir   Norwalk Connecticut Sept. 24th 1793.

The office of Collector for the District of New Haven becoming vacant by the death of Mr Fitch, I take the liberty of offering myself as a candidate for the appointment. If from a consideration of my former services and sacrafices in the common cause of my country, and my qualifications to discharge its duties,[1] you should be pleased, Sir, to favor me with the appointment, it will be accepted with gratitude, and its various duties executed with integrity and punctuality. With the utmost respect I have the honor to be, Sir, Your most Obt & most hum. servt

Hezh Rogers.

ALS, DLC:GW.

1. Rogers had served as an officer in the Continental army from January 1777 to the end of the war, and as surveyor of the port of New Haven from 1789 to his resignation around the beginning of 1793. He did not receive this appointment.

To Charles Carter of Ludlow

Dear Sir   Mount Vernon Sepr 25th 1793

Your letter of the 15th instt having unluckily passed on to Philadelphia before it got to my hands, is the cause of its remaining so long unacknowledged.

I have by the Post of to day written to the Comptroller of the Treasury for most of the other Offrs are absent to obtain, on my acct, one hundred dollars for the use of your Sons in Phila. and hope it will be accomplished; but such is the stagnation of business there and so entirely chang'd is every thing there by the retreat of the Inhabitants & the extention & malignancy of the fever with which it is visited that it is almost impossible from the little intercourse people have with one another to promise any thing on a certainty of having it complied with—Mr Wolcot (the Comptroller) will I am sure do all he can to fulfil your desires and it will give me pleasure if in this instance or in any other I can contribute to your happiness.[1]

My best wishes (in which Mrs Washington joins me) attend Mrs Carter and your family and with very great esteem & regard I am Dr Sir Yr Most Obedt & Affe. H. Ser.

Go: Washington

ADfS, PPRF; LB, DLC:GW.

1. See GW to Oliver Wolcott, Jr., this date. The entry for 20 Dec. 1793 in GW's household account book records the payment of $100 to Wolcott "for so much advanced by him to R. W. Carter, son of Charles Carter of Fredericksburg," and an entry of 17 May 1794 records the receipt of $100 from Carter "in full for so much advanced by Olivr Wolcott Jr Esqr. on the President's accot to R. W. Carter" (PHi). GW also recorded this transaction as an account with Carter in Ledger B, 361.

To Alexander Hamilton

(Private)

My dear Sir   Mount Vernon Sepr 25th 1793

I congratulate you & Mrs Hamilton very sincerely on your recoveries from the malignant fever which prevailed in Philadelphia; and hope you are both restored to perfect health, and that no other of the family has been siezed with the disorder. In these sentiments Mrs Washington cordially unite with me.

From Mr Jefferson who has just passed this[1]—from Genl Knox who has set out for Boston—and from the accts published in the Gazettes—I conceive, that under the most favourable change that can reasonably be expected, the first of November is as soon as business can, with safety, be transacted in the City of Philadelphia; but it appears necessary, at all events, that the heads of Departments should assemble—if not at *that* place, yet in the vicinity of it (say German town) at that time; where I also shall be, if well. My compliments to Mrs Hamilton, & respects to Genl Schuyler & family if you are with them. I am always & with much truth Your Affecte

Go: Washington

ALS, DLC: Alexander Hamilton Papers; LS, in Bartholomew Dandridge, Jr.'s writing, DLC: Hamilton Papers; LB, DLC:GW. The ALS was addressed to Hamilton at Albany. The LS, which was marked "Duplicate," evidently was enclosed with GW's letter to Hamilton of 14 October.

1. Thomas Jefferson stopped at Mount Vernon on 22 September.

To Henry Knox

(Private)

Dear Sir,   Mount Vernon Sep. 25th 1793

I have duly received your letters of the 15th & 18th instt and as the last announces your intention of setting out for Boston the next day I shall add nothing in this letter on business—but shall thank you for the information you have given me—as well private as public; and observe that, it appears to me highly necessary that the heads of Departments should assemble in Philadelphia or the vicinity of it by the first of November at which time & place I shall make it a point to be present. I have wrote to the Secretary of the Treasury to this effect and have communicated the same to the Secretary of State.[1] With very great esteem & regard I am Dear Sir Your Affectionate Servt

Go: W——n

ADfS, DLC:GW; LB, DLC:GW.

1. See GW to Alexander Hamilton, this date. GW probably discussed this topic with Secretary of State Thomas Jefferson when Jefferson visited Mount Vernon on 22 September.

To Tobias Lear

My dear Sir,   Mount Vernon Sepr 25th 1793

I have not written to you since we parted, but had just sat down to do it when your letter of the 13th instt was brought to me from the Post Office in Alexandria.

It gave Mrs Washington, myself and all who knew him, sincere pleasure to hear that our little favourite had arrived safe, & was in good health at Portsmouth—We sincerely wish him a long continuance of the latter—that he may always be as charming & promising as he now is—that he may live to be a comfort & blessing to you—and an ornament to his Country. As a token of my affection for him, I send him a ticket in the lottery now drawing in the Federal City; and if it should be his fortune to draw the Hotel, it will add to the pleasure I feel in giving it.[1]

We remained in Philadelphia until the 10th instt. It was my wish to have stayed there longer; but as Mrs Washington was unwilling to leave me amidst the malignant fever which prevailed, I could not think of hazarding her & the Children any longer by my remaining in the City—The house in which we lived being, in a manner blockaded by the disorder which was becoming every day more & more fatal. I therefore came off with them on the above day, and arrived at this place the 14th without encountering the least accident on the Road.

You will learn from Mr Greenleaf that he has dipped deeply in the concerns of the Federal City; advantageously I think for himself, and I am pleased with it on public ground also; as it may give facility to the operations at that place, at the same time that it is embarking him in a measure which, although it cannot well fail under any circumstances that are likely to happen, may be considerably promoted by men of Spirit with large capitols. He can, so much better than I, detail his engagements, & the situation of things in and about the City, that I shall not attempt to do it at present.[2]

Mrs Washington having decided to let Nelly Custis have her Watch & Chain, is disposed to receive substitutes in lieu there of at about Twenty five guineas price; and leaves the choice of them to you. The plainness of the Watch &ca will be no objection. One hundred and twenty dollars in Bank notes are enclosed for the purchase of them.[3]

If it should be convenient, and perfectly safe for you to engage for me, on reasonable terms, a compleat Black Smith, you would oblige me by doing so. As there are laws in England prohibiting such engagements under severe penalties,[4] and such may exist in other Countries, you will understand me clearly, that, for no consideration whatsoever would I have you run the smallest risk of encountering them. You know full well what kind of a Smith would suit my purposes—it is unnecessary therefore for me to be particular on this head. He must, however, have a character on which you can rely not only as a compleat workman for a Farm, but as an honest, sober & industrious man. If he comes on Wages they must be moderate; & with, or without wages he must be bound to serve me three years, four would be better.

Mrs Washington thanks you for your kind recollection of her request respecting Lincoln, and desires me to assure you of her sincere love for him—in which I Join—and of her friendship & regard for you. In whatever place you may be, or in whatever walk of life you may move, my best wishes will attend you, for I am & always shall be Your sincere friend and Affectionate Servant

Go: Washington

P.S. I have just received a letter from the Earl of Buchan in which he says my letter intended to accompany the Portrait had got safe to his hands, but that he had seen heard nothing of the Picture. If you should, while in New York see the Painter of it, be so good as to mention this circumstance to him, & enquire into the cause of the failure.[5]

The District attorney of New Hampshire has sent his resignation[6]—I am entirely unacquainted with the characters in that line, in that State, and would thank you to name the person whom you think best qualified to succeed Mr Sherburne, & most likely to give general satisfaction.

G. W——n

ALS, CSmH; ADfS, DLC:GW; LB, DLC:GW.

1. In order to raise money for the construction of public buildings in the Federal City, Samuel Blodget, Jr., with the approval of the commissioners, advertised a lottery in January 1793, with the grand prize to be ownership of a hotel to be constructed in the city. Promised for 9 Sept., the drawing was postponed until 23 Sept. (*Gazette of the United States* [Philadelphia], 19 Jan.; *Virginia Chronicle and, Portsmouth & Norfolk General Advertiser,* 21 Sept.). Commencing on that date, the drawings continued into 1794.

2. GW wrote to James Greenleaf on this date: "Understanding from Doctr Stuart, it was not likely you would leave George Town before friday, I take the liberty of giving you the trouble of the enclosed letter to Mr Lear" (ALS, NNYSL). For Greenleaf's arrangement to purchase 3,000 lots in the Federal City, see GW to the Commissioners for the District of Columbia, 20 Aug., n.3.

3. Lear purchased a horizontal gold watch at London in January 1794 (see Lear to GW, 26–30 Jan. 1794, and Ledger C, 4).

4. GW may have had in mind the 1785 "act to prohibit the exportation to foreign parts, of tools and utensils made use of in the iron and steel manufactures of this kingdom; and to prevent the seducing of artificers or workmen, employed in those manufactures, to go into parts beyond the seas" (25 Geo. 3, c.67). See also "An act to prevent the inconveniencies arising from seducing artificers in the manufactures of Great Britain into foreign parts" (5 Geo. 1, c.27 [1718]).

5. GW was referring to the Earl of Buchan's letter to him of 30 June. Lear reported the results of his meeting with the painter Archibald Robertson in a letter to GW of 9 November.

6. See John Samuel Sherburne to GW, 30 August.

From William Powell

Sir					New Haven Septr 25th 1793

Inclosed I have the Honor of forwarding you, the address of a number of the principle Merchants, Traders & other respectable Inhabitants of this City, in my favor for the Office of Collector of this district, who's credibility will bear examination.[1] I have the honor to be with the highest respect Sir Your most Obedient & most humble Servant

Willm Powell

ALS, DLC:GW.

1. This enclosure has not been identified. On 27 Sept. Powell wrote GW another letter, enclosing "the recommendations from the Gentlemen of Derby and Milford, Ports in this District, which are all that are conversant at the Office." The recommendation from Milford has likewise not been found, but the recommendation from Derby, signed by Canfield Gillet, William I. Bellamy, Samuel Hull, William Mansfield, John Howard, Abijah Hull, Richard Mansfield, Jr., Joseph Davis, David Hitchcock, Stone & Lewis, Ebenezer Gracey, Sheldon Clark, William Clark, Jr., Jabez Thompson, and Joseph Whelen, and certified on 25 Sept. by Justice of the Peace John Humphreys that "the aforegoing Persons are all the Principle Merchants in this Port," states that "William Powell of the City of New Haven has ever since the establishment of the Customs under the present Government, been an active and diligent officer and particularly useful in the Collectors Office and for a number of years has uniformly Acted as deputy Collector in the Sickness and absence of the Collector, and we recommend him as a fit person, to succeed the late Jonathan Fitch Esqr. as Collector of this Port and District" (all documents DLC:GW). GW, however, appointed David Austin, Sr., instead of Powell.

Letter not found: to Harriot Washington, 25 Sept. 1793. On 16 Nov., Harriot Washington wrote to GW: "I receiv'd My Honor'd Uncle's letter of the 25 of September."

To Oliver Wolcott, Jr.

(private)

Sir,   Mount Vernon 25th Septr 1793.

Your Letter of the 20th instant came duly to hand. I am much obliged to Colo. Hamilton for sending me a copy of the Memorandum, describing the mode of treating the prevailing fever in his case—& to you for transmitting it.[1] It gave me sincere pleasure to hear that he & mistress Hamilton have got so happily over the disorder—and I hope—Mrs Wolcott[2] & yourself will escape it. The enclosed for Colo. Hamilton, you will be so good as to forward.[3]

An old acquaintance of mine—a respectable character & a staunch friend to the Government of the U. States, has requested of me what you will find in his Letter enclosed.[4] I am anxious to comply with it—but do not, under existing circumstances, well know how to draw the money with regularity from the Treasury, *on my own account;* and therefore take this method of expressing my wish, and leaving it to your judgment to carry it into execution.[5] my compliments to Mrs Wolcott—with esteem & regard, I am Sir, Your very humble Servant

                                        Go: Washington

LS, CtHi: Oliver Wolcott, Jr., Papers; ADfS, DLC:GW; LB, DLC:GW.

1. The copy has not been identified.

2. Elizabeth Stoughton Wolcott (c.1766–1805) had married Wolcott in 1785.

3. See GW to Alexander Hamilton of this date.

4. GW was referring to Charles Carter of Ludlow. On the draft, GW initially wrote "friend," but changed the word to "acquaintance." For the enclosure, see Carter to GW, 15 September.

5. Wolcott advanced $100 to Carter's sons, which GW repaid in December (see 20 Dec. 1793 entry, Household Accounts).

From Thomas Blackburn

Dear Sir   Rippon Lodge[1] [Va.] Sepr 26th 1793.

I take the Liberty of inclosing for your Perusal, some Extracts from a Letter I have just received from a Gentleman of Barbados; the Purport of which appears to me to be interesting to the United States of America: and as it may possibly not yet have come to your Knowledge, I think it my Duty to forward to You the Intelligence without Delay; submitting it entirely to your better Judgment, whether it deserves your Attention. The Writer of the Letter, is a Gentleman in the medical Line, with whom I had the Pleasure of making an Acquaintance, when in Barbados the last Winter, and his Veracity I think may be certainly depended on.

I hope by the Return of my Messenger to hear that you & your Lady are in good Health—Mrs Blackburn joins me in most respectfull Compliments to both.[2] I am, with the most perfect Esteem, Yr obedt humble Servt

                        T. Blackburn

ALS, DNA: RG 59, Miscellaneous Letters.

1. Rippon Lodge was the name of Blackburn's house and estate in Prince William County, at what is now Woodbridge, Virginia.

2. Christian Scott Blackburn (1744/45–1815) was Blackburn's wife.

Enclosure
Extract of a Letter from a Gentleman in Barbados

[Barbados] August 9th 1793

I heartily congratulate your Country on your peace with the Savages; for, from what you tell me, I presume the Indian War is terminated—may this be your last War! but we are not without serious Apprehensions of a rupture between G. Britain & you.

Without troubling You with a detail of many idle & unsupported Tales in circulation, it may be of Use to be informed, that on Tuesday last, (the 6th Instt). an Express arrived from the Governor of Bermuda, requesting Supplies of Ammunition &c., as he apprehended an immediate Attack from America. The Capt. of the Vessell sent Express, deliver'd his letter & message before a large Company at Pilgrim; for Governor Parry having left Barbados on the 21st of July, Mr Bishop, who succeeded him, as President, ⟨ha⟩d made this his first publick Day and had ⟨*mutilated*⟩ out above eighty Cards[1]—the News of course circulated over our little Island, with great rapidity; and was received with the most unfeign'd concern—Among others, Sir Philip Gibbes was a Guest at Pilgrim that Day, and on the next he came to me by 10 in the Morning & passed a long Day with me.[2] We were quite alone—This gave me an Opportunity of discussing the subject with him, & as he is perfectly acquainted with the people in power at Home, what he offers deserves the most serious Attention—Mr Pitt, he is positive, is not willing to quarrall with America, & this pacifick temper is confirmed by his Mother, the avowed Friend of America, and to whose Opinion he pays great Deference:[3] nothing therefore short of real unrepair'd Injury, will provoke the Minister to War, and from the Confidence we have in Wisdom & Integrity of your President & Congress, we take for granted that they will labour to obviate this. But your common People are rather licentious, and as appears by some of your papers, betray the greatest partiality to France—Add to this that the King is unrelentingly vindictive, & woud rejoice to be ⟨j⟩ustified in sending Sword & Fire among you on⟨ce⟩ more.

L, DNA: RG 59, Miscellaneous Letters.

1. Except for a period in 1790, David Parry (d. 1793) of Wales served as governor of Barbados from 1784 to 1793, when he left the island because of declining health. William Bishop (d. 1801), president of the Barbados council, served as interim governor of Barbados, 1793–94, and again, 1800–1801. The governor of Bermuda from 1788 to 1794 was Henry Hamilton (c.1734–1796), formerly the British governor at Detroit during the Revolutionary War. "Pilgrim" probably was Frere Pilgrim Plantation, now a city in south-central Barbados.

2. Sir Philip Gibbes (1731–1815) was created first baronet of Springhead, Barbados, and Faikley, Oxon., in 1774.

3. The mother of British Prime Minister William Pitt (1759–1806) was Hester Grenville Pitt (1720–1803), the widow of William Pitt, earl of Chatham (1708–1778).

To Joseph Harper & Co.

Gentlemen,   Mount Vernon. Septembr 27. 1793.
   Your Letter of the 10th instant enclosing a Memorial dated the 9th, never came to my hands until yesterday.
   I shall transmit both to the Secretary of State, to whom it would have been more regular for you to have applied in the first instance.[1]
   The proofs will be necessary for his inspection & information (if the matter has not been acted upon by the American Minister at Paris) that he may be enabled to report the case fully for my consideration.

                                                Go: Washington

LS (photocopy), Swann Galleries, *Autographs: Americana, artists, entertainers, scientists, industrialists, politicians, explorers, signers, etc.* . . . , 8 June 2000, item 143; LB, DLC:GW; Copy, DNA: RG 76, International Claims: France.
   1. GW's letter to Thomas Jefferson of this date reads, "The enclosed Letter & Memorial came to my hands yesterday, to which I returned an answer of which the enclosed is a copy" (LS, DNA: RG 76, International Claims: France; LB, DNA: RG 59, George Washington's Correspondence with His Secretaries of State). Jefferson responded to GW on 9 October.

To William Wootton Brewer

Sir,   Mount Vernon 29th Septr 1793.
   A Letter from you of the 20th inst: has been received, stating the distressed & truly affecting situation in which you are.[1] Could my ability to do it, keep pace with my sincere desire to relieve the wants of the distressed, the request made in your letter to me would be chearfully complied with; but the numerous & pressing calls upon me for pecuniary aid from real objects of charity, & from those who are more immediately within my own knowledge, are such[2] that I am under the *necessity,* however repugnant to my feelings, of declining to comply with your request[3] but I can have no doubt however, that all those who are acquaintd with your merits and knowing to the circumstances as stated in your letter would readily contribute to make up such a sum as you require to commence business with. sincerely wishing[4] that you may find means to extricate yourself from your present embarrassments, as represented in your Letter, I am Sir, &c.

Df, in the writing of GW and Bartholomew Dandridge, Jr., DNA: RG 59, Miscellaneous Letters; LB, DLC:GW. The draft was addressed to Brewer at Annapolis. In 1799 he submitted a petition to the Maryland legislature praying for an act of insolvency, and the House committee reported in favor of his application (*Votes and Proceedings of the House of Delegates of the State of Maryland. November Session, 1799, Being the First Session of this Assembly* [Annapolis, 1800], 29, 99). His insolvent estate papers from chancery court, 27 Feb. 1800, are in MdAA.

1. Brewer's letter to GW of 20 Sept. has not been found.
2. GW inserted "are such" above the line.
3. GW inserted the rest of this sentence.
4. Dandridge had written "praying," but GW struck that word and wrote "wishing" above the line.

From Charles Carter of Ludlow

Dr Sr   Fredg 29th septr 93

I by Mr Fitz[hugh] of Chatham, reced your kind and Affectionate Letter.[1] ten thousand times I am obliged by this mark of friendship ever greatfully shall I hold it in remembrance. I have the satisfaction to tell you, that by letter of the 15th from my sons, they had got their money, and have by this post, directd them, to let the hundred Dollars you so obligeingly directed the Comptroller Mr Wolcot to pay, lay in case by any unforeseen accident they should be in want, which hope will not be the case. as the sum reced by them of 45£ Va C. this by no means lessens my obligations to you my Friend. I have a letter of the 23d they then were well, but poor Charles, was attending to Mrs Hutchison, & Burgess Ball in the Putrid fever, so that my fears are great.[2] I hope for the best, and must submit to the devine will.

My best wishes in which Mrs Carter most affy joins me attend Mrs Washington and all at Mt Vernon & with esteem & regard I am Dr Sr your much obliged Obt & Affectionate Hble St

Chs Carter

ALS, DLC:GW.
1. See GW to Carter, 25 September.
2. Carter's son Charles Landon Carter and Sidney Evans Howell Hutchinson (d. 1838), the second wife of Dr. James Hutchinson, survived the epidemic. Burgess Ball, Jr. (1773–1793), a son of Lt. Col. Burgess Ball (1749–1800) by his first wife, Mary Chichester Ball, did not.

Bartholomew Dandridge, Jr., to Jonathan Shaw

Sir,   Mount vernon 29 Septr 1793
Your Letter, of the 23d instt has come to the hands[1] of the Presidt who has directed me to acknowledge the receipt of it[.] Your situation therein described is indeed unfortunate, & such as He could wish to better (as nothing gives him more pleasure than to relieve the wants of the distressed, & to encourage industry)—did He conceive it to comport with the various pecuniary calls which he of necessity is obliged to answer, besides objects which are daily presenting themselves & demanding assistance; but so very numerous & urgent are they, that it is impossible that all can be accomodated. These circumstance put it out of his power to afford you the aid you ask, which, in other circumstances, it would give him pleasure to grant. I am Sir &ca
                                                            B. D.

P.S. The two Certificates sent are returned agreeably to your desire.

Df, in the writing of Bartholomew Dandridge, Jr., and GW, DNA: RG 59, Miscellaneous Letters; LB, DLC:GW. Dandridge originally drafted this letter for GW in the first person, but the pronouns of the draft were later changed to refer to the president in the third person.
    1. The remainder of this sentence was inserted on the draft by GW.

From Beverley Randolph

Dear Sir   Chatham[1] [Va.] Sepr 30. 1793.
When I had the Pleasure to see you at Mount Vernon, you express'd a wish to be furnishd, with the Information received, by the Commissrs for treating with the western Indians, from Capt. Wellbank; I therefore inclose you an Extract from my private Journal, which I believe contains the whole of the communication of any Importance made by that gentleman.[2]
    Supposing that the present occlusion of the Public offices in consequence of the dreadful malady which afflicts Philadelphia, would probably prevent your receiving a copy of the Commiss⟨rs⟩ Report. I have also extracted for your Perusal the substance of what pass'd between the Indians & the Commissrs from the 29th of July to the 16th of August. together with a full copy of the

message received on that Day and the Commissrs Reply thereto.[3] with Sentiments of real Respect I am Dr Sir Yr most obdt Servt

Beverley Randolph

ALS, DLC:GW.

1. Chatham, near Fredericksburg, was the home of William Fitzhugh (1741–1809), whose wife, Anne Randolph Fitzhugh, was Randolph's sister.

2. George Welbank (d. 1794) served during the Revolutionary War as a lieutenant in the Loyalist corps of chasseurs commanded by Andreas Emmerich. An associate of William Augustus Bowles, he had resided among the Lower Cherokees since about 1788, and he supported the Shawnee efforts to unite the Southern and Northern Indians. For the enclosed extract, see below.

3. The "Extract from the private Journal of one of the Commissioners for treating with the Western Indians," thirteen pages in Randolph's writing, is in DLC:GW (filed at 14 Aug.). The Indians' speech, dated 13 Aug. but given to the commissioners on 16 Aug., and the commissioners' reply of 16 Aug., are on pages 7 through 13. For those speeches, see *ASP: Indian Affairs*, 1:356–57. The rest of the extract reads: "Mouth of Detroit "July 29th. arrived a second Deputation from the Indian nations assembled at the Rapids of the Miami; with them came Capt Elliot Mr Thos McKee son to Colo: McKee & a Mr [Thomas] Smith. The Indians encamped on an Island call'd Bois blanc opposite to Capt. Elliots House occupied by the comissrs "30th. The Indians came over to the commissrs told them that they were deputed by the nations assembled at the Rapids of the Miami to inform them that the Deputies who met them at Niagara had not explain'd the meaning of the Indians neither had the commissrs been fully explicit with them; they therefore thought it best to put what they had to say into writing. Then handing a Paper said here is the meaning of our Hearts. This Paper was address'd to the Commissrs & was to this Effect.

" 'The Deputies formerly sent to you did not fully explain our meaning we have therefore sent others that you may fully understand the great Question we have to ask you. You know that the Boundary Line which was run between the white People & us at the Treaty at Fort Stanwix was the River Ohio. If you seriously design to make Peace you will immediately remove all your People from our side of the River. We therefore ask you. Are you fully authorized to continue & firmly fix the Ohio River as the Boundary between your People & ours?' This Paper was declared to be signed by the Wyandots, Delawares, Shawanese, Miamis, Mingoes, Patiwatimies, Ottawas, Connoys, Chippeways, & Muncees in behalf of themselves & the whole confederacy & agreed to in full council.

"31st. To the above mention'd Paper the commissrs returned an answer in substance as follows. That they were surprized at the suggestion that in the conference at niagara the Parties did not come to a right understanding— that the Deputies appear'd to be men of sense sober & proper in their conduct, that the commissrs were certainly sufficiently explicit as they had declared in plain words that concessions were necessary on both sides what those concessions should be would be fix'd when they could meet face to face in Council. that they were certain this would be the best way to remove all Difficulties but as the nations had adopted another mode of doing Business & had demanded answers to certain Questions previous to their meeting they would give an explicit answer to the great Question now propo[sed.] It would however be necessary first to look back to some former transactions. The Commissrs then proceeded, acknowleging that the ohio had been fixd on as the boundary by the Treaty at Fort Stanwix in 1768. They then stated the war between Great Britain & america with the subsequent Peace in which the Indian Nations who had taken Part with the King of England not being comprehended it remain'd to establish Peace between them & the United States & that Commissrs had been accordingly appointed to effect this Purpose; after mentioning the Treaty of 1784 at Fort Stanwix with the six nations, that of Fort McIntosh with the Wyandot Delaware Ottawa & Chippewa nations as also that with the Shawanese at the mouth of the great miami the commissrs went on to say, that the commissrs who had conducted their several Treaties had sent the Papers containing them to the great Council of the United States who supposing them satisfactory to the nations treated with had sold large Tracts of the Land thereby ceded & that a great many Families as well French as Americans were now settled on them. But it appearing after some Time that a number of Indians were dissatisfied with the Treaties of Fort McIntosh & Miami governour St Clair was appointed with full Powers to regulate Trade & settle Boundaries between the Indians & the United States in the Northern Department That he accordingly sent messages inviting all the nations concerned to meet him at a council Fire which he had kindled at the mouth of Muskingum but that mischief happening at Place the Fire was put out he therefore kindled another at Fort Harmar where near six hundred Indians of different nations attended; that the six nations then confirmd the Treaty of Fort Stanwix the Wyandots & Delawares that of Fort McIntosh & that some Ottawas Chippewa's Patawatimies & Sacs were Parties to the Treaty at Fort Harmar. The Commissrs then said they had with them all these Treaties as well as the speeches of many chiefs who attended them & who voluntarily express'd themselves satisfied with the Terms; they therefore explicitly declared that it is now impossible to make the River Ohio the boundary. They then endeavoured to show the impracticability of removing People from Lands which had become dear to them in consequence of the Improvements which they had made they also mention'd, as an additional Reason why the Ohio could not now be the Boundary, a sale made by the Wyandots & Delawares to the State of Pennsylvania of a tract of Land lying east of a Line drawn from the mouth of big Beaver Creek on the Ohio due north to Lake Erie & that of this Sale no Complaint had been made. After having thus given a decisive answer to the Question proposed to them; the commissrs stated that the united states wish'd to have confirmed to them all the Lands ceded by the Treaty of Fort Harmar as also a small Tract claim'd by General Clarke for the use of himself & his warriors & that in Consideration thereof the united states would give a larger Sum than was ever given at one Time for any Quantity of Indian Lands since the white People first set their feet on this Island & would moreover give every year a large Quantity of such goods as are best suited to Indian wants. But if the wishes of the united states could not be gratified in their full extent that then the commissioners desired to treat with the Indians for a new Boundary & that for the Quantity of Land which should be ceded they would stipulate a generous compensation not only for a large Sum to be paid at once but for a yearly Rent for the Benefit of themselves & their Children forever. The Commissrs then proceeded, after some general observations on the subject of the right of preemption claimd by the United States as it had formerly been by the King of Great Britain, to declare that by express Authority of the United States they acknowledged the Property or right of soil to be in the Indian nations so long as they desire to occupy the same the united States only claiming particular Tracts of Land as above mention'd & the general Right well known both to the English & americans & call'd the right of Preemption or the Right of Purchasing Lands of the Indian nations disposed to sell to the exclusion of all other white People. The speech of the commissrs was then concluded by a Declaration that they had fully opened their Hearts & by expressing their Hope that another Deputation would shortly lead them by Hand to the Place of Treaty whereby a free intercourse any Difficulties which came in the way of Peace might more easily be removed. The Indians then said they would say a few words in the morning it being now too late.

"August 1st. The Indians & commissrs having met a Wyandot chief said it had been now three years since the united States wanted to speak to them. They heard us yesterday & understood us well. you mentiond the Treaties of Fort Stanwix Beaver Creek & others. Those Treaties were not compleat there were but few chiefs who treated with you. you have not bought our Lands, it belongs to us. you tried to draw off some of us. You mention General Washington. He & you know you have Houses & People on our Lands. you say you cannot move them off & we cannot give up our Land. We are sorry we can't agree. The Line has been fixed long ago. there has been much mischeif done on both Sides. We came here upon Peace & thought you did the same. We shall talk to our Head Warriors. you may return whence you came & tell Washington. The council here broke up, when Capt. Elliot Colo: McKees assistant went to Kakeapalathy a Shawanoe chief & told him the last Part of the speech was wrong, Simon Girtie the Interpreter asserted that he ha[d] given a true Interpretation of what the Wyandot chief said, an explanation took place & Girtie added as follows. Brothers Instead of going Home we wish you to remain here for an answer from us. We have your speech in our Breasts & shall consult our Head warriors The Commissrs then said they would wait to hear again from the council at the Rapids but desired their answer might be without Delay

"August 12th. No official Information being yet received from the Indian council the Commissrs thought it proper for the Purpose of more easy & expeditious communication with the Indian to proceed immediately to the Miami Bay or River. They accordingly wrote to Capt. Ford commanding the Dunmore, the vessel assignd by governour Simcoe for their accommodation, desiring him to be prepared to sail on the next morning. Capt. Ford informd the commissrs that he was instructed to attend them but was to receive his orders from Capt. Bunbury & desired us to speak to him. Capt. Bunbury was immediately applied to & told that gr Simcoe had assigned the Dunmore to our use & that from what the gr & his Secretary had repeatedly said we had a right to conclude she was under our Direction to go when & where we thought proper for the Purpose of the Treaty except to Detroit. He answered he had his orders from governour Simcoe & that from these orders he could not consent that the commissrs or any Deputation from them should go to the Miami Bay or River untill Colo: McKee should give notice that the Indians were ready to receive them but that if the commissrs chose to go to Sandusky he would order the Dunmore to proceed thither. He then read a Passage from gr Simcoe's Letter to him. He was asked if he would give an extract of the Letter containing his orders, he answer'd Mr Storer might take an extract from it. They retired Capt. Bunbury read & Mr Storer wrote down the following words 'The directing the King's vessel to carry them (the commissioners) thither (meaning the mouth of Detroit) she will anchor therefore as conveniently as possible to the Northern shore of the River on the Banks of which they purpose to remain untill they hear from Colo: McKee, the Indians do not wish they should visit the opposite shore.['] Capt. Bunbury although desird by Mr Storer refused his signature to the above extract.

"Augt 13. Being thus prevented from proceeding to the miami Bay the commissrs determined to send a message to the Indians & a Letter to Colo: McKee. In the message to the Indians they complain'd of the great Delays they had met with express'd their sincere Desire for Peace upon just Principles but that if no Treaty was to be held if Peace was not to be obtain'd they desired immediately to know it that they might return Home. In the Letter to McKee after complaining of the unusual Delays which had taken Place the commissrs inform'd him that they had sent runners with a speech to the Indians manifesting their wishes to begin the Treaty immediately expressd their belief that it was in his Power to forward the Business & that his aid therein would be gratefully acknowleged. They then complaind of the improper manner in which the negotiation had been hither to conducted declaring that they must soon close the Business unless substantial Reasons demanded Procrastination & concluded with again requesting his assistance in expediting the Treaty."

Enclosure
Journal Extract about George Welbank's Information

August 13.[1] Capt. Wellbank call'd to see the commissrs & dined with them. As he had lived among the Creek Indian & was conversant with the Cherokees we made inquiry into the causes of their present Dissatisfaction. His information was in substance as follows. That formerly the Creeks in general Council declared that they were willing to confirm to the United States the Lands ceded to them by Treaty as far as the north Fork of the Oconee but not to the South Fork.[2] The Difference between a cession to one Fork & the other he says comprehends a tract of Country about 300 miles long by 70 to 30 miles broad according to the courses of the Rivers. That in June or July 1791 McGillivray wrote to general Knox informing him that the Creeks would not agree to relinquish their Lands Southward of the north Fork. Capt. Wellbank repeated the following as a Passage in McGillivrays Letter. "At our last meeting[3] the articles of the Treaty were explain'd to the nations at large with Respect to the Apilachee or main South Branch of the Oconee it turnd out as I told you it would at New York.[4] They will not agree to that but unanimously agree to the North Fork & hope Congress will require no more." And then he goes on, said Wellbank to describe the Country between the two Forks mentioning the Qualities of the Land as well as its extent. He farther said that Thos. Gegg who is in the commission of the Peace[5] but resides in the cherokee nation gave him a copy of the Letter which is said to have been transcribed from a South Carolina News Paper.[6] The Dispute relative to the Lands lying between the two Forks of the oconee is assigned by Capt. Wellbank as the sole cause of the Creeks having refused to run the boundary line between them & the United States Wellbank farther inform'd that after the Treaty at new york when McGillivray was at new orleans the spanish governour blam'd the Creeks for giving up so much of their Country to the united states. McGillivray said the chiefs had done it. that the governour of New orleans sent among the Creeks Capt. Oliver a Frenchman [in] the Spanish Service who asked the chiefs why they had given away so much of their Land the chiefs laid the blame on McGillivray & he to excuse himself said that when the Treaty was made he was in an interior Part of an Enemy's country & was compeld to give up the Land. That the gr. of New orleans told McGillivray he could not serve two masters he must therefore renounce the Spaniards or the united States; McGillivray then renounced the latter & was going to burn the Commission of Brigadier which he received from the President but the gr. told him that would be improper, if he meant to relinquish it he should return it inclosed in a Letter.[7] These Facts Wellbank says are known to Richard Findleston a half breed of the Cherokee nation now living on Cumberland & was at New Orleans when McGillivray was there.[8] Capt. Wellbank declared that Bowles had not arrived in the Creek Country to his Knowlege as had been reported but that he was really friendly to the united States.[9] He inform'd us that the Spaniards had built a Fort of some strength at the Walnut Hills within the Territory of the United States. that when they began their work the Creeks were about to strike them supposing them to be Americans but on finding them to be Spaniards they permited them to proceed.[10]

Capt: Wellbank says the Cherokees object to the Treaty with Govr. Blount[11] for the following Reasons

1st   That one Line is stated to pass forty miles beyond Nashville when they agreed only for ten miles & that in the Interpretation they were told it was ten miles.

2d   That the Govr promised them 2000 Dollars annually, that they demanded 3000 that the govr. said he had not authority to grant so much but would apply to Congress to allow the third thousand Dollars, when in fact the Treaty only stipulated the annual Payment of 1000 Dollars contrary to the Interpretation to them.

3. That they never agreed to the Road or to the navigation of the Tenessee as mentioned in the 5th Article.

4th   That they did not agree to submit to Congress the Regulation of their Trade as mention'd in the 6th article.

5th   That the Interpreters were bribed by govr. Blount in consequence of which Carey had fled the Country. Capt. Wellbank says that Thompson (who is an Indian) the other Interpreter stands his ground but has in Effect acknowleged the bribery. Thompson said his Fee was 80 guineas. He told some of his acquaintance that he expected to bring in the Value of two Negroes as he had so much due for private services. Wellbank says he charged Carey with Bribery. In Excuse he said he told Thompson that he did not interpret truly but Thompson checkd him saying hold your Tongue it is none of your Business I am a native of the Land Carey spoke this in the presence of Sir Jno: Nesbit & another gentleman of South Carolina.[12] Capt. Wellbank thinks that the united states have not received Just Information of the Dispute with the Cherokees. All the Persons employed he says are Land Jobbers interested to misrepresent. He also says that as soon as govr Blount was appointed governour of that Territory genl Pickens told the Cherokees that a worse man for them could not have been appointed that he loved Land & would all theirs. Capt. Wellbank farther inform'd that three stations are erected in the Ch⟨ero⟩kee Country over the Line settled by Treaty. He particularly mention'd Major Craigs Station at nine mile Creek 20 or 30 miles from Knoxville.

Augt 14th Capt. Wellbank again dined with us. In the Course of Conversation he said that the Business which brought him to the northward was of a commercial Nature relative to the supplying the Indians with goods.[13] That the Creeks were dissatisfied with the high Price of the goods they received from the Spaniards but they would soon obtain Relief for the Chiefs had petitioned the King of Great Britain to have them supplied by his subjects. That an act of Parliament had passed for the purpose &——a Port about seven miles westward of the mouth of Apelichicola River was to be the Place of Entry. That the House of Panton Leslie & Co: at the close of the war in 1783 obtain'd Permission from the King of Spain exclusively to supply the Indians with goods for the Space of ten years which would expire this Summer.[14]

Capt. Wellbank farther inform'd us that the bloody fellow & other Chiefs who went to Philadelphia to represent the grievances of their nation reported on their Return that the President or authority of the States promised Redress. That the nation waited six months & found none. The bloody Fellow then said Congress are Liars general washington is a Liar & governour Blount is a Liar.[15]

AD, in Beverley Randolph's writing, DLC:GW. A second journal of Welbank's information, in Timothy Pickering's writing, is also in DLC:GW. The most significant differences between the two journals are described in notes below.

1. Pickering's journal gives the following background information before the 13 Aug. entry: "Captain Wellbank who arrived at the Miami Rapids with the Cherokees, went thence to Detroit, where Colo. England ordered the schooner Felicity to carry him to Fort Erie: Captain Wellbank requiring a passage, that he might see Governor Simcoe, with whom he had business, or for whom he had letters.

"Capt. Wellbank returned to Detroit in the Chippawa, and came down in her last Sunday, the 11th instant."

2. Pickering here adds, "He does not know what they would be willing to agree to *now*."

3. In Pickering's journal, this reads "last May meeting."

4. McGillivray was referring to the Treaty of New York, 7 Aug. 1790, for which see Proclamation, 14 Aug. 1790, n.5.

5. The corresponding passage in Pickering's journal states that Gegg "has now a Commission of the Peace from Govr Blount." Pickering then adds "n. B. Thomas Gegg is the name of one of the Witnesses to Govr Blount's Treaty with the Cherokees."

6. Here the Pickering journal adds, "He said the letter had some how or other been intercepted; and perhaps (or he believed) had never reached Genl Knox." The quoted passage is a paraphrase of portions of a letter from Alexander McGillivray to Secretary of War Henry Knox of 1 June 1791 that was published in various newspapers with an 18 Aug., Charleston, S.C., dateline (see *Massachusetts Spy: Or, The Worcester Gazette*, 22 Sept. 1791). On 12 Sept. 1791 *Dunlap's American Daily Advertiser* (Philadelphia) printed the following: "We are well assured, that the letter signed by Mr. M'Gillivray, and addressed to the 'Hon. General Knox,' which has recently appeared in several of the newspapers, was never received by that officer."

7. McGillivray and the Spanish governor of Louisiana, Francisco Luis Hector, Baron de Carondelet (c.1748–1807), signed a treaty at New Orleans on 6 July 1792 in which McGillivray renounced the 1790 Treaty of New York made with the United States. For reports of the activities of Pedro Olivier (c.1754–1805) among the Southern Indians, see *ASP: Indian Affairs*, 1:296–97, 304–5, 308, 310. Olivier was an officer in the Louisiana Regiment from 1771 until his death, rising from cadet to captain (brevet lieutenant colonel).

8. Pickering's journal has two additional sentences at this point: "Capt. Wellbank describes McGillivray, as a debauched and mercenary man; and withal extremely timid. He died on the 17th or 18th of last February." Richard Finnelson (Findleston) was a member of the Bird Tribe best known for his association with the Nickajack expedition (see *ASP: Indian Affairs*, 1:288–91).

9. The remaining information in this paragraph is absent from the Pickering journal. William Augustus Bowles (1763–1805), a Maryland Loyalist who organized several filibustering expeditions in Florida, was at this time in Spain, but the *City Gazette & Daily Advertiser* (Charleston) reported on 10 May that "six of the Creek towns, with a number of Cherokees, had declared war against the United States, and were actually marching under the command of Bowles and Galphin, to attack the frontiers," and the report was widely circulated in other papers.

10. Spain had constructed fortifications at the Walnut Hills site, now Vicksburg, Miss., by 1791. Fort Nogales was briefly occupied by the United States as Fort McHenry after the Spanish troops withdrew in accordance with the provisions of the 1795 Treaty of San Lorenzo.

11. This refers to the Treaty of Holston, 2 July 1791 (Kappler, *Indian Treaties*, 2:29–32).

12. James Carey (Cery) accompanied the Cherokee delegation that visited Philadelphia from December 1791 to February 1792, and he was appointed an official interpreter at that time. He was an interpreter and assistant at Tellico Blockhouse in 1797 when William Blount wrote a letter to him that was used as evidence for Blount's 1798 impeachment, and he remained an

interpreter at least as late as 1813 (*Journal of the Senate of the United States of America, Being the Second Session of the Fifth Congress: Begun and Held at the City of Philadelphia, November 13, 1797* [Washington, 1820], 436–37; Kappler, *Indian Treaties*, 2:181). Sir John Nisbet (c.1768–1827) took his title from the estate of Dean in Scotland but had an estate in Berkeley County, South Carolina. He married a daughter of South Carolina state senator William Alston in 1797.

13. At this point the Pickering journal adds "That he wished for peace: but desired that justice might be done to the Indians."

14. For discussion of the concession given to Panton, Leslie & Company by Spain, see Arthur Preston Whitaker, *The Spanish-American Frontier: 1783–1785; The Westward Movement and the Spanish Retreat in the Mississippi Valley* (Gloucester, Mass., 1962), 39–46.

15. Nenetooyah (Bloody Fellow), also known as Iskagua, was a signatory to the 1791 Treaty of Holston. For his visit to Philadelphia as part of a delegation of Cherokee chiefs in January 1792, see Henry Knox to GW, 17 Jan. 1792.

To Edmund Randolph

Dear Sir,   Mount Vernon Sepr 30th '93

The continuation, and spreading of the malignant fever with which the City of Philadelphia is vis[i]ted, together with the absence of the heads of Departments therefrom, will prolong my abode at this place until about the 25th of October—at, or about, which time I shall, myself, (if the then state of things should render it improper for me to carry my family) set out for that City, or the vicinity, say German-Town.

I shall be obliged to you therefore, if you remain at your Post, which I by no means wish you to maintain at the hazard of taking the fever, to keep me advised of the existing state of things in that quarter—& moreover that you would be so obliging (if it should be thought unsafe for me to go into my own house in the City at the time abovementioned) to inquire whether a tolerably convenient lodging for myself, one Gentleman of my family, with three Servants and as many horses could be had in or near German Town. To prevent any misunderstanding of my meaning, I declare explicitly, that it is hired lodgings *only* I will go into—for, unless such can be had, I would repair to one of the most decent Inns.

I have given notice to the heads of departments of these my intentions, requesting their attendance accordingly.[1] The time and Place mentioned.

Have you ever examined with attention, and with an eye to the case, whether the Constitution, or Laws of the Union, give power to the Executive to change the place of meeting of the Legislature in cases of emergency in the recess? for example, whether the spreading of the fever which is so fatal in Philadelphia, thereby endangering the Lives of the members who might assemble there the first Monday in December next, is a case that would come under any provision in either. If you have not, I pray you to do it, and give me the result of your opinion.

Mr Jefferson upon a superficial view of the subject, when here, thought there was no power in either to do this; but the Laws were not examined carefully, and the Constitution is, I believe, silent respecting it.[2] Mrs Washington joines me in best wishes for you, Mrs Randolph, & family. I am, dear Sir, your Affect. Servt

Go: Washington

LB, DLC:GW. A purported ALS of this letter was listed in 1929 as part of the library of Robert Borthwick Adam (*Adam Library,* 3:254–55).

1. See GW to Alexander Hamilton and to Henry Knox, 25 Sept.; GW's notice to Thomas Jefferson probably was given during Jefferson's visit to Mount Vernon on 22 September.

2. Although GW, after much consideration, did not act to change the place where Congress would meet, Congress clarified his authority by passing in its next session "An act to authorize the President of the United States in certain cases to alter the place for holding a session of Congress," 3 April 1794 (1 *Stat.* 353).

From William Claiborne

Sir,   Richmond October 1st 1793

On the 28th of Feby last, I was informed by The Honr. samuel Griffin, That Ferdinand Leigh Claiborne my Eldest son had Obtained an Ensigncy in the Armey of the United States—From my Sons great anxiety to Serve his Country in that Capacity I consented, and in expectation of his being Called into imediate Service, at my request, he disengaged himself from a very Lucrative Business—Not long after, I received information from My friend Mr Griffin that it was probable he would not be Commissiond untill the event of the then proposed Treaty with the Indians was Known,[1] From Feby then to the present time, My Son has remained in great anxiety, unwilling to commence Trade again, untill his destiny was fixed; He is a Youth accustomed to Business from Early life and so great is his Aversion to Continue any longer in a State of idleness, that he has thoughts imediately of entering into the Mercantile line, which will prevent his future Acceptance, shoud a Commission be offer'd him; But on the other hand, such is his inclination to become a Millitary Character (and as its his wish I hope he may be gratified) that if there remain'd Even a probability of his Services being wanting in a Short time he would keep himself in readiness to Act.

Pardon then Sir, the Liberty I am about to take, My Sons hapiness in life, is my greatest Care—His absence would be felt Sensibly, because he is a Comfort to me in my Old Age, but *that,* ah; even his death might happen without my regret, provided it be in his Countrys Cause—He is in his Twenty Second Year and in as much as industry alone, would make him a Useful & worthy Member of Society, (which is the higth of my ambition, & idleness the reverse[)], I wish to see him again in Some Kind of Business—Condicend then Sir, to direct One of your Secretarys to Answer this letter, and Notify me, whether or not he will be Commissiond, & when, and you will Confer on me a distinguishable & Memorable honor, and for which I shall ever be thankful[2]—I have the honor to be With every Sentiment of Esteem & respect, yr Most Obt & very hble Servant,

William Claiborne

ALS, DNA: RG 59, Miscellaneous Letters. The cover, addressed to GW at Mount Vernon, is stamped "RICHMOND, Sept. 30" and "FREE." William Claiborne (1748–1809), the father of William Charles Cole Claiborne, later governor of Orleans Territory, resided at Richmond.

1. Claiborne is referring to the treaty with the hostile Indians of the Northwest Territory held at Sandusky in July and August 1793 (see *ASP, Indian Affairs,* 1:340–61).

2. Bartholomew Dandridge replied to Claiborne in a letter of 4 Oct.: "Your Letter of the 1st inst. to the President of the U.S. has been duly received by him—and in answer there to he has directed me to inform you that the appointment of your Son as an Ensign in the army of the U.S., was only *provisional;* & that his being called into service or not, depended in a degree on the issue of the late proposed treaty with the Western Indians & other circumstances. The President had expected that your Son, together with others who are in the same predicament, with him had been lately called into service by the Secre'y of war; but as this has not been done, & as it is supposed that the army under command of Genl Wayne has moved before this time, the President would not recommend to your Son to wait in expectation of receiving a Commission *Shortly,* & thereby lose any opportunity, which might

present itself, of enterring advantageously into any other employment, as it is more than probable had the public service required it, the Ensigns provisionally appointed would before this, have been notified thereof.

"It is devoutly wished that the present Campaign may terminate so as to admit of the present military Establishment being reduced; in that case many officers who are now in service would necessarily be discharged; but should the event prove contrary to this wish, & an increase of men & of course officers become necessary, those who have before come forward & applied for commissions would certainly be preferred" (ADfS, DNA: RG 59, Miscellaneous Letters; LB, DLC:GW).

From Elizur Goodrich

May it please Your Excellency   New Haven Octr 1 1793

The office of ⟨*mutilated*⟩ in ⟨*mutilated*⟩ being vacant by the death of ⟨*mutilated*⟩ Esquire I have the honour respectfully to solicit that your Excellency would be pleased to confer on me the appointment to succeed him.[1] Should your Excellency consider a complyance with my application, consistent with the public Good I should accept the appointment with unfeigned Gratitude and make it my endeavour to discharge the duties of the office with fidility and for the benefit of my Country. I am with the greatest Veneration and respect your Excellencys humble Servant

Elizur Goodrich

ALS, DLC:GW.

Elizur Goodrich (1761–1849), a graduate of Yale College, was a New Haven lawyer. He served as a Connecticut representative in Congress, 1799–1801, and was reelected to the succeeding Congress but resigned to take an appointment as collector of customs at New Haven. Removed from that office in 1803, he served in the years following as a member of the governor's council, as a judge, and as mayor of New Haven.

1. The endorsement on this letter indicates that Goodrich was "applying for the Collectors Office ⟨Ne⟩w haven—Connt," which had recently come open upon the death of Jonathan Fitch.

From Henry Knox

sir   Elizabeth Town N. Jersey Octr 1. 1793.

I shall go through New York tomorrow for Boston as my days of quarantine expire today. I hope to be in Philadelphia by the 25th instant.

The french fleet excepting the Ambuscade will sail tomorrow from New York upon some cruise unknown.

The surviellant saild on the 29th ultimo for France with dispatches from Mr Genet. and such is his desire that they should arrive safely, that he will in a day or two dispatch the Ceres, an armed brig with duplicates[1]—It is said the fleet is to Winter in New York. still the fever rages in Philadelphia, and still the neighbouring towns take all possible precautions for their own safety. I am Sir with perfect respect and attachment Your humble Servant

H. Knox

ALS, DLC:GW.

1. Genet's letter to the minister of foreign affairs, 19 Sept., discussed his steps to counter Galbaud's attempt "de livrer nos forces et nos Colonies à l'ennemi," and described his hope of defending French rights in the next Congress despite the efforts of Washington, "qui les sacrifie à nos Ennemis." He explained that the people were for France and their opinion differed greatly from that of the government (Turner, *Correspondence of the French Ministers*, 2:242–43).

From Oliver Wolcott, Jr.

Smiths House near Philadelphia
Sir.   October 1st 1793.

I had the honour to receive your Letter of the 25th of September yesterday; in consequence of which I immediately wrote to Mr Carter, that the sum requested should be furnished him at any time on his application. The Letter to Colonel Hamilton I shall not fail to transmit immediately.[1]

The malady which afflicts Philadelphia has not continued to abate in the manner I expected; it seems that the changes from cold to heat, have on the whole increased the virulence of the disorder—among the unfortunate victims of this desolating disease, I mention Mr Samuel Powel with the more sincere regret.

For about ten days a part of the Treasury offices, have been removed to Doct. Smith's house, near the falls of Schuylkill, where the public business is attended to, as well as present circumstances will admit. I am sir, with the most perfect respect & attachment your obedient servant,

Oliver Wolcott Jr

ALS, DLC:GW.

1. Wolcott's letter to Walker Randolph Carter has not been identified. Wolcott is referring to GW's letter to Alexander Hamilton of 25 September.

From John Brown et al.

Sir   Providence Octr 2. 1793

As the office of attorney for the United States for this district is vacant by the decease of William Channing Esqr. permit us to recommend David Howell Esqr. L.L.D. professor of law in the college here,[1] and one of the most approved practitioners at the bar in this State.

This gentlemans literary & professional abilities are generally acknowledged, it also ought to be known that his conduct as Judge of our Superior Court deservedly gaind him great credit and afterwards when attorney gencral for this State, his decided opinions officially given in spirited addresses to both houses of our Legislature in favor of a convention for adopting the federal constitution occasion'd the loss of the office he then held at the next following election.[2]

We shall only add that as we doubt not of his discharging the duties of the office we now sollicit for him with *fidelity* and *ability*, so we have reason to beleive that his appointment would give general satisfaction to the good citizens of this state and in particular to Sir Your freinds & Very Humle Servts

John Brown
Welcome Arnold
Jos. Nightingale of the h⟨ouse o⟩f Clark & Nightingale,
Mr Clark absen⟨t⟩
Thos lloyd Halsey
Jabez Bowen Commissioner of Loans
President of the Rhode Island College Jonathan Maxcy.
D.D.—Enos Hitchcock
Geo. Benson
Nicholas Brown
Wm Peck—Marshall for this district
John francis

LS, DLC:GW. The cover of this letter, which was stamped "Free," was dated at Providence "4 Oct." A note on the cover reads: "The Keeper of the P. Office is desired to forward this to Mount Vernon if there." The letter was initially addressed to Washington at "Philadelphia," which was crossed out and replaced with "at Mount Vernon Virginia." An identical letter of 2 Oct., but with a cover dated at Providence "11 Oct." and directed to Washington at "Mount Vernon Virginia," is also in DLC:GW. That letter was signed by ex-governor William Greene, John Innes Clark, state secretary Henry Ward, William Russell, and Stephen Dexter.

Welcome Arnold (1745–1798), a merchant, represented Providence in the state general assembly. Joseph Nightingale (1748–1797) and John Innes Clark (1745–1808) had been associated in the mercantile firm of Clark and Nightingale since 1768. Thomas Lloyd Halsey (1751–1838) was a Providence shipping merchant who had acted as French consular agent in Rhode Island during the Revolutionary War. Jonathan Maxcy (1768–1820) served as president of Rhode Island College (now Brown University) from 1792 until 1802, when he resigned to become president of Union College in New York. In 1804 he became the first president of South Carolina College, where he remained until his death. Enos Hitchcock (1744–1803), a former Continental army chaplain who received an honorary Doctor of Divinity degree from Rhode Island College in 1788, was pastor of the Benevolent Congregational Church at Providence. George Benson (1752–1836), later a president of the New England Anti-Slavery Society and father-in-law of William Lloyd Garrison, was a partner with Nicholas Brown and Thomas Poynton Ives in the mercantile firm of Brown, Benson, and Ives. He was also clerk of the Providence Baptist Society, for which David Howell acted as legal representative, and he and Howell were further associated together in the Providence Society for Abolishing the Slave Trade (1789) and the Providence Society for Promoting the Abolition of Slavery (1790). Benson's partner Nicholas Brown (1769–1841) was John Brown's nephew and a 1786 graduate of Rhode Island College. He later served many terms in the state legislature and became noted for philanthropy, especially to the college whose name change honored his generosity.

Howell's candidacy had strong support among Rhode Island merchants, but it was opposed by the governor and the collector at Providence. In January 1794 GW nominated Ray Greene to fill the position.

1. Most of the signatories were associated with Rhode Island College, where David Howell also acted as interim president in 1791–92. In addition to Maxcy, the president, John Brown was a trustee and the college treasurer; Bowen was a trustee and the chancellor; Arnold, Nicholas Brown, Clark, Francis, and Nightingale were trustees; Hitchcock was a former trustee and a fellow of the college; and Halsey had a son, Thomas Lloyd Halsey, Jr. (1776–1855), who graduated from the college in 1793.

2. This refers to Howell's defeat in the attorney general election of 1790 (see Howell's statement "To the Freemen of the State of Rhode-Island" in the *Providence Gazette,* 17 April 1790). The Rhode Island legislature in January 1790 passed a bill to call a convention to take into consideration the constitution proposed for the United States.

From Jonathan Trumbull, Jr.

Dear sir   Lebanon [Conn.] 2d Octo. 1793

The prevalence of the distressing and fatal sickness which continues to rage in Philadelphia, induces me to address you with a quere on the propriety of Congress meeting in that City at their approaching Sessions—The unhappy continuance of the Disorder to this period—with the threatning aspect of its Nature & Symptoms, make it more than probable that the City cannot be rendered a healthfull & convenient place for Business for some Months from this time—Under these melancholly circumstances attending that Capital, it would seem that an Occasion exists, sufficiently extraordinary, to warrant the Presidents interposing his discretionary power of making a *special Call* of Congress, to convene *at some other place*, than that to which they now stand adjourned[1]—this I suppose may be constitutionally done, under the urgency of existing Circumstances—fixing on some time—say a few Days—previous to the 1st monday in Decr next—Should this discretionary power not interpose—a majority of both Houses *must* Convene in Phila.—be the Danger what it may—before an Adjou[r]nment can be made to a place of Safety & Convenience.

My Anxiety for the Health & Safety of the Executive & Legislature of the Union—with that of the various Departments of the Goverment, I trust will plead my excuse for troubling you with these hints—I am sure you will credit me when I say, they are made in the sincerity of my Heart[2]—most devoutly praying that the melancholly occasion, as it respects Phila.—may speedily be removed—& that Providence may soon interpose its healing relief & protection to that distressed City—I beg leave to subcribe myself—with unabated respect & regard—sir—Your most Obedient and most humble Servant

J. Trumbull

ALS, DLC:GW; ADf, ViMtvL.

1. Trumbull evidently was relying on the part of Article 2, section 3 of the Constitution that stated that the president "may, on extraordinary Occasions, convene both Houses, or either of them."

2. At this point in his draft, Trumbull wrote the following paragraph, which he then struck: "As to the place of extra Meetg I will say but little—perhaps nothing on the subject from me would be best—I will presume only to

mention—That in casting about, it is probable that the Towns of Baltimore & N. York will occur as the most convenient places—our former experience of the Convenience of the latter place may perhaps be a leadg principle in fixing your Judgment—tho I am sensible objections will be started—but whatever place may be thot best, I [s]hall heartily acquiese."

From Theodore Foster

State of Rhode Island. Providence

Sir,   Octr 3d 1793.

It is with very great Regret that I inform your Excellency of the Death of the late worthy *William Channing* Esqr. Attorney for the United States, within the District of Rhode Island, who died at Newport on the 21st Ulto. He was a firm and able Friend and Supporter of the present National Constitution. He was prudent, discrete and conciliating in his Conduct as a Public Officer: and his private social Virtue such as gained and secured to him the Love and Respect of the People. His Death therefore is to be lamented as *a National Loss.* It is however a Consolation that the Constitution of our Country is such *that it enables your Excellency* to point out that Character, to fill the Vacancy who shall appear to you best qualified to serve the Public—and that *Experience* has shewn that *this Constitutional Indication* of Persons suitable for the Public Confidence is happily calculated to cause Appointments to fall on the best qualified and most meritorious Characters. And on the Presumption that it is always agreeable to your Excellency to receive communications, in Writing, from those acting for the State, in the National Legislature, relative to National Appointments to Office within the State, I take the Liberty of addressing this Letter to you, on the present Occasion.

Many worthy and respectable Persons have mentioned to Me *David Howell* Esqr. L.L.D. Professor of Law in the College, in this Town, and one of the ablest and most esteemed Practitioners of Law, in this State as a Gentleman well qualified for the Office of Attorney for the United States, in this District. I have conversed with him and find that he will serve in the Office if appointed, and I believe his Appointment would give greater Satisfaction than that of any other Person. He possesses one of the best Law Libraries in New England. He has heretofore been Attorney General for the State—While in the Execution of that Office he was called on for his Opinion respecting the Propriety and Expediency of calling a Convention for the Adoption of the present National Constitution and having manfully, ably and boldly advocated that Measure, in Opposition to the then prevalent Party, he was on that Account opposed, at the next Election, when the Office was taken from him, in one of those Paroxisms of Party-Spirit, which sacrifices to the Accomplishment of its Purposes, every thing however good and excellent, in Competition with it. His Superior Literature, his Abilities and his personal Integrity are unquestionable and are generally known. And I have no Doubt of his Disposition firmly and zealously to Support our present happy national Constitution—It may be objected that the Attorney for the District ought to reside in the same Town with the Judge and that therefore he ought to be appointed in Newport. On which I beg leave only to observe that much *the greatest Part* of the National Revenue in this State is raised in the District of Providence, which is of Course the Scene of the most . national Business: That there is daily communication by Water between the Towns of Providence and Newport, so that Letters can be every Day reciprocally transmitted; and that I have not heard of any Gentleman of the Bar, at Newport, by any Means so well qualified as Mr Howell who would probably be willing to undertake the Duties of the Office—and these are Considerations which will have their Weight in the Appointment. With the highest Sentiments of the most respectful Regard and Esteem I have the Honor to be your Excellencys much obliged and most obedient Servt

Theodore Foster.

ALS, DLC:GW.

From Thomas Jefferson

Dr Sir   Monticello [Va.] Oct. 3. 1793.
    I received from mister Gore by yesterday's post the evidence on the aggression committed by mister Duplaine Vice Consul of France at Boston, and it appears fully to establish the fact against him.[1] I have therefore prepared & countersigned a Revocation of his Exequatur, with letters on the subject to him, to mister Genet, & mister Morris; as also instructions to mister

Bankson in what way to make up their several packets. although I know of no circumstance which might change the determination with respect to mister Duplaine, yet I have prepared these papers separately & unconnected with any other business, & put them under a separate cover & instructions to mister Bankson, so that if you should chuse it, the whole will be completely suppressed by your stopping this packet.[2] should you on the other hand think, as I confess I do, that an example of authority & punishment is wanting to reduce the Consuls within the limits of their duties, and should you approve of the papers prepared for that purpose, I must trouble you to stick a wafer in the cover to mister Bankson, & forward it by post. I have the honor to be with the most perfect respect & esteem Dear Sir Your most obedt & most humble servt

Th: Jefferson

ALS, DNA: RG 59, Miscellaneous Letters; ALS (letterpress copy), DLC: Jefferson Papers; LB, DNA: RG 59, George Washington's Correspondence with His Secretaries of State; copy, DLC: Jefferson Papers.

1. The evidence about Antoine Charbonnet Duplaine's resistance to replevy of the schooner *Greyhound* by the U.S. marshal was enclosed in Christopher Gore's letter to Jefferson of 10 Sept. (*Jefferson Papers*, 27:79–82). For discussion of that case, see Cabinet Opinions, 31 Aug., and n.2 to that document.

2. The revocation was issued with a date of 10 Oct. and widely published in newspapers: "The Sieur Antoine Charbonet Duplaine heretofore having produced to me his Commission as vice Consul for the Republick of France, within the States of New Hampshire, Massachusetts, and Rhode Island, and having thereon received from me an Exequatur bearing date the fifth day of June 1793, recognising him as such, and declaring him free to exercise and enjoy such functions, powers and priviledges as are allowed to vice-Consuls of the French Republick by the laws, treaties, and conventions in that case made and provided, and the said Sieur Duplaine having under colour of his said Office committed sundry encroachments, and infractions on the laws of the land, and particularly having caused a vessel to be rescued, with an armed force out of the custody of an Officer of Justice, who had arrested the same by process from his Court, and it being therefore no longer fit nor consistent, with the respect and obedience due to the laws, that the said Sieur Duplaine should be permitted to continue in the exercise and enjoyment of the said functions, priviledges and powers—these are therefore to declare that I do no longer recognise the said Antoine Charbonet Duplaine as vice Consul of the Republick of France in any part of these United States, nor permit him to exercise or enjoy any of the functions, powers or priviledges allowed to the vice Consuls of that Nation—and that I do hereby wholly revoke and annul the said Exequatur heretofore given, and do declare the same to

be absolutely null and void from this day forward" (LB, DNA: RG 59, Domestic Letters).

Jefferson's letters of 3 Oct. to Duplaine and to French minister Edmond Genet announced the revocation and enclosed copies of the evidence on which it was based. His letter of the same date to the American minister at Paris, Gouverneur Morris, directed him to transmit copies of all the material to the French government and "to express to them the very great concern with which the President has seen himself obliged to take a measure with one of their agents, so little in unison with the sentiments of friendship we bear to their nation, and to the respect we entertain for their authority" (*Jefferson Papers*, 27:184–88). For Jefferson's letter of 3 Oct. to Benjamin Bankson, see *Jefferson Papers*, 27:182. Benjamin Bankson (d. 1795) served as a clerk in the office of the secretary of the Continental Congress, in the Senate, and in the War Department before becoming a State Department clerk in the summer of 1793.

From Thomas Jefferson

Monticello [Va.] Oct. 3. 1793.

Th: Jefferson with his respects to the President has the honor to inclose him a commission from the French Executive council to mister Dannery to be Consul for them at Boston, also an Exequatur, countersigned by himself, which will want the Presidents signature, & then the seal of the U.S. with these is a letter to mister Genet, & a cover to mister Bankson directing him what to do.[1] should the whole be approved by the President, he will be so good as to sign the Exequator & then stick a wafer in the cover of the whole to Bankson.

AL, DNA: RG 59, Miscellaneous Letters; AL (letterpress copy), DLC: Jefferson Papers; LB, DNA: RG 59, George Washington's Correspondence with His Secretaries of State.

1. Jean-Baptiste-Thomas Dannery (1744–1806) had served in the French consular service since 1779, most recently as consul at Malaga. After leaving Boston, he was named *commissaire des relations commerciales* at Barcelona in 1799 and finished his career as consul general at Lisbon. The exequatur was issued with a date of 10 Oct. and widely published in newspapers: "The Citizen Dannery having produced to me his commission as Consul for the Republick of France at Boston, I do hereby recognize him as such, and do declare him free to exercise and enjoy such functions, powers, and priviledges, as are allowed to Consuls of the French Republick by the laws, treaties, and conventions, in that case made and provided" (DS, NNGL). A copy of Dannery's commission, 19 Dec. 1792, is to be found in DNA:PCC, item 129.

Jefferson's letter to French minister Edmond Genet of 2 Oct. informed him of the exequatur, suggested that a new commission should be obtained if Dannery was meant to operate outside the bounds of Boston, and reminded him that "all foreign agents are to be addressed to the President of the US. no other branch of the government being charged with the foreign communications" (*Jefferson Papers*, 27:175–76). For Jefferson's letter to Benjamin Bankson, dated 3 Oct., see *Jefferson Papers*, 27:181.

From Thomas Jefferson

Monticello [Va.] Oct. 3. 1793.

Th: Jefferson has the honor to inclose to the President a letter he has received from Mr Bournonville, & his answer. he is in hopes mister Dandridge will be able to translate the letter to the President, & if he approves of the answer he will be pleased to stick a wafer in it, as well as in the cover to mister Bankson.[1]

AL, DNA: RG 59, Miscellaneous Letters; AL (letterpress copy), DLC: Jefferson Papers; LB, DNA: RG 59, George Washington's Correspondence with His Secretaries of State.

1. Charles François Bournonville was second secretary of the French legation at Philadelphia. His letter to Jefferson of 18 Sept. has not been identified, but it evidently complained about the arrest of the British ship *Roehampton*, sent into Baltimore as a prize by the French privateer *L'Industrie*. Jefferson's reply to Bournonville, dated 3 Oct., assured him that if the arrest had been made "on improper grounds," the vessel would be liberated by whichever agency, executive or judicial, had given the arrest order (*Jefferson Papers*, 27:183–84). No cover letter to Benjamin Bankson on this topic has been identified.

From Thomas Jefferson

Dear Sir   Monticello [Va.] Oct. 3. 1793.

I have the honor to inclose herewith the following papers.

1. a Note from mister Coxe which covered a letter from Nassau.[1]

2. a letter from George Nicholas which covered his commission, returned.[2]

3. a letter from mister Gore, relating to mister Duplaine, & the communications between him & Govr Hancock, which I asked at the desire of the Secretary at war, & which are for him.[3]

4. a letter from mister Genet of Sep. 14. which, being merely an answer to one of mine, requires no reply.[4]

5. a letter from mister Genet of Sep. 13. this is an answer to the written and verbal applications made to him on the subject of the William & the Fanny.[5] after being in his hands between two & three months, the Consul at Philadelphia is still too busy to furnish the information I had desired. he is since dead, which of course furnishes a new excuse for delay. this indicates clearly enough that Mr Genet does not mean to deliver them up. however he adds that the information would be useless until we settle what is to be deemed the extent of *the limits of our protection.* as this has never yet been decided, I am not able to answer him until you shall be pleased to determine what shall be proposed on that subject. I think myself that these limits are of great consequence, & would not hesitate the sacrifice of money to obtain them large. I would say, for instance, to Great Britain, "we will pay you for such of these vessels as you chuse; only requiring in return that the distance of their capture from the shore shall, as between us, be ever considered as within our limits: now say for yourself, which of these vessels you will accept payment for." with France it might not be so easy to purchase distance by pecuniary sacrifices: but if by giving up all further reclamation of the vessels in their hands, they could be led to fix the same limits (say 3. leagues) I should think it an advantageous purchase, besides ridding us of an article of account which they may dispute. I doubt on the whole whether any thing further can be effectually done on this subject until your return to the seat of government, or to the place where you will fix for the time.

Mr Genet's answer with respect to his opposing the service of process on a vessel is singularly equivocal. I rather conjecture he means to withdraw the opposition, and I am in hopes my letter to mister Hammond will have produced another effort by the Marshal which will have succeeded. should this not be the case, if military constraint cannot be used without endangering military opposition, this vessel also may become a subject of indemnification.[6]

Mr Bankson writes me word that Genl Moylan's residence being off the Post road, he had been obliged to send an express to him, which was not yet returned. Besides the duplicate dispatches for Gouvernr Morris, I had left in his hands letters for all our foreign ministers & Consuls. he writes me that the communications with Philadelphia had been so much intercepted that he had not yet obtained conveyances.[7]

The death of Wright will require a new nomination of an engraver. if it be left to mister Rittenhouse, I think he would prefer Scott.[8]

Just before I left Philadelphia I received from mister Genet a claim of exemption from tonnage for their vessels which quitted the Cape in distress & made the first ports in the U.S. & particularly as to those which came to Baltimore, the tonnage of which amounted to a large sum. as you were come away, I thought it would shorten the business to send his claim in a letter addressed to the Secretary of the Treasury, but (as he was sick) under cover to mister Wolcott, in hopes they would make a report thereon to you for your consideration.[9] the necessity of these abridgments of formalities in our present distant situations requires that I should particularly suggest to you the expediency of desiring Genl Knox to communicate to the foreign ministers *himself directly* any matters relative to the interpositions of his department through the governors. for him to send these to me from Boston to this place merely that I may send them back to the ministers at Philadelphia or New York, might be an injurious delay of business.

I shall hope to have the honor of a line from you whenever you shall have fixed on the time and place at which you shall decide to reassemble us. I have the honor to be with sentiments of the most perfect respect & attachment Dear Sir Your most obedt & most humble servt

Th: Jefferson

ALS, DNA: RG 59, Miscellaneous Letters; ALS (letterpress copy), DLC: Jefferson Papers; LB, DNA: RG 59, George Washington's Correspondence with His Secretaries of State.

1. See Tench Coxe to Jefferson, 15 Sept. (*Jefferson Papers,* 27:118). Coxe requested that the letter from Nassau attorney general Moses Franks to Coxe's brother John D. Coxe be kept secret and "returned in the course of the Month," with no copy taken.

In a fifth letter to GW of this date, Jefferson had "the honor to inclose to the President a Note to mister Coxe & a letter which is the subject of it. when perused he will ask the favor of the President to stick a wafer into the cover and forward it by post. mister Coxe's note to Th: J. is put into a separate packet among papers to be returned to Th: J." (AL, DNA: RG 59, Miscellaneous Letters). Jefferson's note to Coxe, dated 3 Oct., returned the Nassau letter and commented: "The oppressions of our commerce in the West Indies are really grievous: but it seems best to take no small measure, but to wait for the mass of the matter we expect from the merchants and to require indemnification for the whole" (*Jefferson Papers,* 27:184). The Nassau letter has not been identified.

2. This enclosure, a letter from Nicholas to Jefferson, 25 Aug., evidently declining to serve as federal district attorney for Kentucky, has not been identified.

3. See Christopher Gore to Jefferson, 10 Sept. (*Jefferson Papers,* 27:79–82). In Jefferson's letter of 2 Sept. he had asked Gore "to communicate copies of any memorials, representations or other written correspondence which may have passed between the Governor and yourself with respect to the privateers and prizes which have been the subject of your letters to Mr. Lear" (*Jefferson Papers,* 27:13–14).

4. French minister Edmond Genet's letter to Jefferson of 14 Sept. responded to Jefferson's letter of 7 Aug., which informed Genet that it was "expected" that he would "cause restitution to be made" of prizes brought into American ports after 5 June by the French privateers armed at American ports, and that he would take "efficacious measures to prevent the future fitting out of Privateers in the Ports of the united States." Genet replied that he could not agree to the indemnity and lacked the power to withdraw the privateers' commissions, but that he would try to persuade the privateers to suspend their cruises and change their destinations (*Jefferson Papers,* 26:633–34, 27:112–14; *ASP: Foreign Relations,* 1:184–85).

5. British minister George Hammond had alleged that the ship *William* and brig *Fanny* had been seized within American territorial waters. In two letters to Genet of 29 June, Jefferson directed that he order the French consul to deliver the vessels to their owners or supply evidence to contradict the allegation. Having received no response, Jefferson wrote Genet again on 9 Sept. repeating his request and protesting the delay. To this, Genet responded in the letter of 13 Sept. that Jefferson summarizes here (*Jefferson Papers,* 26:398–99, 27:67–69, 103–6).

6. Genet's letter to Jefferson of 13 Sept. also responded to Jefferson's complaints (in the letter of 9 Sept.) that Genet had interfered with the attempt of "an officer of Justice" to take the prize *William Tell* into custody. Genet observed that the 1778 Treaty of Amity and Commerce prevented the courts from taking cognizance of prizes and that Jefferson's letter of 25 June had stated that the ships were to be in the custody of French consuls until final judgment, but he added that he would direct a compliance with the president's wishes as soon as the court cited the law that gave authority. Meanwhile, Jefferson's letter to Hammond of 9 Sept. had informed him that the president had addressed "the act of opposition made to the Service of legal process on the Brig William Tell, and he presumes the Representations made on the subject to the Minister of France, will have the effect of opening a free

access to the officer of Justice when he shall again present himself with the precept of his Court" (*Jefferson Papers,* 27:67–72, 103–6).

7. See Benjamin Bankson to Jefferson, 23 Sept. (*Jefferson Papers,* 27:145–46). Stephen Moylan (1737–1811) had served during the Revolutionary War as mustermaster general, an aide-de-camp to GW, quartermaster general, and, from 1777 on, colonel of the 4th Continental Dragoons, being breveted brigadier general in 1783. At this time he resided on a farm near West Chester in Goshen Township, Chester County, Pennsylvania. Moylan, who was a justice of the peace, register and recorder for Chester County, and major general of the 3rd Division of Pennsylvania militia, was being offered a commission as federal marshal for the Pennsylvania district. He declined the appointment, but later this year accepted an appointment from GW as commissioner of loans for Pennsylvania, a post he held until his death.

8. Robert Scot (1745–1823), born in Edinburgh, was working as an engraver in Virginia by 1780 and at Philadelphia by 1782. He was commissioned as engraver for the mint on 23 Nov., and his appointment was confirmed by the Senate in December.

9. See Jefferson to Alexander Hamilton, 12 Sept., enclosed in Jefferson to Oliver Wolcott, Jr., 12 Sept. (*Jefferson Papers,* 27:99, 103).

Letter not found: from Edmund Randolph, 3 Oct. 1793. On 14 Oct. GW wrote Randolph: "I have received yours of the 3d instt."

To Alexander Spotswood

Dr Sir,   Mount Vernon October 3d 1793

Sometime before I left Philadelphia I received a letter from you respecting your Son John, and immediately made known (by letter) to Mr Morris your wishes concerning him; but having received no answer to it, I conclude, & think it may be taken for granted, he has not much to expect from that quarter. Indeed Mr Morris & others in that line, have so many applications to them of this kind and have so many friends & relations for whom they wish to provide that those who are strangers to them have little to expect. My advice therefore is, as soon as your Son shall arrive at Philadelphia, for him to call upon Mr Morris and know at once whether he will give him a birth in his Indiaman, or not, for as he has never answered my letter I cannot, again, apply to him on this subject.[1]

Since my arrival at this place your letter of the 15th of September has been presented to me but in reply I can only say that from the moment I embarked in my present walk of life, I resolved, most firmly, never to be under any Promise of an office; or to express any sentiment which could be construed into the most distent intimation of one, until the hour of nomination should arrive; and then, under a full view of the merits and pretensions of the different Candidates to name the person who seemed best qualified for the office; without suffering myself to be influenced in the Smallest degree by my friendship—Relationships—or local attachments of any sort or kind whatsoever.

I do not doubt but that Mr Brooke is a Gentleman of merit, but as your letter is the first intimation I have had that the Naval Office at Hobshole is likely to become vacant, I have made no enquiry as yet into the pretensions to, or fitness of any one to supply his place—whenever this event shall happen Mr Brooke request will be considered with others; and wherever the preponderancy is, there my duty to the public requires me to fix. With my love to Mrs Spotswood and the family, in which Mrs Washington joins me, I remain Dr Sir your Affecte Sert

Go: Washington

LB, DLC:GW.

1. See Spotswood to GW, 27 Aug., and GW to Robert Morris, 5 September.

From David Howell

Providence Octo. 4. A.D. 1793

May it please the President,

As the office of Attorney for the U.S. for this District is vacant by the decease of my lamented Friend Mr Channing, & some Gentlemen have been pleased to recommend me for that place, I flatter myself your Excellencys goodness will excuse the freedom I take in mentioning my readiness to accept the appointment in Case no Gentleman is presented of longer Standing & more merit in the profession of the Law in this State.

The veneration I have always entertained for the Distributor of national Honours in the U.S. will much enhance the value of this appointment.

With ardent wishes for your personal Happiness, & for the prosperity of our dear Country over which you preside, I am your Excellencys real Friend & very humble Servt

David Howell.

ALS, DLC:GW.

From Alexandria, Va., Citizens

[5 October 1793][1]

The Citizens of Alexandria, conceiving it to be at all times the right of the People to declare their political principles, and to express their sentiments upon Subjects which concern the national Interest, met at the Court House on Saturday the 6th October, agreeably to notification, in order to take under consideration the late proclamation of the President of the united States[2] and other subjects which agitate the public mind, and came to the following resolutions thereon:

1st Resolved that our illustrious Fellow-Citizen, George Washington, has, by his well-timed proclamation, given an additional proof of his vigilant attention to his duty, and the welfare of his country; and that it is our duty as well as our interest to conduct ourselves conformably to the principles expressed in the said proclamation, and to use our utmost endeavours to prevent any infringement of them by others: And we hereby declare it is our firm intention so to do.

2d Resolved that it is the interest and duty of these united States to maintain a strict Neutrality towards the belligerent powers of Europe, and to cultivate peace and harmony with all the world by just and honourable means.

3d Resolved that all attempts to subvert the Fœderal Government, to violate it's principles, or to lessen the confidence of the People therein, ought to be firmly and vigorously resisted.

4th Resolved that we are attached to a republican form of Government as being the only one calculated to diffuse true national happiness, and to inspire and cherish those principles and Virtues in the people which are the great Ornaments of human Nature. We reprobate Monarchy, because it tends to oppression, and because, by introducing corruption and depravity, it never fails to destroy those Equal rights to which all Men are, by nature, entitled.

5th   Resolved that every attempt to disunite France and America ought to be opposed, as dangerous to Republicanism.

6th   Resolved that we entertain the warmest gratitude for the generous and important Services of the French Nation during the American revolution; and that we feel the strongest attachment to those principles which have occasioned the glorious contest in which that Nation is Engaged for its own liberty; and we most ardently wish them the complete & lasting Enjoyment of that inestimable blessing which, under divine providence, was secured to us by their timely aid and assistance.

7th   Resolved that the interference of any foreign Minister, of whatever nation, with the Government of this Country will be, at all times, highly improper; but that our gratitude to, and affection for, our good allies, the French People, ought not to be lessened by any indiscretion of their Ambassador. In behalf of the meeting

John D. Orr Secy[3]   John Fitzgerald Chairman

8th   Resolved that a Copy of these Resolves be sent to the President of the United States and that they be published in the Alexandria News-Papers.[4]

DS, DLC:GW; LB, DLC:GW.

On 28 Sept. a "Notice to Republicans" appeared in the *Columbian Mirror and Alexandria Gazette* stating, "It is the wish of many of the Inhabitants of Alexandria, whose Love of Liberty and Republican Government have led them to consider the cause of France, as closely connected with the happiness of America, that some fair and becoming method be adopted for a public declaration of these sentiments," and calling a meeting for that night. Despite its Francophile origins, the meeting evidently discussed the misdeeds of French minister Edmond Genet. According to a letter of 1 Oct. from "A Friend to the People," the "tories of the day" portrayed America as too weak to espouse the cause of France and made attempts "to criminate the conduct of the French minister" that were "treated with contempt by the almost unanimous voice of the assembly." The letter also criticized the "aristocratical faction in America" as "officious propagators of the calumny against Citizen GENET" who wished "to harrass the public mind, between an unshaken attachment to the President on the one hand, and a sympathetic regard to the interests of France, and respect to her representative in America, on the other"(*National Gazette* [Philadelphia], 9 Oct.). A later notice called for the citizens to meet on the next Saturday "for the purpose of considering the report of the Committee appointed last Saturday night" (*Columbian Mirror and Alexandria Gazette*, 2 Oct.).

1. Despite the text of the resolves, Saturday fell on 5 Oct., not 6 Oct., in 1793.

2. This is a reference to GW's Neutrality Proclamation of 22 April.

3. John Dalrymple Orr (c.1772–1816) was an Alexandria physician.

4. There were at least two Alexandria newspapers at this time: the *Columbian Mirror and Alexandria Gazette* and the *Virginia Gazette*. The *Columbian Mirror* printed the resolutions on 9 Oct.; another printing taken from an Alexandria paper of 10 Oct., probably the *Virginia Gazette*, appeared in *Bartgis's Maryland Gazette, and Frederick-Town Weekly Advertiser*, 24 Oct. 1793.

To William Pearce

Mr Pearce,   Mount Vernon Octr 6th 1793

Enclosed is a copy of our agreement with my Signature to it.[1]

Since you were here, Mrs Washington the Widow of my Nephew, who formerly lived at this place, has resolved as soon as we leave it, to remove to her Brother's in the lower part of this State, and will not I believe, return to reside at it again.[2] This will make it more convenient and agreeable, both for yourself and me, that you should live the Winter, at least, at my Mansion house; as it will allow more time for my Carpenters to provide for Mr Crow, and to put the place he lives at in better repair than it now is for yourself, if there should be occasion for you to go there; and this too, under your own inspection.

The right wing to my dwelling house as you possibly may have noticed, & heard called the Hall, (being kept altogether for the use of strangers) has two good rooms below (with tiled floors) and as many above, all with fireplaces. This will accomodate your family (being a larger house) better than Crows; and by being here, you will have the use of my Kitchen, the Cook belonging thereto, Frank the House Servant, a boy also in the House.[3] The Stable, Garden &ca &ca, without any additional expence to me; at the same time that it will, by placing you in the centre of the business, ease you of much trouble; for otherwise, the frequent calls from the Farms, from workmen of different descriptions for Tools, Nails, Iron &ca from the Store—and the particular attention which matters abt the Mansion house will require, would have occasioned you many an inconvenient ride here, the necessity for which will be entirely superceded, as your Mornings and evenings will, of course, be spent where your presence will be most wanting.

As I am never sparing (with proper œconomy) in furnishing my Farms with any, and every kind of Tool & implement that is calculated to do good and neat work, I not only authorize you to bring the kind of Ploughs you were speaking to me about, but any others, the utility of which you have proved from your own experience; particularly a kind of hand rake which Mr Stuart tells me are used on the Eastern Shore of Maryland in lieu of Hoes for Corn at a certain stage of its growth—and a Scythe & Cradle different from those used with us, & with which the grain is laid much better. In short I shall begrudge no reasonable expence that will contribute to the improvement & neatness of my Farms; for nothing pleases me better than to see them in good order, and every thing trim, handsome, & thriving about them; nor nothing hurts me more than to find them otherwise, & the tools & implements laying wherever they were last used, exposed to injuries from Rain, Sun, &ca.

I hope you will endeavor to arrange your own concerns in such a manner as to be here as much before the time agreed on as you conveniently can. Great advantages to me will result from this, by putting the business in a good train before the Fall operations are closed by the frosts of Winter, and all improvements are thereby at an end for that Season. On the other hand, inconveniences to yourself may arise from delay on account of the Weather—Navigation &ca; there having been instances of this River's closing with Ice several days before Christmas which might prevent the removal of yr things in time. That your living at the Mansion may be attended with no more expence to you than if you had gone to the other place (at which Crow now lives) on account of Gentlemen, who now & then call here out of curiosity—as they are passing through the Country—I shall lay in such things as will be necessary for this purpose, and the occasions (which are but rare) may require.

I expect to leave this place about the 28th of the Month for Philadelphia, or the neighbourhood of it; any letter therefore which shall arrive before that time will find me here—afterwards it will have to go to Philadelphia where it had better be directed. I am your friend & Servant

Go: Washington

ALS, ViMtvL.

1. The agreement is dated 23 September.

2. Frances Bassett Washington, widow of George Augustine Washington, evidently was planning to stay with her brother Burwell Bassett, Jr., in New Kent County, Virginia.

3. The cook was Lucy, wife of Frank (Francis) Lee, the house servant.

From Edward Savage

Sir,   London Oct. 6. 1793

I have taken the Liberty to send two prints, the one Done from the Portrait I first Sketch'd in black Velvet, Labours Under Some Disadvantages, as the Likeness never was quite Finished. I hope it will meet with the approbation of yourself and Mrs Washington, as it is the first I Ever published in that method of Engraving.[1]

the Portrait of Docter Franklin which is published as the Companion, is Done from a picture in the Possesion of Mr West, President of the Royal Accademy.[2]

The picture has been Done Some years, and was thought very like at the time when Done.

I have the pleasure to inform you that Booth of those prints are approved of by the artists, Particularly Mr West, whose Friendship and Sivility I have the Honr to Receive. I am Sir With great Esteem your Humbl. Sert

Ed. Savage.

N.B. Please to present my Most Respectfull Compliments to Mrs Washington.

I Expect to imbark for my Native Country about March Next.

ALS, DLC:GW. The cover is addressed to GW "through the hands of Berry Rogers & Berry of New York," a firm of booksellers and stationers.

1. The 1793 mezzotint portrait of GW by Savage can be found in the collections of the National Portrait Gallery (see frontispiece).

2. Benjamin West (1738–1820), the famous historical painter born in America, had succeeded to the presidency of the Royal Academy at London in 1792, and he remained in that position, with the exception of one year, until 1820. The portrait that Savage used for his 1793 mezzotint of Benjamin Franklin apparently was done from a portrait by West that used a painting by David Martin as its source. A Savage mezzotint of Franklin is in the collection of the National Portrait Gallery.

From Moses Brown

Esteemed Friend   Providence 7th 10th Mo. 1793

As the Office of Attorney to the United States is Vacant in this state by the Death of Wm Chaning Esquire I take the freedom to Recommend David Howell Esquire to the President, as a Person

Quallified and Suitable for that Office. His Attention & Faithfulness in his Business I have never heard Called in Question and his superior Abilities are Generaly Acknoledged,[1] and as there are Three of Our Attorneys Members of Congress I know of none who will be Likely to give So General Sattisfaction. With Desires for thy Prosperity & Hapiness I conclude thy friend

                                                        Moses Brown

ALS, DLC:GW; ADf, RHi. Moses Brown (1738–1836) was a textile manufacturer and abolitionist who had served in the Rhode Island legislature before the Revolution.

1. From this point on, the draft reads: "and I beleive the Appointment of him Will give More general Satisfaction than Any Other Attorney in the state who is not a Member of Congress, Bradford, Bourn & Foster being all Low Characters." Attornies Theodore Foster and William Bradford were Rhode Island's senators, and Benjamin Bourne was a representative in Congress.

From Arthur Fenner

Sir,   Providence October 7th 1793.

By the Death of my particular Friend Mr Channing the office of Attoy for this District has became vacant. Mr Howell heretofore a Member of Congress and of late practicing Attorney, has I am informed made great exertions to obtain the appointment, he has procured a Number of Signers in this Town to a Petition or application in his favour, & has written I presume to a Number of his acquaintance in the Middle & Southern States to use their influence in his behalf. I think it my duty on this occasion, as Chief Majistrate of the State to trouble your Excellency with a letter on the subject to give such information as may be necessary to form a right opinion in the Case. Ever since Mr Howell has been known as a political Character he has been Violent in his prejudices and fickle in his opinion—his principles of Government have uniformly changed with his interest he is now very unpopular in this State excepting the Mercantile part who at this time for their interest wish to support him; if he obtains the appointment I believe they will rest assured their purposes will be answerd they have therefore combined to obtain the appointment for him and have induced several Gentlemen of their particular connections to join with them. Its matter of regret that so many attempts have been made to evade & Obstruct the execution of the revenue Laws in this Town and perplex the Collector as have come to the knowledge of the Secretary of the Treasury.[1] The Collector is as faithful attentive and impartial as any Man can be but has need of every assistance and support in the Power of Government to give him to enable him to carry the Laws of the United States into Execution—It is frequently nec[e]ssary for him to have recourse to the District Attoy in construeing the Laws, and has hitherto been happy in placing the utmost confidence in Mr Channing But if Mr Howell is appointed who has now the conducting of Mr Welcome Arnolds Cause again[s]t the Collector (yet undetermined) he perhaps will have some reason to doubt the sincerity of Mr Howells opinion.[2] I am not informed whether the Collector will write to your Excellency on this Occasion or not, but I am warranted in saying that he and Mr Thompson the Naval Officer of this port and Coll Dexter the Supervisor of the District join with me in this opinion I am also informed by good Authority that Mr Ellery the Collector of Newport has given the like opinion freely in decisive terms and I am confident that Judge Marchant if called upon for his sentiments on the subject would decide in like manner.

After saying this much of Mr Howell and Mr Bourne not wishing the appointment I would beg leave to recommend a Gentleman of the Law in this Town, who I have every Reason to believe would be faithful and attentive to the interest of the United States—his Name is David Leonard Barnes he was regularly brought up to the Law in Massachusetts and has been in Practice in that and this State upwards of ten Years he recd his first part of his Legal education under the Honorable William Cushing who has known him from his infancy, and having been acquainted with his practice at the Bar, can give any information respecting his abilities that may be required—I can with confidence say that his being appointed will have a strong tendency to promote the peace and harmony of the different branches of the Government of the United States in this District.[3] General Knox has been here for several days is personally acquainted with both the Gentlemen—has heared their several Characters and will therefore be able on his return to give such further information as may be satisfactory. With every sentiment of esteem I am your Excellency Obedient Friend

A. Fenner.

ALS, DLC:GW.

1. The collector at Providence was Jeremiah Olney. The most notable of his clashes with the Providence merchants involved the court case discussed in note 2 below and a bill of impeachment drawn against him on 31 Jan. but evidently not submitted (see Olney to Alexander Hamilton, 18 March, *Hamilton Papers*, 14:214–18).

2. In early November 1792 Olney had detained the brigantine *Neptune* and its cargo, charging that Welcome Arnold and Edward Dexter had used a "Collusive" transfer of the cargo to avoid customs regulations. Later that month, Arnold commenced a suit against Olney for that detention (Olney to Hamilton, 7 and 28 Nov. 1792, *Hamilton Papers*, 13:25–27, 243–44). The county court found for Olney in December 1792, but Arnold appealed to the Rhode Island Superior Court.

The suit, which was the subject of much correspondence between Olney and Treasury Secretary Alexander Hamilton, was scheduled to be brought before the court on 9 Oct. 1793, but the death of William Channing resulted in a continuance of the case (Olney to Hamilton, 23 Sept. and 21 Oct., *Hamilton Papers*, 15:341–42, 372). The court's decision, rendered in April 1794, went against Olney. Olney then appealed to the U.S. Supreme Court, which found in his favor in August 1796. For a full discussion of the case, see *Documentary History of the Supreme Court*, 7:565–624.

3. David Leonard Barnes (1760–1812), a 1780 graduate of Harvard who had practiced law in Taunton, Mass., since 1783, was one of the attorneys engaged by Olney to defend Arnold's suit. He did not receive this appointment, but in 1801 he was appointed a judge of the U.S. District Court for Rhode Island, a post in which he served until his death.

Letter not found: to John Fitzgerald, 7 Oct. 1793. GW, in a letter of Wednesday, 9 Oct., told Fitzgerald that "I wrote to you on Monday"; on Friday, 11 Oct., Fitzgerald acknowledged a letter "of Monday on private business."

From David Humphreys

(secret & confidential)

My dear Sir. Gibralter Octr 7th 1793.

By my letters of yesterday & to-day to the Secretary of State, you will learn that the Algerines have concluded a Truce with the Portuguese; and that the Algerine fleet has gone into the Atlantic.[1] I think they would not have passed the Streights with all their force, without having *much better Pilots* than usual. In dreading the consequences of surprize to our vessels, I have taken all the means in my power to avert them, by giving the most expeditious & extensive notice to our Countrymen possible.[2]

Conscious as I am, that not a moment has been lost, or exertion withheld on my part, in attempting the accomplishment of your wishes; I entreat, in all events, you will be persuaded of my perseverance in the same line of conduct.[3] Should every attempt prove abortive (as there is but too much reason to fear) perhaps circumstances may occur, which would render it useful to the Public for me to return for a short time to America, to communicate or suggest, in an oral manner, what could not absolutely be so well done by any other means. In that contingency, you might possibly not think it improper to have a discretionary leave of absence lodged for me at Lisbon—Of this, however, you will judge & decide according to the superior lights with which your situation will furnish you. For myself—I do not certainly mention the matter, because I have any desire of returning to America—for I declare most solemnly, I have no personal interest or wish on the subject. With sentiments of the sincerest affection for all around you, I remain, my dear Sir, Your most faithful friend & Hble Servant

D. Humphreys.

ALS, DLC:GW.

1. For Humphreys's letters to Thomas Jefferson of 6 and 7 Oct., see *Jefferson Papers*, 27:196–200. Since 1785, American merchant ships on the Atlantic Ocean had benefitted from a Portuguese naval blockade of the Straits of Gibraltar intended to protect Portugal's commerce with Brazil. However, in September 1793, Charles Logie, the British consul at Algiers, acting on instructions from a government eager to free up Portuguese ships for action against France, assured the Dey of Algiers that Portugal was willing to pay a large sum for a peace treaty, and thus obtained the Dey's consent to a twelve-month truce. The blockade was briefly ended, but by late November, having concluded that the cost of a treaty was excessive, Portugal repudiated the truce and reinstituted the blockade.

2. On 8 Oct. Humphreys issued a notice asking "all Governors, Magistrates, and others concerned in the United States of America. . . . as speedily as possible, to give an universal alarm to all citizens of the United States concerned in navigation, particularly to the Southern parts of Europe, of the danger of being captured by the Algerines in prosecuting their voyages to that destination" (*Dunlap's American Daily Advertiser* [Philadelphia], 25 Dec.).

3. Humphreys is referring to his commission to negotiate a treaty of amity and commerce with the Dey of Algiers (see GW to the Dey of Algiers, 21 March 1793, and n.1 to that document).

To Thomas Jefferson

Dear Sir,   Mount Vernon Oct. 7th 1793

It appearing to me that the public business will require the Executive Officers to be together some time before the meeting of Congress, I have written to the Secretaries of the Treasury & War to meet me at Philadelphia or vicinity—say Germantown— by the first of November, and shd be glad to see you there at the same time. The Attorney General is advised of this also.[1]

In a letter from General Knox of the 24th Ulto who was then at Elizabeth Town performing quarantine before he could be admitted into New York is the following paragraph. "The french fleet is still in New York, in a wretched state of disorganization, which prevents its Sailing. Mr G——t has been low spirited for ten days past. The fleet have been told by him that the Executive of the United States prevent their selling their prizes, & citizen Bompard who belongs to a Club in France as well as all his Sailors, say that they shall represent the matter in its proper colours.[2] I do not find that Mr G——t has promulgated the last letter of the Secretary of State, excepting as to the effect of the measures with the Consuls, which prevent their selling their prizes—Would to God it had been thought proper to publish the letter to Mr Morris—The minds of our own people would have been convinced of the propriety of the measures which have been adopted, and all caval at the meeting of Congress prevented."

I should be of this opinion likewise if there is danger of the public mind receiving unfavourable impressions from the want of information on one hand, whilst the insiduous attempts to poison it are so impudently & unweariedly practiced on the other.

In another letter from Genl Knox dated the first instant at the same place after having lain quarantine from the 19th of September to that date, he says "The french fleet excepting the Ambuscade will sail tomorrow from New York upon some Cruise unknown. The Surviellant sailed on the 29th ult. for France with dispatches from Mr G——t and such is his desire that they should arrive safely, that he will in a day or two dispatch the Ceres, an armed Brig with duplicates.["]

If our dispatch boat should fail, and duplicates are not sent, he will play the whole game himself.

General Knox expects to be back by the 25th of this month.

We are sustaining at this moment, a drought, which if of much longer continuance, will I fear, prove fatal to the Wheat now in the ground—much of which is come up badly, & is diminishing every day for want of Rain. I am sincerely & Affectionately yours

Go: Washington

P.S. The enclosed from Mr Leslie you will know best what to do with. & say to him.[3]

G. W——n

ALS, DLC: Jefferson Papers; ADfS, DNA: RG 59, Miscellaneous Letters; LB, DNA: RG 59, George Washington's Correspondence with His Secretaries of State. The ADfS is dated "Oct. 6th 1793," and the LB bears that date as well. Jefferson docketed the ALS in part, "recd Oct. 15."

1. See GW to Alexander Hamilton, 25 Sept.; to Henry Knox, 25 Sept.; and to Edmund Randolph, 30 September.

2. At this point GW omits about two sentences from Knox's text.

3. Robert Leslie's letter to GW of 24 July 1793 discussed in part his experiments for fixing standard weights and measures in accord with Jefferson's report on weights and measures of July 1790 (for that report, see *Jefferson Papers*, 16:650–74).

From Henry Lee

dear sir Richmond Octr 7th 93.

you will suppose I apprehend that I am rather too solicitous for your possession of the aid of art in threshing out your crops of wheat, when the moment I have understood that the wheat mill will not be adopted by you, I should renew your attention to this subject by informing you, that two english farmers have just arrived here with a model of the machine invented in scotland for threshing out wheat.

It is worked by wind water or horses—Two small horses usually as they say get out six bushels p. hour.

I do not know what the expence of one of these machines will be, but presume not more than 100 dollars will be asked for one fitted for two horses—I have engaged one, when it is completed & proved to be useful by actual experiment, I will then if you choose procure one for mount vernon & send it to you by water. I have the honor to be sir with most affec. respect & regard your ob. st

Henry Lee

ALS, DLC:GW.

From Thomas Sim Lee

Sir   Annapolis Octr 7. 1793

Your Excellency will probably before this letter reaches you, have received from the Secy of War a communication which I made to him on the 18th September last respecting the case of the Ship Roehampton, captured and sent into the Port of Baltimore by the french armed schooner Industry, and which the British Vice Consul alledges to have been illegally taken by reason of the sd schooner's having made some equipments of a military nature in that Port.[1] Not doubting Sir that your determination on the subject of this vessel would in due time reach me through the ordinary channel, I should not have taken this freedom, had not another case occurred which requires me to form an immediate Judgement, how far partial equipments and alterations to vessels originally armed in french Ports, are admissible under the description of reparations, conveniences &c. as mentioned in the 19th article of our treaty with france, which is expressly admitted in extenuation of the prohibitory part of the 7th article of your Excellency's instructions.[2] The papers which I do myself the honour to enclose will explain the case in question—I have requested the Collector of the district of Baltimore to observe the motions of the Privateer mentioned by Mr Thornton, and to acquaint me immediately with any addition of guns or material alteration that he may perceive her to be making[3]—but as by addressing myself as usual to the Secy of State or of War who have both left the seat of government, I should not in all probability obtain your Excellency's ideas in a reasonable time, I trust that you will excuse my taking this method to procure more precise instructions on this point than I can discover in the regulations already issued—As the cases of this kind that may still occur may be various, and some of them may seem such slight infractions as scarcely to require notice, I beg that your Excellency will favour me with the most explicit directions on the subject. I have the honour to be &c.

Tho. S. Lee.

DfS, MdAA; LB, MdAA: Council Letterbook, 1787–1793. Thomas Sim Lee (1745–1819), who served as governor of Maryland from 1779 to 1782 and as a Maryland delegate to the Continental Congress in 1783, was again elected governor in 1792, serving until November 1794. He was also elected governor in 1798, but declined the office.

1. Lee had written Henry Knox on 18 Sept.: "I think it proper to transmit herewith the copy of a Letter just received from the British vice-Consul at Baltimore, as also copies, of two Depositions therein enclosed.

"The circumstances under which this case has been presented to me, do not appear to be such as to justify my interference, and I have accordingly declined interposing until the President shall have had an opportunity of deciding on it and forwarding his Instructions.

"I beg leave to refer you to the Letter of the Council of this State of the 23d of last Month for further information respecting the Privateer by which the Roehampton was captured—I also enclose a copy of my Answer to the British vice-Consul" (DNA, RG 59, Miscellaneous Letters).

Edward Thornton's letter to Lee of 15 Sept. had submitted the depositions of Benjamin Baker, 12 [Sept.], and Warren Lisle Nicoll, 15 Sept., to demonstrate that while at Baltimore, *L'Industrie* "received a very considerable force, and was Completely armed and equipped for successful depredations." Arguing that the ship could not have captured the *Roehampton* without those improvements, Thornton requested that the captured ship be returned to her captain and owners. Lee responded in his letter to Thornton of 18 Sept. that as a previous investigation had failed "to procure Satisfactory information" that *L'Industrie* "had made any material military equipments in Baltimore," the case would be submitted to the secretary of war for GW's decision (all documents, DNA, RG 59, Miscellaneous Letters). For the letter from Council president James Brice to Knox of 23 Aug., see Knox to GW, 27 Aug. (first letter), n.2.

Edward Thornton (1766–1852) became the British vice-consul in Maryland in June 1793 and remained in that post until 1796. Thereafter, he served variously as secretary of the legation at Washington and as chargé d'affaires until he left the United States in 1804. He remained in the British diplomatic service until 1824.

2. The 19th article of the Treaty of Amity and Commerce with France, 6 Feb. 1778, provided that when ships of either party were forced by any "urgent necessity" to seek shelter in the other's ports, they would be permitted "all things needful for the sustenance of their Persons or reparation of their Ships and conveniency of their Voyage; and they shall no Ways be detained or hindred from returning out of the said Ports" (Miller, *Treaties,* 17–18). The "instructions" were the eight rules of neutrality approved by the cabinet opinion of 3 Aug. 1793. The seventh prohibited "Equipments of vessels in the Ports of the United States, which are of a nature solely adopted to war,"

except in certain cases, including "those mentioned in the nineteenth Article of our Treaty with France."

3. Lee presumably enclosed Thornton's letter to him of 3 Oct., which enclosed an extract from a letter from the vice- consul at Norfolk, Va., about the privateer schooner *Republic,* which, Thornton stated, had since arrived at Baltimore with her gunports "covered with a canvass, that their number might not be discovered, these circumstances of concealment (which would be unnecessary if no further equipment were intended) form a strong presumption that her people will endeavor to augment her force in the harbour" (MdAA: Brown Books).

Lee also may have enclosed his reply to Thornton of 7 October. Lee informed Thornton that he had instructed the collector of the district to investigate, and that he would take action according to "the circumstances of the case coupled with the Instructions of the President" (MdAA: Council Letterbook, 1787–1793).

Lee's letter to the collector (Otho Holland Williams) of 5 Oct. stated that Lee had been "informed" that when the *Republic* "came her ports were covered with canvas—this circumstance of concealment lead to a presumption that endeavours will be made to augment her force." The collector, therefore, "should look with any Eye of great circumspection into the conduct of the people on board this vessel," so that if she attempted "to encrease her force by the addition of any sort of Military Equipments . . . measures may be taken to prevent such contravention of the regulations of the Government of the United States" (MdAA: Council Letterbook, 1787–1793).

From Jeremiah Olney

Custom-House, District of Providence
Sir.   7th October 1793.

Permit me respectfully to address you on the subject of appointing a Person to succeed the late William Channing Esquire, deceased, in the Office of District Attorney for the State of Rhode-Island. I have been informed that some Merchants and other respectable Characters have recommended to you David Howell Esquire, to succeed to that Office; and from a full conviction in my Mind that the leading Merchants in this Town have long had, and still have, an undue influence over him, I am induced, Sir, to step forward and discharge (with great deference, and in confidence) what I conceive to be my Duty, by giving this information for your consideration. It appears to me of the first importance that the District Attorney should be a Gentleman of Independent Principles, and that he should co-operate, on all occasions, with the Officers of the Customs, so far as the exercise of their Duty shall be perfectly consistent with the Law, and their Instructions from the principal Officer of the Treasury Department. I should have remained silent on the subject (because I feel a delicacy in an interference) had not the Gentlemen recommended a Man who, I am perswaded, should he be appointed, will for the reason offered, rather embarrass than support me in a just and impartial execution of my Duty; in the exercise of which I have heretofore experienced very great opposition from an unfriendly Disposition manifested by some influential mercantile Characters, who have taken unwearied pains to swerve me from my Duty, and thereby establish practices in this District, which were inadmissible by Law, and which, had they obtained, would have very much endangered the collection of the Revenue; of which the Secretary of the Treasury has a perfect knowledge, and will, if necessary, acquaint you with.[1]

I now beg leave, Sir, most respectfully, to mention David Leonard Barnes Esquire of this Town, Attorney at Law, as a Gentleman well qualified to fill the Office of District Attorney: he ⟨is⟩ justly esteemed for his independent Principles, probity and tallents in the Law, and will do honor to the appointment, should he fortunately obtain it; and who, I am perswaded, will on all occasions, co-operate with the Officers of the Customs in a faithful and impartial executi⟨on⟩ of the revenue Laws, so essential to the support of the National Government. I have the honor to be, Very respectfully, Sir, Your Most Obedt and Most Hume Servant

Jereh Olney Collr

ALS, DLC:GW.

1. For discussion of Olney's differences with the merchants of Providence, see Arthur Fenner to GW, this date, and notes 1 and 2 to that document.

From Nathaniel Skinner

Sir.   Cadiz [Spain] Octr 8th 1793.

I conceive it a duty I owe to a country (of which I have the honor of being a naturalized citizen—& I trust tho' only such as true a freind to its interests as warm a wisher for its every prosperity as tho' it had been my fortune to have the claim of a native of that land of Liberty—America.) to inform Your Excellency of an affair that may materially concern the interests of the United States.

There not being any official American character in this place—I have presumed thus to address & inform Your Excellency.[1]

This morning arrived in this city an express from Gibraltar, informing that in consequence of a peace made & ratified, between the Dey of Algiers & their High Mightynesses of the United provinces & the Queen of Portugal, that al⟨l⟩ cruizers of the latter powers, have orders to treat the Deys subjects as freinds.[2] & on Sunday the [6]th Four frigates three Kebecks & two Brigs belonging to Algiers passed Gibraltar on a cruize to the Westward. Their only prey now is Americans & much I fear that their vile efforts will be too successful, how much Americans are indebted to the intrigues of the courts of England & the powers opposed to the liberties of France, may be easily concluded.

Permit me to add—that the Ship Greenway Amos Oakman Master of Boston belonging to a Mr M. Bicker, was yesterday vessell & cargo condemned, by the court of Admiralty at Caraccas, but which sentence eer it is effectual must be confirm'd at Madrid, an other ship the Rooksby. Jones of Portsmouth N.H. is here also her fate not determin'd, they were taken in consort by a Spanish frigate & sent in here. They were bound from Bordeaux to St Thomas & probably the cargoes are French property. The vessells haveing seen them in Boston, the place of my residence, I doubt not arc American—Oakman & Jones are still confin'd on board their Ships, nor have been suffer'd to communicate with any one—they personally suffer—led by humanity I attempted in passing the ship to speak the centinel level'd & cock'd his musket & had I not retir'd would doubtlessly have executed the orders given.[3]

There are about ten American vessels in this port several of which were about to proceed to the North of Europe with valueable freights. I have a ship with part of a freight on board for there what will be done I know not, copies of the foregoing I shall transmit Your Excellency by various routes, could I individually afford it, or knew wether the expence would be reimburs'd I would send a pass protected vessell with these communications, considering them of such import, the ne⟨mutilated⟩ & my freind whos veracity is undoubted ⟨mutilated⟩ Esqr. Consul to his B.M. assures me ⟨mutilated⟩[4] During my stay in Spain should ⟨mutilated⟩ of consequence transpire it shall be ⟨*mutilated* com⟩municated. The last posts bring acco⟨unts of the⟩ seige of Dunkirk being raised, & of so⟨*mutilated*⟩ the Spanish in Rousillon.[5] The Fr⟨*mutilated*⟩ from hence in a few days on an exp⟨*mutilated*⟩ The American interest not being repr⟨sented⟩ makes the situation of its citizens somew⟨hat un⟩pleasant. I have the honor to be w⟨ith the⟩ most profound respect Your Excellency⟨s *mutilated*⟩ Obedient & Hum⟨*mutilated*⟩

Nathl Ski⟨nner⟩

ALS, DNA: RG 76, Spain, Treaty, 27 Oct. 1795, Vol. 1. This letter was docketed in part, "recd 14 May."

1. Joseph Yznardi, Jr., had been confirmed as consul at Cadiz in February 1793, but he remained in America until March 1794.

2. For discussion of the 12 Sept. truce, see David Humphreys to GW, 7 Oct., and n.1 to that document.

3. The *Greenway* and *Rooksby* were brought into Cadiz on 20 Sept., having been taken by the Spanish frigate *Santa Cathalinda*. The two vessels remained at Cadiz as late as September 1795, when their repair and indemnification for their detention were addressed in Thomas Pinckney's negotiations with Spain (*New-Hampshire Gazette, and General Advertiser*, 9 Nov. 1793; *ASP, Foreign Relations*, 1:539). Amos Oakman (1759–1805) resided at this time in Marshfield, and later in Lunenberg, Massachusetts. Martin Bicker (c.1746–1817) at this time kept a shop on Ann Street in Boston. Nathaniel Jones was master of the *Rooksby*.

4. James Duff (1734–1815) was the British consul at Cadiz. He was made a baronet in 1813.

5. The allied forces who had laid siege to Dunkirk in mid-August 1793 abandoned the siege and retreated toward Furnes on 8 September. Roussillon is a region of France bordering the East Pyrenees and the Gulf of Lion. The Spanish army moved into the region in the summer of 1793 and won a major victory at Truilla on 22 September.

From Nathaniel Skinner

Sir.   Cadiz [Spain] Octr 8[–15]th 1793

I do my Self the Honor to confirm the contents I address to your Excellency of Last Night which was pen'd with so much haste to go by the Mail for Lisbon that I cannot transmit a Copy thereof not having time then to transcribe it.[1]

The purport was that in consequence of at peace being negotiated (by Mr Logie Consul for great Britian[2]) with the Algerines for the Portugeuse for Twelve months the algerine fleet passed the Straits on the 6th bound to the westward on a Cruise which News is this day confirm'd from Various quarters & the additional observations that their High Mightinesses of the united Provinces being included has same foundation.

hear with is inclosed a Letter from David Humphreys Esqr. relative to the Business as said by his Letter to J. Iznardi junr Esqr. Concil for this port but not yet arrived from america, It was handed to James Duff Esqr. his Britannic Magestys Consul for this place, Mr Iznardis patron, who requested me to forward the Same. I hope it may earley reach your Excelencys hands[3]— Americans from the most pleasing, are now in the most disagreable situation here. To go out they have only perpetual slavery in view to remain prehaps long loathsome imprisonment, sad alternative, suc⟨h⟩ are the machinations of the enimes of america & of the liberties of mankind—much clamor has and does still prevail relative to the equi⟨p⟩ments of or by the French in the american Ports notwithstanding Your Excellencys Proclamation relative there to & the opinio⟨n⟩ of the judges relative to the treaties,[4] Pardon me Sir—for presumeing to address you I have no right but as a well wisher to the interests of America of which I have the honor to be a naturalized citizen a resident of Boston, here on commercial affairs and finding a number of my fellow citizens as well as my self in tribulation with no one officially to represent them, the State of Americans vessells in this vicinity is five in Malaga; three in Gibraltar; thirteen in this Port; and advice of many who must be near here if not already captured they having Sail'd previous to some just arrived. the Algerine fleet consists of four Frigates. Viz. one of 44 Guns just off the Stocks, two of 36. one of 28. Three Xebecks of 12. guns each. one, first said to be two Brigs of 22 do. their delination is said to be for Lisbon but which is Little credited, the american Ship Greenway Amos Oakman is Condemnd Vessell & Cargo at the Court of Caracas but which sentence waits the final dicision at Madrid She had on board French property bound from Bordeaux to St Thomas the Cargo condemnd as French the Ship for false declaration the fate of the Ship Rooksby Jones not yet determin'd but presume the cargo being French by information will be condemn'd & no demur on part of the Master the Ship will be releas'd only to be confind here now by pirates her freight &c. to be paid. The Spaniards lament the affair as it will enhance the price of bread so much—their harvest produceing this year little & small Supplies from any place but america, but from thence what can they expect for americans cannot venture that they Love so much & Know so well the sweets of *Liberty* Tho the Temptation may be great. The Brit⟨is⟩h Merchants expect strong convoys will be appointed, as their Vessells are but poorly employ'd in Europe to go to america and be carriers of its p[r]oduce to these parts. Last Nights Post advises of a British Frigate having or being on the eve of Departure from England in which embarks a respected character as Envoy to the American Court, Enclos'd I do my Self the honor to transmit the form of the Treaty Enterd into between the courts of Spain & England. most probably it is already forwarded[5] this & every other step I have taken to forward Information will not I hope be attributed to any unworthier motive than a zeal to throw in what trifle lays in my power to serve the Country I admire—for Commercial Information I annex a List of Americans Vessels in this & adjacent ports[6] & would add that the Premium of Insurance demanded on american & Genoese vessels is Thirty prCent to return Ten should they get in safe, this will of course give an Idea of the apprehended Danger.

9th   Letters in town from Mr Carmichael recommend all americans to proceed home with all dispatch he did not probably Know of this Algriine business & we expect he refers to an other fear.[7]

15th   The wind & some other causes preventing the departure of the vessell—who runs every risk to convey intelligence to America gives me occasion to notice that two of the Algerine frigates cruizing of[f] Cape St Vincents boarded an English Brig who in consequence is performing quarantine at St Lucar, as is also another in Gibraltar who was boarded by a Ship of 22 guns—the advice of which ships sailing was that she passed two days after the fleet.

The Morning Starr—& another New York vessell—are in Carthegena—as advised this day.[8] With the most profound respect I am Your Excellencys Humble Servt

Nathl Skinner

Cadiz Octr 15th 1793.

LS, DNA: RG 59, Consular Dispatches. This letter was docketed in part, "recd 14 May."

1. Skinner was referring to his previous letter to GW, dated 8 Oct. and presumably written on the evening of 7–8 October.

2. Charles Logie became the British consul at Algiers in 1785 and left that post in late 1793 or early 1794.

3. This enclosure was most likely a copy of David Humphreys's letter to Secretary of State Thomas Jefferson of 6 Oct. (*Jefferson Papers,* 27:196–98).

4. Skinner was referring to GW's Neutrality Proclamation of 22 April, and to the charges of John Jay to the grand jury of the circuit court for the District of Virginia, 22 May, and of James Wilson to the grand jury of a special session of the circuit court for the District of Pennsylvania, 22 June, each of which held that proclamation to be consistent with the treaty obligations of the United States (*Documentary History of the Supreme Court,* 2:380–91, 414–23).

5. Skinner was referring to the convention of 25 May 1793, by which Spain and Great Britain joined in an alliance against France (*ASP, Foreign Relations,* 1:277). The enclosed copy has not been identified.

6. The annexed list has not been identified, but for another list of the American vessels at Spanish ports in mid-October 1793, see "Ship News," *Dunlap and Claypoole's American Daily Advertiser* (Philadelphia), 20 Dec. 1793.

7. The remainder of this letter is in Skinner's writing.

8. The brig *Morning Star* remained at Cartagena, Spain, until January 1794 and arrived back at New York on 7 March 1794. Her companion was probably the brig *Mary Ann.* For more on those ships, see Henry Stephens, James Neill, and Ebenezer Rosseter to Don Miguel Gaston, 23 Nov. 1793, *Diary; or, Evening Register* (New York), 7 March 1794.

To John Fitzgerald

Dear sir, Mt Vernon 9: Oct: 1793.

Enclosed is an answer to the resolutions of the Citizens of Alexandria, *which came under a blank cover to me,* & which were ordered to be published in the Gazette of that place. But if the 8th resolution is not published along with the others, nor intended to be so, (which seems probable, as it is separate & distinct) I request, in that case, that the answer may not appear; because I have never taken notice of any resolutions, wherein one of them has not directed, & it has so appeared, that they should be sent to me.[1] considering them without this, as no more than the expression of the sentiments of the meeting to the community, without any particular application. I am &c.

Go. Washington

P.S. I wrote to you on monday,[2] & shou'd be glad to hear from you on the subject of the Letter.

LB, DLC:GW.

1. For the resolutions, see Alexandria, Va., citizens to GW, 5 October. Their publication did include the eighth resolution (see *Bartgis's Maryland Gazette, and Frederick-Town Weekly Advertiser,* 24 Oct.).

2. This letter of 7 Oct. has not been found.

Enclosure
To John Fitzgerald

Sir,   Mount Vernon 8. Octor 1793.

While the public mind is engaged, and in some degree disturbed by various subjects which have arisen, consequent of a War in which most of the European powers are engaged—with the highest satisfaction I have received assurances from many parts of the United States, of the determined resolution of the Citizens thereof to be neutral, thereby securing to themselves the inestimable blessings resulting from peace; & that they will give support to measures, adopted by those to whom they have confided authority for that purpose, which are dictated with an evident regard to their interests, & by a wish to promote the happiness of all the Citizens of the Union. Among those which have been received, the resolutions of my Fellow Citizens of Alexandria, enclosed by you, have contributed not a little to afford me pleasure, and justify the opinion I had entertained of their good sense & patriotism. I request you, Sir, to make known to them my attachment, equally with their's, to a republican system, and as far as my personal endeavours will contribute, they will be employed in supporting the principles of our fœderal Government, and defeating any attempts which might be made to violate them, or to lessen the confidence of the people therein.

I join with them also in expressions of gratitude to the French nation for their timely & important services rendered to these States, and it is my earnest wish that genuine Liberty & equal rights may pervade every Nation of the Earth.

Go. Washington

LB, DLC:GW. This letter was printed in the *Federal Gazette and Philadelphia Daily Advertiser,* 24 Oct., from an Alexandria newspaper of 17 October.

From Thomas Jefferson

Dear Sir   Monticello [Va.] Oct. 9. 1793.

I have the honor of answering, by the return of post, your favor of Sep. 27. recieved this day, inclosing the letter & memorial of messieurs King, Pratt & others, owners of the ship Andrew, & her cargo, desiring the interposition of the Executive on account of the cargo of rice taken by a decree of the general council of L'orient, & of the freight & detention of the vessel.[1] the memorialists seem to expect that an indemnification may be made them by this government out of the monies due from us to France. but this would be an act of reprisal, which the usage of nations would not justify until justice has been required from France, & formally denied. their money in our treasury can no more be taken for this purpose, nor under any other forms, than their vessels in our harbors.[2] it is necessary therefore that the Memorialists make application to the government of France for indemnification, exhibiting the fullest & most authentic proofs. if they will at the same time furnish me with a copy of these, I will instantly write to our minister at Paris, & desire him to give to their claim that firm support which it's justice calls for.[3] the conduct of that government in other cases communicated to us by mister Morris, gives every reason to presume they will do ready & ample justice in the present one. I have the honor to be with great & sincere respect & attachment Dear Sir your most obedt & most humble servt

Th: Jefferson

ALS, DNA: RG 59, Miscellaneous Letters; ALS (letterpress copy), DLC: Jefferson Papers; LB, DNA: RG 59, George Washington's Correspondence with His Secretaries of State.

1. See Joseph Harper to GW, 10 Sept., and enclosure. GW's letter to Jefferson of 27 Sept. also enclosed GW's response to Harper of that date.

2. The debt of the United States to France stemmed from loans made during the Revolutionary War that amounted to over $6 million, including a loan made in Holland but guaranteed by the French court (for a statement of the debt and arrearages thereon as of 31 Dec. 1789, see schedule B of Alexander Hamilton's Report on Public Credit, 9 Jan. 1790, *Hamilton Papers*, 6:112–13). At this time, the United States was making payments on the debt in accordance with a contract of 25 Feb. 1783 (Miller, *Treaties*, 115–22).

3. No further correspondence regarding the memorial from or to Jefferson has been identified.

From Christoph Daniel Ebeling

Sir   Hambro' [Germany] October 10th 1793.

Your Excellency will kindly pardon the liberty I take, to offer You my Description of America. You know, it is the right, as it is the heartfelt pleasure of every freeborn feeling man, to admire the great and good benefactors of mankind. This pleasure I very often enjoyed, when I endeavoured to describe that country, whose daily increasing happiness is principally Your Work and that of those who think and act like You.

I am sensible that my Book is as imperfect, as great were the difficulties wherewith I had to struggle in order to get authentic documents and materials for the same. But my country is to desirous of, and the present times require a more particular knowledge of Your Republic, whose felicity it has much reason to look at with envy. The aspect of so many States enjoying all the blessings, which virtue, wise laws and liberty bestow upon mankind, may have some influence on the councils of our Rulers, now united against liberty, because most of them know but that which degenerated into french Anarchy or british corruption. These reasons induced me to venture an undertaking, which I feel is rather above my forces.

As soon as the Descriptions of the several States are finished, a general Introduction will complete my Work. This is to contain a View of the federal Constitution of the United States, and the History of Your glorious Revolution.

Nothing could be a greater reward of my feeble endeavours than that to be honoured with Your Excellency's protection. I have no other materials for the historical part besides the immortal Franklin's Works, the State-papers published during the Revolution, Adams's and Ramsay's Histories, Gordon's more partial one,[1] and the Journals of Congress from 1774 to 1777, as also those of 1781. If Your Excellency would graciously countenance my Undertaking, perhaps one of the many worthy men who were witnesses to Your deeds, might be enduced to point out to me the defects or errors of the abovementioned Histories and furnish me with more valuable materials.

I shall not presume to ask Your high favour for that purpose, untill my Description of the single States, whereof I also most humbly offer a Copy to Your illustrious Congress, is wholly published, and as I very ardently wish is found not to be quite unworthy of the noble and great subject, it treats of. I have the honour to be with sentiments of the most profound respect Sir Your Excellency's most obedient and most humble Servant

Christoph Daniel Ebeling
Professor of History in the great College at Hambro'

ALS, DNA: RG 59, Miscellaneous Letters. This letter was docketed in part, "need not be answered, 'till his more particular work arrives." Christoph Daniel Ebeling's (1741-1817) *Erdbeschreibung und Geschichte von Amerika: Die Vereinten Staaten von Nordamerika,* published at Hamburg in seven volumes from 1793 to 1816, begins with a volume on New England and ends with the volume on Virginia. He did not complete volumes on the Carolinas or Georgia. No further correspondence with Ebeling has been identified, but GW did receive the first volume of the work (Griffin, *Catalogue of the Washington Collection,* 72).

1. Ebeling evidently was referring to *Works of the Late Doctor Benjamin Franklin: Consisting of His Life, Written by Himself: Together with Essays, Humorous, Moral & Literary, Chiefly in the Manner of the Spectator* (1793); David Ramsay's *The History of the American Revolution* (1789 and other editions); William Gordon's *The History of the Rise, Progress, and Establishment, of the Independence of the United States of America: Including an Account of the Late War; and of the Thirteen Colonies, from Their Origin to that Period* (1788 and other editions); and possibly John Adams, *History of the Dispute with America* (1784).

From Tobias Lear

My dear Sir,   New York October 10th 1793

On my reaching this place yesterday Mr Greenleaf put into my hands your very good & respected favor of the 25 of September, enclosing one hundred & twenty dollars for the purchase of a Watch &c. and a Ticket for my dear little boy, in the Hotel Lottery, which you have had the goodness to give him as a token of your affection.

I feel, my dear Sir, more than I can express for the many proofs of friendship and affection with which you have honored me; and I trust that so long as it may please the Supreme Ruler of Events to continue to me the use of my rational powers I shall never cease to remember with gratitude & affection your goodness to me & my dear boy, and to act in a manner worthy such recollection.

Inexpressibly happy is it for our Country that you left the unfortunate City of Philadelphia before the malignant disorder had seized upon your valuable life. For at all times since we have been a nation your life has been considered by the good Citizens of America as essentially necessary for the prosperity of our public affairs—At the present juncture our existance as a united people is thought to depend upon it—and the universal & warm approbation which your Official conduct, in the late critical state of things, has met with in those parts of the U.S. where I have lately been, shews at once the high confidence which the American people place in & the ardent affection which they bear towards you.

I shall take great pleasure in paying particular attention to your request respecting a Black Smith—and at the same time shall take no steps that can involve me in any difficulty respecting the matter—The Watch &c. for Mrs Washington will be a pleasing commission for me to execute and happy shall I be to know that it gives her satisfaction.

I have the pleasure to inform you that I left my dear boy in fine health, and under every circumstance that could give satisfaction to my mind in an object on which my first hopes & first wishes are placed.

The prospects in my business are more & more flattering as I progress in it—and I have no doubt but if my life & health are preserved, and no *very* untoward circumstances happen, I shall in a few years find myself in a respectable & eligible situation. My business will detain me from sailing for Europe till early in November; and it is not unlikely but that I may find it proper to visit the Federal City before I embark to complete some part of the business of the Company which yet remains unfinished there. In case I should go to the City I shall not be able to leave that part of the Country without seeing Mount Vernon once more.

The disorder which prevails in Philadelphia has given an Alarm to the Eastward beyond conception—and the people there have no idea that Congress will think of meeting in that City at the ensuing Session. The general opinion is, that the President will notify the members of the Circumstances existing—and *recommend* their convening at some other place. New York is the only place I have heard mentioned as the probable one for them to meet at.

I have not yet seen Mr Robinson who took your portrait for the Earl of Buchan, I called at his lodgings but could not see him,

I shall however do it before I leave this place.[1] With respect to the Person to succeed Mr Sherburne, as Atty for the District of New Hampshire I confess I hardly know one who on every & all accounts I could venture to mention; but a further reflection on the subject may enable me to give an opinion.

I must beg you will have the goodness to make my best respects & most grateful remembrance acceptable to Mrs Washington—My love attends the Children—my respects & best regards Mrs F. Washington & her little ones—and Mr Dandridge is rememberd by me with affection & friendship. With every sentiment of gratitude & sincere & respectful attachment I have the honor to be my dear sir Your faithful & affectionate friend & Obedient servant

Tobias Lear

ALS, DLC:GW.
1. For Lear's report of his meeting with the painter Archibald Robertson, see his letter to GW of 9 November.

To Edward Carrington

Sir,   Mot Vernon 11. Octr 1793.
Accompanying this, I send a Letter by post to The Secy of State. I request the favor of you if there should be a probability of its remaining two or three days in the post office at Richmond waiting the regular post to Charlottsville, or on any other accot to have it directly conveyed to mr Jefferson by Express—in which case you will be good enough to let me Know the expense which may be incurred.[1] I am &c.

G. W.

Df, DNA: RG 59, Miscellaneous Letters; LB, DLC:GW.
1. Carrington sent GW's letter of this date to Thomas Jefferson by express and submitted the expense in his letter to GW of 18 October.

From John Fitzgerald

Dear Sir   Alexandria [Va.] 11th Octr 1793
On my return last night from the General Court at Anapolis, I found myself honor'd by two letters from you, one of Monday

on private business, & the other covering your Answer to the resolves of the town meeting, which were enclosed to you.[1]

You will be pleased to observe that the Publick Papers join the Eighth Resolution with the others which, I dont know why, were seperated in the Copy sent, this I presume will render the Answer, to be made public, proper & necessary, which will accordingly appear.

You may be assur'd that I have paid the most direct & strict attention to the subject of your house & Lott & would have wrote you respecting it; but could not bring it to any conclusion[.] The man in possession has not yet return'd from Boston & his family consisting of a Wife & some small Children declaring that an agreement existed between them & Mr Whiting, which gave them a right for some time, they could not say how long, to remain in possession, I should in a Post or two have requested your directions how to act[.] they appear to be an orderly, though poor people, & were extremely distress'd when I told them a few days ago that unless something satisfactory was done in a short time they must be dispossess'd[.] In this state of things I am happy to find that you have other use for the House & that I have not had it in my power to make any agreement for it, by which your intentions can be prevented[.] I am satisfied that no written Contract between your late Agent & those people can appear, to prevent your taking possession whenever you think proper, & the Situation of the poor people will admit of a removal on their part.[2] With sentiments of purest Esteem & Attachment I have the honor to be your mo. Obedt Hble Servant

John Fitzgerald

ALS, DLC:GW.

1. See GW to Fitzgerald, 9 Oct., and enclosure, which replied to the Alexandria citizens' resolutions of 5 October. GW's letter to Fitzgerald of 7 Oct. has not been found.

2. In July GW had asked Fitzgerald to act as his agent for the possible rental to Cleon Moore of GW's townhouse at the corner of Pitt and Cameron Streets in Alexandria, Virginia. Acting on that request, Fitzgerald discovered that a family named Jackson was in possession of the house, and that it was in poor repair (see GW to Fitzgerald, 19 July, and Fitzgerald to GW, 3 Aug.). GW then asked, in a letter of 11 Aug., that Fitzgerald look into the agreement made with the Jacksons by Anthony Whitting and take appropriate action. The missing letter of 7 Oct. apparently informed Fitzgerald that GW was thinking of offering use of the house to Frances Bassett Washington (see her letter to GW, 22 Nov.; GW to her, 15 Dec.; and GW to William Pearce, 23 Dec.).

To Thomas Jefferson

Dear Sir,   Mount Vernon October 11th 1793.

Your dispatch of the 3d with it's several enclosures reached Alexandria on Wednesday evening, and got to my hands yesterday morning.[1]

This afternoon I shall send to the post office the Letters for mister Bankson, with my signature to the Exequatur for mister Dannery, & Letters patent revoking that of mister Duplane. Your letter to the latter, two to the French minister, one to his Secretary mr Bournonville & another to mr Morris being approved are also forwarded.[2]

To a Letter written to you a few days ago, I refer for the time & place mentioned for the meeting of the Heads of Departments, & hope it will be convenient for you to attend.[3] If I do not take a circuitous rout by Frederick-town in Maryland &c. I shall not leave this before the 28th—and in that case should be glad of your company, if it is not inconvenient for you to call. Since writing that letter, however, I have received the enclosed from the Attorney General which may make a change of *place* necessary; but I shall wait further advices before this is resolved on.[4] I have also received a letter from the late Speaker, Trumbull;[5] and as I understand sentiments similar to his are entertained by others— query, what had I best do? You were of opinion when here, that neither the Constitution nor Laws gave power to the President to convene Congress at any other place than where the Seat of Government is fixed by their own act. Twelve days since I wrote to the Attorney General for an official opinion on this head, but have received no answer.[6] If the importance & urgency of the case, arising from a supposition that the fever in Philadelphia should not abate, would justify calling together the Legislature at any other place—where ought it to be? This, if German town is affected, with the malady, involves the Executive in a serious & delicate decision. Wilmington & Trenton are equidistant, in opposite directions, from Philada—both on the great thoroughfare, equally dangerous on account of the infection being communicated to them, & would, I presume, be equally obnoxious to one or the other set of members; according to their situations. Annapolis has conveniences—but it might be thought I had interested & local views in naming this place. What sort of a town then is Reading, & how would ⟨it⟩ answer? Neither Northern nor Southern members would have cause to complain of it's situation. Lancaster would favor the Southern ones most.

You will readily perceive, if any change is to take place, not a moment is to be lost in the notification—whether by a simple statement of facts (among which, I presume, the House intended for them in Philada will be unfit for their reception[7])—and an intimation that I shall be at a certain place   days before the first of December, to meet them in their legislative capacity, or to advise with them on measures proper to be taken in the present exigency. If something of this sort should strike you favorably, draw (& if necessary sign) a proper Instrument to avoid delay, leaving the name of the place blank, but giving your opinion thereon. German town would certainly have been the best place for them to have met in the first instance, there to have taken ulterior resolutions without involving the Executive.

I have no objection to the Director of the Mint, with your concurrence, chusing an Engraver in place of mister Wright.

No report has been made to me relative to the Tonnage of the French Ships from St Domingo.

Major Lenox, I perceive by the papers, is marshall for the District of Pennsylvania.[8]

Limits of Jurisdiction and protection must lie over till we meet, when I request you will remind me of it. I am Your Affecte Servant

Go: Washington

LS, DLC: Jefferson Papers; ADf, DNA: RG 59, Miscellaneous Letters; LB, DNA: RG 59, George Washington's Correspondence with His Secretaries of State. The LS is docketed in part, "recd Oct. 16."

1. The preceding Wednesday was 9 October. Jefferson sent five letters to GW on 3 Oct., and this letter responds to the first four.

2. For these documents, see Jefferson's first three letters to GW of 3 Oct. and notes.

3. See GW to Jefferson, 7 October.

4. This probably is a reference to Edmund Randolph's letter to GW of 3 Oct., which has not been found. Randolph evidently had reported that people in Germantown had died of the yellow fever (see GW to Randolph, 14 Oct.).

5. See Jonathan Trumbull, Jr., to GW, 2 October.

6. See GW to Edmund Randolph, 30 Sept.; Randolph gave his opinion on this question in a letter to GW of 2 November.

7. On the draft and the letter-book copy, the preceding four words are replaced by the word "unfinished."

8. In a letter to GW of 23 Aug., Clement Biddle, the U.S. marshal for Pennsylvania, had announced his intention to resign at the expiration of his term in September. It was agreed that the post would be offered to Stephen Moylan, and, if he declined, to David Lenox. When Jefferson departed Philadelphia in mid-September, he left a blank commission to be completed with one of the two names, and instructed State Department clerk Benjamin Bankson to write GW for instructions if neither of the two accepted (*Jefferson Papers,* 27:117). Although Moylan declined the post in a letter to Jefferson of 19 Sept., Jefferson apparently did not receive that letter until early November, and GW first received a copy with Moylan's letter to him of 21 October. Hence, GW learned of Lenox's appointment (which was dated 26 Sept.) through the newspapers (it was announced in the *Federal Gazette and Philadelphia Daily Advertiser* of 2 Oct.), and it was recorded in his executive journal on 10 Oct. (*JPP,* 241).

David Lenox (c.1754–1828) was a Continental army officer during the Revolutionary War, being wounded and captured at the fall of Fort Washington and serving after his exchange as an aide-de-camp to Gen. Anthony Wayne. He resigned from his post as marshal in 1795. In 1797 Lenox was appointed agent of the United States at London for the protection of American seamen. Lenox became a director of the Bank of the United States in 1805, and in 1807 he succeeded Thomas Willing as president of the bank, serving until the bank's demise in 1811.

From Thomas Sim Lee

Sir   Annapolis Octr 11. 1793

The motive which influenced me to address your Excellency on the 7th Instant must again apologize for my transmitting you the enclosed copies of a letter and depositions received from the British Vice Consul residing in Baltimore [1]—As this gentleman has informed me that no suit has been instituted in the Court of Admiralty respecting the Brigantine mentioned in these papers, I have found it my duty to require the french Vice Consul to take charge of her until your Excellency shall have decided on the case [2]—I have desired Mr Thornton to use all posible diligence in procuring and forwarding to me the additional evidence which he expects to obtain; [3] and which when received shall be transmitted to yr Excellency without delay—but although the allegation of this vessel's having been taken within three miles of our coast has seemed sufficient to authorise the provisionary step I have taken, it is possible that similar representations may be made in cases in which it will be more doubtful whether our rights of Jurisdiction shall have been infringed—Your Excellency will therefore I hope excuse me if I request to be favoured with your idea of the distance within which hostilities are held to be unlawful; for while this point remains unsettled I may expect complaints upon every case that has the smallest chance of procuring the interference of government, and shall in consequence be exposed to great embarrassments[4]—I have &c.

Tho. S. Lee

Df, MdAA; LB, MdAA: Council Letterbook, 1787–1793.

1. The enclosure probably was British vice-consul Edward Thornton's letter to Lee of 8 Oct., which enclosed testimony from the mate and one of the passengers of the brig *Conyngham,* of Derry, Ireland, captured on 29 Sept. by the French privateer *Sans Culottes de Marseilles.* Thornton, who added that the pilot had declared "that the vessel was actually taken by the privateer within three miles of the land" but now "suddenly refused to give his testimony," requested that Lee "adopt such provisional measures as may appear to you most efficacious for facilitating the complete restoration of the vessel and cargo to the lawful owners" (MdAA).

Lee's reply to Thornton of 9 Oct. informed him that the only action Lee could take was to call upon the French consul "to possess himself of the Prize and detain her until the decision of the President shall be made," and then only if no attempt was being made through the courts for "obtaining restitution on the Ground of an illegal capture" (MdAA: Council Letterbook, 1787–1793). Thornton replied in a letter to Lee of 9 Oct. that no suit had been instituted (MdAA).

2. The French vice-consul for Maryland was Francis Moissonnier, who was appointed in June 1793 and replaced in June 1794, although he remained at Baltimore as late as April 1796. For Lee's letter to him of 11 Oct., see MdAA: Council Letterbook, 1787–1793.

3. See Lee to Thornton, 11 Oct. (MdAA: Council Letterbook, 1787–1793).

4. A newspaper account out of Norfolk indicated that the *Conyngham* was "at anchor about four miles from land" when taken (*New-Jersey Journal* [Elizabeth], 16 Oct.). GW discussed the issue of territorial waters in his letter to Lee of 16 October.

To Thomas Sim Lee

Sir,   Mount Vernon 13th Octobr 1793.

The Letter with which your Excellency was pleased to favor me, dated the 7th inst. was received on the 10th—& might have been acknowledged the next day; but I waited the arrival of

Friday's mail[1] in hopes that I should have had a report from the Secretary of War relatively to the Ship Roehampton. Disappointed in this, I am not able to give any opinion thereon, uninformed as I am of the specific articles of charge which have been exhibited by the British Consul. The French minister complains of the detention.[2]

With respect to the second case mentioned in your letter, & those of the British Consuls, I have only to observe that as these Gentlemen are not ignorant that the Custom-house officers in every port are instructed to keep a vigilant watch upon all armed vessels, and the presumption being that they also are not inattentive, there seems to have been no necessity for lodging a complaint unaccompanied with proofs.

It is scarcely possible to give instructions which will embrace every case minutely that may arise during the war—nor do I conceive it essential. Your Excellency will readily perceive by the communications which have been made to you, the *principles* upon which the General Government[3] act in the recess of Congress, respecting the belligerent powers. These principles are to adhere strictly to treaties, according to the plain construction & obvious meaning of them—and, regarding these, to act impartially towards all the Nations at war. Keeping these principles in view & observing the rules which are founded on them—with your disposition to do justice & to preserve this Country in peace—I persuade myself that you can be at no loss—that your decisions will always be right, & I hope they will always be prompt.[4]

Being removed from the public offices—intending when I left Philadelphia not to have been absent from that City more than fifteen or eighteen days, I brought no public papers of any sort (not even the rules which have been established in these cases) along with me—consequently am not prepared at this place to decide points which may require a referrence to papers not within my reach. but as I find cases are daily occuring which call for attention & decision, I have requested the Heads of Departments to attend at Philadelphia—or in its vicinity, by the 1st of next month, whither I shall go & be present myself.[5] With great esteem & regard I am Sir, Your mo: obt humble Servt

Go: Washington

LS, MdAA: Brown Books; ADfS, DNA: RG 59, Miscellaneous Letters; LB, DLC:GW.

1. Friday was 11 October.

2. For the French complaint, see Thomas Jefferson to GW, 3 Oct. (third letter), and n.1 to that document.

3. At this point on the draft, GW initially wrote, "have established for its conduct," but he struck those words out and replaced them with six words that follow on the LS.

4. On 11 Nov. Secretary of War Henry Knox wrote a second response to Lee's letter of 7 Oct., giving the governor a more detailed definition of what augmentations of force were unacceptable (MdAA: Brown Books).

5. See GW to Alexander Hamilton, 25 Sept.; to Henry Knox, 25 Sept.; to Edmund Randolph, 30 Sept.; and to Thomas Jefferson, 7 October.

From Edmund Randolph

Sir   Spencer's[1] October 13. 1793

I did myself the honor of writing to you about ten days ago;[2] since which time we have been in daily hopes and expectation, that a change in the temperature of the air would arrest the progress of the fever. But we are still without rain or cold. Our accounts from Philadelphia are hourly more and more gloomy; whether we consider the number of the deceased, of new patients, or of orphan children. It is confidently reported too, that Dr Rush himself confesses, that in sixteen instances he has seen glandular swellings and other symptoms of the plague, notwithstanding his past publications; and that he even begins to retract his former sanguine declaration, that the disorder was within the reach of medicine. I do not answer for the truth of this; but Dr Shippen this morning said in my presence, that the malady had scarcely any resemblance of the yellow fever; and altho' it did not in strictness accord with the descriptions of the plague in all respects, it had a strong likeness to it; and might with more propriety be classed under that name, than any other in the books of physic. An intelligent Frenchman shortly afterwards affirmed to me, that it was utterly dissimilar from what he had seen in the West-Indies.

In this embarrassing situation I cannot but persuade myself, that congress will not be disposed to sit in Philadelphia; And that Lancaster may *possibly* be chosen for the ensuing session. But be this as it may, I cannot satisfy the anxieties of my family, without carrying them for the present to Lancaster. I prefer this place to Wilmington for many reasons; tho' in fact the latter is so much crouded, that I cannot promise myself any comfortable accommodation there. By this destination, I shall be at hand for any instruction, which you may think proper to give.

To morrow I shall attempt to procure a messenger, who may go to the Post-office in Philadelphia for any letter, which you may perhaps have directed for me. I have the honor sir, to be with the highest respect and sincerest attachment yr mo. ob. serv.

Edm: Randolph.

ALS, DLC:GW.

1. Randolph was staying at the home of Nathan Spencer (1764–1839) at Germantown, Pennsylvania.

2. Randolph's letter of 3 Oct. was acknowledged by GW on 14 Oct., but it has not been found.

To Jonathan Trumbull, Jr.

(Private)

Dear Sir   Mount Vernon Oct. 13th 1793

I was duly favoured with your letter of the 2d instt.

The calamitous situation of Philadelphia makes it necessary that some previous steps should be taken with respect to the meeting of Congress—But of what kind is a serious question. That the President has Power by the Constitution to Convene Congress in *extraordinary cases* admits of no doubt,[1] but that he has power to summon them to meet at an unusual place when the Law, has designated the seat of Government[2] is not merely equivocal, but in the opinion of those with whom I have hitherto conversed on the subject absolutely beyond the powers of the Executive. On the 30th of last month (hearing that the fever rather increased then abated) I wrote to the Attorney General for an official opinion on this point, but have not yet received an answer.

When I left Phila. which was for the purpose of fulfilling a previous engagement of a private nature that made it necessary for me to be at home the 18th of Septr[3] I fully expected to return to the City before the end of the month but the flight of the Clerks from the public Offices which in a manner shut them up and the Head of Departments being also absent my return has hitherto been delayed. But public business of various kinds requiring their attendance I (did some time since) desire them to meet me at Phila. or in the vicinity, the first of next month whither I shall go myself. At the time of my leaving the City with these expectations and till lately, I hoped the fever would be stopped, & the City so purified by the approaching cool Season as to admit Congs with safety by the time appointed—Or Congress to there,[4] if doubts arose then for a quoram to adjourn it to some other place This would have been (for reasons unnecessary to mention) more agreeable to me than to do it myself[5] admitting I had power. But as this is not likely to happen unless a very unexpected change should take place—as I have had no opinion yet from the proper Law Officer of Government on this head—and as you know I wish to hear the opinion of my friends upon all difficult & delicate subjects I would thank you for yours on this—particularly with respect to the place, under present circumstances—least exceptionable.[6] Your letter may meet me at this place—if it does not I may find it on the road—if neither— most certainly at whatever place I shall Assemble the Officers of Governt. I am always & Affly Yours

G. W——n

ADfS, DNA: RG 59, Miscellaneous Letters; LB, DLC:GW.

1. See Article 2, section 3 of the Constitution.

2. GW was referring to "An Act for establishing the temporary and permanent seat of the Government of the United States," 16 July 1790 (1 *Stat.* 130).

3. GW had arranged to meet with William Pearce at Mount Vernon on or about 20 Sept. to complete the process of hiring Pearce as his manager there (see GW to Pearce, 26 Aug., and Pearce to GW, 30 Aug.).

4. The preceding three words are omitted from the letter-book copy.

5. The word "myself" was inserted on the draft and then the letter "m" was crossed out, but the remainder of the word was not stricken. The letter-book copy omits this word.

6. GW originally followed "under present circumstances" not with "least exceptionable," but with more than three lines of written text. Of these lines, only the final words, "of Northern and Southern interests, or convenience," have been retrieved from under the strike.

From Charles Carter, Jr., of Culpeper

Dear Sir   Fredericksburg [Va.] October 14th 1793

The credit you gave me on the purchase of yr property in this place, expired last spring—It is a subject of great regret to me that any delay should have taken place in the fullfilment of my contract, tho' I assure you that circumstances quite unforeseen by me, have occasion'd it[1]—I have made an advantageous sale of my property in this place, in which the lott bought from you is included & could wish that you would execute a deed to Mr Richard Dobson of Cumberland County, (Virginia) for it[2]—I will deposit in yr hands (as a collateral security for the payment of yr money) a bond of General Weedon payable 1st of January 1795 for 432£, tho I am quite certain that I shall be able to make you complete payment in January next—I make you this offer of Genl Weedon's bond, persuaded that it is equivalent to any personal security I could give you—Offer my compliments to Mrs Washington & believe me Most respectfully yrs

Chas Carter Junr

I will assign the bond & deliver it to Howell Lewis if agreable to you—C.C.

ALS, DLC:GW. Carter used the "Junior" to distinguish himself from his uncle, Charles Carter of Cleve.

1. Carter was referring to the double lot (107 and 108) in Fredericksburg on which GW's mother had been housed and on which Carter had been living since 1790. Carter made some payments on his debt, but in 1794 GW forgave the remainder of the debt as a present to his niece and Carter's wife, Betty Lewis Carter (GW to Carter, 29 May 1794).

2. Carter owned town lots 85 and 86 in Fredericksburg, which he conveyed to Richard Dobson in August 1793. Because the title for lots 107 and 108 was confused with the title for lots 111 and 113, which lots were recorded on the indenture for GW's purchase of Fredericksburg lots from Fielding Lewis in 1761, the conveyance of lots 107 and 108 to Dobson was executed by a deed of 3 Feb. 1794 from John Lewis (heir and devisee of Fielding Lewis) and Mary Ann Lewis to Dobson, then of the city of Richmond (Cash Accounts, 1761, n.69, *Papers, Colonial Series,* 7:9–10; Crozier, *Virginia County Records,* 473–74). For the confusion, see Carter to GW, 14 May 1794; GW to Carter, 29 May 1794; and GW to John Lewis, 29 May 1794.

To Alexander Hamilton

Dear Sir,   Mount Vernon 14th Oct. 1793

Enclosed is the duplicate of my last.[1] The calamity which has befallen Philadelphia & seems in no wise to abate renders it more essential than ever for the heads of Departments to Assemble, that proper measures with respect to the public offices &

Papers may be adopted. It is time also, if the President can with propriety interpose, to decide something with respect to the meeting of Congress. But what, is difficult; some being of opinion that there is no power vested in the Executive under any circumstances to change the place of meeting although there is power to call Congress together upon *extraordinary* occasions; Others think, admitting this, the exigency of the case would warrant the measure. It is a delicate situation for the President to be placed in. What would you advise in this predicament? If to call Congress together, where, for the ensuing Sessions? the Public Offices & Papers being difficult & expensive to remove to any distance—and the delicate situation it would throw the Executive into by naming a place far from the present establishment. My wishes would be German town, if the place is free from the fever, for the reasons I have mentioned; but as none can take a more comprehensive view—& I flatter myself a less partial one of the subject than yourself, and as a letter from you *may* reach me before we shall meet, I pray you to dilate fully upon the several points here brought to your consideration.

I shall be at, or somewhere about German town at the time mentioned in the enclosed; and therefore shall only add, what I persuade my self you are already satisfied of, that I am with much truth & sincerity Dr Sir—Your Affectionate

Go: Washington

ALS, DLC: Alexander Hamilton Papers; LB, DLC:GW. The cover of the ALS, which was addressed to Hamilton at Albany, was docketed in part, "Oct. 23. 1793," the date of receipt.

1. See GW to Hamilton, 25 September.

To James Madison

⟨My⟩ dear Sir, (Private)   Mount Vernon 14th Oct. 1793

The calamitous situation of Philadelphia and the little prospect from present appearances of its eligibility to receive Congress by the first monday in Decembr involves a serious difficulty.

It has been intimated by some, that the President ought, by Proclamation, to convene Congress a few days before the above period, at some other place—and by others, (although in extraordinary cases he has power to convene, yet) that he has none to change the place. Mr Jefferson when here on his way home, was of the latter opinion; but the laws were not fully examined; nor was the case at that time so serious as it now is. From the Attorney General to whom I have since written on this subject, requesting an Official opinion,[1] I have received no answer; nor is it probable I shall do it soon, as I believe he has no communication with the Post Office.

Time presses, and the malady at the usual place of meeting is becoming more & more alarming. What then, do you think is the most advisable cours⟨e⟩ for me to pursue in the present exig⟨ency?⟩ Summons Congress to meet at a ce⟨rt⟩ai⟨n⟩ time & place in their legislative capacity? Simply to state facts, & say I will meet the members at the time & place just mentioned, for ulterior arrangements? or leave matters as they are, if there is no power i⟨n⟩ the Executive to alter the place, legally?

In the first & second cases (especial⟨ly⟩ the first) the delicacy of my naming a place will readily occur to you. My wishes are, that Congress could have been assemble⟨d⟩ at German town (to shew I meant no part⟨i⟩ality) leaving it to themselves if there should appear no prospect of getting into Philadelphia soon, to decide on what shd be done thereafter; but accts say that some people have died in German town also, of the malignant fever. Every death, however, is now ascribed to that cause, be the disorder what it may.

Wilmington & Trenton are nearly equidistant from Philadelphia in opposite directions; but both are on the gre⟨at⟩ thoroughfare and equally exposed to danger from the multitude of Travellers & neither may have a Chamber suffic't for the Ho. of Representatives—Annapolis and Lancaster are more secure and have good accomodations; but to name either, especially the first, would be thought to favour the Southern convenience most perhaps might be attributed to local views—especially as New York is talked of for this purpose. Reading if there are proper conveniences at it would favour neither the Southern nor Northern interest most, but would be alike to both.

I have written to Mr Jefferson on this subject[2]—notwithstanding which I would thank you for your opinion, & that fully, as you see my embarrassment. I even ask more, I would thank you (not being acquainted with forms & having no one with me that is.) to sketch some instrument for publication proper for the case you think most expedient for me to pursue in the present state of things, if the members are to be called together as beforementioned. The difficulty of keeping Clerks in the public Offices had, in a manner, suspended business before I left Philada; and the heads of Departments having matters of private concernment which required them to be absent, has prevented my return thither longer than I had intended—but I have now called upon the several Secretaries to meet me there or in the vicinity the first of next month, for which I shall set out the 27th or 28th of the present.

The accounts from that City are really affecting. Two Gentlemen from New York now here (Colonels Platt & Sargent)[3] say they were told at the Swedes ford of Schoolkil by a person who said he had it from Governor Mifflin that by the official report from the Mayor of the City upwards of 3500 had died and the disorder by all accounts was spreading, & raging more violently than ever. If cool weather accompanied with rain does not put a stop to the malady, distressing indeed must be the condition of that City—now almost depolulated by removals & deaths. I am always, and with very sincere regard & friendship Your Affectionate

Go: Washington

I would not have sent you such a scrawl, but really have no time to copy it. I came here to look a little into my own private concerns, but have no time allowed me for this purpose being followed by other matters.

ALS, ViU: George Washington Letters, 1777, 1793; ADf, DNA: RG 59, Miscellaneous Letters; LB, DLC:GW. Where the ALS has been mended, the missing characters are supplied in angle brackets from the draft. The postscript does not appear on the draft or the letter-book copy.

1. See GW to Edmund Randolph, 30 September.

2. See GW to Thomas Jefferson, 11 October.

3. Winthrop Sargent and Richard Platt arrived at Mount Vernon on 12 Oct. and departed on 14 Oct.; Sargent recorded impressions of the visit in his diary: "Saturday 12th. . . . about two and a half miles more the Presidents house at mount Vernon presents itself upon the Left full in view, of elegant and Courtly appearance and the Way to it leads through a Gate upon the Left: a Broad Road on the Right goes to Fredericksburg—Our Reception at mount Vernon was hospitable and polite—from Mrs W——: immediately upon our Arrival; the President having rode out upon one of his plantations: Before Dinner he came in and was pleased to shew us much Civility—we found the place without more Company than the Family, consisting of the President, Mrs Washington Mr Dandridge the presidents Secretary—three Miss Custus' at present, and a Mrs Washington widow of the Presidents Nephew who was in the guards—Dinner was served up in a plain frugal Style and the glass cir-

culated by the President in sufficient Freedom—He always takes his wine at and after Dinner it being his last meal for the Day: Suppers and even a Glass of wine in the Eveg afflicting him with the head ache.

"It was our Intention to have taken Leave after Dinner The President however telling us that if we would dispense with his attentions to us, his Time *even here* being devoted to the public Service almost altogether, he should be very happy in our passing with him a few Days, we have agreed to remain the morrow. . . .

"Sunday 13th. . . . Only a short Time to remain at Mount Vernon I arose early to obtain as much Knowledge as possible of this Seat of our illustrious General and President—The mount itself is very elevated, almost immediately upon the Bank of the Potomack (one mile and three quarters wide at this place) and commanding a most extensive view of the same and adjacent Country upon both Sides of the river—the natural Glacis from the Flanks and Laund in Front is easy and continued to a considerable Distance. The Front towards the waters of Potowmac is of greater Declivity—a small Deer park in that Quarter and a good road to the river with a small Quay or Landing place—about ten thousand Acres constitute the Farm, Seven hundred of which are in Plantations the present Season; cultivated by Slaves of which the President now has full two hundred, better clothed and fed than negroes generally are in this Country—I saw and conversed with many of them in my Walks of this morning who seem well contented in their Situation and much attached to their Master—A very advantageous Situation for a Fortress was pointed out to me by the President nearly opposite to mount Vernon—Commanding perfectly the Channel of the Potowmack both up and down the river to a very considerable Distance—The mansion house which is of wood has been considerably improved since it came into the possession of its present dignified owner—it is about 120 Feet in Length with a capacious open Piazza towards the water supported by a proper number of very lofty and majestic Columns—The Front towards the Country is open and Airy with the Laund before mentioned of neat shorn Grass continuing to the road: upon the Flanks—towards the mansion house are the different Offices, connected therewith by covered Colonnades and constituting handsome and regular Wings—the whole finished in Imitation of Bristol Free Stone; And from the Termination thereof down along the Laund on either Side are continued to the road the deep embowering shades of myrtle Cyprus Cedar and a variety of aromatic 'ever greens'—Into one of those recesses I entered—the feathered Songsters & Turtle Dove had been invited by the Beauties of the Scene—the various Avenues are so artfully contrived as in a very limited Area to afford the most delightful promenades—impervious almost even to the Solar Ray but by small Interstices of Admission purposely disposed upon the Margins—Whilst admiring the hand of Art and Nature in this miniature Labyrinth the great Bell summoned me to Breakfast & I had only Time to observe that upon the Exterior of those Arbours were Kitchen and Flower Gardens abounding in Esculents and much gay and variegated Foliage—a capacious Green house upon the right wing stored with valuable exotics lay in my Passage, offering a high gratification for some Leisure hour of the Day—Around the Breakfast Table were collected the party of yesterday all in health and cheerful—Mrs Washington and the President seem as yet to have suffered but little since the Close of the late War by the ravaging hand of Time—He endures Exercise, unremitted, and even Fatigues of Body and mind very uncommonly for his Season of Life—after a very substantial Repast in which Indian hoe Cake with Butter & Honey seemed the principal Component Parts he withdrew till Dinner at *which* and till late in this Eveg we favoured with his Company—Our Conversation general and the Subject of Politics avoided—I was a little disappointed, coming from the western Country now the Theatre of war and having borne some considerable Part in the unfortunate Campaign of Genl St Clair which is still a Subject of public Discussion that the President did not avail himself of the Information I might have reasonably been supposed capable of imparting—His Silence however upon this head was a good Lesson to me and for *once* I suffered Prudence to assume the Government—his total Apathy to Friendship, all affectionate Attachments, or Encouragement to free confidential Communications should mark the Character of *that* public man who would *appear* immaculate to the jaundiced Eye of a diversified multifarious republican Government—upon the Topics of old Campaigns under the unfortunate General Braddock and his successor Forbes I obtained Information; by Queries however for the President *certainly* is never communicative—He bore a material part under those officers and I learn from him that the British were much indebted to Chance for the possession of Fort 'duquesne' (now Pittsburgh) in the Campaign of [   ] for the French Commandant had dismissed the Indians at a late period when his Enemy was about making winter Cantonment, not having Supplies of Provisions &ca to advance, but Convoys accidentally arriving Forbes pushed on and Acquired his Object without any Opposition—except some Skirmishings which had previously taken place between his advanced Guards and small Parties of Indians; at one of which the President having been sent forward with a Reinforcement, by being mistaken for an Enemy received several Fires from the Guards, that were returned by his own Command and in his Endeavours to correct the mistake between both parties was in extreme Hazard—no Censure however was implied upon him in Consequence as he had taken the proper measures to advise of his Approach.

"Between the President Mr Dandridge and the Ladies we have passed the afternoon and Evening very pleasantly—The Miss Custus' are grand Daughters of Mrs Washington through a first Husband, all of them handsome and agreeable but Nelly who has of Late accompanied her grand mamma in public Life is acknowledged Excellence; with their vocal and instrumental music we have been much Charmed—Mrs the widow Washington is of most amiable person and manners—On the morrow after Breakfast we are necessitated to bid adieu to this honoured assemblage, deeply impressed with a Sense and Esteem for and of the private Virtues and Accomplishments of each and every one of them and with added veneration and respect for the august Chief our illustrious President.

"Monday 14th. This morning after Breakfast—perfectly well satisfied with our Gracious reception we bid Adieu to Mount Vernon" (Diary, 1 Oct. 1793 to 31 Dec. 1795, MHi: Winthrop Sargent Papers).

To Timothy Pickering

Sir, Mount Vernon 14th Octobr 1793.
The numerous & various reports which I have received from people who were not possessed of any *accurate* information with respect to the state of the malignant fever with which Philadelphia is so unfortunately afflicted, and my intention being to return thither, or to it's neighbourhood about the first of next month, have induced me to ask this information from you—and I beg you will advise me as well of the state of the fever in Philada as whether it has extended itself in it's vicinity, German town &c. to which last I have heard it has reached.

Taking it for granted that the fever will not have entirely disappear'd in the City of Philada & the place become quite purified so as to admit the members of Congress to meet there with safety by the first of December, what accommodations could be had for them in German town, if it should be free from infection? If, however, this place should be thought unsafe or improper, what other has been in contemplation for the next Session of Congress? Full information of these matters, & of the prevailing sense of those who have had an opportunity of judging & are best acquainted with the true situation of things in & about Philada is what I very much want, as the accounts we receive here are so opposite & unsatisfactory that we know not on which to rely.

By report we learn that mister Willing (President of the Bank) mister John Ross, mister Jonathan Sergeant, mister Howell, Colonel Franks & many others of our acquaintance have fallen victims to this fatal fever[1]—that near 4,000 have died, & that the disorder is more violent than ever. Is this a faithful representation? I hope your family is out of the way of this dreadful contagion, & that you and mistress Pickering are well.[2] With esteem & regard I am, Sir, Your very humble Servant

Go: Washington

P.S. What sort of a place is Reading? How would it answer for the accomodation of Congress the ensuing Session?

LS, MHi: Pickering Papers; Df, DNA: RG 59, Miscellaneous Letters; LB, DLC:GW.

1. Jonathan Dickinson Sergeant (1746–1793), a lawyer and former congressman, became a member of the committee appointed in September for

the relief of the sick at Philadelphia. He died in early October. It is uncertain which Mr. Howell GW intended to reference. Three men of that name are listed by Mathew Carey as victims of the epidemic, and Oliver Wolcott, Jr., informed GW of another, who recovered (Carey, *Short Account of the Malignant Fever,* 140; Wolcott to GW, 20 Oct.). Although a man named John Ross died during the fever (Carey, *Short Account of the Malignant Fever,* 154), the merchant John Ross, to whom GW probably was referring, survived.

2. Rebecca White Pickering (1754–1828) had married Timothy Pickering in 1776.

To Edmund Randolph

Dear Sir,   Mount Vernon 14th Oct. 1793

Enclosed is the copy of a Letr I wrote to you agreeably to the date—since which I have received yours of the 3d instt—which shews it had not at that time got to your hands.[1]

I sincerely hope your son Peyton is in no danger from the sick person he saw, and that the rest of your family, wherever they be, are in good health.[2] Are you certain that the disorder of which the persons in German town died was the real malignant fever of Philada? For every fever now, of which people die in & about that City, will be so called. I was in hopes Congress might have assembled at German town in the first instance, and there taken ulterior resolutions if the City of Philadelphia *at the time* should be thought unsafe for them to sit in.

I have just received a letter from the Speaker of the late house of Representatives (Trumbull) suggesting the expediency of convening Congress a few days before the first monday in December at some other place than Philadelphia, in order to avoid the necessity of a quoram of both houses meeting there[3]—Similar sentiments I have heard, are entertained by others—Query, what with propriety, can the President do under the circumstances which exist? If the importance, & awfulness of the occasion would justify calling the legislature together at any other place than Philadelphia (on acct of the calamity with which it is visited) where should it be? This question, if German Town is also visited, would involve the Executive in a serious, & delicate decision—Wilmington & Trenton are equidistant from Philadelphia in opposite directions—but both are on the great thoroughfare through the Union—equally liable on that account to receive the Infection—and each, to the members whose distance would be encreased, obnoxious. Annapolis is more out of the Comn & has conveniences—but it might be thought that interested & local views dictated the measure. What sort of a Town is Reading, & how would it answer for the purpose of a Session? Neither Northern nor Southern members would have cause to complain of partiality on acct of its *Situation*. Lancaster would be thought to favour the Southern members most.

You will readily perceive that if a change of place becomes indispensable, not a moment is to be lost in the notification thereof, whether by Proclamation, requiring it—or by a simple statement of facts, accompanied with information that at a certain time and place (which might be blank days before the 1st of December) I would meet the members in their Legislative capacity, or for the purpose of ulterior arrangements. The latter I presume, would be a novel proceeding—the other an illegal Act, if there is no power delegated for the purpose, & either would be food for scriblers; yet, if Philadelphia should Continue in its present unfortunate & alarming state something preliminary seems necessary—I wish you to think seriously of this matter; and not only give me your opinion thereon, but accompany it with what you may conceive a proper & formal instrument for publication for my consideration; leaving the place & time blank thereon, but dilated upon in a letter under the sevel views you may take of the subject; especially too as (I have heard but know not on what ground that) it is made a question by some, whether even the Legislature itself having in this instance fulfilled the powers of the Constitution have now a right to change the places which are established by law—This to me I confess, seems to be a strained Construction of the Constitution and is only mentioned to shew that caution is necessary.

The heads of the Departments you will have no opportunity to advise with on this interesting subject, nor do I suppose you will be in the way of seeing professional men of much eminence, otherwise I should request you to know their sentiments on the *legality*—or *expediency* of Convening Congress otherwise than in Philadelphia. My best wishes attend you, Mrs Randolph & family—and I am, Dr Sir Yours Affectly

Go: Washington

ADfS (photocopy), sold by Christie's, New York, *Printed Books and Manuscripts: Including Americana and Recently Discovered Manuscripts by Ernest Hemingway,* Sale 9364, 19 May 2000; LB, DLC:GW.

1. See GW to Randolph, 30 Sept.; Randolph's letter to GW of 3 Oct. has not been found.

2. Peyton Randolph (d. 1828) later became clerk of the Virginia Court of Appeals and authored six volumes of reports of cases argued before that court.

3. See Jonathan Trumbull, Jr., to GW, 2 October.

Letter not found: from Edmund Randolph, 14 Oct. 1793. On 23 Oct. GW wrote Randolph: "Your letter of the 14th only came by the Post of last night, to Alexandria."

To Oliver Wolcott, Jr.

Sir,   Mount Vernon 14th Oct. 1793

Lest my last letter to Colo. Hamilton should have met some mischance I send a duplicate, & request your care of it;[1] the necessity for the heads of Departments assembling by the first of next month becoming more & more apparent. Philadelphia or vicinity, is appointed for this purpose, where I shall be myself.

Let me know, I pray you, whether the malady with which Philadelphia is afflicted has extended to German town, or neighbourhood. In a word, I would thank you for precise information on this head, for I have not been able to get any. A letter requiring this of the Attorney General is, I presume, still laying in the Post Office as I have received no acknowledgment of it although written & sent from this the 30th of last Month.[2]

On the supposition that the Fever in Philadelphia will not have entirely ceased, & the City Sufficiently purified by the first of December for Congress to Assemble there, what conveniencies would German town afford for this purpose? thereby superceding the necessity of removing the public Offices to a more distant part. If this also should be conceived an unsafe, or an improper place, what other is contemplated for the residence of Congress next Session? full information of the prevailing sense of those who are best acquainted with the true situation of things in and about Philadelphia would be very satisfactory to me, as our accts here are so vague and contradictory that we know not what to rely on.

By report Mr Willing (President of the Bank) Mr Jno. Ross, Mr Jonathen Sergeant, Mr Howell, Colo. Franks, and many others of our acquaintances have fallen victims to the prevailing malignant fever; that near 4000 have died; & that the disorder rages more violently than ever. Are these things true? I hope you & Mrs Wolcot keep your health. with esteem & regard I am, Sir Yr Very Hble Servt

Go: Washington

ALS, CtHi: Oliver Wolcott, Jr. Papers; Df, DNA: RG 59, Miscellaneous Letters; LB, DLC:GW.
    1. See GW to Alexander Hamilton, 25 September.
    2. See GW to Edmund Randolph, 30 September.

To Henry Knox

Dr Sir, Mount Vernon 15th Octobr 1793.

The violence with which (from all accounts I have received) the contagious fever in Philada continues to rage makes it still more necessary than ever that the meeting of the Heads of Departments which I requested you to attend in a letter of the 25th Sept: should not fail to take place by the first of November[1] that, among other things measures may be taken for security of the public offices & Papers. I shall set out from this place in order to meet you & the other Gentlemen in the vicinity of Philada at that time.[2] The heads of Departments being absent the disputes arising between the agents of the Powers at War, and other matters, are transmitted immediately to me.

Should the continuance of the fever in the City of Philada render it unsafe & improper for the members of Congress to assemble there the first of December (& indeed there seems to be no hope of its disappearance by that time) what in that case is to be done? Do you conceive the President is authorised by the Constitution or Laws of the U.S. to interfere in such a case? Altho' the President has power to call Congress together in *extraordinary* cases, it is denied[3] that power is given to change the fixed place of convening[4]—By others it is thought the exigency of the present case wd justify the measure.[5] Indeed it has been made a question by some whether even Congress themselves have this power. I should be glad to have your opinion upon these points as soon as possible, because if the Executive have power no time is to be lost in using it.

Admitting, however, that the President was authorised to convene Congress at any other place than Philada where have you contemplated as most convenient & agreeable to all parties[6] for the ensuing Session—considering it is a temporary measure—that the public offices are established in Phila.—& the papers difficult & expensive to remove? German town would certainly have been preferred by me[7] but, unfortunately, I am told the fever has reached it & several people died therein[8] but all deaths now are charged to acct of the malignt fever. Wilmington & Trenton are equidistant in opposite directions from Philada but situated on the great thoroughfare thro' the Union, and exposed in a great degree to the communication of the infection—& would be equally unsatisfactory to the members whose distance would be encreased. Reading is more out of the way of taking the infection, being off the great road thro' the Country—& could not be complained of by either northern or Southern members on accot of situation. how do you think it would accomdate Congress the ensuing Session?[9] write fully and promptly as I may receive your letter before I shall see you—With very great estm & regard I am—Dr Sir—yr Affecte

G. W———n

Df, in the writing of Bartholomew Dandridge, Jr., and GW, DLC:GW; LB, DLC:GW.

Bartholomew Dandridge, Jr., wrote Oliver Wolcott, Jr., on this date: "As the president is uncertain where Genl Knox is, he directs me to request the favor of you to enquire of the Clerk in his office, & to direct the Letter enclosed herewith for him, accordingly" (CtHi: Oliver Wolcott, Jr., Papers).

1. The rest of this sentence was added by GW.

2. GW inserted the remainder of this paragraph.

3. Following "it," Dandridge wrote, "does not already appear"; GW struck this and inserted, "is denied."

4. The power at issue derived from Article 2, section 3 of the Constitution.

5. GW inserted the preceding sentence. That text is omitted from the letter-book copy.

6. The remainder of this sentence was inserted by GW.

7. GW inserted "by me."

8. The remainder of this sentence is in GW's handwriting.

9. The remainder of the draft is in GW's handwriting.

From Henry Knox

sir   Boston 15 Octr 1793.

since my arrival at this place which was on the 7th instant I have had the honor to receive your favor of the 25th ultimo. I propose to set out on my return on Monday the 21st, and hope to be in the vicinity of the sorely afflicted city of Philadelphia on the or before the 1st of November. I have the honor to be sir with the most perfect respect and attachment Your Most obedient humble Servant

H. Knox

ALS, DLC:GW; LB, DLC:GW.

From Thomas Sim Lee

Sir   Anna[po]lis Octr 15 1793

I do myself the honour to transmit to yr Excelly the copy of a letter from the British Vice Consul residing in Baltimore and of a deposition corroborative of those which accompanied my letter of the 11 Instant respecting the Brig Cunningham.[1]

I enclose likewise the copy of a letter from the same Gentleman on the subject of the Ship Roehampton captured by the french Privateer Industry.[2]

T. S. L.

Df, MdAA; LB, MdAA: Council Letterbook, 1787–1793.

1. British Consul Edward Thornton's letter to Lee of 13 Oct. enclosed a deposition from the pilot aboard the brig *Conyngham* and expressed his hope that the "facts, advanced in this and the former deposition," would be "fully sufficient, to substantial the most important point, and consequently to procure the restoration of the vessel and compensation for its illegal capture and detention" (MdAA).

2. Thornton's other letter of 13 Oct. informed Lee that "The British ship Roehampton . . . was exposed to public sale and purchased by a citizen of the United States, immediately after the suit instituted on behalf of the original owners, had been dismissed from the district Court of the United States." Thornton argued that "The exercise of this right of property, which can only be *justly* founded on the perfect lawfulness of the previous capture . . . must be considered as forming no bar to the claim of the former proprietors, if the illegal equipment of the Privateer Industry be fully substantiated." He also reminded Lee that his previous "requisition for the release of the Roehampton" had been forwarded to the secretary of war in mid-September, and that

the British minister at Philadelphia had earlier announced to the secretary of state that *L'Industrie* had been illegally outfitted at Baltimore. Thornton then requested Lee "to inform me whether the former proprietors may expect to recover their vessel through the exertion of your authority, that in contrary event the whole affair may be fully and finally submitted through his Majesty's Minister to the executive government of the United States" (DNA: RG 59, Miscellaneous Letters). In a longer version of the preceding paragraph that was struck from the draft, Lee summarized this letter and added, "to which I have answered that I have not yet received any instructions from the general government on the subject" (see Lee to Thornton, 15 Oct., MdAA: Council Letterbook, 1787–1793).

From Timothy Pickering

Sir,   Philadelphia Oct. 15. 1793.

The intelligence contained in the enclosed copy of a letter from Mr Storer, seemed to be of sufficient consequence to trouble you with; and I should have transmitted it a week ago; but the sickness in my family, and the death of a favourite son, have prevented me.[1]

To Governor Simcoe's *public* professions of regret &c. at the issue of the treaty, a number of facts may be opposed. These with other communications I hope to have the honour to lay before you, when it shall please God to permit you to return hither with safety.[2]

I have received no further intelligence from Mr Storer. It may be proper for me to say, that I think Captain Ford a man of honour. He is a very sensible man; and whatever information he communicates from Mr *Shehan* may be the more relied on, as they married sisters, and the families lived under one roof. Capt. Ford has come to the States for the recovery of his health.[3]

The applications to Dr Rush, for two or three days past, have sensibly lessened, and the reports from his patients in general, are favourable: whence I hope the destructive fever is abating. It is now beginning to rain, and there is a prospect of its continuance; after which we may expect a cool air and frost that may destroy the fatal contagion. With great respect, I am, sir, your most obedient servant

Timothy Pickering

ALS, DLC:GW; ADf, MHi: Pickering Papers.

1. Charles Storer (1761–1829) of Boston, who graduated from Harvard in 1779 and served for a time as a private secretary for John Adams, acted as sec-

retary for the commissioners, including Pickering, appointed to hold a treaty with the Northwest Indians at Sandusky earlier in 1793. Edward Pickering (1787–1793) died on 10 October.

2. Among the evidence to dispute the good faith of John Graves Simcoe's expressions of regret was an undated [c.23 June–July 1793] memorandum of John Heckewelder to the commissioners, which is now in DLC:GW. Heckewelder reported that missionaries at the Moravian towns stated that the previous winter Simcoe "had positively said: *that there would be no Peace between the Indn Nations & the United States—That the Indians must have the Lands to the Ohio for hunting Grounds—that they would insist on this, & accept of no proposals made to them by the Commissioners Short of this*," and that another officer "had lately said . . . that they yet had some hopes of having all the Country unto the Ohio River joined to Upper Canada."

3. Henry Ford (d. 1793) was captain of the British schooner *Dunmore* on Lake Erie; Walter Butler Sheehan, a nephew of Lt. Col. John Butler, resided near Niagara, where he acted as an interpreter, clerk, and storekeeper for the Indian Department and served for a time as sheriff.

Enclosure
Charles Storer to Timothy Pickering

Sir, New-York 4th October 1793.

Captain Ford[1] & Lady arrived here yesterday: they left Niagara the 13th ulto & came by the way of Oswego. He gives me some information of things which took place after we left that country, and which, as they probably will be new to you, I herewith communicate them.

He says that Talbot,[2] Brant and Shehan[3] had arrived at Niagara some days before he sailed: that they informed the Governor, that as soon as the last message was sent to the Council at the Rapids of the Miami,[4] a party of Indians was dispatched to Detroit River: they crossed at Brown's Town, and arrived at Caldwell's[5] the morning after we sailed; and their object was to take our party prisoners, to cut off our noses and ears, & to detain us as hostages, in hopes thereby to obtain their own terms. They further say that it was very fortunate we did not go to the Miami, as once intended; since the Western Indians went armed into Council, and assuredly would have done us mischief. However, that Captain Bunbury had been severely reprimanded by the Governor, for having misconstrued his orders, in the act of refusing to let the vessel sail when the Commissioners desired it. Captain Ford was also told it was his duty to have sailed had the Commissioners insisted upon it. He has promised me a copy of his orders.[6]

Mr Shehan, in the absence of Colo. Butler, took the direction of the Six Nations: He was therefore early called upon by Colo. McKee to know his mind upon the treaty. He said he went there to treat of peace; that he and the Six Nations were enclined to peace, and should therefore urge it all that lay in their power. In consequence of this he & McKee had a quarrel, and neither he nor Brant were admitted once into the Indian Councils; but were marked out as *Yankies.* They both have declared to the Governor that the Indians were controuled by advice, & urged on to war; and that McKee and sundry traders were at the bottom of it. The Governor had publicly reprobated the conduct of McKee, and the whole proceedings of the Indians, regretting very much that the mission was successless.

Mr Givens[7] also had been severely reprimanded by the Governor for his conduct while with us; & particularly for striking Paine with his drawn sword, on our return to Navy-Hall, for which he was in disgrace.[8]

Brant & Shehan say, before breaking up of the Council at Miami, the Six Nations were called upon to join in the war: that those present said they must first consult their nations: that they had returned, & that Shehan was gone to Buffaloe Creek to attend the Council. And Ford says that they and the Governor were decidedly for their neutrality. When the council broke up, *3000 Indians* went off to strike Wayne. This account is delivered the Governor by Brant, Shehan & Talbot. Captain Ford further adds, that a large party of Western Indians were preparing to attack the Genesee Country: that as soon as the Governor was informed of it, he sent to them positively to forbid it, saying, that as that was the route thro' which he had intercourse with the states, he would stop all presents, supplies &c. to that nation who should send their warriors into Genesee. This broke up the expedition. Ford says the Governor is extremely provoked at the issue of the treaty, and regrets very much he could not see the Commissioners on their return.

I asked Capt. Ford if he had learned what Welbank's business was with the Governor. He says that Shehan informs him, that when Welbank returned to Miami, he related to the Indians that he was sent by the Creeks and Cherokees to know if the Governor of Upper Canada would assist the Western Indians against the states; in which case they would continue their war with Gov-

ernor Blount, & form an extensive league: that Colo. Simcoe
had said he had nothing to do in their dispute with Govr Blount;
that he would not countenance it; nor would he aid the Western
Indians at all against the states. That, however, both had been
exchanged between the Creeks, Cherokees & Western Indians;
and that Welbank had gone southward.[9]

Should Captain Ford communicate any thing further, I shall
duly forward it to you.

Enclosed is a piece of Canada news, which I cut out of one of
their papers on our route. Ford says it was written by some merchant, and not by an officer. Does it not sound something like
Macomb?[10]

I wrote you yesterday, in reply to yours of the first,[11] and am sir
with due respect yr humble servt

Chas Storer.

Copy, DLC:GW. The ALS from which this copy was taken is in MHi: Pickering Papers.

1. Pickering placed a footnote at this point: "Captain of the Dunmore, in
which we made both passages on Lake Erie. T.P."

2. Pickering's footnote at this point reads: "A young officer in Govr Simcoe's
family, & who was sent by him to the council of the Indians at the Miami. T.P."
Thomas Talbot (1771–1853), who was at this time a lieutenant in the British
army, was appointed to be John Simcoe's private secretary in February 1792.
He left Canada in 1794 to take up an army promotion, but in 1800, after rising to lieutenant colonel, he sold his commission to return to Canada, where
he became an important figure in the settlement of Upper Canada.

3. Pickering's footnote at this location reads: "An Assistant of Colo. Butler's, and who attended the same council, as superintendant of the Six Nations. T.P."

4. This is apparently a reference to the commissioners' message of 16 Aug.
(see *ASP, Indian Affairs,* 1:357).

5. Pickering's footnote at this point reads: "Half a mile from Elliots, where
the Commissioners had quartered—T.P." Capt. Matthew Elliott (c.1739–1814)
was an assistant to Alexander McKee. His residence was near the mouth of
the Detroit River. William Caldwell (c.1750–1822), who had been a captain in
the Loyalist Butler's Rangers during the Revolutionary War, was at this time
a merchant active in promoting settlement east of the Detroit River. In 1814
he succeeded Elliott as superintendent of Indians for the Western District.
Brownstown was a Wyandot town located south of where Marsh Creek enters
the Detroit River, in what is now Wayne County, Michigan.

6. For details on this incident, see *ASP, Indian Affairs,* 1:355.

7. Pickering placed a footnote at this point: "Capt. Bunbury & Lieut. Givens were the two British Officers assigned by Govr Simcoe to attend the Commissioners. T.P." James Givins (Givens; c.1759–1846) was at this time a lieu-

tenant in Simcoe's regiment, the Queen's Rangers. In 1797 he was appointed assistant superintendent of Indian affairs for the Home District, and while he continued to serve for a time in the army and later as a militia officer, his main career was in the Indian Department, where he rose to chief superintendent for Upper Canada in 1830.

8. Navy Hall at Newark (now Niagara-on-the-Lake), Ontario, was a group of barracks erected by the British in 1765 and destroyed during the War of 1812. Simcoe used the site as his residence. John Paine was the cook for the treaty commissioners.

9. For documents about George Welbank's activities, including two accounts by Simcoe of their meeting, see Philip M. Hamer, "The British in Canada and the Southern Indians, 1790–1794," *East Tennessee Historical Society's Publications*, 2 (1930): 107–34.

10. The enclosure has not been identified. Storer probably was referring to William Macomb (c.1751–1796), a merchant who lived near Detroit and represented the riding of Kent in the Canadian provincial assembly, 1792–96.

11. Storer's letter to Pickering of 3 Oct. discussed the commissioners' accounts and the yellow fever at Philadelphia (MHi: Pickering Papers). Pickering's letter to Storer of 1 Oct. has not been identified, but Pickering quoted a long paragraph about yellow fever from it in his letter to John Clarke of that date (MHi: Pickering Papers).

From Abraham Forst

Sir   George Town 16th October 1,793

Situated as I am I cannot possibly avoid troubling Your Excellency; and to be brief,

I was brought up & Educated in a genteel Sphere of life, was allways in a State of Affluence, till within a few Years past, but thro' many heavy losses & Sickness, I am now reduced my good Sir to Ask *Aid,* which I take the liberty to do of your Excellency.

I have rec'd from many worthy Bretheren in this respectable town, & Bladensburg Some Aid, as you will perceive by the enclosed Subscription List, & Your distinguish'd name to it Shatter'd as it has become (by handing about) will be the means of Saving an unfortunate man from *total* ruin.[1]

It was my intention to proceed to the Northward, but meeting with encouragement to open a *Lottery office;* I have concluded to remain in this quarter to be Support to the present *Laudable One,* as I have had thoro' experience in that Line in Europe & America.[2]

Yet your Excellency will be pleased to Observe that a plan of that nature, cannot be put into execution without the *usual* means, as it is attended with great expence, but mutual advantage eventually.

Give me leave also to observe respectable Sir, that it'll still produce the means, to enable those Worthy Gentn who are heavy ticket holders to Sell more Speedily to Such advantage as to reimburse themselves for the Losses they have Already Sustained.

There are also many more plans I can point out for general benefit.

I take the liberty to inclose to your Excellency a Certificate, which permit me to request you to have the goodness to *cause* to be *Sealed up,* together with the amo. of whatever Your humanity & generosity may dictate & left with Mr Suter.[3]

I write this respectable Sir in haste, as it is but a Short While Since I heard of your arrival in town. You will be good enough therefore to pardon all incorrectness with your usual Known & much experienced indulgence; for I leave town immediately & Shall not return till Friday next please God.[4]

That the Grand Architect of the Universe may be Your Constant Support & protector in all your undertakings, & Grant You long life, not only for your own & Connections Sake, but as a real blessing to these United States of North America, will be the unremitted prayer of one who is with most profound respect Your Excellencys ever most Faithfull, obedt Humble Servt

Abrm Forst.

If you will have the goodness to cause the additional trouble of an application to Mr Robertson, it may be an additional Satisfaction to your Excellency.

past 3 oC: On finding that you have returned to your Seat permit me to entreat you to return the inclosed &c. for me at Mr Jno. Suter Senr

A.F:

ALS, DLC:GW.

Abraham Forst was a former Masonic officer, having been appointed deputy inspector general for Virginia in 1781. His appointment describes him as a merchant lately from London, and he probably is the man who took the oath of allegiance at Philadelphia in August 1780 as a merchant lately arrived from Eustatia. Forst petitioned the Grand Lodge of Pennsylvania for assistance in September 1791, and at that time offered his services as an accountant or bookkeeper. In 1792 he was employed as a clerk in the Treasury Department (Baynard, *History of the Supreme Council*, 1:72–73; Wolf and White-man, *Jews of Philadelphia*, 100–101, 156, 410; *Builder: The National Magazine of Freemasonry*, 2 [1916]:319; *ASP, Miscellaneous Affairs*, 1:57).

1. The enclosed list has not been identified.

2. Forst was referring to the Federal City hotel lottery (see GW to Tobias Lear, 25 Sept., n.1).

3. John Suter (d. 1794) kept Suter's Tavern in Georgetown.

4. The following Friday was 18 October.

To Henry Lee

(Private)

Dear Sir,   Mount Vernon 16th Oct. 1793.

Since my arrival at this place I have been favoured with your letters of the 17th ulto and 7th instt. For your kind attentions to me I pray you to receive my sincere acknowledgments.

I have always (from the accounts given of it) entertained a high opinion of Colo. Taliaferro's threshing Machine, but knew at the sametime I had no stream that could supply water for one, on any of my Farms. This was confirmed when Mr Payne came hither & examined them.

The model brought over by the English farmers may also be a good one, but the utility of it among careless negros, & ignorant Overseers, will depend *absolutely* upon the simplicity of its construction; for if there be anything complex in the Machinery, it will be no longer in use than a mushroom is in existence. I have seen so much of the beginning & ending of these new inventions that I have almost resolved to go on in the old way of treading, until I get settled again at home, and can attend myself to the management of one.

As a proof in point of the almost impossibility of putting the Overseers of this Country out of the track they have been accustomed to walk in, I have one of the most convenient Barns in this, or perhaps any Country, where 30 hands may with great ease be employed in threshing. I had half the Wheat of the farm stored in this Barn and nothing to do but to lay it on the floor; yet,[1] when I came home about the middle of September, I found a treading yard within 30 feet of the Barn door—the Wheat again removed from the Barn—and the horses treading it out on the ground in an open exposure liable to the vicissitudes of weather. I am now erecting a building for the express purpose of treading. I have sanguine expectations of the utility of it—and if I am not deceived in them—it may afford you some satisfaction when you come into this part of the Country to call & look at it.

I have a grateful sense of your kind offer of Mr Workman. Previous however to the communication I had engaged a manager from the Eastern shore of Maryland[2]—But the impression on my mind is not lessened on that account.

I have not, as you will perceive, touched the subject of Politics in this letter. The reasons are, your letter of the 17th has expressed my ideas precisely of the conduct, & views of those who are aiming I am certain at nothing short of the subversion of the General Government; and that they would do it at the expence even, of plunging the Country in to the horrors of a disastrous war; and because I wish to wait a little longer to see what may be the sense of legally constituted bodies at the meetings about to take place.

The public service requiring it, I shall set off in about ten days for Philadelphia or vicinity. Though unknown to your lady, I beg my respectful compliments may be presented to her.[3] I wish you an agreeable & harmonious Session—and with much truth I am Dear Sir Your Affecte Hble Servt

Go: Washington

ALS, NjMoHP; ADfS, DLC:GW; LB, DLC:GW. The draft, which was heavily revised, in many places differs from the ALS in phrasing but not in meaning. The letter-book copy follows the wording of the draft.

1. On the draft the preceding portion of this sentence reads: "half the Wheat of the Farm was actually stored in the Barn in the straw by my order for threshing; notwithstanding."

2. GW engaged William Pearce in late August (see GW to Pearce, 26 Aug., and Pearce to GW, 30 Aug.).

3. Lee had married his second wife, Ann Hill Carter, in June 1793.

To Thomas Sim Lee

Sir,   George town 16th October 1793.
    I have received your Excellency's Letter of the 11 instant.
    When the British Vice-Consul at Baltimore exhibits all his proofs respecting the capture of the Brigantine Coningham, a

better judgment can be formed than at present, whether this act is an infraction of neutrality. In doing this he ought to make no delay; because there can be no decision before the evidence on both sides is heard.

Three miles will, if I recollect rightly, bring the Coningham within the rule of some decisions, but the *extent* of the Territorial jurisdiction at Sea, has not yet been fixed, on account of some difficulties which occur in not being able to ascertain with precision what the general practice of Nations in this case has been.[1] With very great esteem I am, Sir, Your Excellency's mot Obt Servt

Go: Washington

LS, MdAA: Brown Books; Df, DNA: RG 59, Miscellaneous Letters; LB, DLC: GW.

1. By 8 Nov., GW had determined that until negotiations could be held on the issue, the limits of U.S. territorial waters would be provisionally set at "one sea-league or three geographical miles from the sea shores" (Thomas Jefferson to Certain Foreign Ministers in the United States, 8 Nov., *Jefferson Papers*, 27:328–30). On 10 Nov., Zebulon Hollingsworth, federal district attorney for Maryland, was directed to investigate the *Conyngham* capture, and in April 1794, the ship was ordered returned to its captors for lack of evidence that it had been seized within the three-mile boundary (see *Jefferson Papers*, 27:342–43).

Letter not found: from William Augustine Washington, 16 Oct. 1793. On 21 Oct., GW wrote Washington: "Your letter of the 16th came to my hands the 19th."

From Thomas Jefferson

Dear Sir   Monticello [Va.] Oct. 17. 1793.

I was the day before yesterday honored with your favor of the 7th inst. by post and yesterday I received that of the 11th by express from Colo. Carrington. I will take care to be at Germantown by the 1st of the month. as the ploughing thro the roads of the month of January would be disagreeable with my own horses, I shall send them back from Fredericksburg, for which place I will set out tomorrow (Friday) sennight, in order to take the stage from thence of Monday the 28th this of course will deprive me of the honor of waiting on you at Mount Vernon, but perhaps I may have that of seeing you on the road.

I have carefully considered the question Whether the President may call Congress to any other place than that to which they have adjourned themselves, and think he cannot have such a right unless it has been given him by the constitution or the laws, & that neither of these has given it. the only circumstance which he can alter, as to their meeting, is that of *time* by calling them at an *earlier day* than that to which they stand adjourned, but no power to change the place is given. Mr Madison happened to come here yesterday, after the reciept of your letter. I proposed the question to him, and he thinks there was particular caution intended & used in the diction of the Constitution to avoid giving the President any power over the place of meeting; lest he should exercise it with local partialities.

With respect to the Executive, the Residence law has fixed our offices at Philadelphia till the year 1800. & therefore it seems necessary that we should get as near them as we may with safety.[1]

As to the place of meeting for the legislature, were we authorized to decide that question I should think it right to have it in some place in Pensylvania, in consideration of the principles of the Residence bill, & that we might furnish no pretext to that state to infringe them hereafter. I am quite unacquainted with Reading, & it's means of accomodation. it's situation is perhaps as little objectionable as that of Lancaster, & less so than Trenton or perhaps Wilmington. however I think we have nothing to do with the question, & that Congress must meet in Philadelphia, even if it be in the open feilds, to adjourn themselves to some other place. I am extremely afraid something has happened to mister Bankson, on whom I relied for continuance at my office. for two posts past I have not received any letter from him, nor dispatches of any kind. this involves new fears for the duplicates of those to mister Morris. I have the honor to be with sentiments of the most perfect esteem & attachment, Dear Sir Your most obedt & most humble servt

Th: Jefferson

P.S. mister Randolph's and mister Trumbul's letters are returned.[2]

ALS, DNA: RG 59, Miscellaneous Letters; ALS (letterpress copy), DLC: Jefferson Papers; LB, DNA: RG 59, George Washington's Correspondence with His Secretaries of State.

1. Jefferson was referring to "An Act for establishing the temporary and permanent seat of the Government of the United States," 16 July 1790 (1 *Stat.* 130).

2. GW's letter to Jefferson of 11 Oct. had enclosed Jonathan Trumbull, Jr.'s, letter to GW of 2 Oct., and (probably) Edmund Randolph's letter to GW of 3 Oct. (not found).

From Edward Carrington

Dear sir   Richmond Octo. 18th 1793

Enclosed I have the Honor to transmit a Voucher for the Expence of forwarding your letter to the Secretary of State as requested in yours of the 11th Instant, being thirteen dollars & one third of a dollar.[1] the milage is that which has been established by the Executive of the State, for such Service, & a faithful Express is not to be got lower. I have the Honor to be with the greatest respect your Most Ob. st

                                     Ed. Carrington

ALS (photocopy), sold by Early American History Auctions, Inc., 10 June 2000, item 224; Sprague transcript, with original docket, DLC:GW. The docket reads in part: "Letter from Colonel Carrington and receipt for £4.0."

1. The enclosed voucher has not been identified. GW replied to Carrington on 25 Oct.: "your Letter enclosing the accot of expence incurred in sending an Express to the Secy of State is received; & I now enclose you thirteen Dollars & _, the amot of the accot transmitted by you. I am very much obliged to you for the dispatch & punctuality with which you forwarded my Letters to the Secrey" (Df, DLC:GW).

From Thomas Sim Lee

Sir   Ann[apoli]s October 18. 1793

I beg leave to lay before yr Excellency copies of a letter and depositions received yesterday from the British Vice Consul residing at Baltimore[1]—The Letters I have lately had the honour Sir of addressing to you on similar occasions make it unnecessary for me to explain my object in the present case[2]—I have taken the same provisionary step with regard to the vessel mentioned in the depositions herewith enclosed, as was adopted respecting the Brigantine Cunningham, and although I have not heard from the french Vice Consul, I have no doubt of his paying due attention to my requisitions[3]—I have the Honor &c.

Tho. S. Lee

Df, MdAA; LB, MdAA: Council Letterbook, 1787–1793.

1. The letter from British vice-consul Edward Thornton to Lee of 16 Oct. (MdAA) enclosed the deposition of Peter Walstrum, Edward Matthias, and John Stay, 16 Oct., regarding the capture of the brigantine *Pilgrim* by the privateer *Sans Culottes de Marseilles*. These crewmen testified that the *Pilgrim* was captured near Watts Island, Va., on 6 Oct., "not more than two miles and a half or three miles at most from the shore," and brought into Baltimore on 11 Oct. (P.R.O.: FO 5/1; see also *Counter Case*, 553). Thornton continued by noting that the *Pilgrim* had been advertised for sale and by requesting that Lee "adopt as early as possible the same measures, which you have been pleased to use on a former occasion, for preventing the sale or farther dispersion of the property concerned, until the pleasure of the executive government of the United States shall be known."

2. See Lee to GW, 7, 11, and 15 October.

3. Lee's letter to Francis Moissonnier, 18 Oct., required him to "employ your authority to prevent a transfer or any other act of proprietorship by the Captors until the decision of the President respecting the legality of her capture be obtained" (MdAA: Council Letterbook, 1787–1793). Moissonnier replied that the *Pilgrim* had already been sold, but on Lee's advice he later submitted testimony disputing the alleged illegality of the ship's capture, which Lee forwarded to Secretary of War Henry Knox for GW's consideration (see Lee to Moissonnier, 25 Oct. and 5 Nov., and Lee to Knox, same dates, MdAA: Council Letterbook, 1787–1793).

From Gouverneur Morris

My dear Sir   Paris 18 October 1793

You will see by the Official Correspondence that your orders are complied with, and that your Intentions are fulfilled.[1] Permit me on this occasion to remark that had the People of America been well inform'd of the State of Things on this Side of the Atlantic, no one would have dar'd to adopt the Conduct which Mr Genest has pursued. In reading the few Gazettes which have reach'd me I am surprizd to see so little sound Intelligence.

The present Government is evidently a Despotism both in Principle and Practice. The Convention now consists of ⟨on⟩ly a Part of those who were chosen to frame a Constitution. These after putting under Arrest their Fellows, claim all Power and have delegated the greater Part of it to a Committee of Safety[2]—You will observe that one of the ordinary Measures of Government is to send out Commissioners with unlimited Authority. They are invested with Power to remove Officers chosen by the People and put others in their Place. This Power as well as that of imprisoning on Suspicion is liberally exercis'd. The revolutionary Tribunal establish'd here to judge on general Principles gives unlimited Scope to Will. It is an emphatical Phrase in Fashion among the Patriots that *Terror is the order of the Day.* Some Years have elapsed since Montesquieu wrote that the Principle of arbitrary Governments is *Fear.*[3] The Queen was executed the Day before Yesterday. Insulted during her Trial and reviled in her last moments she behav'd with Dignity throughout. This Execution will I think give to future Hostilities a deeper Dye and unite more intimately the allied Powers. It will silence the Opposition of those who would not listen to the Dismemberment of this Country, and therefore it may be concluded that the Blow by which she died was directed from a Distance. But whatever may be the Lot of France in remote Futurity, and putting aside the military Events, it seems evident that she must soon be governd by a single Despot. Whether she will pass to that Point thro the Medium of a Triumvirate or other smaller Body of Men seems as yet undetermind. I think it most probable that she will. A great and awful Crisis seems to be near at Hand. A Blow is I am told meditated which will shroud in Grief and Horror a guilty Land. Already the Prisons are surcharg'd with Persons who consider themselves as Victims. Nature recoils: and I yet Hope that these Ideas are circulated only to inspire Fear. I am my dear Sir very truly yours

Gouvr Morris

ALS, DLC:GW; LB, DLC: Gouverneur Morris Papers.

1. Morris's most recent dispatches to Secretary of State Thomas Jefferson, both of 10 Oct., discussed Morris's efforts to protect American commerce and announced that the French government had agreed to recall Edmond Genet (*ASP, Foreign Relations*, 1:372–73).

2. On 10 Aug. 1792 the French assembly had called for the election of a national convention to produce a new constitution. That body met in September 1792 and promptly proclaimed the First Republic. For the convention decree of 6 April 1793, establishing a committee of public safety (comité de salut public) "chargé de surveiller et d'accélérer l'action de l'administration confiée au conseil exécutif provisoire, dont il pourra même suspendre les arrêtés," see *Archives Parlimentaires*, 61:373–74. Although the convention ad-

opted a new constitution on 24 June 1793, the French government remained under the control of the provisional convention and its committees during the state of emergency arising out of the European war. As early as June 1793, power struggles within the convention led to the arrest and expulsion of some deputies; by October 1793 France had entered the period conventionally known as the "Reign of Terror."

3. This idea appears in book 3, chapter 9 of Montesquieu's *De l'Esprit des Loix* (1748).

Letter not found: from J. Sandwich, 18 Oct. 1793. On 25 Oct., Sandwich wrote to GW: "I had the honor of addressing you the 18th instant."

From Robert Bowyer

Historic Gallery Pallmall London
19 Octo. 1793.

May it please your Excellency

The utmost apology is due for my presuming to venture upon a repetition of taking the liberty to address your Excellency, who am so perfectly unknown to You, but the high & flattering gratification I reced, from being honor'd with a letter some time since from your Excellency, has embolden'd me to take liberties which otherwise I might not have presumed upon.[1] The cause of my presumption in the present Instance is to beg permission to introduce to your Excellency's Notice, Mr Dowlin, Surgeon, a Gentleman whose abilities in his profession & amiableness of Manners & Character are worthy of the highest Panegyrick.[2] He goes out to settle in that happy Country where every blessing of Felicity & peace must ever be expected, while it has for its patron, the exalted Character I am presuming to address: I must now beg leave to assure Your Excellency that It is my most earnest prayer that every blessing & happiness which this World or that which is to come can bestow may ever be yours. I have the honor to be May it please Your Excellency Your Excellencys Most Obliged & Devoted hble Servt

Robt Bowyer

ALS, DLC:GW.

1. GW had written Bowyer on 8 Jan. 1792, thanking him for an engraving that he had sent.

2. By March 1794 Thomas Dowlin was advertising his services as a "Surgeon and Man-midwife" in Philadelphia. There he claimed to have "studied

under the first medical characters in Europe" and to have "acted in a profes-
sional line for several years on board the largest vessels in the British navy"
(*Philadelphia Gazette and Universal Daily Advertiser,* 14 March 1794). Dowlin
evidently was practicing at Baltimore in 1800 (*The New Baltimore Directory, and
Annual Register: For 1800 and 1801* . . . [Baltimore, 1800], 34).

From Matthew Clarkson

Sir.   Philadelphia October 19. 1793.
   It having pleased Divine Providence to add Doctor Phile, the
naval officer of this port, to the number of those to whom the
present prevailing disorder hath proved fatal, I am induced to
solicit the appointment as his successor.[1]
   Confiding in that protection which hath hitherto preserved
me, whilst upwards of three thousand of my fellow citizens have
been removed into eternity, I shall think myself happy in receiving from you Sir the means of a comfortable support and the opportunity of being further serviceable to my country. I am with
the most perfect esteem Sir Your most obed. humb. servt
                                              Matth. Clarkson

ALS, DLC:GW.
   1. Clarkson did not receive this appointment.

From Thomas Lloyd

                                        Newgate prison in the City of
                                        London Great Britain
                                        October 19th 1793.
To George Washington President of the United states of
America
   The enclosed is a copy of my letter to Thomas Pinckney Minister Plenipotentiary, in which I have solemnly claimed the interference of my country, I send it for your information, trusting
you will direct or recommend as the case may in your judgment
require some effectual measure, by which I may obtain the redress of the injuries I have sustained.[1]
   I transmit a Copy likewise to the House of Representatives of
the United States.
                                              Thomas Lloyd

ALS, DNA: RG 59, Miscellaneous Letters. The cover of this letter indicates that it was sent "per Ship Hunter Captain Hacker Via New York." That ship left London in mid-November and arrived at New York City on 20 Jan. 1794 (*Greenleaf's New York Journal, & Patriotic Register,* 22 Jan. 1794).

Thomas Lloyd (1756–1827) served in the Maryland line and as a quartermaster during the Revolutionary War, and as a clerk in the Treasury, 1781–83. He published editions of proceedings of the Pennsylvania legislature, debates of the Constitutional Convention in Pennsylvania, and *The Congressional Register; or, History of the Proceedings and Debates of the First House of Representatives of the United States of America.*

1. The enclosure was a printed copy of a letter from Lloyd to Thomas Pinckney, 14 Oct. 1793, in which Lloyd requested the United States to intervene on his behalf in regard to his conviction and punishment by a British court for attempted escape from the Fleet Prison (where he had been imprisoned for debt) and for publication of a libel (DNA: RG 59, Miscellaneous Letters). For a more detailed record of the case, see *The Trial of P. W. Duffin, and Thomas Lloyd, a Citizen of the United States of America and an Officer in the Late American Army; for a Libel in the Fleet-Prison* (London, 1793), which Lloyd had published. According to a 14 Nov. 1799 application by Lloyd for the position of assistant clerk to the Pennsylvania House of Representatives, he was imprisoned for 1,187 days (broadside, NHi). For Pinckney's explanation of his response to Lloyd, see Pinckney to Secretary of State, 11 Nov. (DNA: RG 59, Despatches from U.S. Ministers to Great Britain).

From Gouverneur Morris

My dear Sir   Paris 19 October 1793

I had Hopes untill last Evening that the Persons who are to go out as Commissioners from hence would have embarkd with Captain Culver, but Circumstances have delay'd the Appointment. The Plan which was in Agitation and which will probably be carried into Effect is to send over three or four Commissioners one of whom will be charg'd with Letters of Credence but instructed to conform to the Directions of the Board. It is probable that the new Minister immediately on being presented will ask you to aid in securing the Person and Papers of the old one. My public Dispatch of this Day contains a remote Hint to lead the Investigation of the Secretary of State. I did not chuse to be more particular because You can both give and take the Informations you chuse.[1]

I have favor'd or rather excited the Idea of this Proceedure for the following Reasons. First such a public Act will place in a contemptible Light the Faction connected with Mr Genet. Secondly the Seizure of his Papers by exposing his Connections with *prime Movers* will give a Lesson of Caution to others. And thirdly the Commissioners who exercise this high handed Authority will on Reflection feel the Necessity of respecting your Government lest they should meet a similar Fate. Having alarm'd their Apprehensions as to the Effect which Mr Genet's Imprudence might produce, and knowing the public and *private* Views of the *Parties* I have insinuated the Advantages which might result from an early Declaration on the Part of the new Minister that as France has announced her Determination not to meddle with the interior Affairs of other Nations so he can know only the *Government* of America. In Unison with this Idea, I told the Minister that I had observed an overruling Influence in their Affairs which seem'd to come from the other Side of the Channel, and at the same Time had traced the Intention to excite a Seditious Spirit in America. That it was impossible to be on a friendly Footing with such Persons, but that at present a different Spirit seemd to prevail &ca &ca &ca. This Declaration producd the Effect I intendd. The Minister has himself the wish to go out as plenipotentiary and Mr Otto his principal Secretary having the same wish they will I beleive endeavor while they stay to put things in good Train here[2]—It may be an important *judicial* Question how far A Minister is protected by the Law of Nations after the Arrival of his Successor. In my opinion the same Principles which exempt him from the municipal Law subject him to the will of his Sovereign and of Course the Aid given to the new Minister is not an Act of the *judiciary* but of the *executive,* perform'd as an *Ally* and *friend* and is meerly *discretionary*—I find that this Commission will endeavor to get Hold of the Debt from America to france by Anticipation:[3] if no other Reasons militated against the *Advance* the Advantage of a Pledge to satisfy Damages our Citizens may sustain during the present Violences is considerable and will not I presume be overlook'd. I am my dear Sir very truly yours

Gouvr Morris

ALS, DLC:GW; LB, DLC: Gouverneur Morris Papers.

1. William Culver, who commanded the sloop *Hannah* out of Philadelphia, had been entrusted with carrying the dispatches asking Morris to request the recall of French minister Edmond Genet (Thomas Jefferson to Delamotte, 26 Aug., *Jefferson Papers,* 26:759). Morris sent this letter and his official dis-

patches by Culver's ship, which arrived at Philadelphia in mid-January 1794 (*Gazette of the United States and Evening Advertiser* [Philadelphia], 14 Jan. 1794). Morris wrote in his letter of this date addressed to Secretary of State Thomas Jefferson that the French foreign minister had "assured me that Genet should be *punished*. I replied that the United States had only ordered me to ask his recall, and I could go no further. The idea is to send over a commission of three or four persons, and to authorize that board to send him over a prisoner. . . .

"It is probable that the successor of M. Genet may ask the interposition of our Government in the discussions likely to arise. I have given assurances to the extent of what our laws and constitution may authorize. You will be able to measure better than I can that extent, and, at any rate, this hint will be kept secret, for that is, as you will readily see, of the utmost importance" (*ASP, Foreign Relations,* 1:374–75).

2. Louis-Guillaume Otto, comte de Mosloy (1754–1817), formerly chargé d'affaires for the French legation in the United States, became chef de la première division politique of the French foreign ministry in January 1793. After falling out of favor during the Reign of Terror, he resumed his diplomatic career in 1798. In the preceding part of this paragraph, Morris evidently was referring to the new French foreign minister, François Louis Michel Chemin Deforgues, rather than to the new minister to the United States.

3. For the contract for the payment of America's debt to France, 25 Feb. 1783, see Miller, *Treaties,* 115–22. Genet had already proposed an advanced payment on that debt (see GW to Thomas Jefferson, 5 June, n.1), and he renewed the effort in November (see the report on Genet's debt proposal enclosed in Alexander Hamilton to GW, 23 Nov.).

From William Pearcc

Sir   Kent County [Md.] October 19th 1793

I Recevd you Letter with a Coppy of our Agreement[1]—you Inform me that I am to Live this winter at your mansion House which I shall Like Very well as it will be giving me an oppertunity of Giting acquainted with the Business there—But after that If it should be agreeable to you I had Rather Live in the house you intended for me as I have Several small Children and I should Like to keep them at A distance from the Black ones. and I thougt I saw a great many at your mansion house I have spoke for the plows and Expect to bring Them down with me and the other things you mention—As you Intend to leave home and probable will not be there when I go Down I will thank you to Leave me Every Instruction That you may think Nessessary—for their is some of your Business I fear I shall be at *a Loss* at first as to the management of your farms I Hope I shall Give you Sattisfaction However I shall use my utmost Indevours to Do it, for I do assure you that I would not miss Giveing you Sattissfaction for twice the sum I am to Receive—I am makeing Every Exertion In my power to Git my Business Setled and to git in Readiness to Come as soon as I possable Can, But my people has Been Very Sick and people are Generaly so—that hands ware not to be hired, but I hope I shall be ready to git Down before frost Set in, I have been Looking out For a Carpenter that I thought would Suit you But I cannot git one to Come that I think would do nor a man to Look after your house people, Dichers &c.[2]—In your Letter you did not say wheather you Had got Either of them—I will still be upon the Look out for such Carractors as you first mentiond & will Ingage them Conditionaly If I Can meet With such as I think would suit and If you think proper to write and should not be suited and I should git Such men I will bring them down with me. I am Sir with the Greatest Resect Your Humbe Servt

William Pearce

ALS, DLC:GW.

1. See GW to Pearce, 6 October.

2. GW had suggested in his letter to Pearce of 25 Aug. that if Pearce were to become superintendent of Mount Vernon, he should look for a new carpenter.

From Robert Rutherford

Dear Sir   Fredericksburgh [Va.] October 19th 1793

The direful Contagion at Philada precludes Congress, I therefore beg leave to mention as the prevailing opinion, that you will recommend some place as a rallying point for the representatives of the people where they Can Resolve to proceed on the business of the Session. I write in haste from this place impressed with every sentiment of respect, and Confidence in your enlarged prudence, and far superior Judgment, while I have the honour to be with great Esteem and every good wish My Dear Sir Your Most obedt Hble Sert

R. Rutherford

ALS, DNA: RG 59, Miscellaneous Letters.

From James Abercrombie

Sir, Philada Octr 20th 1793.

The death of Dr Frederick Phile the late Naval Officer of this State, occasioning a vacancy in that department, I beg leave to offer myself a Candidate for the appointment.

I forbear to trouble your Excellency with testimonials in my favor, as I flatter myself those recommendations which upon my application for the Treasuryship of the Mint, I presented to Coll Hamilton, will operate with equal force on the present occasion.[1] I shall therefore only assure your Excellency, that If I am so happy as to obtain your approbation and patronage, my best abilities shall unremittingly be exerted, to discharge the duties of the office with fidelity and accuracy.[2] I have the honor to be, Your Excellency's, Most obedt hble Servt

Jas Abercrombie

ALS, DLC:GW.

1. Alexander Hamilton had enclosed the recommendations, which have not been identified, in his letter to GW of 11 April 1792.

2. Abercrombie did not receive this appointment.

From Frederick Augustus Conrad Muhlenberg

Providence Township, Montgomery County [Pa.]
Sir, Oct. 20th 1793.

Lt Col. Solomon Bush, who has the Honor of being personally acquainted with You intends solliciting for the Appointment of naval Officer, for the Port of Philada in the Room of Dr Phile deceased, & considering his Service & Sufferings during and since the late War, I take the Liberty of assuring You that I know no one whom I can more cheerfully recommend than him, & that I verily believe, as far as my Knowledge extends that he would give general Satisfaction to the Merchants of Philadelphia amongst whom he is well acquainted. I have the Honor to be with the most unfeigned Respect Sir Your most obedient humble Servant

Fredk A. Muhlenberg

ALS, DLC:GW.

From Oliver Wolcott, Jr.

Smiths House, Falls of Schuylkill [Pa.]

Sir,   October 20th 1793

I have had the honour to receive your Letter dated the 14th instant[1] and have lost no time in obtaining the best information in my power, on the several questions therein stated.

The malady with which the City is afflicted, has been progressive, from the time of your departure, untill Monday the 14th instant, at which time it had nearly extended through the City—Several small remissions have been observed during that period, all of which were confined to cool days, when the wind was in the northern quarter[2]—whenever the wind has shifted towards the South, the number of the sick & the mortality have invariably increased. On monday there was a slight fall of rain—which was succeeded by cool days and several frosty nights—the mortality of course greatly diminished and but few comparatively fell sick—the three last days have been more warm, and the unfavourable effects, are at present rather increasing.

From repeated observations it may be infered that the cause of the malady still exists—that its activity is increased by heat & diminished by cold—and that the City will not be purified and rendered safe, untill after heavy rains or severe frosts.

It was very lately Doct. Rush's opinion that the disorder was more *violent* & more *fatal,* than at the time of its first appearance in the City.

Nothing certain is known of the number of victims; for some time, information on this point was carefully concealed; but from *data* which cannot be very erroneous—I judge that more than four thousand persons, have died.

Mr Willing was for some time sick, but has recovered, Mr John Ross, has resided in the country, and is I presume well; Mr Sergeant & Colo. Franks are dead—several gentlemen of the name of Howell have died, & among them a relation of Mr Rawle who was much esteemed—the accountant of the War Department, has been indisposed, but he has recovered and is now in the Country.[3] There is no point on which the public opinion is more unsettled, than in respect to the degree of danger which attends any given position in the vicinity of Philadelphia. It is certain that some gentlemen of good sense and those not deficient in firmness on ordinary occasions, have removed from the villages and estates in the neighbourhood of the City, to more interior situations—a greater number who have not removed, remain at home compleatly insulated from society.

I have regularly obtained good information of the state of the City, and the adjoining places, and it is my opinion that the disorder is generally if not solely communicated by specific contagion—that its ravages have been confined to no age, sex, or temperament—and that it has affected those classes of citizens most extensively, who have been most exposed to intercou[r]se with each other—I mention in proof of this opinion, that six Clerks of the Treasury Department, seven persons employed by the Collector of the Customs—a number of Clerks in the different Banks and three persons in the Post Office have fallen victims—several others have been affected, who have recovered—being in the whole, a very great proportion of all those who have been exposed—A number of persons, belonging to, or resident in the Country, have contracted the disorder by occasional visits to the City—Mr Powel doubtless lost his life in consequence of a humane visit to his house in town, to provide for the accomodation of a favourite servant. The malady moreover appears to be contagious by having been constantly observed to extend and diverge, from infected places. though it is now spread nearly through the City, yet there are some neighbourhoods where it has not yet appeared.

There has all along been a considerable diversity of opinion, in respect to the cause, nature and manner of communicating the malady. some have supposed that it was generated in the City—certain facts have however, been recently stated to me, by men of indisputable honour, which leave no doubt on my mind that it was introduced by an American Vessell, with French passengers & property from Hispaniola—It has also been asserted on respectable authority, that there has been no instance of the disorder being communicated to any person, who has constantly resided out of the City. I must admit that of the numbers, who have died in the villages and places adjacent to the City, I have known of no instance where the person affected, had not visited the City—if the observation should be found true in the latitude it has been made, it would militate with the opinion, which I have advanced and would go far to prove, that a residence near the City, admitting the malady to continue, would be absolutely safe.

The Philadelphians will not abandon their present expectation, that the City will be purified and safe before the meeting of Congress, without painful reluctance—in that event it would be their wish and that of the people adjacent that Congress should convene, as near as possible to the City. Lancaster, Wilmington & Germantown have been mentioned—it is supposed that the latter place would under all circumstances afford the best accomodations.

I have made full enquiry & entertain no doubt that the town is free from contagion—it is certain, that at present, not an individual is affected with the prevailing malady.

I have conversed with a Majistrate of the place and am informed by him & other persons, that if events should render it necessary, every exertion will be made to accomodate Congress and the public Officers—the School House, with the adjoining buildings, may in my opinion, at a small expence, be fitted up & attired, so as to afford tolerable accomodations for the two houses & their immediate Officers.

I have called at the house of the Attorney General near Germantown, and was informed that he was at Lancaster, but was expected soon to return—it was suggested that your Letter had been recd and that measures had been taken for engaging a house, the result of which, were not known.[4] Col. Hamilton is in New Jersey, on his way to this place, I shall therefore retain the Letter to him, untill his arrival.[5] Genl Knox is I presume from the best information I can obtain, at Boston, to which place, I shall address the Letter transmitted to me by Mr Dandridge, which has been just received.[6]

It has been just told me, that Doct. Phile, the Naval Officer is dead; though unfounded reports are often circulated I fear that this is true. I have the honour to be with the most perfect respect Sir, your most obedt & humble servant

Oliver Wolcott Jr

ALS, DLC:GW; ADfS, CtHi: Oliver Wolcott, Jr., Papers.

1. The draft specifies that Wolcott received GW's letter "On the evening of the 17th instant."

2. The draft says "western quarter."

3. Jacob Roberts Howell (d. 1793), a lawyer, notary public, and city council-

man, was William Rawle's brother-in-law, having married in 1788 Elizabeth Burge (b. 1767), a sister of Rawle's wife, Sarah Coates Burge (1761–1824). Joseph Howell, Jr., served as accountant of the War Department from 1792 to 1795.

4. Wolcott was referring to GW's letter to Edmund Randolph of 30 September. See Randolph to GW, 22 Oct., for his efforts to engage a house for GW.

5. This was a duplicate of GW's letter to Alexander Hamilton of 25 September.

6. Wolcott was referring to GW's letter to Henry Knox of 15 October.

From Thomas FitzSimons

Sir   Philada 21. October 1793.

The death of Mr Phile the late Naval Officer of this district haveing left a vacancy in an important Office I beg leave to Call your attention to my worthy friend Mr Clymer on Whose Capacity for executeing the duties of that office it is Unnecessary for me to make any observation. he has for some time been determined on resigning the Appointment he at present holds and only waited till the business was properly Arranged and time was afforded to find a proper Sucessor.[1]

It would be presumption in me to Suggest any reasons that should induce the President to give him this appointment in preference to many others who will apply for it.

I will only take the liberty to add that it would gratify a Great Number of people in this City who are Among the most respectable And the Most Zealous Supporters of Government. With the Greatest respect I am Sir Yr Mo. hble Servt

Thos FitzSimons

ALS, DLC:GW.

1. George Clymer did not resign his post as supervisor of the revenue for Pennsylvania until around June 1794, and there is no evidence that he made any direct application to become naval officer at this time.

From John Graff

Sir,   [Pennsylvania] October 21. 1793

Your Excellency will no doubt before the receipt of this be informed of the death of the late naval Officer Fred. Phile—

Having had the honor to represent the Collector of the District of Pennsylvania (whose name is in the list inclosed) since the Year 1784 untill this date under the regulations of sd state & since under our happy Constitution I trust with Integrity am emboldened to sollicit a nomination for the Office above named[1]— Almighty God having visited the City of Philada with a great Calamity prevents me at this time to offer recommendations such as I hope would be satisfactory, the Citizen in the mercantile line being dispersed in this & neighboring States, shall take the liberty of forwarding further recommendations as soon as may be[2]—With great Respect & Esteem am Your Excellencys Most Obt huml. Servt

John Graff

ALS, DLC:GW.

John Graff (born c.1760), who served in the Philadelphia militia during the Revolutionary War, continued to work as a weigher and deputy collector of customs until 1811 or 1812.

1. Graff's application file contains three undated recommendations (two of which are labeled "No. 3" and "No. 5") reading (with slight variations of style): "The Subscribers recommend John Graff Dy Collr of the Distr[i]ct of Pennsylvania as capable & worthy of Trust to fill the office of Naval Officer, vacant by the Death of Fred. Phile late Naval Offr" (DLC:GW). Collector of Customs Sharp Delany appears as a signatory on the unnumbered recommendation.

Delany also wrote a separate letter to GW, dated 17 Nov.: "Mr John Graff being advised by his Friends to solicit for the Naval Office at his Request I take the Liberty of Informing Your Excellency, that he has acted as my Deputy for a Number of Years, and has conducted himself with Honesty and Ability" (DLC:GW).

2. Apparently, two recommendations were submitted with this letter, and Graff submitted additional recommendations with his letter to GW of 14 November. The three recommendations remaining in Graff's application file contain the names of ninety-eight individuals and firms. He did not, however, receive the appointment.

From Ludwell Lee and Roger West

Sir   Fairfax County [Va.] 21st Octr 1793

We do ourselves the honor of enclosing to you an address signed by about five hundred of the most respectable Landholders, Merchants, & Inhabitants of this County—It is with pleasure we execute the desire of our fellow Citizens in forwarding to you this token of their approbation esteem & confidence, so justly merited on your part, and so freely given on theirs. We have the honor to be with the highest respect Sir Yr most Obedient, Humble Servants

Ludwell Lee

R: West

LS, in Ludwell Lee's writing, DLC:GW.

Ludwell Lee (1760–1836), a son of Richard Henry Lee, was a lawyer who served three terms in the Virginia House of Delegates, 1787–90, and represented Prince William and Fairfax counties in the Virginia Senate, 1792–1800.

Enclosure
Address from Fairfax County, Va., Citizens

[Fairfax County, Va., c.21 October 1793]

To George Washington President of the United States of America

Whilst the people of America, are so generally signifying to you Sir, their perfect approbation of your Proclamation; enjoining on the part of the Citizens of the United States, a strict neutrality, towards the belligerent Powers of Europe;[1] we should have remained silent, under this general approbation, & not have troubled you, with our sentiments, did we not conceive, that the present crisis, calls loudly on all those, who feel for the dignity of their Government, to speak out, the language of their hearts—When foreigners, shall be so far forgetful, of the respect they owe, to the Sovereignty of the Community, in which they reside, as to threaten an appeal, to the Body of the People, from the decisions, & conduct of those, with whom the people have entrusted, that part of it, which relates to their foreign connections; & in despite of the public authority, prohibiting the contrary; shall arm & equip Vessels of war in our Ports, for the purpose of capturing the property of Nations with whom we are at Peace;[2] which things can only have for their object, internal confusion, and all the calamities, of external warfare; that a stop may be put, to proceedings so hurtful, & so dangerous, we think it the duty, of the Citizens, to let their Sentiments be publicly known—Impressed with this truth, we the Subscribers, Landholders & Inhabitants of Fairfax County, have presented ourselves before you, and beg leave to assure you; that, as in all your conduct as Presiding Majistrate of these United States, we have seen you pursuing, with firmness & propriety, the good of Mankind, & the solid glory, & interests of your Country; and in no instance, we conceive, more truly honorable to yourself, or more serviceable, to us, than in the conduct, you have caused to be pursued, towards the Nations of Europe now at war; we shall hold ourselves bound to oppose, all attempts that shall be made, to disturb the Peace, or injure the Independance, & dignity of the Government, over which you preside, by the machinations of foreigners, or the intemperate actions, of discontented Individuals, of our own Country—We trust, that in speaking thus, we do but proclaim, the Ideas of every well intentioned Citizen of America, for all have felt, & we trust, will long continue to feel, the blessings of an Administration, where wisdom, temper, & firmness, have so conspicuously presided.

Signed by about five hundred Inhabitants And by their desire forwarded by.[3]

Ludwell Lee
R: West

DS, DLC:GW; LB, DLC:GW. The DS is in Ludwell Lee's writing. This address was dated 22 Oct. when published in newspapers such as the *Baltimore Daily Intelligencer,* 2 November.

1. See Neutrality Proclamation, 22 April.

2. For the charge that French minister Edmond Genet had threatened to appeal some of GW's decisions to the people, see Genet to GW, 13 Aug., and n.4. For the controversy over the arming of French privateers, see memorandum from Alexander Hamilton, 15 May, and notes 1 and 3 to that document. A circular letter of 24 May from Secretary of War Henry Knox to the state governors had announced GW's prohibition of the practice (see Knox to GW, 24 May, n.2).

3. The 500 signatures are not on the DS. GW responded to this address in a letter to Lee and West of 24 October.

From Stephen Moylan

Sir   West Chester [Pa.] Octobr 21st 1793

the communication between the City and country is So much interupted that I am uncertain whether my Letter to the Secretary of State has ever reached him, I take the Liberty of inclosing a copy therof, that you Sir may Know the reason of my nonacceptance of the Office of Marshal which you was pleased to Offer to me[1]—an Office is now vacant by the death of Fred-rick Phyle naval Officer if you will please to confer it on me I will exert myself in fullfilling the duties of it Whether you think me worthy of this favor or not you may be assured Sir; it will make no alteration in the Sentiments of esteem and respect, which a long acquaintance with your virtues has indelibly impressed on the mind of Sir your obedient and much obliged humb. Servt

Stephen Moylan

ALS, DLC:GW.

1. In the enclosed copy of his letter to Thomas Jefferson of 19 Sept., Moylan wrote "that nothing but the narrowness of my circumstances makes me decline accepting this honorable office, I had but little time to gain information respecting its income if I thought the emoluments of it were at present Such, that with a Rigid Oeconomy I coud mentain my familly I most certainly woud accept of it, but from the little information I can procure, the income does not exceed 400 dollrs ⅌ annum—I hold an office under the State which brings me about that Sum, which with the product of a Small farm enables me to rub thoro Life in this country with decency it woud not do in the City." Moylan also asked that Jefferson "Lay this before the President" (DLC:GW). Jefferson's docket on the original letter indicates that it was received by him on 4 Nov. (*Jefferson Papers*, 27:137–38).

From Peter Muhlenberg

Sir   Philadelphia County. Octobr 21st 93

Having understood that a vacancy has taken place in the naval Office, by the Death of Dr Phile I presume to sollicit the appointment to that Office, provided The President conceives me qualified for it—I will not trouble The President with enumerating the motives which occasion the solicitation, and will only beg leave to mention, That if I had not been prevented by the Indian War, from removing my Family to the Western Country, where I have some property in Lands—I should not have become troublesome with my solicitation—But as I am situated at present; not having added to, but diminishd my little fortune during the War, and not having it in my power to return with propriety to the only occupation or calling I was brought up to[1]—I wish to serve my Country as well as myself in some way or other, untill I can with safety retire with my Family to the Ohio. I have the Honor to be with the highest Respect Sir your most Obedt humble Servant

P: Muhlenberg

ALS, DLC:GW. John Peter Gabriel Muhlenberg (1746–1807), a former Revolutionary War general and vice-president of Pennsylvania, was at this time a Pennsylvania congressman. He did not get this appointment, but he was named collector of customs for Philadelphia in 1801.

1. Muhlenberg had been a Lutheran minister before the war.

From Timothy Pickering

Sir,   Philadelphia Oct. 21. 1793.

I have been honoured with your letter of the 14th relatively to the fever which has raged so fatally in this city. "Accurate information" of its state it may be impossible to obtain. But I am warranted by Doctor Rush's opinion, grounded on his own practice and the information of other physicians, *that there is an abatement of it by at least one half.* For a number of days preceeding the last ten days, I was frequently at Dr Rush's, when his house was always thronged with applicants for assistance or advice: I sat an hour with him yesterday, and not one new application was made. One of his young men said that on Saturday a French physican of the hospital at Bush-Hill, told him they had then but three dangerous cases there.[1]

About *Three Thousand* persons have died in the city and suburbs, since the beginning of August; of whom perhaps 2800 may have died of the yellow fever. Of the persons you mention by name, Mr Willing & Mr John Ross are alive and well. Mr J. Sergeant, Mr Howell a lawyer, brother in law to Mr Rawle,[2] & Colo. Franks, are dead; as well as many other valuable citizens. Mr Powell's death was long since announced in the news-papers.

Of the multitude that have died, I believe full three fourths have fallen victims to bad practice, and absolute neglect. This neglect was such, that nearest relatives have abandoned each other. Many physicians persisted in the *stimulant* plan of cure, against the evidence of their senses. Yet at length, when themselves attacked by the disease, they have resorted to Dr Rush's mode— bleeding and purging. One of them (Dr Currie) in particular, in a publication of the 17th of September, pronounced bleeding & purging in the yellow fever, to be *certain death.* He has lately fallen sick, and rescued himself from the grave by *bleeding & purging!*[3] Some others (probably most or all now) bleed & purge but either inadequately, or counteract their effects by then giving bark and laudanum! To this last mentioned practice, the pious Dr Sproat, one of his daughters, his son the Major (formerly aid to Genl Hand) and his wife, have lately fallen sacrifices.[4] In short, multitudes have been the unhappy victims of *ignorance* & *pride.* Dr Kuhn early pronounced the disease to be *putrid* & *debilitating.* Dr Stevens (who attended Colo. Hamilton) confirmed his errors: and they had many followers.[5] Kuhn soon fled to a safe distance from the city: but has left his first opinion uncontradicted. That Rush's opinion was right, is confirmed by writers of indisputable authority, as well as large experience here. He, it is true, has lost a number of patients: but worn down with fatigue, he was not able to see divers of them at critical periods. From observation in my own family, of those who died as well as those who lived, I am *perfectly convinced* that terrible as the disease has proved, the cure of it, in common subjects, is *short* and *easy, if no time be lost in bleeding and purging,* according to the degree of inflamation. In a letter I lately wrote you, I mentioned the death of one of my sons:[6] the other death in my family was of a maid servant. Eight have had the disease. Besides which, Mrs P. & myself, without being confined, have experienced *new sensations* which we can attribute only to the contagion, of the fever. On my return from Canada, I found, unexpectedly, my family in the city; and a son and servant sick. Under such circumstances, it was impossible for me to find a house in the country for their reception, and I could not abandon them. And when we had all been exposed to the contagion, I feared to remove from the physician on whom I could depend. Numbers have removed with the infection, and died in the country. This in a few instances has happened in Germantown: but the disease has not otherwise been there.

If this city should remain infected till December, Germantown will not furnish accommodations for Congress: 'tis *crouded* with citizens of Philadelphia. Reading is a large village, containing several hundred houses, with a large courthouse that might do for the house of Representatives; and probably some room elsewhere in the town might be found for the Senate. I have several times thought on the ensuing session of Congress; but indeterminately on the safety of their meeting here the beginning of December. Dr Rush thinks that by that time the city will be free of the contagion, here and there a solitary instance excepted, from which there can scarcely be any hazard.[7] This is a well known fact—That a considerable encrease of cold, even during a single day, has constantly been marked by a abatement of the number of deaths. If then in the height of the contagion, its effects were suspended by a day's cold, we may reasonably conclude that a continuance of cold with rains, which we may expect in November, will *destroy it*. And this is Dr Rush's opinion.

I do not know what sentiments are entertained relative to the meeting of Congress. I will see Judge Peters and the Attorney General, and transmit you their opinions by the next post. I will afterwards write you weekly or oftener on the state of the disease, from which you will be able to determine what course to pursue. But I would entreat you not to return hither yourself so soon as the beginning of next month—nor to any place in the neighbourhood for you would be illy accommodated. I am with the most sincere respect, sir Your obedt & humble servant

Timothy Pickering

ALS, DLC:GW; ADfS, MHi: Pickering Papers.

1. Jean Devèze (1753–1829), a doctor trained at Bordeaux and Paris who had spent many years as a military surgeon in Saint Domingue, was one of the refugees from that island who arrived at Philadelphia in early August. He later published *An Enquiry into, and Observations upon the Causes and Effects of the Epidemic Disease, Which Raged in Philadelphia from the Month of August till towards the Middle of December, 1793* (Philadelphia, 1794) and, after his return to France, *Traité de la Fièvre Jaune* (Paris, 1820).

2. The draft has "Jacob Howell."

3. In a letter addressed to Andrew Brown, editor of the *Federal Gazette*, and dated 17 Sept., Dr. William Currie (1754–1828), a founder of the Philadelphia College of Physicians and member of the American Philosophical Society, argued that two fevers were present in Philadelphia: "the infectious or yellow fever" and "the common remittent or fall fever." He declared that the mode of treatment advised by Dr. Benjamin Rush was proper only with the remittent fever and meant "certain death" when applied to the yellow fever (*Federal Gazette and Philadelphia Daily Advertiser*, 17 Sept.). Later, however, his *Treatise on the Synochus Icteroides, or Yellow Fever: As It Lately Appeared in the City of Philadelphia* (Philadelphia, 1794) stated that "Blood-letting generally afforded relief in all cases, when the activity of the arterial system was evident," and endorsed "mercurial purges" in conjunction with the blood-letting (pp. 40–42).

4. James Sproat (1722–1793), a graduate of Yale College in 1743, served as minister of Philadelphia's Second Presbyterian Church from 1769 until his death on 18 October. His daughter Anne [Nancy] Sproat (c.1767–1793) died on 23 September. William Sproat (1756–1793), James's son, served as an officer in the Pennsylvania Regiments of the Continental army from Janu-

ary 1777 to November 1783, rising in rank from lieutenant to captain. He served as aide-de-camp and brigade major for Brig. Gen. Edward Hand during the Sullivan expedition in 1779 and at Yorktown in 1781. After the war, William Sproat became a merchant in Philadelphia; he died on 11 October. Maria Thompson Sproat (1767–1793), a daughter of John Thompson of Cecil County, Md., had married William Sproat in October 1792.

At this point on the draft, Pickering wrote and struck out the following: "One German Clergyman [John Winkhause of the German Calvinist Church] & two Catholic Priests [Francis A. Fleming and Laurence Graessl] have also died. Mr [Joseph] Pilmore is sick but, recovering. Mr [Robert] Blackwell about a week since went from the city to Gloucester where he has fallen sick."

5. Dr. Adam Kuhn's view of the "Putrid Fever" was published in the *Federal Gazette* of 11 Sept. as an extract of a letter dated 7 Sept. and signed A.K. In a postscript to that letter, printed in the *Gazette* of 12 Sept., Kuhn cited Dr. Edward Stevens in support of the application of cold baths. Stevens's opinion about the fever was given fuller expression in a letter to Dr. John Redman, published in the *Gazette* of 16 September. He recommended treating the disease with rest and efforts to mitigate the symptoms, and strongly opposed the use of "drastic cathartics."

6. See Pickering to GW, 15 October.

7. On this date Benjamin Rush noted in a letter to his wife, "If the weather continues to increase in coldness, and above all if we should have a few days' heavy rain joined with it, the disease will be driven from the city in a few weeks. A few scattered cases may perhaps exist from carelessness or accident during the winter" (Butterfield, *Rush Letters,* 2:720–21).

From Richard Dobbs Spaight

Sir   North Carolina Newbern 21st Octr 1793

In September I received a letter from the Collector of Wilmington informing me that the Captain of the Privateer, Vanqueur de Bastille had carried his prize the British Sloop Providence, down to the bar of Cape Fear river and had there shifted her guns &c. from on board the Vanqueur de Bastille to the prize sloop, proceeded to sea with her and was then cruizing off that Harbour, the Schooner was sent back again to Wilmington.[1]

I felt myself extremely mortified that a proceeding of that nature should take place in any port within this State after I had taken every step in my power to prevent it.

In pursuance of the instructions received from the Secretary of War of the 16th and 21st of August I immediately dispatched orders to the major of New Hanover Militia, to order the Vanqueur de Bastile to leave the port. and that should the aforesaid Sloop or any other privateer fitted out of the United States send or bring in any prize or prizes into the port of Wilmington, to secure her or them to be delivered to the former Owners, or to the Consul of the Nation to whom they belonged and to order the privateer or privateers to depart the port immediately.[2]

On the 15th instant I received letters from Col: Benjm. Smith of Brunswick County and Major Wright of New Hanover informing me that the said Sloop had arrived at that port, and brought with her a Spanish brig her prize, that they had agreable to my orders made some dispositions to Secure the prize. but had been prevented by the officious interposition of some evil disposed persons in Wilmington who sent down a boat in the night to give Captain Hervieux information of their intentions, who in consequence of it sent his prize to sea, where she remained about eight miles to the southward of the Bar; that Colonel Smith had given orders to Captain Hervieux to leave the port. who gave in excuse for his not complying with them, that he had put in there in distress and could not go to sea, till his people had recovered, and his Vessel was refitted, together with some other reasons mentioned in his letters to Coln. Smith and Major Wright.[3] From the deposition marked No. 2 it appeared to me that the Vessel was really in a distressed Situation⟨.⟩ I therefore wrote to those Gentlemen that as the instructions I had received did not comprehend a case of that nature that they might permit her to remain in port for such time as was absolutely necessary to refit her for sea and then to compell her to depart—as the prize was without the port on the high seas I did not conceive myself at liberty to give orders to send after her. indeed from her force (she carries 8 Guns and from 20 to 30 Men) it could not be easily done as there is no armed vessel in the State, but I instructed them that if she should return into port again to use every means in their power to take and secure her for the Original Owners.[4]

Captain Hervieux previous to his receiving the information from Wilmington had put on board of the revenue Cutter Captain Cook a chest containing (it is said) betwe⟨en⟩ thirty and forty thousand dollars which he had taken out of the Spanish prize on its arrival at Wilmington it was seized by the revenue Officers and placed in the hands of the Mareshall. I have wrote to Major Wright to give the Mareshal orders to keep the money secure till proper application is made for it by the former Owners or the Consul for Spain and if no such application should be made, untill such time as I should receive further instructions from you respecting what is to be done with it.[5]

The Schooner Vanqueur de Bastille lies at one of the Wharfs at Wilmington quite dismantled and unrigged and no person on board of her who can be made to comply with that part of your instructions of obliging her to leave the port under these circumstances I should be glad to know what is to be done with her.

As this business is a national one it is expected that the General Government will pay every expence attending it at the same time it may be requisite that this State should advance in the first instance the monies necessary for the Amunition pay and subsistance of such part of the Militia as may be called into service to execute the instructions of the President of the United States. I shall therefore apply to the Council to authorize me to draw on the treasury of this State for such sums as may be wanted. I shall likewise be glad to be informed in what manner the State is to be reimbursed by the United States, the monies which may be occasionally advanced.

I really feel myself ashamed of the Conduct of the New hanover Militia as related by Major Wright. I shall direct him to take such steps as are pointed out by the laws of the State to punish them for their disobedience of his orders.[6]

That you may be fully acquainted with the real state of the Case I have sent you enclosed copies of Col: Smith and Major Wrights letters and of the other papers which accompanied them. I have the Honor to be with due respect Sir Your Mo. Obt Servant

Richd D. Spaight

LB, Nc-Ar: Governors' Letterbooks.

1. See James Read to Spaight, 6 Sept. (Nc-Ar: Governors' Letterbooks). The *Providence,* captured by *Vainqueur de Bastille* in June, was fitted out as the French privateer *L'Aimée Marguerite.*

2. Secretary of War Henry Knox's circular letter to the governors of 16 Aug. directed them to order an immediate departure from their ports of the privateers that had been fitted out in American ports (including the *Vainqueur de Bastille*) and to seize any prizes that they brought in. His circular letter of 21 Aug. directed that the prizes be restored to their owners (see Knox to Tobias Lear, 17 Aug., n.1).

Spaight wrote Maj. Thomas Wright, who was also sheriff of New Hanover County, on 16 Sept.: "In June last I wrote a letter to the Colonel of New Hanover County containing sundry instructions respecting the fitting out of armed vessels in the port of Wilmington to act as privateers on behalf of the parties at War; But from a late occurence which has happened at that place and which I have been informed of by the Collector, I am sorry to find that my orders on that head have been quite unattended to. Under these circumstances I feel myself under the necessity of applying to some other Officer of that County (for it would be useless to give further orders to a man who has already disobeyed those which he has received) to prevent if possible any other acts which may tend to a violation of the neutrality which the United States have embraced and to carry into effect as far as in our power the instructions of the Executive of the United States respecting this important object, I have therefore thought proper to address myself to you and to request that you would undertake the business and carry into effect as far as you possibly can the different instructions which shall be communicated to you on this head.

"No Vessel whatever must be allowed to be fitted out for the purpose of acting as a privateer on behalf of any of the parties at War—should any attempt of the kind be made you will with the aid of such part of the militia of the County as you may deem necessary seize upon the Vessel or Vessels and keep them in safety till further orders, giving me at the same time information in writing with a particular statement of the facts.

"No armed vessel which has been or shall be originally fitted out in any port of the Unites States as a cruizer or privateer by either of the parties at War is to have asylum in any ports of the United States—and in case of any vessel within the foregoing description should arrive in the port of Wilmington you will order her to depart immediately, and in case of refusal you will take effectual measures to oblige her to depart. force is not to be resorted to untill every proper effort has been previously made to procure the early departure without it.

"And in case any such Vessel shall have sent or brought subsequent to the 5th of August last or should hereafter bring or send any prize or prizes into the port of Wilmington, you will with the aid of the Militia secure such prize or prizes for the purpose of restoring them to the former Owner."

Spaight finished by specifically directing Wright's attention to the case of the *Vainqueur de Bastille* and her prize, and by directing him to keep good accounts of the expenses, which would be "born by the General Government" (Nc-Ar: Governors' Letterbooks).

3. In addition to describing his unsuccessful efforts to secure the prize ship, Benjamin Smith's letter to Spaight of 11 Oct. pointed out that in New Hanover County "the right of their Officer to order them out has been questioned," and asked what punishment he could apply if "the infection" should spread to his county. He also requested the governor's "command respecting the Privateer & Prize," noting that the privateer could easily be taken—the captain having declared "that he cannot go, or oblige his men to go out in a Vessel that he is sure would sink"—while the prize was anchored within sight

of land. "The Captain has hopes that under his particular circumstances you will permit him to bring her in—Whether you will think his case not included in the Instruction of the Executive of the United States & that as the Citizen of an allied friendly power he has a right to comfort & Shelter in our Port when in distress must be left to your own wisdom. . . .From the Inhabitants of Wilmington I apprehend no exertion can be expected" (Nc-Ar: Governors' Correspondence).

Thomas Wright's letter to Spaight of 12 Oct. explained that after he "Warned the officers of Militia in Town to have in readiness 25 Men to go down the River" as soon as "necessaries" could be provided, "only four persons obeyed the Orders given manay of them declaring they would not render any assistance in Such a case." Even had he obtained a sufficient crew, however, the prize would have escaped, as the French captain was warned by a Wilmington citizen. "I hope your Excellency will deem it expedient to check by Proclamation such Conduct . . . otherwise it will be useless here to make any efforts to Suppress any Acts whatsoever inconsistent with our duty as a Neutral Port." Wright went on the describe the seizure from the privateer captain of a chest which the captain's lawyers were attempting to reclaim. "I have thought it my duty to say agreeable to your Orders that as it is undoubtedly a part of the Prize, and as the former Owners are Confined so that no delivery can be made to them, it must be delivered to the orders of the Consul of Spain" (Nc-Ar: Governors' Correspondence).

The prize was the Spanish brig *San Josef,* or *San José* (see Josef de Jaudenes and Josef Ignacio de Viar to Thomas Jefferson, 26 Dec., *Jefferson Papers,* 27:625–28, and Bee, *Reports of Cases,* 29–34).

The French commander, François Henri Hervieux (born c.1767), wrote Smith on 7 Oct. and then sent him a second letter of that date, conveying the same information but adding a stronger protest of the government's policy, to be substituted for the first. The "other reasons" were the seizure by "the Officers of the Customs or others the Servants of the fœderal Government" of a trunk containing his commission and dispatches as well as some $30,000 to $40,000 belonging to himself and his crew, without the restoration of which he was unwilling to sail (Nc-Ar: Governors' Correspondence). No letter from Hervieux to Wright has been identified.

4. In the deposition, dated 4 Oct., Drs. Nathaniel Hill and James Larogue asserted that "but two able bodied Seaman remained in health" on board *L'Aimée Marguerite;* ship carpenters John Telfair and William Keddie testified that the ship was in need of structural repair; and mariner Joseph Brown declared "that the Jib is unfit for use, & that in general the Sails and Rigging are in such a Situation that the Vessel is unfit to proceed to Sea without fresh Supplies thereof" (Nc-Ar: Governors' Correspondence). Spaight's instructions regarding *L'Aimée Marguerite* were given in a letter to Wright of 17 Oct., in which he added, "if the prize should attempt to return if possible have her secured" (Nc-Ar: Governors' Letterbooks).

5. Capt. William Cooke commanded the revenue cutter *Diligence.* The directions about the money were contained in Spaight's letter to Wright of 17 Oct. (Nc-Ar: Governors' Letterbooks). The trunk was in the possession of

the deputy marshal at Wilmington, John Blakeley (d. 1797). See Spaight to Blakeley, 31 Oct., Nc-Ar: Governors' Letterbooks; and Blakeley to Spaight, 3 Nov., Nc-Ar: Governors' Correspondence.

6. In Spaight's letter to Wright of 17 Oct. he had written: "as to the Militia under your command refusing to obey your Orders; I think either the laws of the State or those of the Union sufficient to punish them for their neglect or refusal, see the 11th Sec: of the Militia law of this State and the 28th Chap: of the 1st Session of the 2nd Congress" (Nc-Ar: Governors' Letterbooks).

The 11th section of the 1786 militia law prescribed a fine of ten pounds for those "who shall neglect or refuse on Call or Alarm given, to appear at such Times and Places as shall be appointed by his Captain or other Officer," and allowed courts-martial for more serious refusals (James Iredell, *Laws of the State of North-Carolina* [Edenton, N.C., 1791], 594–95). The 28th chapter, "An Act to provide for calling forth the Militia to execute the laws of the Union, suppress insurrections and repel invasions," 2 May 1792, provided that militia who failed to obey a call-up by the president were subject to forfeiture of pay and to courts-martial (1 *Stat.* 264–65).

To William Augustine Washington

My dear Sir:—   [Mount Vernon, 21 October 1793]

Your letter of the 16th came to my hands the 19th and the Post by which this goes is the first that has occurred since.[1]

As one of Mr. Stone's carpenters is a White lad, and two of them but green hands, I decline employing them,—I have already more white people about my house than are governed properly in my absence—tho' for the sake of getting an honest, skilful & industrious person to superintend my carpenters I would have added one more,—Two is too many; especially as one of the Negroe's (as well as the White lad) can have but little knowledge of the trade they profess.[2]

I thank you for the trouble you have had in this business and with much truth am Your affect'd friend and Uncle

GEO WASHINGTON

L, printed in Stan V. Henkels, *Revolutionary Manuscripts and Portraits* (catalog 683; 1892), item 678.

1. The letter of 16 Oct. has not been found.

2. For William Augustine Washington's effort to find a carpenter for GW, see his letter to GW of 3 Sept., and n.1 to that document.

From Joseph Wharton

sir   Philada October 21st 1793.

My condition in life, through unmerited sufferings, which brought upon me the sacrifice of faithfull industry for many years, deprived me of the means of supporting an aged wife, and five Children—whose Characters are, in just estimation of my fellow Citizens, eminent for their virtue, and respectability.[1]

It is not for the honor of Truth, that my failings should be withheld from your knowledge, nor do I suppose, that the conduct of a Citizen, who once partook of your esteem, hath been undiscovered to you. But, as the great Doctor Franklin said, "that part of a Truth, is sometimes worse, than the whole Truth"[2]—so may my infirmities have been exagerated, without those extenuations, which Charity would have mollified, and which good Men deplored. Those sufferings, and the consequent distresses to *those,* who ought *not* to have felt them—drove me to a temporary excess—which, however injurious to a once well earned reputation, brought it's own remedy, by the severest contrition. It hath God! to grant me fortitude, to withstand the only temptation, that ever sullied my fair fame: and I have a well founded hope, that it will never revisit me, either to my friends anxiety, or my own dishonor. There are Men Sir, whose afflictions, cramp their virtues—whose confidence becomes annihilated, and constrains them to acts, which their very Souls abhor. This, unfortunately, has been my case. For, having formerly had the closest connection, with most of the trading Gentlemen in the United States, as well as with the principal Merchants in Europe—and foreseeing no prospect of reganing my station in the Commercial line, nor of aiding those Ties, who are nearest to me—*I fell.* It is not, nor ever was, the lot of humanity, in such scenes of complicated misery, which I have endured for nineteen years, "to bring the mind, instantly, to its' condition": It was not mine. For it requires time, and an exertion, not common, and scarcely known, to recover a firm dignity of conduct, and lament over a fatal secession from it.

I have had the honor of a small correspondance with your Excelle⟨ncy⟩ respecting our quondam friend Colonel Mercer, and I have enjoyed the felicity of your favor at my House—on board my Ship, and at the Tables of your particular acquaintance, in this *once* blessed City.[3] nor have my principles been adverse, but on the contrary, always flow from the purest motives, to the sacred Rights of my Countrey—which in fact, was the cause of my Ruin.

Thus having presumed to lay my circumstance, and my change of life, before your rational and humane disposition—I beg leave to offer myself a Candidate for the Naval Office of the District, vacant by the death of Mr Frederick Phile. And, if it is expedient, that a powerfull recommendation, should preced appointment; I have not the least doubt of procuring signatures pleasing to your Excellency, and honorable to myself—nor shall competent security be unobtained from those, who are equally wealthy as they zealously disposed to serve me. I foresee but one obstacl⟨e⟩ in my progress of Recommendation, and that is, the extremely scattered residence of my fellow citizens in this calamitou⟨s⟩ affliction.[4]

I beg leave to sollicit your favorable acceptance of my application, and to pardon the freedom of this tedious narrative— which is written solely, that I may recover you⟨r⟩ esteem, favor and confidence. I am Sir, with the grest Respect Your most ob: hl. Ser⟨vt⟩

Jo. Wharton

ALS, DLC:GW.

Joseph Wharton (1733/4–1816) of Philadelphia was a Quaker merchant who suffered large losses in the American Revolution.

1. Wharton married Sarah Tallman (b. 1740) in 1760. Their five surviving unmarried children were Thomas Parr Wharton (1763–1802); Nancy (Ann) Wharton (1770–c.1852), who married James Cowles Fisher in 1804; Sarah Wharton (1772–1847), who married Jonathan Robeson in 1795; Martha Wharton (1774–1861); and Eliza Wharton (1781–1869).

2. Wharton may have had in mind Benjamin Franklin's "Remarks on a late Protest against the Appointment of Mr. Franklin as Agent for this Province," in which he wrote: "A falshood may destroy the innocent; so may *part of a truth* without *the whole;* and a mixture of truth and falshood may be full as pernicious" (Franklin, *Political, Miscellaneous, and Philosophical Pieces* . . . [London, 1779], 413).

3. GW's diary entry for 12 Oct. 1774 notes that he "Dined at Mr. Josh Whartons" (*Diaries*, 3:285). For the correspondence regarding Col. George Mercer, see GW to Wharton, 15 Sept. 1779.

4. Wharton did not receive the appointment.

From Nathan Beers

Sir   New Haven 22 Octr 1793

Among the number of Persons who have offered themselves as Candidates for the Office of Collector for this Port, I beg leave to mention to your Excellency my desire of that appointment— As by the Laws of These States the present duty of the Collector devolves on the Surveyor, I have been lead to suppose that the appointment will not be made untill the Meeting of Congress in December next, at which time I hope to forward such information respecting my Charracter and Services, as I flatter myself will have some weight with your Excellency, if they do not I cannot wish or desire the appointment. I am with due respect your Excellencys most Obedient & Humble Servant

Nathan Beers

ALS, DLC:GW; Copy, CtNhHi. The copy lacks the dateline and salutation.

Nathan Beers (1753-1849), a Connecticut paymaster during the Revolutionary War, retired from the army in June 1783 but served for a time as agent for settling regimental accounts. He was a charter member of the Connecticut Society of the Cincinnati and in 1793 its treasurer. He did not receive the desired appointment.

From Archibald Engle

Sir   Philada County Oct. 22, 1793.

The office of naval officer for the District of pennsylvania being vacant by the death of the much & justly regretted Dr Phile—I beg leave to offer myself to your Excellencys notice for that office—I also beg leave to inform you—that I have acted as Deputy naval officer of this District since the adoption of the present Constitution & for several Years before under the State Government—and flatter myself I have gained the favor & good will of the mercantile Interest & Such officers of Government as Superintend this office—any of whom I believe would cheerfully declare & approve of my abilities for the due & faithful discharg⟨e⟩ of the duties of the office—I am Sir wi⟨th⟩ Sentiments of the greatest respect your Excellencys Most obedient & very hble s⟨ert⟩

Archibald Engle

ALS, DLC:GW.

Archibald Engle (d. 1796) had been a clerk in Frederick Phile's office since about 1783 (see Engle affidavit, 29 July 1789, DLC:GW). He was not appointed naval officer, and at the time of his death he was a deputy collector of the revenue for the district of Pennsylvania.

From Samuel Hanson (of Samuel)

Sir   Alexandria [Va.], Octr 22d 1793
    Finding that the Emoluments of my Office (about 400 Dollars per annum) are, with the utmost Economy, entirely inadequate to the support of my family, I am constrained to quit Alexandria; and mean to give in my resignation the 15th next month.[1]
    I thought it necessary to inform you of my intention, in order that my Successor may be appointed against that day.
    Mr James McRea means to become a Candidate for the place.[2] In favour of that Gentleman, I take the liberty of adding my public testimony to the recommendations from many others which he will have the honour to lay before you. with perfect respect and Esteem, I am Sir your most obedient Servant
                                        S. Hanson of Saml

ALS, DNA: RG 59, Miscellaneous Letters.
    1. Hanson was surveyor for the port of Alexandria.
    2. See James Mease McRea to GW, 23 October. James Mease McRea (d. 1809) acted for several years as Virginia's searcher for the port of Alexandria. He had applied unsuccessfully for the position of surveyor in June 1789.

From Edmund Randolph

Sir   Spencer's [Germantown, Pa.] October 22. 1793.
    On my return from Lancaster, I found, that Major Franks had agreed to let you have his house. But the terms are excessive; being no less than 150£ per annum, or for a shorter period, not under six months, at the same rate. Except a looking-glass or two, and a few pictures, he will not suffer any of the furniture to remain; tho' I have prevailed upon his agent to permit a couple of beds and some chairs and tables to continue, until you can accommodate yourself from some other quarter. But I have made no conclusive bargain; leaving this and the other house, which

I mentioned in my last letter, and adjoins the school-house lot, free for your choice.[1] Dr Bensel declines renting his house.[2]

The best road from the main Baltimore road to German Town is from Darby to the *black-horse* at the seven mile stone, on the Lancaster road: from thence to Righter's ferry on Skuylkill, which is about two miles from German Town.

We are flattered with a report, that the cold weather has given a stroke to the fever; but the authority, upon which it is circulated, is not conclusive with me. I have the honor, sir, to be, with the highest respect, and sincere attachment yr mo. ob. serv.

Edm: Randolph.

ALS, DLC:GW.

1. Randolph's letter to GW of 14 Oct. has not been found. GW's accounts for 22 Nov. record, "Contingt Exps. pd Wm Bringhurst, sent by Mr. Randolph express to Colo. Franks at Nazareth with a letter relative to renting his house in Germn town for the Presdt [$]15.67" (Household Accounts; see also Account Book, 2 Sept. 1793–4 April 1794, DLC:GW). The Franks house, at 5442 Germantown Avenue, is now known as the Deshler-Morris House and is preserved by the National Park Service. Isaac Franks (1759–1822) served during the Revolutionary War in the quartermaster department and as an ensign in the 7th Massachusetts Regiment. After the war, he became a broker at Philadelphia, and he became colonel of the Philadelphia County militia in 1794.

GW recorded in his account book for 26 March 1794 that he paid Franks $75.56 "in full for house rent &c. at Germantown" (Household Accounts). The house near the schoolhouse evidently was that belonging to Frederick Herman (see Randolph to GW, 28 Oct., and n.2 to that document). GW stayed there briefly before he took up residence at Franks's house.

2. Randolph most likely was referring to Dr. Charles Bensell (1725–1795), whose house was at the corner of Germantown Avenue and School House Lane.

From John Fitzgerald

Sir   Alexandria [Va.] Octor 23d 1793

Hearing this Morning that the Surveyor of this District was about to resign,[1] I could not in justice to the Individual, or my own sense of propriety in the Office which I have the honor to hold, forbear solliciting your attention to Mr Vincent Gray; who was Mr Lee's Deputy & continues to be mine[.][2] his constant & Vigilant attention, his strict impartiallity, & his knowledge of the business, entitle him in my estimation to a decided preference to any who may claim this appointment, & I will venture to say that in the performance of the duties of his office, he has constantly had the most minute regard to the public good, whilst in the other hand his Deportment has been such as to give the highest possible satisfaction to the Mercantile Interest with which of course the business was transacted[.][3] Added to this the business will in future be under the same Roof, which is the Mode in every large Seaport to the Northward, & will prevent an amazing delay to Owners & Masters of Ships, who often have, after their business with the Collector is done, to seek for a length of time after the Surveyor from whom they have nothing to get but a Certificate of admeasurement, & the fees of the Surveyor at this Port are inadequate to a constant attention to that duty.

If any doubts should remain on your mind respecting this application, I have only to request that you would lay it before the immediate Head of the department who is soon to meet you, & I am persuaded is well acquainted with the merits of this Gentleman, & will by his observations strengthen the subject of my request.[4] With most perfect Esteem I have the honor to be Sir your mo. Obedt Servant

John Fitzgerald

ALS, DLC:GW.

1. See Samuel Hanson to GW, 22 October.

2. Fitzgerald was collector for the port of Alexandria. Gray wrote GW on this date: "Being informed that Colo. Hanson intends to resign his office as Surveyor of this District, I take the liberty, from my knowledge of the duties of that Department, to offer my self as his Successor, should you think me qualified to execute the duties of that office" (ALS, DLC:GW).

3. A letter of this date signed by thirty-three Alexandria citizens and mercantile firms informed GW: "We the Subscribers beg leave to mention that Mr Vincent Gray (who since the commencement of the Fœderal Government has acted as Deputy Collector) is by his knowledge in that Line of Business, as well as by his good Conduct in every Respect, well qualified to fill that office, and that we humbly conceive the Appointment of him thereto, will greatly conduce to the Ease & Facility with which mercantile Business may be conducted in this place" (LS, DLC:GW).

4. Fitzgerald wrote to Secretary of the Treasury Alexander Hamilton on 20 Nov. to announce that he had given a temporary appointment as surveyor to Gray. He added, "The President will of course have some conversation with you on the subject of filling up this vacancy. Mr. Gray has been strongly recommended for that purpose; as you must have a knowledge of his talents and assiduity for some years past, I shall only assure you, that, in my opinion, the appointment of him will not only tend to give general mercantile satisfaction here, but also to the stability and perhaps the increase of Revenue" (*Hamilton Papers,* 15:403).

From Samuel Fraunces

Hond Sir   Philada 23d October 1793

I received your letter last Evening[1]—and it gives me the greatest Satisfaction that my conduct meets your approbation—was any accident to happen in the Famely it would not be for want of my care and attention I strictly adhere to your directions in every point—The House is clean and ready for your return and every thing in proper order—I long to see you home where I think you will be as safe as any where—as our Neibourhood is entirely clear of any infection—The Fever still continues to abate in the City but rages in Southwark & other out parts—You mention if any of the Famely should be taken ill to take advice which cannot be done as there i⟨s⟩ no Person of any consequence left but I hope we shall want none as your direction is quite sufficient—several Famelys however begin to return as it is thought they may with Safety—I Knew that the President lent Mr Osborn Money[2] & in consequence made an enquiry before I received your Letter, & found none but fifteen dollrs with his distressed Wife which She took to the Hospital with her his Trunk and some of his Cloaths are here which I detained untill I heard from you—The Trunk is locked what is in it I do not know[3]—Mrs Emerson is well and gives her duty to Madam but She is much oppressed in Spirits— Yr dutifull Servt

Samuel Fraunces

ALS, DLC:GW.

1. This letter has not been found.

2. On 9 Sept. William Osborne, a steward in GW's household who died during the yellow fever epidemic, had been given a loan of $100 "by order of the President, to be repaid in one year" (Household Accounts; see also Account Book, 2 Sept. 1793–4 April 1794, DLC:GW).

3. Mrs. Osborne subsequently complained that things had been taken from Osborne's trunk and indicated doubts about Fraunces's honesty (see Mrs. William Osborne to GW, 7 June 1794, DLC:GW).

From Richard Henry Lee

Dear Sir,   Alexandria [Va.] Octr 23d 1793

Having been informed that you designed to go northward in a few days, and finding Mrs Lees recovery to be too slow for the purpose of seeing you at Mount Vernon as we travelled homewards;[1] I had fixed on this day, with my Son Ludwell to pay our respects to you. But, to my very great mortification and disappointment, I was attacked with a fever last Night, the consequence of the influenza that has afflicted me for some days past; and which deprives me of the happiness that I this day proposed to myself. It realy gives me infinite concern to find, even a few, for I am sure they are very few; who appear disposed to disturb the peace of our country under the feigned pretext of favoring the cause of liberty in France. I call it feigned because I think that a very careless Observer of what passes, must have seen, for some time past, that the Contest in France has been less for liberty than for Jacobinism or Anarchy, to favor the views of ambition and avarice. As well might it be said that supporting O. Cromwell was defending the cause of liberty, when he had destroyed it by erecting a despotism in his own country! But the very Men who talk in favor of french liberty acknowledge our inability to go to War, and yet they are inconsistent enough to counsel a conduct that must inevitably produce it! It appears to me, from some of Mr Genets late proceeding, that Jacobine like, he wishes from the atrocity of his own conduct, to force others into such intemperance as might at once justify and excuse himself.

Give me leave to assure you Sir that to hear of your health and happiness will always contribute greatly to mine; being with the most unfeigned affection dear Sir your friend and servant

Richard Henry Lee

ALS, PHi: Gratz Collection.

1. Lee married his second wife, Anne Pinckard (d. 1796), widow of Thomas Pinckard and daughter of Thomas Gaskins, Sr., in 1769.

From William MacPherson

Sir   Chester October 23d 1793

Under the most sensible impressions of gratitude to you Sir for the appointment I now hold, the duties of which I hope I have discharged in such manner, as to merit your approbation, and that of my fellow Citizens—beg leave to offer myself as a Candidate for the Naval office of this District, vacant in consequence of the unfortunate Death of Doctr Phile[1]—I trust

Sir I shall not appear presumptious or over greedy in making this request—The naval office being consider'd a superiour Grade in the Customs—I feel an honest ambition to receive this further mark of your goodness Sir, which I shall value in the highest degree; as it will be an evidence of my conduct having been such, as to merit your approbation. I have the honor to be with the most perfect respect your most obedient Servt

W. Macpherson
Surveyor District of Pennsylvania

ALS, DLC:GW.

1. GW appointed MacPherson to this post (see GW to the United States Senate, 9 and 27 Dec.).

From James Mease McRea

Sir.   Alexandria [Va.] 23d October 1793

In consequence of the Resignation of Colo. Hanson late Surveyor of this port I have been induced to offer myself a Candidate for that office.[1] Not having the honor to be personally Known to you Sir, I have obtaind the recommendation of a few Gentlemen of this place, who are mostly of the longest standing, and who are I beleive mostly Known to you, in my favour, which I have the honor to inclose herewith[2]—If the time had been longer since I was made acquainted with Colo. Hansons resignation, I shoud have added many more Signatures to my recommendation—I have only to add in favor of my application, that I am a Young Man, and have a growing Family and That previous to the Adoption of our present Government, I held the office of Searcher, under the State Government for several years, the duties of which was very similar to those of the Surveyor—In my application for Recommendations I have not generally apply'd to persons engag'd in Active Commerce, conceiving that such as I have Chosen were more likely to appoint or recommend, a person whose Conduct in office woud, be guided by an attention to The Interst of the Government as well as the ease of Individuals. I have the Honour to be with the greatest respect Sir your Most Obedient and Very Humble Servant

James M. McRea

ALS, DLC:GW.

1. See Samuel Hanson to GW, 22 October.

2. The enclosed document of this date, signed by Elisha C. Duke, Samuel Hanson, Charles Little, William Herbert, Robert Townsend Hooe, Robert Mease, Jesse Taylor, Daniel Roberdeau, James Craik, Roger West, and Richard Harrison, recommended McRea as "a gentleman" who "has been so fortunate by his Integrity and Industry as to have acquir'd the Esteem of his Fellow Citizens—And we think him well qualifyed to fill the office of Surveyor of this port in such a manner as to give general satisfaction" (DLC:GW). On 5 Nov. McRea wrote GW again to enclose a nearly identical recommendation signed by Charles Simms, Benjamin Dulany, and George Gilpin (DLC:GW). He did not, however, receive the appointment.

To Stephen Moylan

Sir   Mt Vernon Oct. 23d 1793

Your letter of the 21st was handed to me last Night. As I expect to be in the vicinity of Philadelphia (German town I believe) on the first of November I shall decline saying any thing on the subject of your application 'til then—It being my invariable custom to possess myself of the circumstances of every case before I decide on a nomination to the office[1]—With esteem & regard I am Sir Yr very Hble Servt

G. W——n

ADfS, DNA: RG 59, Miscellaneous Letters; LB, DLC:GW.

1. GW did not offer Moylan the post he was seeking, but he did nominate him to be commissioner of loans for Pennsylvania (see GW to the United States Senate, 5 Dec.).

From Timothy Pickering

Sir,   Philadelphia Octr 23. 1793.

I wrote you by Monday's post.[1] That afternoon I went to see Mr Peters; and had the pleasure to find that your accommodation and a suitable provision for Congress had engaged the attention of him and divers other citizens of Philadelphia who were scattered in the adjacent country. They have had some consultations on the subject; and will continue them until suitable provision shall be made; of which he has promised to give me early information.

It is Mr Peters's opinion that the city will be perfectly safe for the assembling of Congress the first week in December: but lest it should be otherwise, competent provision will be made at Germantown. He says that a number of the citizens of Philadelphia are preparing to quit Germantown, for places on the river where they can better receive and dispose of their fall goods. These removals & the other measures which he and his fellow citizens will take, will make room for the members of Congress. He says also, that an Academy and an adjacent building at Germantown will answer very well for the meeting of the two houses of Legislature⟨.⟩ Their first object will be to provide for you the most convenient house the adjacent country will afford, to which, if you think proper you can soon resort. I will give you the earliest notice when this provision is made.

As I mentioned in my last, the fever has not been known in Germantown, except with persons who had carried the infection from the city. And Mr Peters mentioned a remarkable fact—That from all such deaths in the country, not a single instance had been known of the infection being communicated. On my way to Germantown yesterday, I spoke of this circumstance to a reputable man whom I knew, and who lives near Fair-Hill: He confirmed it by many[2] instances which he said had fallen under his own knowledge. By this it would seem, that persons not previously contaminated by the impure air of the city, were not susceptible of the disease.

My ride to Germantown yesterday was on purpose to see the Attorney General: but he was not at home.

I am waiting for an answer from the Mayor to a letter I wrote him last evening, requesting authentic information of the number of deaths, and of the present state of the disease.

I have sent my servant a second time for the Mayor's answer: but he does not return; and the closing of the mail being at hand, I must conclude now, and write again by the next post.[3] I am most respectfully sir, Your obedient servant

Timothy Pickering

ALS, DLC:GW; ADfS, MHi: Pickering Papers.

1. See Pickering to GW, 21 October.

2. On the draft, Pickering initially wrote "near seventy," but he struck those words out when he revised the sentence.

3. A note written on the draft reads: "Afterwards recd the Mayors answer, and inclosed it in another letter of this date, to the President" (see below).

From Timothy Pickering

Sir,   Post Office Philaa Oct. 23. 1793
    Since sealing my letter of this date, my servant has brought me an answer from the Mayor, which I enclose. I am surprized at the number of deaths from Oct. 11th to the 22d. I will continue to advise you of the state of the disease, as often as I can obtain any new information. very respectfully yr most obedt servt

Timothy Pickering

ALS, DLC:GW.

Enclosure
Matthew Clarkson to Timothy Pickering

Sir   Philada Oct. 23—1793
    I think it may be concluded that the state of the mortal sickness is become more favorable, this appears from the decrease of funerals in the City generally, and at the Hospital at Bush-Hill It is not possible to ascertain, with any degree of precission the degree in which it has abated.
    The general appearance is pleasing, the Physicians have fewer applications from new patients, the proportion of those who recover is abundantly greater than at the commencement of the disease. The general Countenance of these Citizens who remain, has changed, there is an obvious difference in their looks, a cheerfulness hath taken place of a general gloom which not long since overspread every face; several Shops & stores which were shut up, are again opened.
    I have herewith sent you a New York paper in which I find a pretty accur[at]e Account of the funerals from the first of August to the 11th October, this is the best which can at present be obtained.[1] since that time the funerals amount to about[   ]to the present day. I am very respectfully Sir—Your most obt servt

Matth. Clarkson

Particulars since the 11⟨th Oct⟩ober

Christ Church	19	
St Peters	17	43
St Pauls	7	

Germ. Lutheran	110	
Calv:	48	158
Friends		56
Romans		34
Methodists		18
Potters field		313

642 to 19th October[2]

You will observe that returns from some of the Congegrations are not included in the above—for which may be added to that period—say 58—which will make the whole from the 11th to 19 inclusive 700.

Note the Potter's Field return is up to the 22d and inclusive.

ALS, DLC:GW.

1. The "List of Burials in the several Grave Yards in the City and Liberties of Philadelphia, from August 1, to October 11, 1793, inclusive," printed in the *New-York Daily Gazette,* 19 Oct., showed 2,737 burials.

2. The numbers actually add to 622. A more comprehensive list of burials from 1 Aug. to 9 Nov., published in the *Federal Gazette and Philadelphia Daily Advertiser,* 18 Nov., records 4,031 burials—3,328 from these cemeteries, and the rest from locations not reported here, most notably the Presbyterian cemeteries.

To Edmund Randolph

Dear Sir,   Mount Vernon 23d Oct. 1793

Your letter of the 14th only came by the Post of last night, to Alexandria, & this is sent thither to day, that it may go by tomorrow's Mail, & thereby reach you as soon as the nature of the case will admit.[1]

As you have given no positive opinion respecting the Power of the Executive to change the place for Congress to meet at, & as it is uncertain what will be the result of this business; I am really at a loss to decide which of the three houses mentioned in the P.S. to your letter of the above date would best suit me, or whether either of them wd.

If from the present state of the malady, with which Philadelphia is visited, & there is an unfavorable prospect of its ceasing, Germantown should be thought unsaf⟨e⟩ &, of course an ineligable spot for Congress ⟨to⟩ sit in, or meet at even in the first i⟨n⟩stance, *any kind* of lodging & board would suffice for the short stay I sho⟨uld⟩ have to remain there, especially as all the time not e⟨m⟩ployed in business with the heads of Dep⟨art⟩ments & yourself might be spent in li⟨ttle⟩ excursions to places at a small dist⟨ance⟩ therefrom—of course all idea of furnishing, & keeping a house myself, (being entirely unprovided with Servants or means of any sort) ought to be banished entirely if it be practicable—& some rooms, even in a tavern, (if I could be retired in them) taken in preferrence. On the other hand, if my stay there is likely to be of any continuance, then, unquestionably Colo. Franks' (if to be had) wd suit me best—because most commodious for myself, & the entertainment of Company—& next to this Bensel's.

This is the light in which the matter strikes me, at this distance—but as you are on the spot—know more precisely than I possibly can do, the real state of things—and besides, have been in the way of hearing the various opinions of People on the subje⟨ct⟩ of what Congress ought to d⟨o,⟩ I would leave much to your judgment. I shall set out so as to be in Germantown, or thereabouts, the first of November, if no difficulties are encountered on the Road—As there can be but a short interval between your receipt of this letter, & my arrival, any place might do for my first reception.

It is not in my power to dispatch a servant before me—I shall have but two neither of which can be spared for such a purpose—these with five horses—Mr Dandridge & myself—form the total of my family & equipage.[2] It would be very convenient for me therefore to meet a letter from you at Wilmington, that I may know better how to proceed from thence—& where to cross the Schuylkill.

My best wishes, in which Mrs Washington unites, attend you Mrs Randolph and family—we are glad to hear that your apprehensions on acct of Peyton have subsided. With sincere esteem & regard I am yours Affecte

G. W——n

ADfS, DNA: RG 59, Miscellaneous Letters; LB, DLC:GW. The text in angle brackets is taken from the letter-book copy.
    1. Randolph's letter to GW of 14 Oct. has not been found.
    2. The remainder of this paragraph was written below the signature on the draft and apparently considered initially as a postscript (since it is followed by the words "My best wishes &ca as above"). However, it was then marked for inclusion at this point, and it appears in this location on the letter-book copy.

From Solomon Bush

Alexandria [Va.]
May it please your Excellency—   Octr 24th 1793
    The Naval Office for the Port of Philadelphia being vacant by the Death of Doctr Phile, Permit me to solicit the same, assuring your Excellency that shou'd I be honourd with the Appointment no endeavours shall be wanting in Me, to give satisfaction, and fill the duties of the Office.

    I humbly beg leave to call your Excellencys attention to my present situation, confiding in your well known goodness for the liberty I take, some time since I was comfortably establish'd in England in a beneficial Medical employment in which I continued untill the Death of An aged Father called Me to my Country to take charge of three helpless Orphan Sisters whose tender years demanded my Protection, and to return again to Europe to my Practice when the wounds I receivd in the service of my Country became so troublesome as to render it impossible, and during The last Winter I underwent another operation having half of my thigh bone extracted, this has injured my Constitution so much, as to put it out of my power, to follow the practice of Medicine. thus am I situated with a Wife and family, three Sisters, and an unfortunate Brother, who was deprived of his reason (in a Campaign to the Southward under Genl Green) all looking to Me for support;[1] pardon my mentioning these circumstances, but I trust your Excellencys well know Goodness will excuse—I shoud have endeavour'd to laid many recomendations from the Merchants, and others of the Port of Philadelphia, but at present there is no communication with that unfortunate City, and my Friend Mr Robert Morris is at a distance—I beg leave to Inclose a Letter from that Gentleman on a former occasion; when I was in Nomination as first Secretary to the Board of Treasury under the former Congress; that Board being dissolved the appointment fell through.[2] I have honour to subscribe your Excellency Obdt Hble Servt

S. Bush

ALS, DLC:GW.

Bush wrote GW again on 12 Nov. promising, "as it has pleasd Providence to releive that unfortunate City from their late Calamity and the Citizens again returning to their homes shou'd your Excellency think it necessary, I will endeavour to obtain Recomendations of my Charecter, Conduct, and Attachment to our happy Goverment and cheerfully lay the same before you" (DLC:GW), but he did not obtain the appointment.

1. Bush may have been referring to his half-sisters Richea Bush (1765–1844), Margaret (Pier, Peggy) Bush (1770–1799), and Elkali (Eleanor) Bush (1772–1830), who married Moses Sheftall of Georgia in 1792. Bush married Ann (Nancy) Marshall (d. 1818), daughter of Christopher Marshall, Jr., of Philadelphia, in 1791. They had one son, Mathias. After Bush's death (1795), she married Dr. William Currie in 1796.

2. This letter has not been identified. Bush had applied to be secretary of the Board of Treasury in December 1780 (Bush to Continental Congress, 8 Dec. 1780, DNA:PCC, item 42).

From Alexander Hamilton

Sir,   2½ Miles from Philadelphia Octobr 24. 1793.

I arrived at my own house yesterday evening, where I found your letter of the 14 instant; having previously received that of the 25 of September, by the circuitous route of Albany, the evening before my departure from New York.

As to the right of the President to convene Congress out of the ordinary course, I think it stands as follows—"he may on *extraordinary occasions* convene both houses of Congress or either of them"—These are the words of the Constitution.[1] Nothing is said as to *time* or *place*—nothing restrictive as to either—I therefore think they both stand on the same footing. The discretion of the President extends to *place* as well as *time*. The reason of the thing as well as the words of the Constitution, would extend it to both. The usual seat of the Government may be in possession of an enemy—it may be swallowed up by an earthquake.

I know of no law that abriges in this respect the discretion of the President—if a law could abrige a constitutional discretion of either branch.

But the doubt with me is whether the "extraordinary occasion" mentioned in the constitution be not some unforeseen oc-curence in the public affairs, which renders it adviseable *for the public service,* to convene Congress at some *time* different from that which the Constitution or some law has established—in other words, to anticipate their ordinary meeting—to have a *special* session, for a *special object of public business* out of the prees-tablished course.

I doubt therefore whether the circumstance of a contagious disease existing at the seat of Government be a constitutional ground for convening Congress at *another place,* but at the same *time,* they had premeditated.

And I know that there are respectable opinions against the power of the President to change the place of meeting in such a case; so as I think to render it inexpedient to take the step.

But the President may *recommend* a meeting at some other place, as a place of preliminary rendezvous for the members of the two houses, that they may informally concert what further the exigency may require—and my *present opinion* inclines in fa-vor of such a measure.

The question then would be, what place is the most eligible?

Obvious reasons render it desireable that it should be as near Philadelphia as may consist with the motive for naming such a place—(to wit)—the safety of the members—I—Innovation upon the existing arrangement with regard to the seat of Gov-ernment, ought to be avoided as much as possible—II. Congress may think it necessary for regularity to go within the limits of the City (tho' but for an hour) to give legality by some summary act to another place of Meeting—and with this view it will be convenient to meet at no great distance from the City. III. The place recommended may influence the place of session—The President and heads of Departments ought to be near Con-gress, but they cannot be long remote from their offices, and a removal of the public offices for one session would be in many ways an evil. Lastly—The less the President in such case departs from the preestablished course, the less room there will be for cavil.

All these reasons would operate in favor of German town, if competent only to the *momentary* accommodation of Congress. Mr Peters & some other gentlemen affirm that it is. I have myself great doubt on the point, and I have not had time to examine, but I cannot help paying deference to the opinion of those who assert it's competency.

There is, however, another consideration not unworthy of attention. Experience seems to decide satisfactorily that there would be due safety at Germantown; but it is very probable, this would not appear to be the case to the members generally. The alarm appears to be greatest in proportion as you go furthest from the seat of the disease. Yet I should hope the Presidents recommendation stating the *fact* as evidenced by experience would appease the apprehensions of the parties concerned.

If Germantown should not be found adequate, on the score of accommodation, Trenton, Reading, Lancaster & Wilmington are the places which present themselves to choice as most eligible. Nothing more notherly or southerly ought to be thought of. A place in Pennsylvania will best please the Pennsylvanians. They would be very jealous of Trenton, and they would have some, tho' less jealousy of Wilmington. Lancaster would afford better accommodations than Reading. Wilmington would I apprehend be the most agreeable of these places to Congress.

But I am, upon the whole, of opinion that it will be best to make Germantown do if possible. It will be time enough to decide when you arrive—and the interval will be employed to examine the ground.

Mrs Hamilton & myself are very sensible to the obliging interest you have manifested on our recovery. Exercise & Northern air have restored us beyond expectation. We are very happy that Mrs Washington & yourself escaped. I have the honor to remain &c.

A. Hamilton

LB, DLC:GW.

1. Hamilton is quoting from Article 2, section 3 of the Constitution. The emphasis is his.

To Ludwell Lee and Roger West

Gentlemen,   Mount Vernon 24 Octor 1793.

The address of the Landholders & Inhabitants of Fairfax County, forwarded to me by you, has been received.[1]

It is a source of much pleasure to me to find my Fellow Citizens of Fairfax among those spirited republicans of the United States, who declare to the world their firm determination to support the Government they have chosen for themselves, & to oppose with manly resolution any attempts to weaken the public confidence therein, or to interrupt the repose they now enjoy, or a state of peace to which their interest & happiness are so closely allied.

In fulfilling the duties which are attendant on the trust with which my Country men have honored me, my highest gratification is in meriting & receiving their approving voice; I therefore request you to communicate to the Citizens of Fairfax the pleasure I derive from their approbation of my public conduct, and to assure them of my constant and unremitted attention to the promotion of the prosperity and happiness of my Fellow Citizens of these States.

Go. Washington

LB, DLC:GW. This reply was published in newspapers such as the *Baltimore Daily Intelligencer,* 2 November.

1. This address came enclosed in a letter from Lee and West to GW of 21 October.

To Richard Henry Lee

Dear Sir,   Mount Vernon 2⟨4⟩th Octr 1793

Your favor of yesterday the 23d[1] was handed to me upon my return from my usual ride, & almost at the moment I was setting down (with company) to dinner, which prevented my acknowledging the receipt of it by your servant.

I am sorry I shall not have the pleasure of seeing you & your Lady before I return to the Northward, and regret the cause. On sunday,[2] if I can previously arrange some business that presses, I shall commence my journey, and if I can render you any service whither I am going, I should be happy in doing it.

On fair ground, it would be difficult to assign reasons for the conduct of those who are arraigning, & constantly (as far as they are able) embarrassing the measures of government with respect to its pacific disposition towards the Belligerent Powers in the convulsive dispute which agitated them but their motives are too obvious to those who have the means of information, & have viewed the different grounds they have taken to mistake their object. It is not the cause of France (nor I believe not of liberty) they regard; for could they involve this Country in War (no matter with whom) & disgrace, they would be among the first and loudest of the clamourers against the expence and impolicy of the measure.

The specimens you have seen of Mr G——ts sentiments & conduct in the Gazettes, form a small part only of the agregate; but you can judge from these to what test the temper of the Executive has been put in its various transactions with this Gentleman. Tis probable, the whole will be exhibited to public view in the course of the next Session of Congress—delicacy towards his Nation, has restrained doing it hitherto. The best that can be said of this agent is, that he is entirely unfit for the Mission on which he is employed, unless, contrary to the express & unequivocal declaration of his Country (wch I hope is not the case)—made through himself—it is meant to involve ours in all the horrors of an European War. This, or interested motives of his own—or having become a dupe, & the tool[3] of a Party, formed on various principles but to effect local purposes, is the only solution that can be given of his conduct.

I sincerely wish that Mrs Lee & yourself may soon & effectually recover your healths & with very great esteem & regard I am—Dear Sir Your Most Obedt & Affecte Hble Servant

Go: Washington

ADfS, ViMtvL: Chapin-Gould Collection; LB, DLC:GW. The date on the draft was altered and is not clear. GW docketed the draft "24 Oct. 1793," and the letter-book copy is dated "Octr 24th 1793." However, when Stan V. Henkels sold a purported ALS in 1921, he reported the date as 25 Oct. (*ABPC*, 28:930).

1. GW struck out the original text at this point and inserted "yesterday" above the line; he later added "23d" on top of the original strikeout but did not cross out "yesterday."

2. The following Sunday was 27 October.

3. The letter-book copy has "fool."

From Nicholas Lewis

Sir   Albemarle [Va.] October 24th, 1793

I have the Honour, to transmitt You Sundry Resolves entered into by a considerable proportion of the Inhabitants of the

County of Albemarle, & I have Sir assumed thus far in conformity to the last of Said enclosed Resolutions. I am Sir With great
respect your very Humble Servt

                                         Nicholas Lewis

ALS, DLC:GW; LB, DLC:GW.
     Nicholas Lewis (1734–1808), uncle of Meriwether Lewis and grandson of
Nicholas Meriwether, had been involved in managing Thomas Jefferson's financial affairs from 1781 to 1792.

Enclosure
Resolutions from the Albemarle County, Va., Citizens

                         [Charlottesville, Va., 10 October 1793]
     At a numerus meeting of the free men of the County of Al-
bemarle in the State of Virginia, at the Town of Charlottesville
on the tenth day of October, one thousand seven hundred and
ninety three, being the day appointed by Law, for holding Court,
within the said County on which day they had been requested
to attend for the special purpose of taking into consideration
the political subjects that now engage the Publick attention, and
the matter being opened to them the following persons were
appointed a committee, to draw up resolutions declaratory of
their sentiments, Viz., Wilson C. Nicholas, Nicholas Lewis, William Woods, Thomas M. Randolph[,] Robert Jouett, Peter Carr,
James Kerr, John Key, Bernard Brown, Bazaleel Brown, William
Clark, Edward Moore, Samuel Dyer[,] Samuel Murril, Thomas
Garth, Joseph J. Monroe, & John Carr, who then retired and
proceeded to appoint, Nicholas Lewis, their Chairman & John
Carr Secretary, who came to the following resolutions, unanimously & having presented them to the People, were unanimously agreed to.[1]
     It is conceived that all Power is vestered in the hands of the
People from which it follows that all the Power which is exercised by any man or men, being derived from the people, they
have a right to direct the tendency and to declare the objects,
towards which, it ought to be pointed; It being considered impossible that the people can be too watchful of their liberties, it
is expedient for them to adopt some mode, by which they may
declare their wishes and opinions, relative to the great questions
which now employ the attention of this Country, It is considered
the more necessary at this particular crisis, when it is common

for some men actuated probably by motives different from those of the bulk of the nation, to give their own notions and wishes as those of the People.

It is thought prudent to avoid this danger by entering into resolutions declaratory of the true sence of this County.

Resolved, that our Constitution ought to be supported against every effort that may be made to subvert it, and that all who entertain any such designs ought to be viewed as the Enemies of their Country.

Resolved that we ought carefully to avoid, by all proper means, disputes with any foreign nation whatever, as injurious to the welfare of this infant Country.

Resolved that the past services of our worthy fellow Citizen George Washington, President of the United States, entitle him to our highest respect and gratitude, and that the executive ought to be supported, in the exercise of those Powers, entrusted to them for the benefit of the People.

Resolved, that the generous support and great services rendered us by the French, in our efforts for independance, entitle them to our warmest wishes & earnest Prayers for their success.

Resolved that attempts to disunite the People of France and the people of America ought to be reprobated by the Lovers of Liberty and Equality, as they are encouraged by those who hate them.

Resolved, that those who make such attempts ought to be detested by all honest republicans, as they tend to lessen our esteem for the principles of our own Government from which we should never deviate.

Resolved, that our Connection with France is a beneficial and glorious one, that to brake it off would be a great stride towards an alliance with some power unfriendly to the spirit of our Government, that such a connection ought to be warmly opposed, as it would tend to distroy our Present Government, and to introduce in its stead one unfriendly to the principles, we wish to Cherish.

Resolved, that the French revolution ought to be earnestly espoused by those who are friends to the generous principles which produced it, that it ought to be the more particularly favoured at this conjuncture, when there is such a combination of Tyrants to distroy it, that we have the more reason to interest ourselves, as we have great fears, that there are in our Country, men of Monarchical principles, unfriendly to the cause which gave birth to an event, that may serve to open the eyes of all mankind, to their natural and inherent rights.[2]

Resolved, that the intention of the Presidents proclamation was laudable, that as the Power of declaring peace or War, is not vested in him, the exercise of such Power, would be userpation, and contrary to the general tenor of his conduct, that it is illiberal under these circumstances to attribute, to him any such unconstitutional designs without manifest intention.[3]

Ordered that the foregoing resolutions be forthwith Published in the national Gazett, and the Publick Papers of Virginia,[4] and a fair Copy thereof transmitted by the Chairman, to the President of the United States.

Nicholas Lewis, Chairman
John Carr Secretary

DS, in John Carr's writing, DLC:GW; LB, DLC:GW.

John Carr (b. 1753), a younger brother of Thomas Jefferson's brother-in-law Dabney Carr, was deputy clerk for Albemarle County from 1793 to 1805 and clerk of the circuit court from 1809 to 1819.

1. William Woods (1738–1819) was a Baptist minister who completed Nicholas's term in the Virginia House of Delegates, 1799–1800. He later moved to Kentucky. Thomas Mann Randolph (1768–1828), Thomas Jefferson's son-in-law, represented Virginia in the U.S. Senate, 1793–94, and in the U.S. House, 1803–7. An infantry colonel in the War of 1812, Randolph was governor of Virginia, 1819–22. Robert Jouett (c.1756–1796) was a Revolutionary War officer and a lawyer. Peter Carr (1770–1815), Jefferson's nephew, served four terms in the Virginia House of Delegates, 1801–4, 1807–8. James Kerr, who lived in the Ivy Creek area and was a county magistrate, became county sheriff on this date. Brothers Bernard Brown (1750–1800) and Bazaleel Brown (1754–1829) were Revolutionary War veterans who lived near White Hall and Doyles River. They were both county magistrates. William Clark[e] (d. 1800) and Edward Moore (d. 1808) represented Albemarle County in the Virginia House of Delegates at this time, Clark serving 1790–93, and Moore, 1792–95. Clark was also a magistrate, and Moore became one in 1794. Thomas Garth (c.1740–1812) and John Key (d. 1811) were formerly stewards for Thomas Jefferson. Garth was a county magistrate. Key, a former magistrate, became county coroner on this date and county sheriff in 1795. Samuel Dyer (1756–1839), a Revolutionary War veteran, was a merchant. Samuel Murrell (1756–1836) was a Revolutionary War veteran, a county magistrate, and in 1794 a militia major. In 1806 he moved to Barren County, Kentucky, where he served in the state legislature and as a presidential elector. Joseph Jones Monroe (1771–1824) was a brother of James Monroe and son-in-law of James Kerr.

2. The preceding resolutions generally follow a draft for such resolutions created by James Madison and James Monroe in late August. For their role in regard to the Albemarle County resolutions, see Resolutions on Franco-American Relations, c. 27 Aug., and Monroe to Madison, 25 Sept., *Madison Papers*, 15:76–80, 121–22.

3. This resolution evidently was addressing the issues raised by "Helvidius" (James Madison) in five essays printed in the *Gazette of the United States* (Philadelphia) from 24 Aug. to 18 Sept. (*Madison Papers*, 15:66–74, 80–87, 95–103, 106–110, 113–20). "Helvidius" responded to what he saw as dangerous claims of executive authority made by "Pacificus" (Alexander Hamilton) in an essay printed in the *Gazette* of 29 June (*Hamilton Papers*, 15:33–43), first by denying that those claims were valid and, second, by denying that GW's Neutrality Proclamation involved any such claim of authority.

4. The resolutions were not printed in the Philadelphia *National Gazette* before that paper was discontinued, after the issue of 26 October. They were, however, printed in *Dunlap's American Daily Advertiser* (Philadelphia), 4 December.

From James Madison

Dear Sir   Orange [Va.] October 24th 1793.

Your letter of the 14th instant did not arrive till sunday night,[1] and being not then at home, I did not receive it till last night. I now lose not a moment in complying with its request; tho' I foresee it cannot reach you before you will have left Mount Vernon, and before you will probably have made up a final determination on some if not on all the questions proposed. These are

1. Ought the President to summon Congress at a time and place to be named by him? or,

2. If the President has no power to change the place, ought he to abstain from all interposition whatever? or

3. Ought he to notify the obstacle to a meeting at Philadelphia, state the defect of a regular provision for the exigency, and suggest his purpose of repairing to [   ] as a place deemed most eligible for a meeting in the first instance?

4. What is the place liable to fewest objections?

From the best investigation I have been able to make in so short a time, the first expedient, tho' most adequate to the exigency, seems to require an authority that does not exist under the Constitution and laws of the U. States.

The only passage in the Constitution in which such an authority could be sought is that which says "The President may, on extraordinary occasions, convene both Houses, or either of them."[2] But the obvious import of these terms is satisfied by referring them to the time only at which the extraordinary meeting is summoned. If indeed they included a discretion as to the place as well as the time, it would be unnecessary to recur to the expedient of altering the time in order to get at an alteration of the place. The President could as well alter the place without interfering with the time, as alter the time without interfering with the place. Besides; the effect of a change as to place would not be in all respects similar to a change as to time. In the latter case, an extraordinary session running into the period of an ordinary one, would allow the ordinary one to go on under all the circumstances prescribed by law. In the former case, this would not happen. The ordinary part of the Session would be held out of the place prescribed for it—unless prevented by a positive act for returning to it.

The obvious meaning here assigned to the phrase is confirmed by other parts of the Constitution. It is well known that much jealousy has always appeared in every thing connected with the residence of the General Government. The solicitude of the Constitution to appease this jealousy is particularly marked by the 1st paragraph of section 6th & the 3d paragraph of section 7th of article I. The light in which these paragraphs must be viewed cannot well be reconciled with a supposition that it was meant to entrust the Executive alone with any power on that subject.[3]

Laying aside the Constitution and consulting the law, the expedient seems to be no less inadmissible. The act of July 1790 "establishing the temporary & permanent seat of the Government of the U.S." cannot be understood to leave any such power in the President. And as the power, if exercised so as to interfere with the provision relating to the temporary seat, might beget an alarm lest, in the hands of a President unfriendly to the permanent seat, it should be turned on some pretext or other against that arrangement, prudential reasons unite with legal ones, for avoiding the precedent.[4]

The 2d mode of treating the difficulty would seem to be best, if the danger at German Town were out of the way. A voluntary resort to that place might be relied on; and the members of the Legislature finding themselves together and with the President, might legalize the necessary steps, or if that should be thought wrong might deliberate and decide for themselves on the emergency. But as the danger might defeat such an expectation, it results that,

The 3d expedient is called for by the occasion; and being sufficient, is all that can be justified by it.

The 4th point to be considered is the delicate one of naming the place.

In deciding this point, it would seem proper to attend *first* to the risk of the infection. This consideration lies, as you observe, against Trenton & Wilmington: *secondly,* to Northern and Southern jealousies. This applies to N. York and Annapolis: *thirdly,* to the disposition of Pennsylvania, which is entitled to some regard, as well by her calamity, as by the circumstance of her being in possession of the Government.

In combining these considerations we are led to look for some place within the State of Pennsylvania not materially different from Philada in relation to North and South. Lancaster and Reading appear to have occurred. With the former I am but little acquainted. The latter I never saw. If the object of the Executive should be merely to put Congress in the most neutral situation possible for chusing a place for themselves, as would have been the case at German Town, Reading seems to have the better pretensions. If the object should be to provide a place at once marking an impartiality in the Executive, and capable of retaining Congress during the Session, Lancaster seems to claim a preference.

If the measure which my present view of the subject favors, should be deemed least objectionable, something like the following form might be given to it.

"Whereas a very dangerous and infectious malady which continues to rage in the City of Philada renders it indispensable that the approaching Session of Congress should be held, as well as the Executive Department be for the present administered, at some other place: And whereas no regular provision exists for such an emergency; so that unless some other place be pointed out, at which the members of Congress may assemble in the first instance, great embarrasments may happen: Under these peculiar circumstances I have thought it incumbent on me to notify the obstacle to a meeting of Congress at the ordinary place of

their Session; and to recommend that the several members assemble at [   ] in the State of [   ] at which place I shall be
ready to meet them. G.W. P.U.S.["]

With sentiments of the highest respect and attachment I remain, Dear Sir, your affectionate humble servant

Js Madison Jr

ALS, DLC:GW; ADfS, DLC: Madison Papers.

1. The previous Sunday was 20 October.

2. Madison is quoting from Article 2, section 3.

3. The first paragraph of section 6 reads: "The Senators and Representatives shall receive a Compensation for their Services, to be ascertained by
Law, and paid out of the Treasury of the United States. They shall in all
Cases, except Treason, Felony and Breach of the Peace, be privileged from
Arrest during their Attendance at the Session of their respective Houses, and
in going to and returning from the same; and for any Speech or Debate in
either House, they shall not be questioned in any other Place."

The third paragraph of section 7 reads: "Every Order, Resolution, or Vote
to which the Concurrence of the Senate and House of Representatives may
be necessary (except on a question of Adjournment) shall be presented to
the President of the United States; and before the Same shall take Effect,
shall be approved by him, or being disapproved by him, shall be repassed
by two thirds of the Senate and House of Representatives, according to the
Rules and Limitations prescribed in the Case of a Bill."

4. For this act of 16 July 1790, see 1 *Stat.*, 130.

From Edmund Randolph

Sir   Spencer's [Germantown, Pa.] October 24. 1793.

My messenger, who carried into Philadelphia yesterday the letter, which I had the honor of addressing to you at Baltimore,[1]
brought from the post-office your favor of the 14th instant. It is
but lately, that I could procure an intercourse with it: but he will
go in again tomorrow, in order to convey this letter, and receive
any others, which you may have thought proper to write to me.

I have travelled over the subject of your interposition as to the
place for the next session of congress: but have not been able to
complete my remarks on paper. They will be ready at your arrival at German-Town. In the mean time, I beg leave to suggest
the result of my reflections, as being adverse to a call of congress
from the executive. It seems to be unconstitutional. It is also unnecessary at this moment; for if the two houses should happen

to meet within the limits of Philadelphia on the first monday in december, they may adjourn to some other place: if they do not meet, then the President will stand justified to convene them; inasmuch as a failure to meet in the present posture of public affairs on the appointed day will, by producing a well-grounded apprehension, that they may not assemble for a long time, of itself create an *"extraordinary occasion"*. Some days may be lost, if the members may not have come into the neighbourhood; but not many more, than by an adjournment of their own to a new place. By my mode the object will be accomplished in an easy and natural course: by a summons from the President serious discontents may be excited.

I ought however to inform you, sir, that the governor of Pennsylvania, (whose authority is, so far as the constitution of this state goes, nearly the same with yours,) will probably call his legislature a few days before the regular meeting to German Town, instead of Philadelphia. Mr Dallas thinks, that he may do so with safety; but the question is to be submitted to the attorney-general.[2] He tells me, that Mr Rawle is of opinion, that altho' you should convene congress, they must assemble in the first instance at Philadelphia. I intended to have consulted with him and Mr Lewis; but having heard from Major Lenox, that Colo. Hamilton came home last night, I shall postpone going over to them until I can converse with him. But in pursuance of your instruction, I inclose, what appears to be a proper proclamation, if my sentiments should unfortunately not accord with your decision.

Concerning the place; I can with certainty give you the characters of such of the towns in this state, as you have named. German Town cannot accommodate congress with tolerable satisfaction; it will be surcharged with the assembly and congress together; it is not willing to enter upon the task; and a great part of the very furniture, which would be used, would be drawn from Philadelphia itself—I called at Reading on saturday last; and Judge Rush, who lives there asserted, and I believe from my examination, with truth, that it could not accommodate congress.[3] The public building might answer well enough, but if the President should carry them to a place, where houserooom and supplies would be scanty, because the demand is unexpected, multitudes would feel sore—Lancaster is able and willing to provide for congress in every shape; and I hope to receive in a day or two a statement of the arrangements, which can be made for their reception. In this place the Pennsylvania members will concur, and probably in no other out of Philadelphia. It is an universal persuasion, that, unless Lancaster be chosen, New-York will be revisited by congress—Your observation on Annapolis is too striking not to command an instantaneous assent. Wilmington and Trenton, besides being thoroughfares, are beyond the limits of Pennsylvania, who thinks herself intitled by a kind of compact to retain the temporary seat of government within its own bosom.

There can be no doubt of several persons dying in, and about German Town, with the yellow fever.

Dr Rush has written to Dr Shippen, that he may advertize for the commencement of the medical lectures about the first day of december; as the disorder has abated.[4] This may be the case; but many discerning men think differently. I have the honor, sir, to be, with the highest respect, and true attachment yr mo. ob. serv.

Edm: Randolph

ALS, DLC:GW.

1. Randolph was presumably referring to his letter to GW of 22 October.

2. No opinion from Pennsylvania Attorney General Jared Ingersoll regarding a move of the Pennsylvania legislature has been identified. Governor Thomas Mifflin wrote two Philadelphia physicians on 31 Oct. asking if it would be safe for the legislature to meet at Philadelphia, and received a reply that the disease had "so rapidly declined" that "at the time appointed" the legislature should be able to meet "without being under any apprehensions of danger from the contagion" (*Diary; or, Loudon's Register* [New York], 8 Nov.). Alexander James Dallas, secretary of the Commonwealth of Pennsylvania, did, however, write Randolph on 1 Nov. reporting that he and Ingersoll agreed that in such extraordinary circumstances the president did have the right to change the place at which Congress met, although he hoped that a change would prove "unnecessary" in this instance (PHarH: Executive Correspondence, 1790–99).

3. Jacob Rush (1747–1820), who graduated from the College of New Jersey in 1765, was an associate justice of the Pennsylvania Supreme Court and president of the third judicial district at Reading. The previous Saturday was 19 October.

4. William Shippen, Jr., had written Benjamin Rush earlier in October proposing to advertise lectures for December or January (see Rush to Mrs. Rush, 11 Oct., Butterfield, *Rush Letters*, 2:712–13). Later, Shippen announced, in an advertisement dated 31 Oct., that the medical lectures of the University

of Pennsylvania would commence on 9 Dec. (*Independent Gazetteer, and Agricultural Repository* [Philadelphia], 23 Nov.).

Enclosure
Draft for "A Proclamation By the President
of the United States"

[c.24 October 1793]

Whereas the situation of public affairs requires, that the ensuing session of congress should not be postponed beyond the first monday in december next, being the day appointed by the constitution of the United States for the assembling thereof; and there is reason to doubt, whether the city of Philadelphia, the temporary seat of government, which for some time past hath *laboured under*[1] a contagious fever, may on that day be fit for their reception: I do therefore, by virtue of the power, in me vested by the said constitution, to convene congress on extraordinary occasions, by these presents convene the senate and house of representatives of the United States, at [   ] in the state of [   ] on the [   ] day of [   ] next: And I do accordingly hereby notify to the members of the said senate and house of representatives respectively, then and there to attend for the dispatch of legislative business.

Given under my hand, and the seal of the United States this [   ] day of [   ] in the year of our lord 1793 and of Independance the seventeenth.

Qu: Altho' the above is in the best form, which occurs to me, does it not exhibit many objections to the thing itself, if it be really the best form?

D, in Edmund Randolph's writing, DLC:GW.

1. Above "*laboured under*," Randolph inserted "*been visited with*," although he did not strike the former phrase.

From J. Sandwich

Sir   Fruit Hill Columbia County Georgia 25th Oct. 1793

I had the honor of addressing you the 18th instant from Wrightsboro' being then on a journey but least any accident shod happen to that Letter—I beg to repeat my observes that fumigating with Tobacco will stay the effects of the present dreadful disorder—This was done during the plague of London & the Tobacconists shops were all exempt.

The steam from Vinegar with rue steeped in it is used whereever the Goal distemper is suspected to raje. I have the honor to subscribe sr. Your very Obdt Servt

J. Sandwich

ALS, DLC:GW.

From Edward Stevens

Sir   Culpeper [Va.] October 25th: 1793

Inclosed are some Resolutions which the Yeomanry of the County of Culpeper have lately entered into, and which they have enjoined on me to Transmit to you. I am with the highest Respect Sir Your very Obedt hum: Servt

Edward Stevens. Chairman

ALS, DLC:GW; LB, DLC:GW.

Enclosure
Resolutions from Culpeper County, Va., Citizens

Culpeper County [Va.] 21st day of October 1793

At a meeting of the Yeomanry of Culpeper County, at the Courthouse on Monday the 21st day of October 1793.[1] the following resolutions were adopted.

Resolved 1st That all attempts to Subvert the federal Government or violate its principals ought to be firmly and vigorously resisted.

2. That a continuation of the union between France and America is necessary to the existance of the liberties of both: all measures therefore which may be or have been adopted for the purpose of exciting a prejudice against the French nation or the Citizens of France are dangerous to the welfare of America, and are injurious to the cause of liberty.

3. That it is the interest of the united States to promote peace and harmony with all nations by just and honourable means and that the executive authority ought to be supported in the excercise of its constitutional powers for enforcing the laws.

4. That the patriotic wisdom and tried virtue of the president of the united states Entitle him to the highest confidence as well as lasting gratitude of his country to whose present peace liberty and happiness he has so largely contributed.

5. That we are attached to the federal Government, that we are attached to peace so long as it can be maintained on honourable grounds, that we are attached to the French nation and feel a disposition to render them every service consistant with existing treaties, that we hate monarchies and more intimate connexions with them as productive of the worst of evils.

Attest, Robt W. Peacock Secy[2]   Edward Stevens Chairman

DS, DLC:GW; LB, DLC:GW. These resolutions were printed in the *Virginia Herald, and Fredericksburg Advertiser,* 14 Nov., which included two orders not on the copy sent to GW: "That a copy of the foregoing resolutions be transmitted to the President of the United States, by the chairman of the meeting, and that he sign the same in behalf of this meeting," and "That the proceedings of this meeting be published in the *Virginia Herald.*"

GW replied to these resolutions in a letter to Stevens of 16 Nov.: "The resolutions of the Yeomanry of Culpeper, announcing their determination to resist all attempts to destroy the fœderal Government, or violate its principles, bespeak a laudable interest in the national prosperity. Among the means of accomplishing the general happiness, peace with all nations is an obvious policy. It is our duty too to remember the services of the French Nation, & to pursue the republican spirit of our Constitution.

"In whatever degree I may be conceived to have contributed to the public welfare, it is very acceptable to me to know that my conduct is approved by the Yeomanry of Culpeper." (LB, DLC:GW).

1. The call for this meeting was issued on 2 Oct. in opposition to a circular letter of James Mercer and others calling for a district meeting at Fredericksburg on 7 October. At the Fredericksburg meeting, strongly pro-French resolutions were introduced but rejected in favor of resolutions calling for the subject to be considered in county meetings (*Virginia Herald, and Fredericksburg Advertiser,* 3 Oct.; *Virginia Gazette, and General Advertiser* [Richmond], 16, 23 Oct.; James Monroe to Thomas Jefferson, 14 Oct., *Jefferson Papers,* 27:236–37).

2. Robert Ware Peacock (born c.1770) was a Stevensburg, Va., lawyer. By 1801, when he was admitted to practice before the Supreme Court, he had moved to Washington, D.C. In 1805 he escaped from the jail there, where he was being held on a forgery conviction (*National Intelligencer, and Washington Advertiser,* 29 March 1805), and thereafter no record of him has been found.

From Rayner Taylor

Octr 25 Philadelphia
No. 96 north sixth street
Sir,   between Arch and Race streets
That Philanthrophy which marks your character, encourages me to take the liberty of addressing you, particularly as a stranger lately settled in this City; the intention of which is to request the honour of your Name as a subscriber to an Anthem I am now publishing, particulars of which are mentioned in the Federal Gazette.[1]

I left the city of Annapolis a few months ago at the desire of Mr Reinagle, who was formerly my scholar, and who wished me to settle here as a teacher of Music to succeed him in that Business; but the unhappy calamity has deprived me of all business, and having no other employment I have been advised to compose the work in question, which, from the opportunity I have had of acquiring my profession in the first seminary in England, and Thirty years experience, I flatter myself will not be found unworthy public encouragement, particularly if honoured by your approbation.

I will no longer tresspass on your Time and begging pardon for this intrusion am Sir Your most obedient and most humble servant

Rayner Taylor.

ALS, DLC:GW. The composer Rayner Taylor (1747–1825) was educated at the King's Singing School in London. After a career as church organist and music director for theaters in England and Scotland, Taylor emigrated to the United States in 1792. Before his move to Philadelphia in 1793 he was organist at St. Anne's Church in Annapolis. He was for many years the organist at St. Peter's Church in Philadelphia.

1. The *Federal Gazette and Philadelphia Daily Advertiser,* 24 Oct., printed an advertisement, dated 23 Oct., for "Sacred Music. Proposals, for printing by Subscription, An ANTHEM, Suitable to the present occasion, for public and private worship. The Music composed by RAYNER TAYLOR, Teacher and Professor of Music, Philadelphia. The price to subscribers—One Dollar."

To Francis Willis, Jr.

Sir,   Mount Vernon 25th Octr 1793
Your letter of the 4th of Augt had to go to Phila. & come back, before I received it.

The mistakes which have happened respecting the Negros of the late Mrs Saml Washington are somewhat singular; and it is not a little surprizing after the first mistake had happened, and so much pains had been taken to account for, & set it right, that *now* after a lapse of five or Six years the whole matter should assume quite a different face. it should be Discovered at this late hour that that lady *herself* had no right to the Negros. which, by the bye, I believe possession *alone* wd have given her.[1]

If I had ever intended to avail my self of the Law for my *own* benefit (which made me heir to those Negros) I would not have relinquished my claim without a thorough investigation of the subject of defective title. For presuming tha⟨t⟩ all Law is founded in equity and being under a conviction tha⟨t if⟩ Mrs Washington had survived her husb⟨and⟩ she would have released nothing to which she would have been entitled by law, I saw no injustice or impropriety upon the ground of reciprocity of receiving for my Brother's Children that which in the other case would have been taken from them—But not having finally resolved in my own Mind (as you may readily infer from my long silence) whether to take from Mrs Washington's family for the benefit of my Brothers only daughter (who from the involved State of his Affairs had left her by his Will a very small pittance; and the obtainment of that, even doubtful) the whole, or only part of what the law entitled me to, I let the matter rest til your second letter had revived the Subject.[2]

I now, in order to close the business finally, have come to the following conclusion. Pay me one hundd pounds which I shall give to my Niece for her immediate support, and I will quit claim to *all* the Negro's which belonged to Mrs Saml Washington, & will releas⟨e⟩ them accordingly[3]—I am Sir &ca &c.

ADf, ViMtvL; LB, DLC:GW. The text in angle brackets is supplied from the letter-book copy. GW wrote the draft on the back of an apparently unrelated address leaf to "The President of the United States Mount Vernon Virginia."

1. Willis was executor of the estate of Susannah Perrin Holding Washington, the last wife of GW's brother Samuel Washington. The "first mistake" was Willis's sale of five slaves whom she had bequeathed to a son, but who should have been inherited by GW (see Willis to GW, 24 Sept. 1788). Willis's letter to GW of 4 Aug. 1793 explained that those slaves really belonged to the estate of her brother, who had not conveyed them to her.

2. For a copy of Samuel Washington's will of 9 Sept. 1781, see Berkeley County, W.Va., Will Book 1, pp. 237–39. GW was one of Samuel Washington's

executors and had contributed much to the support of Samuel's children, including the daughter, Harriot.

3. Willis replied to GW on 9 Dec.: "About forty days after date I received your favour,[4] I waited the present opportunity to answer it, I accept your offer to put an end to a business that has given me much trouble & uneasiness, & will most certainly soon send the money by some safe opportunity" (ALS, DLC:GW).

To John Cowper

Sir,   Mount Vernon 26. Octo. 93.

I have in my possession a bond of yours, assigned to me by Mr Jno. Lewis, for £146.13.4d—payable with interest the 18. day of may last. I should be glad if you would cause it to be discharged as soon as convenient, as I am in want of the money.[1]

Tomorrow I shall leave this for the vicinity of Philada. the money may be sent by any of the Delegates of this State; or in any other manner more convenient to yourself. I am &c.

                                              Go. Washington.

LB, DLC:GW.

1. This debt stemmed from Cowper's purchase of land in North Carolina owned jointly by GW and the heirs of Fielding Lewis (see George Augustine Washington to GW, 7 Dec. 1790, and n.7; Indenture with John Cowper, 17 May 1791, and n.1). Cowper did not reply at this time, so GW wrote him again on 27 Jan. 1794 mentioning this letter and continuing, "as I have not heard from you on the subject, I presume the letter never reached your hands.

"My want of money urges me, Sir, to beg that you will cause the bond to be discharged with all convenient dispatch" (DfS, sold at auction by Christie's, 1995). Cowper then indicated that payment might not be made until the end of June 1794, and GW did not receive payment until September 1794 (see GW to Cowper, 9 March and 4 Sept. 1794; GW to John Lewis, 8 Sept. 1794).

To John Francis Mercer

Sir,   Mount Vernon 26. October 1793.

Since my arrival at this place from Philada the attachmt of which the enclosed is a copy has been served upon me. I wish to be informed by you how I am to proceed in this business, & what steps, if any, are necessary to be taken by me in consequence thereof.[1] Notwithstanding the directions you have given to the contrary, there rarely comes a Collector who does not present (mingled with my own) Clerk's notes on accot of your brother's Estate, & these, in my absence, are paid by my Manager. I hope your orders will be so pointed in future as to prevent any more coming against me, or my being subject to the paymt of monies for which I receive no benefit.[2]

I brought the bond of your deceased Father, & the Mortgage of your brother with me from Philada for the purpose of surren-dering them to you when the conveyance of the Land to me is made complete; & I beg to know from you whether my signature to that instrument (as it is so drawn) is, in the opinion of profes-sional men, necessary.[3] I shall not appear too pressing I hope to get this business finally closed when, besides the desire natural to me to leave nothing open that can be settled, it has become necessary, that I may take some measures with respect to the Land. I am &c.

Go. W.

Df, ViMtvL; LB, DLC:GW.

1. The enclosed document has not been identified. From Mercer's reply of 30 Nov., it apparently was connected to John Henshaw's bill of complaint about land purchased from George Mercer's estate.

2. For GW's connection with the estate, see Statement concerning George Mercer's Estate, 1 Feb. 1789. John Francis Mercer's response of 30 Nov. 1793 promised to repay these charges.

3. For discussion of John Mercer's bond and James Mercer's mortgage, which GW had acquired as part of his wife's share of her daughter's estate, see GW to James Mercer, 18 March 1789, and n.1 to that document. On the uncompleted conveyance of Montgomery County, Md., land to GW, see GW to John Francis Mercer, 7 Aug., and n.1 to that document, and John Francis Mercer to GW, 15 Aug., and n.2 to that document.

From Edmund Randolph

Sir   Spencer's October 26. 1793.

I had this moment the honor of receiving your letter of the 23d instant by a special messenger from Philadelphia. As he is impatient to return, and I mean to write a duplicate for Elkton, I will trouble you with but a short communication.

At Baltimore and Elkton, two letters of different dates are waiting for your arrival; one written on the 23d, the other on the 25th instant. Since the writing of the last, Colo. Hamilton came hither; and I find, that he concurs in the opinion, which I have given to you in my letter of the 25th that the President cannot constitutionally convene congress, to a different place *as yet*. But he informed me, that he had explained himself in a letter to you for Baltimore.[1]

The disorder is supposed to be better in Philadelphia; but in the suburbs, both North and South, it rages with its ancient vehemence. I cannot therefore believe it possible, for the Ensuing session to be held in that city. I shall go over to German Town this afternoon, and will make an arrangement for your temporary accommodation, adapted to the uncertainty of the position, which congress may take, and leaving you still in possession of the right to choose between Franks's house, and the lodgings near the schoolhouse. Major Lenox, the new marshal, purposes to meet you at Wilmington; and by him I will transmit an account of what I have done. My letter at Elkton compares the different places, which have been named, and mentions a route to German Town; which, however, Major Lenox thinks, that he can improve.[2] I have the honor, sir, to be, with the highest respect, and sincere attachment yr mo. ob. serv.

Edm: Randolph

ALS, DLC:GW.

1. Randolph evidently was referring to his letters to GW dated 22 and 24 October. Alexander Hamilton's letter to GW was dated 24 October.

2. The suggested route is in Randolph's letter of 22 Oct., while the comparison of places is in his letter of 24 October.

From Elizabeth Foote Washington

Sir   Hay-Field [Va.] octo. 26th 1793.

Docter Stuarts stay here was so short the other day & he appear'd to be in such hast to be gone, that mr Washington apprehends he may not have been so circumstantial in his detail of Mr Washingtons case as is necessary, for the cancer Docter to form his judgment on, therefore we have taken the liberty to trouble you with another, as you were so good to mention to mr Washington when you were here, that if he would state his case that you would get mr Dandridge or some other to apply to the Docter respecting it. mr Washingtons objection to going to Pennsylvania or any where from home, arises from his want of eye-sight, & if the Medicine to be given is any ways violent in its operation it affects mr Washingtons nerves in such a degree, that he requires much quiet & not the least noise, for he has already taken so much Medicine during this unfortunate disease—that we are almost alarm'd at the thoughts of giving him any violent medicine at all, indeed several times in his weak state he fell down in all appearence dead, & I fear'd never to recover. am Sir with great esteem your very Hle Sert

Elizabeth Washington

ALS, ViMtvL.

To William Pearce

Mr Pearce   Mount Vernon 27th Oct. 1793.
    Your letter of the 19th came duly to hand. Tomorrow I leave this for Philadelpa or the vicinity of it; where, when you have occasion to write to me, direct your letters.
    As you seemed to be in doubt whether a proper character could be engaged in the part of the Country you live in, to look after my Negro Carpenters; and (having much work to do in their way, & not being willing to leave matters at an uncertainty, I have engaged the person who superintends them at present to look after them another year. He is a good workmen himself, and can be active; but has little authority (I ought to have said command, for I have given him full authority) over those who are entrusted to him—and as he is fond of drink, tho' somewhat reformed in this respect, I place no great confidence in him. He has, however, promised so to conduct himself, as that there shall be no cause for complaint—I thought it was better, therefore, to engage him than to run any hazard.[1] I have engaged no person to look after the house People, Ditchers &ca in place of the one now occupied in that business; and unless a very active & spirited man could be had, it will scarcely be essential while you reside at the mansion house yourself. The old Man that is employed in this business is, I believe, honest, sober, well meaning, and in somethings knowing; but he wants activity & spirit; and from not being accustomed to Negros, in addition thereto; they are under no sort of awe of him—of course do as they please. His wages are

low, Twenty pounds pr Ann. only—Under this statement of the case you may do as shall seem best to yourself. If he is to go, he ought to know it seasonably: his time is up at Christmas; & nothing betwn us has past either as to his going, or staying.[2]

I shall, before you remove, or by the time you may arrive at Mount Vernon; give you full directions, & my ideas upon the several points which may, between this & then, occur to me. In all things else you must pursue your own judgment, having the great outlines of my business laid before you.

After having lived the ensuing winter at the Mansion house you will be better able to decide than at the present moment, how far your convenience, my interest, and indeed circumstances, may render your removal to the other place more eligable. I shall readily agree to either. Materials are now providing for building a house for Mr Crow; whose house it was first proposed you should live in for him to remove to. There are a great number of Negro children at the Quarters belonging to the house people; but they have Always been forbid (except two or 3 young ones belonging to the Cook, & the Mulatto fellow Frank in the house, her husband; both of whom live in the Kitchen) from coming within the Gates of the Inclosures of the Yards, Gardens &ca, that they may not be breaking the Shrubs, and doing other mischief; but I believe they are often in there notwithstanding: but if they could be broke of the practice it would be very agreeable to me, as they have no business within; having their wood, Water, &ca at their own doors without.

The season has been remarkably sickly, generally, but my family, except a few slight touches of the intermittant fever—chiefly among the blacks—have shared less of it, than I find from report, has been felt in most other places. I am Your friend &ca
Go: Washington

ALS, ViMtvL.

1. GW's agreement with Thomas Green is dated 25 Oct. (ViMtvL). In the next year Green's conduct remained so unsatisfactory that GW repeatedly urged Pearce to find a replacement, but Green left of his own accord in September 1794.

2. GW was referring to James Butler, who left Mount Vernon around September 1794.

From "A Citizen of Virginia"

Sir.   Virginia *28 Octr 1793.*

The question, no doubt, has often occurred to you; "where will the Congress meet"? "by their adjournment," which is law to them, at Philadelphia; but, by a physical necessity, more injurious, than law itself, at Philadelphia, they cannot meet. you, Sir, as President of the United States, by the impolitic and narrow jealousy of the Constitution, have a right to convene Congress; but, not to appoint the place. but, in this instance, the Salus populi, which is literally at Stake, is the suprema lex, & must prevail. the crying necessity not only suspends the law, but, quoad hoc, rides over the constitution & tramples it underfoot. clear as this is, still you may feel yourself under a dilemma, because illiberal cant & prompt opposition never suffer an occasion to escape, that affords an opportunity of exercising petulance, & vociferating abuse—to offer to you advice, who, no doubt, will adopt the fittest expedient, may seem presuming; I have therefore suppressed my name, which, at your desire, shall nevertheless be communicated. The expedient, I would with all deference to your better judgement recommend, is, "to write a circular letter to each member of Congress, setting forth the difficulty of the case, (if there be in truth any in it) & proposing different places for their choice, Alexandria, George Town Baltimore, Annapolis, New york, or any other that you may please to enumerate, in order to extract from each of them an opinion of the properest place; & whichever place the majority fixed on, at that place let them be convened"—this may be done by Proclamation, and shelter the executive from any charge of infracting the Constitution, by the assumption of powers, not warranted by the Constitution— should this proposal meet with your approbation, there will be just time enough, to carry it into execution, for, from this day there are five weeks, before the meeting of Congress.

Your goodness and condescension will excuse this obtrusion of my sentiments on you, even if they be erroneous, from my supposing a constitutional embarrassment where there is none, & impute it to my zeal, "to suggest any expedient in this crisis," which my weak Judgement leads me to suppose, may in any the smallest degree, tend to the facilitation of government—with every Consideration of respect & esteem for your private & public Character I remain your fellow Citizen—& faithful Servant—

"A Citizen of Virginia"

AL, DLC:GW.

From Philip Richard Fendall

Dear Sir   Alexandria [Va.] 28th October 1793.

The office of Surveyor of this District being vacant, by the resignation of Mr S. Hanson;[1] I take the liberty of recommending Mr Vincent Gray to you as his Successour.

Mr Gray has acted as deputy Collector for several years, and his conduct has been such as to give the highest satisfaction to the Mercantile interest. I am so well convinced of his integrity and knowledge of the business that I can venture to assure you, that if he is so fortunate as to succeed, he will do credit to the appointment. with due respect I have the Honor to be, Dear Sir your most obedt Servt

Phil. Rd Fendall

ALS, DLC:GW.

1. See Samuel Hanson to GW, 22 October.

From Timothy Pickering

Sir,   Philadelphia Oct. 28: 1793.

I have the pleasure to inform you that the mortal fever which has raged in this city, is prodigiously reduced. A fortnight ago, from 10 to 14 were daily buried in *Friends'* burying ground: but in the last *Five* days only *three* in the whole have been buried there. Among the German Lutherans, the reduction appears by the following list—

Oct. 22d buried 19
23 —— 10
24 —— 8
25 —— 8
26 —— 5
27 —— 1

Of the burials among Friends, half were not of their society: but permission was obtained to bury in their ground.

Last night we had a frost: I found ice in my yard the 5th of an inch thick. We may expect a continuance or frequent repetition of Frost, which must destroy the contagion. The rapid decrease of the sickness within a few days, well warrants that conclusion. Nevertheless, I am of my first opinion, that it will not be expedient for you to come to the city yet: tho' divers of the inhabitants are returning.

Not having been informed whether a house has been provided for you in the neighbourhood, I shall ride to-day or to-morrow to see Mr Peters about it. I hope by the next post to inform you that the provision is made.

Shops are opening, business increasing, and the countenances of the citizens look cheerful.

I am happy to communicate such pleasing news; and remain most respectfully sir, your most h'ble servant

Timothy Pickering

ALS, DLC:GW; Copy, MHi, Timothy Pickering Papers.

From Edmund Randolph

Sir　　　　　　　　　　　　　　Spencer's October 28. 1793.

By the time, when this letter is delivered to you by Major Lenox, you will have received the different letters, which I forwarded to you at Baltimore and Elkton, stating, among other things, what I had done concerning your lodgings.[1] Colo. Franks not being in town, and his agent not being willing to let the house for any period, short of six months, I could not combine the objects, which you have in view so effectually, as to conclude an arrangement with the German Clergyman near the schoolhouse.[2] I wish the accommodation was complete; but it is certainly the best, which can be had. I have agreed for three rooms, and two beds for yourself and Mr Dandridge, and breakfast and tea in the afternoon, at ten dollars each per week. I was afraid, that your servants would have been obliged to lodge three or four hundred yards from you; but this morning I engaged board for them on the lot, adjoining your rooms.[3] Should you want another room,

I am pretty well satisfied, ('tho I do not know it absolutely) that it may be procured. Your horses are to be at Mr Feree's stable about two hundred yards from the schoolhouse.[4] The only remaining difficulty is dinner; for the clergyman cannot go so far, as this meal. A tavern-keeper was to see, if he could get a cook; in which case he would send a dinner to your lodgings. I shall settle with him to morrow, and can give him the information, with which Major Lenox has furnished me, respecting such a servant. I have the honor, sir, to be with the highest respect and sincere attachment yr mo. ob. serv.

Edm: Randolph.

ALS, DLC:GW.

1. See Randolph to GW, 22, 24, and 26 October.

2. An entry for 18 Nov. in GW's accounts records that he "pd Fred: Herman in full for 1½ weeks board & lodging of the President & B.D.—Candles &c. per rect—[$]37.94." (Household Accounts; see also Account Book, 2 Sept. 1793–4 April 1794, DLC:GW). Frederick Herman, a native of Holland who had come to the United States in 1786, was a pastor of the Germantown Reformed Church and teacher at the Germantown Academy. His house, built about 1766, still stood in 1915 at 130 West School House Lane in Germantown (Charles F. Jenkins, *Guide Book to Historic Germantown* [Germantown, Pa., 1915], 79–80).

3. On 18 Nov. GW paid John Merkel $15.82 "for boardg & lodging Lewis & Austin 1½ weeks—& for washg" (Household Accounts; see also Account Book, 2 Sept. 1793–4 April 1794, DLC:GW).

4. Joseph Ferree (c.1729–1804), who represented Lancaster County in the Pennsylvania general assembly, 1770–74, moved to Germantown in 1775. He was a trustee of the Germantown Academy. On 2 Jan. 1794 GW paid Ferree $24.64 for stabling GW's horses at Germantown (Household Accounts; see also Account Book, 2 Sept. 1793–4 April 1794, DLC:GW).

From Philip Filicchi

Sir, Leghorn [Italy] 29 Octr 1793.

The Court of Tuscany having taken the greatest notice of the application I made in favor of the American Brig Minerva Captain Joseph Ingraham consign'd to my Commercial House, I have thought that Your Eccellency would be pleased to be acquainted with it.[1] I therefore have the Honor to enclose a translation of my Letter to the Governor of Leghorn, and of the Answer of the Prime Minister for Foreign affairs to the representation made by

His Eccellency. I remain with the greatest respect Your Eccellency's Most hble & devoted Servt

(Signed,) Philip Filicchi.

Copy, DNA: RG 59, Consular Dispatches. The copy probably was sent via William Seton of New York, to whom Filicchi wrote on this date, in part: "I think
that the President of the United States will be pleased to find that the Court
of Tuscany has been so solicitous to afford every protection to the American Vessell, tho the United States have nobody here authorized to support
the Interest of the People of America—if you think proper you may forward
the enclosed to General Washington" (DNA: RG 59, Consular Dispatches).
Philip Filicchi (Feliechy; d. 1816) was nominated to be consul at Leghorn in
1794, and he served until 1798.

  1. The *Minerva,* owned by Thomas Smith of New York, was captured in
November 1793 by an Algerian corsair, and both ship and crew remained
captive at Algiers in February 1794 (see *Daily Advertiser* [New York], 19 March
1794; *American Apollo* [Boston], 6 Nov. 1794). Joseph Ingraham was redeemed
by the U.S. government in 1796, although he remained in Algiers with the
consul at that time (*United States Chronicle* [Providence, R.I.], 17 Nov. 1796).

Enclosure I
Philip and Anthony Filicchi to the Governor of Leghorn

Leghorn [Italy] 21 Octr 1793.
  We have the Honor to lay before Your Eccelency a Copy of the
Certificate of the Oath taken in New York by every Individual of
the Crew of the American Brig the Minerva (as well as the Extract of the Articles of Navigation, by which every Seaman who
without leave of the Captain is absent from the Vessel for the
space of 48 Hours loses every right to claim his Wages).[1] Alexander Haterton Mariner having incurred this penalty has enter'd
into His Britannic Majesty's service on board of the Frigate the
Meleager. Several days after an Officer of the said Frigate came
to demand the Man's Wages, declaring moreover that he would
in this Port take away by force from the said Brig Minerva that
navigates under the Colours of the United States of America,
the Mate, & one, or two more Men whom he asserts to be born
in England, not valuing that these People having been since naturalized Americans have volontarily given up the Privelege of
being consider'd as Englishmen.[2]
  Lest a violence of this kind should take place in spite of the
Laws, We, to whom the Vessel is consign'd, have thought it our
Duty to have recourse to the Protection of Your Eccelency, &

the more so, as the Vessel would be disabl⟨ed⟩ to proceed in her intended Voyage, if the Threats of the English Officer were to be realiz'd, as there being no American Sailors to be found in Leghorn, the Captain would be oblig'd to take Foreigners, who would be liable to be taken away from him when at Sea, & lose thus both Vessel & Cargo. General Washington will be pleas'd to find that even without the assistance of an American Consul, notice has been taken of his Circular in which he requests protection for the American Colours.[3] We remain with the greatest respect Your Eccellency's Most humble & obt Servts

Philip & Anty Filicchi

Copy, DNA: RG 59, Consular Dispatches.

1. These enclosures have not been identified.

2. When the *Minerva* sailed from Leghorn in November, its mate was Edward Smith (born c.1772). He was captured with the ship at that time and redeemed from Algiers in 1796 (see *American Apollo* [Boston], 6 Nov. 1794; *Minerva, & Mercantile Evening Advertiser* [New York], 3 Nov. 1796). The *Meleager*, which carried thirty-two guns, was launched in 1785 and wrecked in 1801.

3. The Filicchis evidently were referring to Secretary of State Thomas Jefferson's circular letter to Consuls and Vice-Consuls of 21 March 1793 (*Jefferson Papers*, 25:415–18).

Enclosure II
Antonio Serristori to the Governor of Leghorn

Florence [Italy] 23 Octr 1793.

Having spoken to Lord Hervey, & shewn him Your Eccel⟨ys⟩ Letter dated the 21 inst. as well as the Paper No. 1, therein a⟨n⟩nex'd, he has inform'd me by writing that he has represented t⟨he⟩ matter to the Commander of the Squadron who is now in t⟨he⟩ City, & who has written to the Commander in his Absence ordering him not to take any Step against the America⟨n⟩ Vessel.[1] I remain &c. Your humble Servt

(Signed,) Anthony Seristori.
Minister for Foreign affairs

Copy, DNA: RG 59, Consular Dispatches.

Antonio Serristori was councillor of state for Tuscany from 1748 until at least 1794.

1. John Augustus Hervey (1757–1796), styled Lord Hervey, was the British envoy to Tuscany, 1787–91, and minister, 1791–94. The commander of the

British squadron at Leghorn was Capt. William Young (1751–1821), a career naval officer who was promoted to captain in 1778 and ultimately rose to the rank of vice admiral (Filicchi to William Seton, 29 Oct., DNA: RG 59, Consular Dispatches). According to a letter from Filicchi to Seton of 11 Nov., the *Minerva* "went away undisturbed" (DNA: RG 59, Consular Dispatches).

From Gouverneur Morris

Paris 29. October 1793

I take the liberty of introducing to the acquaintance of General Washington a person highly deserving of his Notice: Monsieur de Volney who will have the Honor to deliver this letter goes out to acquire in America an Addition to his Stock of knowledge.[1] His Conversation equally pleasing and instructive will I trust agreably relax some of your careful Hours. I am happy in the opportunity he gives me of presenting him and of assuring you of my Esteem and respect.

LB, DLC: Gouverneur Morris Papers.

1. Constantin-François Chasseboeuf. Volney (1757–1820) was a French writer most noted for *Les Ruines; or Méditation sur les Révolutions des Empires* (2 vols. [Geneva, 1791]), which attacked political despotism. He was arrested for debt in November and hence postponed his contemplated visit to America. However, he did make an extended visit to America beginning in October 1795 and stayed at Mount Vernon in July 1797 (see GW to George Washington Parke Custis, 23 July 1797).

From Robert Townsend Hooe and David Ross

George Town 31st Octr 1793.

Sir

We have according to your appointment[1] at the instance of the Commissioners of the City of Washington examined their Accounts, and find themselves charged to the State of Virginia £30.000. the State of Maryland £27.000 and for Lots and other articles sold £6.005.14.9. Amounting to the Sum of £63.005.14.9. And we find vouchers of Expenditure, up to the 30th Instant, to the Amount of £50.502.9.9.¼ including the purchase of the Quarry of White Stone, leaving a Balance in Mr William Deakins's hands their Treasurer £12.500.4.11.¾, of whic⟨h⟩ £6.743.12.10.½ is Cash in hand, the Balance consists of an Order in his favor on the State of Virginia not yet received. It may not be improper to add that besides this balance there is £15.000 of the Donation of the State of Virginia not yet drawn for.[2] And the Commissioners have already sold Lots to the Amount of £89.568.9.8.¼ payable by installments and including a contract, with one of the purchasers to build ⟨A⟩nnually Ten Houses for seven years, each House to cover at leas⟨t⟩ 1200 square Feet of Ground.[3] We have the Honor to be Sir with the greatest Respect Yr Most Obt Servts

R. T. Hooe
David Ross

Copy, DNA: RG 42, Records of the Commissioners for the District of Columbia, Proceedings, 1791–1802.

A note preceding the copy of this letter states that Hooe and Ross "made their report to the President, a Copy thereof they delivered the Commissioners, and is as follows."

1. For the appointment see GW to Ross and Hooe, 9 September.

2. In 1790 the Virginia legislature had agreed to advance $120,000 to the federal government for the construction of public buildings at the Federal City, payable in three equal yearly installments (Va. Statutes, 13:125).

3. This contract was made with James Greenleaf on 23 Sept. (see GW to the Commissioners for the District of Columbia, 20 Aug., n.3).

From Jonathan Trumbull, Jr.

Dear sir   Lebanon [Conn.] 31st Octo. 1793

By some unaccountable delay, the Letter with which you have favored me, of the 13th inst. did not reach me 'till the 30th.

While writing mine of the 2d of this month, the doubt which you have been pleased to mention, respecting the Law of Congress, fixg the seat of Government, occurred to me; but turng to the Law, I found the 5th sec: mentions—"That prior &ca *all offices* attached to the Seat of Government shall be removed to Phila. &ca at which place, the session of Congress *next ensuing* shall be held." the 6th Sec: mentions "That in *the Year 1800*—the Seat of Government shall be transferred &ca and *all offices* &ca shall be also removed" &ca but not a word of the Legislature— by which it would seem, *it* is left to its own adjournments, and the discretion of the President *on extra Occasions.*[1]

Indeed I conceived that the Constitution in granting this discretion, must have contemplated *place,* as well as *time* of meet-ing—because the necessity for its exercise, might be grounded equally in one as the other—Witness the existing instance—the first that has occurred.[2]

Moreover the Constitution must be paramount to the Law in such Cases: otherwise the power granted may be so controuled as not to be sufficient to surmount the necessity of the occasion[3]—the like necessity may also exist under other circumstances—such as, the total destruction of the City by fire, or other means, its being in complete possession of an Enemy—& other insur-mountable calamities which might occur—In all which cases, if the Law fixing the Seat of Govermment must rise superior to the Constitution, the discretionary Power of the President, calculated to afford a remedy under such exigencies, must be futile, & prove totally inadequate to the purposes for which it was intended.

I also considered that should doubts arise, they would be eas-ily obviated by reflecting, that this exercise of discretion could not be dangerous; because it would be in the power of Congress, as soon as met, to remedy the Evil, should they apprehend any, by an immediate adjournment to where-ever they might judge proper—besides it is calculated to remedy an existing inconve-nience & danger to themselves, which in its nature, is only tem-porary, & is hoped to prove of but short continuance.

As to the Place of meeting, I am very sensible it will be an ob-ject of delicacy to decide—When I took the liberty to suggest the hints I gave to you, this difficulty presented itself; and I was then almost tempted to add a word on that head, but was repressed by the fear of assuming too much—I therefore now mention—what I before thought—that in casting about, it is probable the Towns of Baltimore & New York will present themselves to your Mind as the most convenient places. to the latter I am sensible Objections will be started by some; notwithstandg its superiour advantages perhaps for the present temporary Occasion—to ob-viate therefore these objections to New York, should they appear with weight—and to save any uneasiness in the minds of our southern Brethren from that Quarter, I have thought for myself, (& in this I have been joined by others)—that I should perfectly acquiesce in Baltimore—I should mention the expedient of con-vening Congress somewhere in the vicinity of Philadelphia, and leave the final decision of *Place* to their determination; but that I fear, such Event may occasion disputes & delay—not to say heats perhaps—which might prove much more detrimental to our general Interests, than your fixing at once a place by your own Judgment & discretion—I most sincerely hope, that, whatever place is appointed, the melancholly occasion of leaving Philadelphia may speedily be removed—and that Congress may soon be able to return to that City again. With real regard & respect, I am, most most affectionately, Dear sir Your Obedient & obliged humble servant

J. Trumbull

P.S: Before closing this Letter, we are gratified with much more favorable Accounts from Phila. than for some time past—I really hope they may prove true—and that circumstances in that distressed City may continue to meliorate, so that you may have complete relief from your present dilemma on that Score. Yours as above—

ALS, DLC:GW; ADf, ViMtvL.

1. Trumbull was referring to "An Act for establishing the temporary and permanent seat of the Government of the United States," 16 July 1790 (1 *Stat.* 130).

2. On the draft the text in this paragraph was written as an insertion to be placed in front of a sentence that does not appear in the ALS: "This View of the Law—compared with the constitutional Power of the Presidt satisfied my mind—& occasioned my writing as I did." Trumbull evidently was referring to Article 2, section 3 of the Constitution, which stated that the president "may, on extraordinary Occasions, convene both Houses, or either of them."

3. At this place on the draft, Trumbull wrote the following before revising and then striking it: "as in this Instance particularly calls for the Exercise of Discretion."

Letter not found: from J. Des Moulins, 1 Nov. 1793. On 6 Jan. 1794, Moulins wrote to GW: "I humbly presume to remind your Excellency, of...a long Letter from Wilmington on the 1st of last Novr."

From Edmund Randolph

Novr 2. 1793.

The attorney general of the United States has the honor of submitting to the President of the United States the following considerations on the power and propriety of convening congress to a place, different from the city of Philadelphia.

The constitution declares, that "neither house, during the session of congress, shall, without the consent of the other, adjourn for more, than three days, nor to any other place, than that, in which the two houses shall be sitting."[1]

The residence-act directs, that the session "of congress next ensuing the present (that is the session in July 1790) shall be held" in the city of Philadelphia;[2] and the adjourning order of both houses, at the close of every session, since they began to sit in Philadelphia, has made no mention whatsoever of *place*.

Hence it is correct to infer, not only that Philadelphia was the place, intended by congress for their next session; but also, that the constitution and residence-act have rendered that city, at least until the year 1800, the constant place of session; unless it be changed in some constitutional way.

How can such a change be effected?

By a new law, a concurrent vote of both houses, even without the intervention of the President, or by a summons from the President.

The past conduct of the legislature shews their opinion of their own power, to fix a temporary place for the session of congress. If it were now a question, whether by a new law the *permanent* seat of government might be altered, much could be urged in opposition upon constitutional grounds. But the temporary seat stands upon a less solemn basis.

Had the constitution been silent as to the place for the sessions of congress, they would have possessed inherently a right to assemble, wheresoever they pleased. But it is more than silent: it recognizes that right; and restricts it in no respect, until the permanent seat shall be established. For the temporary is not contemplated by the constitution—it makes no part of the ten miles square—it requires no cession from particular states—it is liable to no exclusive legislation. It is true indeed, that the temporary seat was said out of doors, at the time of the passing of the residence-act, to be a condition of the permanent: that is, Pennsylvania was to enjoy the benefit of congress until the year 1800, as preliminary to the final position on Potomack. Be this as it may, the judgment must turn upon the rules of construction. These inform us no where of this supposed condition: in 1800, the government is to be transferred to the fœderal city, without regard to any place, *from* which it is to go; and after 1800, the public offices attached to the seat of government, will absolutely cease to be exercised elsewhere.

It may therefore be concluded, that by a new *law*, congress may choose a new spot for the temporary seat of government.

Nor does the residence-act abridge the power of the two houses to adjourn to a different place, even without the consent of the President; or in other words, they may so adjourn by a mere vote, instead of a formal law. For, altho' it is thereby established, that the offices, attached to the seat of government, among which is comprehended that of President, are to remain at Philadelphia; it is practicable for congress, notwithstanding the inconvenience, to carry on their business, without the presence of those offices, with *all* their papers, or more than are necessary for the matters immediately in hand.

In like manner may the place be varied, whensoever an extraordinary occasion shall arise, which justifies the President to convene congress. It must be admitted, that he will generally find the last place of session most proper for their meeting on his call: Yet if the last place must be adhered to at all events, the power of convening may be often annihilated in substance. For example: the extraordinary occasion may consist in a foreign invasion; and the last place of session may be in the hands of the enemy. In such a case, the President may surely mark out both time and place. If therefore an extraordinary occasion may sometimes signify place, as well as time; the President, being the judge of the nature of that occasion, may name the place, according to his discretion, as soon as he has decided the time.

Between the act of the two houses, and his own interposition, the President will be compelled to elect; should the misfortune of Philadelphia continue to oppress it; and indeed it ought rather to be said, that this is the moment for determining, whether he will leave the place for the next session to the will of congress in the first instance, or will now convene them to a place of his own choice.

The objections appear so strong against the latter expedient, as to give a clear preference to the former. What are extraordinary occasions, are left to the decision of the President; who may pronounce definitively and without controul upon them. No individual, nor either body of legislation can refuse to comply with the summons. This power therefore, like all others of a supreme nature, ought to be exercised with caution.

It would be impossible to enumerate every species of extraordinary occasion. The most obvious definition would be such a situation of public affairs, as requires the meeting of congress at an earlier day, than that, on which they would meet of course. For if they were bound by their own adjournment, or by the operation of the constitution, or of some law, to meet sooner than, or as soon as, they could assemble under a call from the President, it would be in general inexpedient to superadd a call.

With this criterion of an extraordinary occasion, it may be asked, whether any exists independent of the contagion? It cannot but be answered, that some such does exist. The contagion then may be viewed under two aspects; either as a cause for calling congress, or as a cause for changing the place of session. It might perhaps amount to a cause for calling congress, if we were to advert, only to the expence of double public offices—the danger of keeping the public archives in so exposed a city, and a well grounded reluctance in the President to be responsible for ordering them to another place, not designated by, but contrary to law—the difficulty to public creditors in procuring payments from the treasury—the propriety of legalizing many acts, concerning the revenue performed at the custom-houses, removed, as they are, from the port of Philadelphia—the interruption to the sessions of the district courts, confined as they are by law to Philadelphia; and to other topics, like these.[3] But the entire energy of them is taken away, when it is notorious, that congress will come together, in pursuance of their own adjournment sooner than the President could collect them.

Undoubtedly the contagion may be a cause for changing the place of session. But how wide is this idea from a cause for calling congress? It would approach to an absurdity to contend, that the malignant fever in Philadelphia, by being a reason for congress, (if they are to meet) meeting at some other place, is of itself a reason, why they should meet. In fact, the extraordinary occasion must arise, before the place can be thought of; for the power of fixing the place is not given to the President *expressly,* but merely as an incident to the great necessity, which induces the President to convene congress. And this distinction deserves the more attention; as the constitution, while it suffers him to interpose on a disagreement of the two houses as to time, has not submitted to his umpirage their disagreement as to place.[4]

And what harm can be done, by leaving things in their usual channel? Perhaps by the first monday in december next, Philadelphia may be restored to health, and freed from infection. It is possible, that on the appointed day a quorum of both houses may enter its limits, and adjourn to some other spot, or be content to remain. If none of these events should happen during the first day, then an extraordinary occasion will be created. For the legislative concerns of the U.S. will not admit delay; and it will be fairly presumable, that there will be no certainty of a session before a distant day. A proclamation for convening congress may therefore issue immediately afterwards.

Upon the whole, It seems adviseable for the President not to convene congress *now*. This opinion may be fortified by other subordinate considerations: the exercise of a doubtful power excites clamor—some members nay a majority may prefer Philadelphia under all its embarrassments—it may be conceived to be an unnecessary cruelty to that depressed city, *as yet,* to transfer congress elsewhere.

If at length, however, a place must be selected by the President, he will probably ask himself, whether he means it for a previous consultation of the members, or for the absolute sitting of congress. For the former purpose, German Town is sufficiently convenient. But it will not escape the President's observation, that this exercise of authority will be so feeble, as to betray a suspicion, that he himself distrusts his right to fix the place, and therefore consigns it to congress. Besides it may be easily conceived, that the representations from the different states will be very disproportionate at the commencement of the session; and it will be fortunate, if any accidental majority should be deprived of the opportunity of rivetting an improper place of session. Nay farther: if one place if countenanced for a moment by the President, it will prevent every other place from making preparations; and then congress must go to some large town, New-York or Baltimore, where they can be received at the shortest notice.

But if instead of a place for previous consultation, the President should seek one adapted to the full session, and Philadelphia be excluded, New-York, Trenton, Wilmington, Baltimore,

Annapolis, German-Town, Reading, and Lancaster come into competition.

A general objection applies to the first five. They are out of Pennsylvania, which is intitled by law, as the law now stands, and by equity too, to the temporary residence. If this once passes into another state, its return will be very difficult; or if it should return, a precedent will be established, which will press at a future day, with great force, on the removal to the fœderal city. It will be argued, that the residence-act had no other sanction, than an ordinary law, since it could be so easily dispensed with for the sake of a seeming public utility.

But against those five towns, individually taken, these things may be excepted. New-York will awaken old jealousies, and may not be without her hauteur—Trenton is a thoroughfare; considerably exposed to infection, if it exists in Philadelphia; and from its past pretentions to the seat of government in its neighbourhood may also agitate the minds of some. If Wilmington is equal to congress, it is also a thoroughfare. Baltimore and Annapolis would be to the Pennsylvanians, as odious, as New-York would be to the friends of Potomack.

As to the towns in Pennsylvania, Lancaster is first in rank. It is able and willing to accommodate. Reading, as Judge Rush asserts, cannot undertake such a task—German Town, in spite of all, that may be said, cannot accommodate congress satisfactorily. The timid will shrink from the neighbourhood of Philadelphia, they may with reason apprehend the return of the fever in the spring; and with certainty they may expect old beds and furniture from Philadelphia, which remained in many infected houses. The fare and rooms will be wretched; the distance, which the members will have to travel thro' unpaved streets in a muddy season, will be dreadful; the high prices, which will be demanded by the people for putting themselves out of the way, will disgust, when the entertainment is so indifferent; the foreign ministers will be crouded into dirty hovels; and a place of worship in the English language is scarcely to be found. These disadvantages cannot be counterbalanced by access to the public offices; as the papers, wanting for congress from them, may be put in a compass, not very bulky.

Altho' the foregoing sentiments are designed to dissuade the President, if he interferes at all, from interfering in an indecisive manner; yet as the sense of Several members as to the place will be known, it will no doubt be treated with due respect.

However it will be a very questionable policy for the President to recommend to them, even informally, any thing preliminary; because in his intercourse with public men on public subjects, he ought to be seen only as a public man himself; and because the steps, which the exigency of the moment may dictate, will be so obvious to the members, that an intimation from him will be deemed useless, if not intrusive.

If any thing is permitted to be said, as from the President, by individuals to their friends, ought it to go farther than this: that if from the appearance of things on the second day it shall be proper to convene congress by a special act, he will do so, and at a different place. This communication may serve to bring the members into the neighbourhood.

Edm: Randolph

ADS, DLC:GW.

1. Randolph was quoting from Article 1, section 5 of the Constitution.

2. Randolph was referring to "An Act for establishing the temporary and permanent seat of the Government of the United States," 16 July 1790 (1 *Stat.* 130).

3. Section 1 of "An Act to regulate the Collection of the Duties imposed by law on the tonnage of ships or vessels, and on goods, wares and merchandises imported into the United States," 31 July 1789, had specified that Pennsylvania would be a single district, with Philadelphia the "sole port both of entry and delivery," and that the naval officer, collector, and surveyor "shall be appointed, to reside at the said port of Philadelphia" (1 *Stat.* 32). Section 3 of "An Act to establish the Judicial Courts of the United States," 24 Sept. 1789, stated that the district court for Pennsylvania would be held at Philadelphia (1 *Stat.* 73–74).

4. Article 2, section 3 of the Constitution, which gave the president the power to convene Congress "on extraordinary Occasions," also stated that "in Case of Disagreement between them, with Respect to the Time of Adjournment, he may adjourn them to such Time as he shall think proper."

From Hannah Fairfax Washington

Sir   Nov: 2d: 1793:

On reconsidering Your Acct I think it but reasonable (as I am to be allow'd interest) that I shou'd also pay it (for the last ten Years) on the Acct thought to be due from our estate of £16.6. As

I did agree to pay You the principal, I will certainly allow the interest for the above term of Yrs. If that Acct had been presented by any other; than from One of my Brothers Executors, I wou'd not have paid it, but I thought as He had been so kind as to leave me a Legacy, I wou'd lose some pounds, rather than dispute it, tho I knew Mr Washington had paid it off, many Yrs Ago.[1]

Your Acct of £52.7.1. I am very willing to have deducted out of the £94.8. due me, as interest on my Bro: Legacy. Mr F. Fairfax told me the other Day, as He shou'd indemnify You for paying me the Interest, on my legacy, there was not the least necessity for my giving a Bond.

As to the debt thought to be due, from Mrs Bushrods Estate I cannot think of paying it. I might just as soon pay any other persons Acct off, as Hers. You was misinformed about Mr Washingtons being a Legatee, it is true His Children were, but several of them are Married, & have receiv'd their Legacies long ago. Were not the Legatees, assur'd She had paid the Acct Herself, & think there must have been an omission in not giving her credit, they wou'd willingly refund, each their share, & pay it. They have reason to think so, knowing She was never easy, if She owed a Shilling to any One, till She paid it, & had allways Money by Her at least ever since I knew Her, which was upwards of twenty Years.[2] I am Sir Yr very Hble Serv:

H: Washington

ALS, ViMtvL.

1. The account being discussed here has not been found. It apparently was connected to the estate of George William Fairfax, who died in 1787 leaving Hannah Fairfax Washington a legacy of "five hundred pounds currt money of...Virg[ini]a." GW, who between 1773 and 1775 had overseen George W. Fairfax's affairs in America, was designated as one of his executors and had delivered the news of Hannah's legacy, but he declined to serve. See Samuel Athawes to GW, 20 July 1787; GW to Warner Washington, 9 Nov. 1787; and GW to Athawes, 8 Jan. 1788 (*Papers, Confederation Series,* 5:263–65, 425–26; 6:14–15).

2. Mildred Washington Bushrod (1720/1–1785) was a sister of Hannah Fairfax Washington's husband, Warner Washington (1722–1790). In her will she bequeathed to her brother Warner "all the Horses and money I have in my Possession at my Death as well money due me and not heretofore disposed of" (Will Book 5, pp. 85–86, ViWnFreCh).

From the Commissioners for the District of Columbia

sir   George Town 3d Novm. 1793

Colo. Hooe and Majr Ross's report, which they have inclosed you will inform you of the result of their examination of our accounts; that with the Treasurer stands in the place of a cash account, is accurate and authorized by our warrants, which are justified by Vouchers—these were all compared and did not take up two days—The Gentlemen went farther and have given a general state of Funds, this part is not so precise, it gives a general Idea, and was added under an impression; that you might perhaps think proper to publish it—not that they urge it, and we have no desire at all that it should be done[1]—We have much more pleasure in being able to inform you, that we have a prospect by negociations with the Banks, to keep in Credit till May, even if Virginia should disappoint us; and then Mr Greenleaf's payment and Loan; if not extended, coming on, things may be pushed with vigour a year longer.[2]

We have concerned in an application for a chartered Bank on such a system that we hope the City may be bennefitted by its Gaurrantee for the payment of Interest instead of the deposit of productive Funds required by Dutch Capitalists. to give the out lines of the whole would be too lengthy, but it appears to us a sober plan.[3]

Permit us to request your order on Virginia for her last payment—We are advised the Taxe's are now coming in, and we wish to make the demand early in the Session. We are &ca

Th. Johnson
Danl Carroll
Comrs

P.S. Colo. Deakins has just now receivd a Letter from Mr Hopkins informing him that the executive of Virginia has granted an order on the Secretary of War for 10.000 Dollars.

Copy, DNA: RG 42, Records of the Commissioners for the District of Columbia, Letters Sent, 1791–1802.

1. See Robert Townsend Hooe and David Ross to GW, 31 October. For background to this audit, see D.C. Commissioners to GW, 5 Sept., and n.2 to that document.

2. In an agreement of 23 Sept., James Greenleaf had contracted with the commissioners to purchase 3,000 lots in the Federal City at £25 each, to be paid in seven annual installments commencing on 1 May 1794. In addition, Greenleaf agreed to loan monthly £1,000 current money of Maryland, commencing on 1 May 1794 and continuing until the public buildings "now erected" were completed, or until 1 Jan. 1800 (see GW to the Commissioners for the District of Columbia, 20 Aug. 1793, n.3).

3. For the passage by the Maryland legislature of a bill to establish a bank in the District of Columbia, see Daniel Carroll to GW, 9 Dec., and n.2 to that document.

From Alexander Hamilton

Sir,   Fair Hill[1] [Pa.] Novembr 3d 1793.

Not having been in condition to attend you yesterday, and (though free from fever) yet not being well enough to go abroad immediately, I have concluded to submit to you by a line the result of my further reflections on the subject of my last letter.[2]

I believe it will be altogether safe for the ensuing session of Congress to be held at Philadelphia, and that the good of the public service requires it, if possible. Under the existing prospect, I do not think it would be adviseable for the President to give the business a different direction by any preliminary step. But as the apprehensions of distant members will probably be too much alive it is desirable they should if possible be brought into the vicinity of Philada *some days* before hand to examine and judge for themselves. It is likely they will then be satisfied that they can safely sit in the City. If otherwise, their sentiments concerning another place can be collected as a guide to the President.

To effect this end I would advise that circular letters be written (say by the Atty General, the Secy of State not being here) to the respective members informally recommending to them as on the part of the President to repair to Germantown and it's vicinity some days not more than a week prior to the day for the meeting of Congress, giving the reasons for this recommendation.

I prefer this to any public act, because there is an inconvenience in giving any sort of formality to an unauthoritative proceeding.

An objection to the proceeding is that the remote southern

members cannot be reached in time but the answer to this is that they will probably come forward of course to some neighbouring State, New York Delaware or Maryland, & letters for them may be lodged in each. With true respect & attachment I have the honor to be sr

Alexr Hamilton

LB, DLC:GW.

1. Fair Hill was located roughly three miles from Philadelphia along the Germantown Road.

2. See Hamilton to GW, 24 October.

From Tobias Lear

My dear Sir,   New York November 3d 1793

Presuming that you are now in German Town, agreeably to the arrangement which you informed me you had made for that purpose, when I had the honor of seeing you at Mount Vernon, I shall address this letter to you at that place; and have taken the liberty to enclose two copies of some observations respecting the River Potomack, the Country about it and the City of Washington, which I have noted down since my return to this place from George Town.

My object in writing these observations is to have some copies of them printed, that I may have it in my power, while in Europe, to give a more particular account, to such as may wish it, of that part of the Country which I have chosen for my establishment, than they may, as yet, have been able to obtain.

I have not had time to go so much into the detail on this subject as I wished. My view in these notes has been to give such facts respecting the Potomack and the City as may be important to be known, in the first instance, to those who may turn their attention to that quarter. My own knowledge of that part of the Country was too limited to allow me to depend altogether upon that for a statement of facts. I have, therefore, as you will observe, had recourse to others on whose authority I could rely—and I have found Mr Jefferson's notes on the State of Virginia, and some extracts, which I met with, from the Report of the Committee appointed by the Merchants of George Town & Alexandria

which is said to be founded on the actual observations made by
order of the Directors of the Potomack Company of great use
to me.[1] I have given these observations in as plain and simple
language as I was capable of doing, beleiving, if I had been able
to dress them up in a captivating garb, that it would not be best
to do so. A naked state of facts is all that is necessary to recommend the Potomack or the Country about it. All comparisons
or reflections that might look like raising the Potomack by the
depression of any other place, I have carefully avoided.

The friendship with which you have honored me, and the indulgence you have always shewn towards such attempts as I have
made to be serviceable to myself or others, emboldens me, my
dear Sir, to ask the favor of your perusing the enclosed, and rec-
tifying such errors of fact as may appear therein, and to return
me one of the Copies with your sanction of the statement being
founded in truth, *if you shall feel yourself perfectly free to do so.*

In the copies I may have printed, or otherways, I shall make
no improper use of the sanction you may be pleased to give of
the truth of the statement. I wish it only for my own satisfaction,
that I may feel confident in what I relate; for altho' it will not be
mentioned in the printed copies by whom the observations are
made; yet as that may hereafter be known, and possibly while I
am at a distance from this Country, the truth of the statement
may be questioned by persons who may be interested in depre-
ciating subject of these notes, I shall feel gratified by having it
in my power to convince those who may be interested in obtaining the truth, that they have been inspected by one whose situation has given him the best opportunity of knowing the circumstances of the Country, and who would not suffer a statement to
have his sanction unless supported by truth.

At the present moment, which I know must be a busy one with
you, I would not presume to offer a thing of this kind for your
inspection, but under a full beleif that the subject is so well understood by you that a single perusal will enable you to pass sentence upon it.

Finding that my business in Europe will first require my presence in Great Britain, I have engaged my passage in the American Ship Fanny, bound to Glascow, which is expected to sail
about the 10th of this month; but I think it probable she may be

detained a few days longer. She is a regular Trader to Glascow &
a very fine Ship. An extension of our business will probably occasion my stay in Europe to be longer than I at first contemplated.
This has obliged me to protract the time of my sailing beyond
what I expected, in order to make my arrangements to comport
with the time which I may be absent.

As I shall go to Scotland from the circumstance of the Ship in
which I am to sail being the first American Vessel bound from
this place to Great Britain, it is my intention (if nothing should
occur to make it proper for me to go to London *immediately* on
my arrival) to visit some of the principal Manufactories of Scotland where such goods are fabricated as suit our market; altho'
I shall have letters from some respectable merchants of this
place to their correspondents; yet I shall esteem it a great favor if
you will have the goodness to give me letters of introduction
to the Earl of Buchan & Sir John Sinclair, who from their situations in that Country may be able to give me much useful
information.

Upon enquiring for Mr Robinson, who took your portrait for
the Earl of Buchan I am informed that he is now up the River;
but is expected home in a day or two, when I shall, without fail,
see him respecting the portrait.[2]

I have been so closely engaged in my own business since my
return from George Town, that I have had but little opportunity
of mixing in Society and learning the prevailing opinion of the
day on politics. I have heard enough, however, to know that the
conduct of Mr Genet, in the publication of his correspondence
with Governor Moultrie and his letter to Mr Jefferson, is very
much disapproved.[3] Indeed so warm appears to be the censure
of those I have heard speak on the subject, that I am not without
apprehension that the operation of party, added to the general
indignation expressed at his conduct, may lead to some impru-
dent step towards Mr G. personally, which might be productive
of unpleasant circumstances in a national view.

The British Packet arrived here this day; but she brings no
accounts so late as have been brought by other vessels from
Europe.

The Accounts of the disorder in Philadelphia having been
checked by the weather give great pleasure but still there are

strong expressions of anxiety on account of your being so near the City while any signs of the disorder remain in it. Since the abatement of the disorder it seems to be a general opinion here that Congress will sit in Philadelphia.

A man by the name of Jacob Baur, has for some days past been importuning me to mention to you his wish to fill the place about your person lately occupied by William. He says he was for several years Valet de Chambre to the late Lord Barrymore, and occasionally acted as his Butler. He shewed me a certificate give him by Lord B. in which he recommends him as an honest, sober & most valuable servant. His present occupation is hair dresser at the Tontine Coffee House. I have made no enquiries respecting the man here, and shall not do it unless it is your wish to get a person of this description.[4]

Since my return to this place I have received several letters from my friends in Portsmouth which give me the pleasing information of my darling boy being in fine health & as full of spirits and activity as ever. The interest which you have ever taken in the welfare of this little fellow leads me to beleive that this account will be acceptable to you—and to Mrs Washington I am likewise sure it will give pleasure.

I presume Mrs Washington is not with you at German Town; but whether she is or not, I must beg the favor of being presented to her in terms of the liveliest respect & gratitude. My young friends about her have my best wishes for their health & happiness and will always be remembered by me with sincer regard.

I shall do myself the honor of writing to you again before I sail, if anything should occur worthy of being communicated to you. With sentiments of the highest respect and unbo⟨und⟩ed attachment I have the honor to be, my dear Sir, Your grateful & affectionate servant

Tobias Lear.

ALS, DLC:GW; ADf, PWacD: Sol Feinstone Collection, on deposit at PPAmP. The last three paragraphs of the ALS do not appear on the draft.

1. The first American edition of Thomas Jefferson's *Notes on the State of Virginia* was published at Philadelphia in 1788. The report of the committee, signed by Robert Peter and nine others, was dated 7 Dec. 1789 and published as a one-page broadside at Alexandria, Virginia.

2. For Lear's report of his meeting with the painter Archibald Robertson, see his letter to GW of 9 November.

3. William Moultrie's letter to Edmond Genet of 5 Sept. and Genet's reply of 15 Oct. appeared in *Diary; or, Loudon's Register* (New York), 22 Oct., and other papers. Moultrie asked Genet about the reports that he had threatened to "appeal to the people" in his dispute with GW. Genet replied by stating that he would ask Congress for "the severest examination of all my official measures, and of every particular step which may be supposed to have been an attempt, upon the established authority of the American Republic." This examination would refute the "falsehoods, which a dark and deep intrigue has laid to my charge," and show that "if I have complained officially, and in no other way of the conduct of certain officers of the Federal Government, whose intentions appeared to me both destructive of liberty, and favourable to our enemies: if I have declared that their tameness, that their small measures in the common danger which menaces free nations, did not appear to me to be consistent with the sentiments of their fellow-citizens, with the true interests of their country: if I have expressed without disguise, my grief at seeing General Washington, that celebrated hero of liberty, accessible to men whose schemes could only darken his glory: if by this boldness, I have made myself the mark for all the resentment their utmost perfidy can occasion, I have never forgotten, what I owe to the supreme head of the executive of a great people, who were the first to open the career to freedom, the first to proclaim the Rights of Men, and whose existence is as dear to us, as ours is necessary to them."

A translation of Genet's letter to Thomas Jefferson of 27 Oct. appeared in *Diary; or, Loudon's Register,* 30 Oct., and other papers. Genet protested GW's dismissal of Antoine Charbonnet Duplaine as French vice-consul at Boston, "because the constitution of the United States has not given the President the right which he now appears desirous to exercise." Genet argued that once a diplomatic officer was admitted, he could be dismissed only by the sovereign who had sent him.

4. On 5 March 1793 Jacob Baur advertised himself in New York as a ladies' hairdresser "Just arrived from London" (*Diary; or, Loudon's Register,* 9 March). GW employed Baur as a valet and butler from late December 1793 to November 1794 (see GW's testimonial for Baur, 4 Nov. 1794). After leaving GW's employ, Baur resumed his occupation as a hairdresser at 61 Liberty Street in New York (*Daily Advertiser Extraordinary* [New York], 9 Dec. 1794). Richard Barry (1769–1793), tenth earl of Barrymore, was a Whig member of Parliament from 1791 until his death in March. GW's former valet William Osborne, who had given notice in August, died during the yellow fever epidemic.

Enclosure
Observations on the Potomac River

[c.3 November 1793]

Observations on the River Potomack—the Country about it—
and the City of Washington.

The River Potomack forms a junction with the Bay of Chesapeak 150 miles from the Sea. From thence to the head of tide-
Water is about 160 miles.

"This River is 7½ miles wide at its mouth; 4½ at Nomony Bay;
3 at Aquia; 1½ at Hollowing-Point; 1¼ at Alexandria—and the
same from thence to the City of Washington, which is within
3 miles of the head of tide Water. It's soundings are 7 fathoms
at the mouth; 5 at St Georges Island; 4½ at Lower Matchodic; 3
at Swan's Point—and the same from thence to the City." (Mr Jef-
fersons Notes on Virginia)[1]

From the Capes of the Chesapeak to the City of Washington
is upwards of 300 miles; but the navigation is easy and perfectly
safe. ["]A vessel of 1200 Hogsheads of Tobacco has loaded at and
sailed from Alexandria, and one of 700 at George Town—which
is above the City.["] [(]Report of Committee[)]

At the City the water rises four feet in a common tide.

From the City of Washington to Cumberland, a flourishing
town at the head of the River, is about 230 miles as the River
runs.

Early in life General Washington contemplated the opening
of this River from tide water to its source, so as to render it navigable for such vessels as were suitable for carrying the produce
of the Country to the shipping ports below. His public employments in the part of the Country through which the Potomack
and its branches run, had given him a more complete knowledge
of this River than almost any other man possessed at that time
and his mind was strongly impressed with its future importance.
But the period for undertaking a work of such magnitude had
not yet arrived. The Country was then but sparsely inhabited;
Canals & Locks but little understood, especially in America and
but few men of property were willing to embark in an undertaking, the cost of which they could not clearly calculate, and the
profits of which were to many doubtful. General Washington

however kept the object steadily in view, waiting until time & circumstances should enable him to bring it forward with a prospect of success. The war with Great Britain took place about the time when the importance of this object began to be understood and a willingness to embark in it began to appear among men of property. Until the close of that war nothing, however, could be attempted in the business. But no sooner had a happy termination of it enabled General Washington to retire from his high public station, than he resumed this object which had so long before occupied his mind. He found Gentlemen of the first property and respectability in the neighbourhood of the Potomack, both in Virginia & Maryland, ready to engage in the enterprize. In the year 1784 a Company was formed for the purpose of removing the obstructions and opening the navigation of the River from its source down to Tide-Water—and an act of incorporation passed by the Assemblies of Virginia & Maryland, authorizing the Company to take the necessary measures for carrying into effect the objects for which they were corporated—and granting to them *forever* the tolls which may arise therefrom; which tolls are fixed by the same law that empowers the Company to undertake the business. The sum agreed upon to complete the navigation was fifty thousand pounds sterling, divided into five hundred shares of one hundred pounds each, to be paid by such instalments and at such times as the Directors of the Company Shd find necessary for the prosecution of the work. Ten years were allowed to the Company to finish the business.[2]

The Company have prosecuted their work with great success; And, what is not common in undertakings of this nature, they will complete it for something less than the sum subscribed. The rate of toll being fixed, and knowing with some accuracy the quantity of produce that is now brought by land from those parts of the Country which will of course throw the same upon the River, they have a certainty of receiving a handsome per Centage on their Capital in the first opening of the River (even without calculating upon the articles which will be sent up the River)—and the increase will be almost incredible—Those who know the Circumstances of the Country best, and some who are not among the most sanguine with respect to the profits of this undertaking, have no doubt of the Capital's producing fifty per Cent annually in less than ten years from the time of the Tolls commencing.

The principal work in completing the above mentioned navigation is at the Great Falls, 14 miles above the City of Washington—at the Little Falls 4 miles above said City, and in clearing the River between these two falls. At the Great Falls the water falls 72 feet in one mile and an half—and at the Little Falls 36 feet 8 inches in about two miles. At the former there will be 6 and at the latter 3 locks. The Locks at the Little Falls will be finished this season and fit for use; those at the Great Falls are in forwardness—and with the clearing the bed of the River between the two Falls, will be completed next year. This will finish the navigation of the main River from Cumberland down to tide water, and enable the Company to receive the reward of their expense & labour. Bateaux carrying from 150 to 200 barrels of flour already pass from Cumberland to the Great Falls—and many thousand barrels of flour have actually been brought in boats to the latter place during the present year.

Besides the main River of the Potomack, its numerous & extensive branches offer the prospect of transporting to the main River, and from thence to the Shipping ports, an immense quantity of produce.

The following are the principal Streams which empty into the Potomack, above tide water, and the distances to which they are navigable in their natural state, from their conflux with the Potomack—*Patterson's Creek,* which falls into the River ten miles below Cumberland, is navigable twenty miles above its mouth; *The South Branch,* seventeen miles below Cumberland, navigable one hundred miles; Cape Capeon, sixty miles below, is navigable twenty miles; *Connocochegue,* ninety miles below, is navigable twenty four miles; *Opecan,* one hundred & twenty five miles below, is navigable twenty five miles from its mouth, and within a few miles of Winchester, which, after Lancaster, is the largest inland town in the United States; The *Shannandoah,* one hundred & thirty miles below, runs into the Country at right angles from the Potomack near two hundred miles—and the navigation of it for one hundred & fifty miles of that distance is but little interrupted: The chief obstru[c]tion is where it enters the Potomack, and so trifling is that compared with the great advantages of this noble branch, that its removal, and clearing other parts, will not cost more than twenty five thousand dollars. The Potomack Company have already made a beginning on this work. The *Monocosy* one hundred & fifty miles below Cumberland, is navigable thirty miles above its mouth. This branch is within two miles of Frederick Town in Maryland, one of the largest inland towns in the United States.[3]

These several Streams as well as the main River, pass through a Country not exceded in fertility of soil and salubrity of air by any in America, if by any in the World. And no part of America can boast of being more healthy than the Potomack in general.[4]

The number of inhabitants living in the several counties of Virginia & Maryland which touch upon the Potomack or its Branches, amount to upwards of three hundred thousand, according to the Census taken by order of the General Government in 1791. They are all, or so nearly so that not one fiftieth part can be excepted, Cultivators of the Soil. It is therefore easy to conceive that they must send an immense quantity of Produce to the Shipping ports on the River. But still so extensive is the Country through which the Potomack and its branches pass, that it is yet but thinly settled. Its inhabitants are however very rapidly increasing as well by imigration as by the natural course of population.

The Productions of the Country consist of Wheat—Indian Corn or maize, Rye—Oats—Tobacco—Potatoes, Beans—Peas—and in short of every article that the best farming lands are capable of producing. Hemp & Flax are cultivated here and yield large quantities. The Land is rich in pasturage—most parts of it admirably adapted to sheep—and a heavy growth of Timber fit for ship building, as well as for every other purpose, is found here. There is near Cumberland, and within 10 or 12 miles of the River, a tract of country that abounds with very large white pine trees suitable for masts of Ships: some of these trees are from 5 to 6 feet diameter and run up one hundred feet without a limb.

Slate, Marble, Freestone of the red & gray portland kind and Iron Ore are found in abundance on the Banks of the River. Several large Iron works are already established which furnish Bar Iron & Castings of an excellent quality. Limestone abounds everywhere. Of coal too there is an inexhaustible quantity near

Cumberland laying on the Banks of the River—and in other parts at no great distance from it; from whence in future not only all the towns and manufactories on the River may be supplied; but it will become a capital article of exportation.

There is in the River a great plenty of very fine fish. Large quantities of shad and Herrings are annually taken here and exported to the West Indies.

From the preceding observations it is easy to conceive that the Commerce of this River cannot be inconsiderable: And a single view of the Situation upon which the City of Washington is laid out, points out that spot as the most eligible on the River for a large commercial town.

The City of Washington lays in Latitude 38_ 53' it is situate on the East side of the Potomack about 4 miles from the head of tide water, and extends down the River nearly four miles, to an angle which is formed by the junction of the Eastern Branch with the Potomack; it then runs along the Eastern Branch for more than two miles. Its general width is about one mile and three qua⟨rters.⟩

The Eastern Branch affords one of the finest harbours for Ships imaginable. It is more than a mile wide at its mouth, and holds nearly the same width for almost the whole distance to which the City extends upon it; it then narrows gradually to its head, which is about ten miles from its conflux with the Potomack. The Channel of this Branch lays on the side next the City; it has in all parts of it, as far as the City extends, from 20 to 35 feet of Water. Above the City it is only navigable for small craft. The Channel is generally so near the City that a wharf extended 40 or 50 feet from the Bank will have water enough for the largest Ships to come & discharge or receive their Cargoes. The land on each side of the Branch is sufficiently high to secure shipping from any wind that blows. And one very important advantage which this Branch has, as a harbour, over all extensive Rivers which freeze and are liable to be broken up suddenly by freshes or land floods, is, that, on account of the short distance to which it extends into the land, no rapidity of current is ever occasioned by freshes; and while Vessels in the main River, if they should happen to be caught there by the ice, are liable to receive great injury, and are sometimes totally lost by it, those in the Branch lay in perfect security: it has also the advantage of being open some days earlier in the spring and later in the winter than the main River at George Town and the upper parts of the City. The River generally shuts up about Christmas and is open again the latter part of february or very early in March. Sometimes there are only short interruptions by ice through the winter—and sometimes it happens that it is not closed so as to prevent the navigation during the winter. This was the case last winter.

The main Channel of the Potomack opposite the City, running near the Virginia Shore, that part of the City which lays on the Potomack has only a small Channel carrying from 8 to 12 feet of water, until you come within about _ of a mile of George Town, when the Channel turning between Mason's Island and the City, gives a depth of water from 20 to 30 feet close in with the shore of the City. This renders the water lots within that small space very valuable; for any ships that come up the River may here lay within twenty yards of the City; and the Bateaux which bring the produce of the Country down the River may at all times come here deep loaded as the⟨y⟩ come down, whereas they could not go thus loaded down to the Eastern Branch, unless in very smooth weather.

Before a particular description of the Spot &ca on which the City of Washington is laid out, be given, it may not be improper to note the constitutional and legal ground upon which the location of the City is made.

The Constitution of the United States grants to Congress the power "to exercise exclusive legislation in all cases whatsoever, over such district (not exceeding ten miles square) as may by cession of particular States, and the acceptance of Congress, become the seat of the Government of the United States."[5]

In conformity with this Constitutional power the following Act was passed on the 16th of July 1790—

"An Act for establishing the temporary and permanent Seat of the Government of the United States.

Section 1st Be it enacted by the Senate and House of Representatives of the United States of America in Congress assembled, That a district of Territory, not exceeding ten miles square, to be located as hereafter directed in the River Potomack, at some place between the mouths of the Eastern Branch and Connogochegue, be, and the same is hereby accepted for the permanent

Seat of the Government of the United States: Provided nevertheless, that the operation of the laws of the State within such district shall not be affected by this acceptance, until the time fixed
for the removal of the government thereto, and until Congress
shall otherwise by law provide.

Sect. 2d And be it further enacted, that the President of the
United States be authorized to appoint, and by supplying vacan-
cies happening from refusal to act or other causes, to keep in
appointment as long as may be necessary, three Commissioners,
who, or any two of whom, shall, under the direction of the President, survey, and by proper metes and bounds define and limit
a district of Territory, under the limitations abovementioned;
and the district so defined, limited & located, shall be deemed
the district accepted by this Act for the permanent Seat of the
Government of the United States.

Sect. 3d And be it enacted, That the said Commissioners or
any two of them, shall have power to purchase or accept such
quantity of land on the eastern side of the said River, within the
said District, as the President shall deem proper for the use of
the United States; and according to such plans as the President
shall approve, the said Commissioners or any two of them, shall
prior to the first monday in December, in the year one thousand
eight hundred, provide suitable buildings for the accommodation of Congress, and of the President, and for the public Offices of the Government of the United States.

Sect. 4. And be it enacted, That for defraying the expense of
such purchases and buildings, the President of the United States
be authorized and requested to accept grants of money.

Sect. 5. And be it enacted, That prior to the first Monday in
December next, all offices attached to the seat of the Government of the United States, shall be removed to, and until the
said first monday in December one thousand eight hundred,
shall remain at the City of Philadelphia, in the State of Pennsylvania, at which place the session of Congress next ensuing the
present shall be held.

Sect. 6. And be it enacted, That on the said first Monday in
December in the year one thousand eight hundred, the seat of
the Government of the United States, shall, by virtue of this Act,
be transferred to the District and place aforesaid. And all Offices attached to the seat of Government, shall accordingly be

removed thereto by their respective holders, and shall, after the said day, cease to be exercised elsewhere; and that the necessary expense of such removal shall be defrayed out of the duties on imposts & tonnage, of which a sufficient sum is hereby appropriated." [6]

Upon examining the ground within the above described limits, and taking into consideration all circumstances, the President fixed upon the spot upon which the City has been since laid out, as the most proper for erecting the public buildings which are authorized to be prepared by the foregoing Act.

But the Eastern Branch being made one of the boundaries within which the District of ten miles square was to be laid out, an amendment of the preceding act was thought necessary, so as to include a convenient part of the said Branch and the land of the South Eastern side of it within the said District of ten miles square. A formal Act for that purpose was accordingly passed on the third day of March 1791. By this means the Commissioners were enabled so to lay off the District of ten miles square, that the Centre thereof is made the centre of the spot on which the City is laid out as nearly as the nature & form of the ground of the City will permit. The District of ten Miles square thereby includes the River Potomack for 5 miles above & the like distance below the middle of the City—and extends into the State of Virginia about three miles over the River.[7]

The whole Area of the City consists of upwards of four thousand Acres. The ground is on an average about forty feet above the water of the River. Altho' the whole taken together appears to be nearly a level spot, yet it is found to consist of what may be called wavy land—and is sufficiently uneven to give many very extensive and beautiful views from various parts of it, as well as to effectually answer every purpose of cleansing and draining the City.

Two Creeks enter the City, one from the Main River, the other from the Eastern Branch, and take such directions as to be made to communicate with each other by a short Canal. By this means a water transportation for heavy Articles is opened into the heart of the City.

No place has greater advantage of water either for the supply of the City or for cleansing the streets than this ground. The most obvious source is from the head waters of a Creek which

seperates the City from George Town. This Creek takes its rise
in ground higher than the City, and can readily be conveyed
to every part of it. But the grand object for this purpose which
has been contemplated by those best acquainted with the Country hereabouts and the circumstances attending it, and which
has been examined with an eye to this purpose by good Judges,
is the Potomack. The water of this River above the Great Falls,
14 miles from the City, is 108 feet higher than the tide water. A
small Branch, called Watt's Branch, just above the falls, goes in a
direction towards the City. From this Branch to the City a Canal
may be made (and the ground admits of it very well) into which
the River, or any part of it, may be turned and carried through
the City. By this means the Water may not only be carried over the
highest ground in the City; but if necessary over the tops of the
Houses. This operation appears so far from being chimerical,
that it is pronounced by good judges, who have examined the
ground through & over which it must pass, that it might be effected for perhaps less money than it has and will cost the Potomack Company to make the River Navigable at the Great &
Little Falls—and to clear the bed of the River between them.

Should this be effected the produce of the Country will naturally be brought through it, and the situation afforded thereby
for Mills and Manufactories of every kind that require the aid
of Water, will be most excellent, and commensurate with any
object.

The public buildings for the accommodation of the Congress
and the President of the United States are begun—and progress
with much spirit. They are on a scale equal to the magnitude of
the objects for which they are preparing—and will, agreeably
to the plans which have been adopted, be executed in a style
of architecture chaste—magnificent & beautiful. They will be
built with beautiful white Stone which is pronounced certainly
equal if not superior to the best portland Stone, by persons who
have been long experienced in working the first quality of the
Portland Stone. The quantity of this Stone is fully equal to any
demand that can arise for it. That used for the public buildings
is from an Island about 20 miles[8] below the City, which has been
purchased by the Commissioners, and from which, and a tract
of land laying on the River in the neighbourhood of it (the right
of getting stone from which for 20 years has also been purchased

by the commissioners) it is supposed that enough of this Stone may be obtained to answer every demand, however great.

Besides the buildings for the accomodation of the Government of the United States, a very superb Hotel is erecting, the expense of which is defrayed by a lottery the Hotel being the highest prize. This building, with all its accommodations and dependencies, will perhaps be equal to any one of the kind in Europe.

The Original proprietors of the land on which the City is laid out, in consideration of the great benefits which they expected to derive from the location of the City, conveyed, in trust, to the Commissioners, for the use of the public & for the purposes of establishing the City, the whole of their respective lands which are included within the lines of the City, upon condition, that, after retaining for the Public any number of Squares that the President may think proper for public improvements or other public uses, the lots shall be fairly and equally divided between the public and the respective proprietors.

By this means the public had possession of upwards of ten thousand lots from which funds are to be raised to defray the expense of the public buildings (in addition to [   ]⁹ dollars given by the States of Virginia and Maryland for that purpose)— and to effect such other things as it may be incumbent on the public to do in the City—Between three & four thousand lots have been already disposed of by the Commissioners, and the average price at their public sales has exceded two hundred & forty dollars per lot. The price of lots has lately risen very much— and a great increase is still expected as the object comes to be more investigated & better known.

After furnishing very ample funds for the accomplishment of every object in the City on the part of the public, a large surplus of lots will remain the property of the City, which hereafter may, and undoubtedly will be so applied as to defray the annual expenses incident to the City—and the Citizens and their property thereby be free from a heavy tax which is unavoidable in other large Cities.

Among the many advantages which will be derived to this City, over almost all other large Cities, from the Circumstance of its being originally designed for the Capital of a great Nation—may be ranked as the foremost, the width of the Streets—(none of which are less than ninety feet, & from that to one hundred & sixty) and the attention which will be paid to leveling or regulating the Streets, upon a general principle, in the first instance, in such a manner as to avoid any future inconvenience to such buildings as may be erected in the early establishment of the City—and to give that declivity to them in the several parts of the City as will readily and effectually carry all filth into the common Sewers—These circumstances are of the highest importance as they affect the health and the lives of the inhabitants.

Besides the advantages which the City of Washington will have from its being the Seat of the Government of the United States—from its being within a few miles of the Centre of the Territory of the United States from North to South, and nearly the Centre of population—and from the immediate commerce of the Potomack—it will receive an immense benefit from its intercourse with the Country west of the Allegany Mountains through the River Potomack, which offers itself as the most natural and the nearest Channel of Commercial intercourse with that very extensive and rich Country.

At present the land carriage between the navigable Waters of the Monongahelia (a fork of the Ohio) and the navigable Waters of the Potomack is less than forty miles, and a good waggon Road is open between the two waters. Men of judgement on the subject of inland navigation have examined the ground between the highest branches of the Potomack and those of the Ohio, and have been decidedly of opinion that the land carriage between the two places, where boats may come to each, can be reduced to fifteen miles, and they have found nothing to convince them but that these waters may hereafter be made to communicate with each other.

The Settlers on the Ohio & Mississippi will of course carry their heavy produce to a market down those Rivers; but their returns will be most natural through the Potomack; for they cannot ascend the Western Waters without great expense and much loss of time, the current there being so rapid that a sharp boat with six oars can scarcely ascend fifteen miles per day.

The fur and peltry trade of the great Lakes may be brought to the City of Washington, through the Channel of the Potomack, four hundred miles nearer than to any other shipping port to which it has hitherto been carried.

Mr Jefferson, in his notes on the State of Virginia, mentions this subject in the following words,

"The Potomack offers itself under the following circumstances for the trade of the Lakes and the Waters Westward of Lake Erie. When it shall have entered that Lake it must coast along its southern shore on account of the number and excellence of its harbours; the Northern tho' shortest having few harbours and those unsafe. Having reached Cayahoga, to proceed on to New York it will have eight hundred and twenty five miles and five portages; whereas it is but four hundred and twenty five miles to Alexandria its emporium on the Potomack, if it turns into the Cayahoga and passes through that, Big Beaver, Ohio, Yahogany (or Monongahelia & Cheat) and the Potomack, and there are but two portages; the first of which from Cayahoga to Big Beaver may be removed by uniting the sources of these waters which are Lakes in the nighbourhood of each other and in a Champain Country: The others, from the waters of the Ohio to the Potomack, will be from fifteen to forty miles, according to the trouble which shall be taken to approach the two navigations. For the trade ⟨of⟩ the Ohio, or that which shall come into it from its own waters or from the Mississippi, it is nearer through the Potomack to Alexandria than to New York by five hundred & eighty miles, and is interrupted by one portage only. There is another circumstance of difference. The lakes themselves never freeze; but the communications between them freeze; and the Hudson's River itself is shut up by ice three months in the year; whereas the Channel to the Chesapeak leads directly to a warm climate, the southern parts of it very rarely freeze at all, and whenever the Northern do, it is so near the sources of the Rivers, that the frequent floods to which they are liable, break the ice up immediately, so that vessels may pass through the winter subject only to accidental and short delays." [10]

In addition to the foregoing remarks it may be only necessary to say, that there is not a River in America capable of being rendered more secure from an attack by water than the Potomack. Its banks are every where high and bold, with the Channel often not more than two hundred yards from the Shore. Diggs' point, about ten miles below the City of Washington, is remarkably well calculated for a Battery; as all vessels coming up the River must present their bows to that point for the distance of three quarters of a mile;[11] and after passing, their sterns are equally exposed for about the same distance; the middle of the Channel there is not more than two hundred yards from the point.

It may not be amiss to subjoin the following extracts from the Laws of Maryland, and the terms and conditions for regulating the materials and manner of the buildings and inprovements on the Lots in the City of Washington.

Extract from the Act of the Assembly of Maryland, entitled "An Act for opening and extending the navigation of the River Potomack," in which the Shares are made real Estate.

"Be it enacted, That foreigners shall be and are hereby enabled to subscribe for and hold Shares in the Potomack Company." [12]

Extract from an Act of the General Assembly of Maryland, entitled "An Act concerning the Territory of Columbia, and the City of Washington.

Be it enacted, That any foreigner may, by deed or will, here-after to be made, take and hold lands within that part of the said Territory which lies within this State, in the same manner as if he was a Citizen of this State, and the same lands may be conveyed by him and transmitted to, and be inherited by his heirs or relations, as if he and they were Citizens of this State Provided, That no foreigner shall, in virtue hereof, be entitled to any further or other privilege of a Citizen." [13]

"Terms and Conditions declared by the President of the United States, for regulating the materials and manner of the Buildings and Improvements on the lots in the City of Washington.

1st   That the outer and party walls of all houses within the said City shall be built of Brick or Stone.

2d   That all buildings on the streets shall be parallel thereto, and may be advanced to the line of the Street, or withdrawn therefrom, at the pleasure of the improver: But where any such Building is about to be erected, neither the foundation or party-wall shall be begun without first applying to the person or persons appointed by the Commissioners to superintend the buildings within the City, who will ascertain the lines of the walls to correspond with these regulations.

3d   The wall of no house to be higher than forty feet to the Roof in any part of the city; nor shall any be lower than thirty five feet on any of the Avenues.

4th   That the person or persons appointed by the Commissioners to superintend the Buildings may enter on the land of any person to set out the foundation and regulate the Walls to be built between party and party, as to the breadth and thickness thereof: Which foundation shall be laid equally on the lands of the persons between whom such party-walls are to be built, and shall be of the breadth and thickness determined by such person proper: and the first builder shall be reimbursed one moity of the charge of such party-wall, or so much thereof as the next builder shall have occasion to make use of, before such next Builder shall anyways use or break into the Wall—The charge or value thereof to be set by the person or persons so appointed by the Commissioners.

5th   As temporary conveniences will be proper for lodging workmen and securing materials for building, it is understood that such may be erected with the approbation of the Commissioners: But they may be removed or discontinued by the special order of the Commissioners.

6th   The way into the Squares being designed in a special manner for the common use & convenience of the occupiers of the respective squares. The property in the same is reserved to the public, so that there may be an immediate interference on any abuse of the use thereof by any individual, to the nuisance or obstruction of others. The proprietors of the lots adjoining the entrance into the Squares, on arching over the entrance and fixing gates in the manner the Commissioners shall approve, shall be intitled to divide the space over the arching and build it up with the range of that line of the square.

7th   No vaults shall be permitted under the streets, nor any encroachment on the footway above by steps, stoops, porches, cellar doors, Windows, ditches or leaning Walls; nor shall there be any projection over the Street, other than the eves of the Houses, without the consent of the Commissioners.

8th   These regulations are the terms & conditions under and upon which conveyances are to be made, According to the deeds in trust of the lands within the City." [14]

AD, in Tobias Lear's writing, DLC:GW. This document, with a few mostly minor alterations, was printed as *Observations on the River Potomack, the Country Adjacent, and the City of Washington* (New York, 1793). The differences that affect content are indicated in notes below.

1. See Jefferson, *Notes on the State of Virginia*, 5. Lear's citations for this paragraph and the next paragraph are in the left margin of the document.

2. For a summary of GW's involvement with the Potomac River Company, see GW to Benjamin Harrison, 10 Oct. 1784, editorial note. For the act,

passed by the Maryland legislature on 28 Dec. 1784 and by the Virginia legislature on 4 Jan. 1785, see GW and Horatio Gates to the Virginia Legislature, 28 Dec. 1784, enclosure II.

3. In the printed version, this paragraph is footnoted with the following information: "Report of the Committee appointed by the Merchants of George-Town and Alexandria, which, being founded on the actual observations made by order of the Directors of the Potomack Company, may be deemed authentic" (p. 10).

4. In the printed version, the preceding sentence is replaced with a similar claim: "and few parts of *America* can boast of being equally healthy with the banks of this river, and the adjacent country" (p. 10).

5. Lear is quoting from Article 1, section 8 of the Constitution.

6. See 1 *Stat.* 130.

7. For this act, see 1 *Stat.* 214–15.

8. This is "40 miles" in the printed version (p. 20).

9. This blank is filled in the printed version as "192,000 dollars," of which $120,000 came from Virginia and $72,000 from Maryland (p. 21).

10. For this text, see Jefferson, *Notes on the State of Virginia*, 14–15.

11. In the printed text this distance is given as "three miles" (p. 26). Digges Point is the site of what is now Fort Washington National Park, in Prince Georges County, Md., across the Potomac River from Mount Vernon, north of where Piscataway Creek enters the river.

12. This act was passed 21 Dec. 1790 (*Md. Laws 1790*, ch. 35, sec. 4).

13. This act was passed 19 Dec. 1791 (*Md. Laws 1791*, ch. 45, sec. 6).

14. Lear here reproduces GW's second proclamation of 17 Oct. 1791 (see Proclamation, 17 Oct. 1791, n.1).

To Howell Lewis

Dear Howell,   German Town [Pa.] Novr 3d 1793.

The short time I was with you, and the hurry into which I was thrown by the pressure of many matters, public & private, prevented my mentioning many things wch ought to have been communicated to you before I left home; but I shall do it by letter as they may happen to occur to me.

I have already told you, that the Corn is to be gathered without loss of time as soon as circumstances will permit. When this is done, let all that is intended for the uses of the respective Plantations be put into Corn houses by itself; and the overplus into other Houses. As there is but one Corn house at Muddy hole, Davy must put all that grows at that place into it—I hope the quantity will exceed 150 Barrels; but if it should fall short of it, that quantity must be made up from the field he tended at

Dogue Run. after which, the residue of that field of his, may be lofted along with McKoys Corn. Let McKoy put 180 Barrels into one of his Corn houses for the use of the Farm, & the residue in the other. Crow may put 250 Barrls in one house, and the residue in another; And Stuart may do the same—that is—put 250 barrls in one house, and all that remains in the other.[1] Tell all of them that I exhort them most earnestly to be extremely careful of the Corn. I know this article will fall short of my demands for it; & I know not where it is to be bought, or where to find money if I did. Unless you can buy Oats, the horses at the Mansion house must be fed with Corn & Bran, & that sparingly, except the five horses which are to come this way with your Aunt. Have an eye that Martin does not neglect them; nor spare the Curry comb. He wants looking after. The Corn with which these five horses are fed should be ground into small homony, & if Bran was mixed with it, it would be none the worse, & would go farther. The Horses on the different Farms, tell the Overseers, must be kept in good heart (notwithstanding the sparing use of the Corn) as they will have a great deal of heavy plowing to do this Fall & Winter; which, not being sure I fully explained to all of them, I herewith enclose a list; with which you will furnish each of them that is with so much as relates to his own business.[2]

As a house will be built for Crow at the place marked out (not far from the Barn) the Corn house near to the one in wch he now lives, ought to be removed to the Barn, & set in uniformity with the other, before the Corn is lofted (if it can be done conveniently) and as there is no Spring near to the house which is to be built for Crow, a Well should be dug in the Barn lane, opposite to the centre of that house, & exactly half way between the same and those which will be opposite to it for the Negros. My ideas on this head have been explained to Thos Green, as to the spot. This Well need be no larger in the diameter than is sufficient to contain a Pump, which it must receive; & the size proper for this you must enquire into. I should think Thomas Davis & Nuclus must have ingenuity enough to sink this Well as I hope & expect it will be very shallow after they have laid the foundation (with Brick) for the Overseers house; but if they have any doubts themselves of their sufficiency, employ the Well digger in Alexandria, who sunk the Well at the Mansion house lately; & if it is to be done by him, let it be undertaken immediately[3]—For Wa-

ter found at this season of the year, & especially after so parch-
ing a drought, may be depended upon. This is a good reason for
its being done soon, by whomsoever it is undertaken.

I directed the Miller to put up 6 Hogs for forward Bacon, &
to call upon McKoy for Corn to feed them. I always forgot to tell
the latter to send it, & possibly it has been neglected. enquire
into, & see that it is done.[4]

As I am almost certain I shall want feed next year, both for
man & beast, more than I have made this; and as a good deal of
my Wheat (unless it surprisingly alters from the Rain which has
lately fallen here, & I hope with you) tell Mr Stuart & Mr Crow
(whose Wheat I think was worst) that if they could sow a part
of that which is most missing with Rye, if to be had, it will be a
pleasing thing to me. I mean such parts of the fields only as are
not likely to produce Wheat next year with any prospect of success—It is not too late to sow Rye, & the Straw will be useful for
thatching sheds, for the Cover of my Cattle; which I should wish
to do before the winter, next after this which is now approaching, sets in.

If you cannot get Oats, about ten bushels of old Corn ought
to be reserved for feeding the horses with, which are to come
this way some days before they set out otherwise travelling them
after being fed upon new corn may be the loss of some of them
on the road, besides the detention it would necessarily occasion
to your Aunt.

Just before I left home I discovered that the Carters & Wag-
goner, in order to get their horses easily of mornings, turned
them into the Clover lot by the quarter. forbid this absolutely.
They have injured it considerably already, by eating it so bear as
for the frosts to kill the roots, but will ruin it entirely if they are
suffered to continue this practice any longer.

When the Potatoes are taken up, tell Butlar to have the tus-
sicks of course grass or Broom, & large Weeds (which I noticed
in the lower part of that lot) taken up also; that the ground, when
sown next Spring, may be in better condition for the Oats &
clover which is to be put in it.

Whenever the weather appears to be settled, and the morning
promises a good day, get Peter & Martin, or Charles (for I know
not what he does) and take every thing out of the Store that requires to be aired—cleaned from Mould, and the other injuries

they are sustaining—and when thoroughly cleaned and dried, returned & put away again together with the other things in that place; with that regularity and order that whatever is wanted from thence may be seen & got at without difficulty. When this is done, take an exact inventory of the whole (even to minute things) and send it to me. that I may know what is there. The Valeses (that is things like Portmanteaus) which contain my marquie & other things, ought all to be opened, wiped clean, and dried. The Trunks, belonging to my camp equipage should be served the same way, (the Keys you will find in my writing table). and in short every thing rescued from the disorder and injury which they seemed to be undergoing. The Nails where they are not in whole Casks shd be counted (which is soon done by counting 125 & putting the same weight of nails in the other scale & keep doubling of them until you get 1000 in a scale; after which you will soon ascertain the whole number of thousands in the Cask[)]. I sent, (not a great while ago) a considerable quantity of Paint from Philadelphia to Mount Vernon; but do not recollect to have seen any in the store. enquire for this, and let it be put there for safety (if it can be stowed there conveniently) or kept under a lock the key of which is in the box; for unless this is done there will be a flemish account of it when it is wanted for use.[5]

Before I left home I directed old Jack to clean the Seed loft over the green house thoroughly, that the several Bins might be in order for the reception of Oats or other Grain, in quantities, which might be placed there for Spring seeding. To put the Casks which had Timothy & orchard grass seeds by themselves, so as to be known—and all the empty Casks by themselves, & as much out of the way as they could be. See that this is done, & tell Butler it is my wish as soon as his Potatoes are up, & secured in the manner already mentioned to you; I desire he will immediately thresh out all the Oats at the Mansion—on the Barn floor if it can be spared by the work people—measure & put them in the Seed loft above mentioned, & inform me of the quantity. Those in the Corn loft, if any remains after the others are threshed, might be threshed also; as I want all I have for seed; being of a good kind. The Straw after the Oats are taken from them, may be still cut for the Work horses as usual, but Bran or chopped Corn must be mixed therewith, to give the more nourishment to them.

As the Corn house at Crows is of framed work, & not heavy, while empty, it may be removed on Rollers; and as Mr Stuart pretends to be well acquainted with the manner of doing this work having been frequently engaged therein, consult him, as well as Green on this business—Stuart says there is a gum tree on the Farm he is at, that will make excellent rollers—Let these be got from thence & well made, that they may serve for other purposes hereafter. It will naturally occur to you that this work (if done at all this season) ought not to be delayed until the ground gets soft, for that would encrease the labour four fold, if not render it impracticable at all. And speaking of this I will mention a proverb to you which you will find worthy of attention all the days of your life; under any circumstances, or in any situation you may happen to be placed; and that is, to put nothing off 'till the morrow, that you can do to day. The habit of postponing things, is among the worst in the world—doing things in season is always beneficial—but out of season, it frequently happens that so far from being beneficial, that oftentimes, it proves a real injury. It was one of the sayings of the wise man you know, that there is a season for all things, and nothing is more true; apply it to any Occurrence or transaction in life. I am Your sincere frie⟨n⟩d and Affectionate Uncle

Go: Washington

P.S. If you could get a fair rope for the Well by the Quarter it would be desireable. I directed Peter two or three times to make enquiry for one at the Rope Makers in Alexa., but I do not know the result of it.[6]

As your Aunt may wish to see my letters to you, always show them to her. Yrs as above

G.W.

ALS, owned (1970) by Mrs. Robert P. Oldham, Carpinteria, California.

1. Henry McCoy, Hiland Crow, and William Stuart were GW's overseers for the Dogue Run, Union, and River farms at Mount Vernon.

2. The enclosed list has not been identified.

3. This well was constructed opposite the greenhouse between July and November 1792 (see GW to Anthony Whitting, 1 July and 25 Nov. 1792). GW's accounts indicate that in October 1792 Robert Brockett was paid £28.14.6 "for digging & walling a Well" (Ledger B, 347). Robert Brockett (c.1751–1829), a native of Scotland, arrived at Alexandria from Ireland in 1785 and advertised his services as a stonecutter and bricklayer. He remained in Alexandria until his death.

4. The miller at Mount Vernon was Joseph Davenport.

5. A Flemish account is one in which the value is less than expected, an unsatisfactory or bad account.

6. GW may have been referring to James Irvin, who was a rope-maker at Harper's Wharf in Alexandria in the 1780s and 1790s (Miller, *Artisans and Merchants of Alexandria,* 1:226).

From Thomas Jefferson

[Germantown, Pa.] Tuesday Nov. 5. 1793.

Th: Jefferson with his respects to the President sends for his perusal some of the letters which had been accumulating at his office, & which he received yesterday.[1] he will wait on the President to-day to translate the Spanish papers sent by mister Short, as also with some other letters in foreign languages.

Th: J. sends to the President a supply he received yesterday of paper, of which the President will be pleased to take any proportion he may have occasion for. he sends him wafers also & wax, & could furnish him copying ink, but he believes the President has no press here. Th: J. did not understand yesterday whether any meeting was desired to-day or at any other particular time.

AL, DNA: RG 59, Miscellaneous Letters; LB, DNA: RG 59, George Washington's Correspondence with His Secretaries of State.

1. The enclosures included a letter from William Carmichael and William Short to Jefferson, 15 Aug., enclosing copies of their correspondence with Diego de Gardoqui about accusations that Spanish agents were exciting Indian animosity toward the United States (*Jefferson Papers,* 26:668–71); a letter from Short to Jefferson, 20 Aug., enclosing a copy of the convention between Spain and Great Britain signed at Aranjuez, 25 May (*Jefferson Papers,* 26:732; for the convention, see *ASP, Foreign Relations,* 1:277); Thomas Pinckney's letter to Jefferson of 27 Aug. discussing his efforts to assist Philip Wilson, whose ship *Mentor* had been destroyed by British vessels near Cape Henlopen in 1783 (*Jefferson Papers,* 26:770–71); Pinckney to Jefferson, 28 Aug., enclosing both his correspondence with Lord Grenville about the rights of neutral vessels and the slowness of admiralty decisions on vessels seized and a letter from Thomas Digges discussing a plot to counterfeit American currency (*Jefferson Papers,* 26:776–82); a letter from David Humphreys to Jefferson of 1 Sept. reporting his plans to leave for Gibraltar and miscellaneous news (*Jefferson Papers,* 27:4–5); a letter from Ezra Fitz Freeman to Jefferson, 5 Sept. (not identified), enclosing Abraham Freeman to GW, 5 Sept.; Stephen Moylan to Jefferson, 19 Sept., notifying that he would not accept his appointment as federal marshal for Pennsylvania (*Jefferson Papers,* 27:137–38); Christopher Gore to Jefferson, 21 Oct., discussing grand jury proceedings in the case of the

French privateer *Roland* (*Jefferson Papers,* 27:261); Tobias Lear to Jefferson, 1 Nov. (not identified), enclosing a representation by Keyran Walsh (Walch) of the brig *Maria* about his capture by a French frigate and recapture by a British privateer; and two letters from Elias Vanderhorst to Jefferson, 1 and 3 Sept., discussing the improper capture of American vessels and their detention in British ports (DNA: RG 59, Dispatches from U.S. Consuls in Bristol; abstracted in *Jefferson Papers,* 27:10–12, 29). GW's receipt and return of these letters is recorded in his journal under the date 4 Nov., GW having made no entry for 5 Nov. (*JPP,* 244–46).

From Richard O'Bryen

Most Excellent Sir   Algiers November the 5th 1793.

In consequence of the Portugeese obtaining a cessation of hostilities with this regency, the Algerine corsairs has captured ten american vessels the masters and crews, amounting to one hundred and five subjects of the United States—are employed as captive slaves on the most laborious work. the[y] are in a distressed and naked situation.[1]

Mathias Skjoldebrand Esqr: the Swede Consul has befriended them by advancing them money to relieve theire present necessities. We hope you will order him to be reimbursed, and also paid for his generous advance in the ransoming of George Smith, one of the subjects of the United States.[2]

The british Nation, the natural and inviterate enemies of the United States, has brought about this truce or ½ peace for Portugal in order to alarm our commerce and prevent the United States from supplying the French in theire present glorious contest for liberty.

A Portugee frigate is at present at Algiers relative to theire peace. I have reason to believe the[y] will obtain their peace for one million of dollars not including presents or the redemption of sixty five Portugee captives—The Algerine corsairs consists of ten sail mounting from 40 guns to 16. Those of Tunis consists of twenty corsairs mounting from 24 guns to—8.

The corsairs of Algiers and Tunis in consequence of the Portugee truce has became masters of the western ocean, and will of course prove very detrimental to the commerce of the United States to Europe the fatal consequences of those american vessels being captured I presume is fully evident to Your Excellency's known wisdom & penetration.

Your Excellency will perceive that the United States has at present no alternative then to fit out with the greatest expedition thirty frigates and corsairs in order to stop those sea-robbers in capturing american vessels. Fifteen of these vessels would be sufficient for a defensive war in order to guard the streights of Gibralter and prevent the algerine and tuniseien corsairs even if combined from visiting the westen ocean—but in order to convince the Barbary states of the force and vigilence of American corsairs it would be requisite the other fifteen american corsairs should be employed in the Meditteranian in order to destroy many of the corsairs of the Barbary states and oblige them to make a peace on somewhat honourable terms with the United States.

We should have accepted of the terms offered the United States by the Dey of Algiers which be assured Most Excellent Sir was raisonable considering what other Nations pays.[3] But I am affraid that that favorable opportunity is irrevocably lost. But depend Sir that the Dey would wish to be at peace with the United States provided we paid equal to what the Dutch Swedes or Deans pays. We should be at peace with all the Barbary states. Our colours free and respected and no subjects of the United States slaves[.] You must needs think Sir that in case of the United States fiting out this proposed fleete that those subjects of the U.S. which has been nearly nine years in captivity that the[y] would when redeemed be a very valuable acquisition to the American corsairs, for by theire known experience of the wayes and manuvres of those crafty people, would in a great measure depend, the desired effect in captureing the corsairs of this Regency.

Humanity towards the unfortunate american captives I presume will induce Youre Excellency to coopperate with Congress to adopt some speedy and effectual plan in order to restore to liberty and finally extricate the American captives from their present distresses. I am with the most profound respect Your Excellencys Most obedient and faithfull servt.

Rd OBrien
Late Master of the ship Dauphin
of Philadelphia, captured in July 1785.

American captives in Algrs 10 captured in July 1785[4]—105 captured in October 1793 115 total. Cruisers going out in quest of more.

Copy, DNA: RG 46, Third Congress, 1793–95, Senate Records of Legislative Proceedings, President's Messages; LB, DNA: RG 46, Transcribed Reports and Communications Transmitted by the Executive Branch to the U.S. Senate, 1789–1819. GW enclosed this letter to the United States Senate and House of Representatives, 3 March 1794. The copy was certified as a "True Copy" by George Taylor, Jr., chief clerk of the State Department, 31 March 1794.

1. For discussion of the 12 Sept. truce between Portugal and Algiers, see David Humphreys to GW, 7 Oct., and n.1. For a list of the ten American ships and crews taken in October 1793, see *American Apollo* (Boston), 6 Nov. 1794.

2. Mathias Skjöldebrand, the Swedish consul at Algiers, was the older brother of Pierre Eric Skjöldebrand, who acted as an American consul at Algiers from June 1796 to August 1797. George Smith, a member of the crew of the schooner *Maria* out of Boston, taken in July 1785, was redeemed in March 1793 (see David Humphreys to GW, 5 May 1793, n.1; *American Apollo* [Boston], 6 Nov. 1794).

3. In a letter to Congress of 28 April 1791, O'Bryen had claimed that "the United States may obtain a peace with this regency for fifty or sixty thousand pounds sterling, all expenses included" (*ASP, Foreign Relations*, 1:129–30).

4. O'Bryen was here reporting the number of captives who had neither died nor been redeemed in the period since 1785. For the names of those six members of O'Bryen's crew on the *Dauphin* and four members of the crew of the *Maria*, as well as the crew members redeemed or dead, see *American Apollo* (Boston), 6 Nov. 1794.

From the Germantown, Pa., School Trustees

Sir   [Germantown, Pa.] Novr 6th 1793

The trustees of the public School of German-town have the honor to wait upon the President with a respectful tender of the school buildings for the accommodation of Congress, should they convene at this place.[1]

To judge of the other inhabitants of German-town from our own motives, it cannot be questioned they would on this occasion strive to make it as convenient a residence as possible.

On the permanence of our general Government and the safety of it's supporters and defenders, rests, under God in our view, whatever we hold most valuable.

It has been our fortune, Sir, to see you in many Seasons of difficulty & danger, always surmounting them, & even now fortifying with your presence, the good spirit of the Union, lately humbled by the calamity in Philadelphia; an aleveviation of which we participate, doubtless in common with the Survivors of the City, in consequence of your propitious return to this State.

LS, in Henry Hill's writing, DLC:GW; LB, DLC:GW. This letter was printed in the *Federal Gazette and Philadelphia Daily Advertiser,* 8 November. Samuel Ashmead (1731–1794), a Philadelphia County judge, also represented Philadelphia County in the Pennsylvania general assembly, 1782–83 and 1789–90. Christian Schneider (died c.1802) was a leather dresser. Samuel Mechlin (1730–1817) was a tanner.

1. The trustees' minutes indicate that on 2 Nov. the signatories were constituted a committee authorized to offer the buildings for the use of Congress at a rent of $300 per session (*A History of the Germantown Academy* [Philadelphia, 1910], 121).

To the Germantown, Pa., School Trustees

Gentlemen,   [c.6 November 1793]

The readiness with which the Trustees of the public School of Germantown tender the buildings under their charge, for the use of Congress, is a proof of their zeal for furthering the public good; and doubtless the Inhabitants of Germantown generally, actuated by the same motives, will feel the same dispositions to accommodate, if necessary, those who assemble but for their service & that of their fellow citizens.

Where it will be best for Congress to remain will depend on circumstances which are daily unfolding themselves, & for the issue of which, we can but offer up our prayers to the Sovereign Dispenser of life & health. His favor too on our endeavours— the good sense and firmness of our fellow citizens, & fidelity in those they employ, will secure to us a permanence of good government.

If I have been fortunate enough, during the vicissitudes of my life, so to have conducted myself, as to have merited your approbation, it is a source of much pleasure; & shoud my future conduct merit a continuance of your good opinion, especially at a time when our Country, & the City of Philada in particular, is visited by so severe a calamity, it will add more than a little to my happiness.

Go. Washington

LB, DLC:GW; Df (incomplete), in Thomas Jefferson's writing, DLC: Jefferson Papers. The draft does not contain the final paragraph, but otherwise differs from the letter-book copy only in minor ways. This letter was printed in the *Federal Gazette and Philadelphia Daily Advertiser,* 8 November.

From Thomas Jefferson

[Germantown, Pa.] Nov. 6. 1793.

Th: Jefferson has the honor to inclose several letters for the perusal of the President.[1] when he wrote to the Governor of Kentuckey, on a former intimation from the Spanish representatives, there was no probability that the intervention of military force would be requisite, and as far as illegal enterprizes could be prevented by the peaceable process of law, his writing was proper.[2] it is proper now, so far as the same means may suffice. but should military coercion become necessary, he submits to the President whether a letter from the Secretary at war should not go, Th: J. having avoided any order of that kind in his letter.[3]

AL, DNA: RG 59, Miscellaneous Letters; LB, DNA: RG 59, George Washington's Correspondence with His Secretaries of State.

1. Jefferson enclosed for approval four letters that he had written on this date: to Spanish representatives José Ignacio de Viar and José de Jaudenes, informing them that the governor of North Carolina was being written to about their protest of the seizure of a Spanish ship by the French privateer *Vainqueur de la Bastille;* to Henry Knox, directing him to give "proper instructions" to the governor "for executing the decisions of the government in cases of this description"; to Viar and Jaudenes, informing them that the governor of Kentucky was being directed to prevent the project of four Frenchmen who, Viar and Jaudenes had warned, were going to Kentucky "to procure some hostile enterprize from our territories against those of Spain"; and to Isaac Shelby, directing his attention to the Frenchmen, "that they may not be permitted to excite within our territories or carry from thence any hostilities into the territory of Spain," the "coercion" to be peaceable if possible, by force if necessary (*Jefferson Papers,* 27:310–14). GW approved the letters and returned them to Jefferson (*JPP,* 246–48).

2. See Viar and Jaudenes to Jefferson, 27 Aug., and Jefferson to Shelby, 29 Aug. (*Jefferson Papers,* 26:771–73, 785–86).

3. Jefferson wrote a second letter to Henry Knox on this date, enclosing his letter to Shelby of this date to be forwarded with instructions from Knox to Shelby about the use of military force (*Jefferson Papers,* 27:311). Knox wrote Shelby on 9 Nov. that if the "usual course of the laws . . . should be ineffectual, I am instructed by the President of the United States to request that your Excellency will use effectual military force to prevent the execution" of

the Frenchmen's plans (DNA: RG 46: Transcribed Reports and Communications Transmitted by the Executive Branch to the U.S. Senate, 1789-1819).

Letter not found: from Howell Lewis, 6 Nov. 1793. On 10 Nov. GW wrote Lewis: "Your letter of the 6th instt came duly to hand."

From Thomas Jefferson

[7 November 1793]

Mr Smith supposes the bill he incloses must be laid before Congress.[1] on a former suggestion of the same kind Th: J. being able to find nothing which rendered it necessary, consulted the Attorney General, who was of opinion it was not necessary, but promised make more diligent enquiry.[2] the result will now be asked of him by Th: J.

AL, DNA: RG 59, Miscellaneous Letters; LB, DNA: RG 59, George Washington's Correspondence with His Secretaries of State. Bartholomew Dandridge, Jr., docketed the AL as "7. Novr 1793," the same date that appears on the letter-book copy.

1. The enclosed bill was an act of the governor and judges of the Southwest Territory "requiring persons holding monies arising from fines and forfeitures imposed for the punishment of public offenders, taxes on proceedings in law and equity, on the probate of deeds, on the registering of grants for land, and the issuing marriage and ordinary licenses . . . to account for and pay the same," 13 March 1793 (Carter, *Territorial Papers,* 4:242–43).

2. See Jefferson's third letter to GW of 19 June, and notes 2 and 3.

From Thomas Jefferson

Nov. 7. 1793.

The Secretary of State having received from the Secretary of the territory South of the Ohio a report of the Proceedings of the Governor of that territory from Mar. 1. to Sep. 1. 1793. has examined the same and Reports to the President That he finds nothing therein which will require his immediate agency.[1]

Th: Jefferson

ALS, DNA: RG 59, Miscellaneous Letters; ALS (letterpress copy), DLC: Jefferson Papers; LB, DNA: RG 59, George Washington's Correspondence with His Secretaries of State.

1. For this report, see Carter, *Territorial Papers,* 4:453–57.

To the Earl of Buchan

German Town in the State of Pennsyla
My Lord,   8th Novr 1793
   Mr Lear, The Gentleman who will have the honr of putting
this letter into your hands, I can venture, & therefore shall take
the liberty, to introduce as worthy of your Lordships civilities.
He has lived seven or eight yrs in my family as my private Secretary, and possesses a large share of my esteem & friendship.
Commercial pursuits have taken him to Europe & a desire to
visit some of the Manufacturing towns in Scotland carries him
first to that Country. A wish while there to pay his respects to
Your Lordship, with whom he knows I have been in corrispondence, must be my apology for recommending him to your notice especially as it will afford me a fresh occasion to assure you
of the high esteem & respect with which I have the honor to be
Your Lordships Most Obedt & Very Hble Serv⟨t⟩
                                        Go: Washingt⟨on⟩

ADfS, DLC:GW; LB, DLC:GW; Copy, MHi: Miscellaneous Collection.
   The ALS of this letter was offered for sale by Sotheby's (London), *English
Literature and History: Comprising Printed Books, Autograph Letters and Manu-
scripts,* 15 Dec. 1988, Lot 185. The catalog states that Buchan wrote on the
address panel: "I happened to be at some little distance from home when Mr.
Lear arrived at Dryburgh Abbey, & such were the Allarmist feelings of the
Country created by the Mountbankism of Pitt he was strictly examined by my
Clerk & forced to show the Presidents handwriting before he was admitted to
remain!" For Lear's account of his reception by Buchan, see his letter to GW
of 26–30 Jan. 1794.

To Tobias Lear

My dear Sir   German Town [Pa.] 8th Novr 1793
   I arrived at this place at the time appointed—to wit—the 1st
inst. but did not receive your letter of the 3d until yesterday for
want of a regulr Comn with the P. Office and this too at a time
when as you have well suppos'd I was immerced in the consideration of Papers from the different Departments after a separa-
tion from the heads of them almost two Mo.
   I have, however, run over your observations on the Potomac
Navigation &ca &ca—and in a hasty manner, as I went along at
the first reading made the notes & remarks which are returned

with one of the copies.[1] The statement made by you in all other respects accord with my ideas of facts as far as a recolln of them will enable me to pronounce; nor can I controvert by evidence even those which it would seem that I had queried by my remarks. Had I more leizure and especially if I could have had recourse to my papers, I might have been more correct in some things but as the 10th is the day appointed for your Sailing & that happening to be on a Sunday a chosen day by Sailors for commencing thier Nautical movements I did not incline to miss the Post of this day to return your observations and to furnish the letters you have asked for.[2]

It gives me sincere pleasure to hear that Lincoln continues well as I am sure it will do the family at Mount Vernon who must remain there until it is known what Congress will do; for 'till then I move like a snail with every thing on my back.

I do not *yet* know whether I shall get a substitute for William: nothing short of excellent qualities & a man of good appearance, would induce me to do it. and under my present view of the matter too, who would employ himself otherwise than William did—that is as a Butler as well as a Valette for my wa⟨nts⟩ of the latter are so trifling that any man (as Willm was) would soon be ruined by idleness who had only them to attend to—Having given these ideas—if your time will permit I should be glad if you would touch the man upon the strings I have mentioned—probe his character deeper—say what his age appearance & Country is—what are his expectations & how he should be communicated with, if, upon a thorough investigation of matters you should be of opinion he would answer my purposes well for Kennedy is too little acquainted with the arrangement of a Table, & too stupid for a Butler, to be continued if I could get a better.[3]

I once more, & I suppose for the last time before you sail, bid you adieu; my best wishes wherever you go will accompany you, for with much truth I am Your sincere friend & Affecte Servant

Go: Washington

ADfS, DLC:GW; LB, DLC:GW.

1. GW's undated "Notes, or Remarks upon Mr Lear's Observations" read: "Page 1st. The general idea I had entertained of the distance from the mouth of Potomack to the Capes of Delaware was, that it is short of 150 miles, but I never had any data to govern it. Therefore can neither confirm nor contradict this opinion.

"The River Potomack at the Mouth can be little, if any, short of 12 miles.

"5th. I cannot undertake to say that the streams of water here enumerated are navigable in their *present* state the distances which are mentioned, nor can I contradict it. that they may be made *so* a *much greater distance* I have not the smallest doubt from my former knowledge of them; and probably the activity of the navigation may have produced this agreeable discovery already; for this work unfolds every day surprizingly.

"8th. Does not the City of Washington extend more than two miles on the Eastern Branch? the Plan will decide this.

"16th. The Island from whence the freestone is taken is 40 Miles below the City.

"17th. The Streets also are given up by the Proprietors of the Land in the City as well as the sqrs.

"The two states give 192,000 Dolars—Virg. 120,000 & Maryland 72,000.

"19. In the Mississipi three times Six hands could not ascend the stream 15 miles pr day.

"20. If Philadelphia has hitherto been a shipping Port for the fur & Peltry of the lakes the difference of 400 miles will not apply—to Canada & New York it would.

"21. The Channel at Digges point is not Twenty *feet* from the shore. A Vessel can approach no otherwise than with her bow to a battery at that place for at least three miles; and present her stern *unavoidably* the same distance when She passes it—and the whole width of the Channel at that place scarely exceeds 300—I am sure not 400 yard⟨s.⟩" (AD, ICU).

2. See GW to the Earl of Buchan and GW to John Sinclair, both this date.

3. Patrick Kennedy entered GW's service before May 1793, when he was paid two months' wages, and he probably left GW's service around May 1795, when he was paid wages "in full" (Household Accounts).

To John Sinclair

Sir,   German Town near Philada 8th Novembr 1793

Mr Lear who will have the honor of presenting this letter to you has lived many years in my family & is a person for whom I have a particular esteem.

Having lately engaged in a Commercial Scheme he goes to Europe for the facility of his Plan & being desirous of visiting some of the principal Manufactures in Scotland I take the liberty of giving him this letter of introduction to you, being persuaded he would be grateful for any information he should receive from you in any matter relative to this business.

You will find him intelligent and well disposed I am sure (as far as he is acquainted) to answer any enquiry of yours respect-

ing things in this Country. With great respect I have the honor
to be Sir Your Most Obedt H. Ser.

Go: Washington

ALS, P.R.O.: Chatham Papers; LB, DLC:GW.

From Charleston, S.C., Merchants

Charleston So. Carolina 9th November 1793
The Memorial of James & Edward Penman & Co., North &
Vesey and Jennings & Woddrop of Charleston South Carolina
merchants Sheweth

That your Memorialists, deeply impressed with the deplorable
situation to which many of the Inhabitants of St Domingo, now
residing in this City with their families, have been reduced, from
Affluence, to Want of the necessaries of Life, undertook to send
a Small Vessel, with a confidential Shipmaster, to bring off some
little Matters for their Subsistan⟨ce⟩ and at same time to see if
the Country was in that situation that Vessels could be sent with
safety, and a certainty of bring⟨in⟩g off farther Supplies.

That in consequence thereof, they on the 18th of August last,
dispatched the Schooner Pilot B⟨*mutilated*⟩ Trial, an American
Bottom, under Command of Captn Archi⟨bald⟩ Thompson, an
American Citizen, with a Cargo of Rice, flo⟨ur⟩ and Pork, with
orders to call at St Marcs and Port au pr⟨ince⟩ and take onboard
*whatever property might be offered for Relie⟨ving⟩ the unfortunate per-
sons now in this State,* but advising h⟨im⟩ at same time, and also
our Correspondents Messrs James Gra⟨nt⟩ Forbes & Co. of Port
au prince "That in our sincere Wishes to be aiding in procuring
some little Supplies for those unhappy people here, We meant to
run no Risk ourselves, nor that ⟨*mutilated*⟩ or any others should in
any shape do so, of offending against ⟨*mutilated*⟩ Laws which, unknown to us, might be made, or of drawing ⟨the⟩ Resentment of
the Ruling Powers; that 'though Humanity was deeply imprinted
in our nature, and we had never met greater occasion to exercise
it, yet it was not to be expected at perils to ourselves or friends." [1]

That your Memorialists have been rendered very uneasy at receiving no direct Intelligence of this Vessel for some time, but
have lately had open Letters sent them from New providence,
advising that not only the Vessel had been laid hold of by the

Commissioners, but the captain and your Memorialists' Correspondent, James Grant Forbes, had been put in confinement at Port au prince, on *Suspicion* of *intending* to bring off Property for Persons here.

That having candidly mentioned the Truth, they are ignorant of the reasons which can have led to such a procedure: As American Citizens, they understood they had a right, both by existing Laws and Treaties, to send their Vessel to a french Port which had always been open to American Vessels, and to bring away their own, or the Property of others, not absolutely forbid by any Law or Proclamation, of which they avow their Ignorance, and which it is evident, by their Letters and Instructions they did not mean to offend against.

They therefore humbly request your Interference with the proper persons for Relief of Mr Forbes and captain Thompson and also for Redelivery of their Vessel and Cargo with Damages And Your Memorialists &ca &ca

Jas & Ed. Penman & Co.
North & Vesey
Jennings & Woddrop

DS, ViW: Tucker-Coleman Papers. This memorial was sent to Thomas Jefferson by Edward Rutledge. Jefferson submitted it to GW on 3 Dec., and GW returned it to Jefferson the same day (Rutledge to Jefferson, 9 Nov., *Jefferson Papers*, 27:336–37; *JPP*, 263–64).

The partnership of ship chandlers Edward North (d. 1798) and Joseph Vesey (1747–1835) was formed before 1790 and dissolved in early 1797. The mercantile partnership of Daniel Jennings (d. 1793) and John Woddrop (1756–1828), probably formed about 1785, ended 1 Jan. 1799.

1. Shipmaster Archibald Thomson resided at 66 East Bay in Charleston. James Grant Forbes (1769–1826) served as an army officer during the War of 1812, went as envoy in 1821 to receive the relinquishment of the Floridas from the Spanish authority in Cuba, and later in 1821 was appointed United States marshal for the Florida territory. His *Sketches, Historical and Topographical, of the Floridas; More Particularly of East Florida* was first published at New York in 1821.

From Jacob Dūrang

sir   Philadelphia Novr 9th 1793

Being informed that your Excellency was desirous to employ a Person, who could Shave, dress Hair, and otherwise wait upon you, in your Chamber, I have Presumed, to Address you upon that Subject; I Concieve myself, Sir, Competant to Such duty, and I trust, that I should be happy, in giving full Satisfaction was I to be favored with the Station, I therefore Present myself with *hope* for that Purpose.

With respect to my Moral Character, I have Nothing to fear, And if it shall appear to you, that I am a Man who may Answer the Purpose; I have it in my Power, to produce recommendations from Gentlemen of the first respectability in the City of Philadelphia.

I am a Married Man, by birth a German, Can speak English & French, so as to Understood, I would wish to be, sir, at your Command

Jacob Dūrang

LS, DLC:GW. Jacob Dūrang, father of the actor and dancer John Dūrang, was born near Strasbourg in the Alsace and served for a time as a surgeon in the French army. He came to Pennsylvania in 1767 and lived at Lancaster and York before moving to Philadelphia around 1781. He was a barber and surgeon, residing in 1793 on Fifth Street.

From Tobias Lear

My dear Sir,   New York November 9th 1793

A thousand times after my letter to you, enclosing Observations on the Potomack &c. had gone, did I wish to recall it: for the more I reflected on your situation at this moment, in point of business, the more did I see the impropriety, as well as the unfriendliness of my adding to that burthen, which I could not but know was at least as great as it ought to be, and more especially as mine was a business in which the public was not interested. I have been ever since distressed on that account. And the good letter with which I have been this day honored from you, has not removed my uneasiness on that score; altho' it is to me another proof of that attention towards me which has already made too deep an impression on my mind for time or any event to erase. I say it did not remove my uneasiness; because I was convinced by it and the notes & letters accompanying it, that it must have taken up more of your time than I had, upon any grounds, a right to ask for at this busy moment. My thanks & gratitude, my very dear & honored Sir, are too small to offer for all your goodness to me: But they are all I have that can be acceptable to you.[1]

I have seen Mr Robertson, who took your portrait for the Earl of Buchan, and he tells me that he sent it to his Lordship, by way of Glascow, more than six months since; but he had never heard whether it got to hand or not—and says he is much distressed to learn that the Earl had not receivd it when his letter to you was written—and that he shall not rest until he has ascertained its fate.[2]

I have got all the information of & about the man whom I mentioned in my last, that time & circumstances have permitted me to do. He is a tolerably well sized & well made man of about 5 feet 8 or 9 inches—and about 30 years of age—a German by birth—speaks the french language well—dresses Ladies' & Gentlemen's hair very well.[3]

The account which he gives of himself is—that he lived for upwards of four years with Lord Barrymore as his Valet de Chambre and occasionally acted as his Steward. Finding that the Expenses to which Lord B. was subjected from his stile of living & other extravagances would not allow him to pay his domestics so regularly as their necessities required, he thought best to quit him; and as a Mr Cox, who had superintended the building a Theatre for Lord Barrymore, was about to come to Philadelphia for the purpose of attending the building the new Theatre there, he thought it a good opportunity of trying his fortune in this Country[4]—and was, after he got to Philadelphia, fixed upon as a suitable person to keep the Coffee rooms in the New Theatre; but the use of that Theatre having been postponed—he found it necessary to resort to other means for a living—and followed the business of hair dressing there for some months, 'till Mr Hyde came to this place to keep the Tontine Coffee House when he came here with him & has been since the hair dresser of the Coffee House. He says he understands the duties of a Butler well—and can set out a table in as handsome a manner as any man: But he is not acquainted with marketing or providing for a family—He would prefer acting as Valet & Butler to having the duty of one only. He would not undertake the business for less than *two hundred & fifty dollars* per year. Thus far the man says of & for himself. His price I tell him puts him out of the question; if every thing else should answer.

Mr Hyde seems to be the only person who knows anything particular about the man here. He says he is a sober, steady, neat man—He has lived in the Coffee House ever since Hyde has kept it—Hyde says he thinks the man capable of doing those things which he professes—and from his own knowledge of the kind of person who would be servicable & agreeable to you, Hyde says he could venture to recommend this man.

The foregoing is all I can collect respecting Jacob Baur & therefrom it must be left with you, my dear Sir, to decide. Should you think any thing further of him, Mr Hyde seems to be the only person capable of giving information here.

Tomorrow, wind & weather permitting, I shall sail—and let me visit whatever clime I may—or let whatever will be my situation, I shall never fail, my dear & honored Sir, to implore the best of Heaven's blessings for your health & happiness—I feel more for your goodness towards me than I can or ought to express to you—Accept every thing that a grateful heart can give & present me, if you please, in the most respectful & dutiful manner to Mrs Washington. With truth & sincerity, I always shall be your devoted & affectionate friend & servant

Tobias Lear.

ALS, DLC:GW.

1. See Lear to GW, 3 Nov., and GW to Lear, 8 November.
2. See the Earl of Buchan to GW, 30 June.
3. In his letter to GW of 3 Nov., Lear had mentioned that Jacob Baur was interested in becoming GW's valet.
4. The Earl of Barrymore's Theater at Wargrave was opened in 1789. The foundation of the New Theatre on Chesnut Street in Philadelphia was laid in May 1792, and the theater was opened with a concert in February 1793, but dramatic productions did not begin there until February 1794. Before his association with Barrymore, Cox reputedly was associated with the Theatre Royal at Covent Garden (John Robert Robinson, *The Last Earls of Barrymore, 1769–1824* [London, 1894], 47).

From Richard Chichester

Honod & very Dear Sir   Newington [Va.] 10th November 1793.

I've to Apologise for this intrusion on Your time, with an Address of So trivial A Nature—And make No Doubt of Your Excuse, when You hear of my Afflicted Situation—I am and have been for Near three Years last Past, in So low a State of health, almost daily Expecting the Dissolution of my body, and cannot Depart in Peace without endeavouring to undeceive You, and

Acquit myself of the charge of Misdemeanor against Your Property, of Which I'm entirely inocent: And ever did most cordially despise every Appearance of Meaness.

Through the Medium of Colo. Burgess Ball, I've lately understood that you have been inform'd, that I was the Person who kill'd your Tame Deer (a large black buck) about Two or three years ago,[1] which hath wounded my feelings beyond expression, for you to Possess Such an Idea of my Principles—I Therefore take the liberty to Assure You of my Inocence of the charge, and Declare most Solemnly in the Presence of the Searcher of all hearts, before Whom I'm in daily expectation of being Summon'd to Render An Acct of the Deeds done in the body, that I never even Saw a Deer of that description Since my Existance in the World, Nor Did I ever directly or Indirectly, to my knowledge, Injure my Neighbour, or Any Person Whatever, in Any Such like Respect—Truly I Should view Any Person of that conduct, in the light of a thief and a Rober. The colour of Such a Deer would ever be a Sure Defence against a Shott from myself or Any of my family.

A certain Charles Dodson, a Tenant on Ravensworth, was the Person that kill'd your black buck, at least he told me himself that he kill'd a large Deer of that Colour Just about the time I heard of the Loss of Yours—It was without doubt Judg'd by the Neighbourhood, and himself, to be Your Deer, as the Colour prov'd him Not a Native of this Country, And we All had heard of Your Receiving Such Deer.[2]

As Soon as I Recd Mr Dodsons Information as Above, I gave Major George Washington a State of the case in Writing, And did not Suppose there was A Person in the World capable of giving you Such an Information Against me, without Any foundation—However, my trust is, that Your Acquaintance with my General Character for Almost Thirty Years last Past, Will induce you to give credit to my Solemn Declaration of Inocence at this late Period of my life—Which will Add much to the Satisfaction and Peace of Mind of One Who ever did, and I hope ever Shall during life, Revere Your Name And Person, As a fellow Citizen, And An Instrument in the hands of Divine Providence in Establishing the happy Independence of America.

Tho' I never expect the happiness of Seeing You Again on the Stage of Action, Your Prosperity and happiness in time And through Eternity will ever be Remember'd at the throne of Grace by Dr Sir Yr Most Obt & very H. Servant

Richard Chichester

ALS, DLC:GW. This letter was addressed to GW at Mount Vernon.

1. For GW's acquisition of tame deer for Mount Vernon, see GW to Benjamin Ogle, 17 Aug. 1785; Ogle to GW, 12 July 1786; Benjamin Grymes to GW, 24 April 1786; and GW to George William Fairfax, 25 June 1786.

2. Charles Dodson (d. 1805) resided near Chichester as early as 1782 and remained in Fairfax County until his death. Ravensworth was the name of a 21,996-acre tract granted to William Fitzhugh in 1694. The tract, north of Mount Vernon and west of Alexandria, was by this time divided up into various plantations and quarters.

To Howell Lewis

Dear Howell   German Town [Pa.] 10th Novr 1793

Your letter of the 6th instt came duly to hand,[1] and I received pleasure in learning from it, that you participated in the fine rain I travelled in on the Road, and that the Wheat began to shew the effect of it. I hope the second rain which fell here about the middle of last week extended also to that quarter. admitting this, and that the quantity was equal to what we have had here, I persuade myself it must have put the ground in a good state for plowing & that no time will be lost in which the horses can be spared from other work, to expedite this business for it is of essential importance to have the fields mentioned to you in my last,[2] broke up in the course of the Fall with as little encroachment on winter as may be, that the ground may be turned again in the Sprg.

Send me that Bills of Scantling, or copies of them, and when I see the amount of Taylers I will provide some way or other to pay it.[3] Let every precaution be taken to prevent thefts, or other injury being committed on the Plank Shingles, or Scantling; and particularly to guard them against fires.

As my Wheat Crop is the most important of all, to me, Continue to inform me how it comes on in all your letters; and whethe⟨r⟩ there is any prospect of the forward sowing, which was so much injured by the drought, ever being thick enough. What I mentioned in my last about sowing Rye, I still wish to have done, unless the change is so great for the better, that a full Crop of Wheat may be expected from the bare parts which I then alluded to; & my reason for it is, as I then mentioned, that I may have Rye straw for Thatching shed⟨s⟩ for Cow houses &ca next year. Take particular notice of the drilled wheat, & let me know how it comes on; and how the Corn is likely to yield; at least how it turns out as this business advances. What is gathered and measured in the course of the Week ought always to be noted in the Weekly report; for the Great object of these reports is to let me know the occurrences & true state of things on the Farms once a week; & none can be more interesting than the ascertainment of the Crops.

Whenever the quantity of Clover Seed (for I perceive you have been threshing it) is known, let it be locked up safe, and inform me of the quantity.

Patt had better be struck of[f] the Mansion house list altogether, and if there be a younger one there who has never had a child she may come to the Mansion ho. in her place.[4]

The old Bull commonly called the Callico Bull (now at Stuarts, if not already brot to the Mansion house) I would have brot there; that he may this Winter receive the benefit of the litter from the Stables. And it is my earnest wish tell Butler that 12 of the best Cows I have might breed from him before he goes hence & be heard of no more. I do not mean 12 in addition to what is now at Mansion house but twelve in all.

Tell the Overseers that I will submit to no excuse for deficient reports—it is these I look to for proper statements—and will Submit to no neglect—they shall be responsible for their reports.

Enquire what is become of the Corn Tubs which were at Dogue run, Muddy hole, & River Farm, that new ones were wanting for those places, as I see by the Coupers Report. It is a most shameful thing that conveniences of this sort which ought to last for years are suffered to go to destruction after once or twice using, & then new ones are to be provided.

I request, as soon after the receipt of this letter as an opportunity shall present from Alexandria, or elsewhere, that you would write in my name to Lawrence Washington to come immediately to Mount Vernon, in order to proceed on to this place or Philadelphia with your Aunt, as it will be proper for you to remain at my house until Mr Pearce shall arrive there, which he has given me reason to hope wou'd be by the middle of next month, though it may possibly be later; for without you are there to deliver things over to him, and give him information of matters, especially of those about the Mansion house, and put him in possession of the Keys &ca (which I do not incline to leave with Butler) he will have to grope in the dark for every thing; and set out at last in a wrong track perhaps. I repeat my desire therefore that you would write immediately to Lawrence to come down, & send letters by different conveyances, that the chances of getting one to him may be multiplied & if possible rendered certain. I am Your Sincere friend and Affectionate Uncle

Go: Washington

ALS, NNGL.

1. This letter has not been found.

2. See GW to Lewis, 3 November.

3. GW may have been paying for some of the construction at Frances Bassett Washington's Clifton Neck farm, whose overseer was a man named Taylor (see her letter to GW of 21 July 1793 and GW's letter to Pearce of 19 Jan. 1794).

4. The dower slave Patt (born c.1775) was a daughter of Doll, a laborer on Ferry Farm in 1786. Patt was moved to Union Farm, where she died in 1798 or 1799, leaving a son, Jesse, who was born about 1793.

From Edmund Randolph

(Private)

Sir.   Spencer's [Germantown, Pa.] Novr 10. 1793.

After I parted from you last night, I obtained a promise from Mr Dunlap, the printer, to bring out on monday his file of newspapers.[1] This renders it unnecessary for me to continue my request as to yours. But while I am thus led to recollect, that you meditate a visit to the city to morrow, permit me to suggest one consideration. The mayor and the physicians dissuade people from returning yet, and especially in great numbers. You will hardly be at your door, before your arrival will be rumoured abroad; and multitudes, who will not distinguish between a momentary stay, and absolute residence, will be induced by your example to croud back, and carry fresh, and therefore more vulnerable subjects into the bosom of infection. The consequences may be the more serious, as we have not yet learned, that any radical precautions have commenced, for purging the houses and furniture. It is strengthened too in a degree, from the uncertainty of the malady, under which the soldiers from St Domingo labour, and of the effect, which the late warm days may have had upon the disorder. Nor can I conceal a fear, which I have often heard expressed, by the friends of yourself and the government, that your indifference about danger might push you perhaps too early into Philadelphia.

I have Examined the addresses, resolutions and answers, which are now returned. In many of them, the proclamation is called a declaration of neutrality; And therefore confirms the opinion, that the speech ought, (as it clearly may) put this paper upon its true, and a satisfactory footing.

What has been published concerning it, united with numberless misrepresentations in other instances, determined me some months ago to begin a history and review of your administration. I had made some progress in it; and should have advanced further, had I not found some difficulty in asking from the secretary of state access to the public archives, without communicating at the same time my object. However, had it not been for the interruption, which has been given for some time past to every business, connected with Philadelphia, I should have persevered, and endeavoured to procure the means of full and accurate information. The essay of Agricola convinces me of the importance of such a work, upon public as well as other interesting considerations; and let my future arrangements be, as they may, I shall not relinquish it.[2] But I am extremely apprehensive, that the pestilence of Philadelphia will reduce the practice of the law within the city to such a modicum, as to force me to think of reestablishing my self in Virginia. For altho' I do not doubt, that were I to go into as large field, as some others of the bar here, my share of profit would content me; yet as that cannot be done, consistently with my office; the share, which I had, must be considerably diminished. Whatever delay may proceed from this circumstance, the work itself shall proceed; and I have now taken the liberty of saying thus much to you, in confidence, only to prepare the way, if on some occasion I shall find it necessary, to beg the communication of any particular information.

I will thank you for the Virginia gazette, containing Agricola; as I wished to write to Colo. Carrington, and enclose to him some remarks, which may tend to disabuse the public mind. I have the honor, sir, to be, with a sincere and affectionate attachment yr mo. ob. serv.

Edm: Randolph.

ALS, DLC:GW.

1. John Dunlap (1747–1812), formerly editor of the *Pennsylvania Packet* (Philadelphia) and printer to Congress from 1778 to 1789, was at this time editor of *Dunlap's American Daily Advertiser* (Philadelphia). The following Monday was 11 November.

2. Five essays authored by James Monroe and signed "Agricola" appeared in the *Virginia Gazette, and General Advertiser* (Richmond), 4 Sept., 9 Oct., 30 Oct., 13 Nov, and 4 December.

Of the three essays published by this date, the first indicted the exposure by John Jay and Rufus King of French minister Edmond Genet's statement that he would appeal to the American people. Monroe called the exposure an effort by "the enemies of the French revolution, who are likewise notoriously the partizans for Monarchy. . . . to separate us from France, and to bring about a more intimate connection with Britain" using "the popularity of the President . . . as a precious means for its accomplishment."

The second essay began with the question, "Should America and France be parted, what other friend or ally remains for either nation upon the face of the globe?" and went on to argue that the natural alliance of the two republics had been brought to crisis by "many acts of outrage" committed by the United States against France. Among the acts were the choice of a minister to France "wedded to monarchy, opposed to the great principles of the French Revolution, and odious to those who conducted it"; the Neutrality Proclamation, which "manifested towards France a disposition unfriendly, and towards Britain a spirit of conciliation," and was "unconstitutional and . . . unwarranted"; the "Pacificus" essay, "published apparently from behind the curtain, and by a secretary of the government," which denied France merit for her assistance in the American Revolution and "charged her with the crime of aggression upon all the powers now invading her territories"; the "withdrawal of the money from Holland, which was destined for payment of the French debt"; and the disclosures of Jay and King.

The third complained of American "complaisance and condescension" in the face of Great Britain's fomenting of Indian hostilities and its refusal to return frontier forts, contrasting the "patience and humility" shown to her with the "unfriendly and irritating policy" applied toward France (*Papers of James Monroe*, 2:641–43, 646–50, 652–54, 659–63; 665–67).

From Anonymous

Sir   Novr 11th 1793 Boston Lincoln Shire [England]

The purport of this Epistle will I presume apologize for the liberty I take in addressing you.

By the accounts we receive from Philadelphia we are inform'd that a dreadful disease rages there which proves fatal to most people, & that the Contagion probably will spread to other parts of the Country; an Idea has occurr'd to me that this Malady may be obviated, & I therefore think it my duty to communicate it to Society.

It will be needless of me to point out the method of Cure for those who labor under this Disease, as the well known Abilities of Dr Rush renders that unnecessary, but I wish to suggest a method of stopping its further progress, which must be done by destroying the specific Contagion on which it depends, & this may be obtain'd by one of the following means, by changing the state of the atmosphere, or by Decomposing the Infectio⟨us⟩ matter. It is a well known fact that when a Putrid Fever prevails in Hospitals, Jails or Ships, the means used for destroying its effect is by the Combustion of Pitch &c. or by firing Gun powder in the tainted Rooms. This method of Cure admits of no other explanation than that the Gases which are the product of Decomposition of the Inflammable matter, by Combustion decomposes the Contagious matter, what corroberates this opinion, the Plague (which differs only in a degree of violence from the Putrid Fever) which raged in London in 1665 disappeard by a Fire breaking out & consuming a great number of Houses, & those dreadful Conflagrations which often happen at Constantinople generally puts a stop to the Plague there; these are some of the reasons which has induced me to hope that if the following means are used they may be attended with happy Effects.

Lay long trains of Gun powder in the Streets & fire them, Tar Barrels or Timber smear'd with Tar may be piled in more open places & burnt for a considerable time, a similar method may be follow'd in the Houses, Gun powder may be fired & Pitch or the Resinous Gums may be burnt, even in the Chamber of the Sick, Camphor, Gum Benzoin &c. with Steams of Vinegar, will not only tend to eradicate the Infection but will prove refreshing to the Patient.

It is ascertain'd that Contagious matter does not rise very high in the Atmosphere, nor is it carried to any great distance, but the more it is diffused the more inert it becomes, & exerts itself with greater violence when in a confined state, & adheres more tenaciously to some Substances than to others, such as Woolen, Furs &c., this points out the necessity of using such things as little as possible about the Sick person & the admission of plenty of fresh Air. Nitre being join'd with the Combustible that may be used will be of service, as it yields by burning, great quantity of Vital or Dephlogisticated Air, which will greatly promote the Conflagration & at the same time contribute to the Salutariness of the Atmosphere.

If these suggestions shou'd have the honor of meeting with your Excellency's approbation & shou'd in any degree ⟨*mutilated*⟩ the impending Calamity I shall think myself extremely ⟨*mutilated*⟩. I am your Excellency's most obet Humle Servant

W. C——.
M.D.

AL, DLC:GW. The cover, addressed to GW at "Philadelphia America," is marked "Inland Postage paid."

From Alexander White

Sir   Woodville[1] [Va.] 11th November 1793

It is with real pleasure I obey the commands of a respectable meeting of the Citizens of Frederick County, in communicating the enclosed Resolutions expressive of the result of their deliberations. I am with sentiments of the most perfect respect Sir Your Obt Servant

Alexr White

ALS, DLC:GW; LB, DLC:GW.

1. Woodville, White's country estate, was near Winchester, Virginia.

Enclosure
Resolutions from Frederick County, Va., Citizens

[Winchester, Va., 5 November 1793]

At a numerous meeting of the Inhabitants of Frederick County at the Court House in Winchester on Tuesday the fifth day of november 1793 for the purpose of taking under Consideration the Proclamation of the President of the United States, declaring the neutrality of the said States in the present European War—Alexander White is appointed Chairman and John Peyton Clerk.[1]

Resolved that in the opinion of this meeting the late Proclamation of the President declaring the neutrality of the United States and enjoining a conduct friendly and impartial towards all the Belligerent Powers of Europe was a well timed Constitutional measure, and holds a conspicuous place among the many great and important services rendered by him to his native Country.

Resolved that this meeting consider it as an incumbent duty to express their approbation of the said Proclamation, and of the measures which have been pursued for enforcing the same, as a tribute justly due to the Wisdom, the vigilance, and unremitted attention of our Fellow Citizen in the discharge of the important Duties of his high Office, more especially as attempts have been made to censure his Conduct therein, and to induce a belief that it does not accord with the general Sentiments and Wishes of the American People—This meeting are duly impressed with the important truth "That the Sovereignty of the United States is vested in the People"—but it being impracticable to exercise that Sovereignty either in their individual or collective capacity—they have wisely instituted Governments, General and particular, and have transferred to them every power deemed necessary to secure Peace and Liberty and promote the general Welfare.

Resolved that it is through the several Departments of Governments alone that the Will of the People can be manifested or their power exerted. That the Officers of those Departments (although amenable to the People for their Conduct in the various ways prescribed by the Laws and Constitutions of the Union and of the several States) in the exercise of their proper functions ought to be respected and obeyed—That an appeal to the People at large in opposition to any Constitutional Act of Government is inconsistent with the principles of Civil Society, and in all cases would prove destructive of that Peace and Order for the support of which Governments are instituted—That should the ministers or agents of Foreign nations appeal or propose to appeal from the decisions of the Excutive of the United States in matters respecting their mission, to any other Department of Government, or to the People; every attempt of that kind ought to meet the most pointed disapprobation of the Citizens of the United States as a measure evidently tending to introduce civil dissention, discord, and corruption; and finally to endanger the existence of the Government itself.[2]

Resolved that this meeting retain a grateful remembrance of the distinguished Services rendered to our Country by the

French nation—that they wish to cultivate her Friendship and Alliance, to see her Government assimilated to our own by the establishment of a free Republic as the best foundation of her prosperity and an additional cement of our union.

Resolved as the opinion of this meeting that the United States are not bound by the existing Treaties with France to engage in the present War against any of the European nations—That such a measure would prove destructive of the dearest interests of America without rendering any essential service to France— On the contrary that she would be thereby deprived of the advantages she now recieves from our neutrality.

Resolved that a Copy of the several foregoing Resolutions be forthwith transmitted to the President of the United States And that they also be published in the Winchester Gazettes.[3]

Teste   Alexr White Ch: M.
John Peyton Clk

DS, DLC:GW; LB, DLC:GW.

1. GW's Neutrality Proclamation was dated 22 April. John Peyton (c.1757–1804), a son-in-law of Virginia congressman Robert Rutherford, was clerk of the Superior Court at Winchester and had been clerk of the Frederick Parish vestry.

2. This resolution refers to accusations about the conduct of French minister Edmond Genet (see Genet to GW, 13 Aug., and n.4).

3. The resolutions were printed in *Bowen's Virginia Centinel and Gazette; or, the Winchester Repository*, 11 November.

From Elias Boudinot

Dear Sir   Elizabeth Town [N.J.] Novr 12th 1793
The troubling you to read the enclosed oration may perhaps need an Apology, undoubtedly the liberty I have taken, to address it to you, without your express permission, renders one absolutely necessary.[1]

A number of concurring Circumstances, added to the subject & design prompted me to it, and a dependance on your known Candor & Friendship makes me hope, it will not give Offence.

Mrs Boudinot joins me in the most respectful & affectionate Compliments to Mrs Washington. I have the honor to be with every Sentiment of Duty & respect Dr Sir Your most Obedt Hble Servt

Elias Boudinot

ALS, DLC:GW.

1. Boudinot enclosed *An Oration, Delivered at Elizabeth-Town, New-Jersey, Agreeably to a Resolution of the State Society of Cincinnati, on the Fourth of July, M.DCC.XCIII. Being the Seventeenth Anniversary of the Independence of America* (Elizabeth-Town, N.J., 1793). The publication included a dedication in the form of a letter to GW, dated 4 July: "The great respect due to your public character, as the first servant of a Nation of Freemen, greatly heightened by a knowledge of the amiableness of your deportment in private life, have been additional arguments with me to dedicate an Oration to you, which, however inadequate to the purpose, was designed to promote a reverence for that happy revolution, in which divine Providence has been pleased to make you so peculiar an instrument.

"A frequent recurrence to the first principles of our constitution, and from thence to inculcate the necessity of a free, firm, and energetic government, in which Liberty shall rise superior to licentiousness, and obedience to the Laws become the best evidence of attachment to the Independence of our common Country, cannot but meet with your approbation.

"This is the great object designed by instituting the Anniversary of the Fourth of July, one thousand seven hundred and seventy-six, as a Festival, to be sacredly observed by every true American. This is the Day, chosen by the Defenders of our Country, your friends and companions in arms, to meet together and rejoice in the recollection of past labors, while they receive the glorious reward of their services, by looking forward to the increasing prosperity of the union, secured by their united exertions.

"It arose from a desire, that this Jubilee might be improved, to continue those principles to posterity, which led them to arm in defence of their most invaluable privileges, that the Society in this State instituted an Oration on this Anniversary, to commemorate the successful result of their sufferings, and to perpetuate a constitution founded on the Rights of Men, as Men and Citizens.

"You, Sir, as their Head, must enjoy, in a very peculiar manner, the contemplation of these blessings, and to you every attempt in this important service will be most properly dedicated.

"Long may you personally experience their benign effects—Long may you live to testify, by a successful practice, the truth of the theory established by your struggles in the cause of universal Liberty" (pp. iii–iv).

The *Oration* remained in Washington's library at the time of his death (Griffin, *Catalogue of the Washington Collection*, 31).

From Gouverneur Morris

My dear Sir   Paris 12 Novr 1793

Monsieur de la forét calld just now while I was at the Ministers' to inform me that he shall probably leave Paris ToMorrow Morning I therefore write this as an *Introduction* to you and proceed to give a hasty Sketch of the Form in which the Business now stands. A Commission is named (the Appointments not yet gone through the Forms) to consist of four Persons. The Minister is a Mr Fauchèt Secretary of the executive Council a young Man of about three and thirty whom I hav⟨e n⟩ot yet seen but he is said to possess Genius and Information. The Secretary of Legation is a Mr Leblanc a Man of about fifty and who was lately at the Head of the Police Department in this City. Him also I am as yet unacquainted with but he is mention'd to me as a prudent sensible Man. Mr de la forét goes out as Consul General and Mr Petrie his friend and Companion as Consul in the Port of Philadelphia.[1] These two will undoubtedly draw together and will probably sway the Conduct of the Commission for the Minister is to take no important Steps without being previously authoriz'd by the Board. I understand that a Kind of Etiquette has been establish'd by which the Con⟨suls⟩ as not being properly diplomatic Characters are not receivd or invited with the Minister and I perceive that there is a strong Wish to enjoy the exterior Respect of Office as well as the solid Authority. I cannot pretend to judge nor even to guess how far any thing of this Sort consists with the general Rules which you may have found it proper to establish but I think I can perceive that the two Consuls expect to govern the Commission by two Means One their greater knowlege of our Country and Laws and Inhabitants The other a Perswasion to be inculcated on the Minister and Secretary that they enjoy the Confidence of our Government. Perhaps a little Vanity may also be for something in the Business, but your Judgment will well discern Motives and therefore I only give Hints. I think that Mr de la forét and his friend being Men of Understanding will endeavor to keep things in a Line of Prudence and Propriety therefore being uncertain (at present) as to the personal Characters of the other two it seems to be well that the Board be kept steady by the Anchors we are acquainted with and as the others unfold themselves it will appear what Reliance can be plac'd on them. The Minister, in the Conference I had with him just now, has again reiterated the Assurance that he and the other Members of this Government have the most sincere Desire to be on the most cordial Terms with us and I am the more dispos'd to beleive in these Assurances because America is the only Source from whence Supplies of Provisions can be drawn to feed this

City on which so much depends.[2] The coming Winter will be I beleive dreadful and the Spring (should the War continue) must open with partial Scarcities if not general Want. To the Sufferings unavoidable from many other Causes no small addition will be made by the Laws limiting Prices which must endure till they shall be shatterd to Peices by the iron Hand of Necessity. God bless you my dear Sir I am very truly yours

Gouvr Morris

ALS, DLC:GW; LB, DLC: Gouverneur Morris Papers.

1. Antoine René Charles Mathurin de La Forest was officially appointed consul general to the United States on 15 November. He was recalled in June 1794. Jean Antoine Joseph Fauchet (1761–1834), who was received as minister plenipotentiary from France on 22 Feb. 1794, was replaced in June 1795. After he returned to France, he wrote a book translated in America as *A Sketch of the Present State of Our Political Relations with the United States of North-America* (Philadelphia, 1797). From 1783 to 1792 Jean-Baptiste Pétry (1757–1838) filled posts as consul at Wilmington, N.C., and Charleston, S.C. He was received as consul at Philadelphia in February 1794, and his exequatur was revoked in July 1798. Pétry was first secretary of the French legation to the United States from 1804 to 1810, and he was appointed consul at New Orleans, 1815; consul general at Washington, 1819; and consul general at Madrid, 1823. Georges-Pierre Le Blanc returned to France in June 1794.

2. Morris probably was referring to the French foreign minister, François Louis Michel Chemin Deforgues.

From John Rutherford

Lauder-east-mains [Scotland],
Hon. Sir   November 12th 1793.

The very high esteem I have ever had for your excellency, as a Personage of the greatest abilities and integrity, encourages me to present you with this. It becomes me, as a stranger, to ask pardon for this my freedom, but I am fully persuaded that such are your views of Humanity, and of the Duties which we owe to each other as fellow citizens of the great theatre of the Universe that I shall readily obtain remission. Having no acquaintance on the great continent of America, I thought proper to apply to the fountain-head, not doubting but that I should acquire the necessary information from so exalted a character. I was informed by a person, who had read an American Paper, that a Person of the name of Andrew Mien, son of Andrew Mien in Maryland, died some time ago, possessed of a considerable fortune without Heirs. He was a native of North-Britain, had been in America for many years, and joined the united forces of that country during the late unhappy contest with Great-Britain. Andrew Mien Senior was married to a Native of America, and his son was born there. As my Wife is Sister to Andrew Mien Senior, I should consider it as the highest obligation, would your excellency cause inquiry be made whether such a person is dead or living.[1] A line directed to John Rutherford, Lauder-east-mains, near Lauder, by Edinburgh, North-Britain, by your excellency's order, would be deemed a singular honour and favour, by, Hon. Sir, Your excellency's most obedient, and most humble servt &c.

John Rutherford.

ALS, DLC:GW. The letter, which was stamped "KELSO," was addressed to GW at New York.

1. Rutherford evidently was referring to the family of Andrew Mein (died c.1770) of Talbot County, Md., who married Ann Walker. GW asked Maryland congressman William Vans Murray to look into this matter, and Murray wrote GW on 16 May 1794 to report that Andrew Mein "resided in Talbot County on the Eastern shore of Maryland—He died about twenty years since—& left a son who came to the age of twenty one about three years since & died—leaving a will by which a few legacies excepted he devised a landed & other property of near five thousand pounds value to Mr Peter Edminston, his Executor of Caroline County, E. Shore of Maryland. This young gentlemen (Mr Mein) was heir to Mr Andrew Mein—and had the sole right to the estate—The family of Mein is now extinct in Maryland—This information I have obtained from Doctor Potter of Caroline County who was well Known to young Mein.

"I have written to the Executor Edminston but he has not yet answered my letter" (ALS, DLC:GW).

Peter Edmondson subsequently reported to Murray, "Mr Andrew Mein has been dead about twenty years last fall, he left a widow and one son, he willed all his estate to his Son, he lived till he was about twenty-two years old—he died & Willed all his real estate to me both in America & Scotland there was a small farm near Edinburgh which his father willed to him which I have understood was worth between six or seven hundred pounds Sterling—Mr Andrew Mein Junior's mother died Some years before he did—There did not appear that old Mr Mein left any personal Estate—he was also a good deal in debt There is also a british debt now depending in the General Court should it be recovered will take all the lands that old Mr Mein left" (quoted in Murray to GW, 4 June 1794, DLC:GW).

Bartholomew Dandridge, Jr., replied to Rutherford in a letter of 18 June 1794: "In answer to the enquiry made in your Letter of the 12 Novr '93 to the President of the United States, he has directed me to transmit to you the copies of two letters herewith enclosed, which contain all the information the President can obtain relative to Mr Mien. These letters are from a member of the Congress of the United States from the State of Maryland, & the information may be relied on. The public occupations of the President do not permit him to spend much time in enquiries of this nature" (ViMtvL).

Resolutions from Shenandoah County, Va., Citizens

[Woodstock, Va. 13 November 1793]

At a meeting of sundry Inhabitants of Shanandoah County, at the Courthouse in Woodstock on Wednesday the 13th day of November 1793 for the purpose of taking into consideration, the Proclamation of the President of the United States declaring the Neutrality of the said States in the present European War, William Aylett Booth, was appointed Chairman, & Richard Tutt Clerk.[1]

1 Resolved, as the opinion of this meeting, that it is at all times the right, and at Certain periods the Indispensable duty of the people, to declare their opinions on Subjects which concern the national Interest, and that in the present Important crisis the Exercise of that duty is perhaps rendered indispensable, by the prevailing practice of declaritory resolutions, in places where the Inhabitants can more easily assemble and consult, than in the Country, but where Interests & political opinions different from those of the great body of the people may happen to predominate, from where there may be danger of unfair and improper inferrences concerning the general sense of the people.

2 Resolved, that the Constitution of the United States having been dopted by the free sufferage of the people, ought to be firmly and Vigorously supported against all direct, or indirect attempts that may be made to subvert, or violate the same.

3 Resolved, that it is the Interest of the United States of America, to cultivate peace and harmony with all the world by Just and honorable means, and that our Executive authority, ought to be supported in the Exercise of its Constitutional Powers, for enforcing the Laws and securing to us this Inestimable blessing.

4 Resolved, that the known patriotism, wisdom, & tried virtue of the President of the United States entitle him to the highest confidence, as well as lasting gratitude of his County, to whose present, peace, liberty and happiness he has so largely Contributed.

5 Resolved, that the many important services rendered to these United States in their late arduous struggle for Liberty, by the French nation, ought ever to be remembered and acknowledged with gratitude, and that the Spectacle exhibited to us by the glorious and sevier contest she is now engaged in, for her own liberty, ought and must be peculiarly interesting to the wishes of every one, who considers the true interest of america.

6 Resolved, that all attempts under whatever aspects they may appear to Alienate the good will of the People of America, from the cause of liberty and Republican Goverment in France, have an evident tendency to subvert the principles of their own goverments, and manifest designs which ought to be narrowly watched & seasonably counteracted.

7 Resolved, that any endeavours to dissolve the connection between these United States, and France, must be obviously attempted with a view to forward a more intimate union, and Connection of the former, with great Brittain, as a leading step towards assimilating the American goverment to the form and Spirit of the British monarchy, and that these apprihensions will be greatly strengthened if it shall appear that the Active Zeal displayed in propagating prejudices against the French nation, and Revolution have proceded from persons either disaffected to the American Revolution, or of known monarchial principles, and that for any foreign Court to attempt by any means to prohibit our exporting our produce, or abridging our Commerce with any other nation than their own, Contrary to the Laws of Nations are hostile to the Interests of these United States, and is an infringment of the rights of an independant and Neutral Nation.[2]

8 And, finally resolved that all foreign Ministers to these United States ought to negociate the object of their Mission with the President; and if at any time a difference in opinion should happen, on the Exposition of Treaties, or other Subjects, the same ought to be stated by such minister to the Goverment of his nation that on a discussion betwen the two goverments, an amicable adjustment may be effected and peace & friendship preserved, and all applications of a Minister in such a case to the people, who act with foreign nations only by their representatives in the different departments of the goverment, are highly improper and tend to create parties and dissentions amongst us, and that if a Minister shall adopt such improper conduct on

any occasion, Although the application ought to be treated with contempt by the people, yet it should not affect his nation, unless it shall avow and Justify his conduct therein, We therefore declare our disapprobation of certain Attempts in late newspaper Publications, to make alledged behaviour of that kind in the minister of the French nation, if any such really existed, the means of withdrawing our affection either from the President or our respectable allies.[3]

Resolved. that a copy of the several forgoing resolutions be inserted in the several newspapers in the United States,[4] and that a fair Copy be Sent the President.

Richard Tutt, Clerk   William Aylett Booth, Chairman

DS, DLC:GW; LB, DLC:GW. The numbers of the resolutions were added in a different writing than the rest of the DS. The resolutions are numbered in the letter-book copy.

1 William Aylett Booth (1754–1820) represented Shenandoah County in the 1790 session of the Virginia House of Delegates and served as sheriff and county treasurer, 1799–1801.

2 The instructions of 8 June authorizing British warships and privateers "to stop and detain all ships loaded wholly or in part with corn, flour, or meal, bound to any port in France" had been published in American newspapers by late August (*ASP, Foreign Relations*, 1:240; *General Advertiser* [Philadephia], 29 Aug.). For a summary of other restrictions on American commerce, see Secretary of State Thomas Jefferson's report to Congress of 16 Dec. (*ASP, Foreign Relations*, 1:300–304).

3 For the charges that French minister Edmond Genet had threatened to appeal to the people certain decisions of GW, see Genet to GW, 13 Aug., and n.4 to that document. "Agricola" (James Monroe) had argued in a Richmond newspaper of 4 Sept. that the publication of these charges was designed to "compel" the American people "to decide between their attachment to" GW and "their obligations to France, as well as their veneration for the great principles of liberty, upon which her revolution is founded" (see *Papers of James Monroe*, 2:642, and Edmund Randolph to GW, 10 Nov., n.2).

4 These resolutions were printed in *Bowen's Virginia Centinel and Gazette; or, the Winchester Repository*, 2 [Dec.].

From Richard Snowdon

Newton Gloucester State of New Jersey Novbr 13th 93

The Author of the enclosed Volume presents it to the Worthy President of the United States as a Small Tribute of that affectionate esteem which he with many thousands bear for his

Person whose merit both as a Hero and Citizen hath captivated the feeling Heart that thrills with exalted pleasure at the loved name of Washington.[1] As the Author is one of the People called Quakers he cannot consistent with his profession make use of a Style that custom hath established in what is called the Polite World Shall therefore confine himself to the feeling Language of the Heart and that mode of expression which he hath been educated in And notwithstanding Providence hath placed him in the humble Walks of Life he is firmly persuaded that like the Widows Mite it will be no less acceptable on that account And shall now take the Liberty to conclude this address in the Words of Dr Young as they accord with the Sentiments of his own Heart viz.

"Farewel! thro' boundless ages fare tho⟨u⟩ well! The dignity of Man and blessing of Heaven be with thee! The broad Hand of the Almighty cover thee! Mayst thou Shine when the Sun is extinct⟨!⟩ Mayst thou live and triumph when time Expires"[2] is the Ardent wish of thy Sincere friend and Admirer

Richard Snowdon

ALS, DLC:GW. Richard Snowdon (Snowden; 1753–1825) was the author of *The American Revolution; Written in the Style of Ancient History* (2 vols., Philadelphia, 1793–94); *The Columbiad, or, a Poem on the American War, in Thirteen Cantoes* (Philadelphia, 1795); and *The History of North and South America, from Its Discovery to the Death of General Washington* (2 vols., Philadelphia, 1805).

1. Snowdon enclosed the first volume of his *American Revolution*. GW wrote Snowdon on 4 Dec. to acknowledge its receipt: "I have received, and thank you for the first vol. of the American Revolution—I shall read it, I am persuaded, when my leizure will allow me with not less pleasure because it is 'written in the style of ancient history'—I thank you also for the favorable sentiments & good wishes you have expressed for me" (ADfS [photocopy], NjMoHP).

2. Snowdon is quoting the English poet Edward Young (1683–1765). The passage, with "quenched" in place of "extinct," appears in the section called "The Dignity of Man Resumed" in the later editions of Young's *The Centaur Not Fabulous. In Six Letters to a Friend, on the Life in Vogue* (see, for example, *The Works of the Reverend Edward Young, LL.D. Rector of Wellwyn in Hertfordshire, and Chaplain in Ordinary to His Majesty* [4 vols., London, 1765], 4:177–78).

From the Inhabitants of Womelsdorf, Pa.

Ihro Excellenz!   [13 November 1793][1]

Möchten Sie doch unsere aus Dankbarkeit und Gehorsam
entstehende Freudensbezeugungen, in diesem glücklichen Au-
genblick da wir die persönliche Gegenwart von Ihro Excellenz
genießen, in Dero angebornen und gewöhnlichen Güte an-
zunehmen belieben.

Die kluge und mit glücklichem Erfolg gecrönte Thaten, die Sie
unter dem Schutz des Allerhöchsten Wesens in dem lezten glor-
reichen Krieg ausgeführt haben, das Glück und Zufriedenheit
das wir unter Dero Regierung seither in Friedenszeit genießen,
und das lezthin so wohl überlegte und zum rechten Zeitpuncte
anempfohlene Neutralitäts-System, ermuntert alle Menschen
aufs Neue zur Hochachtung und Liebe gegen Sie. Die Einwoh-
ner dieser Gegend werden niemals unterlassen, langes Leben
und Gesundheit von Gott für Sie zu erbitten.[2]

Printed, *Neue Unpartheyische Readinger Zeitung, und Anzeigs-Nachrichten* (Lancaster, Pa.), 20 Nov. 1793.

1. The newspaper account, dated 14 Nov., stated that the inhabitants of
Womelsdorf hosted GW "Gestern Abends" (yesterday evening) and took the
opportunity to hand him this address.

2. The newspaper reported that GW replied to the address—which
thanked him for his deeds during the Revolution, the happiness enjoyed under his government in time of peace, and his well-timed proclamation of
a well-considered neutrality system—as follows: "Die Aufmerksamkeit die
Sie mir erze[i]gen, und der Beyfall von meinen Bemühungen, giebt mir das
größte Vergnügen"—that the attentiveness shown him and their approbation
of his efforts gave him the greatest pleasure.

From Mary Atlee

[14 November 1793]

the tears of distress, Could never give pleasure To the Friend
of Mankind; the humane, Illustrious president: From his Be-
neficence, mine would Cease to flow; the unhappy Mary atlee
Casts herself upon your Bounty sir, she asks but the means of
subsistance.

AL, DLC:GW. The date is taken from the docket of the letter.

To Mary Atlee

14th Novr 1793.

The President wishes Mrs Atlee to be assured that, his disposition to prevent tears of distress from flowing, is far beyond his means to accomplish; and that he should be extremely happy if the latter were adequate to the numerous calls that are made upon the former.

Mrs Atlees case being entirely unknown to the President—Her application of course, is not well understood by him.

ADf, DLC:GW; LB, DLC:GW. The draft is docketed in part, "To Mrs or Miss Mary Atlee." The copyist initially wrote "German Town" on the dateline in the letter book, but crossed that out and wrote "Lancaster." GW left Germantown on 12 Nov. for Lebanon, Pa., to view the canal being constructed by the Schuylkill and Susquehanna Navigation Company near Quittapahilla Creek, and he returned via Lancaster, arriving back at Germantown on 16 November. GW was at Womelsdorf, Pa., on the evening of 13 Nov. and spent several hours at Reading, Pa., on 14 November. See *JPP*, 251; *Neue Unpartheyische Readinger Zeitung, und Anzeigs-Nachrichten* (Lancaster, Pa.), 20 Nov. 1793.

From John Graff

Sir, Germantown [Pa.] Novemr 14. 1793.

Your Excellency will have received a letter of the 22d Ulto containing two papers of the same import with those now inclosed.[1]

I was desirous of paying my respects to you Sir, & arrived here with that intent, but your Excellency's being from this place has occasioned my troubling you with the present—Many Citizen of the mercantile line have not yet returned to Philada which has occasioned the inclosed not to be as full as would have been.[2] With Sentiments of the greatest respect am Your Excellencies Most Obt hume Servt

John Graff.

ALS, DLC:GW.

1. Graff evidently was referring to his letter to GW of 21 October.

2. For discussion of the enclosures, see Graff to GW, 21 Oct., notes 1 and 2.

From George Clinton

Sir   New York 15th Nov.

In my last letter dated the 8th September (and to which I ⟨*mutilated*⟩ yet been favored with an answer) I have omitted to mentio⟨n⟩ the French vessel, called the Republican, a prize to the Brit⟨ish⟩ frigate Boston, had departed, and was without the reach of my a⟨*mutilated*⟩ previous to the receipt of the Letter from the Secretary of war, directing her detension.[1] It will appear from the communications which ⟨*mutilated*⟩ in the first instance, on the subject of this vessel, that I had (under an impression that conformably to the 17th article of our Treaty with France, which declares that no vessel aught to receive any shelter or refuge in any of the Ports of the United States, she appearing both in ⟨the⟩ character of a prize, and Tender to the above mentioned Frigate being brought in here by one of her officers and part of her crew) I directed her immediate departure[2]—I now enclose copies of a corespondence which has lately taken place, between me and the minister of France, respecting a vessel which was reported to me as repairing in this port, whose appearances indicated as if she was intended for military purposes,[3] as this case is nearly if not exactly similar to the one reported in my last letter, I conceive it proper to desist from doing any thing farther therein, until I shall receive your advice on the subject. I am with the greatest respect & esteem,

Geo. Clinton

LB, N-Ar: Papers of George Clinton.

1. Clinton had asked for guidance regarding the *Republican* in his letter to GW of 30 July. Secretary of War Henry Knox replied on GW's behalf in a letter to Clinton of 2 Aug., but the surviving letter-book copy of that document has been so damaged that the advice given is not clear (N-Ar: Papers of George Clinton). On 3 Aug., however, Knox wrote Clinton to report that Secretary of State Thomas Jefferson had asked the British minister to have the vessel detained (N-Ar: Papers of George Clinton).

2. Clinton was referring to the correspondence enclosed with his letter to GW of 30 July. For the 17th article of the Treaty of Amity and Commerce of 1778, see Miller, *Treaties*, 16–17.

3. The enclosed copies of Clinton's letter to Edmond Genet of 9 Nov. and Genet's response to Clinton of 11 Nov. have not been identified. Clinton asked Genet about reports of a sloop under French colors in the East River that "appears as if intended for military purposes." Citing Genet's previous

assurances that he would stop the fitting out of privateers in U.S. ports, Clinton claimed to "have a confidence" that the vessel was either non-military or being fitted out without Genet's knowledge, but added, "it has become my duty to make enquiry into the object of her equipments, I have therefore to request of you to give directions to the officer having charge of her, not to leave the wharf until this can be Affected" (N-Ar: Papers of George Clinton). Genet replied that the vessel under repair was the schooner *Carmagnole*, which he had renamed *Columbia*. The ship, initially fitted out by private citizens as a privateer, was now to be used as an "advice boat, and the Military preparations ⟨which you are⟩ informed are making on board her, have absolutely no other object ⟨than⟩ to enable her to act on the defensive" (N-Ar: Papers of George Clinton; DLC: Genet Papers).

From Jean Louis Du Rumaine

Edenton caroline Du Nord
15. 9bre 1793.

Monsieur Le president,

Les malheurs Sans nombre que j'ai éprouvé et L'absolue detresse à La quelle je Suis reduit me forcent à avoir Recours à La commiseration Du congrès.

Victime de L'insurrection arrivée dans Le quartier de jacmel isle de St Domingue, je m'embarquai en juillet dernier avec mon épouse enceinte de huit mois, Sur une goelette Venant à edenton caroline Du Nord. j'avais été assez heureux pour Sauver des mains des Brigands quelque peu d'argent, mes couverts de Table et Environ Sept milliers de caffé que j'avais dans un magasin au bord de mer. Les corsaires anglais m'ont Enlevé En Route mon argent et mon argenterie, pour comble le malheur La goelette a fait côte au cricot, et mon caffé n'a pu m'être remis que Tres avariè; arrivé à ma destination je me Suis conformé à La Loi, on a verifié Le poids du caffé, La Seule grace que L'office ait pu m'accorder a été de me donner pour Le payement des droits un delai de 4. mois en fournissant caution. ce delai est prêt décheoir et a peine puis-je Trouver du caffé Somme Suffisante pour payer Les droits. je me Trouve par La privé de la Seule Ressource Sur La quelle je fondais mon existence et celle de ma famille. j'ai cru dans cette circonstance accablante devoir m'adresser au congrès, et Vous Supplier, Monsieur Le president, de Vouloir bien y appuyer ma reclamation.[1] j'attens ce bienfait de L'humanité avec La quelle Vous avez Traité Tous Les malheureux insulaires.

je Suis avec un profond Respect, Monsieur Le president, Votre Tres humble et très obeissant Serviteur.

jean Louis Du Rumaine

ALS, DNA: RG 59, Miscellaneous Letters.

1. A second letter from Du Rumaine of this date, addressed to GW and Congress, relates the same sad story of fleeing from the Santo Domingo insurrection with a pregnant wife and child, losing his money and silver to English privateers, and arriving at Edenton, N.C., with coffee so damaged that it would not pay the customs fees. Then, noting that if he had landed at one of the larger American cities he might have benefited from the charity offered to refugees in those towns, Du Rumaine requests that Congress remit the duty on his coffee: "Si au Lieu d'être à edenton, mon Sort m'avait conduit à philadelphie, Baltimore, charlestoun, et Enfin dans Les autres endroits ou L'humanité des americains s'est Si bien deployée en faveur des français Victimés au moins j'aurais participé à La genérosité des états unis; mais, pour comble d'infortune, je me Trouve forcé de demeurer dans une ville denuée de Ressources, ne pouvant m'en eloigner avec une femme et un Enfant Sans des moyens pecuniaires qui me manquent absolument.

"c'est dans cette circonstance accablante que je prens La Liberté d'avoir récours au congrès, pour Lui demander La remise des droits attachés aux 7200 ⟨livres⟩ de caffé que j'ai introduit dans La Ville d'edenton. cette faveur me mettrait à même de fournir à ma femme et à mon enfant Les choses nécessaires à Leur existence jusqu'á mon depart pour St. Domingue.

"je Supplie Monsieur Le prèsident et Messieurs Les membres Du congrès de faire attention qu'il Est des cas ou des magistrats équitables font ceder La Loi aux circonstances, et qu'il n'en Est point de plus favorable que celle ou L'humanité Se Trouve interressée. j'attens Tout de ce Sentiment qui fait Le premier ornement de Tous Les peuples policés" (DNA: RG 59, Miscellaneous Letters).

GW submitted this letter to Secretary of State Thomas Jefferson, whose response is reported in his letter to GW of 15 December. On 7 March 1794 Congress passed "An Act for the remission of the duties arising on the tonnage of sundry French vessels which have taken refuge in the ports of the United States," remitting "duties on the tonnage" of vessels that were "compelled" to flee Cap Français (1 *Stat.* 342).

From Thomas Mifflin

Sir   Philada 15th November 1793

As the period prescribed for the next session of Congress, approaches, I was solicitious to ascertain, whether the accomodations, directed to be prepared for that body, by the Legislature of Pennsylvania, would be compleated in due season: and I have the pleasure to communicate to you the answer of the Commissioners in the affirmative.[1] I am, with perfect respect Sir Your mo: obedt Servt

Tho. Mifflin

LS, DNA: RG 59, Miscellaneous Letters; Df, PHarH: Executive Correspondence, 1790–99; LB, PHarH: Executive Letterbooks.

1. By "An Act to provide for the accommodation of the Congress of the United States," approved on 11 April, the Pennsylvania General Assembly granted $6,666.67 to the commissioners of Philadelphia County "for the purpose of enlarging the building at present occupied by the two Houses of the Congress . . . *Provided, however,* That the commissioners aforesaid shall prepare, in the room of the Senate of the United States, a gallery, calculated for the admission of the citizens of the United States to hear the debates of that House . . ." (*Pa. Acts,* 1792–93 session, 375–76). In the enclosed letter of 14 Nov., Philadelphia commissioners Thomas Hopkins, Isaac Howell, and George Forepaugh wrote Mifflin: "we can with certainty asure thee that the accommodations for Congress will be ready in time, except the Gallery, which, on account of the Malignant disorder, and scarcity of Carpenters, we could not compleat, and thought it best to finish the more immediately accommodating parts" (DNA: RG 59, Miscellaneous Letters).

From the Provisional Executive Council Of France

Au Nom de la République Française   [le 15 Novembre 1793]

En vertu de la Loi du quinze août 1792. qui attribue au Conseil exécutif provisoire toutes les fonctions de la puissance exécutive et du Décret de la Convention Nationale du 21 septembre suivant, lequel maintient les autorités publiques qui étoient en activité à cette dernière époque,[1]

Nous les Citoïens formant le Conseil exécutif provisoire de la République, aux Etats-unis de l'Amérique Septentrionale. Très-chers grands-amis et alliés. Sur les plaintes qui nous ont été portées, par votre ordre contre Edmond Genet,[2] ci-devant Ministre plénipotentiaire de la République Française près de vous, nous avons résolu de vous donner une satisfaction entière en désavouant formellement sa conduite et en le remplaçant par le Citoïen Joseph Fauchet secrétaire actuel du Conseil exécutif, pour resider auprès de vous en qualité de Ministre plénipotentiaire. Nous espérons qu'il justifiera l'opinion que nous avons de son Zèle et de son patriotisme. Nous lui recommandons de saisir avec empressement toutes les occasions de vous rendre sa personne agréable, et de vous convaincre de l'attachement et des bonnes intentions du peuple Français.

Nous vous prions Très-chers grands-amis et alliés d'ajouter une entière créance à tout ce qu'il sera chargé de vous dire de la part de la République française, Elle desire sincèrement concourir aux avantages et à la prosperité des Etats-unis et resserrer de plus en plus les liens de l'amitié et de la fraternité entre les deux peuples. Ecrit à Paris le 25. Brumaire, L'an 2eme de la République française une et indivisible (le 15. Novembre 1793, Vieux Stile).

Les Citoïens formant le Conseil exécutif provisoire de la République française,

Deforgues
Dalbarade
J. Bouchotte
Gohier
DesTournelles
Paré
Par le Conseil exécutif provisoire
Desaugiers Secr[étai]re par interim

DS, DNA: RG 59, Communications from Heads of Foreign States, Ceremonial Letters.

François Louis Michel Chemin Deforgues (1759–1840) became minister of foreign affairs on 21 June. Jean Dalbarade (1743–1819) became minister of marine and colonies on 13 April. Jean-Baptiste Noël Bouchotte (1754–1840), a career soldier, became minister of war on 4 April. Louis Jérôme Gohier (1746–1830), a Breton lawyer, became minister of justice on 20 March. Louis Grégoire Des Champs Des Tournelles (1746–1794) became minister of finance on 13 June. Jules François Paré (1755–1819) became minister of interior on 20 August. All these ministers served until 1 April 1794, when the ministries were abolished and replaced by twelve executive commissions. The document announces that, in response to American complaints, they have replaced Edmond Genet with Joseph Fauchet as minister plenipotentiary to the United States. Desaugiers, formerly head clerk in the secrétariat, began functioning as interim secretary for the council by July. He was officially appointed interim secretary in November, and he continued as such at least until February 1794 (*Recueil des actes du Comité de salut public*, 5:462, 8:690, 10:753).

1. For the "Loi Concernant la formule des actes de la Puissance exécutive" of 15 Aug. 1792, see *Lois, et actes du gouvernement* (8 vols., Paris, 1806–1807), 6:47–49. The decree of 21 Sept. 1792 stated that there was no other constitution than that adopted in the first assemblies, continued provisionally "les autorités" until otherwise organized by the convention, and abolished the monarchy in France (*Gazette Nationale de France*, 22 Sept. 1792).

2. For GW's decision to request the recall of French minister Edmond Genet, see Cabinet Opinion, 23 August. For Thomas Jefferson's letter to Gou-

verneur Morris of 16 Aug. listing the complaints Morris was to make to the French government, see *Jefferson Papers*, 26:697–715.

From Burgess Ball

Dear sir,   Leesburg [Va.] 16th Novr 93.

We have been here about ten days, and are now tollarably fix'd.

I have been making Enquiry about Buck Wheat, and have given notice that I will give 2/ ℔ Bush: (a Price the Merchts told me I might purchase for) but, from the Scarcity of Corn, which now sells @ 12/ ℔ Barrell, I fear I shall not be able to get the Buck wheat for less than 2/6—For this price I'm sure I can get any quantity in a very short time, and if I can get it @ 2/ I shall be very glad—My Mill has taken in but very few Bushills—If you are willing I shou'd give 2/6, or whatever price, or quantity you may think proper, I shall be happy in executing your directions—If you'll send me on Bank notes, I will negotiate them here, and, if they shou'd not be made use of, they shall be return'd. Please write me as soon as convenient.

I am happy to hear that Philada is almost reliev'd from the misfortune it has so long been afflicted with—I hope you run no risque. Wishing you every filicity, I am with the highest Esteem Dr sir Yr. mo: Obt servt

B: Ball

P.S. My Wife & Miss Milly (who is with us) desire their respects &c.[1] B: B.

ALS, DLC:GW. The cover is stamped "ALEX Nov. 18"

1. GW's niece Mildred Gregory Washington was a sister of Ball's wife, Frances Washington Ball.

From Thomas Jefferson

[16 November 1793]

Th: Jefferson with his respects to the President has the honor to inclose for his information the following letters written in consequence of the two last consultations preceding his departure. there being quadruplicates of most of them, the trouble of looking over them will be proportionably diminished to the President.

Nov. 8. four letters to the foreign ministers on the *extent* of our jurisdiction[1]
   10. Circular to the district-attornies on the *same* subject and on the mode of settling the cases which arise.[2]
   do four letters to the foreign ministers on the mode of settling the cases which arise of captures within our jurisdiction[3]
   *do to Messrs Viar & Jaudenes, covering answer of Govr of Kentuckey as to military enterprizes projected there, & the information of the Govr of N. Carolina as to the Spanish prize carried in there.[4]
   †13. to mister Hammond on the inexecution of the treaty.[5]
   †   to Govr Moultrie on Mr Genet's suggestion of military enterprises projected.[6]
   *   to Judge Morris, inclosing Fitz Freeman's petition.[7]
   14. to mister Hammond on the Roehampton & Industry.[8]
       to the District Attorney of Maryland on the brig Coningham.
       to d[itt]o on the condemnation of the Roehampton & Pilgrim by the Fr. Consul[9]
   15. to d[itt]o of Pensylvania on the Ship William.
       to mr Genet on same subject
       to mister Hammond on same subject.[10]

*these are on subjects not referred to our consultation.
†these were in consequence of determinations at our consultations, but the letters, being in plain cases, were not communicated for inspection to the other gentlemen, after they were written.
there are some other letters agreed on, but not yet copied.

AL, DNA: RG 59, Miscellaneous Letters; AL (letterpress copy), Jefferson Papers; LB, DNA: RG 59, George Washington's Correspondence with His Secretaries of State. The AL is undated, but GW's executive journal records receiving it on 16 Nov. (*JPP*, 251–52), and Bartholomew Dandridge, Jr.'s, docket on the document reads, "From the Secy of State 16. Nov: 1793."

1. For this circular letter, sent to the ministers of Great Britain, France, the Netherlands, and Spain, see *Jefferson Papers*, 27:328–30. It announced that while the extent of American territorial waters was being decided, a limit of one sea league, or three miles, would be in force.

2. For this circular letter, see *Jefferson Papers,* 27:338–40. The attorneys were instructed to try to get the parties to agree on arbiters to ascertain whether the seizure was legal, or if the parties could not agree to arbitration, to take depositions for transmission to the executive.

3. For this circular letter, see *Jefferson Papers,* 27:340–42.

4. For this letter and Kentucky Governor Isaac Shelby's letter to Jefferson of 5 Oct., see *Jefferson Papers,* 27:196, 345–46. For the North Carolina information, see Richard Dobbs Spaight to GW, 21 Oct., and notes. On these topics, see also Jefferson to GW, 6 Nov., and n.1 to that document.

5. For this letter to British minister George Hammond, see *Jefferson Papers,* 27:353.

6. This letter relayed to South Carolina governor William Moultrie French minister Edmond Genet's information that two persons were equipping a vessel at Charleston to seize Turtle Island [Tortuga Island], "and there to put to death all the French who shall remain faithful to their country. . . . The same line of Conduct being proper for us between parties of the same nation engaged in civil war, as between different nations at war," GW expected Moultrie "to prevent every preparation of hostilities . . . against countries or people with which we are at peace" (*Jefferson Papers,* 27:356).

7. For this letter, see *Jefferson Papers,* 27:355. For its subject, see Abraham Freeman to GW, 5 Sept., and n.2 to that document.

8. Jefferson's letter to Hammond of 14 Nov. informed him that the *Roehampton* would not be restored, but promised to institute a new inquiry into whether the French privateer *L'Industrie* had been illegally equipped in American ports and to take appropriate action if such was found to be the case (*Jefferson Papers,* 27:368–73). Secretary of War Henry Knox had written to Maryland Governor Thomas Sim Lee on 12 Nov. requesting a report on whether *L'Industrie* had augmented her force, and on 23 Nov. he wrote Lee that *L'Industrie* should be reduced if she had (MdAA: Brown Books).

9. For Jefferson's two letters of 14 Nov. to Maryland district attorney Zebulon Hollingsworth, see *Jefferson Papers,* 27:374–75. Jefferson desired Hollingsworth to bring the case of the *Conyngham* "to final settlement" in accordance with the instructions given in Jefferson's circular letter of 10 Nov. and to investigate whether the French consul at Baltimore, Francis Moissonnier, had, contrary to Jefferson's remonstrances to Edmond Genet and his threat to revoke exequaturs, "undertaken to try and condemn" the *Roehampton* and *Pilgrim* "and to order their sale."

10. Jefferson's letter of 15 Nov. to Pennsylvania district attorney William Rawle directed him to proceed with the case of the *William* according to the instructions given in Jefferson's circular letter of 10 November. His letters to Hammond and Genet informed them that he had so instructed Rawle (*Jefferson Papers,* 27:382–85).

From Henry Knox

sir   Falls of Schuylkill [Pa.] 16 Nov. 1793

I have the honor to submit two letters of Major Genl Wayne one dated the 17th of Septr and the other the 5th of October with a variety of enclosures, including the proceedings of the Court martial upon Ensign Morgan.[1]

In addition to the information contained in these papers, I am informed that the late Lt Jennifer who was cashiered,[2] arrived at Pittsburg from Head quarters who says that General Scott arrived at Fort Washington on the 7th Octr a few hours after Genl Wayne had marched, with nearly six hundred mounted voluntiers, and that as many more were expected hourly. I have the honor to be with the highest respect sir your obedient Servt

H. Knox

ALS, DLC:GW; LB, DLC:GW.

1. Gen. Anthony Wayne's letter to Knox of 17 Sept. reported his receipt of the commissioners' letter of 23 Aug. notifying of the failure of their peace talks with the Indians. Regretting that the commissioners had not accepted as final the Indians' answer of 31 July, "but rather chose to place Confidence in a Mr Matthew Elliot, an artful designing–interested man--*the partner of Colo McKee* who was apprehensive that we shou'd receive intelligence *too soon,* & be better prepar'd for a forward move, in due season & before the Grass shou'd fail," Wayne described his preparations for that move: calling on Maj. Gen. Charles Scott to join him with troops at Fort Jefferson, ordering quartermasters and contractors to collect their means of transportation, and creating a list of appointments and reorganizing his army. Wayne questioned the "propriety" of his acting on John Morgan's court-martial, as it had originated before Wayne was called into service, and he enclosed the proceedings for GW's decision. In response to Knox's order, Wayne enclosed a determination on the relative ranks of captains in his army. In addition he enclosed various items about the Chickasaws: letters from Piomingo to Gen. James Robertson and from Robertson to Wayne, and the report of Lt. William Clark, who was given charge of stores sent to the tribe (Knopf, *Wayne,* 272–75).

Wayne's letter to Knox of 5 Oct. reported the arrival of three companies of troops totaling about 170 men and some damaged clothing, on which he enclosed a report. Wayne faulted Col. John Clark for "Neglect of duty & disobedience of Orders" in the forwarding of men and supplies and enclosed a letter from Maj. Isaac Craig as evidence. Wayne reported a shortage of auxiliary forces, only 36 guides and 360 mounted volunteers, enclosing copies of his correspondence with Governor Isaac Shelby and with General Scott about the Kentucky mounted volunteers, and adding that he had even ordered a draft of militia with "but little hopes of success." Moreover, in addition to the "considerable number of Officers & men sick & debilitated from fevers & other disorders incident to all Armies," his legions had been struck with influenza, with a reduction in force illustrated by an enclosed general return of the legion. As a result Wayne would "not be able to advance beyond Fort Jefferson with more than Twenty Six Hundred regular Effectives, Officers included." Nonetheless, his plans were to "advance tomorrow with the force I have, in order to gain a strong position about Six miles in front of Fort Jefferson, so as to keep the Enemy in Check." Wayne believed that the "present apparent tranquility on the fronteers" was evidence that the enemy was collecting to attack his army; by his movement, they might "probably be tempted to attack our lines. . . . They can not continue long embodied for want of provisions, & at their breaking up they will most certainly make some desperate effort, upon some quarter or other–shou'd the Mounted Volunteers Advance in force, we might yet compel those haughty Savages to sue for peace before the *next opening* of the Leaves, be that as it may–I pray you not to permit present appearances to cause too much anxiety either in the minds of the President or yourself on account of the Army. . . . You may rest assured that I will not commit the Legion Unnecessarily" (Knopf, *Wayne*, 275–77).

2. Daniel St. Thomas Jenifer killed Ensign William Pitt Gassaway in a duel in March 1793 and was dismissed from the service on 10 Sept. 1793.

To Nicholas Lewis

Sir,   Germantown [Pa.] 16th Novemr 1793.

While I acknowledge that all power is derived from the people, and that the Federal Government has been instituted for their happiness, I cannot but unite in the attachment expressed by the freemen of Albemarle to the Constitution of the U. States.[1] Harmony with foreign Nations is a blessing which we ought to prize & to cherish; & from a desire of cultivating it the proclamation was issued.[2] Such a measure became the more eligible, as it neither cancelled nor weakened our obligations to the French Nation.

Go. Washington

LB, DLC:GW. This letter was printed in the *Virginia Gazette, and General Advertiser* (Richmond), 25 December.

1. GW was referring to the resolutions of Albemarle County, Va., citizens, 10 Oct., enclosed in Lewis's letter to GW of 24 October.

2. GW's Neutrality Proclamation was dated 22 April.

From the Saint Marc (Saint Domingue) Council

                                                    A St marc, isle St Domingue,
Monsieur le Président,   le 16 9bre 1793. 2e
    Nous avons l'honneur d'adresser à votre excellence un ex-
emplaire du Traité fait entre les paroisses de St marc, des ver-
rettes et de la petite rivière, Section de la colonie française de
St Domingue.[1] L'un de ces articles tend à rappeller ceux de
nos freres qui chassés ⟨par⟩ le despotisme des Commissaires Polverel & Sonthonax ont trouvé un asile chez la genereuse nation
dont vous avez assuré l'indépendance. Il est digne d'elle et de
⟨vous⟩ de leur donner le Signal de la résistance à l'opression, en
leur transmettant notre voeu et notre exemple. Le témoignage
de bienveillance et d'humanité que vous donneres tant à nous
qu'à nos freres refugiés et déportés, a les invitant à venir recon-
querir leurs propriétés, ajoutent, S'il est possible, aux Sentiments du profond respect avec lequel nous Sommes, De votre
Excellence, Les très humbles & très obéissants Serviteurs.
    Les members du Conseil de Paix & d'union Séants à St marc.

                                                    F. Trinquart
                                                    Presidt
                                                    Gornail aîné
                                                    Morel
                                                    ⟨Niel⟩
                                                    Bretton des Chappelles

LS, DNA: RG 59, Miscellaneous Letters.
    Edmund Randolph's endorsement with this letter reads: "Feby 7. 94. Sent
to the French Gentlemen of *St Domingo* at Mrs Dunn's Phila."
    An F. Trinquart was in Philadelphia in 1798 (*Porcupine's Gazette* [Philadel-
phia], 12 July 1798). The last signer may have been Jean-Baptiste François
Bretton des Chapelles (1739-1795), who moved to Wilmington, Del., before
his death.
    1. The enclosed "treaty," which the writers claim contains an article that
may encourage Saint Domingue refugees in the United States to return to
the island and fight oppression, has not been identified.

From Harriot Washington

                            Fredericksburg [Va.] November the 16, 1793
    I receiv'd My Honor'd Uncle's letter, of the 25 of September[1]
and am now seated, to return him a thousand thanks, for the

money he was so obleiging as to send me. Aunt Lewis informed me, that you mentioned in your last letter to her,[2] if the fever in Philadelphia did not abate, that Aunt Washington would spend the winter at Mt Vernon, and if she did, you would send for me. I shall be very much pleased if you do, for I am very anxious to se yourself and Aunt Washington. About a week ago Cousin Carter was so unfortunate, as to lose her youngest child.[3] she is soon a going to Culpepper, and as she is very lonesome, she has perswaded me to go with her, but Aunt Lewis desire'd me to let you no, if you could contrive her word, about a forghtnight or three week, before I go to Mt Vernon, she will pay a visit to Cousin Carter and I should return with her. I acquainted Brother Lawrence with your request. Aunt Lewis and Cousin Carter join me in love to you and Aunt Washington. I am Honor'd Uncle Your affectionate Neice

Harriot Washington

ALS, ViMtvL.

   1. This letter has not been found.

   2. This letter has not been found.

   3. Betty Lewis Carter's deceased child was Mary Willis Carter, who was born in July 1793.

Drafting GW's Annual Address, 18–28 Nov. 1793

EDITORIAL NOTE

Although the journal of GW's presidential proceedings for 1793 recorded only a single cabinet discussion on 23 Nov. about his annual message, according to notes made by Secretary of State Thomas Jefferson, the cabinet discussed the subject at four meetings held on 18, 21, 23, and 28 Nov. (*JPP*, 257; *Jefferson Papers*, 27:399–401, 411–13, 428, 453–56).

It seems most probable that documents I–III, which lay out topics to be communicated in the annual address or other messages, were prepared in anticipation of the meeting on 18 Nov., where the cabinet "took up the discussion of the subjects of communication to Congress." That meeting, however, stalled at the very first topic, the presentation on GW's Neutrality Proclamation of 22 April. Attorney General Edmund Randolph "read the statement he had prepared" (possibly document IV), but Secretary of the Treasury Alexander Hamilton "did not like" Randolph's text. Hamilton expressed his belief "that the Presidt. had a right to declare his opinion to our citizens and foreign nations that it was not the interest of this country to join in the war and that we were under no obligation to join in it." While Hamilton conceded that the declaration "would not legally bind Congress . . . he was against any expln. in the speech which should yeild that he did not intend that foreign nations should consider it as a declaration of neutrality future as well as present." Randolph and Jefferson "opposed the right of the Presidt. to declare any thing future on the qu. shall there or shall there not be war? and that no such thing was intended." After discussion, in which GW "declared he never had an idea that he could bind Congress against declaring war, or that any thing contained in his proclmn. could look beyond the the first day of their meeting, his main view was to keep our people in peace," GW decided that Hamilton "should prepare a paragraph on this subject" for consideration.

Hamilton presented that paragraph (Document VI) at the meeting on 21 Nov., explaining that his intention was "to say nothing which could be laid hold of for any purpose, to leave the proclamation to explain itself." In the discussion that followed, Hamilton "entered pretty fully into all the argumentation of Pacificus" and went so far as to argue that "the constn. having given power to the Presidt. and Senate to make treaties, they might make a treaty of neutrality, which should take from Congress the right to declare war in that particular case, and that under the form of a treaty they might exercise any powers whatever." Randolph opposed that position, believing that "an act of the legislature would be necessary to confirm" any treaty provisions touching on legislative powers, and Jefferson contended that the president and Senate could only "carry into effect by way of treaty any powers they might constitutionally exercise." On the proclamation, then, Randolph and Jefferson supported Randolph's phrasing, while Hamilton and Secretary of War Henry Knox supported Hamilton's. GW "said he had but one object, the keeping our people quiet till Congress should meet, that nevertheless to declare he did not mean a declaration of neutrality in the technical sense of the phrase, might perhaps be crying *peccavi* before he was charged. However he did not decide between the two draughts."

Meanwhile, the secretaries apparently were preparing additional materials for the speech in the areas covered by their departments (see documents V and VIII; document VII also may be such an item or, despite being recorded under the date 22 Nov., an earlier general outline). On 23 Nov., with Hamilton absent due to ill health, the cabinet finally moved on to other matters. Jefferson opposed a "proposition to Congress to fortify the principal harbors," and "It was amended by substituting a proposition to adopt means for enforcing respect to the jurisdiction of the US. within it's waters." Jefferson also opposed a proposal for "the establishment of a military academy," on grounds that "none of the specified powers given by the constn. to Congress would authorize this," and that issue was deferred. GW "acknowledged he had doubted of the expediency of undertaking the former, and as to the latter, tho' it would be a good thing, he did not wish to bring on any thing which might generate heat and ill humor." At this meeting it was agreed that Randolph would draft the annual address and Jefferson the other messages.

Randolph's final draft, which was presented to the cabinet on 28 Nov., has not been identified, but document IX apparently is his outline for that draft. The only debate that Jefferson recorded was on the military academy, since "The clause recommending fortifications was left out." Hamilton, Knox, and Randolph all supported the academy recommendation, and GW "said he would not chuse to recommend any thing against the constitution, but if it was *doubtful,* he was so impressed with the necessity of this measure, that he would refer it to Congress, and let them decide for themselves whether the constn. authorized it or not. It was therefore left in." According to Jefferson, "No material alterations were proposed or made in any part" of Randolph's draft.

For the final version of the message, see GW to the United States Senate and House of Representatives, 3 December.

I
Alexander Hamilton's Outline for GW's Annual Address to Congress

[November 1793]

Objects to be communicated in Speech & Messages

I Proclamation
II Embarrassments on carrying into Execution the princi-

ples of neutrality; necessity of some auxiliary provisions
by law—

III   Expectation of indemnification given in relation to illegal
        captures—

IV   State of our affairs with regard to G. Britain
                                        to Spain
                                        to France—claim
        of *Guarantee*[1]—propositions *respecting Trade*—

V   Indian affairs—
                failure of Treaty[2]—state of expedition under Wayne
                prospects with regard to Southern Indians—

VI   Prudence of additional precautions for defence; as the
        best security for the peace of the Country—
                1 fortification of principal sea ports
                2 Corps of efficient Militia—

VII   Completion of settlement of Accounts between the United
        and Individual States:[3] Provision for ballances—

VIII   Provision for a sinking fund—

IX   Our revenues in the aggregate have continued to answer
        expectation as to productiveness but if the various objects
        pointed out and which appear to be neccesary to the pub-
        lic Interest are to be accomplished it can hardly be hoped
        that there will be a necessity for some moderate addition
        to them—

X   Prolongation of the Dutch installment by way of
        Loan—terms.[4]

XI   Provision for the second installment due to the Bank of
        U. States—[5]

XII   for interest on the unsubscribed debt during the present
        year. Quære

XIII   Communication of the state of cessions of Light Houses.
        The Cession in various instances has not been intire; it
        has reserved a partial right of jurisdiction for *process;* con-
        sequently is not strictly conformable to law—[6]

XIV   Commissary to receive issue & account for all public stores
        would conduce much to order & œconomy.[7]

AD, DLC:GW.

    1. By articles 11 and 12 of the Treaty of Alliance with France, 6 Feb.
1778, the United States guaranteed to France "the present Possessions of
the Crown of france in America as well as those which it may acquire by

the future Treaty of peace," that guarantee to take effect "in case of a rupture between france and England . . . the moment such War shall break out" (Miller, *Treaties,* 39–40). For previous discussion of the meaning of that guarantee in the context of the 1793 European conflict, see GW to the Cabinet, 18 April; Thomas Jefferson to GW, 28 April; and Edmund Randolph to GW, 6 May.

2. Hamilton was referring to the treaty with the hostile Indians of the Northwest Territory held at Sandusky in July and August (see *ASP, Indian Affairs,* 1:340–61)

3. See the Commissioners for Settling Accounts between the United States and the Individual States to GW, 29 June.

4. On the prolongation of the Dutch loan approved by Congress on 14 Sept. 1782 (*JCC,* 23:575–80), see Wilhelm and Jan Willink, Nicholaas and Jacob Van Staphorst, and Nicholas Hubbard, to Hamilton, 1 May (*Hamilton Papers,* 14:364–67).

5. For the $2 million loan, see GW to Alexander Hamilton, 9 May 1792. On 4 June 1794 Congress passed "An Act providing for the payment of the second instalment due on a Loan made of the Bank of the United States" (1 *Stat.* 372).

6. Section 1 of "An Act for the establishment and support of Lighthouses, Beacons, Buoys, and Public Piers," 7 Aug. 1789, made the United States responsible for all expenses accruing in the "necessary support, maintenance and repairs of all lighthouses," but only if the lighthouse were "ceded to and vested in the United States . . . together with the lands and tenements thereto belonging, and together with the jurisdiction of the same" (1 *Stat.* 53–54). Some states, however, proved reluctant to cede jurisdiction for the issuance of civil and criminal process (see Tench Coxe to Hamilton, 3 and 19 Jan. 1793, *Hamilton Papers,* 13:447–48, 503–4). Ultimately, Congress, by an act of 2 March 1795, provided that cessions "with reservation, that process civil and criminal, issuing under the authority of such state, may be executed and served therein" would "be deemed sufficient," and that such process might be "served and executed" even where the state had made a full cession of jurisdiction (1 *Stat.* 426).

7. GW did not make this recommendation in his annual address, but it was the subject of his second message to Congress of 7 Jan. 1794.

II
Edmund Randolph's List of Topics to be Communicated to Congress

[November 1793]

Heads of subjects to be communicated to congress; some at the opening, others by messages.

1. The proclamation, and the reasons for issuing it, together with an observation on the French treaty.

2. The selling of prizes in our ports.

3. The engagement concerning compensation for vessels, captured under certain circumstances.[1]

4. The propriety of vesting the fœderal courts with power to aid the executive in cases of capture.

5. The enaction of a particular penalty against consuls of foreign nations, opening courts in the United States.

6. The necessity of providing means for commanding respect from foreign vessels, which are refractory.

7. To submit to congress, whether it be better to rest the jurisdictional claim into the sea, as it stands, or to assert A particular distance by law.

8. The abortive attempt to treat with the Western Indians.

9. The situation of the U.S. with respect to
France
Great Britain and
Spain

10. Military intelligence.
quæ

11. To provide some other place for the sessions of congress, in case that of their last sitting should be improper &c.

12. Has any loan been affected, which ought to be communicated?
Quæ: whether Mr Genet's propositions as to commerce are to be sent to the senate *executively,* or to *congress?*[2]

13. The memorial on the guarantee.[3]

AD, DLC:GW.

1. For GW's commitment to make compensation for vessels seized by French ships equipped in U.S. ports, see Cabinet Opinion on French Privateers and Prizes, 5 Aug., and Thomas Jefferson's letters of 7 Aug. to French minister Edmond Genet and to British minister George Hammond (*Jefferson Papers,* 26:633–35).

2. For discussion of Genet's proposition about payment of the French debt, see the enclosure with Alexander Hamilton to GW, 23 November.

3. For discussion of the guarantee, see Hamilton's outline, November 1793, n.1.

III
GW's Notes on the Annual Address to Congress

[November 1793]

Sundry matters to be communicated for the information of Congress—either in the Speech at the opening of the Session, or by Messages thereafter, as shall be thought best.

Proclamation, informing the United States of the actual State of things as they stood between them and the Powers at War.[1]

State of Our application respecting the surrender of the Western Posts.[2]

Additional Instructions of his Britanic Majesty relative to Corn &ca in Neutral Vessels.[3]

State of matters as it respects our Negociation with Spain, relative to Territory and the Navigation of the River Mississipi.[4]

Corrispondence with Mr Genet, Minister from the French Republic.

The impediments which have taken place in the intended Ransom of our Citizens, captives in Algiers—& treaty with the Barbary States.[5]

Treaty attempted with the Western Indians, and the result of it.[6]

March of the Army in consequence of it—delayed by the suspension we were held in thereby

State of matters as they relate to the Creeks and Cherokees—& to the Frontiers of Georgia and the South Western Territory.

Would not a trade on *Public* ground, with *all* the bordering tribes of Indians (if they can once be made sensible of their folly by the Superiority of our arms) be an effectual mean of attaching them to us by the strongest of all ties, Interest.

The utility of establishing proper Arsenals unfolds itself more & more every day. And the propriety of a Military Accademy for teaching the Art of Gunnery & Engineering, can scarcely be doubted. A War, at any time, would evince the impropriety of such a neglect.

Might it not be expedient to take off the Tax upon the transportation of News Papers &c.?[7]

An Act of the Legislature, So. West of the Ohio, Passed Novr 20th 1792—Deposited in the Secretary of States Office.[8]

As both Representatives & President are newly chosen, and it is their first meeting, may it not be a good occasion, & proper for the latter to express his sentiments of the honor conferred on by his fellow Citizens. The former is an augmented body—The times are critical—and much temper, & cool deliberate reflection is necessary to maintain Peace with dignity & safety to the United States.

Appointments, during the recess of Congress to be laid before the Senate.

AD, DLC:GW. An unidentified writer (probably Edmund Randolph) placed a check mark next to all but the last paragraph.

1. GW was referring to his Neutrality Proclamation of 22 April.

2. On the stalled effort to obtain British evacuation from western forts, see Cabinet Opinion, 7 Sept., and n.8 to that document; Record of Cabinet Opinions, 22 Nov.; and *Jefferson Papers,* 27:353.

3. For the additional instructions of 8 June, see Thomas Jefferson to GW, 15–16 Sept., n.4. See also the cabinet opinions of 31 Aug. and 7 Sept. for the U.S. response to unofficial news of these British orders.

4. For this, see GW's first message to the U.S. Senate and House of Representatives of 16 Dec. and notes to that document.

5. On this topic, see Jefferson's Report on Morocco and Algiers, 14 Dec., enclosed with GW's second message to the U.S. Senate and House of Representatives of 16 December.

6. GW was referring to the unsuccessful treaty with the hostile Indians of the Northwest Territory held at Lower Sandusky in July and August (see *ASP, Indian Affairs,* 1:340–61).

7. GW apparently was referring to section 22 of "An Act to establish the Post-Office and Post Roads within the United States," 20 Feb. 1790, wherein the conveyance of newspapers by mail was charged at "one cent, for any distance not more than one hundred miles, and one cent and a half for any greater distance" (1 *Stat.* 232–39).

8. This act, which the territorial secretary thought needed congressional approval, authorized the county courts to levy a tax for the construction of courthouses and prisons and to defray other legal costs (see Jefferson's third letter to GW of 19 June, and n.2 to that document).

IV
Edmund Randolph's Draft for GW's Annual Address to Congress

[November 1793]
As soon as the European war had embraced those nations, with which the U.S. have an extensive commercial intercourse,

there was reason to apprehend, that this intercourse might be interrupted, and our disposition for peace drawn into question, by the suspicions, usually entertained by belligerent powers. It seemed therefore to be my duty, to admonish my fellow-citizens, of the consequences of a contraband trade, and of hostile conduct towards any of the parties; and to obtain, by a declaration of the existing legal state of things, an easier admission of our right to the immunities, belonging to our situation. Under these impressions, the proclamation, which will be laid before you, was issued.[1]

It did not escape notice, that our treaties with France might probably produce claims for the performance of many important stipulations, contained in that instrument.[2] But these, so far as their fulfilment might depend upon the opinions and authority of the executive, could not with propriety be considered, as clashing with the proclamation; and they have been accordingly fulfilled.

Several prizes, taken by the French ships of war and privateers, were brought into our ports, under the permission, given by the treaty of commerce; and being there, they have been sold by the captors. Howsoever salutary a prohibition or restriction of this practice might have been; it appeared to be a subject, more fit for a provision by law, than for the interposition of the executive.

On other occasions, when the jurisdiction of the U.S. has been infringed by captures within the protection of our territory, or by captures, made by vessels, commissioned or equipped in our ports, I have not refused to restore them; and I have also, in many instances, ordered the vessels, so equipped, to be reduced from their military preparations. But, notwithstanding every precaution, some of those captures were attended with such circumstances, as to render it proper for me to undertake, what is expressed in a communication to the ministers of foreign courts, resident here, concerning compensation.

It would however, have been very acceptable to me, if the constitution of the fœderal courts would have suffered me to consign to their decision many cases, upon which I was compelled to act definitively. Even now perhaps, it may be expedient to extend their cognizance of captures, as well to the ascertaining of facts by a jury, when the executive shall, for its own information, request it; as even to the making of restitution when restitution shall be due. The want of aids, like these, induced me to adopt a system of rules, of which copies will be presented to you.[3]

Nor is it less urgent, that some particular penalty should be enacted against those foreign consuls, who shall open courts within the U.S. for the condemnation of vessels, captured from their enemy. The means, which are in the hands of the executive for repressing this assumption of power, will not be always equal to the mischief, which may spring from it.

But with the wisest legislative institutions on these subjects, and with the greatest vigilance of the public officers against their violation, a respect to the authority of the U.S. cannot be insured from foreign vessels of force, without an ability to coerce them. On some of the waters of the U.S., a few forts have been adapted to effectual service; but on others, none are to be found.

Among other arrangements, which the posture of public affairs demands, it seems adviseable to define the extent of protection and jurisdiction from the coast of the U.S. into the ocean. Different nations have established different pretensions into the sea. For the present, no greater distance has been assumed by the U.S., than a marine league, which is the shortest distance, claimed by any nation. It remains therefore for congress to determine, whether it be better to rest this unsettled point, upon explanations and adjustments, which may be made thro' the channel of negotiation, or to prescribe the range, to which the right of the U.S. shall be hereafter asserted.

AD, DLC:GW.

1. Randolph was referring to GW's Neutrality Proclamation of 22 April.

2. Randolph was referring to the Treaties of Amity and Commerce and of Alliance, both 6 Feb. 1778 (Miller, *Treaties*, 3–44).

3. For GW's unsuccessful attempt to obtain guidance from the Supreme Court, see Cabinet Opinion, 12 July, and n.4; Thomas Jefferson to GW, 18 July, enclosure; Jefferson to GW, 19 July, n.1; and Supreme Court Justices to GW, 8 August. For the system of rules, see Cabinet Opinion on the Rules of Neutrality, 3 August.

V
Henry Knox's Draft for GW's Annual Address to Congress

[c.19 November 1793][1]

The efforts which have been made without the desired effect, to adjust, by an amicable negociation, all causes of difference with the hostile Indians north of the Ohio, will I trust, be found demonstrative of the sincere dispositions of the United States for peace, upon moderate and equitable terms, and also, of their liberal intentions, of rendering more comfortable, the condition of their ignorant and barbarous neighbours.

I have directed that all the papers relatively to the pacific overtures to the said Indians, together with the result thereof, should be laid before you for your information upon the subject.[2]

If after the fairest experiments peace is unattainable upon reasonable grounds, it appears to be incumbent on the United States to use decisively, such degrees of their force, as shall be competent, as well to the immediate protection of their exposed citizens, as to the exemplary punishment of those tribes, which obstinately persevere in their cruel depredations upon our frontiers.

The season for military operations having been occupied by negociations, the public force will not probably be able to undertake any considerable enterprizes in a wilderness, during the remainder of the Year.

A return of the troops in service will be laid before you, by which, it will be perceived that the numbers authorized by law, are materially deficient, notwithstanding the recruiting, has been continued to the present time. It will be a subject of consideration, whether the establishment shall be completed by additional encouragements, or whether powerful aids of militia shall be afforded to accomplish the public objects.[3]

The situation in the southwestern frontiers will also claim the serious attention of Congress. A statement upon this subject, together with the papers on which it is founded will be laid before you in order that you may be enabled to judge of the measures which it may be proper to adopt on the occasion.[4] At the same time means may be devised for the prompt punishment of bandittie Indians belonging to tribes in peace with us, it would appear to be indispensible, that the laws should be so strengthened, that our own violators of the peace, and existing treaties, should not escape with impunity, & thereby bring down upon innocent men women and children all the horrors of savage retaliation, and also involve the United States in an unjust War.

I have directed the secretary of War also to lay before you a statement of the present situation of the public Magazines and Arsenals.[5] Although it will appear, that the war like apparatus and stores, contained are respectable, yet motives of prudence, require that large augmentations should be made thereto. During the recess of Congress I conceived it to be my duty to direct that some essential articles should be provided, and some repairs made, which might be required at a time and under circumstances when they could not be obtained. The expences incurred for these Objects, will be stated in the estimates for the ensuing year, for which appropriations will be requisite.

Although it be deemed that neither our interests nor any other circumstances require us to become parties to the existing war among the European powers, yet it is an obligation of the highest nature, which every Nation owes to itself, to be provided at all times, in full abundance, with the means necessary for its own preservation, and defence.[6] Hence it is submitted to your wisdom whether the exposed situation of some of the principal Seaports of the United States do not require that species of fortification which would secure them from insult or surprize. Applications for this purpose have been made to me by several of the excutives of the individual states, but as there was no law authorizing the measure it could not be undertaken.[7] Its propriety however is too apparent to require any arguments to enforce it.

Being upon the subject of our defence I feel myself impelled by a sacred love for my country, and by a solemn conviction of the importance of the object—again to suggest the propriety of establishing that bulwark of liberty and national security an energetic Militia. To act in all emergencies as the advanced Guard of the Country behind which the great body of the people by their representatives should have time and opportunity afforded them to take such arrangements as the situation of affairs might demand. With an adequate body of free citizens properly organized the United States would be in a condition to meet and dissipate those events, which sometimes arise in the affairs of men, and for which being unprepared, the happiness and the liberty of societies have too frequently been overturned and ruined.

AD, DLC:GW; ADf, NNGL: Knox Papers.

1. Knox docketed the retained draft of this document as "Submitted the President Nov. 1⟨9⟩, 1793." The "Dec. 1793" docket on the document in GW's papers probably refers to the 3 Dec. 1793 date of GW's address to the United States Senate and House of Representatives, which included most of the ideas contained in the document. Check marks corresponding to each paragraph appear in the margins of the document in GW's papers.

2. For the papers about the unsuccessful treaty at Lower Sandusky submitted to the Senate on 4 Dec., see *ASP, Indian Affairs,* 1:340–61.

3. Knox's "Statement of the Non Commissioned Officers and Privates in the service of the United States," 4 Dec., showed a deficiency of 1,259 soldiers from the establishment of 5,120 (DLC:GW).

4. Knox submitted this statement to the Senate on 16 Dec. (*ASP, Indian Affairs,* 1:361–468).

5. Knox sent a return of ordnance, arms, and military stores, dated 14 Dec., to the Senate on 16 Dec. (*ASP, Military Affairs,* 1:44–60).

6. At this point on the retained draft, Knox continued with the following text, which he then struck out: "It is for this reason that I conceive Wisdom dictates that not only our arsenals and magazines should be well provided but also that is important, that definitive arrangements should be taken for the purpose of fortifying some of our principal Seaports. Applications have been recently made to me for this purpose by several of the executives of the individual states, but the measure being unauthorized by law it could not be undertaken."

7. On the retained draft, the text between this point and the previous note is written on a separate page.

VI
Alexander Hamilton's Draft of a Statement on the Neutrality Proclamation for GW's Fifth Annual Address to Congress

[c.21 November 1793]

It is greatly to be lamented, for the sake of humanity, that the flame of War, which had before spread over a considerable part of Europe has within the present year extended itself much further; implicating all those powers with whom the United States have the most extensive relations. When it was seen here, that almost all the maritime Nations either were, or were likely soon to become parties to the War, it was natural that it should excite serious reflections about the possible consequences to this Country. On the one hand, it appeared desireable, that no impressions in reference to it should exist—with any of the powers engaged, of a nature to precipitate arrangements or measurs tending to interrupt or endanger our peace.[1] On the other, it was probable, that designing or inconsiderate persons among ourselves might from different motives embark in enterprizes contrary to the duties of a nation at peace with nations at war with each other; and, of course,[2] calculated to invite and to produce reprisals and hostilites. Adverting to these considerations, in a situation both new and delicate, I Judged it adviseable to issue a Proclamation (here insert the substance of the Proclamation)—The effects of this measure have, I trust, neither disappointed the views which dictated it, nor disserved the true interests of our Country.

AD, DLC:GW; ADf, DLC: Alexander Hamilton Papers. The document at DLC: Hamilton Papers is an earlier draft that contains numerous emendations and stricken passages. The draft at DLC:GW, which contains far fewer changes, was docketed by GW. This draft evidently was prepared for the cabinet meeting of 21 Nov. (see editorial note above).

1. On the earlier draft, Hamilton first wrote: "On the one hand, it was not impossible that the unfounded jealousies of some of the powers concerned might have led hastily to measures injurious to our rights and tending to implicate us in hostility," but he deleted that text and substituted the language used here.

2. In the earlier draft, Hamilton initially finished this sentence with the phrase, "to occasion reprisals detrimental to our well dispos ed citizens."

VII
Thomas Jefferson's Notes for GW's Annual Address to Congress

[c.22 November 1793][1]

Notes

cases where individuals (as Henfield &c.) organize themselves into military bodies within the U.S. or participate in acts of hostility by sea, where *jurisdiction attaches to the person.*[3]

Text

The Constitution having authorised the legislature exclusively to declare whether the nation, from a state of peace,

What is the present legal mode of *restraint*? binding to the good behavior? military restraint? or what? or can the act only be *punished* after it is committed?

shall go into that of war,[2] it rests with their wisdom to consider Whether the restraints already provided by the laws are sufficient to prevent individuals from usurping, *in effect*, that power, by taking part, or arraying themselves to take part, by sea or by land, while under the jurisdiction of the U.S. in the hostilities of any one nation against any other with which the U.S. are at peace?

Vessels originally constituting themselves cruizers here, or those so constituted elsewhere & augmenting their force here, may they be seized & detained? by what branch of the government? e.g. the Polly or Republican at N.Y. the Jane at Philada the Industry at Baltimore. Their Prizes. may they be restored? e.g. the Lovely lass, Pr. Wm Henry, Jane of Dublin, the Spanish prize &c.[4]

Whether the laws have provided with sufficient efficacy & explicitness, for arresting & restraining their preparations & enterprizes, & for indemnifying their effects?

Captures within our waters, by whom to be restored? e.g. the Grange, the William, the Providence, the William Tell &c[5]

Whether within the territory of the U.S. or those limits on it's shores to which reason & usage authorize them to extend their jurisdiction & protection, & to interdict every hostile act, even between hostile nations, the partition of the National authority between the civil & military organs is delineated with sufficient precision to leave no doubt which of the two is justified, & is bound to interpose?

Cases of the Betsey, and American Vessel & Swedish cargo. the Maxwell, vessel & cargo Swedish.[6]

Whether either & Which of them is authorized to liberate our own property or that of other peaceable nations, taken on the high-seas & brought into our ports?

merely an intimation to establish all these cases with the judiciary.

Whether all such of these interferences as may be exercised by the judiciary bodies with equal efficacy, with more regularity, and with greater safety to the rights of individuals, citizen or alien, are already placed under their cognisance, so as to leave no room for diversity of judgment among them, no necessity or ground for any other branch to exercise them, merely that there may not be a defect of justice or protection, or a breach of public order?

for a specification of some of these duties see Jay's & Wilson's charges.[7] are they all sufficiently provided with specific punishments?

Offences against the Law of Nations. Genet's conduct is one. by that law the President may order him away. has the law provided for the efficacy of this order?

And Whether the duties of a nation at peace towards those at war, imposed by the laws and usages of nature, & nations, & such other offences against the law of nations as present circumstances may produce, are provided for by the municipal law with those details of internal sanction and coercion, the mode & measure of which that alone can establish?[8]

other subjects
Proclamation
Report of balances between the states.
Western Indians
Creeks.
Provision of arms *made*, & to be made.
subsequent.   Genet's conduct
             England. inexecution of treaty.
                     interception of our provisions.

Spain.   boundary & navigation of Missisipi.
protection of Southern Indians.

AD, DLC:GW; AD (letterpress copy), DLC: Jefferson Papers.

The AD has check marks corresponding to each paragraph of "Text" and each topic of the "other subjects"; the letterpress copy does not.

1. Jefferson recorded this document in his summary journal of public letters under the date 22 Nov. (DLC: Jefferson Papers; see *Jefferson Papers*, 27:423).

2. The power to declare war is given to the legislature in Article 1, section 8.

3. Gideon Henfield was tried in July 1793 on charges that he had violated his duty as a citizen by serving, contrary to GW's Neutrality Proclamation, aboard the French privateer *Citoyen Genet*. For the trial and Henfield's acquittal on 29 July, see *Federal Cases*, 11:1099–1122.

4. For the detention of the French privateer *Republican* (formerly *Polly*) at New York, see George Clinton to GW, 9 June, and n.4, and Cabinet Opinion, 12 June. For the case of the British privateer *Jane* at Philadelphia, see Thomas Mifflin to GW, 5 and 10 July, Cabinet Opinion, 12 July, and notes. For the French privateer *L'Industrie*, see Henry Knox to GW, 27 Aug. (first letter), n.2, and Thomas Sim Lee to GW, 7 Oct., and notes. The *Lovely Lass, Prince William Henry,* and *Jane* (of Dublin) were prizes of the French privateer *Citoyen Genet* (see Cabinet Opinion, 5 Aug., and notes 4 and 10). The Spanish brig *San Josef* was prize to the French privateer *L'Aimée Marguerite* at Wilmington, N.C. (see Richard Dobbs Spaight to GW, 21 Oct., and n.3 to that document).

5. For the *Grange,* see Memorandum from Jefferson, 26 July, and n.5, and Edmund Randolph's opinion on the *Grange,* 14 May (*Jefferson Papers,* 26:31–36). For the *William,* see Cabinet Opinion, 7 Sept., and n.3 to that document, and George Hammond to Jefferson, 5 June (*Jefferson Papers,* 26:199–201). For the *William Tell,* see Cabinet Opinion, 7 Sept., and n.3 to that document; Clinton to GW, 8 Sept., n.1; and *Counter Case,* 595.

6. The *Betsey* was captured in late June by the French privateer *Citoyen Genet* and taken to Baltimore, where it was condemned as a legal prize by the French consul Francis Moissonnier on 9 July. Meanwhile, the ship's owners both appealed to the government and began litigation seeking to reclaim their property. GW's administration refused to intervene, pending completion of the judicial process. Ultimately, the Supreme Court ruled in the case of *Glass v. Sloop Betsey* that federal courts had jurisdiction over such cases and that foreign nations did not have the right to erect courts of admiralty on United States territory, unless under special arrangement by treaty (*Documentary History of the Supreme Court,* 6:296–355). The *Maxwell* was taken in August by the French privateer *Sans Culotte* and brought into Baltimore. There, in accordance with the instructions given in Secretary of War Henry Knox's circular letter to the governors of 16 Aug. (see Knox to Tobias Lear, 17 Aug., n.1), the Maryland council had the ship seized for restoration to its owners, an action that Moissonnier protested (Thomas Jefferson to Henry Knox, 22 Aug.; Thomas Sim Lee to Jefferson, 3 Sept.; Jefferson to Lee, 13 Sept., *Jefferson Papers,* 26:740; 27:25–26, 108).

7. Both these charges were given in response to attempts to enforce the Neutrality Proclamation. For Supreme Court Justice John Jay's charge of 22 May to the grand jury of the United States Circuit Court of Virginia and Supreme Court Justice James Wilson's charge of 22 July to the grand jury of the United States Circuit Court of Pennsylvania, see *Documentary History of the Supreme Court*, 2:380–91, 414–23.

8. Jefferson wrote the remaining words of this document upside down at the bottom of the "Notes" column.

VIII

Alexander Hamilton's Draft of a Statement on Financial Affairs for GW's Fifth Annual Address to Congress

[November 1793]

The Commissioners charged with the settlement of Accounts between the United & the Individual States completed that important business within the time limited by Law; and the ballances which they have reported have been placed upon the Books of the Treasury. A copy of their Report bearing date the [   ] day of [   ] last will be laid before Congress for their information.[1]

The importance of the object will justify me in recalling to your consideration the expediency of a regular and adequate provision for the Redemption and Discharge of the Public Debt. Several obvious considerations render the œconomy of time, in relation to this measure, peculiarly interesting and desireable.

It is necessary, that provision should be also made for paying the second installment of the loan of two Millions from the Bank of the U. States agreeably to the terms of that loan; the first having been paid, pursuant to the provision for that purpose made during the last session.[2]

on the first day of June last an installment of 1000000 of florins became payable on the loans of the U. States in Holland. This was adjusted by a prolongation of the period of reimbusement, in nature of a new loan at an interest of 5 per Cent, for the term of ten years. The charges upon this operation were a commission of *three* per Cent.[3] It will readily be perceived that the posture of European affairs is calculated to affect unfavourably the measures of the U.S. for borrowing abroad.

The productiveness of the public Revenues hitherto has continued to equal the anticipations which were formed of it; but it is not expected that it will prove commensurate with all the objects which have been suggested. Some auxiliary provisions will, therefore, it is presumed, be requisite; but these it is hoped can be made consistently with a due regard to the convenience of our citizens, who cannot but be sensible of the true wisdom of encountering a small present addition to their contribution for the public service, to avoid a future accumulation of burthens.

AD, DLC:GW.

1. On this commission, see Robert Barnwell to GW, 27 April 1789, and n.1. The initial authorization of 7 May 1787 had been amended and continued by acts of 5 Aug. 1789, 5 Aug. 1790, 23 Jan. 1792, and 27 Feb. 1793 (*JCC*, 32:262–66; 1 *Stat.*, 49, 178–79, 229, 324). The commissioners' report to GW was dated 29 June 1793.

2. For the agreement on the terms of this loan, 25 June 1792, see *Hamilton Papers*, 11:560–63. "An Act providing for the payment of the First Instalment due on a Loan made of the Bank of the United States" was approved on 2 March 1793 (1 *Stat.* 338). Congress approved an act providing for payment of the second $200,000 installment on 4 June 1794 (1 *Stat.* 372).

3. Hamilton wrote the remainder of this paragraph in the left margin and marked it for insertion at this point. Another note (in Edmund Randolph's writing) above that marginal text reads: "add Military repairs and purchases." The payment due on 1 June was the first installment of the Dutch loan approved by Congress on 14 Sept. 1782 (*JCC*, 23:575–80). On the prolongation of the loan, see Wilhelm and Jan Willink, Nicholaas and Jacob Van Staphorst, and Nicholas Hubbard to Hamilton, 1 May (*Hamilton Papers*, 14:364–67). There the commission fee is stated to be 3½ percent.

IX
Edmund Randolph's Outline for GW's Annual Address to Congress

[c.28 Nov. 1793][1]

Heads of matter, to be communicated to congress, either in the speech, or by message, as collected from the notes of the President, and the other gentlemen.

advised speech—	I. The acknowledgment to the people, which the reelection of the President would naturally excite
add—speech	II. The proclamation

do   1. Referring to the time, when it
            issued.

do   2. Assigning the motives of it
            to be

    do   1. to quiet the suspicions of
                foreign powers;

    do   2. and to prevent the citizens
                of the U.S. from hostile
                conduct.

            3. Accomplishing these ends

    do   1. by indicating the existing
                legal state of things:

    do   2. by admonishing the citizens
                of the U.S. against the conse-
                quences of contraband, and
                engaging on either side of
                the war:

                3. but not interfering with the
                treaty between the U.S. and
                France.

III. The measures flowing from, or sug-
      gested by, the war.

            1. The French have brought their
            prizes into our ports in pur-
            suance of the treaty and sold
            them without prohibition; this
            being thought a fitter subject
            for the legislature, than the
            executive.

            2. In other respects, the President
advd speech.   has formed principles involv-
            ing the belligerent powers, into
            a system of rules;

            3. And he has been also com-
            pelled to undertake the
To be under the   compensation for vessels,
head of Genet.   captured under certain illegal
            circumstances.

            4. to recommend auxiliary provi-
            sions to the legal code and

the constitution of our courts
concerning war and foreign
nations, in the following cases:

1. To add to the legal code

    1. by a more explicit penalty

advd. speech.

    on individuals under the
    jurisdiction of the U.S.,
    taking part in the war:

    2. by a like penalty on and
    suppression of all unau-

do

    thorized preparations
    within the U.S. for expedi-
    tions and enterprizes upon
    any belligerent party.

    3. by saying, whether the civil
    or military power shall

do

    liberate the property of
    American citizens, or that
    of peaceable nations, un-
    justly taken, and brought
    into our ports:

    4. by saying, whether the civil
    or military power shall
    interpose, in case of the

do

    violation of the protection
    of the U.S. on the rivers
    or sea; submitting it at the
    same time to congress,
    whether it be better to rest

To be referred to
head of the Genet.

    the jurisdictional claim of
    the U.S. into the sea, as it
    stands, or to assert by law
    a particular distance into
    the sea.

    5. by a particular penalty

advd speech.

    against the consuls of
    foreign nations, opening
    courts in the U.S.

    6. and in general, by fixing
    penalties, and establishing

advd speech.	internal coercion, against such violations of the law of nations, as circumstances may from time to time produce.
advd speech	2. To add to the constitution of the courts, by vesting them with power to aid the executive in cases of capture
	5. to provide means of defence, and of enforcing our national rights, against foreign nations,
advd speech.	1. by furnishing arsenals with arms, &c. in addition to those already in the public stores:
advd speech.	2. by providing means for maintaining the jurisdiction of the U.S. on its waters
advd speech.	3. by establishing corps of efficient militia: and
To be examined by the constitution and touched in a general way	4. by the creation of a military academy.
	IV. To represent the situation of the U.S. with in the speech.
General allusion in the speech—To go by message.[2]	respect to foreign powers:
	1. To France[3]
advd	1. The claim whatever it is of the guarantee.
advd—two messages one to Senate the other to house of reps	2. The propositions concerning trade; and
advd	3. Mr Genet's conduct, including the notification of a reimbursement out of the French debt, for the compensation, stipulated on certain captures.
	2. To Great-Britain[4]
advd	1. The inexecution of the treaty as to the Western posts.

advd	2. The interception of our provisions, under the additional instructions of the King, and vexations of commerce
	3. To Spain[5]
advd	1. The negotiation as to territory, and the Mississippi
advd	2. The protection of the Southern Indi⟨ans⟩ qu: convention for giving up fugitives.
	4. To the Barbary States.[6]
Suspended till	1. The state of the treaty with them.
	2. The impediments in ransoming the year American prisoners at Algiers.
	V. To lay before congress the following fiscal matters:
advd speech	1. The completion of the accounts between the U.S. and individual states.
advd speech.	2. The prolongation of the Dutch instalment by way of loan; and the terms.
	3. The pecuniary arrangement, which are necessary; to wit:
advd speech	1. a moderate addition to the revenues.
do	2. a supply to the sinking fund.
do	3. a provision for a second instalment, due to the bank of the U.S.
que:	4. a provision for the interest on the unsubscribed debt, during the present year.
do	5. The expence attending the military repairs made, and the purchase of warlike stores—

do	6. The expediency of taking off the tax on News-papers.

VI. To communicate Indian affairs.

advd speech.	1. The failure of the treaty with the Western Indians
advd speech	2. The progress of the expedition under General Wayne.
advd speech	3. The situation of the Southern Indians, as connected with the frontiers of Georgia, and the South Western territory, so far as it may not have been detailed under the head of Spain.
advd speech.	4. The expediency of carrying on trade with the Indians on public ground.

VII. Miscellanea, not reducible under any of the preceding heads.[8]

advd message.[7]

1. State of the cessions of light-houses.
2. The propriety of having a commissary, who may receive, issue, and account for, all public stores.
3. The act of the legislature of the SouthWestern territory.

AD, DLC:GW. The docket for this document, in GW's writing, reads: "Attorney-General Mr Randolph—Drawn in to heads from the Materials enclosed—for the Speech to Congress. in December 1793."

1. The date "Dec. 1793" on this document is not in Randolph's writing. According to Thomas Jefferson's notes of cabinet meetings, it was agreed on 23 Nov. that Randolph would draft GW's speech, and on 28 Nov. he submitted a draft, to which "No material alterations were proposed or made" (*Jefferson Papers,* 27:428, 453–56). As at least one phrase in this outline, "maintaining the jurisdiction of the U.S.," arose from an amendment agreed to on 23 Nov., this outline was surely crafted between 23 and 28 November.

2. A bracket is drawn on the page to indicate that this marginalia refers to all entries under section IV.

3. GW discussed U.S. relations with France in his message to Congress of 5 December.

4. GW addressed these topics in his message to Congress of 5 December.

5. Relations with Spain were communicated in GW's first message to Congress of 16 December.

6. U.S. relations with the Barbary States was the subject of GW's second message to Congress of 16 December.

7. A bracket is drawn on the page to indicate that this marginalia refers to all entries under section VII.

8. The topics in this section do not appear in the annual message. For the first two, see Alexander Hamilton's Outline, November 1793, and notes 9 and 10; for the third, see GW's Notes, November 1793, and note 8.

From Alexander Hamilton

Treasury Deparmt Novemr 18. 1793

The Secretary of the Treasury respectfully submits to the consideration of the President of the United States, a communication from the Commissioner of the revenue of the 6th instant, transmitting two proposals respecting the masons work for repairing the Tybee Lighthouse in Georgia.[1]

From the measures, which have been taken, it appears improbable that better terms are obtainable, and from such means, as are possessed, of judging, there is no reason to conclude that they are not reasonable. Under these circumstances, and considering the distance, it is submitted, as the opinion of the Secy, expedient to close with the proposal of John Armour.[2]

A. Hamilton.

LB, DLC:GW.

1. In a letter of 31 Aug. to Savannah collector John Habersham, John Armour offered to "do the Brick-layers work to Tybee Light House" for $250, adding, "that is to say, I will do every thing in fitting the Iron work that ought to be expected from a Brick layer" (DNA: RG 26, Lighthouse Deeds and Contracts, 1790–1812). The other enclosures have not been identified.

2. Bartholomew Dandridge, Jr., replied to Hamilton in a letter of 26 Nov., returning the enclosures and informing him "that the President thinks it proper that the proposal of John Armour for doing the masons work . . . should be accepted" (DLC:GW). According to the letter-book copy of Armour's proposal, GW's signature of approval was dated 23 November.

From Alexander Hamilton

Treasury Departmt Novr 19. 1793.

The Secretary of the Treasury respectfully submits to the consideration of the President of the United States a letter from the Commissioner of the revenue of the 15 instant, transmitting two proposals respecting the Carpenters work of the Tybee Lighthouse in Georgia.[1]

The Secretary agrees in sentiment with the Commissioner of the revenue that it is for the interest of the United States to close with the second proposal of Adrianus van Denne.[2]

A. Hamilton

LB, DLC:GW.

1. The enclosed letter has not been identified. It evidently transmitted Adrianus Van Denne's letter of 31 Aug. addressed to Savannah collector John Habersham, which offered to deliver the carpentry work with "a hanging stair case" for £160 sterling, or "a plain Square stair case" for £110 sterling (DNA: RG 26, Lighthouse Deeds and Contracts, 1790–1812).

2. Bartholomew Dandridge, Jr., replied to Hamilton on 26 Nov., returning the enclosures and informing him "that the President thinks it proper that the proposal . . . of Adrianus Van Denne for doing the wood work, with the *plain stair case,* should be accepted" (DLC:GW). According to the letter-book copy, the proposal was marked by GW, "Approved with the plain stair case," and signed on 23 November.

From John Marsden Pintard

Sir   Madeira 20th November 1793

Mr Lear under date of the 20th of August last desiers me to Ship for you two pipes of wine by the first opportunity that would Sail from this port for Philadelphia after the Receipt of His letter. He Requests me also to address my letters to you as he was about leaving your family in a few weeks after the date of his Letter to form a Commercial Establishment at the new City of Washington on the Potomack. In consequence of which I now have the Honor to Inform you that By this Conveance the Sloop Lively Capt. Stephen Moore I have Shiped two pipes of choice old wine for you to the address of Mr Joseph Sims of Philadelphia amounting to £76 Sterling as per Invoice herewith enclosed. which I wish Safe to hand and to your liking.[1] The American Ship John of Boston Sailed from this a few days ago for

India. I shiped by her to the Care of Mr Benjamine Joy owner & Passenger on board a pipe of very choice old wine with directions to him to Ship it to the Care of thomas Russell of Boston from India It amounts to £40 Sterling being Cased as per Invoice enclosed.[2] the freight to Boston will be £15 Str. I have desired Mr Russell to Hold it at your disposall if you think proper to take If not He has my directions How to dispose of it. If you Conclude on taking it you will be So obliging as to Settle with Mr Joseph Sims for the amount thereof as well as the amount of the two pipes I now Ship you by the Sloop Lively. Should you not think proper to take the pipe that is gone to India you will be So obliging as to Inform Mr Russell So that he may otherwise dispose of it as I have directed him Mrs Pintard[3] begs her Best Respects May be presented to you and Mrs Washington and I have the Honor to be with profound Respect Sir Your Most obedient and very Humble Sert

John M. Pintard

ALS, DLC:GW; ALS, duplicate, DLC:GW. The cover of the duplicate is stamped "York Feb. 1."

1. This invoice, dated at Madeira 20 Nov., listed "2 Pipes Old particular Madeira Wine at £ 38," for a total charge of "£ Stg 76:0:0" (DLC:GW). Joseph Sims (c.1760–1851) was a merchant on Water Street in Philadelphia. The sea captain Stephen Moore resided on Penn Street in Philadelphia. The arrival at Philadelphia of Moore's ship *Lively* from Madeira and St. Eustatius was noted in the *Philadelphia Gazette and Universal Daily Advertiser,* 25 Jan. 1794.

2. The version of this invoice that was sent with Pintard's ALS has not been identified. According to the copy of both invoices that accompanied the duplicate, it was dated 12 Nov. and charged "£ Stg 40:0:0" for "1 Painted pipe Cased of Choice Old particular Madeira wine" (DLC:GW). For the delivery of this wine to GW in late 1795, see Benjamin Joy to Bartholomew Dandridge, Jr., 4 Nov. 1795, DLC:GW; Thomas Russell to Dandridge, 26 Nov. 1795 and 2 Jan. 1796, DNA: RG 59, Miscellaneous Letters; and Dandridge to Russell, 23 Dec. 1795, ViMtvL.

3. Elizabeth Naomi Pintard, originally from Ireland, had married John Pintard at Madeira in 1785. The two divorced by 1803, when he remarried, and she married Silas Talbot in 1808.

From Post Vincennes Citizens

(Translation)

Post Vincennes [Northwest Territory] 20 Novr 1793

The Petition of the Inhabitant of Post Vincennes humbly sheweth,

That your petitioners having lately heard of the publication of the Laws of Congress, made for the regulation of the Commerce with the Indians, and of your proclamation in congress forbidding any person whomsoever to establish himself upon lands belonging to them;[1] being ignorant whether we are comprised therein; wishing to second as much as possible, the good and just intentions of the United States; and to avoid drawing on ourselves any reproach, by precipitating the views we had of going upon Lands, which those same Indians gave to us as soon as the Peace between them and the United States should permit, we would submit to the Equity of Congress, this exposition of our Titles to those Lands in the hope that that Tribunal will guarantie to us the peaceable possession by a solemn act, and by that means enable us to commence an establishment, which we have for some time had in contemplation, and so flattering, after having groaned within the limits of a small village.

In 1742, sometime after the foundation of this post, the natives of the Country made the french and their Heirs an absolute gift of the lands lying between the *point above* (pointe copée en haut) and the river blanche, below the village, with as much land on both sides of the Wabash as might be comprised within the said limits. At first the ignorance of the value of these Lands was the reason why there have been no authentic writings concerning this Donation; but such as were in existence, an unfortunate Register carried off with several other consequential papers; afterwards the war of 1759 prevented the obtaining of them. However the Doners ratified the Gift in all the Councils which have since been held; both with the officers of France, and with those of his Britannic Majesty, and when the English Agents in 1774, came to purchase lands of the Indians, the Donors at that time also ratified anew the said Donation. We observe that at the time of the purchase made by the English, as they wished to deceive the unfortunate Indians, by inserting in the contract, both sides of the river instead of one, which the latter consented to dispose of, they would not subscribe to it.[2]

The last year in Councils, the first which have been held between the United States, and these Indians, they unanimously
spoke of this donation in these Terms. "Americans this is the
first time I have come to see you, and to hearken to you. I shall,
however, tell you the Truth. Our Fathers gave to the French and
their Heirs, all the lands from *la* pointe *coupée* and the river
blanche on both sides of the Wabash river; to enable them to
live, and for the pasturage of their animals. The French and us
are but one people; Our bones are mingled in this earth: We are
not now come to take it from them. On the contrary we say that
all those who are here dwell here. These lands are theirs. We
have never sold Lands. I do not think that there is a son capable
of selling the Grave of his mother; were we to sell our lands the
Grand Source of Life, would be displeased, for we should also
sell the Bones of our Fathers, and the roebucks, and we should
die with hunger. I do not come to jest with you, or to ridicule
our brethren the french. I refer to the writings for which our
Fathers have given to the French. Writings properly drawn never
deceive. Tell the Great Chief, what I have just said. They are our
unanimous sentiments." [3]

It would doubtless be advantageous to us also to state here in
detail the endless difficulties we have surmounted; the dangers
we have braved on the part of the Indian enemies of our neighbors, because we were not willing to abandon this Country; The
reiterated and expensive Efforts we have used since our establishment, to keep our neighbors within the limits of moderation and
to prevent their inroads on our brethren; The favorable disposition towards the United States in which Genl Clarke found us,
as well as our neighbors by the means of our Councils; In a word
the considerable losses we have experienced, principally because
we had fraternised with the americans, and took the advantage
of supporting our rights with them: But we had rather appeal to
the Equity of the United States, than to all these considerations,
however dear they may be to our recollection; persuaded as we
are, that Congress will dissipate our doubts by an act, in which
regard will be had to these circumstances; to the little knowledge we possess of affairs of this nature; to the antiquity of our
titles; and above all to our truly deplorable situation.

D (extract of translation), DNA: RG 46, Third Congress, 1793–95, Senate
Records of Legislative Proceedings, President's Messages. The caption on

this document states that it was "signed by Pierre Gamelin & 15 others." The document was "Faithfully translated from the Original by Go. Taylor Jr 4 apl 1794" and enclosed with GW's message to Congress of 15 April 1794. The House of Representatives referred the document to a committee, which submitted a report on 30 April, but the report was tabled (for the report, misdated 3 April, see *ASP, Public Lands,* 1:27).

1. The petitioners were referring to "An Act to regulate Trade and Intercourse with the Indian Tribes," 1 March 1793 (1 *Stat.* 329–32).

2. The congressional committee rejected the inhabitants' claim based on the 1742 grant, arguing that the grant had not been produced, that its extent could not be ascertained, and that, as the grant was to the French government and not the inhabitants, their individual claims had already been acknowledged and any surplus belonged to the United States by right of cession from France to Great Britain and from Great Britain to the United States. The extent of the land ceded by the Indians in 1742 remained unclear. Although the 3 Aug. 1795 Treaty of Greenville reserved to the United States "The post of St. Vincennes on the river Wabash, and the lands adjacent, of which the Indian title has been extinguished," the 7 June 1803 Treaty of Fort Wayne conceded, "it has been found difficult to determine the precise limits of said tract as held by the French and British governments" (Kappler, *Indian Treaties,* 2:41, 64). Boundaries were agreed on at that treaty. The "English agents" were probably the representatives of the Wabash Land Company, which purchased land bordering the Wabash River in October 1775 (see *ASP, Indian Affairs,* 1:338–40). Point Coupee on the Wabash River was about twenty miles above Post Vincennes.

3. The petitioners were referring to the treaty with the Wabash and Illinois Indians concluded at Post Vincennes, 27 Sept. 1792 (see *ASP, Indian Affairs,* 1:338). Sentiments similar to those quoted appear in the remarks of a "Peankeshaw Chief" reported in the proceedings of the treaty (Buell, *Putnam Memoirs,* 358–59).

Record of Cabinet Opinions

[22 November 1793]

At sundry meetings of the heads of departments & Attorney General from the 1st to the 21st of Nov. 1793. at the President's several matters were agreed upon as stated in the following letters from the Secretary of state. to wit.

Nov. 8. Circular letter to the representatives of France, Gr. Brit. Spain & the U. Netherlands, fixing provisorily the extent of our jurisdiction into the sea at a sea-league.[1]

10. Circular do to the district attornies, notifying the same, & committing to them the taking depositions in those cases.[2]

same date. Circular to the foreign representatives, notifying how depositions are to be taken in those cases.

the substance of the preceding letters were agreed to by all, & the rough draughts were submitted to them & approved.[3]

Nov. 14. to mister Hammond, that the U.S. are not bound to restore the Roehampton.[4] this was agreed by all, the rough draught was submitted to & approved by Colo. Hamilton & mister Randolph. Genl Knox was absent on a visit to Trenton.

10. letters to mister Genet & Hammond, & the 14. to mister Hollingsworth for taking depositions in the cases of the Coningham & Pilgrim.[5]

15. do to Genet, Hammond & mister Rawle for depositions in the case of the William.[6]

14. do to Hollingsworth to ascertain whether mister Moissonier had passed sentence on the Roehampton & Pilgrim.[7]

these last mentd letters of the 10th 14th & 15th were as to their substance agreed on by all, the draughts were only communicated to mister Randolph and approved by him.

Nov. 13. to mister Hammond. enquiry when we shall have an answer on the inexecution of the treaty.[8] the substance agreed by all. the letter was sent off without communication, none of the Gentlemen being at Germantown.

22. to mister Genet. returning the commissions of Pennevert & Chervi because not addressed to the Presiden.

same date. to do enquiring whether the Lovely lass, Prince William Henry & Jane of Dublin have been given up, and if not, requiring that they be now restored to owners.

these were agreed to by all as to their matter, and the letters themselves were submitted before they were sent to the President, the Secretary of War & the Attorney General, the Secretary of the treasury absent.[9]

same date. to mister Gore for authentic evidence of Dannery's protest on the President's revocation of Duplaine's Exequatur.[10] the substance agreed to by all. the letter sent off before communication.

Th: Jefferson
H. Knox
Edm: Randolph
Alexandr Hamilton

DS, in Thomas Jefferson's writing, DLC:GW; D (letterpress copy), DLC: Jefferson Papers. Jefferson dated the letterpress copy and wrote the signers' initials on it.

1. For this letter, see *Jefferson Papers*, 27:328–30.

2. For this letter, see *Jefferson Papers*, 27:338–40.

3. For this letter, see *Jefferson Papers*, 27:340–42.

4. For this letter, see *Jefferson Papers*, 27:368–73.

5. For Jefferson's letters of 10 Nov. to Genet and to Hammond about the *Conyngham* and the *Pilgrim,* and his letter of 14 Nov. to Zebulon Hollingsworth, see *Jefferson Papers*, 27:342–43, 374. After considering the depositions gathered, the administration ruled in April 1794 that the *Pilgrim* had been illegally taken and was subject for compensation, but that the case of the *Conyngham* had not been proven (see Edmund Randolph to George Hammond, 5 April and 21 June 1794, *Counter Case*, 580–83).

6. For these letters, see *Jefferson Papers*, 27:382–85.

7. For this letter, see *Jefferson Papers*, 27:375.

8. For this letter, see *Jefferson Papers*, 27:353.

9. For these letters, which GW approved on 22 Nov. (*JPP*, 255–57), see *Jefferson Papers*, 27:413–15. After Genet offered an explanation of his conduct in a letter to Jefferson of 3 Dec., the exequaturs of John Pinevert (c.1746–1805) to be vice-consul at New London and Paul Arnold Cherui to be vice-consul at Alexandria were granted on 24 Dec. (see *Jefferson Papers*, 27:479–80, 618). Cherui returned to France in late 1796. Pinevert remained vice-consul at New London at least into 1797.

10. For this letter, see *Jefferson Papers*, 27:416.

To Thomas Jefferson

Dear Sir,   22d Novr 1793.

I think Colo. Humphrey's in one of his letters to you, refers to his to me, for some article of News. I see nothing therein that we have not had before; but send it nevertheless, for your perusal.[1]

Can any thing be said, or done, respecting the Marquis de la Fayette? I send the letter that you may give it another perusal.[2] I send a letter also from a French Gentleman in New York offering his Services as Engineer &ca.[3] We may want such characters! A civil answer therefore may not be amiss to give him, although he cannot be employed *now,* nor never indeed[4] he is well qualified.

Are resignations deposited in the Office of State? If they are I send one just received.[5] Yours always

Go: Washington

ALS, DLC: Jefferson Papers; ALS draft, PPRF; LB, DNA: RG 59, George Washington's Correspondence with His Secretaries of State. Jefferson docketed the ALS as received on 22 November.

1. In David Humphreys's letter to Jefferson of 13 Sept., he wrote: "I write the general News, which is of great importance, to the President" (*Jefferson Papers*, 27:106–7). GW here enclosed Humphreys's letter to him of 13 September.

2. For a translation of Lafayette's letter of 15 March to the princesse d'Hénin, sent to GW in John Barker Church's letter of 16 Aug., see Jared Sparks, *The Life of Gouverneur Morris with Selections from His Correspondence and Miscellaneous Papers* (3 vols., Boston, 1832), 1:406-10.

3. This enclosure has not been identified.

4. On the ALS draft, GW wrote "unless" instead of "indeed," and the LB also has "unless."

5. This enclosure has not been identified.

From Henry Knox

Sir   Philadelphia 22 Nov. 1793

General Stewart declines the office of Inspector He says he would have done the same by the naval office, and that he was induced to make the application to please his father in Law; but that he intended this day to have come to me to withdraw it, as his commercial prospects are exceedingly Good—At the same time he is grateful for the offer.[1]

I submit a letter from Ensign John Morgan being another speciman of his indecorum. In this he objects to the proceedings of the Court Martial which have been received, as not being "the original proceedings" of the Court. I submit this letter to-day in order that if you should judge proper that the validity of those objections may be considered to morrow.[2] I have the honor to be sir with the highest respect your humble Servt

H. Knox

ALS, DLC:GW; LB, DLC:GW.

1. Walter Stewart reconsidered (see Alexander Hamilton to GW, 30 Nov. and 5 Dec.), and on 9 Dec. GW nominated him to be surveyor and inspector of the revenue for Philadelphia. Stewart served in that post until January 1796. Stewart's father-in-law was Blair McClenachan (d. 1812), a wealthy Philadelphia merchant, shipowner, and banker, who served in the Pennsylvania House, 1790–91 and 1795, and in the U.S. House, 1797–99.

2. Ensign John Morgan's letter to Knox of 20 Nov. has not been identified, but an extract certified by War Department clerk John Stagg, Jr., was enclosed with Knox's letter to Anthony Wayne of 29 Nov.: "It was my wish Sir to have had my trial in Philadelphia not only as a Justice due to me, but that I might have a Man of abilities and Candour and one conversant in the Law, as a Judge Advocate. (An Officer much wanted in the Amercan Army.) The one appointed on my trial I have been under the necessity to expose, as very

deficient in these respects—In consequence of his incapacity &c. manifested in various instances a number of Officers amongst whom was all or most of the Members of the Genl Court Martial petitioned to General Wayne the appointment of another, after my trial was at an end. I mention these circumstances to you because even the original proceedings of the Court are very defective on these accounts and because Ensign Hyde has not transmitted to your Office a true copy of the proceedings as you will see when you shall have the opportunity of comparing the two together. I therefore beg leave to insist that you direct him to send forward the original proceedings to your Office agreeably to the articles of War—Section Administration of Justice Article 24th & as I insisted to him he should for the above reasons—This Article expressly and wisely declares that 'Every Judge Advocate or Officer officiating as such at any General Court Martial shall transmit with as much expedition as the opportunity of time & distance of place can admit, *the original* proceedings & sentences of such Court Martial to the Secretary at War.' General Waynes well know honour Talents & Character render it unnecessary for me to declare that I mean no disrespect to him for the appointment of such an ignorant & incapable Man as Ensign Hyde to the Judge Advocateship—There are few Officers of Talents & Honour in our Army who have been bred to the Law; & of those few I do not know one who can be induced to accept of the Appointment under the present regulation—Indeed the Articles of War require alterations and amendments in several respects; if the public good and Justice to Individuals be their object" (MiU-C: Wayne Papers).

At the cabinet meeting on 23 Nov., GW "Put the proceedings of the Court Martial on the trial of Ensign Morgan, & his letter to the Secy. of War, into the hands of the Attorney General to consider the legality of his complaint &c." (*JPP*, 257). Edmund Randolph reported his conclusions in his letter to GW of 24 November.

From Frances Bassett Washington

Dear & honord Sir   Mount Vernon November 22d 1793

My Aunt expecting soon to receive a summons to attend you in Philadelphia,[1] I take the liberty by her hand to offer a request to your consideration, one however which I almost fear all the friendship you have shewn me, will not justify me in making but confiding as I do, in your judgement & in your kindness, I trust you will tell me, if you think me wrong, & rather ascribe my errors to inexperience than to a wilful intention of acting imprudently—I must also assure you, that however you may think proper to decide, I shall most chearfully acquiese in your opinion—the request which I beg leave to make is, that while the repairs are making to your house in Alexandria (which you have been so good as to offer me for a habitation) the roof may be taken off, & another story added, this I hope will not increase the expence considerably, & woud afford me exactly the accommodation I most wish for—my circumstances I am very certain will not justify me in anything more than a very moderate stile of living, & I hope I have considerd nothing more in my ideas of settling myself—to retain a few of the indulgencies I have been accustomd to, & to give my Children good educations is all that I wish—with devout prayers to the bestower of all blessings, long to continue to you health & happiness, I subscribe myself, dear Sir, your grateful & affectionate

Frances Washington

ALS, ViMtvL.

1. Martha Washington joined GW at Philadelphia by mid-December.

To Richard Chichester

Dear Sir,   German Town [Pa.] 23th Novr 1793.

On the 21st instt I was favored with your letter of the 10th.

I am very sorry that so trivial a matter as that related in it, should have given you one moments pain. There must have been some misconception on the part of Colo. Burgess Ball if he understood that I had been informed it was you, who had killed my English Buck; for no such information that I can recollect ever was given to me. I had heard before the rect of your letter but how, is more like a dream than reality, that that particular Deer was killed on Ravensworth. Nor did I ever suppose that you would have been so unneighbourly as to kill any of my Deer knowing them to be such; but as they had broke out of the Paddock in wch they had been confined & were going at large—and besides consisted as well of Country as English Deer I wished to protect them as much as I was able and upon that principle, and that alone, declined giving the permission you asked to hunt some of my Woods adjoining to yours—knowing that they did not confine themselves within my exterior fences—and moreover that, when Hounds are in pursuit no person could distinguish them from the wild Deer of the Forest.[1] I thank yo. for yr kind wishes—& am sorry to hear you are in such bad health yourself & sincerely wish you may be restored to that which is good—My Compliments to Your Lady & Mrs McCarty[2] & I am Dr Sir Yr Obedt Hble Servt

G. W——n

ADfS, DLC:GW; LB, DLC:GW. GW initially dated this letter the "25th," but when writing a "3" over the "5" he neglected to strike "th."

1. For GW's refusal of permission to hunt, see Chichester to GW, 6 Aug. 1792, and GW to Chichester, 8 Aug. 1792.

2. Chichester's wife, Sarah McCarty Chichester (d. 1826), was the daughter of Daniel (d. 1792) and Sinah Ball McCarty (1728–1798).

From Alexander Hamilton

November 23d 1793.

The Secretary of the Treasury presents his respects to the President. He regrets extremely that the state of his health does not permit him to attend the President today. He has the honor to enclose a report on two of the letters to Mr Genet, & would have embraced the third respecting the protested bills, if it had been in his power.[1] But no inconvenience can in this case ensue, as the supposed mistake with regard to the funds already promised has been adjusted, and the enclosed report embraces and answers the question of advance upon a future fund. The report would have been more full & precise, if my situation had permitted, but my frame is so disordered as almost to unfit me for business.

LB, DLC:GW.

1. The third letter from, not to, French minister Genet was probably Genet's second letter to Thomas Jefferson of 15 Nov., which complained that some of the drafts given to suppliers were refused by the Treasury on the grounds that the funds put at his disposal in the month of November were exhausted and the budget for 1794 had not been completed (*Jefferson Papers,* 27:382). For Hamilton's explanation of the Treasury's action, see his letter to GW of 2 December.

Enclosure
Report on Edmond Genet's Debt Proposal

Treasy Departmt Novemr 23. 1793.

The Secretary of the Treasury upon two Letters from the Minister plenipotentiary of France to the Secy of State severally bearing date the 11. & 14 of November inst. respectfully reports to the President of the United States as follows.[1]

1. The object of these Letters is to procure an engagement that the bills which the Minister may draw upon the sums, which according to the terms of the Contracts respecting the French

debt would fall due in the years 1794 and 1795, shall be accepted on the part of the United States, payable at the periods stipulated for the payments of those sums respectively.[2]

The following considerations are submitted as militating against the proposed arrangement.

I. According to the view entertained at the Treasury of the situation of the account between France and the U. States, adjusting equitably the question of depreciation, there have already been anticipated payments to France equal or nearly equal to the sums falling due in the course of the year 1794.

II. The provision by law for discharging the principal of the French debt contemplates only loans.[3] Of those, which have been hitherto made, the sum unexpended is not more than commensurate with a payment which is to be made on the first of June next upon account of the Capital of the Dutch Debt.[4] It is possible that a fund for this payment may be derived from another loan; but it is known to the President that from advices recently received full reliance cannot be placed on this resource; owing to the influence of the present state of European Affairs upon the measures of the U. States for borrowing.[5] It need not be observed that a failure in making the payment referred to would be ruinous to the credit of the U. States.

The acceptance of the bills of the Minister of France would virtually pledge the only fund, of which there is at present a certainty, for accomplishing that payment. And as this is a matter of strict obligation, directly affecting the public credit, it would not appear adviseable to engage that fund for a different object, which if the ideas of the Treasury are right, with regard to the state of our account with France, does not stand upon a similar footing.

It would be manifestly unsafe to presume upon contingencies, or to enter into engagements to be executed at distant periods when the means of execution are uncertain.

But as there appears to be a difference of opinion between the Minister of France and the Treasury with regard to the state of the account between the two countries, it is necessary that something on this head should be ascertained. With this view the Secretary of the Treasury will proceed without delay to take arrangements for the adjustment of the account.[6]

Alexandr Hamilton
Secy of the Treasy

LB, DLC:GW; LB, DNA: RG 59, Domestic Letters; Copy, DLC: Jefferson Papers; Copy, FrPMAE: Correspondence Politique, États-Unis, Supplement, vol. 20; Copy (French translation), FrPMAE: Correspondence Politique, États-Unis, vol. 39. Jefferson enclosed this report in his letter to Genet of 24 Nov., and it was submitted to Congress with GW's message of 5 Dec. and published by order of the House (*A Message of the President of the United States to Congress Relative to France and Great-Britain. Delivered December 5, 1793. With the Papers therein Referred to* . . . [Philadelphia, 1793], 97–98).

1. For Edmond Genet's letter to Thomas Jefferson of 11 Nov., and his fourth letter to Jefferson of 14 Nov., see *Jefferson Papers*, 27:347–48, 364–65 (translations of both letters are in *ASP, Foreign Relations*, 1:185–86).

2. For the contract for payment of the French debt, 16 July 1782, see Miller, *Treaties*, 48–58.

3. See section 2 of "An Act making provision for the [payment of the] Debt of the United States," 4 Aug. 1790 (1 *Stat.* 138–44).

4. The Dutch loan of five million guilders approved by Congress on 14 Sept. 1782 (*JCC*, 23:575–80) was to be paid in five installments commencing in June 1793. The first of these payments had been met by a new loan of two million guilders, and the second, due on 1 June 1794, was also finally met with a new loan (see Wilhem and Jan Willink, Nicholaas and Jacob Van Staphorst, and Nicholas Hubbard to Hamilton, 1 May and 27 Dec. 1793, *Hamilton Papers*, 14:364–67, 15:593–96).

5. The Dutch bankers Wilhem and Jan Willink, Nicholaas and Jacob Van Staphorst, and Nicholas Hubbard advised in a letter of 1 July received by Hamilton in late October: "The demands for money by the European belligerant Powers will continue to be so great and pressing, and force them to such sacrifices in the Charges, as will render highly improbable the success for a long time to come, of Loans for ye. U.S. under five pr. Ct. interest" (*Hamilton Papers*, 15:47–49).

6. Hamilton wrote Genet on 26 Nov., "It appears indispensable to adjust disagreeing Ideas with regard to the State of the Account between France and the UStates. . . . With this view I have instructed the Accounting Officers of the Treasury to proceed in the business as soon as there shall appear some person on your behalf to cooperate in it" (*Hamilton Papers*, 15:411).

From David Humphreys

(Secret & confidential)

My dear Sir.   Alicant [Spain] Novr 23d 1793.

By my letter of the 19th to the Secry of State, & particularly by that of this date to him (of which I forward Duplicates) you will find that the Dey of Algiers has refused to grant a Passport for me to come to Algiers.[1] All hopes of any accomodation by negotiation for the present are therefore at an end. To use the Dey's own expression, "he would not treat with us, even if we were to lavish Millions."

It seems unfortunate that my full Powers had not arrived at the time, or soon after, the notice did of their being in preparation, in order that an experiment of treating might have been made before these late innovations had taken place at Algiers: but it was exceedingly fortunate, arriving when they did, that I was obliged by the Instructions of the Secretary of State to go to Gibralter to settle Mr Barclay's accounts [2]—otherwise the property of the U.S. now with us would in all probability have been lost, & other disagreeable consequences might possibly have ensued.

It is now some consolation, that the money is at hand, to be applied (at least a part of it) to the immediate cloathing & comfort of our naked & distressed Countrymen who are in captivity. I hope & trust that my arrangements herein (which will be more fully explained in my next letter to the Secry of State) will meet with your approbation;[3] and that I may have the satisfacton of knowing that to be the case—That circumstance, in addition to the consciousness of having attempted to do my duty, will be the only compensation I can ever receive for no small portion of fatigue, anxiety & distress, that I have experienced in the course of this business.

When I arrive at Madrid, I shall disclose the whole state of affairs to Mr Carmichael & Mr Short, and shall be influenced very much by their advice in respect to the ulterior measures which ought to be pursued. I need not mention to you, my dear & most respected General, that a naval force has now (to a certain degree) become indispensable; or that the future reputation of the U.S. in Europe & Africa will depend very much, & for a very great length of time, on the success of our fleet at its very first appearance on the Ocean. For this effect, it will not, I am confident, escape your recollection that the whole Nation ought, from every sentiment of patriotism, liberty & humanity, to be roused into exertion, as one Man.[4] Whether, in the midst of such an afflicting national calamity, the resources of Religion ought not to be called into our aid, by setting apart a day of solemn fasting & prayer, throughout the U.S., to implore the blessing of Heaven on our arms, and for the liberation of our fellow Citizens from Slavery, you can best determine.

It will doubtless be thought expedient to publish some Proclamation, Manifesto, or Statement of facts—Forcible truths set home to men's feelings are apt to have an effect. It is time to awaken mankind from the Lethargy of Ages.

How far considerable preparations can be made for offensive war, under a public idea of only furnishing convoys to our merchantmen, I do not know—but this would probably be the only way by which we could hope to catch some of the Corsairs seperated, & perhaps out of the Mediterranean. I will not be remiss in my endeavours to make combinations with any Nation in similar circumstances, & to keep you informed of the result. Adieu, my dear General, and believe me, in offering my best respect to Mrs Washington and our friends. Your most affe and devoted Servant

D. Humphreys

P.S. I leave the discussion of the policy & agency which brought about those inauspicious truces to a more convenient occasion.[5]

This ought to be the time (& I hope to God it will) for extinguishing all the little affects of party spirit among ourselves.

D.H.

ALS, DLC:GW; ALS (duplicate), DLC:GW.

1. For Humphreys's letters to the Secretary of State of 19 and 23 Nov., see DNA: RG 59, Despatches from United States Ministers to Portugal (see also *ASP: Foreign Relations*, 1:413–14).

2. The powers and credentials for Humphreys's mission to Algiers and the instructions for him to go to Gibraltar were sent with Thomas Jefferson's letter to Humphreys of 21 March, which was carried by Nathaniel Cutting. Cutting, who was directed to proceed via London to consult first with Thomas Pinckney on the "Algerine Business," did not arrive at Lisbon until 28 Aug., while Jefferson's subsequent letter to Humphreys of 30 March, which mentioned that Cutting was bringing the credentials, was received by Humphreys in early May (*Jefferson Papers*, 25:420–22, 468–69; 26:60; 27:4–5).

3. Humphreys discussed his arrangements for the care of the Algerine prisoners in his next two letters to the Secretary of State (received by Edmund Randolph), 7 and 25 Dec. (DNA: RG 59, Despatches from United States Ministers to Portugal; see also Humphreys, *Life and Times of David Humphreys*, 2:191–92; *ASP: Foreign Relations*, 1:418–19).

4. On the duplicate, Humphreys underlined the words "whole Nation" and "as one Man."

5. Humphreys was referring to the September truce between Portugal and Algiers (see Humphreys to GW, 7 Oct., and n.1 to that document) and to a

truce negotiated about the same time between the Netherlands and Algiers (see Edward Church to Jefferson, 12 Oct., *Jefferson Papers,* 27:230–35).

To Alexander White

Sir,   Germantown [Pa.] 23d Novemr '93.

The advantages which result from a state of peace & amity (preserved upon respectable conditions) with all nations—and particularly when applied to our Country, yet in its infancy, are too striking to need elucidation; & such as must be obvious to the least accurate enquiry into the subject.

To secure these advantages to the United States, it was thought expedient to pursue a friendly & impartial conduct towards the belligerent powers; & with a view to this object, and to the advancement of the prosperity of these States, the proclamation declaring the actual state of things was thought right & accordingly issued—and I am pleased to find the measure approved by the enlightened Citizens of Frederick County.[1]

I cherish a grateful recollection of the distinguished services rendered to our Country by the French Nation, & unite my wishes to those of my Fellow Citizens of Frederick, that it may establish a Government for itself upon those principles, which are best calculated to make it happy.

If in the discharge of the duties attendant on the trust committed to me by my Fellow Citizens, my conduct should meet their approbation, it will be my highest glory—& I am happy to have it approved by the Citizens of Frederick County.

Go. Washington

LB, DLC:GW. On 7 Dec. White submitted a copy of this letter for publication in order to "effectually communicate the sentiments of the President" to his fellow citizens. In the newspaper printings that have been identified, the letter bears the date 25 Nov. (see, for example, the *Daily Advertiser* [New York], 24 Dec). It has not been determined whether the letter sent was so dated or whether the date was erroneously transcribed by White or by the first publishing newspaper.

1. GW was replying to the resolutions of Frederick County, Va., citizens of 5 Nov., enclosed in White's letter to GW of 11 November. The proclamation was the Neutrality Proclamation of 22 April.

To Burgess Ball

Dear Sir,   German Town [Pa.] 24th Novr 1793.

I have duly received your letter of the 16th Instant, from Leesburgh.

In answer to which, respecting the purchase of Buck Wheat, I send you a Bank note for two hundred dollars; being more disposed to give two & six pence pr Bushel in Loudoun than depend upon the purchase here, & the uncertainty of getting it round in time. What the Waggonage of it to my house from thence (as fast as it is bought, for that I make a condition, in order that *no disappointment* may happen) will be, I know not; but with a view to place the matter upon an *absolute certainty* I had rather give three & six pence for it, delivered at Mount Vernon, than encounter delay, or trust to contingencies; because, as it forms part of my system of Husbandry for the next year, a derangement of it would be a serious thing; for which reason, a small difference in the price can be no object when placed against the disconcertion of my plans: especially too, as I am persuaded you will purchase, & transport the B. Wht for me on the best terms you can.

Four hundred & fifty bushels, or call it 500, is the quantity I shall want; and more money shall be sent to you as soon as I know your prospects, and the expenditures of what is now forwarded. For the reasons I have already assigned, I must encounter *no disappointment;* if therefore your prospects (as you proceed in this business) are not so flattering as those detailed in your letter, inform me of it in time, that I may supply my self from hence before the frost sets in.

The malady with which Philadelpa has been sorely afflicted, has, it is said, entirely ceased; and all the Citizens are returning to their old habitations again. I took a house in this town when I first arrived here, & shall retain it until Congress get themselves fixed; altho I spend part of my time in the City.

Give my love to Mrs Ball & Milly, and be assured of the sincere esteem and regard with which I am, Dear Sir Your Affecte Servt

Go: Washington

ALS, PHi: Dreer Collection; ADfS (photostat), ViMtvL; LB, DLC:GW.

From George Clinton

Sir   New York 24th November 1793

I have recently received a Letter from the Secretary of War dated the 12th and also another dated the 13th[1] Instant in Answer to mine of the 8th of September last.

On recurring to my Correspondence with the Minister of France a Copy of which was enclosed in that letter it will appear that my Object was to procure the departure of the privateers Petit Democrat and Carmagnole Agreeably to your decision communicated to me in a letter from the Secretary of War dated the 16th of August;[2] but as it was mentioned to be your desire that forcible Measures Should not be resorted to until every other effort had been tried, I thought it proper to Submit to your Consideration the Measure proposed by the French Minister—In the interim the Petit Democrat departed from this harbour without any Augmentation of her Military equippments So far as my knowledge extends. The Carmagnole Still remains here, And it Seems is the Vessel to which my letter of the 15th refers. I now transmit a Second letter which I have written to the French Minister on this Subject And his Answer,[3] And have only to request to be informed whether Any farther interferences on my part is expected.[4]

As I Shall in a Short time Set out for Albany to Attend the Meeting of our Legislature I take this opportunity of Apprising You of it in Order that if any Arrangements are thought Necessary which may require my personal Attention they may be concerted before my departure, As it is Uncertain whether I Shall return to this City before Spring. I am with Sentiments of the highest Respect Your most Obedient Servant

Geo. Clinton

Copy, DNA: RG 46, Third Congress, 1793–95, Senate Records of Legislative Proceedings, President's Messages; LB, N-Ar: Papers of George Clinton. This document was enclosed with GW's message to the United States Senate and House of Representatives of 5 Dec. 1793.

1. The letter-book copy gives this date as "15th," which is correct. Secretary of War Henry Knox's letter of 12 Nov. was a circular announcing that GW "conceived it best as far as shall concern the Executive powers to take the distance of a Sea league, for the Limits of the protection of the United States. . . . within which all hostilities are interdicted." Governors were requested in case they "should take possession of any vessel upon an allegation of her having

been captured within our Limits . . . to Cause the attorney of the United states within your State to be notified thereof, in order that he may take the proper Steps for the Examination of the necessary witnesses upon the affair." In addition, each governor was instructed "that if any Privateers, which have been illegally fitted in any of our ports, should by any circumstances be constrained to come into any of the ports" of his state, "they may be permitted to make no repairs whatever, but on the Condition of their divesting themselves of all warlike equipments." After disarming, they were "permitted to make any repairs belonging Solely to a commercial Vessel" (the LB of this letter in N-Ar: Papers of George Clinton is severely damaged, so the quotations are taken from the intact LS of Knox to Joshua Clayton, 12 Nov., De-Ar: Executive Papers; see also Knox to Thomas Mifflin, 12 Nov., DLC; Knox to Henry Lee, 12 Nov., Vi; and Knox to Arthur Fenner, 12 Nov., R-Ar). For Knox's letter to Clinton of 15 Nov., see Clinton to GW, 8 Sept., n.2.

2. For a summary of Knox's circular letter of 16 Aug., see Clinton to GW, 2 Sept., n.7.

3. In his letter to French minister Edmond Genet of 21 Nov., Clinton enclosed a copy of Knox's letter of 15 Nov., adding, "you will perceive it to be the sense of the President, that the vessel should be intirely devested of her warlike equipments and which from the readiness you are pleased to express, to conform to the views of the federal government, I cannot doubt will on the receipt hereof be complied with, and that until this is effected, you will not permit her to leave the harbour."

Genet replied on 23 Nov.: "The fresh requisitions which have lately been transmitted to you respecting the schooner Columbia formerly called the Carmagnole, are only a continuation of the system which has been observed towards me from the very commencement of my mission, and which evidently appears to be calculated to baffle my zeal, to fill me with disgust, and to provoke my country to measures dictated by a just resentment, which would accomplish the wishes of those whose politics tend only to disunite America from France, the more easily to deliver the former into the power of the English, warned by this conjecture which is unfortunately but too well founded, instead of proving to you, as I could easily do, that the orders which have been given to you are contrary to our treaties, to the conduct of the Federal government even towards the British nation, whose packets, and a great number of merchant vessels, I am well informed have been permitted to arm for defence in their ports. to the bonds of friendship which unite the people of both Republics and to their mutual Interest, since the vessel in question is intended to serve as an advice boat, in our Corespondence with the French Islands, which by our treaties you are bound to guarantee, and in whose fate your prosperity is no less interested than ours; I will give orders to the Consul and to the French Commodore of the road, to conform themselves to every thing that your wisdom, may think proper to direct" (both N-Ar: Papers of George Clinton).

4. GW received this letter on 26 Nov., and his secretary Bartholomew Dandridge, Jr., wrote Knox on that date: "By the President's order B. Dandridge has the honor to enclose herewith a letter just reced from the Gov. of New

York, with his correspondence with mister Genet respecting the Carmagnole. The President desires you will take them into consideration, & prepare such answer to the Govrs letter as to you may seem proper" (DLC:GW). For Knox's action, see his letter to GW of the same date.

From Thomas Jefferson

Nov. 24. 93.

Th: Jefferson with his respects to the President returns the inclosed. he will mention M. de la Fayette to mister Pinckney in a letter he is now about to write, to go by the William Penn on Thursday.[1]

The other paper was inserted in Brown's paper of Friday, probably by the governor.[2]

AL, DNA: RG 59, Miscellaneous Letters; LB, DNA: RG 59, George Washington's Correspondence with His Secretaries of State.

1. The enclosure was Lafayette's letter to the Princess Hénin of 15 March, which GW had transmitted in his letter to Jefferson of 22 November. Jefferson wrote to Thomas Pinckney on 27 Nov., "We wish to hear from you on the subject of M. de la Fayette, tho we know that circumstances do not admit sanguine hopes" (*Jefferson Papers*, 27:450–51). The following Thursday was 28 November.

2. Jefferson was referring to the letter from Philadelphia commissioners to Thomas Mifflin, 14 Nov., regarding their preparations for the accommodation of Congress (see Mifflin to GW, 15 Nov., n.1). The commissioners' letter was published in Andrew Brown's *Federal Gazette and Philadelphia Daily Advertiser* of 22 November.

To William Pearce

Mr Pearce, German Town [Pa.] 24th Novr 1793.

On my way to this place (about the last of Octr) I lodged a letter for you in the Post Office at Baltimore, which I hope got safe to your hands, although I have not heard from you since.[1]

I shall begin, now, to throw upon Paper such general thoughts, and directions, as may be necessary for your government when you get to Mount Vernon; and for fear of accidents, if transmitted to you thro' any other channel, will deposit them in the hands of my Nephew, Mr Howell Lewis, who will remain (though inconvenient to me) at that place until your arrival there, that he pray put you in possession, and give you such information into matters as may be useful.

As my farms stand much in need of manure, and it is difficult to raise a sufficiency of it on them; & the Land besides requires something to loosen & ameliorate it, I mean to go largely (as you will perceive by what I shall hand to you through Mr Lewis) upon Buck Wheat as a Green manure (Plowed in, when full in blossom)—for this purpose I have requested a Gentleman of my acquaintance in the County of Loudoun, above Mount Vernon, to send to that place in time 450, or 500 bushels of this article for Seed.[2] And as I do not wish to go largely upon Corn, it is necessary I should sow a good many Oats; my calculation (allowing two bushels to the acre) is about 400 bushels wanting. Not more than the half of which can I calculate I have of my own, for Seed next Spring, & therefore if you could carry round with you two hundred, or even 300 bushels to be certain; of those which are good in quality, & free from Onions, I will readily pay for them and the accustomed freight. That I may know whether to depend upon yr doing this, or not, write me word; that in case of failure with you, I may try to obtain them through some other channel. I am Your friend & Servant

Go: Washington

ALS, ViMtvL. The cover, which is addressed to "Mr William Pearce of Hopewell near Chester Town Maryland," is stamped "FREE."

1. See GW to Pearce, 27 October.
2. See GW to Burgess Ball, this date.

From Edmund Randolph

Sir. German Town [Pa.] November 24th 1793.

Upon the proceedings against Ensign Morgan two questions may arise. The first is, whether the President, as the constitutional commander in chief of the army, ought to pass his judgment on them; and if he ought, the second will be, whether the sentence of the court-martial is supported by the testimony, and the articles of war.

When the subject was opened yesterday for consideration, and I had the honor of expressing to you my sentiments in favor of your interference, I went upon general principles, drawn from your official relation to the army, without having had an opportunity of consulting those articles. But now, after having examined them, I am induced by the rules *"for the administration of justice"* to a contrary opinion[1]—By the second article of that head; general courts martial are to be ordered, as often as the cases may require, by the general or officer commanding the troops; and in this instance Mr Morgan's court martial has been ordered by General Wayne. The article further declares, that no sentence of a court martial shall be carried into execution, until after the whole proceedings shall have been laid before the *said* general, or officer commanding the troops for the time being. Who is meant by the said general? The general, who had ordered the court martial: This construction is enforced by several considerations. Altho' the President is the constitutional commander in chief, he will seldom be the commander in the field, and he being therefore necessarily absent from the scene of action, the arrest of an officer would be continued contrary to the spirit of the sixteenth article of the same head, by the time spent in sending backwards and forwards to him.[2] Again; the proceedings are to be laid before the general, or the officer; that is, before the one or the other, as the one or the other may be in the command. The exception, by which no sentence of a general court martial *in time of peace,* extending to the dismission of a commissioned officer, shall be carried into execution, until the whole proceedings shall be laid before congress, does not affect a case *in time of war.* Consequently in this time of war, the proceedings against Mr Morgan are to be laid before the same officer, before whom they would have been laid under the preceding clause of the article; that is, General Wayne. And such is the language which follows: "All other sentences["] (that is, except those extending to life or dismission in time of peace, or a general officer, in time of peace or war) "may be confirmed and executed by the officer ordering the court to assemble, or the commanding officer for the time being, as the case may be["][3]—The oath, taken by the members of a court martial prohibits them from divulging the sentence of the court, until it shall be published by the *commanding officer;*[4] in no manner intimating thereby, that the publication of it is to depend upon the will of another—Farther: in the 13th article of the same head, it is directed, that no commissioned officer shall be cashiered or dismissed from the service, excepting by order of Congress, or by the sentence of a general court martial. Now if we suppose that the President, not being in the field, has succeeded Congress in this particular; (as we must suppose, to prevent a link in the chain from being broken) there appears to be a contrast between him, and the actual commander in the field.

Copy (extract), in the writing of John Stagg, Jr., PHi: Wayne Papers; copy (letterpress copy of extract), PHi: Wayne Papers. The copy is signed with the following certification: "The foregoing is an authentic extract from the original, compared by, Jno. Stagg Junr Chf Clk War Department Novr 29th 1793." This opinion was enclosed in Henry Knox's letter to Gen. Anthony Wayne of 29 Nov.: "The President has had the subject [the court-martial of Ensign John Morgan] under his consideration, and for the reasons contained in the opinion of the Attorney General herein enclosed, he has directed me to return you the said proceeding in order that you may pass your judgment thereon" (PHi: Wayne Papers). Wayne confirmed the court-martial verdict in his general orders of 31 Dec. (PHi: Wayne Papers).

1. The articles of war established by the Continental Congress in 1776 were modified on 31 May 1786 by the repeal of section 14 and its replacement with twenty-seven "rules and Articles for the Administration of justice" (*JCC,* 30:316–22).

2. Article 16 provided that "No Officer or Soldier . . . shall continue in his confinement more than 8 days, or until such time as a Court-Martial can be assembled" (*JCC,* 30:319).

3. This quotation is taken from article 2.

4. This oath is ordered in article 6.

From John Armstrong

Honored Dear Sir   Carlisle [Pa.] 25th Novr 1793

Please to accept my sincere Congratulations on the reputed State of your good health & safe return to our Afflicted Capitol, or the invirons thereof.

The design of this letter which ought to have been much sooner addressed, is to tender my Cordial thanks & acknowledgments of your Excellencys friendly rememberance of my son in the appointment proposed to him—of which thro' an accidental delay in his correspondence, I knew nothing until a short time before your last setting out to Mount Vernon. his non-acceptance I find gave him some pain for certain reasons distinct from the change of his residence to that of New York, which he thinks would not correspond to his circumstances in life; and which I hope he may in some degree have explain'd in the acknowledgments incumbent upon him.[1] It has been amongst my wishes for and advices to him, to keep a constant eye to the common dictates of providence, seeking resignation in Such Station as most naturally presented itself however private it might be, and I trust he has in a good degree began to see the propriety thereof, and the Sovereign disposal of men & things which this world presents to the observation of every day! his elder brother who never looked for any thing out of the sphere of his own profession, and which former bad health had even obliged him to lay aside, is now called forth to deliberations of a very important kind for which he hath few possitive quallifications beyond the native Simplicity and firmness of his mind, yet such is the course of human conduct.[2]

In regard to our Western Affairs, a Solemn Silence at present prevails—if Genl Wayne has carried out 3000 effectives, from the consideration of more discipline & better appointments, there is much to hope he has reach'd the Villages near the begining of this month. If a general Action should take place it is not likely to be obstinate, as the Novelty joined to the terror of the Horse has a tendency at once to intimidate & discomfit the Enemy, who in my opinion have no rational motive at all for a general engagement except their numbers far Exceed our computation; their present estimation of their own Superiority at Arms may prove a Stimulas to produce a general battle, but if they persist, (the circumstances of light & ground being favourable) the Stimulas I hope will prove a Snare to these inflated men.

Publick prayers have been offered in these parts for the Success of our little Army—the preservation of our Country & the Capitol of this state from wasteing & contagious diseases—and the Governor I see has recommended another day of the like Ser⟨*illegible*⟩ which may be more generally attended to—this to be sure is both laudible & highly expedient, but pity it is, where the holy Bible may be so easily consulted that this devout prescription should appear to be wanting in a Capital Article—as of the merits & intercession of jesus Christ, the proclamation sayeth nothing! without a special respect thereto (if revelation be true) the other good things mentioned therein can avail nothing— but the people we hope will make this necessary Supplement.[3]

The late afflictive Visitation of God to the inhabitants of Philada is truly Alarming & ought to awaken not only the reflexion of Pennsylvania, but of every State in the Union—nor is the limittation of the infection to that spot (as is generally reported) less extraordinary, from which we are not unnaturally led to augur some good to this country—happy however at the present in hearing not only of a gradual abatement of this malignant disease for more than a month past, but now of it's total abolition.

I should but improperly offer to touch the publick difficulties of the present moment and can only express my earnest wishes that together with the country where you preside you may be safely carried through the political intricacies that either now or hereafter may fall in the way—You were Sir, I firmly believe providentially called to this checkered task, and in a diligent attention not only to your official, but Christian duty, have cause to be of good Courage, not because of an imperfect discharge of these duties, but because the lord reigns & will do all his pleasure, who can carry you through this maze of things, with honor and dignity to the end. And this dear Sir in the simplicity of truth is the habitual desire of your frail but invariable friend

John Armstrong

ALS, DLC:GW.

1. In April 1793 John Armstrong, Jr., was offered an appointment as surveyor of the revenue for New York City, a position he briefly accepted and then resigned (see Tobias Lear to GW, 8 April, and n.8).

2. James Armstrong (1748–1828), a physician and judge, was elected to represent Pennsylvania in Congress, 1793–95.

3. Pennsylvania Governor Thomas Mifflin's proclamation of 14 Nov. read: "WHEREAS it hath pleased Almighty GOD to put an end to the grievous Calamity, that recently afflicted the City of Philadelphia; and it is the Duty of all, who are truly sensible of the Divine Justice and Mercy, to employ the earliest moments of returning Health, in devout expressions of penitence, submission, and gratitude: THEREFORE I have deemed it proper to issue this Proclamation; hereby appointing THURSDAY, the *Twelfth Day of December* next, to be holden throughout the Commonwealth, as a Day of general Humiliation, Thanksgiving, and Prayer. AND I earnestly exhort and entreat my Fellow-Citizens, to abstain on that Day from all their worldly Avocations; and to unite in Confessing, with contrite Hearts, our manifold sins and transgressions; in acknowledging, with thankful adoration, the mercy and goodness of the Supreme Ruler and Preserver of the Universe,—more especially manifested in our late deliverance; and in praying, with solemn zeal, that the same mighty Power would be graciously pleased to instill into our Minds the just

principles of our duty to Him, and to our Fellow Creatures;—to regulate and guide all our actions by his Holy Spirit;—to avert from all Mankind the evils of War, Pestilence and Famine;—and to bless and protect us in the enjoyment of Civil and Religious Liberty. AND all officers of the Commonwealth, as well as all Pastors and Teachers, are, also, particularly requested to make known this Proclamation, and, by their example and advice, to recommend a punctual observance thereof, within their respective jurisdictions and congregations:—so that the voice of the People, strengthened by its unanimity, and sanctified by sincerity, ascending to the Throne of Grace, may there find favor and acceptance" (*Federal Gazette and Philadelphia Daily Advertiser,* 18 Nov.).

From Joseph Barrell

Pleasant Hill[1] Charlestown,
Much Respected Sir,   state Massts, Nov. 25th 1793
By Major Sargeant, I have taken the liberty to send you, the only intire Sea Otter Skin, brought to this Country, which was procured by the Columbia & Washington, on the North West Coast of America; the first American Vessels that ever visited that Coast, or went round the Globe.[2]
If you will please to Accept it as a seat for your Sadle, you will very much gratify One, who is with the highest Respect, and most sincere esteem Your most Obedient and very humble Servant
Joseph Barrell

ALS, DLC:GW.

1. Pleasant Hill, a house designed by Charles Bulfinch in 1792, was Joseph Barrell's country seat. The property was sold to Massachusetts General Hospital in 1816 and altered for use as one of the first insane asylums in the United States (see Nina Fletcher Little, "Early Buildings of the Asylum at Charlestown, 1795–1846, Now McLean Hospital for the Mentally Ill, Belmont, Massachusetts," *Old Time New England,* 59 [October–December 1968], 29–52).

2. Barrell was one of a group of merchants who decided profit was to be made in trading sea otter furs from the northwest coast of America to the Chinese. In September 1787 they sent the ship *Columbia* and sloop *Lady Washington* around Cape Horn to the northwest coast and then on to China. The ships returned to Boston in August 1790 (*Connecticut Courant, and Weekly Intelligencer* [Hartford], 16 Aug. 1790). Winthrop Sargent left Boston on the morning of 28 Nov. and arrived at Philadelphia in the evening on 12 Dec. (Diary, 1 Oct. 1793 to 31 Dec. 1795, MHi: Winthrop Sargent Papers).

From Stephen Cross

Sir   Newbury port [Mass.] November 25 1793
    Inclosed is A Coppy of my last letter to the Secretary of the
Treasury and his answer thereto, since which I have waited more
than a year but have receiv'd nothing ferther from him, and
Concluding that in the Multiplisity of Buisness he has forgoten
boath me and his promis.[1] Therefore I now take the liberty of
addressing your Excelency, requesting your attention and reconsideration of my Case I am not insencible that it is in your power
to remove any Officer of the Customs or Revenue without giveing any reason. But this power I conclude you will not exersise
without a suffisiant reason operating in your own Mind. But that
maters may be misrepresented, or such a Construction put upon
A Persons Conduct as may lead to A wrong Judgement espesial
when it is by those who are ameing at Revenge, had You been
fully knowing to my whole conduct, and the temper and views of
those who inform'd against me, I cannot but think it would have
appeared to you in a verry differant light. although I was not
gratified with an Information who my accuser was, I have good
reason now to think who the person was which was the principal mover, and most offisious. And who I have reason to think
was actuated by A malisious and revengful temper, and for no
other reasons that I can conceive of but the following Viz: first
I was ever a Zealous opposer of the British Goverment in their
measures against this Countrry. And this person though lately
crept into life and importance in his own esteem, his Connections fully attached to the British and of course Inemical to me.
Second when I wanted assistance of Councill either in my private or Offsial capasity I did not Imploy him but another person
whom I Esteeme his Supriour. And third my Brother[2] & myself
had A matter in Law in which this person was Imploye against
us in which he used his utmost indevour to destroy my Brothers Reputation, and prevent me from obtaining my Just due in
booth which he failed and to his great Mortification as it planly
appeard. And fourthly I could not be prevailed on to imploy
A Friend of his as an officer in the Customs who I deemed unworthy and unfit for the trust, and although he has since been
imployed yet I believe it is evident to all who has been witness to
his Conduct that he is not a sutable Person.

These are the only reasons I can think of which Indused him to use all his Contrivance to stir up every person he could perswade to joyn him in A representation to the Secretary of the Treasury against me. And although he failed with most of those with whom he took much pains and earnestly soliseted to joyn him, (as some have since Inform'd me) and who dispised him for this Conduct, Yet I conclude he prevailed with some persons that were disafected for my strict attention to the Law and not Constureing it agreeable to their wish and in the Close watch I kept on their movements of those persons I had reason to suspect of fraudelant designs agains the Revenue. That this person Who had been seeking accaison against me should be Particularly pointed out by the Secretary to take depositions respecting my deportment in Office. And as I have been Informed had A private interview with that Mr Joseph Whittemor before the examination as (I suppose) to state the questions, and forme the answers. And to make A great perade invited most of the Merchants in the Town to attend an examination against me, all of which rejected and despised his invitation except three Persons, one of which was his Brother in law, and the person with whom my Brother and myself had the law sute before mentioned and one of the persons I had reason to suspect had defrauded the Revenue, and either he or his partner I suspect be Informers against me.[3] And what was the enquiry, the questions will Shew. And no other part of my Conduct enquired into, as they had no hope of any thing which would serve their perpose, but must all terminte in my favour. And what was found against me, why really this and this only Viz. one of the under Officers had left in my hand A sum of money for me to divide with the Naval officer & Surveyer (and this was done of his own free will accord and without my ever makeing any proposal, or changing A word with him on the subject) and afterward when I found this was represented to my disadvantage I had paid it to him.[4] this together with my imploying some of my own connections and against whome no one pretended were unfit or their Conduct improper: is the great Crime for which I have been removed from Office, not being even called on for my defence.[5] And was ordered to deliver up the Bonds I had taken for duties and without that allowance, which the Law would have given my family if my removal had been by Death.

In my own justification I do now Sir assert that I did not look on my Office as A sinecure, but I ever attended to the duties of office in my own person I cast the duties on all goods, wrote all Bonds for duties and made the first entry with my own hands. I received and payed all monies, (except fees) administered the oaths required by Law, and in the presence of the Naval officer, and never allowed it to be done by him (and that in my absence) These matters I never Intrusted to any other person. I gave Bond in season, and to acceptance for my faithfull performance of the duties of my Office. And no person can support an accusation of intemperance against me. If my conduct had been different in any or all these maters I might have expected notice would have been taken of me, Whether all those now in office can say thus much of themselves and support It, I leave to those whose Buisness it is to enquire. Or whether the old adage yet holds good, that one man may better Steal A Hors than another look over the Hedge.

In support of my faithfull Conduct in office I appeal to all those who have been knowing thereto, and to a Letter wrote by some of the principall Merchanst in this Town to Mr Goodhew one of our Representatives in Congress and which was laid before the Secretary & also A letter wrote by some of the principal stockholders in this Town to the Secretary A coppy of one of them I have been since favoured with, and been told the purport of the other.[6] And even to the Secretary himself respecting those matters which Came under his knowledge. And I challange all who have been acquainted with me from early life to fix on me one act of injustice or fraud. And suerly if I had been charged in a Court of Judicature with a crime of the most hanious nature, and even if it had been proved upon me yet all my other conduct through life would have in some measure pleaded a mitigation of some degree of punishment or at least pity for me (if not for me) yet for my inocent family espesially if they must be great sharers in the punishment. And although I have committed no breach of law or of trust or done any act of fraud either to the Publick whose servant I was or to any private pe⟨rson⟩ what ever, and that no officer in the United states kept a more Regular office pa⟨id⟩ greatetr attention to the duties of it kept closer to the law or gave better satisfaction to the Merchants. To the truth of what I now assert I dare appeal to all, even my enemies and that my conduct should be contrasted with the person now holding the office I dare to challange,[7] yet punished I feel myself to be, and that with severity, and my inocent family which are dependant on me for support are sharers in my punishment and we are fallen on a sacrifice (as I verrily believe) to malice and revenge. And if Inocence and A faithfull discharge of the duties of any office can plead for a reconsideration, I think myself Intitled to it. And if you Shall think to do it, And enquire respecting my general carrecter, Mr Goodhew and Judge Holten, as well as Mr Wingate of New Hamshire, will be able to inform you what it has been and now is.[8] To the two last mentioned Gentlemen I have communicated all that has past between the Secretary and me on this mater. And on A reconsideration I flatter myself that my conduct will appear in a differant light from what it did when I was removed from office. And on your Considering the Importance of this matter to me and my family I flatter myself you will excuse me for thus troubleing you. And I dout not of that Justice you shall find me intitled to as a faithfull servant of the Publick. And if their should be an opening that you will replace me in some Situation to serve the Publick as well as my own family, which will be accepted with gratitude. By your Excellcy most Obedient Humble Servant

Stepn Cross

ALS, DNA: RG 59, Miscellaneous Letters.

1. Cross enclosed his letter to Alexander Hamilton of 18 Oct. 1792 and Hamilton's reply of 29 Oct. 1792 (both DNA: RG 59, Miscellaneous Letters). Cross wrote, "I do not aprehend the President actuated by any other motive than the Publick good," but protested that his "conduc⟨t⟩ in this matter has been misjudged." He then posed fourteen questions (beginning, "What law have I violated") to lay out his grievances and finished by reviewing his long career of public service to question whether "this is my demerrit and the reward I ought to have for all my past servises." Hamilton replied, "I duly receved your letter of the 18th instant, to which I shall reply at the first moment of sufficient leisure. It will be communicated in the mean time to the President."

2. Cross's brother Ralph Cross (1737/8–1811), an officer of the Massachusetts militia during the Revolutionary War, was employed as a weigher and gauger at Newburyport. He was appointed collector of customs there in 1802.

3. The documents alleging Cross's misconduct, which were submitted with Hamilton's letter to GW of 23 April 1792, have not been identified. Joseph Whittemore (Whitmore; 1743–1821) was a gauger and weigher at Newbury-

port. According to a later letter from Cross seeking an appointment from then-president Thomas Jefferson, his enemies "resorted to a matter with one of the Gaugers respecting his fees, though it was a matter which no way concerned the Public" (Cross to Jefferson, 20 Sept. 1802, DNA: RG 59, Letters of Application and Recommendation during the Administration of Thomas Jefferson, 1801–1809).

4. The naval officer at Newburyport was Jonathan Titcomb; the surveyor was Michael Hodge. Cross addressed this issue in the third question of his 18 Oct. 1792 letter to Hamilton: "had not the under officers a right to give the other Officers their whole pay or any part of it if they pleased, and what danger of abuse would arise there from if they did The money represented to be stoped by me I believe Mr Whittemore himself will own was voluntary left in my hands without any agreement made or suggested by me or by my proposal."

5. In addition to his brother Ralph, Cross employed his son Stephen Cross, Jr. (1760–1834), at the Newburyport customs (as an inspector) and apparently employed a second son there as well. In the thirteenth question of Cross's 18 Oct. 1792 letter to Hamilton, he wrote: "What could be the reason of an enquiery whether some of the under officers were not my near connections, was there any Impropriety in appointing them, or was it not A disgust some person took on discovering my sons privately watching A Vessell where I suspected A Fraudelant design which I always ordered when I suspected such design. it is a satisfaction howeve to me that those People do not Pretend any neglect or Improper conduct in either of them."

6. Neither the letter to Benjamin Goodhue nor that to Hamilton has been identified.

7. Cross had been replaced by Edward Wigglesworth, who retained the office until 1795.

8. Samuel Holten (1738–1816), a physician by training, had been a judge of the Essex court of common pleas since 1775 and was also a justice of the court of general sessions. A former Massachusetts delegate to the Continental Congress, he was at this time a congressman. Paine Wingate (1739–1838) was a former senator and at this time a congressman from New Hampshire.

From Henry Knox

Sir.   November 26th 1793

I have the honor to submit to you, a copy of a letter transmitted this day to the Governor of New York, and which is in pursuance of the rules heretofore adopted—Colonel Hamilton was present and approved of it, and it does not appear that any other answer can be given to the Governor's letter of the 24th, than to acknowledge the same, and adhere to the letter of to day.[1] I have the honor to be, Sir, with the highest respect, Your most obedt Servt

H. Knox

LS, DLC:GW; LB, DLC:GW.

1. Knox was responding to a letter from Bartholomew Dandridge, Jr., of this date, enclosing George Clinton's letter to GW of 24 Nov. regarding the French privateer *Carmagnole,* and conveying GW's instructions that Knox "prepare such answer to the Govrs letter as to you may seem proper" (DLC: GW). Knox enclosed his first letter to Clinton of this date, which acknowledged Clinton's letter to GW of 15 Nov. about the *Carmagnole* and informed Clinton that, "As this vessel was originally fitted in a warlike manner in the United States she was named in my letter to your Excellency of the 16th August, as one which was to be denied asylum in our ports.

"But if she divests herself entirely of her warlike equipments, which are her offensive qualities, she may then be permitted to make any repairs not belonging to a vessel of war, as mentioned in my letters of the 12th and 15th November. This divestment is an indispensible condition" (DLC:GW).

Knox wrote a second letter to Clinton on this date to acknowledge the letter of the 24th. He informed the governor: "I am instructed to say that the rules which have been transmitted to your Excellency were formed upon the most mature deliberation, and considered as indispensible for the preservation of our neutrality—that they have been measured out impartially as far as any cases have been known to the Executive of the United states.

"That the letter which I had the honor to transmit this day respecting the Carmagnole is conclusive as to her case" (N-Ar, Papers of George Clinton).

The *Carmagnole* apparently remained at New York until 7 Jan. 1794, when she sailed, along with two French frigates, "on a private expedition" (*Greenleaf's New York Journal & Patriotic Register,* 8 Jan. 1794).

Letter not found: from Richard Dobbs Spaight, 26 Nov. 1793. On 13 Dec., Bartholomew Dandridge, Jr., sent to Henry Knox "a Letter from the Govr of North Carolina of 26 Nov. 93 to the President."

To Elias Boudinot

Dear Sir,   Philadelphia 27th Novr 1793.

I have been duly favoured with your letter of the 12th instt and the Pamphlet which accompanied it. I am sensible of the honor you have done me in the Address, and am grateful for the flattering expression of it.

Sure I am, I shall peruse the sentiments which you have breathed in the Pamphlet with pleasure as soon as my leizure will allow me to read it. At present I am occupied in collecting & arranging the materials for my communications to Congress.

With best wishes for the health & happiness of Mrs Boudinot & yourself and with very great esteem & regard I am—Dear Sir Your Most Obedt Hble Servt

Go: Washington

ALS (photocopy), American Art Association, *Autograph Letters and Documents, Including Important Portions of the Collections of Alexander W. Hannah of Pasedena and Joseph Husband of Nantucket,* Dec. 2–3, 1926, item 320; ADfS, PWacD: Sol Feinstone Collection, on deposit at PPAmP; LB, DLC:GW.

To George Clinton

(Private)

Dear Sir,   Philadelphia 27th Novr 1793

Not having the letters at hand, I am unable to refer to dates; but the one with which you were pleased to favour me, dated sometime in September, did not reach my hands before I had left this City. Immediately, however, upon the receipt of it (at my own house in Virginia) I put it under cover to the Secretary of War with directions to answer it conformably to the rules which had been adopted for Government in such cases; but before my letter got to this place he also had left it, for Boston. This being the true state of the case will, I hope, apologize for your being so long without an acknowledgment of the first letter, whilst those of subsequent date have been answered with more promptitude.[1]

Whenever it shall be perfectly convenient to you,[2] I would thank you for a statement of our joint concern in the Mohawk Land—that is—for information of what Lots have been sold, and what remain on hand, with the numbers of each.[3] My compliments & best wishes attend you, Mrs Clinton[4] & the family—& with real regard & friendship I am—Dear Sir Your Affecte & Obedt Servt

Go: Washington

ALS, owned (1982) by James F. Ruddy, Rancho Mirage, Calif.; ADfS, DNA: RG 59, Miscellaneous Letters; LB, DLC:GW.

1. GW is responding to Clinton's letter of 24 Nov., which made reference to his earlier letters to GW of 8 Sept. and 15 November. GW received the 8 Sept.

letter at Alexandria on 14 Sept. and sent it to Secretary of War Henry Knox in a letter of 16 September. Knox's replies to Clinton's letters of 8 Sept. and 15 Nov. are dated 15 Nov. and 26 Nov. (see Clinton to GW, 8 Sept., n.2, and Knox to GW, 26 Nov., n.1).

2. On the ALS the remainder of this paragraph was underlined at a later date, apparently subsequent to the letter's sale in 1977 (see Charles Hamilton Galleries, Inc., Auction 103, 24 Feb. 1977, item 266).

3. For discussion of the 6,071 acres along the Mohawk River that Clinton purchased in 1784 on behalf of himself and GW, see GW to Clinton, 25 Nov. 1784, and Indenture with Jedediah Sanger, 22 July 1790, source note. For information about Clinton's reply to this inquiry, see GW to Clinton, 25 Dec., n.1.

4. Clinton married Cornelia Tappan (1744–1800) in 1770.

To Thomas Jefferson

[27 November 1793]

Enclosed is another Specimen of Mr Genets Indecent conduct towards the Executive Government of the U. States.[1]

AL, DLC: Jefferson Papers. Jefferson docketed this note as "recd Nov. 27. 93."

1. GW probably enclosed the correspondence between Edmond Genet and George Clinton that Clinton had sent with his letter to GW of 24 Nov. (see note 3 to that letter).

From Thomas Jefferson

Nov. 29. 93.

Th: Jefferson has the honor to inclose to the President some letters brought by the Rider yesterday afternoon, & which he found on his return home in the night.[1]

AL, DNA: RG 59, Miscellaneous Letters; LB, DNA: RG 59, George Washington's Correspondence with His Secretaries of State.

1. According to GW's journal, these enclosures were letters "From Thos. Pinckney Esqr. of the 25 Sept. 93," regarding Pinckney's efforts to secure the release of Lafayette and the conditions of Lafayette's imprisonment; "from Ditto—27 Septr.—enclosing duplicate of one of 25th," about British capture of vessels, copper for the Mint, and the ship *Laurens* of Charleston seized by a French privateer; and "from Rob. Morris, Dist. Attorney for New Jersey, dated 25 Nov. 93," about the case of Clarkson Freeman (*JPP*, 259–60). For those letters, see *Jefferson Papers*, 27:149–51, 158, 439–43.

From Henry Knox

Sir   War Department Nov. 29. 1793

I know not what dependence to place upon the second paragraph of the following intelligence just received from Major Craig, dated Pittsburg 22d November, but it is my duty to communicate it.

"By accounts from Kentuckey, it appears that the army was on the 18th of October six miles advanced of Fort Jefferson—and that a small party escorting either Forage or Commissary stores, commanded by Lieut. Lowrey, had been attacked—Lieut. Lowrey killed, and the party defeated.[1]

"By account this moment arrived via of Niagara, and Genesee, it appears that our army has had a general engagement with the enemy, and has obtained a complete victory". I am Sir with great respect Your obedt servt

H. Knox

LS, DLC:GW; LB, DLC:GW. The LS is in the writing of War Department clerk Jacob Hoffman.

1. Maj. Gen. Anthony Wayne gave a report of this incident in his letter to Knox of 23 Oct.: "Lieut. Lowry, of the 2nd Sub Legion & Ensign Boyd of the 1st. with a Command consisting of about Ninety Non Commissioned Officers & privates (having in charge twenty waggons belonging to the Q M Generals department loaded with Indian Corn, & one of the Contractors loaded with stores) were attacked in the morning of the 17th. Instant about seven miles advanced of Fort St. Clair by a party of Indians, those two Gallant young Gentlemen . . . together with thirteen Non Commissioned Officers & privates bravely fell, after an obstinate resistance, against superior Numbers, being abandoned by the greater part of the Escort, upon the first discharge.

"The savages killed or carried off about seventy horses, leaving the waggons & stores standing in the road, which have all been brought to this Camp without any other loss or damage except some triffling articles" (Knopf, *Wayne,* 279).

From Thomas Marshall

Sir   Woodford County, Buck-pond[1] [Ky.] Novr 29th 1793

I have taken the liberty of inclosing you a publication which appeard in the Lexington paper of the 16th of this Month. It is said to be written by a gentleman, an acquantance of yours, who is at the head of a very powerful party in this Country. I shall make no farther observation on the subject, only that I am really affraid that something is brewing in this country that may end disadvantageously to the United States as well as to us.[2]

I wish my suspicions may have no other foundation than a wachful jealousy grounded on the knowledge of some past transactions of a very suspicious nature. I have the honor to be with the most respect esteem Sir Your most obedient Servant

T: Marshall

ALS, DNA: RG 59, Miscellaneous Letters.

1. Buck Pond, Marshall's Kentucky plantation, was about one and a half miles east of Versailles.

2. Marshall evidently enclosed the resolutions agreed to by the Democratic Society of Kentucky at a meeting in Lexington on 11 Nov. (*Kentucky Gazette* [Lexington], 16 Nov.). For a summary of those resolutions, see Citizens West of the Allegheny Mountains to GW and Congress, December 1793, source note.

From William Thornton

sir   Wilmington (Delaware) November 29th 1793.

I have lately been informed that your Secretary, Mr Lear, has taken his departure for England, on private Business, and as I imagine the multiplicity of your Engagements, and the extent of your Correspondence will require a Substitute I take the liberty of tendering my Services; yet with a degree of hesitation mixed with Confidence. I hesitate, lest my Abilities may not be equal to all that might be requisite; but I should rest much Confidence in my Endeavours to render Satisfaction, and to prove myself worthy of the Trust reposed in me. While, however, I solicit this Trust I cannot be ignorant of a Circumstance that might operate to my disadvantage. My Situation in Life has precluded me from the honor of being but very partially known to you, and I must request a reference to one of my Friends. I had the pleasure of residing for some years in the same House with Mr Madison, to whom I should with much Satisfaction submit my Reputation.[1]

I am well aware, Sir, that numerous applications are made to you upon Occasions of this sort, and I reluctantly trouble you with this, but my desire to dedicate my time to you and my Country, would not permit me to be silent. Whatever may be your Determination in this Instance it cannot lessen my wish to serve you to the utmost of my power, nor affect the sincerity with which I have the honor of declaring myself your respectful, and affectionate Friend &c.[2]

William Thornton

ALS, DLC:GW.

1. While at Philadelphia from 1787 to 1790, Thornton stayed at Mary House's boarding establishment, also used by James Madison.

2. GW replied to Thornton on 3 Dec.: "thank you for your obliging offer to supply the Office lately occupied by Mr Lear. I am persuaded it would have been ably filled with your abilities—but previous to the departure of that Gentleman my arrangements were made in favor of Mr Dandridge, who is now in the exercise of the Office of private Secretary" (ALS, DLC: William Thornton Papers).

From Alexander Hamilton

Sir,   Treasury Depart: Nov: 30. 1793.

Inclosed I have the honor to transmit a letter which I have received from General Stewart on the subject of his proposed appointment.[1]

I should conceive it consistent with a reasonable construction of the general intent of the Law to allow the indulgence which his situation requires. With perfect respect I have the honor to be &c.

Alexr Hamilton

LB, DLC:GW.

1. Walter Stewart's letter to Hamilton of 27 Nov. has not been identified, but according to the entry in GW's journal for 2 Dec., it stated "that in his present situation he doubted whether the law constituting the office of Surveyor wou'd allow him, being concerned in commerce vessels &c. to hold that office. Says, however, if he *can* be allowed to act in that office *now,* he can he thinks acquit himself of all mercantile concerns in about 7 months. Promises to make no new engagements in trade, & to wind up the old ones as soon as possible" (*JPP,* 262).

From Thomas Jefferson

Nov. 30. 1793.

Th: Jefferson presents his respects to the President & incloses him some letters just received.[1]

Mr Pinkney's & mister Morris's information relative to the doing & undoing the decrees of the National assembly, in the case of the ship Lawrence and some other expressions in mister Morris's letter seem to render it proper to lower the expression in the message purporting the *just & ready redress of wrongs* on the high sea afforded by that government, which Th: J. will accordingly attend to.[2]

AL, DNA: RG 59, Miscellaneous Letters; LB, DNA: RG 59, George Washington's Correspondence with His Secretaries of State.

1. According to GW's journal for this date, the enclosures were Gouverneur Morris to Jefferson, 25 June, "enclosing a correspondence with Mr. Le Brun, respecting an outrage committed by the crew of a french privateer, upon that of an American vessel called the little Cherub and the repeal of the Decree of the Nationl. Conven. of 9 May 93 exempting American vessels from seizure &c."; and Richard Söderstrom to Jefferson, 30 Nov., "covering a copy of one to him from the Consul General of Sweden, at Algiers, dated 7 augt. 93 mentioning the miserable situation of some American captives there, and expressing a willingness to endeavour to have them released" (*JPP*, 260). For the texts of these letters, see *Jefferson Papers*, 26:363–69, 27:466.

2. The French national convention on 9 May 1793 had passed a decree authorizing the seizure of "merchant vessels which are wholly or in part loaded with provisions, being neutral property, bound to an enemy's port, or having on board merchandise belonging to an enemy." A protest from Morris, however, produced a decree of 23 May "that the vessels of the United States are not comprised in the regulations of the 9th of May" (both, *ASP, Foreign Relations*, 1:244). Morris's letter to Jefferson of 25 June discussed Morris's protest of a subsequent decree of 28 May, repealing the decree of 23 May. The *Laurens* left Charleston at the end of January, bound for London, and was seized by a French privateer in March and taken into Le Havre, where a court voided the seizure (*City Gazette & Daily Advertiser* [Charleston], 1 Feb., 28 May, 13 July). Morris wrote that the object of the decree of 9 May and subsequent decree of 28 May was "to effect the Confiscation of a large Cargo belonging to Citizens of the State of South Carolina, and which has been sometime since acquitted at Havre . . . . The Captors then declar'd that they would obtain a Decree for the Confiscation" (*Jefferson Papers*, 26:364).

Thomas Pinckney's letter to Jefferson of 27 Sept., which Jefferson had enclosed in his letter to GW of 29 Nov., included a letter from the English consignees of the *Laurens* that added decrees of 1 and 27 July to the three mentioned by Morris and asked Pinckney's assistance in recovering the ship for its American owners (*Jefferson Papers*, 27:158; for the decrees of 28 May [misdated 29], 1 July, and 27 July, see *Daily Advertiser* [New York], 9 Dec.).

Jefferson did revise his first draft for GW's message to Congress on relations with France and Great Britain, 5 Dec., to eliminate the reference to "ready redress" (see note 1 to that document).

From Henry Knox

Sir   War Department Nov. 30. 1793

I have the honor of submitting to you, a letter with enclosures from Major General Wayne—dated on the 23d of the last month—and I also submit the draft of a letter proposed to be sent to Ensign Morgan.[1] I have the honor to be, with the greatest respect Sir Your very obedt servt

H. Knox
Secy of War

LS, DLC:GW; LB, DLC:GW.

1. Maj. Gen. Anthony Wayne's letter to Knox of 23 Oct. stated that the army's march had been temporarily halted "Six Miles advanced of Fort Jefferson" by a shortage of supplies, reported the deaths of Lieutenant John Lowry and Ensign Samuel Boyd, enclosed returns including that of the mounted volunteers recently arrived at Fort Jefferson, discussed intelligence of Indian movements, noted the effect of influenza on the army, complained of the want of officers, and reported the acceptance of one resignation and the arrest of three officers (Knopf, *Wayne*, 278–81).

Bartholomew Dandridge, Jr., replied on behalf of GW, writing Knox on 1 Dec.: "By the President's command; Bw Dandridge has the honor to return to the Secy of War General Wayne's Letter of the 23d Octobr with it's enclosures—also the Letter intended for Ensign Morgan; & to inform the Secretary that if the facts stated in the last mentioned letter are unequivocal, the President approves thereof" (DLC:GW).

On 7 Dec. Knox replied to Wayne's letter of 23 Oct.: "I am instructed to say that the President approves of your intended Winters position as far advanced of Fort Jefferson, towards the Miami Villages as you shall judge proper—Such a position it is expected will in a certain degree have the same effects to alarm the Indians for their own safety as one at the Miami Villages and to push them to a greater distance and perhaps enable you to strike some severe blow in their unguarded moments during the Winter.

"The measures which you have taken to obtain a full supply of provisions appear proper and energetic, and on a full supply will depend your security and the maintenance of your posts . . ." (PHi: Wayne Papers; see also Knopf, *Wayne*, 289–90).

Knox's letter to Ensign John Morgan has not been identified, but Morgan quoted from it in his letter to Wayne of 4 Dec.: "that the Propriety . . . of the Presidents deciding upon the Proceedings being questionable, according to the Articles of War, he had taken the opinion of the Attorney General of the United States, which concuring with his own he directed the Proceedings to be returned to you [Wayne] with *an order* that you should judge definitively on them" (PHi: Wayne Papers).

From John Francis Mercer

Sir   West River [Anne Arundel County, Md.] Nov. 30. 93.

On my arrival at this place from Virginia where I had been long detained by domestic circumstances as melancholy as they were unexpected, I found a letter from you[1]—The Deed from the several parties to You for the Land in Montgomery has been long executed agreably to the Laws of this State, & I will bring the original with me to the meeting of Congress[2]—I have drawn upon you in favor of Doctor James Steuart for four hundred dollars on acct of his part of this Land which by my calculation is below the sum you will have to pay, the ballance however I shall settle in Philadelphia.[3]

The answers to the Bill of Hanshaw my Brother Robert informs me, was detain'd by my brother James, under an impression that they were insufficient.[4]

The circumstances of the fees improperly Charged to you, have not arisen from any neglect of mine, I am persuaded, but suspect that they have been made on a process instituted under the direction of my late Brother agt Lord Dunmores Estate, & which was committed entirely to his care,[5] I will however on seeing you repay the same, & can only regret that you have by the ignorance of inattention of any person been perplexed or injured by these or similar charges. With the greatest respect I have the honor to bc &c.

                                          John F. Mercer

ALS, DLC:GW.

    1. GW wrote Mercer on 26 October. The "melancholy" event was the death of Mercer's half-brother James Mercer on 31 October.

    2. On GW's acquisition of the Montgomery County, Md., land, see GW to Mercer, 7 Aug., and n.1 to that document, and Mercer to GW, 15 Aug., and n.2. For continuing problems with the deed, see GW to Mercer, 10 March 1794, and Mercer to GW, 13 April 1794. Mercer represented Maryland in Congress from 5 Feb. 1792 to 13 April 1794.

    3. GW's account book records in the entry for 10 Dec. 1793: "The President's accot proper, pd a draft of Jno F. Mercer in favr of Jas Stuart [$]400" (Household Accounts; see also Account Book, 2 Sept. 1793–4 April 1794, DLC:GW).

    4. John Henshaw's bill of complaint was related to his purchase in 1774 of land from the estate of George Mercer, for which GW was a trustee. GW's answer has not been found, but for his response to the bill of complaint, see

GW to John Francis Mercer, 23 July 1792, and GW to Bushrod Washington, 30 April 1794. Robert Mercer (1764–1800) was John Francis Mercer's youngest brother.

5. John Murray (1732–1809), fourth earl of Dunmore, served as governor of Virginia from 1771 to 1776. The process instituted against the Dunmore estate may have been the action for recovery of a debt that James Mercer was planning in 1792 (see James Mercer to GW, 20 Feb. 1792).

To the Commissioners for the District of Columbia

Gentlemen   Philadelphia 1st Decr 1793

Your Letter of the 3d of last Month came to me by the Post of yesterday with the George Town mark of the 27th of November. What caused such delay in forwarding it, you better than I, can explain. For the reason mentioned therein it is to be regretted.[1]

I shall not lose a Post in transmitting the enclosed Order (to you) and wish it may be in time to produce the desired effect at the Treasury of Virginia.[2]

I am glad to hear your prospect with the Banks will enable you to look forward with well grounded hope of another vigorous operation next year, without depending upon the offers of Dutch Capitalists. I hope & expect, that all things will work well. With great, & very Sincere esteem & regard I am Gentlemen Your Most Obedt Hble Servt

Go: Washington

LB, DNA: RG 42, Records for the Commissioners for the District of Columbia, Letters Sent, 1791–1802, vol. 1; LB, DNA: RG 42, Records for the Commissioners for the District of Columbia, Letters Sent, 1791–1802, vol. 2; ADfS, DLC:GW; LB, DLC:GW.

1. In GW's draft and his letter-book copy, the first part of this sentence is rearranged, and the clause "that it did not come to hand sooner" is added to the end of the sentence.

2. GW wrote to Virginia treasurer Jaquelin Ambler on this date: "Be pleased to pay Messrs Johnson Stuart & Carroll Commissioners of the Federal buildings on the Patomac or to their order, or the order of any two of them, the third instalment of the monies granted by the State of Virginia towards the said buildings" (ALS, Vi; LS draft, DLC:GW; LB, DLC:GW).

To Thomas Jefferson

Dear Sir, Philada 1st Dec. 1793.

Is there no clue to Mr Morriss meaning respecting Monsr Merlino?[1] The next paragraph of his letter is enigmatical to me, from the want of my recollecting perfectly the subjects alluded to. What are the orders given him which he will implicitly obey, and which were, according to his acct, received so very opportunely?[2] Has not a letter of his of subsequent date to that laid before me yesterday, acknowledged the receipt of the Plans of the Federal City.[3]

There can be no doubt since the information which has come to hand from our Ministers at Paris & London of the propriety of changing the expression of the Message as it respects the Acts of France.[4] And if any bad consequences (which I declare[5] I see no cause to apprehend) are likely to flow from a *public* communication of matters relative to G. Britain it might be well to revise the thing again in your *own* mind, before it is sent in; especially as the Secretary of the Treasury has, more than once declared, and has offered to discuss & prov⟨e⟩ that we receive more Substantial benefits (favors are beside the question with any of them, because they are not intended as such) from British regulations with respect to the Commerce of this Country than we do from those of France; antecedant I mean, to those of very recent datc. Wc should be very cautious *if this be the case* not to advance any thing that may recoil; or take ground we cannot maintain well.[6] Yours always

Go: Washington

ALS, DLC: Jefferson Papers; ADfS, DNA: RG 59, Miscellaneous Letters; LB, DNA: RG 59, George Washington's Correspondence with His Secretaries of State. Jefferson docketed the ALS as received on 1 December.

1. GW's questions refer to Gouverneur Morris's letter to Jefferson of 25 June, which Jefferson had submitted to GW in a letter of 30 November. About Jean Marie François Merlino (1738–1805), who represented Ain as a delegate to the National Convention, Morris wrote: "In a Letter written long since I mention'd to you Sir that I was in Quest of Monsieur Merlino. I have since found him and convers'd with him. He is immensely rich but seems to have been the Father of his own Fortune, amass'd (as Fortunes frequently are) without rendering the Possessor respectable. If I can judge from his Countenance, the Enquiry was set on Foot in the Hope of negative Answers, and the Affirmative is of Course not pleasing. Certain it is that he shew'd no Inclina-

tion to spare to the Necessities of Nephews a Part of his own Abundance, but this is the less reprehensible in that he treats himself no better than his needy Relatives." Jefferson, who wrote on Morris's letter, "Who is Mr. Merlino?", was unable to answer this question (*Jefferson Papers,* 26:364, 369).

2. GW's question actually applies to the next two paragraphs of Morris's letter, which read: "Your Favor of the twentieth of April reach'd me two Days ago and now I have those of the eighth of that Month and twelfth and fifteenth of March. To the Contents of the last mention'd Letter I shall pay all due Attention whatever Opportunities can be found or made for the Purpose. I am happy to find by what you say in the Begining of yours of the twelfth of March, that your Sentiments accord so entirely with those which I had the Honor to express in mine of the twenty second of August, and that the Conduct which I had thought it proper to pursue is thereby justified. My Correspondence with Mr. Short will have shewn you Sir that I have been very far from questioning the Principles which you state; And I perfectly agree that there is little Difficulty or Embarrassment in the application of clear Principles, when the Facts are clear. But while Events are doubtful the Feebleness of human Foresight may I hope be pardon'd for Hesitating where Things of vast Moment depend on Steps to be immediately taken. A Man of no little Eminence in the late Revolutions and who has since left France urg'd me much to go away, shortly after the tenth of August. As I had not (and have not) any Reason to question, either on my own Account or on that of my Country, the Sincerity of his advice I could only examine the Ground of his Judgment, which has always been esteemed a good one. We differed in Opinion but this Sentiment he express'd strongly. 'In your Case, said he, I would go to England or Holland and from thence state the existing Facts, and ask my Court to decide at once on my Conduct, without waiting for future events.' As it was clear from hence that his Reflections turn'd principally on my personal Situation, I told him that my Conduct would be influenced by Considerations totally different, and therefore conceiving it most conducive to the Interests of the United States I should stay.

"In the present Moment you will observe, Sir, by the public Papers, that a Majority of the Departments declare themselves against the Authority of the present Convention, after the Arrestment of their Fellow Members, just as in the Month of June last a similar Majority declar'd their Execration of the Attempts on Louis the sixteenth; but who will venture to tell us what August is to produce? No small Part of France is in open War with the Rest, and wherever the Insurgents arrive it appears that the whole Country is friendly to them; so that if one were to Judge by what passes in that quarter, France would be nearly unanimous in the ReEstablishment of Royalty should they come on in Force to Paris. Then the establish'd Principle of Administration would undoubtedly be, that all which has been done within the last Year was an abominable Usurpation &ca. &ca.; And without questioning our Principles of Government, they might dissent from the Application of them by a subtle Distinction between the Voice of a Nation and what would then be call'd the Voice of a Faction. Under Circumstances of this Sort I am particularly happy to have receiv'd your Orders, which I shall implicitly obey. Accept I pray you my sincere Thanks for having given them so opportunely" (*Jefferson Papers*, 26:364–65).

Jefferson replied to GW's inquiry on 2 Dec. by enclosing the letters sent to Morris, of which the letter of 12 March contained the relevant "orders" about how Morris should respond to transition in the form of French government (*Jefferson Papers*, 25:367–70).

3. Jefferson had sent plans of the Federal City to Morris via London, probably early in January 1793 (see Jefferson to Morris, 12 March 1793, and Jefferson to Thomas Pinckney, 30 Dec. 1792, *Jefferson Papers*, 25:367–70, 24:802–4). However, no acknowledgment of receipt by Morris has been identified.

4. GW was referring to Jefferson's first draft for GW's message to Congress on U.S. relations with the various powers of Europe (see GW to the United States Senate and House of Representatives, 5 Dec., n.1; and Jefferson to GW, 30 Nov.).

5. Both the draft and the letter-book copy have "still declare."

6. In the draft and the letter-book copy, this sentence ends with the words "cannot support."

From Alexander Hamilton

Treasury Dept Decemr 2d 1793.

The Secretary of the Treasury on the letter from the Minister plenipotentiary of France to the Secretary of State of the 15 instant,[1] respectfully makes the following report to the President of the United States.

It is true as alleged by the Minister that certain drafts of his on the Treasury have not been admitted.[2]

Some of them were predicated upon the fund engaged to him in November; but one of them for twenty thousand dollars was expressed to be upon the funds which should be at the disposal of France in Jany 1794.

With respect to the first kind an accidental error occasioned the temporary exclusion of some drafts, which were within the proper limit. The clerk charged with registering the bills as presented had noted one as for Forty thousand dollars, which was afterwards found to be for only fourteen thousand, whereby the fund stipulated appeared to have been exceeded, when in fact there was yet a balance. But as soon as the error was discovered, the consequences were rectified.

The draft expressed to be upon funds to be at the disposal of France in January 1794, was refused, because it was not warranted by any previous arrangement, or even notice.

The funds by arrangement put in the disposal of the Minister were *definite* vizt, one million and five hundred thousand livres payable on the third of September last, deducting Ninety four thousand five hundred six dollars and ten and a half cents to be paid for bills drawn by the Administration of St Domingo, and one million of livres payable on the fifth day of November following. The precision given to this arrangement will be seen by the copy of my letter to him of the 24. of July last, herewith communicated.[3] no other arrangement was made.

The Minister ought not to have operated upon the accessory fund of interest, for two reasons—first, because the terms of the arrangement with him did not include it—Secondly, because it could only have been properly considered as payable *of course* if it had been mutually understood as absolutely becoming due, unaffected by any antecedent payment; whereas the Minister had been informed, that the advances which had been made were supposed to have exceeded the sums due, according to the stipulated course of payment.[4]

It need only be added that to preserve order in money transactions it is essential to proceed with regularity; that an unauthorised latitude of drawing upon the Treasury could not without impropriety & inconvenience be countenanced by it, and that it was reasonable to expect that Mr Genet, being at no greater distance than New-York, would not have undertaken to exceed the limit concerted with him without previous notice & consent.

Alexr Hamilton
Secy of the Treasy

LB, DLC:GW; LB, DNA: RG 59, Domestic Letters; copy, (letterpress copy), in the writing of Thomas Jefferson, DLC: Jefferson Papers; LB, FrPMAE: Correspondence Politique, États-Unis, Supplement, vol. 20. The letterpress copy of this document is of the copy that Jefferson enclosed to Genet in his letter of 6 Dec. (see *Jefferson Papers*, 27:487–88).

1. Hamilton was referring to Edmond Genet's second letter to Jefferson of 15 Nov., which complained that some of the drafts that he had given to suppliers were refused by the Treasury on the grounds that the funds put at his disposal in the month of November were exhausted and the budget for 1794 had not been completed (*Jefferson Papers*, 27:382).

2. At this point in Jefferson's copy and the letter-book copy at DNA, a one-sentence paragraph appears: "These Draughts were of two descriptions."

3. For Hamilton's letter to Genet of 24 July, see *Hamilton Papers*, 15:124–25. The September and November payments were the annual installments on the 1782 French loan of eighteen million livres and on the 1782 Dutch loan

of ten million livres, respectively. For the deduction made for paying bills drawn by the administration of Saint Domingue, see Hamilton's conversation with Edmond Charles Genet, 27 June 1793 (*Hamilton Papers,* 15:29–30).

4. Hamilton's letter to Genet of 24 July informed the French minister that according "to our view of the state of our account with France, the payments already made exceed the installments which have heretofore fallen due" (*Hamilton Papers,* 15:124–25).

From Thomas Jefferson

Dec. 2. 1793.

Th: Jefferson with his respects to the President has the honor to send him the letters & orders referred to in Mr Morris's letter, except that of the 8th of April, which must be a mistake for some other date, as the records of the office perfectly establish that no letters were written to him in the months of March & April but those of Mar. 12. & 15. & Apr. 20. & 26. now inclosed. the enigma of Mr Merlino is inexplicable by any thing in his possession.[1]

He incloses the message respecting France & Great Britain. he first wrote it fair as it was agreed the other evening at the President's. he then drew a line with a pen through the passages he proposes to alter, in consequence of subsequent information (but so lightly as to leave the passages still legible for the President) and interlined the alterations he proposes. the *overtures* mentioned in the first alteration, are in consequence of it's having been agreed that they should be mentioned in general terms only to the two houses. the numerous alterations made the other evening in the clause respecting our corn trade, with the hasty amendments proposed in the moment had so much broken the tissue of the paragraph as to render it necessary to new mould it. in doing this, care has been taken to use the same words as nearly as possible, and also to insert a slight reference to mister Pinckney's proceedings.[2]

On a severe review of the question whether the British communications should carry any such mark of being confidential as to prevent the legislature from publishing them, he is clearly of opinion they ought not. Will they be kept secret if secrecy be enjoined? certainly not, & all the offence will be given (if it be possible any should be given) which would follow their complete publication. if they could be kept secret, from whom would it be? from our own constituents only, for Gr. Britain is possessed of every tittle. Why then keep it secret from them? no ground of support for the Executive will ever be so sure as a complete knowlege of their proceedings by the people; and it is only in cases where the public good would be injured, and *because* it would be injured, that proceedings should be secret. in such cases it is the duty of the Executive to sacrifice their personal interests (which would be promoted by publicity) to the public interest. the negociations with England are at an end. if not given to the public now, when are they to be given? & what moment can be so interesting? if any thing amiss should happen from the concealment, where will the blame *originate* at least? it may be said indeed that the President *puts it in the power* of the legislature to communicate these proceedings to *their constituents;* but is it more their duty to communicate them to *their constituents,* than it is the President's to communicate them to *his constituents?* and if they were desirous of communicating them, ought the President to restrain them by making the communication confidential? I think no harm can be done by the publication, because it is impossible England, after doing us an injury, should *declare war* against us merely because we tell our constituents of it: and I think good may be done, because while it puts it in the power of the legislature to adopt peaceable measures of doing ourselves justice, it prepares the minds of our constituents to go chearfully into an acquiescence under these measures, by impressing them with a thorough & enlightened conviction that they are founded in right. the motive too of proving to the people the impartiality of the Executive between the two nations of France and England urges strongly that while they are to see the disagreeable things which have been going on as to France, we should not conceal from them what has been passing with England, & induce a belief that nothing has been doing.[3]

Th: Jefferson

ALS, DNA: RG 59, Miscellaneous Letters; ALS (letterpress copy), DLC: Jefferson Papers; LB, DNA: RG 59, George Washington's Correspondence with His Secretaries of State.

1. Jefferson here replies to GW's letter to him of 1 Dec. inquiring about the meaning of some passages in Gouverneur Morris's letter to Jefferson of 25 June (for those passages, see notes 1 and 2 to GW's letter). In fact Jefferson had written, but not recorded, a letter to Morris on 8 April in which he asked him to inquire about some dies for medals made at Paris.

His letter to Morris of 12 March discussed the "principles" that supported the legitimacy of the new French government—"We surely cannot deny to any nation that right whereon our own government is founded, that every one may govern itself according to whatever form it pleases, and change these forms at it's own will. . . . The will of the nation is the only thing essential to be regarded"—discussed repayment of the debt owed to France, and urged Morris "to improve every opportunity which may occur in the changeable scenes which are passing, and to seize upon them as they occur, for placing our commerce with that nation and it's dependancies, on the freest and most encouraging footing possible."

His letter to Morris of 15 March desired him to "avail yourself of every opportunity of sounding the way towards" Lafayette's "liberation." The letter of 20 April directed Morris to obtain an "immediate decision" from the man offered employment as chief coiner for the Mint and discussed neutrality. The letter of 26 April enclosed GW's Neutrality Proclamation for presentation to the French government (*Jefferson Papers,* 25:367–70, 387–89, 519–20, 575–76, 591–92).

2. See GW to the United States Senate and House of Representatives, 5 Dec., and notes. For the draft here submitted, see *Jefferson Papers,* 27:474–79. Jefferson's first draft of the message had been discussed at a cabinet meeting on 28 Nov. (see *Jefferson Papers,* 27:453–56).

3. According to Jefferson's notes, at the cabinet meeting of 28 Nov., Alexander Hamilton had objected to the initial draft of this message as unfair to Great Britain. Even after editing, "He still was against the whole, but insisted that at any rate it should be a secret communication, because the matters it stated were still depending. These were 1. the inexecution of the treaty 2. the restraining our corn commerce to their own ports and those of their friends." Although Hamilton's desire for secrecy was supported by Henry Knox and in part by Edmund Randolph, GW "took up the subject with more vehemence than I have seen him shew, and decided without reserve" that both sections "should go in as public" (*Jefferson Papers,* 27:454–55).

To Thomas Jefferson

Dr Sir   Phila. 2d Decr 1793

I am very well satisfied with the train things are in. You will recollect that the Proclamation, Rules and other things are referred to in the Speech[1]—I shall depend upon there being got ready at your Office.[2] Yours &ca

Go: Washington

ALS, DLC: Jefferson Papers. A note by Jefferson at the bottom of this document reads: "answer to note of this day respecting publication of proceedgs with Gr. Britn."

1. GW is discussing the preparation of his annual address to the Senate and House of Representatives, which was delivered on 3 December. For the

proclamation, see Neutrality Proclamation, 22 April; for the rules, see Cabinet Opinion on the Rules of Neutrality, 3 August.

2. Jefferson replied on this date, "Th: Jefferson with his respects to the President has the honor to inclose him three copies of the Proclamation & of the Rules.

"Having only heard the speech re[a]d, he cannot recollect it perfectly enough to decide by memory what documents it requires from his office, and therefore is obliged to ask of the President if any more be requisite?" (AL, DNA: RG 59, Miscellaneous Letters; LB, DNA: RG 59, George Washington's Correspondence with His Secretaries of State).

From Thomas Mifflin

Sir   Philadelphia December 2d 1793

In consequence of a letter from the Secretary at War, stating the suggestion of the French Minister, relative to the design of the Refugees, who, according to his information, were about to embark from this Port for Jeremie, or Cape St Nichola Mole, in the Ship Delaware, and the Goillette Betsey;[1] I have instituted an enquiry on the subject; the result of which I have now the honor to communicate, in the report of the Master Warden of the Port of Philadelphia. I am, with perfect respect, sir, Your Excellencys Most obedient Servant

Tho. Mifflin

LS, DNA: RG 59, Miscellaneous Letters; LB, DNA: RG 59, Domestic Letters; Df, PHarH: Executive Correspondence, 1790–99; LB, PHarH: Executive Letterbooks; Copy, DLC: Jefferson Papers. An endorsement with the LS notes that it was "recd 2d Decr."

1. British forces had captured Saint Domingue ports Môle-Saint-Nicolas and Jéremie in September. In a letter to Secretary of State Thomas Jefferson of 25 Nov., French minister Edmond Genet passed on reports that 200 colonists were leaving Baltimore for Jéremie while two ships were loading at Philadelphia for the Môle. Genet claimed to have proofs that the surrender of the Môle had been abetted by a conspiracy of some residents. He suggested that the people embarking intended to join the "traîtres" at those locations, and also stated that American vessels were carrying supplies to the rebels (*Jefferson Papers*, 27:436–39). Secretary of War Henry Knox's letter to Mifflin of 29 Nov. requested, on behalf of GW, "your Excellency's attention to this circumstance, and that if the persons alluded, or any others, should appear to be forming a military expedition, or enterprize within the State of Pennsylvania, that you would please to cause them to be stopped, and prevent their design—But, if it should appear that they are returning to their homes, or departing elsewhere, in a peaceable manner, it is considered that

it would neither be lawful nor proper to detain them" (PHarH: Executive Correspondence, 1790–99).

Enclosure
Nathaniel Falconer to Thomas Mifflin

Sir,   Wardens Office Philadelphia 29th November 1793.

In Obedience to Your Excellency's Letter of this Morning,[1] I have seen Mr Jacob Shoemaker, one of the Owners of the Ship Delaware; he informs me that they intend their ship for Cape Nichola Mole, and expected to take a Number of passengers, if they Offered; but they Assure me, only one person has as Yet engaged his passage in the Ship Delaware; I have requested of Mr Shoemaker and Captain Art, that whatever French Men, may engage their passages, that they will bring them to me, in Order to declare the Object of their Voyage.[2] I have also been with the Owners of the Goillette, Betsey, who are Reed and Ford;[3] who inform that She is not Bound to Jeremie nor the Mole, but Chartered by a French Gentleman for Guadaloupe, to go there in Order to bring off his property, Some passengers are going in her for that Island. You may rest Assured, I will pay every attention to those Vessels; and if I can discover any thing like Armament, I shall give Your Excellency immediate Notice of it. I am Your Excellency's most Obedt Humble servt

Nathaniel Falconer,
Master Warden of the port of Philadelphia

Copy, DNA: RG 59, Miscellaneous Letters; LB, DNA: RG 59, Domestic Letters.

1. Mifflin also enclosed to GW a copy of this letter, in which Mifflin repeated Knox's request and directed: "You will be pleased, therefore, with great Caution, to make such enquiries, as are Calculated to produce Satisfactory evidence on this Subject; and report the result with all Convenient dispatch. The Owners of the Vessels, as well as the persons on Board of them, will, I presume, give a Candid statement of the Object of the Voyage; but I do not mean to Confine You to those Sources of information" (DNA: RG 59, Miscellaneous Letters).

2. Jacob Shoemaker was a partner with John James in the mercantile firm of James & Shoemaker at 25 N. Water Street in Philadelphia. The sea captain James Art resided on Front Street in Philadelphia. He was still captain of the *Delaware* in February 1794, when the ship was taken by a privateer out of Bermuda and condemned in the admiralty court at Montserrat (see Fulwar Skipwith to Edmund Randolph, 1 March 1794, DNA: RG 46, Third Congress,

1793–95, Senate Records of Legislative Proceedings, President's Messages; and *Greenleaf's New York Journal, & Patriotic Register,* 22 March 1794).

3. John Reed and Standish Forde (1759–1806) were partners in a mercantile firm on S. Front Street in Philadelphia from 1781 until Forde's death. At this time they were advertising freight or passage on the schooner *Betsy and Hannah,* bound for "Point Peter" (Pointe-à-Pitre), Guadeloupe (*Federal Gazette and Philadelphia Daily Advertiser,* 25 Nov.).

From James White

[Augusta, Ga.] December the 2 179[3][1]

May it please your Exelency this is my third Letter to you in Which I gave you A true State of my Case[2] as thay have Misd Your perusal I Shall Trouble you with this I Early Ingaged In the Cause of Independancey and was Imployed in making of Cannon and Bullets for which the British Disstroyd all my Tools Stock and provisions to the Amount of 200 pounds Worth at the Lowest Calcullation this I Could have Born But our own Armey Came and Sat Down on my plantation and Staid thare Six Months in which time thay Did not Leave me A rail Nor A tree to Make a rail of Which Abloiged me to Sel my plantation for which I Received 5233 Contonantal Dollars of the omishons May the 20 1777 and April the 11 1778[3] I moved out into the State of North Carolinah whare the whole of it wood not purchase Me one Bushel of Corn I was Informd thare was A man appointed by Congress to take it and Give me Sumthing in Lew that mite purchase Bread for my family Who was plaisd in the wild woods whare was not A grub taken Up I traviled Down to him which was more then 200 miles Distance but he wood not take it on Saying he had wrot to Congress to apoint a man in Every County to take it in as it Hurt the Back peopel by Coming all the way Down to Him I had to Return towards home with my money but Was Soon Convins'd it was no money Calling at A tavern for a feed for my horse and Self telling the Landlord I had No money But them omissions that was Cald in of which I wood Give his own Asking But he Said he would not Give me A grots worth for the full of A washen tub of That Sort of Money Travilling on till night it Being Dark I lost my way and was Abloiged to Lay in the woods with Hunger and Cold for my Compny YOUR Exellency may Judg of my thoughts About the Congress but hoping under This New Constestution to have Sum Justice Dun me

I wrote to the Speaker Mr Mulenburg who Informd me It was in the power of Congress to make me whole if they had Gon A littel farther and told me wheather thay wood make me Whole or not it mite have prevented my troubling your Exellency with my Scrowls[4] The Congres has Been Very Lavish in heeping their Greautuites and Anuieties upon Barron Steubain who Did Not A whit more for Independanc⟨e⟩ Then my Self[5] he Lost nothing All I had was taking away By the Brittish and by our own Army as Above He Did Teuterd the Armey I Made Cannon and Bullets I Do not Plead for Gifts or Rewards for Gods Sake Let me have my Just Dew if You will Not Make me up the Lose of my Tools Make Good Your Resolutions and Suffer me not To Live Wretched Now to wards the Decline of Life for I have Labourd at a Grait Dissadvantaige Not Being Abel to purchase me A set of Tools Sence the British Distroyed Mine I Might have Been A very Servisable ma⟨n⟩ To my Country Being Very Capebel of performing Many of the Macannackel Arts But I fear I ha⟨ve⟩ Intruded two mutch upon your patience when I Reflect Our Country Suffaring for the want of A true Standard of Weights and measures I Canot but Pray Your Exell⟨ency⟩ To Appoint Sum Suteable person to Exammen Weights and Measures it wood prevent mutch Defraud Among the pooerer Sort of peopel the wellfair of Which Depends Mutch upon Your Exellincy Good Conduck the Experionce of Which is Highly Aplaud By all Ranks of peopel Whatsocvcr this from your Humbel petissioner

James White

Pray Sir If you think A poor mans Case worth Notice and Send mee A line or two Direct to Mr John Smith printer in Agusta Richmon County State of Georgia.[6]

ALS, DNA: RG 59, Miscellaneous Letters. The cover bears the notations "Free" and "Augusta Decr 19th."

1. White wrote "1792," rather than 1793, but the document is docketed "2d Decr 1793" and filed with other December 1793 letters.

2. One of White's earlier letters, docketed by GW as "without date" but apparently written between August 1790 and December 1792, is filed with this letter in DNA: RG 59, Miscellaneous Letters. In the earlier letter, White, then of Guilford County, N.C., asked GW "to Lay A true State of my Case before the Congress and See if I must Loose all or not." He told the same story, but added more about his problems. Upon returning from his trip, White wrote, he met with a friend "who agread to Let me have 297 Acres of Land for the Sum of three hundred pounds hard money he to wait without interest until the year 1788 the State of North Carolinah Striking a paper Currency put it

out of my power to Comploy with the agreement my friend Sence Dead his heirs Now Calling upon me for prinsopel and interest Which will amount to much higher Sum then the place will Bring altho I have improved it with A good gristmill and Sawmill Dwelling house and other Nessasery buildings. . . . I plead for Nothing But what in Justice I ought to Get that is the Congress wood make Good their Resolves that the Barrer of these Dollars in my possession might Receive A spanish mild Dollar or the Vallue thereof in Gold or Silver I Did Expect when I Receivd them Dollars and Gave my property to the full Value of that mutch Gold or Silver I Cood have pas'd them from me for the Like Currency But the Congress makeing them Good for nothing has Left me in A very Deploreable Situation as I must of Consequence turn of the place I am now on or otherwise pay the money Above Contracted which is out of my power unless Congress make their Money Good." White's other letter to GW has not been found.

3. In White's earlier letter he wrote: "Apploying to your Exelencey to know wheather I Could git Any thing for the Dammages you told me I Shood bee paid for every farthings worth that our armey Distroyd by apploying to the Quarter master Genral Green the Valueation was So low that it wood not moove me out to Carolinah I was forsd to Sell my plantation for the Sum of two thousand Pounds Congress money the Dammages in Clueded which was All of the Dates May the 20 1777 and 11th April 1778." The plantation apparently was in the vicinity of Valley Forge, as White also wrote that GW "had Sum personal Views of my Suffrings at the Valey forge." In 1777 and 1778 a man named James White did own a plantation in Charleston Township, Chester County, Pa., adjoining the Schuylkill River near Valley Forge (*Pennsylvania Gazette,* 11 June 1777; *Pennsylvania Packet or the General Advertiser,* 1 Sept. 1778).

4. In the earlier letter, White wrote that he had "alread wrote to two of the members of Congress Mr Gilman and Mr Mulenberg all to no purpose." Frederick A. C. Muhlenberg served as speaker of the House of Representatives for the first federal Congress, from 1 April 1789 to 3 March 1791.

5. By an act of 4 June 1790, Congress granted Steuben an annuity of $2,500 for life (6 *Stat.* 2)

6. John Erdman Smith (c.1756–1803) printed an Augusta, Ga., newspaper, initially called *The Georgia State Gazette or Independent Register* and at this time *Georgia. The Augusta Chronicle, and Gazette of the State,* from September 1786 until his death.

From Sundry Frenchmen in a Philadelphia Jail

Monsieur   A philadelphie ce 3. Décembre 1793
    Je prend La Liberté de vous Ecrire La presente pour Réclamer aupres de vous La justice a LEgard des peines Et traveaux que L'on nous fait Subir dans vos prisons innocemment, En Bravant Les Loix de La Republique francaise qui Déffend de punir au-

cun Citoyen francais de deux maniere Si votre Ministre veut nous faire périr icy, afin que nous ne puissions pas nous justi-fier devant notre patrie; vous pouvez dans vos Etats nous tirer des fers afin que nous puissions nous procurer les moye⟨ns⟩ De rejoindre nos Drapeaux que nous n'avons pas voulu quitter pour Entrer dans La Légion du Citoyen Genet, voila Le Sujet qui nous tien⟨t⟩ Dans Les fers: En quittant notre patrie La Municipalité de Brest nous a fait prêter Serment de ne pas quitter nos Drapeaux Et nous L'avons juré Et Le jurons Encore de ne Les quitter qu'a La mort; Si nous avons quitté notre vaissaux, c'est par L'ordre Du Ministre qui nous a Désarmé En nous arrêttant les vivres a Bord Et nous a Refusé La Subsistance En ville pour nous forcer a prendre party dans une Lègion inconnüe de La Républiqu⟨e⟩ francaise C'est a ce Sujet qu'a notre arrivé nous nous Sommes presenté devant vous pour vous annoncer notre arrivé En vous Demandant La Subsistance Lorsque vous nous avez donné une ordre pour porter immédiatement au Consul francais pour faire rentrer Les troupes qui Etoit Sortit pour nous arrêter, dès que le Consul Eut fait la Lecture de vos ordres il a chifonné le Billet D'un air de mépris Et nous fit passer pour des Laches déserteur⟨s⟩ Sans nous Laisser justifier devant La justice voila trois mois que nous Souffrons Sans Espoir d'En Sortir Si nous Etions Coupables Le Ministre nous auroit bien vite fait passer En france pour nous faire punir mais comme il n'a que Des in-justc dénonciation contre nous il cherche a nous faire périr dans Les fers par La fain La froideur Et La misére En nous mêlant parmi des criminels Et nous faire Subir Les traveaux de galéres avec Les marques de mérite Et d'Encienneté de Service portant Lhabit Militaire de La nation francaise dans vos galéres Sans Distinction. Nous Sommes avec Respect Les Republiquains fran-cais prisonniers

Maurice Matelota Bettuy aide Canonnier
Tholomé Sergent Conquete Segonde
du Clot Caporalle metre
jan pier Reboure contre metre
marjan pinare gabies de grand hune
augustin ville cartü maitre
jean Baptiste verrier
pignatelle canonnier
La combe

LS, in the writing of Bettuy, DNA: RG 59, Miscellaneous Letters. These men, who were among those arrested as deserters from the French ships at New York City (see George Clinton to GW, 2 Sept., and Thomas Mifflin to GW, 2 Sept.), complain of their imprisonment, explaining that they had refused to join the Légion du Citoyen Genet because they had taken an oath at Brest not to abandon the regiments they joined there. In consequence, they were forced to leave the ships when their provisions were cut off in an attempt to coerce their enlistment in the legion. They complain that they have been held for three months among common criminals without any chance to defend themselves in court or any hope of release. GW referred their complaint to Secretary of State Thomas Jefferson, who communicated it to Pennsylvania Governor Thomas Mifflin (*JPP*, 267). On 13 Dec. Mifflin wrote Pennsylvania Chief Justice Thomas McKean, informing him that complaints had been made about the imprisonment and asking him "to investigate the grounds for the allegation; and to inform me, what steps have been, and will be taken, with respect to the commitment, confinement, trial, or discharge of the prisoners." Mifflin also sent a copy of his instructions to McKean to French minister Edmond Genet and invited his comments (PHarH: Executive Letterbooks). For Genet's response, see Jefferson to GW, 21 Dec., and notes.

To the United States Senate and House of Representatives

[3 December 1793]

Fellow Citizens of the Senate, and of the House of Representatives

Since the commencement of the term, for which I have been again called into office, no fit occasion has arisen for expressing to my fellow Citizens at large, the deep and respectful sense, which I feel, of the renewed testimony of public approbation. While on the one hand, it awakened my gratitude for all those instances of affectionate partiality, with which I have been honored by my Country; on the other, it could not prevent an earnest wish for that retirement, from which no private consideration should ever have torn me. But influenced by the belief, that my conduct would be estimated according to its real motives; and that the people, and the authorities derived from them, would support exertions, having nothing personal for their object, I have obeyed the suffrage which commanded me to resume the Executive power; and I humbly implore that Being, on whose

Will the fate of Nations depends, to crown with success our mutual endeavours for the general happiness.

As soon as the War in Europe had embraced those Powers, with whom the United States have the most extensive relations; there was reason to apprehend that our intercourse with them might be interrupted, and our disposition for peace, drawn into question, by the suspicions, too often entertained by belligerent Nations. It seemed therefore to be my duty, to admonish our Citizens of the consequences of a contraband trade, and of hostile Acts to any of the parties; and to obtain by a declaration of the existing legal state of things, an easier admission of our right to the immunities, belonging to our situation. Under these impressions the Proclamation, which will be laid before you, was issued.[1]

In this posture of affairs, both new & delicate, I resolved to adopt general rules, which should conform to the Treaties, and assert the priviledges, of the United States. These were reduced into a system, which will be communicated to you.[2] Although I have not thought myself at liberty to forbid the Sale of the prizes, permitted by our treaty of Commerce with France to be brought into our ports; I have not refused to cause them to be restored, when they were taken within the protection of our territory; or by vessels commissioned, or equipped in a warlike form within the limits of the United States.[3]

It rests with the wisdom of Congress to correct, improve or enforce this plan of proceedure; and it will probably be found expedient, to extend the legal code, and the Jurisdiction of the Courts of the United States, to many cases which, though dependent on principles, already recognized, demand some further provisions.

Where individuals shall, within the United States, array themselves in hostility against any of the powers at war; or enter upon Military expeditions, or enterprizes within the jurisdiction of the United States; or usurp and exercise judicial authority within the United States; or where the penalties on violations of the law of Nations may have been indistinctly marked, or are inadequate; these offences cannot receive too early and close an attention, and require prompt and decisive remedies.

Whatsoever those remedies may be, they will be well administered by the Judiciary, who possess a long established course of investigation, effectual process, and Officers in the habit of executing it.

In like manner; as several of the Courts have *doubted,* under particular circumstances, their power to liberate the vessels of a Nation at peace, and even of a citizen of the United States, although siezed under a false colour of being hostile property; and have *denied* their power to liberate certain captures within the protection of our territory; it would seem proper to regulate their jurisdiction in these points.[4] But if the Executive is to be the resort in either of the two last mentioned cases, it is hoped, that he will be authorized by law, to have facts ascertained by the Courts, when, for his own information, he shall request it.

I cannot recommend to your notice measures for the fulfilment of *our* duties to the rest of the world, without again pressing upon you the necessity of placing ourselves in a condition of compleat defence, and of exacting from *them* the fulfilment of *their* duties towards *us.* The United States ought not to endulge a persuasion, that, contrary to the order of human events, they will for ever keep at a distance those painful appeals to arms, with which the history of every other nation abounds. There is a rank due to the United States among Nations, which will be withheld, if not absolutely lost, by the reputation of weakness. If we desire to avoid insult, we must be able to repel it; if we desire to secure peace, one of the most powerful instruments of our rising prosperity, it must be known, that we are at all times ready for War. The documents, which will be presented to you, will shew the amount, and kinds of Arms and Military stores now in our Magazines and Arsenals: and yet an addition even to these supplies cannot with prudence be neglected; as it would leave nothing to the uncertainty of procuring a warlike apparatus, in the moment of public danger.[5]

Nor can such arrangements, with such objects, be exposed to the censure or jealousy of the warmest friends of Republican Government. They are incabable of abuse in the hands of the Militia, who ought to possess a pride in being the depositary of the force of the Republic, and may be trained to a degree of energy, equal to every military exigency of the United States. But it is an inquiry, which cannot be too solemnly pursued, whether the act "more effectually to provide for the national defence by

establishing an uniform Militia throughout the United States"
has organized them so as to produce their full effect; whether
your own experience in the several States has not detected some
imperfections in the scheme; and whether a material feature in
an improvement of it, ought not to be, to afford an opportunity
for the study of those branches of the Military art, which can
scarcely ever be attained by practice alone?[6]

The connexion of the United States with Europe, has become
extremely interesting. The occurrences, which relate to it, and
have passed under the knowledge of the Executive, will be exhibited to Congress in a subsequent communication.[7]

When we contemplate the war on our frontiers, it may be truly
affirmed, that every reasonable effort has been made to adjust
the causes of dissention with the Indians, North of the Ohio.
The Instructions given to the Commissioners evince a moderation and equity, proceeding from a sincere love of peace, and
a liberality, having no restriction but the essential interests
and dignity of the United States.[8] The attempt, however, of an
amicable negotiation having been frustrated, the troops have
marched to act offensively. Although the proposed treaty did
not arrest the progress of Military preparation; it is doubtful,
how far the advance of the Season, before good faith justified
active movements, may retard them, during the remainder of
the year. From the papers and intelligence, which relate to this
important subject, you will determine, whether the deficiency
in the number of Troops, granted by law, shall be compensated
by succours of Militia; or additional encouragements shall be
proposed to recruits.

An anxiety has been also demonstrated by the Executive, for
peace with the Creeks and the Cherokees. The former have
been relieved with Corn and with clothing, and offensive measures against them prohibited during the recess of Congress.
To satisfy the complaints of the latter, prosecutions have been
instituted for the violences committed upon them. But the papers, which will be delivered to you, disclose the critical footing
on which we stand in regard to both those tribes; and it is with
Congress to pronounce, what shall be done.[9]

After they shall have provided for the present emergency, it
will merit their most serious labours, to render tranquillity with
the Savages permanent, by creating ties of interest. Next to a

vigorous execution of justice on the violators of peace, the establishment of commerce with the Indian nations in behalf of the United States, is most likely to conciliate their attachment. But it ought to be conducted without fraud, without extortion, with constant and plentiful supplies; with a ready market for the commodities of the Indians, and a stated price for what they give in payment, and receive in exchange. Individuals will not pursue such a traffic, unless they be allured by the hope of profit; but it will be enough for the the United States to be reembursed only. Should this recommendation accord with the opinion of Congress, they will recollect, that it cannot be accomplished by any means yet in the hands of the Executive.

Gentlemen of the House of Representatives

The Commissioners, charged with the settlement of Accounts between the United and Individual States, concluded their important functions, within the time limited by Law; and the balances, struck in their report, which will be laid before Congress, have been placed on the Books of the Treasury.[10]

On the first day of June last, an instalment of one million of florins became payable on the loans of the United States in Holland. This was adjusted by a prolongation of the period of reimbursement, in nature of a new loan, at an interest of five per cent for the term of ten years; and the expences of this operation were a commission of three prCent.[11]

The first instalment of the loan of two millions of dollars from the Bank of the United States, has been paid, as was directed by Law. For the second it is necessary, that provision should be made.[12]

No pecuniary consideration is more urgent, than the regular redemption and discharge of the public debt: on none can delay be more injurious, or an œconomy of time more valuable.

The productiveness of the public revenues hitherto, has continued to equal the anticipations which were formed of it; but it is not expected to prove commensurate with all the objects, which have been suggested. Some auxiliary provisions will, therefore, it is presumed, be requisite; and it is hoped that these may be made, consistently with a due regard to the convenience of our Citizens, who cannot but be sensible of the true wisdom of encountering a small present addition to their contributions, to obviate a future accumulation of burthens.

But here, I cannot forbear to recommend a repeal of the tax on the transportation of public prints. There is no resource so firm for the Government of the United States, as the affections of the people guided by an enlightened policy; and to this primary good, nothing can conduce more, than a faithful representation of public proceedings, diffused, without restraint, throughout the United States.[13]

An estimate of the appropriations, necessary for the current service of the ensuing year, and a statement of a purchase of Arms and Military stores, made during the recess, will be presented to Congress.[14]

Gentlemen of the Senate, and of the House of Representatives.

The several subjects, to which I have now referred, open a wide range to your deliberations; and involve some of the choicest interests of our common Country. Permit me to bring to your remembrance the magnitude of your task. Without an unprejudiced coolness, the welfare of the Government may be hazarded; without harmony, as far as consists with freedom of sentiment, its dignity may be lost. But, as the Legislative proceedings of the United States will never, I trust, be reproached for the want of temper or of candour; so shall not the public happiness languish, from the want of ⟨my strenuous and warmest co-operation.

Go: Washington.⟩

AD[S] (fragment), DNA: RG 46, Third Congress, 1793–95, Senate Records of Legislative Proceedings, President's Messages; Copy, RG 233, Third Congress, 1793–95, House Records of Legislative Proceedings, Journals; LB, DLC:GW; Translation (French), DLC: Genet Papers. The last page of the AD[S] is missing; the words in angle brackets are taken from the copy.

The letter-book copy states that at 12 o'clock on this date, GW, attended by his cabinet, "proceeded to the Senate chamber, where finding both Houses of Congress assembled, he deliver'd to them the following Speech," and that Bartholomew Dandridge, Jr., delivered to Congress copies of the proclamation and rules mentioned in the address (see notes 1 and 2 below).

This speech was printed in the *General Advertiser* (Philadelphia), 4 Dec., and other newspapers.

1. GW is referring to his Neutrality Proclamation of 22 April.
2. See Cabinet Opinion on Rules of Neutrality, 3 August.
3. See Cabinet Opinion on French Privateers, 3 August.
4. Richard Peters, the federal district judge for Pennsylvania, had ruled in the cases of the British vessels *William* and *Fanny,* allegedly seized within territorial waters, that his court did not have jurisdiction (*Federal Cases,* 9:57–62, 17:942–48). In the case of the sloop *Betsey,* an American vessel with a Swedish

cargo, the federal district judge for Maryland, William Paca, had accepted an argument that article 17 of the Treaty of Amity and Commerce with France precluded his court from exercising jurisdiction. In 1794, however, the Supreme Court, in the appeal of the *Betsey* case, ruled that U.S. district courts did have such jurisdiction (*Documentary History of the Supreme Court*, 6:296–355).

5. For the return of ordnance, arms, and military stores, 14 Dec., sent to the Senate by Secretary of War Henry Knox on 16 Dec., see *ASP, Military Affairs*, 1:44–60.

6. For the militia act of 8 May 1792, see 1 *Stat.* 271–74. This portion of GW's message was referred to a House committee, which reported back on 24 March 1794 opposing any amendment of the act, because "they have their doubts how far Congress can, consistent" with the Constitution, "make any important alterations or amendments to the present law; and as the right of training the militia is constitutionally reserved to the States, if they can be impressed with the importance of exercising this power, and directing its operation, more especially to the light infantry and grenadier companies of each regiment, an efficient force may be thereby created, and equal to any that can probably be obtained by any additional law of the United States" (*ASP, Military Affairs*, 1:66). The reference to study of the military art was evidently intended to recommend a military academy (see Drafting GW's Annual Address, 18–28 Nov. 1793, editorial note; and Edmund Randolph's Outline for GW's Annual Address, c.28 Nov.).

7. See GW to the United States Senate and House of Representatives, 5 December.

8. For these instructions, issued by Secretary of War Knox on 26 April, see *ASP, Indian Affairs*, 1:340–42.

9. For the papers submitted to the Senate by Secretary of War Knox on 16 Dec., see *ASP, Indian Affairs*, 1:361–470. The prohibition of offensive operations against the Creek Indians appeared in Knox's letter to Georgia governor Edward Telfair of 30 May (*ASP, Indian Affairs*, 1:364).

10. See Commissioners for Settling Accounts Between the United States and the Individual States to GW, 29 June. The report was submitted to Congress on 5 Dec. (*ASP, Miscellaneous*, 1:69).

11. The payment due on 1 June was the first installment of the Dutch loan approved by Congress on 14 Sept. 1782 (*JCC*, 23:575–80). On the prolongation of the loan, see Wilhem and Jan Willink, Nicholaas and Jacob Van Staphorst, and Nicholas Hubbard, to Hamilton, 1 May (*Hamilton Papers*, 14:364–67).

12. For the $2 million loan, see GW to Alexander Hamilton, 9 May 179.2. For the payment of the first installment, see Alexander Hamilton to GW, 12 March 1793. On 4 June 1794 Congress passed "An Act providing for the payment of the second instalment due on a Loan made of the Bank of the United States" (1 *Stat.* 372).

13. GW apparently was referring to section 22 of "An Act to establish the Post-Office and Post Roads within the United States," 20 Feb. 1790, wherein

the conveyance of newspapers by mail was charged at "one cent, for any distance not more than one hundred miles, and one cent and a half for any greater distance" (1 *Stat.* 232, 238).

14. For Secretary of the Treasury Alexander Hamilton's report on estimates for 1794, 21 Dec. 1793, communicated to the House on 23 Dec., see *Hamilton Papers*, 15:552–81.

Bartholomew Dandridge, Jr., to Thomas Jefferson

4. Decr 93

Bw Dandridge has the honor to inform the Secy of State that Congress adjourn at 1 o'Clock to day, so that no message can now go. By the President's order B. D. also informs the Secy that the Presidt wishes, if practicable, a meeting may be had with the Gentlemen—in order that the papers intended to have been sent to day, may go to Congress as early tomorrow as possible.[1]

AL, DNA: RG 59, Miscellaneous Letters; LB, DNA: RG 59, George Washington's Correspondence with His Secretaries of State.

1. See GW to the United States Senate and House of Representatives, 5 December.

From Gimat

A Bordeaux Le 5 Xbre 1793.
Lan 2eme de la Republique fransaise

Monsieur Le president;

Daprés Touttes Les marques des Bontés que vous avés daigné me prodigué pandant Le siege diork & dont je suis demuré jusqua presant penetré de Reconoisance & Celles que vous avés particulieremant pour mon frere qui a Eu Lhoneur de servir sous vos ordres pandant Les dernieres années de la Guerre de votre pays.

Permetés moy de man faire un Titre pour vous demander un Grasse, qui Est Celle dagréer Les Lettres incluses pour y faire donner Cours par La premiere ocasion qui Ce presantera, vous Randerois heureuse une famille Reconoisante qui Est dans Le plus profond Chagrain Sur Les Nouvelles indirectes quelle a Re-

cues Sur Le Sor de mon frere, Lincertitude ou je suis particulieremant de landroit ou il Est Nan ayant point Recû des Nouvelles depuis un an! me fait prandre La Resolution & La liberté,
monsieur Le presidant, de vous prié tres instamant de vous faire
informé Cy Gimat ou sa fame sont Randus a philadelphia, ou
sils Sont Encore Sur Leur hab[itati]on de la martinique & de
donner vos ordres a faire que Le presant paquet parviene a Lun
ou a Lautre.[1]

Pardones monsieur Le presidant, a mon Extraime sancibil-
itté & a mon impatiance de Conoitre La destinée dun frere que
J'aime Tandremant, Cy je prands La liberté de madresser directemant a vous, pour massuré l'arrivêe a sa destination du presant paquet inclux, qui interoisse Toutte ma famille.

Agrées je vous prie avec ma Reconoisance Le Tres profont
Respect avec Lequel Je suis Monsieur Le presidant Votre tres
humble & tres obeisant Serviteur

Gimat
Cadet

P. S. Le plus Gros des paquets Conserne La famille de Mad[am]e
de Gimat il Est de son interoit particulié quil parviene Bien sure-
mant au Neg[ocian]t a ladresse du quel il Est, jause me flatté
monsieur Le president que vous aurois La maime Bonté pour
Lui que pour Celui qui Regarde directemant Madame de Gimat & qui vous voudrés Bien doné vos ordres afain qu'il soît
acheminé par Les premieres ocasions.

Madame piemon porteur de la presante Est un habitante
du port au prince apartenant a une famille de plus justemant
Distînguée & qui prand La vois de votre pays pour se Randre
dans Le sien, permetés moy monsieur Le president de La Con-
cigné dans Ma Lettre Comme une damme veritablemant Respectable; Ele interesse autant par ses malheurs que par Touttes
Ses Calittés agreables, je sais Combien Touts ses Titres sont
Grands auprés de vous, J'ause vous prié, monsieur Le president
Ci Le quas Le Requiert, de faire pour Ele Ce que vous pour-
riés faire pour moy Ci Des sirconstances me Raprochant de vous
Conjouintemant avec mon frere G. qui ne Sera pas moins san-
cible a vos Bontés.[2]

ALS, DNA: RG 59, Miscellaneous Letters. The writer, a brother of Jean Joseph, chevalier de Gimat, evidently had been at the siege of Yorktown during

the Revolution, since he thanks GW for kindnesses rendered at that time, but he has not been otherwise identified.

1. The enclosed packets of letters for delivery to Jean Joseph Gimat or his wife have not been identified. Gimat was dead, having been mortally wounded in an engagement on Martinique in June 1793, and his wife has not been identified.

2. The bearer of this letter, whom Gimat recommends to GW as a respectable woman of distinguished family, was probably Marie Madeleine Rossignol Bancio Piémont (born c.1764), widow of Jean-Baptiste Marie Pierre Bancio Piémont (1752–1791), a former member of the Port-au-Prince council. Having reached Philadelphia, she enclosed the packet with a letter to GW of 12 March 1794 (signed Rossignol Piémont) offering regrets that her health deprived her of the opportunity to deliver it personally.

From Alexander Hamilton

Decemb: 5 1793.

The Secretary of the Treasury presents his respects to the President to inform him that he has reason to believe General Stewart has removed the obstacles to his appointment.[1]

LB, DLC:GW.
1. For the obstacles, see Hamilton to GW, 30 Nov., n.1.

From David Lenox

Sir   Philadelphia 5th Decemr 1793
I feel myself in a very delicate situation respecting the subject on which I am about to address you.

The Death of Mr Thomas Smith has made a vacancy in an Office to which I conceive my abilities equal & for which I beg leave to apply.[1]

I declare to you Sir that I think the Appointment with which you have favored me equally honorable,[2] but there are circumstances which to me would make a change very agreeable. Should I be so fortunate as to succeed to my wishes, my best endeavours shall not be wanting to execute the Duties of the Office with justice to the Public & reputation to myself. I have the honor to be With every sentiment of Respect Sir Your Most Obedt Servt

D. Lenox

ALS, DLC:GW.

1. Thomas Smith, commissioner of loans for Pennsylvania, died on 3 December. Other applicants for his position included Matthew Clarkson, who wrote GW on 4 Dec. (DLC:GW), Jonathan Smith, for whom Richard Peters wrote on 5 Dec., and William Nichols, who wrote on 6 Dec. (DLC:GW), but GW nominated Stephen Moylan for the post on 5 December.

2. Lenox had been appointed U.S. marshal for Pennsylvania in early October. His nomination was sent to the Senate on 27 Dec. and confirmed on 30 Dec. (*Senate Executive Journal*, 142–44).

From Richard Peters

Dear sir   Philada Decr 5. 1793

The Office of Comr of Loans for Pennsilvania is vacant by the Decease of Mr Smith who married my Sister & has left little or Nothing behind him but a good Name, many Friends & a Wife & seven Children several of whom are in their Minority.[1] On hearing of his Death I thought of Nothing on the Subject but lending my Assistance from my own Resources towards the Support of that Part of the Family with whom I am connected. But it has been suggested to me that the Public may be well served, & some Provision ensured to the Family, if the Office were bestowed on Jonathan Smith the Son of the late Comissioner who will be assisted by a younger Brother. Both these have been in the Office many Years & are perfectly acquainted with the Business. They are both well known in the Treasury Department, Jonathan is near 30 years of Age & every Way qualified as to Abilities & Intigrity.[2] The one who would assist him is equalled by very few young Men in a Multitude of Acquirements & excellent Qualities. I know that the Appointment would give great Pleasure to very many of the Citizens of this State who valued Mr Smith & deem him the Father of the Loan Office here, having brought it from small Beginnings, to extensive Usefulness, by his Address & great Attention—Private or compassionate Considerations I am well aware are only secondary in Affairs of public Duty. But they do not fail to have an Effect on the public Mind where the public Interest is also served. They have had their Influence on me, who have indeed only private Feelings as immediate Motives for giving you this Trouble. But no such Considerations would bias me if I were not firmly convinced that the Office would be better executed by J. S. assisted as he will be, than by any other Person; as he has Capacity equal to any other & in Addition much Experience in the Bussiness. Having stated to you the Circumstances I leave to you, without Anxiety, the Result. I know that altho' you do not neglect such Considerations as I have mentioned, you are the best Judge of their Coincidence or Disagreement with your public Duties. I am sir with the most respectful Esteem your obedt Servt

Richard Peters

ALS, DLC:GW.

1. Mary Peters (d. 1797) married Thomas Smith before 1776. One son, Richard Peters Smith (d. 1797), became a merchant and an officer of the American Philosophical Society. The chemist Thomas Peters Smith (c.1777–1802) may have been another son.

2. Jonathan Smith may be the man who appears in the 1796 Philadelphia directory as a scrivener at 100 Union Street, a few doors down from the family home at 110 Union Street.

To the United States Senate

United States,

Gentlemen of the Senate,   December the 5th 1793.

I nominate Stephen Moylan, to be Commissioner of Loans for the State of Pennsylvania; vice Thomas Smith, deceased.[1]

Go: Washington

LS, DNA: RG 46, Third Congress, 1793–95, Senate Records of Legislative Proceedings, President's Messages—Executive Nominations; LB, DLC:GW.

1. On receiving this message, the Senate "Ordered, That it lie for consideration," but they took up the nomination the next day and approved it (*Senate Executive Journal*, 140–41). On that date (6 Dec.) GW's secretary Bartholomew Dandridge, Jr., wrote Thomas Jefferson: "By direction of the President Bw Dandridge has the honor to send to the Secretary of State a resolution of the Senate of yesterday's date; & to request that a Commission agreeably thereto, may be made ready for Stephen Moylan" (DNA: RG 59, Miscellaneous Letters).

To the United States Senate and
House of Representatives

United States [Philadelphia], Decemb. 5th 1793
Gentlemen of the Senate, and of the House of Representatives.

As the present situation of the several Nations of Europe, and especially of those with which the U.S. have important relations, cannot but render the state of things between them and us matter of interesting inquiry to the legislature, & may indeed give rise to deliberations to which they alone are competent, I have thought it my duty to communicate to them certain correspondences which have taken place.

The Representative and Executive bodies of France have manifested generally a friendly attachment to this Country; have given advantages to our commerce & navigation; and have made overtures for placing these advantages on permanent ground; a decree however of the National Assembly, subjecting vessels laden with provisions to be carried into their Ports, & making enemy goods lawful prize in the vessel of a friend, contrary to our Treaty, tho' revoked at one time, as to the U.S. has been since extended to their vessels also, as has been recently stated to us—Representations on this subject, will be immediately given in charge to our Minister there, and the result shall be communicated to the legislature.[1]

It is with extreme concern I have to inform you that the proceedings of the person whom they have unfortunately appointed their Minister Plenipy here, have breathed nothing of the friendly spirit of the Nation which sent him. their tendency on the contrary has been to involve us in war abroad, & discord & anarchy at home. So far as his Acts, or those of his agents, have threatned our immediate commitment in the war, or flagrant insult to the authority of the laws, their effect has been counteracted by the ordinary cognisance of the laws, and by an exertion of the powers confided to me. Where their danger was not imminent, they have been borne with, from sentiments of regard to his Nation, from a sense of their friendship towards us,[2] from a conviction that they would not suffer us to remain long exposed to the action of a person who has so little respected our mutual dispositions, and, I will add, from a reliance on the firmness of my fellow citizens in their principles of peace and order. In the mean time, I have respected and pursued the stipulations of our Treaties, according to what I judged their true sense; and have withheld no act of friendship which their affairs have called for from us, & which justice to others left us free to perform. I have gone further. rather than employ force for the restitution of certain vessels which I deemed the U.S. bound to restore, I thought it more adviseable to satisfy the parties by avowing it to be my opinion, that if restitution were not made, it would be incumbent on the U.S. to make compensation.[3] The papers now communicated will more particularly apprize you of these transactions.[4]

The vexations and spoliation understood to have been committed, on our vessels and commerce, by the cruizers & officers of some of the belligerent powers, appeared to require attention, the proofs of these however not having been brought forward, the description of citizens supposed to have suffered were notified, that on furnishing them to the Executive, due measures would be taken to obtain redress of the past, and more effectual provisions against the future.[5] Should such documents be furnished, proper representations will be made thereon, with a just reliance on a redress proportioned to the exigency of the case.

The British Government having undertaken, by orders to the Commanders of their armed vessels, to restrain generally our Commerce in Corn and other provisions to their own ports & those of their friends, the instructions now communicated were immediately forwarded to our Minister at that Court. In the mean time some discussions on the subject, took place between him & them. these are also laid before you; and I may expect to learn the result of his special instructions in time to make it known to the legislature during their present session.[6]

Very early after the arrival of a British Minister here, mutual explanations on the inexecution of the Treaty of peace were entered into with that Minister. these are now laid before you for your information.[7]

On the subjects of mutual Interest between this Country & Spain, negociations & conferences are now depending. The public good requiring that the present state of these should be made known to the legislature *in confidence only,* they shall be the subject of a separate & subsequent Communication.[8]

Go: Washington

DS, DNA: RG 46, Third Congress, 1793–95, Senate Records of Legislative Proceedings, President's Messages; Df, in Thomas Jefferson's writing, undated, and with numerous emendations, some of which are written on a slip of paper pasted over parts of the second and third paragraph on the first page, DLC: Jefferson Papers; Df (letterpress copy), in Jefferson's writing but partially overwritten at a later date, dated in ink "Dec. 5. 93.," and copied before the emendations noted above, DLC: Jefferson Papers; Df, in Jefferson's writing with three sets of emendations, undated, and bearing the note, "this shews my original draught, and the alterations made in it at our council at the President's Nov. 28. 93.," DLC: Jefferson Papers; Df (letterpress copy), in Jefferson's writing, undated, without note or most emendations, DLC: Jefferson Papers; Copy, DNA: RG 233, Third Congress, 1793–95, House Records of Legislative Proceedings, Journals; LB, DLC:GW; Copy (French translation), FrPMAE: Correspondence Politique, États-Unis, vol. 39.

At a cabinet meeting on 23 Nov., it was agreed that Jefferson would prepare a draft of this message. At a meeting on 28 Nov., Jefferson agreed to make several alterations to his first draft in the face of cabinet members' objections, and he made additional changes after receiving Gouverneur Morris's reports critical of France (see Jefferson's Notes of Cabinet Meetings, 23 and 28 Nov., *Jefferson Papers*, 27:428, 453–56; and Jefferson to GW, 30 Nov.). Jefferson enclosed his final draft (the one with the pasted alterations) in his first letter to GW of 2 December. The DS sent by GW to Congress followed Jefferson's final draft with only minor variations. Significant differences between Jefferson's first draft and the message sent by GW to the U.S. Congress are noted below. For the text of Jefferson's final draft and a more detailed treatment of the draft variations, see *Jefferson Papers*, 27:474–79).

This document was printed in the *General Advertiser* (Philadelphia), 6 Dec., and other newspapers.

1. In Jefferson's first draft, this paragraph originally read, "The several Representative & Executive bodies in France have uniformly manifested the most friendly attachments to this country, have shewn particular favor to our commerce & navigation, & as far as yet appears have given just & ready redress of the wrongs to our citizens & their property irregularly taken on the high seas, & carried into their ports." Criticism by Hamilton and others, along with the information contained in Morris's dispatches, forced Jefferson to revise this paragraph.

A French decree of 19 Feb. had opened French colonial ports to American ships, provided that produce carried by such ships be charged the same duties as borne by French vessels, and suggested negotiations with Congress for mutual reductions in duties (*ASP, Foreign Relations*, 1:147). For discussion of the French decree of 9 May and the subsequent alterations, see Thomas Jefferson to GW, 30 Nov., n.2). GW's information about the re-extension of that decree to U.S. vessels came from Gouverneur Morris's letter to Jefferson of 25 June (*Jefferson Papers*, 26:363–69).

2. At this point Jefferson's first draft contains the phrase "& favors, ancient & recent." Jefferson replaced that phrase with "towards us" in response to

Alexander Hamilton's objections to the draft presented at the cabinet meeting of 28 November. The phrase remained, however, in the letterpress copy.

3. For this decision, which was communicated in letters of 7 Aug. from Jefferson to French minister Edmond Genet and British minister George Hammond (*Jefferson Papers*, 26:633–35), see the cabinet opinions of 3 and 5 August.

4. For the enclosed documents, certified by Jefferson as authentic copies on 4 Dec., see *ASP, Foreign Relations*, 1:142–88.

5. This notification was given by a circular letter of 27 Aug. from Jefferson to various American merchants, which was widely reprinted in the newspapers (see *Jefferson Papers*, 26:767–69).

6. Jefferson's original rendition of the preceding paragraph, prior to several corrections made at the behest of the cabinet, read, "The undertaking to restrain generally our commerce of corn & other provisions to their own ports & those of their friends by an express order of their government, being an infraction of our natural rights, unfounded in reason, inconsistent with the candor of our conduct towards them & excused by·no want of these articles themselves, the representations on that subject now communicated were forwarded to our minister at their court. by these you will percieve that we may expect final information thereon in time for the legislature to consider whether any provision will be necessary on their part for securing an indemnification to our agriculture & commerce for the losses sustained by this interception of their produce." For the documents enclosed, see *ASP, Foreign Relations*, 1:239–43.

7. For these documents, see *ASP, Foreign Relations*, 1:188–238.

8. See GW's first message to the United States Senate and House of Representatives of 16 December.

Bartholomew Dandridge, Jr., to Childs & Swaine

Gentlemen,   Philadelphia 6 December 1793

I am directed by the President of the United States to inform you that the business to which he is necessarily obliged to attend does not permit him to read the public prints which are *now* brought to him. He therefore desires you will not consider him as a subscriber for the Supplement to the daily Advertiser[1]—& that you will discontinue to transmit it to him. I am Gentlemen your most Obt Sert

B. Dandridge

LB, DLC:GW.

1. Francis Childs (1763–1830) and John Swaine (1762–1794) were printers of the *Daily Advertiser* (New York City).

From Robert Denny

Sir   Annapolis Decr 6th 1793

I am favor'd with a letter from the Comptroller of the United States, dated the 28th ulto inclosing me a Commission from your Excellency as Collector of the Customs at this port.[1]

permit me Sir, to return you my thanks for this distinguished favor, But as Auditor of the State of Maryland, I am prohibited by an Act of the legislature from holding any office under the General Government, And the legislature of the United States having also, by their Act, precluded an Officer of the Customs, almost, from pursuing any other business,[2] that contrary to my wishes, being obliged to relinquish one of the appointments, in Justice to myself, from prudential motives, I am induced to decline the Acceptance of that with which you have honored me, I have therefore returned the Commission, and hope from the peculiar circumstances of the case, I shall stand fully justified to your Excellency.

the Salary allowed me as Auditor of this State is indeed small, but it appears that the emoluments arising as Collector of the Customs at this port is much less, and very inadequate to the exigencies of a family, independent of other resources.[3]

To fill an office in one of the Executive departments of this rising Republic is one of my first wishes, and if your Excellency should be pleased to honor me with a future trust, I shall endeavor to execute it agreeably to the intentions of the appointment, according the best of my abilities. I have the honor to be with much respect your Excellencys most Obedient & Hble Servt.

                                        Robert Denny

ALS, DNA: RG 59, Miscellaneous Letters.

1. The letter to Denny from Comptroller Oliver Wolcott, Jr., has not been identified. GW had signed Denny's commission on 23 Nov. (*JPP*, 257).

2. The applicable Maryland law was "An ACT to prohibit members of congress, or persons in office under the United States, from being eligible as members of the legislature or council, or holding office in this state," 30 Dec. 1791 (*Md. Laws 1791*, ch. 80). In "An Act supplementary to the act, entitled, 'An act to provide more effectually for the collection of the Duties imposed by law on Goods, Wares and Merchandise, imported into the United States, and on the Tonnage of Ships or Vessels,'" 2 March 1793, Congress had forbidden

collectors from owning ships, acting as ships' agents, or being "concerned directly or indirectly in the importation of any goods" (1 *Stat.* 336–38).

3. By "An ACT to settle and pay the civil list and other expences of government," 23 Dec. 1792, Maryland's auditor was paid a salary of £200 for the year (*Md. Laws 1792*, ch. 78). The compensation of collectors was determined by fees as set out in "An Act to provide more effectually for the collection of the duties imposed by law on goods, wares and merchandise imported into the United States, and on the tonnage of ships or vessels," 4 Aug. 1790, and added to by "An Act relative to the compensations to certain officers employed in the collection of the duties of impost and tonnage," 8 May 1792 (1 *Stat.* 145–78, 274–75).

From Julbin and Rapelling

Monsieur Wasginethon   Philadelphie ce 6. Decembre 1793
Président des Etats Unis
de L'Amérique

Victimes de l'horrible Despotisme q'exercent à Saint Domingue, deux hommes aussi méchants que pervers, et Pressés par le Sentiment qu'inspirent les premiers besoins de la vie, en l'absence des moyens pour les Satisfaire, Deux Colons Infortunés enhardis, par L'Exemple de vos Vertus viennent avec confiance en epancher l'expression dans votre Ame Généreuse autant que Sensible et Solliciter auprès de vous quelques Secours, en attendant que des Circonstances plus heureuses leur permettent de retourner dans leurs foyers. Ils Sont avec Le plus profond respect, Vos très humbles & tres obeissants Serviteurs
                                        Julbin; et Rapelling

ALS, DNA: RG 59, Miscellaneous Letters. The letter is docketed in part: "asking pecuniary aid." No reply has been identified.

From Laurent De Saxÿ and Laurent De Verneüil

A Néwcastel Ce 6 Decembre 1793

Votre Bienfaisance et votre humanité Monsieur, nous Sont assés connüe, pour nous faire Espérer que vous tendrez Une main Secourable á deux meres de familles charger De quatres Enfants, dont L'ainée n'a que huit ans Echappés Nuitament aux Sattélites des commissaires Civils qui avoients donnés L'ordres, De nous Egorgés Aprés avoir fait Embarqués il y a un an nos maris,[1] Nous avons donc été forcés de fuir de nos habitations Pour nous refugiér dans votre paÿs, ou nous sommes arrivée sans moÿens N'y aucunes Ressources, nous Sommes descendüe a philadelphie Le premier D'aoust En arrivant quelques personnes s'emploÿerent pour Nous procurér quelques Secours, ce que nous ôbtimmes De la caisse de Bienfaisance, mais m'alheureusement Nous n'umes Ses secours que jusqu'au premier Séptembre, Epoque á laquel nous avons quitté Philadelphie, parcequ'il y faisoit trop chers vivre Et que les loÿer ÿ sont aussi Excéssivement chers Nous Croÿons qu'il nous en couteroit moins icÿ,[2] nous Nous trouvons Monsieur dans Le plus grand Embaras faute de moÿens il ne nous reste que Deux portugaises pour tout Bien á L'entré de L'hiver et N'aÿant pas Les moÿens de nous procurer les Vétements nécéssaires Pour nous méttre á l'abrÿ du Grand froids ainsÿ que Nos m'alheureux Enfants, s'es en vous seul Monsieur, que nous Espérons persuadez que vous nous donnerai quelque Sécours,[3] ayant Lâme Sensible, si vous Etes pére, vous s'entiraÿ combien notre Situâtion est D'ouloureuses puis ceque nous sommes á la véille de n'avoir Pas dequoy subvenir á L'existance de ce qui nous reste De plus chers aux monde, Pardon Monsieur de vous Importuné en vous faisant part de nos m'alheurs honnoré moy je vous prie d'une reponce et veuillez je vous prie la mettre Sous Le couvert de Mr Cameron á Newcastel pour mêtre remises, soÿez je vous prie Persuadez de toutes notre Reconnoissance, elle ne finira qu'avec la vie de celle qui a L'honneur Dêtre tres parfaitemente Monsieur Votre tres humble et tres ôbte servante,

Laurent De Saxÿ
Laurent De Verneüil

LS, DNA: RG 59, Miscellaneous Letters.

These two women also wrote a very similar letter to GW, dated 10 Dec. (DNA: RG 59, Miscellaneous Letters). The little information added by that letter is recorded in the notes below.

According to a subsequent letter to GW of 8 May 1794, in which they requested assistance to return to Saint Domingue, Laurent De Saxÿ and Laurent De Verneüil were sisters from the towns of La Borgne and Gros Morne in what is now Haiti. Saxÿ apparently did not return at that time either, as she wrote George Read on 26 Aug. 1794 asking aid for the next winter (Read, *Life of George Read*, 554–55). At least some of the Saxÿ family were apparently residents of Philadelphia in 1808 (see "Marriage Registers at St. Joseph's Church, Philadelphia, Pa.," *Records of the American Catholic Historical Society of Philadelphia*, 20 [1909]:46).

1. According to the letter of 10 Dec., the women's husbands were military officers: "lun ôficier aux Régiments du cap [evidently Saxÿ], et Lautre ôfficier Dartillerie." Verneüil had been ordered out of the colony in December 1792 and was in France, where in August 1794 he criticized the Saint Domingue commissioners before the national convention (*Recueil des actes du Comité de salut public,* 10:260; *Gazette Nationale ou Le Moniteur Universel* [Paris], 24 Aug. 1794).

2. The comparable sentence in the letter of 10 Dec. continues by noting that their expectations were wrong because things were just as expensive at New Castle: "mais nous étions dans L'erreur car á peu de choses prés nous paÿons les choses aussi Chers."

3. For GW's response to this request for aid, see his letters of 26 Dec. to George Read and to Saxÿ and Verneüil.

Cabinet Opinion

[7 December 1793]

At a meeting of the heads of departments & Attorney Genl at the President's on the 7th of Dec. 1793.

Mr Genet's letter of Dec. 3. questioning the right of requiring the address of Consular commissions to the President was read. it is the opinion that the address may be either to the U.S. or to the President of the U.S. but that one of these shoud be insisted on.[1]

A letter from James King was read, dated Philadelphia Nov. 25. 1793. complaining of the capture of his schooner Nancy by a British privateer & carried into N. Providence, and that the court there has thrown the onus probandi on the owners, to shew that the vessel & cargo are American property. it is the opinion that mister King be informed that it is a general rule that the governmt should not interpose individually, till a final denial of justice has taken place in the courts of the country where the wrong is done; but that, a considerable degree of information being shortly expected relative to these cases, his will be further considered & attended to at that time.[2]

The Secretary of state informed the President that he had received a number of applications from mister Genet on behalf of the refugees of St Domingo who have been subjected to tonnage on their vessels & duties on their property on taking asylum in the ports of this country, into which they were forced by the misfortunes of that colony. it is the opinion that the Secretary of state may put the petitions into the hands of a member of the legislature in his private capacity to be presented to the legislature.[3]

Th: Jefferson
Edm: Randolph
Alexandr Hamilton
H. Knox.

DS, in Thomas Jefferson's writing, DLC:GW.

1. For Edmond Genet's letter to Thomas Jefferson of 3 Dec., see *Jefferson Papers*, 27:479–80. Jefferson had informed Genet in a letter of 2 Oct. that "by our constitution all foreign agents are to be addressed to the President of the US." When Genet questioned that view in a letter to Jefferson of 14 Nov. and failed to address the commissions of two vice-consuls according to those instructions, Jefferson returned the commissions with his second letter to Genet of 22 Nov., telling him that GW would "issue no Exequatur to any Consul or Vice consul not directed to him in the usual form" (*Jefferson Papers*, 27:175–76, 363–64, 414–15). Jefferson's reply to Genet of 9 Dec. followed this cabinet opinion (*Jefferson Papers*, 27:500–502).

2. King's letter to Jefferson of 25 Nov. has not been identified. Jefferson's reply to King of 7 Dec. was in accord with the cabinet opinion (*Jefferson Papers*, 27:491). James King (1751–1832) was a Philadelphia merchant.

3. French minister Edmond Genet had written at least three letters to Jefferson supporting the remission of tonnage duties for the vessels of Saint Domingue refugees, 1 and 29 Oct. and 25 Nov. (*Jefferson Papers*, 27:172–73, 280–82, 435). Jefferson approached William Vans Murray on this subject (see Jefferson to GW, 15 Dec.), and on 7 March 1794 Congress passed "An Act for the remission of the duties arising on the tonnage of sundry French vessels which have taken refuge in the ports of the United States" (1 *Stat.* 342).

From William Moultrie

Sir   Columbia [S.C.] 7th December 1793

I have the Honor of transmitting to you the Resolves of the Legislature of this State together with a Number of Affidavits, setting forth that Certain Persons in this State have been enlisting Men for the Service of the French Republic to go on an Expedition against a Power not at War with the United States—the Investigation of the whole Business is fully expressed in the Report of the Committee.

In the Message with which the Resolves & affidavits were sent to me, I am desired to request, that the names of the several Witnesses will not be known—the Necessity of this Secrecy is obvious.[1] I have the Honor to be with great Respect & Esteem, Sir, your most obedient & most humble Servant

Willm Moultrie

ALS, DNA: RG 59, Miscellaneous Letters; Copy, DNA: RG 46, Third Congress, 1793–95, Senate Records of Legislative Proceedings, President's Messages; LB, DNA: RG 46, Transcribed Reports and Communications Transmitted by the Executive Branch to the U.S. Senate, 1789–1819. This letter evidently was not sent until 9 Dec. or later, as all of its enclosures bear attestations of that date. On 15 Jan. 1794 GW submitted to Congress this letter and enclosures (along with Genet's statement on the matter to Thomas Jefferson, 25 Dec.) "as being connected with the correspondence, already in your possession, between the Secretary of State and the Minister plenipotentiary of the French Republic" (LS, DNA: RG 46, Third Congress, 1793–95, Senate Records of Legislative Proceedings, President's Messages; see also *ASP, Foreign Relations*, 1:309–11).

1. This paragraph appears as a postscript in the copy and letter-book copy. The copy of the letter and enclosures in Senate Records includes a certification by State Department chief clerk George Taylor, Jr., 14 Jan. 1794, that the documents were "truly copied from the originals (except the omission of certain names agreeably to the letter of December 7th 1793, from Governor Moultrie)." Those copies omit the names of the persons giving affidavits.

Enclosure
Resolves

state of South Carolina
In the House of Representatives December 6th 1793

The Committee to whom was referred the business of examining unto and ascertaining the truth of a Report—That an Armed force is now levying within this State by Persons under a foreign Authority without the pemission and Contrary to the express prohibition of the Government of the United States and of this State.

Report—

That they have made diligent Enquiry respecting the truth of this report and have collected such Evidence relating thereto as was immediately within their reach—That your Committee are perfectly satisfied from the information on the Oaths of divers credible Persons which they have received—That William Tate, Jacob R. Brown William Urby Robert Tate, Richard Speake Citizens of this State and other Persons unknown to your Committee also Citizens of this State have received & accepted military Commissions, from M. Genet Minister Plenipotentiary from the

Republic of France to the United States of America Authorising them and instructions requiring them, to raise, organise,
train and Conduct Troops within the United States of America[1]—That the avowed purpose for which these Troops are now
raising is to rendezvous in the State of Georgia and from thence
to proceed into the Spanish Dominions with a view to Conquest
or plunder as their Strength might enable or opportunity might
tempt them That in the Event of a French Fleet approaching
the Coa[s]ts of the Southen States a junction and co:operation
with it is contemplated by the Persons abovementioned But that
tho this was the avowed Object of these Troops and their Leaders among themselves from the injunction to conceal the whole
System from persons not initiated and the Subordination established to Mr Genet, the author of the plan and the Source of
Authority to the Officers—It is probable that the Corps when
raised must yeild to any change of destination which the Judgment or inclination of M. Genet may point out to them: That
several of the Persons above named received together with their
Commissions instructions by which they were to regulate their
enrollments of Men Stating the pay, rations, Cloathing, plunder
and division of conquered Land, to be allotted to the officers
and Men who should enter into this Service and marking the
proportions of the Acquisitions to be reserved to the republic
of France. That the persons abovenamed in pursuance of the
powers vested in them by the said Commissions and in obedience to the instructions of M. Genet and his Agents particularly
M. Mangourit who signed some of the papers[2] have proceeded
by themselves and by their Agents without any Authority from
the United States, or from this State to enroll numbers of the
Citizens of this State whom they deluded with the hopes of plunder and the Acquisition of riches in the Service of the Republic
of France to be subject to the orders of M. Genet the Minister
plenipotentiary of France.

That Stephen Drayton and John Hamilton also Citizens of
this State have made application to the Good Citizens thereof
to engage in this scheme of raising Men in this State for the
Service of France to Act under the orders of M. Genet, and to
commit Acts of hostility against nations at peace with the United
States of America, and have avowed that they acted by the Authority of M. Genet the Minister plenipotentiary of the Republic of France:[3] That upon the whole of the information which

your Committee have been able to obtain This is a daring and dangerous attempt by a Foreign Minister to intermeddle in the Affairs of the United States, to usurp the powers of Government and to levy Troops in the bosom of the Union without the Authority and contrary to the express Sense of the Government of the United States and in Violation of the Laws of Nations.

That the direct tendency of these measures of the foreign Minister is to disturb the internal tranquility of the United States and to involve them in hostilities with Nations with whom they are now at peace, which sound policy requires should be preserved.

That in the Opinion of your Committe this attempt is the more dangerous, and alarming as many Citizens of the United States, have been thereby Seduced from their duty by insiduous Arts practised on their kindred Affection to the french Republic and have been drawn into a Scheme in the execution of which they have usurped the functions of Government and exercised the power of the sword which the wisdom of the Constitution hath vested exlusively in the Congress and President of the United States—That this Committee therefore recommend that the Governor of this State be requested to issue his proclamation forbidding all persons from enrolling any of the Citizens of this State and prohibiting the Citizens from enlisting under any Officers or for any purposes not previously Sanctioned by the Government of the United States or of this State And also forbidding all unlawful Assemblages of Troops unauthorized by Government,[4] And that the Governor be requested to exert the whole public force to the utmost extent if necessary to insure obedience to his proclamation.

That in the oppinion of this Committee the said William Tate Jacob R. Brown Robert Tate, Stephen Drayton John Hamilton and Richard Speke have been guilty of Hight Crimes and Misdemeanours and they recommend that the Attorney General and Solicitors be directed forthwith to institute or cause to be instituted and conducted prosecutions in the proper Courts of Law against the said William Tate Jacob R. Brown Robert Tate, Stephen Drayton John Hamilton and Richard Speke for accepting or engaging to accept Commissions from a foreign power to raise Troops within the United States and for going about within the State levying or Attempting to levy Troops and for seducing and endeavouring to seduce the Citizens of this State to enroll themselves for foreign Service to commit Acts of hostility against Nations with whom the United States are at peace without the permission of the Government and contrary to the proclamation of the President of the United States declaring these States to be in a State of Nutrality and Peace—That Copies of the Evidence collected by this Committee together with the proceedings of this House thereon be forwarded immediately to the President of the United States and to the Executives of the State of North Carolina and Georgia for their information.

Resolved Unanimously that this House do concur in the said Report.

Ordered that the Report and Resolution be sent to the Senate for their concurrence.

By order of the House
John Sandford Dart C. H. R.[5]

Resolved unanimously that this House do concur with the House of Representatives in the foregoing Report and Resolution.

Ordered That the Report and Resolution be sent to the House of Resolution.

By Order of the Senate
Felix Warley C. S.[6]

A true Copy, and which I Attest

John Sandford Dart
Clerk of the House of Representatives
Columbia December 9th 1793

Copy, DNA: RG 59, Miscellaneous Letters; Copy, DNA: RG 46, Third Congress, 1793–95, Senate Records of Legislative Proceedings, President's Messages; LB, DNA: RG 46, Transcribed Reports and Communications Transmitted by the Executive Branch to the U.S. Senate, 1789–1819.

1. For a copy of William Tate's commission of 15 Oct. 1793, see "Mangourit Correspondence," 599. Jacob Roberts Brown (1731–1805), originally from Virginia, was a former Continental army officer who represented the Newberry District in the South Carolina general assembly. At a hearing to determine whether he should be stripped of his seat, Brown claimed that he had taken the proposed commission under consideration but had ultimately refused to accept the commission, which he burned (*State Gazette of South-Carolina* [Charleston], 19 Dec.). Richard Speake (1753–1834) served as a private in the Revolutionary War. He was a brother-in-law of Robert Tate (d. 1803), who served as a captain of South Carolina dragoons in 1781. The charges against these men were supported by four af-

fidavits given to committee members Henry William DeSaussure (1763–1839), Timothy Ford (1762–1830), and James Green Hunt (d. 1794) on 2 December.

Thomas Wadsworth (1755–1799), who represented Laurens County in the South Carolina Senate, 1791–97, testified that Urby had said he had a commission, which Wadsworth "understood was for Foreign Service," and was authorized to raise troops to be commanded by William Tate. Wadsworth also testified that Brown had shown him a paper outlining details of the proposal and asked if Wadsworth would advise him to "engage in this Business." Wadsworth "understood that the Source of all Power & the Spring of Action in this Business, was Mr Genet" and "that the Business was to be conducted secretly."

Thomas Farrar (1754–1833), a former Continental army officer, at this time a sheriff for Washington District and later a representative of the Pendleton District in the South Carolina Senate, testified that William Tate had showed him two papers signed by Genet, one appointing Tate "a Colonel in the Service of the French Republic" and the other "being a Plan for the Formation of a Military Corps." Tate told Farrar that he was enlisting men "to march to South America & attack the Spanish Dominions."

Thomas Brandon (1741–1802), a colonel in the South Carolina militia who had served five terms in the South Carolina general assembly between 1776 and 1790, testified that Robert Tate had "urged him to accept an appointment in a Body of Troops that was to be raised in this State under French Commissions—which Troops were to go on an expedition against the Spanish possessions on some part of the American Continent."

Jacob Rumph (1752–1812), a militia lieutenant colonel who represented Orange County in the general assembly, testified that he met two men, one of whom, thinking he was of "the party for enlisting and ⟨r⟩aising Men for the French Service," offered to show Rumph his commission, which Rumph refused. The two said "they were to have their rendezvous in Georgia" and asked whether Rumph had seen "Captn Tate" (certified copies of all depositions, DNA: RG 59, Miscellaneous Letters; see also *ASP, Foreign Relations*, 1:310–11). The committee subsequently employed Farrar to secure the papers of these men, but he was unsuccessful (*State Gazette of South-Carolina* [Charleston], 28 Dec.).

2. Michel Ange Bernard de Mangourit (1752–1829) was the French consul at Charleston from 1792 to 1794. In 1796 Mangourit was appointed as chargé des affaires to the United States, but the appointment was withdrawn after the American minister in France, James Monroe, protested (Monroe to Timothy Pickering, 4 and 15 Aug. 1796, *ASP, Foreign Relations*, 1:741).

3. John Hamilton probably was the man who had served as a lieutenant and adjutant of the 1st South Carolina Regiment during the Revolutionary War. This charge was supported by the 3 Dec. affidavit of Laurence Manning (1756?–1804), a Revolutionary War officer who represented Claremont County in the South Carolina general assembly. Manning testified that Drayton and Hamilton called at his house "& mentioned to this Deponent as a very advantageous Plan that was a foot to get as many Men as possible to

agree to assemble by small Parties upon some of the Shores near Charleston or elsewhere & that a french Fleet was to attend for the Purpose of receiving them and that the Object was to make a Descent upon some of the Spanish Islands that would be a very Lucrative Conquest if effected." Manning, who "understood" that Drayton and Hamilton "were acting under the Authority of the Minister of the French Republic at the Time," refused Drayton's offer of "a pretty high Commission" because of "Doubts of the Legality of the Undertaking in as much as it would be inconsistent with the Proclamation of the President of the United States" (Copy, DNA: RG 59, Miscellaneous Letters; see also *ASP, Foreign Relations,* 1:311).

The committee submitted the affidavits to the justices of the state supreme court, who issued warrants for the arrest of Drayton and Hamilton. The two were bound over to answer charges at the next federal court at Columbia. Meanwhile, the committee authorized Col. Wade Hampton to seize papers from the two men, which he did by "breaking open the locks" of their trunks "with all the delicacy and tenderness possible due to the citizen of a free country." Hampton found in Hamilton's possession papers containing "military regulation for the American revolutionary legion, intended to be raised under the auspices and by the authority of Mr. Genet in America." On 17 Dec. the South Carolina House adopted the committee's report calling for the transmission of those papers to GW (*State Gazette of South-Carolina* [Charleston], 28 Dec.). No such transmission has been identified.

For Drayton's challenge to the actions and authority of the committee, which included a lawsuit asking damages, see his letter of 10 Dec. in the *City Gazette & Daily Advertiser* (Charleston), 14 Dec., and Alexander Moultrie, *An appeal to the people, on the conduct of a certain public body in South-Carolina, respecting Col. Drayton and Col. Moultrie* (Charleston, 1794). A grand jury at the May 1794 U.S. circuit court at Columbia indicted Drayton but returned no bill against Hamilton (*City Gazette & Daily Advertiser,* 17 May 1794).

4. A copy of Governor Moultrie's proclamation to this effect, dated 9 Dec., appears with the copy of this report in senate records.

5. John Sandford Dart (1741?–1798), a merchant who represented Christ Church in the 1775 Provincial Congress and the 1782 session of the South Carolina general assembly, served as clerk of the general assembly from 1783 to 1797. The remainder of this document is in a different handwriting.

6. Felix Warley (1749?–1814), a Revolutionary War officer, served as clerk for the South Carolina Senate from 1785 to 1801. The following attestation is in Dart's writing, which is different from those of the copyists.

From Francisco Rendon

sir   Madrid December the 7th 1793

Having Constantly in my memory the many marks of Esteem with which you honoured me while my residence in the United states; and take for granted that you will hear with pleasure any thing which may Contribute to my wellfare and happiness—I take the liberty to acquaint you that Tho' I have been for some years past in a very disagreable ⟨situation⟩ and which has prevailed upon me to ⟨declined⟩ all my Correspondence with my american friends I am now again in a very diferent Circumstances Clear'd from the darkness of my past ⟨mist⟩.

⟨The King⟩ my Mastter well Informed at last of my services by His Excellency D. Diego de Gardoqui, has been pleased to honoured me with the appointment of the Intendence of ⟨*illegible*⟩ new orleans and all the other establishments of that part of America, Declearing to me also the fun[c]tions and honours of Intendent of his majesty's Army. This honorable Commission affords to me a great satisfaction not only on account of my advancement and the service I may be able to render to my Contry, but the Circumstances of been placed so near neighbour to the United states which I may probable find occasion to shew to the Inhavitants of them my sincere disposition to Contribute in any manner to their happiness as well as to Establish a perfect harmony with those of the Possessions of my sovereign.

The City of my residence will be that of New orleans where (if pleased to god) I hope to arrive Early in the spring next, and where I expected to receive your Commands with the agreable news of your perfect health and that of Mrs Washington to who I beg you to present my best respects; and you sir be assured of the true affection and respect with which I am and shall be for ever your most obedt and most humble servt

Francisco Rendon

ALS, DLC:GW.

Francisco Rendon came to the United States from Cuba in 1779 to serve as secretary to Juan de Miralles, Spain's unofficial representative to Congress. After Miralles's death in April 1780, Rendon succeeded him as unofficial representative, and in 1785 and 1786 he served as secretary to Diego de Gardoqui, Spain's first official representative to the United States. Rendon served as Spain's intendant in Louisiana from 1794 to 1796, and subsequently as intendant in Zacatecas, Mexico, 1796–1810, and Oaxaca, Mexico, 1814–16 and 1818–21.

From the United States House of Representatives

Sir,   [7 December 1793]

The Representatives of the people of the United States, in meeting you for the first time since you have been again called by an unanimous suffrage to your present station, find an occasion which they embrace, with no less sincerity than promptitude, for expressing to you their congratulations on so distinguished a testimony of public approbation; and their entire confidence in the purity & patriotism of the motives which have produced this obedience to the voice of your country. It is to virtues which have commanded long and universal reverence, and services from which have flowed great and lasting benefits, that the tribute of praise may be paid, without the reproach of flattery; and it is from the same sources, that the fairest anticipations may be derived in favor of the public happiness.

The United States having taken no part in the War which had embraced in Europe the powers with whom they have the most extensive relations, the maintenance of peace was justly to be regarded as one of the most important duties of the magistrate charged with the faithful execution of the laws. We accordingly witness with approbation and pleasure the vigilance with which you have guarded against an interruption of that blessing, by your proclamation admonishing our Citizens of the consequences of illicit or hostile acts towards the belligerent parties, and promoting by a declaration of the existing legal state of things, an easier admission of our right to the immunities belonging to our situation.[1]

The connexion of the United States with Europe has evidently become extremely interesting. The communications which remain to be exhibited to us, will, no doubt, assist in giving us a fuller view of the subject, and in guiding our deliberations to such results as may comport with the rights and true interests of our Country.

We learn, with deep regret, that the measures dictated by a love of peace, for obtaining an amicable termination of the afflicting war on our frontier, have been frustrated; and that a resort to offensive measures has again become necessary.[2] As the latter, however, must be rendered more satisfactory in proportion to the solicitude for peace manifested by the former, it is to be hoped they will be pursued under the better auspices on that account, & be finally crowned with more happy success.

In relation to the particular tribes of Indians, against whom offensive measures have been prohibited,[3] as well as all the other important subjects which you have presented to our view, we shall bestow the attention which they claim. We cannot, however, refrain at this time, from particularly expressing our concurrence in your anxiety for the regular discharge of the public debts, as fast as circumstances and events will permit; and in the policy of removing any impediments that may be found in the way of a faithful representation of public proceedings throughout the United States,[4] being persuaded, with you, that on no subject more than the former, can delay be more injurious, or an œconomy of time more valuable; and that with respect to the latter, no resource is so firm for the Government of the United States, as the affections of the people, guided by an enlightened policy.

Throughout our deliberations we shall endeavour to cherish every sentiment which may contribute to render them conducive to the dignity, as well as to the welfare of the United States; and we join with you, in imploring that Being on whose will the fate of nations depends, to crown with success our mutual endeavors. Signed by order, and in behalf of the House

Frederick Augustus Muhlenberg
Speaker.

Attest
John Beckley—Clerk.

LB, DLC:GW; Copy (French translation), DLC: Genet Papers; Copy (French translation), FrPMAE: Correspondence Politique, États-Unis, vol. 39.

1. This refers to GW's Neutrality Proclamation of 22 April.

2. This is a reference to the failed treaty negotiations with the northwest Indians.

3. On the prohibition of offensive measures against the Creek Indians, see GW to the United States Senate and House of Representatives, 3 Dec., and n.9.

4. This responds to the recommendation in GW's annual message, delivered 3 Dec., for a repeal of the tax on transportation of public prints.

To the United States House of Representatives

Gentlemen,   [7 December 1793]
    I shall not affect to conceal the cordial satisfaction, which I derive, from the Address of the House of Representatives. Whatsoever those services may be, which you have sanctioned by your favor, it is a sufficient reward, that they have been accepted as they were meant. For the fulfilment of your anticipations of the future, I can give no other assurance, than that the motives, which you approve, shall continue unchanged.
    It is truly gratifying to me to learn, that the proclamation has been considered, as a seasonable guard against the interruption of the public peace.[1] Nor can I doubt, that the subjects, which I have recommended to your attention, as depending on legislative provisions, will receive a discussion suited to their importance. With every reason, then, it may be expected, that your deliberations, under the divine blessing, will be matured to the honor and happiness of the United States.

Go: Washington.

Copy, DNA: RG 233, Third Congress, House Records of Legislative Proceedings, Journals; LB, DLC:GW.
    1. GW is referring to his Neutrality Proclamation of 22 April.

From Joshua Gayle

Honerabl. Sir,   Virginia Decer 8th 1793
    Your Excellency has a Tract of Land laying in Gloucester County on North River, I have heard You have a mind to Sell it, if so, be please'd to let me no Your lowest price in Cash or Credit and the Terms of Credit, as I would wish to purchase if the Terms can be made Agreeable,[1] the Land is at present in a bad Sitiuaten Distuate of Houses fenceses & all in Willdderness, which point I will referr you to Colol John Page, being Acquinted with the same.[2] I am sir, Your Excency Mos. Obet Hbe Sert

Joshua Gayle

ALS, DLC:GW. Joshua Gayle resided in Mathews County, Va., which was formerly Kingston Parish, Gloucester County.
    1. Gayle was referring to the tract of about four hundred acres on Back River (a branch of North River) that GW acquired from John Dandridge in

1789 (see Dandridge to GW, 27 Oct. 1788, and source note). GW apparently did not receive Gayle's letter until early February 1794. He responded in a letter to Gayle of 13 Feb. 1794: "My lowest price for the Land I hold on the North river, in Gloucester County, in Virginia, is One thousand pounds, estimating dollars at six shillings. about this sum the land actually stands me in at this moment, & I shall advance the price in proportion, at least to the interest of the above sum, at any time hereafter.

"If credit is required, it may be obtained for two, three, or four years—paying Interest on the purchase money" (LB, DLC:GW).

GW did not sell the property at this time.

2. GW did inquire of John Page about Gayle's financial status. After investigating, Page reported a favorable opinion about Gayle's honesty and ability to pay (Page to GW, 30 March 1794, DLC:GW).

From Daniel Carroll

Sir, George Town Decr 9th 1793

Mr Hoban is desirous of forwarding to you a sample of Free Stone found on your Land (about Mount Vernon), on or near the River—Captn Butler has offerd to take charge of it[1]—Mr Hoban says, that it is harder than the Bath Stone from the sample, which was taken from the outSide, & probably will be found better on getting into the quarry.

I have the pleasure to inform you, that several persons from England, are allmost weekly reaching this place—Besides farmers, there are some in the Mechanical & Commercial line with property.

The proposd Bank Bill has passd our General Assembly[2]—Messrs Johnson & Stuart were to have been here at this time; In consequence of a letter from Mr Greenleaf, who intends to be with us about the 15th Instant the meeting has been postpond to that time[3]—Yr favor of the 1st Instant is come to hand.[4] I have the honor to be with sentiments of the greatest Respect, Sr yr Most Obt & very Hble Servt

Danl Carroll

ALS, PHi: Gratz Collection; Sprague Transcript, DLC:GW.

1. Captain Butler may have been John B. Butler, master of the sloop *George*, which operated in 1793 as a packet between Philadelphia and the Virginia ports of Norfolk and Alexandria.

2. The bill to establish a bank in the District of Columbia passed the Maryland Senate on 23 Nov. and the Maryland House on 5 Dec. (*Votes and Proceedings of the Senate of the State of Maryland. November Session, 1793.* . . . [Annapolis,

1794], 10; *Votes and Proceedings of the House of Delegates of the State of Maryland. November Session, 1793. . . .* [Annapolis, 1794], 56–57). For its provisions, see "An ACT to establish a bank in the district of Columbia," 28 Dec., *Md. Laws 1793*, ch. 30.

3. The letter from James Greenleaf has not been identified.

4. See GW to the Commissioners for the District of Columbia, 1 December.

To the United States Senate

Gentlemen of the Senate,   United States, Decemb: 9th 1793.

I nominate Walter Stewart, to be Surveyor for the District of Philadelphia, and Inspector of the Revenue for the port of Philadelphia; vice William McPherson, appointed Naval Officer. and, Daniel Lionel Huger, of South Carolina, to be Marshall for the District of South Carolina; vice Isaac Huger, resigned.[1]

Go: Washington

LS, DNA: RG 46, Third Congress, 1793–95, Senate Records of Executive Proceedings, President's Messages—Executive Nominations; LB, DLC:GW.

1. The Senate approved these nominations on 10 Dec. (*Senate Executive Journal,* 141). GW's secretary Bartholomew Dandridge, Jr., wrote Secretary of State Thomas Jefferson on that date to convey GW's request that Jefferson have the commissions prepared (DNA: RG 59, Miscellaneous Letters). Daniel Lionel Huger (1768–1798), Isaac Huger's second son, served as marshal for about one year, resigning in late November or early December 1794.

From the United States Senate

December the 9th 1793[1]

To The President of the United States.

Accept, Sir, the thanks of the Senate for your Speech delivered to both Houses of Congress at the opening of the session.[2] Your reelection to the chief magistracy of the United States gives us sincere pleasure.[3] We consider it as an event every way propitious to the happiness of our Country; and your compliance with the call, as a fresh instance of the patriotism which has so repeatedly led you to sacrifice private inclination, to the public good. In the unanimity which a second time marks this important national act, we trace with particular satisfaction, besides the distinguished tribute paid to the virtues and abilities which it recognizes, another proof of that just discernment, and constancy of sentiments and views, which have hitherto characterized the Citizens of the United States.

As the European powers with whom the United States have the most extensive relations were involved in war in which we had taken no part; it seemed necessary that the disposition of the Nation for peace should be promulgated to the world, as well for the purpose of admonishing our Citizens of the consequences of a contraband trade and of acts hostile to any of the belligerent parties, as to obtain by a declaration of the existing legal state of things, an easier admission of our rights to the immunities of our situation, we therefore contemplate with pleasure, the proclamation by you issued, and give it our hearty approbation.[4] We deem it a measure well timed, and wise; manifesting a watchful solicitude for the welfare of the Nation and calculated to promote it. The several important matters presented to our consideration will, in the course of the Session, engage all the attention to which they are respectively entitled; and as the public happiness will be the sole guide of our deliberations, we are perfectly assured of receiving your strenuous & most zealous cooperation.

John Adams, Vice President of the U. States,
and Presidt of the Senate.

LB, DLC:GW; Df, DNA: RG 46, Third Congress, 1793–95, Senate Records of Legislative Proceedings, President's Messages.

The draft is in two parts: a report of the committee appointed to draft the address and a list of "Motions for Amendment." A notation on the committee report states that it was "adopted as amended." The amendments are indicated in the notes below.

1. The letter-book copy is dated 9 Dec. 1793, headed by a note which reads, "At twelve o'Clock, agreeably to appointment, the Senate waited on the President at his House and presented the following." The message was approved by the Senate on 9 Dec., at which time Senators Pierce Butler and Oliver Ellsworth were designated to "wait on the President of the United States, and desire him to acquaint the Senate at what time and place it will be most convenient for him that the foregoing address should be presented." The address actually was delivered to GW at noon on 10 Dec. (see *Journal of the Senate*, 6:14–15; *JPP*, 265; and GW to U.S. Senate, 10 Dec.).

2. See GW to the United States Senate and House of Representatives, 3 December.

3. A substitute for the preceding two sentences was proposed but not adopted: "Called again by the general Suffrage of your Country to resume

the executive power, to which from your distinguished Virtues and eminent Services you were justly entitled, the Senate of the United States express to you their sincere Congratulations for this renewed Testimony of public Approbation."

4. The preceding long sentence was substituted by amendment for the following text: "The Proclamation which you issued during the recess of Congress, with reference to the war in Europe, has our entire approbation." The sentence refers to GW's Neutrality Proclamation of 22 April.

To Lund Washington

Dr Lund,   Phila. Decr 9th 1793.

Doctr Tate being among those who had fled from the City during the raging of the Yellow fever I was unable to lay the Statement of your case before him till his return when he sent the enclosed opinion with a request that I would read, & forward it to you.[1]

As soon as I had done so, I sent Mr Dandridge to his lodgings in order to desire him to proceed immediately to Alexandria in the Stage of this day with out waiting to hear from you, but behold he had left town again not to return before Wednesday.

I thought it best, for the reasons he assigns to loose no time; and because I think his charge (even if his expences are added which I presume will be the case) is a very reasonable one for he can not be absent much short of 15 days from his practice in these parts.

I shall repeat this request as soon as he returns—giving you notice of it in the meanwhile—My Complimts to Mrs Washington—and with every wish for Yr speedy & perfect recovery I am Dr Lund Yr Affe. frd

                                              Go: Washington

ADfS, PPRF; LB, DLC:GW.

1. The enclosure has not been identified. James Tate (d. 1813), a surgeon of the 3d Pennsylvania Regiment during the Revolutionary War, practiced medicine in Philadelphia and Bucks County. In June 1794 he successfully treated GW for a skin complaint that GW believed to be cancerous (see GW to Thomas Pinckney, 25 Feb. 1795, DLC:GW).

From Hugh Williamson

Sir   Edenton [N.C.] 9th Decr 1793.

You will readily believe that I am extremely desirous of being near my Children so as to have an Eye on the Progress of their Education and this cannot well be in Carolina where the State of the Climate proves unfavourable to the means of Learning. With this Impression I take the Liberty to intimate that a respectable Employment viz. any Office by the immediate nomination of the President and at the Seat of Government would be acceptable to me. Some Office may chance to be erected or may become vacant to the Duties of which I might not be unequal. In such Case, if my name should be thought of, I have only to promise for myself Diligence and Fidelity, of the other necessary Talents you are a much better Judge. I have also to observe that as Offices to which large Salaries are attached generally require superior Talents and are at the same Time Objects of Competition and Envy, my Ambition does not aspire to such Places.

You will be pleased to excuse the Liberty I have taken in this Intimation and to be assured that I am with the most profound Respect Your most obedient and very humble Servant

Hu. Williamson

ALS, DLC:GW.

From Carl Andreas Kierrulf

Monsieur le Président
Votre Excellence   Philadelphie ce 10 Dec. 1793

Pour m'annoncer digne de Votre faveur, j'ai crû le meilleur moÿen d'être de Vous donner le Tableau d'un Caracter dans les suivants Papiers, qui font voir mon Portrait, et mes ésperances de profiter de votre faveur.[1]

Un autre que moi, Vous fera plus des compliments: moi au contraire je Vous éstime au point de croire, que des mots vuides du sens ne conviennet pas à un Caracter si Grand, comme le Votre—Les faits, et la vérité toute nue, voila ce qui convient d'etre éntendû du premier homme de notre siècle—Une réputation si bien établie est au dessus de mes éloges, et n'en a pas besoin; et en Vous donnant justice, je ne fait que répeter les éxpressions des interressé des hommes à l'Estime universelle, qui se sont donné les premiers places dans la République des lettres—Je sais tout ce que l⟨'⟩Amérique, que tout le monde enfin, réspirant le Civisme, Vous doit: j'en suis charmé, et souhaite tous les succés en accord avec vos sentiments connûs, et vos vûês Patriotiques? Je récommande la contenûe de mon réquête dans Votre souvenir, et Vous demande comme juge de ma conduite et de mes pensées, étant avec le plus profond estime et dévouement Monsieur le Président de votre Excellence Le plus soumis serviteur

Charles André Kierrulf

ALS, DNA: RG 59, Miscellaneous Letters.

In a second letter to GW, undated but docketed in part "Decr 1793," Kierrulf described himself as a pensioner of Russian empress Catherine the Great, "suedois de nation, Republicain par principes, et Patriot par instinct," and asked for a meeting with GW (ALS, DNA: RG 59, Miscellaneous Letters). During the years 1789 to 1793, Carl Andreas Kierrulf (b. 1755) had authored several tracts opposing Gustav III of Sweden. Earlier in the year he had been arrested, and his arrival in America was in consequence of his expulsion from Sweden. In 1796 Kierrulf advertised in New York City that, having been a minister in his native country, he intended to publish "a Sermon in the English, French, and German Languages, of the True Doctrine of Jesus Christ our Redeemer." During the years 1795–96, Kierrulf spent time on the island of Saint Bartholomew, but otherwise he remained in the United States until late 1799, when the Swedish consul passed on reports that the "rascal" Kierrulf had departed for Sweden. Kierrulf's request to be repatriated was, however, rejected, and in 1803 he was in Russia (*Argus. Greenleaf's New Daily Advertiser* [New York], 17 Aug. 1796; Nils William Olsson, "Extracts from Early Swedish Consular Reports from the United States," *American Swedish Historical Foundation Yearbook* [1967], 35; Erik Wikén, "Prästmannen Carl Andreas Kierrulf," *Personhistorisk Tidskrift*, 83 [1987], 105–7; "Kjerrulf," *Svenskt Biografiskt Lexikon,* 32 vols. to date [Stockholm, Sweden, 1918—], 21:235).

1. The enclosed papers included a petition addressed to GW and Congress in which Kierrulf characterized himself as "Un *Martir* enfin de *la Liberté*," gave an extended account of his sufferings at the hands of kings and aristocrats in Sweden and elsewhere in Europe, and concluded by asking to be supported as a professor of moral philosophy: "Voila l'ab[r]egé de ma vie; car ma plus grande faute étoit de n'avoir pas voulû lire une Priere scandaleuse et prophane pour la Guerre la plus injuste da[n]s mes Eglises 1788 et 89 *Mr Le President* et *Mr Membres* de L'Assemblée Nationale. Quelle moyen donc de douter de Votre assistence? Ouvrer moi seulement une Carrière d'etrê utile et je payera mon séjour. Je sois Maitre ou *Docteur en Philosophie* depuis 1775 J'ai frequenté des Academies 10 années de suite. J'ai composé des dissertations Theologiques et Moraux—J'ai fait mes Etades dans la Philosophie

et la Politique, et cela selon les enseignements des premiers dans la Republique de Lettres, *Helvere, Montesquieu,* et l'Esprit des Anciens et Modernes Autheurs, ont pris l'ascendant sur mon Esprit; et je me sois formé après ces hommes aux lumières des qui Votre Grand Philosophe Franklin, a scû se faire un Guide et un Ange Tutelaire de cette Hemisphœre Libre. Je sçais Allemande, et ayant été engage dans les Offices Publiques en Resteur et Curé; je pourrois aussi y etrê employe. Encore, versé dans la Science la plus interressante, et d'une necessité absolue pour former des Citoyens, je m'offre pour enseigner publiquement en Latins et en Allemande La Philosophie Pratique ou la Morale d'une façon à etrê mis en ouvre comme raisonable, celeste, ravissante et d'une utilité réciproque dans la Societé. Je sçais qu'un Proffeseur de la Morale manque ici, je n'en sois point surpris; mais bien qu'on ne se donne pas la peine d'employer les hommes capables à former les hommes après les premiers modeles et selon leur destination pour dévenir bons et virteux Citoyens, et pas une bonté intrinseque de l'Ame dévenir propres pour la jouissance d'une autre vie, pour la quelle ils sont ici. Les Reflexions ici viennent en foule—mais pour finir, je m'addresse au Congress d'un Peuple Libre, aussi activ pour encourager les hommes sçavants qui viennent ici, que les *Egoistes,* les *Aristocrates,* les *hommes passions* et *L'Esprit Traitre Mercantile* se fait un plaisir de les impecher à s'établir, de les noircir, et de les abandonner à leur sort; insouciants du bien etrê de la Republique" (SwSR: Americana, vol. 1).

On 20 Dec. 1793 Secretary of State Thomas Jefferson wrote Kierrulf informing him that GW had "referred to me the letter you wrote him inclosing a paper addressed to Congress" and advising that he should direct his application to a member of Congress, as "the mode of conveying this paper to Congress . . . cannot be through the President" (*Jefferson Papers,* 27:595–96). Kierrulf had submitted the petition by 20 Feb. 1794, when the Swedish consul made a copy, but it did not come up in the House of Representatives until 7 April 1794, when it was tabled (*Journal of the House,* 6:242).

From Stephen Sayre

Sir.   [c.10 December 1793]

I do myself the honor of inclosing the Copy of a Letter, which I address'd to your Excellency, in 1789.[1]

I trouble you with it, to remind you, of having, long since, had some expectations of being employ'd, in an object, which, has for many years, occupy'd my thoughts & my time.

As Congress seem disposed to fulfill your expectations by building a certain number of Ships, for our defence; I beg to be brought into your remembrance, so as to have a fair opportunity of recommending myself, as able to conduct our naval force, be it what it may.

The Science of Ship building has been my favorite amusement—and during the late war, I found opportunity of making some experiments—I built two Ships in St Petersburg, of 1200 Tons each, which, tho' of pine timber, have made several Voyages to India—have proved strong—profitable as to freight, & swift sailors, tho' rigg'd with Masts & Spars, so as to require, only half the number of men, necessary for other Ships, of the same Tonnage. They were built, after my own draughts which I found, on comparing them with those of Mr Peck of Boston, exactly on the same principle—this he acknowledged, at our first interview—having never seen each other till after the war.[2]

Since that period, I have been, for some three weeks, in Plimouth, Portsmouth, & Chatham, employing every hour in observations on their Ships, their Dockyards &c. Were the United States to follow the same useless, and expensive mode, in our naval Establishments, they will find the Sums enormous.

I can build Frigates—costing no more than those of 36 guns, now in use in England, that shall defend themselves against those of 74 guns.

But since the Country must have a Navy, or rather some naval force for our immediate safety: I have communicated an improvement to General Knox—such as would, if press'd with danger, & the necessity of our utmost exertions, make us the only naval power on the Seas—*I can build Ships which cannot be taken by Ships now in use.*[3]

I am ready & wish for opportunity, to prove the fact to demonstration. I believe the General will tell your Excellency, if ask'd the question, that the fact appears evident the moment the principle is known. One days experiment will however decide the question. I am with great Respect your Excellenceys most sincere &c. &c.

Stephen Sayre

ALS, DNA: RG 59, Miscellaneous Letters. Although undated by Sayre, this letter carries a docket of "Decem. 1793" and is marked "File Dec. 10. 1793."

1. Sayre's letter to GW of 3 Jan. 1789 sought appointment as a commissioner to establish a naval force for the United States or as U.S. consul general for England. The enclosed copy evidently was made from a retained draft and differs somewhat from the letter sent to GW, but the basic content is the same (DNA: RG 59, Miscellaneous Letters).

2. Sayre arrived at St. Petersburg, Russia, in April 1780 and left in October 1781. While there, he wrote John Adams about his shipbuilding venture (see

Sayre to Adams, 21 Oct. [1 Nov.] 1780 and 30 Dec. 1780 [10 Jan. 1781], *Papers of John Adams*, 10:321–23; 11:36–39). John Peck (c.1726–1790), of Boston and later Kittery, built a number of ships during the Revolutionary War and was celebrated as a naval architect.

3. Sayre's communication to Henry Knox has not been identified. He wrote Knox again on 16 Dec., "asking a declaration, favouring the object I have lately communicated to you" and adding, "Have I not a right to expect you, to state this important improvement, as far as it strikes your understanding, and as far as prudence dictates, to the President of the United States. If Congress should resolve to build any number of ships, for our safety and defence, ought not the President to know, in time, that there is, in this City, a man who is capable of building them, on the highest stage of improvement?" (NNGL: Knox Papers). Knox replied to that letter on 18 Dec. offering to meet with Sayre (NNGL: Knox Papers).

Letter not found: to Robert Taylor, 10 Dec. 1793. On 30 Jan. 1794, Taylor wrote to GW: "I was favoured with two letters from you under date of the 10th and 17th December."

To the United States Senate

Gentlemen   [10 December 1793]

The pleasure, expressed by the Senate, on my reelection to the station, which I fill, commands my sincere and warmest acknowledgments. If this be an event, which promises the smallest addition to the happiness of our country, as it is my duty, so shall it be my study to realize the expectation.

The decided approbation, which the Proclamation now receives from your house, by completing the proof, that this measure is considered, as manifesting a vigilant attention to the welfare of the United States, brings with it a peculiar gratification to my mind.[1]

The other important subjects, which have been communicated to you, will, I am confident, receive a due discussion; and the result will, I trust, prove fortunate to the United States.

Go: Washington

ALS, CStbK; LB, DLC:GW. The ALS is undated. Although the letter-book copy is dated 9 Dec. 1793, GW delivered this message to senators on 10 Dec. (see U.S. Senate to GW, 9 Dec., n.1).

1. GW is referring to his Neutrality Proclamation of 22 April.

To Alexander Hamilton

Dear Sir,   Philadelphia 11th Decr 1793

I was led the other day to reflect, whether I had ever put into your hands the last, as well as the first letter, which A.G. Frauncis wrote to me concerning the Warrants.[1] Finding no trace of any remarks from you to me, I take it for granted, that I omitted to do with respect to the last, what I had done with respect to the first. But being uncertain, how far the new matter, which is suggested, may be thought worthy of your attention, I have concluded to forward it to you; and when you have read it, you will return it to Dear Sir Yours sincerely

Go: Washington

ALS, DLC: Alexander Hamilton Papers; LB, DLC:GW.

1. GW was referring to letters of 30 July and 19 August, in which Andrew G. Fraunces complained about Hamilton's role in the nonpayment of certain warrants for Revolutionary War debt held by Fraunces. For Hamilton's report on the first letter, see his letter to GW of 9 August.

Bartholomew Dandridge, Jr., to Thomas Jefferson

December the 11. 1793.

By the Presidents order Bw Dandridge has the honor to transmit the enclosed papers relating to the truce between Portugal & Algiers, to the Secretary of State[1]—& to inform the Secretary that the President wishes him to prepare such information respecting the same as may be necessary to be made public—and as considerable expence has been incurred in the conveyance of said intelligence to the Goverment of the U.S. to consider what communication shall be made thereupon to Congress.[2]

AL, DLC: Jefferson Papers; ADf, DNA: RG 59, Miscellaneous Letters; LB, DNA: RG 59, George Washington's Correspondence with His Secretaries of State. Jefferson endorsed this letter as "recd Dec. 10. 93," but GW's journal of proceedings confirms that 11 Dec. is the correct date (*JPP*, 266).

1. The enclosures, which Jefferson had submitted for GW's information on this date, included William Carmichael and William Short to Jefferson, 29 Sept., acknowledging letters and discussing their prior correspondence; Edward Church to Jefferson, 8 Oct., giving his opinion that England and Spain intend eventually to "Crush" the United States, and suggesting a commercial

agreement involving Portuguese wines and U.S. fish; Church to Jefferson, 12 Oct., reporting the truce between Portugal and Algiers; David Humphreys to Jefferson, 26 Sept., announcing his arrival at Gibraltar; and Humphreys to Jefferson, 6 and 8 Oct., both about the truce between Portugal and Algiers (*JPP*, 266; *Jefferson Papers*, 27:152–53, 161–63, 196–98, 220–23, 230–35).

2. Jefferson's report to GW on this subject, dated 14 Dec., probably was submitted on 15 December. GW conveyed that report to Congress on 16 December. The expense involved the charter of an express vessel (see Jefferson to Alexander Hamilton, 12 Dec., *Jefferson Papers*, 27:507).

From Henry Knox

Sir. War Department, December 11th 1793.

I have the honor to submit to you, some new propositions from the Six Nations of Indians, relatively to boundaries; and a Map, by which they explain their meaning, by black lines drawn up the River Muskinghum, and round certain spots at the mouth of the Scioto, Fort Washington, and General Clark's Trace at the falls—And, I also submit two journals.[1] I have the honor to be, Sir, with the highest respect, Your most obedt Servt

H. Knox

LS, DLC:GW; LB, DLC:GW.

1. The map has not been identified. The journals were most likely the records of proceedings of the councils at Buffalo Creek on 8 and 10 Oct. (see *ASP, Indian Affairs*, 1:477–78). Israel Chapin wrote Knox on this date to clarify the Indians' views, which were "imperfect, as stated in the written account of the proceedings." The Indians, Chapin wrote, had "agreed to propose a boundary line, which should comprehend all the settlements made by the people of the United States over the Ohio, together with the whole of the land eastward of Muskingham as high up as the portage from the head of this river to Cayahoga, and southward of a line running from that portage to the Pennsylvania line, northward and eastward of Venango: as marked in the map which they gave me, & which I have delivered to you. The detached spots marked on the map along the Ohio, appearing small, and not to comprehend all our settlements, I asked the Chiefs for an explanation. They then said, that it was meant to comprehend all our settlements, with good pieces of land about them, so as to make good farms for the settlers. With respect to the grant to Genl Clarke, they appeared to mean that the whole of that land should be confirmed, for him & his warriors" (NHi: Henry O'Reilly Papers). For Knox's reply to the Indians of 24 Dec., see Knox to GW, 23 Dec., n.1. General Clark's Trace was a route between Post Vincennes and the Rapids of the Ohio River made during George Rogers Clark's Wabash campaign of 1786 (see "Denny Journal," 313).

To Thomas Pinckney

Dear Sir,   Philadelphia 12th Decr 1793

You would oblige me by giving the letter & Roll herewith sent for Mr Young a safe, and as speedy a conveyance as you can, without saddling him with Postage.[1]

Although I believe the enclosd letter from Mr Keith Wray is little more than the child of imagination, I would notwithstanding, thank you for directing one of your domestics to enquire into the truth of the information which it contains.[2]

This letter will be handed to you by Mr Willm Morris, third Son of Mr Robt Morris, to whom for domestic occurances of a private nature, I shall refer you—those of another kind you will, of course receive from the Secretary of State.

I pray you to offer my best respects, in which Mrs Washington joins to Mrs Pinckney & accept assurances of the sincere esteem & regd with which I am &ca

Go: W——n

ADfS, DLC:GW; LB, DLC:GW.

1. See GW to Arthur Young, this date, and n.2 to that document.

2. The enclosure, which has not been identified, concerned a box that supposedly had been lodged for GW at a banker's house in London. Pinckney reported the results of his investigation in his letter to GW of 1 Feb. 1795. Keith Wray, whom Pinckney describes as a wharfinger, appears in the London directories of this period as a merchant at 6 Tower Dock.

To Arthur Young

Sir,   Philadelphia 12th Decembr 1793

I wrote to you three months ago, or more, by my late secretary and friend, Mr Lear;[1] but as his departure from this Country for Great Britain, was delayed longer than he or I expected, it is at least probable that that letter will not have reached your hands at a much earlier period than the one I am now writing.

At the time it was written, the thoughts which I am now about to disclose to you were not even in embryo; and whether, in the opinion of others, there be impropriety, or not, in communicating the object which has given birth to them, is not for me to decide. My own mind reproaches me with none, but if yours should view the subject differently, burn this letter and the draught which accompanies it, and the whole matter will be consigned to oblivion.

All my landed property East of the Apalachian Mountains is under Rent, except the Estate called Mount Vernon. This, hitherto, I have kept in my own hands; but from my present situation; from my advanced time of my life; from a wish to live free from care, and as much at my ease as possible during the remainder of it; & from other causes which are not necessary to detail, I have, latterly, entertained serious thoughts of letting this estate also—reserving the mansion house farm for my own residence—occupation—and amusement in agriculture—provided I can obtain what in my own judgment, and in the opinion of others whom I have consulted the low Rent which I shall mention hereafter—& provided also I can settle it with *good* farmers.

The quantity of ploughable land (including meadows)—the relative situation of the farms to one another; and the division of these farms into seperate inclosures; with the quantity & situation of the Woodland appertaining to the tract, will be better delineated by the sketch herewith sent (which is made from actual surveys, subject nevertheless to revision & correction) than by a volume of words.[2]

No estate in United America is more pleasantly situated than this—It lyes in a high, dry & healthy country, 300 miles by water from the Sea—and, as you will see by the plan, on one of the finest Rivers in the world. Its margin is washed by more than ten miles of tidewater; from the bed of which, and the enumerable coves, inlets & small marshes with which it abounds, an inexhaustable fund of rich mud may be drawn as a manure; either to be used seperately, or in a compost, according to the Judgment of the farmer. It is situated in a latitude between the extremes of heat & cold, and is the same distance by land & water, with good roads & the best navigation (to &) from the Federal City, Alexandria & George town; distant from the first twelve, from the second nine, and from the last sixteen miles. The federal City in the year 1800, will become the seat of the general Goverment of the United States. It is increasing fast in buildings, and rising into consequence; and will, I have no doubt, from the advantages given to it by nature, and its proximity to a rich interior country and the western territory, become the emporium of the United States.

The Soil of the tract I am speaking, is a good loam, more inclined however to Clay than sand. From use, and I might add abuse, it is become more & more consolidated, and of course heavier to work. The *greater* part is a greyish clay—some part is a dark mould—a very little is inclined to sand—and scarcely any to stone. A husbandmans wish would not lay the farms more level than they are, and yet some of the fields (but in no great degree) are washed into gullies, from which all of them have not, as yet, been recovered.

This River, which encompasses the land the distance above-mentioned, is well supplied with various kinds of fish at all seasons of the year; and in the Spring with the greatest profusion of Shad, Herring, Bass, Carp, Perch, Sturgeon &ca. Several valuable fisheries appertain to the estate; the whole shore in short is one entire fishery.

There are, as you will perceive by the plan, four farms besides that at the Mansion house: these four contain 3260 acres of cultivable land—to which some hundreds more, adjoining, as may be seen, might be added, if a greater quantity should be required—but as they were never designed for, so neither can it be said they are calculated to suit tenants of either the first, or of the lower class; because those who have strength & resources proportioned to farms of from 500 to 1200 acres[3] (which these contain) would hardly be contented to live in such houses as are there on—and if they were to be divided and subdivided, so as to accomodate tenants of small means—say from 50 to one or 200 acres, there would be none; except on the lots which might happen to include the present dwelling houses of my Overlookers (called Bailiffs with you), Barns, & Negro Cabins. Nor would I chuse to have the woodland (already too much pillaged of its timber) ransacked for the purpose of building many more. The soil, howevr, is excellent for Bricks, or for Mud walls; and to the buildings of such houses there wd be no limitation, nor to that of thatch for the cover of them. The towns already mentioned (to those who might incline to encounter the expence) are able to furnish scantling, plank and shingles to any amount, and on reasonable terms; and they afford a ready market also for the produce of the land.

On what is called Union farm (containing 928 acres of arable & Meadow) there is a newly erected Brick Barn equal perhaps to any in America, & for conveniences of all sorts particularly for sheltering & feeding horses, cattle &ca scarcely to be exceeded any where. A new house is now building in a central position, not far from the Barn, for the Overlooker; which will have two Rooms 16 by 18 feet below and one or two above nearly of the same size. Convenient thereto is sufficient accomodation for fifty odd Negroes (old & young); but these buildings might not be thought good enough for the workmen, or day labourers of your Country. Besides these, a little without the limits of the farm (as marked in the Plan) are one or two other houses very pleasantly situated; and which, in case this farm should be divided into two (as it formerly was) would answer well for the Eastern division. The buildings thus enumerated are all that stand on the premises.

Dogue run farm (650 acres) has a small but new building for the Overlooker—one room only below, and the same above, about 16 by 20 each; decent and comfortable for its size. It has also covering for forty odd negroes, similar to what is mentioned on Union farm. It has a new circular barn now finishing on a new construction; well calculated, it is conceived, for getting grain out of the straw more expeditiously than in the usual mode of threshing. There are good sheds also erecting, sufficient to cover 30 work horses and Oxen.

Muddy hole farm (476 acres) has a house for the Overlooker, in size & appearance, nearly like that at Dogue run; but older[4]. The same kind of covering for about thirty negroes—and a tolerable good barn, with stables for the work horses.

River farm which is the largest of the four, and seperated from the others by little hunting Creek (contains 1207 acres of ploughable land)—has an Overlookers Ho. of one large & two small rooms below, and one or two above; sufficient covering for 50 or 60 Negroes like those beforementioned. A large barn & stables (gone much to decay, but will be replaced next year with new ones).

I have deemed it necessary to give this detail of the buildings that a precise idea might be had of the conveniences and inconveniences of them; and I believe the recital is just in all its parts. The Inclosures are precisely, and accurately delineated in the plan; & the fences now are, or soon will be, in respectable order.

I would let these four farms to four substantial farmers, of wealth & strength sufficient to cultivate them; and who would insure to me the regular payment of the Rents; and I would give them leases for seven or ten years, at the rate of a spanish milled dollar, or other money current at the time, in this country, equivalent thereto, for every acre of ploughable & mowable ground within the Inclosures of the respective farms, as marked in the plan; and would allow the tenants during that period to take fuel; and use timber from the Woodland to repair the buildings and to keep the fences in order; until live fences could be substituted in place of dead ones; but in this case no subtenants would be allowed.

Or if these farms are adjudged too large, and the Rents of course too heavy for such farmers as might incline to emigrate, I should have no insuperable objection against dividing each into as many small ones as a society of them, formed for the purpose, could agree upon among themselves; even if it shd be by the fields as they are now arranged (which the plan would enable them to do)—provided such buildings as they would be content with, should be erected at their own expence,[5] in the manner already mentioned. In which case as in the former, fuel, & timber for repairs, would be allowed; but as an inducement to parcel out my grounds into such small tenements, and to compensate me at the sametime for the greater consumption of fuel & timber, & for the trouble and expence of collecting small Rents, I should expect a quarter of a dollar pr acre in addition to what I have already mentioned. But in order to make these small farms more valuable to the occupants, and by way of reimbursing them for the expence of their establishment thereon, I would grant them leases for 15 or 18 years; although I have weighty objections[6] to the measure, founded on my own experience of the disadvantage it is to the Lessor, in a Country where lands are rising every year in value. As an instance in proof, about 20 years ago I gave leases for three lives, in land I held above the blue Mountain, near the Shanondoah River, Seventy miles from Alexandria or any shipping port, at a Rent of one shilling pr Acre (no part being then cleared) and now land of similar quality in the vicinity, with very trifling improvements thereon, is renting currently at five & more shillings pr acre & even as high as 8/.[7]

My motives for letting this estate having been avowed, I will add, that the whole (except the Mansion house farm) or none, will be parted with, and that upon unequivocal terms; because my object is to fix my income (be it what it may) upon a solid basis in the hands of *good* farmers; because I am not inclined to make a medley of it;[8] and above all, because I could not relinquish my present course without a moral certainty of the substitute which is contemplated: for to break up these farms—remove my Negroes—and to dispose of the property on them upon terms short of this would be ruinous.

Having said thus much, I am disposed to add further, that it would be in my power, and certainly it would be my inclination (upon the principal above) to accomodate the wealthy, or the weak handed farmer (and upon reasonable terms) with draught horses, & working mules & Oxen; with cattle, Sheep & Hogs; and with such impliments of husbandry if they should not incline to bring them themselves, as are in use on the farms. On the four farms there are 54 draught horses, 12 working Mules,[9] and a sufficiency of Oxen, broke to the yoke—the precise number I am unable at this moment to ascertain as they are comprehended in the agregate of the black cattle. Of the latter there are 317. Of sheep 634 of hogs many, but as these run pretty much at large in the Woodland (which is all under fence) the number is uncertain. Many of the Negroes, male & female, might be hired by the year as labourers, if this should be preferred to the importation of that class of people; but it deserves consideration how far the mixing of whites & blacks together is advisable; especially where the former, are entirely unacquainted[10] with the latter.

If there be those who are disposed to take these farms in their undevided state, on the terms which have been mentioned; it is an object of sufficient magnitude for them, or one of them in behalf of the rest, to come over & investigate the premises thoroughly, that there may be nothing to repro[ac]h themselves or me with if (though unintentionally) there should be defects in any part of the information herein given—or if a society of farmers are disposed to adventure, it is still more incumbent on them to send over an Agent for the purposes abovementioned: for with me the measure must be so fixed as to preclude any cavil or discussion thereafter. And it may not be malapropos to observe in this place, that our Overlookers are generally engaged, & all the arrangements for the ensuing Crops are made before the first of September in every year; it will readily be perceived then, that if this period is suffered to pass away, it is not to be regained until the next year. Possession might be given to the Newcomers at the Season just mentioned to enable them to put in their grain for the next Crop; but the final relinquishment could not take place until the Crops are gathered; which, of Indian Corn (maiz) seldom happens 'till toward Christmas as it must endure hard frosts before it can be safely housed.

I have endeavoured as far as my recollection of facts would enable me, or the documents in my possession allow, to give such information of the actual state of the farms as to enable persons at a distance to form as distinct ideas as the nature of the thing is susceptible short of ones own view. and having communicated the motives which have inclined me to a change in my System, I will announce to you the origin of them.

First—Few Ships, of late, have arrived from any part of G: Britain or Ireland without a number of emigrants, and some of them, by report, very respectable & full handed farmers. A number of others, they say, are desirous of following; but are unable to obtain passages; but their coming in that manner, even if I was apprised of their arrival in time, would not answer my views for the reason already assigned—and which, as it is the ultimatum at present, I will take the liberty of repeating—namely— that I must carry my plan into *complete* execution, or not attempt it; and under such auspices too as to leave no doubt of the exact fulfilment—and

2dly because from the number of letters which I have received myself (& as it would seem from respectible people) enquiring into matters of this sort, with intemations of their wishes and even intention of migrating to this County, I can have no doubt of succeeding[11]—But I have made no reply to these enquiries, or if any, in very general terms, because I did not want to engage in corrispondences of this sort with persons of whom I had no knowledge, nor indeed leizure for them if I had been so disposed.

I shall now conclude as I began, with a desire, that if you see any impropriety in making these sentiments known[12] to that class of people who might wish to avail themselves of the occasion, that it may be mentioned.[13] By a law, or by some regulation of your government, Artizans I am well aware, are laid under

restraints; and for this reason I have studiously avoided any overtures to Mechanics although my occasions called for them—But
never having heard that difficulties were thrown in the way of
Husbandmen by the Government, is one reason for my bringing
this matter to your view—a 2d is, that having, yourself expressed
sentiments which shewed that you had cast an eye towards this
Country, & was not inattentive to the welfare of it, I was led to
make my intentions known to you, that if you, or your friends
were disposed to avail yourselves of the knowledge, you might
take prompt measures for the execution. and 3dly I was sure if
you had lost sight of the object yourself, I could, nevertheless rely
upon such information as you might see fit to give me, and upon
such characters too as you might be disposed to recommend.

Lengthy as this epistle is, I will crave you patience while I add,
that it is written in too much haste, and under too great a pressure of public business at the commencement of an important
session of Congress to be correct or properly digested. But the
season of the year & the apprehension of Ice are hurrying away
the last vessel bound from this Port to London. I am driven
therefore to the alternative of making the matter known in this
hasty manner, & giving a rude sketch of the farms, which is the
subject of it—or to encounter delay, the first I preferred. It can
hardly be necessary to add, that, I have *no* desire that any formal promulgation of these sentiments should be made.[14] To accomplish my wishes, in the manner herein expressed would be
agreeable to me, and in a way that cannot be exceptionable wd
be more so. With much estm & regd—I am—Sir Yr Most Obedt
Servt

Go: Washington

ALS, PPRF; ADfS, DLC:GW; Copy, in Bartholomew Dandridge, Jr.'s writing,
ViMtvL; LB, DLC:GW. GW made many revisions on the ADfS, the most significant of which are reported in the notes below.

1. See GW to Young, 1 September.

2. The enclosed sketch was a version of the map reproduced as Fig. 3, with
somewhat variant reference notes. It also was the basis of the printed map
published in *Letters from His Excellency General Washington, to Arthur Young, Esq.
F.R.S. : Containing an account of his husbandry, with a map of his farm; his opinions
on various questions in agriculture; and many particulars of the rural economy of the
United States* (London, 1801), facing p. 1. The printed map is shown in this
volume as Fig. 2.

3. An insertion marked on the draft here specifies "of ploughable land."

Fig. 2. "A map of General Washington's farm of Mount Vernon from a transmitted drawing by the General," in *Letters from His Excellency General Washington, to Arthur Young, Esq. F.R.S., containing An Account of His Husbandry, with a Map of His Farm; His Opinions on Various Questions in Agriculture; and Many Particulars of the Rural Economy of the United States* (London, 1801). (Library of Congress, Geography and Map Division.)

...ght be formed. — The greater
...of it is already reclaimed—
...it. -

...cleared and in cultivation,
...tleman's seat. -

...ould be sub-divided, it might
...f the River.

A Map of General Washington's Farm, of MOUNT VERNON from A Drawing transmitted by the General?

Road to Alexandria 9 Miles from Mt Vernon

E

Scale
100   200   300

Field No 7
150 Acres

Field No 5
130 Acres

Field No 4
155 Acres

E

Field No 6

RIVER FARM

C

D

Common Pasture, about
211 Acres

Field No 2

Field No 3

A

C

RIVER

LITTLE HUNTING

4. On the draft, GW initially continued this sentence with the words "and not quite as good," but he struck that phrase.

5. At this point on the draft, GW substituted the words that complete this sentence for several lines that he initially had written but struck out: "materials for which, and on moderate terms are to ⟨*illegible*⟩ be had from the market Towns already mentioned and at which they would find a ready sale for the produce of their farms—If they could accomodate themselves with houses made of Brick Clay or Clay made with their own hands or at their own expense there would be no limitation to the number nor to the straw necessary to thatch them—and"

6. GW initially wrote on the draft that he had "an almost insuperable objection," but he revised the sentence.

7. GW was referring to his lands in Berkeley County, Va. (now Jefferson County, W.Va.). In 1789 nine Berkeley County lots were under lease for three lives (Ledger B, 281–85). All of these leases were made between 1769 and 1776, and only the most recent, that of Samuel Bailey at £10 for 183 acres, called for a rent of more than a shilling per acre (see List of Tenants, 18 Sept. 1785, and source note and notes 1–8, *Papers, Confederation Series*, 3:256–61).

8. On the draft, GW wrote: "medley of the business, i.e., renting some & keeping others."

9. An asterisk is placed at this point on the draft to suggest insertion of the phrase "since increased to 30."

10. The draft and both copies use the word "unaccustomed" instead of "unacquainted."

11. See, for example, Lory to GW, 27 Dec. 1790; Hugh O'Connor to GW, 22 Sept. 1791; Robert Sinclair to GW, 12 Dec. 1791; and Heinrich Matthias Marcard to GW, 5 Aug. 1793.

12. On the draft, GW initially continued at this point with "in a manner liable to no exception in your own ju," but he struck that text. He then placed similar sentiments following "avail themselves of"—writing "it (& I will add in a manner unexceptionable)"—but he struck that text as well.

13. The draft and both copies have "may never be mentioned" here. Young's reply of 2 June 1794 assured GW that there was no impropriety in the request.

14. Young's reply of 2 June 1794 reported that he had found little interest in "*hiring* in America tho' very many were eager to become proprietors there." He did, however, state that were it not for the passage "which precludes my taking any publick step to procure such tenants as you describe," he would have "little doubt" of success (DLC:GW).

Bartholomew Dandridge, Jr., to Henry Knox

13 Decemr 1793

By the Presidents command Bw Dandridge has the honor to send to the Secretary of War—a Letter from the Govr of North

Carolina, of 26 Nov. 93 to the President, covering depositions respecting the Spanish prize carried into Wilmington by Capt Hervieux—& to inform the Secretary that the President wishes him to take such measures thereupon as may seem to him adviseable.[1]

ADf, DLC:GW; LB, DLC:GW.

1. The enclosed letter and depositions have not been found. For information about the *San Josef,* carried into Wilmington as prize of the French privateer *L'Aimée Marguerite,* see Richard Dobbs Spaight to GW, 21 Oct., and n.3.

From Henry Knox

War Department December 13th 1793

The Secretary of War respectfully submits to the President of the United States the following statement relatively to the South Western Frontiers of the United States as connected with the State of Georgia and the Creek Indians and the Territory of the United States South of the Ohio and the Cherokee Indians.

That in the month of November 1792. James Seagrove a temporary Agent held a conference with the lower Creeks, at which were present upwards of One thousand Men, Women, and Children. That the objects of this conference were to confirm the treaty which had been made with them at New York and by administering to their necessities, they being greatly in want of Corn & Clothing to attach them more firmly to the interest of the United States.[1]

That as the said Indians expressed themselves with great gratitude for the kindness they received, a hope was indulged that beneficial consequences would flow from the measure, especially as it was directed that the said Agent should repair both to the lower and upper Creek Towns in order to tranquillize their minds upon past, and prevent any misconceptions respecting the future conduct of the United States.

But on the eleventh day of March these prospects were clouded by a party of about thirty of the Seminoles (some of them living to the Southward of the Territory of the United States) who plundered a store upon the St Mary's River of a large quantity of goods and killed several persons.[2]

This outrage being followed by some others excited a general alarm on the frontiers of Georgia. The Governor of that State called into service considerable bodies of Militia, Horse, and Foot for the protection of the exposed inhabitants.

That upon the receiving information of the aforesaid event, the President on the 30th of May directed that the Governor of Georgia should be informed that from considerations of policy at this critical period relative to foreign powers and during the pending Treaty with the Northern Indians, it was deemed adviseable for the present to avoid offensive expeditions into the Creek Country. But that from the circumstances of the recent depredations on the frontiers of Georgia, it was thought expedient to increase the force in that quarter for defensive purposes, and therefore the Governor was authorized to call into service in aid of the Continental Troops One hundred horse and one hundred foot of the Militia of the said State.

That as it did not appear that the whole of the Creek Nation were disposed for or engaged in hostility, it was considered that the above force was sufficient for the purposes designated.

That the case of a serious invasion of Georgia by large bodies of Indians must be referred to the provisions of the Constitution.[3]

That on the 10th of June the Governor of South Carolina was requested to afford aid to Georgia, in case that it should be seriously invaded by large bodies of Indians.[4]

That a Magazine of two thousand Arms and a proportionable quantity of Ammunition and some other military Stores have been established in Georgia as a provisional measure in case the said State should be invaded, the said articles in that event being subject to the order of the Governor.

That on the 12th of June the Governor transmitted information of an intended expedition into the Creek Country, to consist of a body of about Seven hundred Volunteers and on the 18th of the same month he transmitted the result thereof, by which it appeared that the said Volunteers commanded by General Twiggs proceeded to the Oakmulgie, about forty miles distant from the Oconnee and from circumstances of their provisions being nearly exhausted, many horses tired[5] and other adverse events they returned on the 12th of the Month.[6]

That on the 13th of August the Governor transmitted information that he had convened a Council of General Officers on the subject of reducing the five inimical Towns in the Creek Nation; the propositions to, with the answers of the Council he transmitted for the purpose of being laid before the President of the United States.[7] That in an answer to the said letter dated the 5th September, the Governor was informed that as an offensive expedition against the Creeks of the nature and under the circumstances mentioned was a subject of great and complicated importance to the United States, it had engaged the serious consideration of the President, and as the deliberate result thereof he utterly disapproved the measure at that time as being unauthorized by law—as contrary to the present state of affairs, and as contrary to the instructions heretofore given upon the subject.[8]

That on the 2d of October the Governor transmitted the information of Two Officers who commanded an expedition against a Creek Town which they surprized on the 21st of September and killed Six Warriors and took eight Women and Children Prisoners.[9]

That it appears from the representations of James Seagrove that the Indian Town which was surprized as before mentioned on the 21st of September was situated on the Chatahoochee River and called "The little Oakfuskie" that the people belonging to it were among the most friendly of the Creeks and no way concerned in stealing of Horses, they being under the direction of the White Lieutenant.[10]

That it has been the opinion of James Seagrove communicated in his various dispatches, that notwithstanding the outrage of the 11th of March last and the subsequent Conduct of some of the Banditti that the main body of the Creek Nation are desirous of remaining at peace with the United States. That in pursuance of his directions from the President of the United States and his own opinion he had been endeavouring for some months past to make arrangements to go into the Creek Nation for the purpose of obtaining the punishment of the Banditti Indians who have committed the outrages aforesaid and of more closely attaching the Creeks to the United States.

That he had made an agreement to meet a number of friendly Indians on the Oakmulgie River about the 30th of September and with them to proceed into the Indian Towns for the purposes aforesaid. But the expedition of the 21st of September and the violent threats of a number of lawless Whites on the frontiers of Georgia had prevented him. Some of these people appear to oppose every effort for peace and ardently desire a War.

That by his letter of the 21st October it appears that two parties were preparing to go to War against the Creeks, the result of which has not yet been known.[11]

That the information of the Governor of Georgia to James Seagrove dated the 26th of August last, to wit "that under the law of the United States as well as for the security of this state, the government of Georgia cannot recognize the establishment of peace without having Commissioners at the Treaty" is a matter which requires serious notice.[12]

It is to be observed that the Governor of Georgia has not organized the hundred horse and hundred Militia foot, which he was authorized to do by the President on the 30th May last; but instead thereof he has kept up considerable bodies of mounted Volunteers of the Militia, of which no Returns have been received; but which perhaps may be nearly or quite five hundred Men. The payment of these troops will probably amount to a very large sum of Money, and it may become a question of importance whether the United States are responsible for their payment; the circumstances of the case being duly considered.

It is suggested in the papers which accompany this statement, that it is highly probably that it is owing to some of these troops that Mr Seagrove has been hitherto restrained from adjusting amicably the causes of difference with the Creek Nation; and also probably that it was a part of them who surprized the little Oakfuskie Town.

From a review of the representations contained in the letters of James Seagrove, Major Gaither (the commanding Officer) and Constant Freeman herewith submitted, it will appear that the Creeks are generally disposed for peace, but that there is too much reason to apprehend that the unjustifiable conduct of certain lawless Whites on the frontiers of Georgia will prevent that desireable event from being realized.[13]

The present state of this part of the frontier involves national considerations of great magnitude—whether viewed as relative to the expence which has been incurred during the the past summer, of which payment will most probably be demanded of the United States—whether with regard to the claims of the Governor of Georgia of a right of interference in any treaty with the Creeks, which is presumed to be contrary to the Constitution of the United States—or whether with regard to a War with the powerful tribes of the Creeks, with the long and almost unlimited train of collateral and consequent evils attendant thereon—a measure which perhaps may be avoided, if means could be devised to keep the bold and turbulent of both sides in order.

Of the Territory of the United States South West
of the Ohio and the Cherokees.

That it will appear from the papers relative to the Cherokees on the files of Congress that in the Year 1792 a partial disposition for war existed among the Cherokees being chiefly confined to the five lower Towns so called embracing to the utmost one third of that Nation or Six hundred and fifty Warriors.[14]

That however by the abilities and assiduity of Governor Blount this disposition in the commencement of the Year was greatly changed and the said five Towns were supposed to be desirous of an accomodation.

That while this business was negociating a party of armed Men under Captain John Beard, who had been called into service by Governor Blount—with a view of protecting the Settlers, did on the 12th of June in defiance of their orders cross the Tennessee and surprize and kill a number of our best friends among the Indians at the moment Governor Blounts messengers were among them.[15]

This violent outrage, so disgraceful to the United States, has been followed by several others and the South Western Territory is involved in a War with the Cherokees which as it relates to the above event must be considered as highly unjust. It is to be apprehended and regretted that from the prejudice against Indians on the frontiers, it is but too probable that the perpretators of these violences will escape unpunished—Such measures, as the laws authorize, have been directed,[16] but as yet no result has been transmitted.

Great bodies of Militia have been brought into service on this occasion in order to guard against the effects of savage retaliation. Much expence has been already incurred nor is it yet terminated. For however hostilities shall be restrained by the severity of the Winter yet they may be expected to break out with renewed violence in the spring.

The evil seems to require a remedy. But no Indian peace will be permanent unless an effectual mode can be devised to punish the Violators of it on both sides. It will be with an ill grace that the United States demand the punishment of Banditti Indians, when at the same time the guilty Whites escape with impunity. All which is respectfully submitted

H. Knox
secy of war

DS (letterpress copy), DNA: RG 233, Third Congress, 1793–95, House Records of the Office of the Clerk, Records of Reports from Executive Departments; Copy, DNA: RG 233, Third Congress, 1793–95, House Records of the Office of the Clerk, Records of Reports from Executive Departments. Knox submitted the DS to Congress in a communication of 16 Dec. "giving a view of the Southwestern frontiers, as connected with the Creeks and the State of Georgia, and the Southwestern territory of the United States and the Cherokees." That communication, including this letter, is printed in *ASP, Indian Affairs*, 1:361–468.

1. For the Treaty of New York, 7 Aug. 1790, see Kappler, *Indian Treaties*, 2:25–29. James Seagrove reported that the conference "hath gone favorable, beyond my most sanguine expectation. . . . Peace and friendship with the United States they confirm, and declare pointedly against joining the Northern tribes, or any others, *red* or *white*, against us" (Seagrove to Knox, 22 Nov. 1792, *ASP, Indian Affairs*, 1:336).

2. For reports of this raid, see Edward Telfair to Knox, 3 April, and Seagrove to Knox, 17 March, *ASP, Indian Affairs*, 1:368, 373–74.

3. For Knox's letter of 30 May to Georgia Governor Telfair, see, *ASP, Indian Affairs*, 1:364.

4. For Knox's letter of 10 June to South Carolina Governor William Moultrie, see *ASP, Indian Affairs*, 1:366.

5. The copyist wrote "died."

6. For Telfair's letters to Knox of 12 and 18 June, see *ASP, Indian Affairs*, 369–70. John Twiggs (1750–1816), a Richmond County planter and businessman, had been a Georgia militia officer since the Revolutionary War and ranked at this time as major general.

7. For Telfair's letter to Knox of 13 Aug. and the enclosed report of the council of general officers of 8 Aug., see *ASP, Indian Affairs*, 1:370–71.

8. For Knox's letter to Telfair of 5 Sept., see *ASP, Indian Affairs*, 1:365.

9. For Telfair's letter to Knox of 2 Oct. and the enclosed reports to Telfair by Lt. Col. William Melton, 26 Sept., and Capt. Jonas Fauche, 28 Sept., see *ASP, Indian Affairs*, 1:372–73.

10. This information appeared in Seagrove's letter to Knox of 9 Oct. (*ASP, Indian Affairs*, 1:411–12).

11. Seagrove's letters to Knox of 17 March; 19 and 30 April; 24 May; 14 June; 6 and 31 July; 13 and 21 Aug.; 3, 5, 6, and 17–22 Sept.; and 9, 14, and 21 Oct., with their various enclosures, appear in *ASP, Indian Affairs*, 1:373–417.

12. This quotation comes from William Urquhart's letter (on behalf of Governor Telfair) to Seagrove of 26 Sept., not 26 Aug. (see *ASP, Indian Affairs*, 1:412).

13. For Maj. Henry Gaither's letters to Knox of 7, 17, and 19 April; 6 and 23 May; 9, 11, and 14 June; 15 and 20 July; 28 Aug.; 3 and 23 Sept.; and 11 Oct., with enclosures, see *ASP, Indian Affairs,* 1:417–25. For letters to Knox of 4, 11, 18, and 25 Sept. and 2, 7, 14, and 21 Oct. from Capt. Constant Freeman, Jr., who had been sent to Georgia in July as a War Department agent, see *ASP, Indian Affairs,* 1:425–29.

14. Knox apparently was referring to the enclosures of Charles Pinckney to GW, 30 Sept. 1792, which were enclosed by Knox to the House of Representatives on 7 Nov. 1792 and to the Senate on 21 Nov. 1792 (*ASP, Indian Affairs,* 1:225, 316–17).

15. For reports of this event, see Knox to GW, 16 July, and n.1 to that document. John Beard (Baird), who was commissioned a captain of militia in 1790 and 1792, represented Knox County in the territorial general assembly, 1794–95.

16. See Knox to William Blount, 26 Aug. (*ASP, Indian Affairs,* 1:430–31).

From Nicholas Pariset

Sir   Trenton [N.J.] December 13th 1793.

I flatter myself with a hope that you will pardon the liberty I have taken to dedicate to your Excellency this Small performance.[1] my labour Shall be amply rewarded if it meets with Your Excellency's approbation.

I purpose presenting it to the Congress for their acceptance as the "Book of the Discipline of the Cavalry of the United States." I am with great Respect, Your Excellency's Most obedient humble servant

Nas Pariset

ALS, DLC:GW. The docket for this letter reads in part, "13th Dec. 1792," but 1793 is evidently the correct date.

1. Pariset was referring to *The American Trooper's Pocket Companion: Being a Concise and Comprehensive System of Discipline for the Cavalry of the United States,* which he published at Trenton in 1793. The dedication, which appears in the form of a letter to GW, dated "December, 1793," reads: "NOTHING could justify my Temerity in offering to your EXCELLENCY a Work so little proportioned to your enlightened Talents in the Art of War, but your EXCELLENCY's known Disposition to patronize every well-meant Endeavour.—My Presumption in presenting it to the Public proceeds solely from Devotion and Zeal for the Service of my Fellow-Citizens of the United States.

"The Utility of an invariable and uniform Plan of Exercise and Discipline for the rising Cavalry of the States, appeared to me obvious.—Assisted by some Years Experience in that Service, I have presumed to digest a System, as concise and comprehensive as a Subject so extensive in itself would permit.— Should this my present Performance fail of receiving your EXCELLENCY's Approbation (which to me would be above all other Eulogium) I flatter myself that your EXCELLENCY will pardon me in favour of the Motive that induced me to undertake it."

From Thomas Jefferson

Dec. 14. 1793.

Th: Jefferson has the honor to inform the President that the Spanish papers are now all ready. he sends him a set for his examination & will send two others Monday morning. he also sends the draught of the message he would propose, with the blank filled up which had been left in it whenever the President is satisfied about it, either with or without amendments, Th: J. will have copies made out.[1]

The Algerine papers will not be ready till tomorrow when they shall be submitted to the examination of the President.[2]

AL, DNA: RG 59, Miscellaneous Letters; LB, DNA: RG 59, George Washington's Correspondence with His Secretaries of State.

1. Jefferson sent a draft for GW's first message to the United States Senate and House of Representatives of 16 Dec. (see *Jefferson Papers*, 27:519–20). The day in the dateline is left blank on Jefferson's draft. The "Spanish papers" were the enclosures with that message. The next Monday was 16 December.

2. For Jefferson's report on Algiers, see the enclosure to GW's second message to the U.S. Senate and House of Representatives of 16 December.

From Henry Knox

Sir,   War Department December 14th 1793.

I have the honor to submit a Return of the Ordnance, Arms and Military stores in possession of the United States.[1]

It resulted from the casual circumstances of the late War, that these stores were accumulated principally at the following points, Viz: New London in Virginia[2]—Philadelphia—West Point on Hudsons river—and Springfield on Connecticut River; all of which perhaps, excepting Springfield, are improper places for permanent Magazines.

The important characteristics for magazines and arsenals, seem to be perfect security against enemies, internal and external, blended with an easy access by water. The expence of land transportation of heavy articles for a series of years, compared with that by water, renders the latter quality indispensible for a Magazine.

The Situation of New London being destitute of Water communication with the Ocean, is not a proper place for a permanent magazine, and it would seem therefore necessary that some other position should be sought on James River, more suitable for the erection of proper buildings.

It may be questionable whether a populous City is a proper place for the repository of large quantities of Military stores on account of the accidents to which such places are liable by fire and other causes. Hence it is intended that a part of the stores now deposited in Philadelphia shall be removed to some safe position, higher up the Delaware.

West Point on Hudson River, although a precious link in the chain which binds the States together, has on account of the well known navigation of that river, and the easy access from the Ocean, been considered as an improper place for an extensive magazine. For this reason part of the surplus stores have been removed temporarily to Albany.

During the late War a number of valuable brick buildings were erected at Carlisle in Pennsylvania, as well for the reception of stores, as to accomodate a number of Workmen in the Ordnance Department, but these buildings were not much used, after the apprehensions of invasions subsided owing to the expence and delay occasioned by the land transportation. The same causes still prevent their use in any considerable degree.

The situation of the United States would seem to require that three capital Magazines should be established permanently, one for the Southern, one for the Middle, and one for the Eastern States, with such subdivisions as may be deemed indispensible for General use.[3]

It would also seem to be a dictate of sound national policy that the United States should always possess, one hundred thousand arms placed in their respective Arsenals, and that the battering and field Artillery, and ammunition should be in ample proportion.

It is presumed that all the Cannon, Arms, and ammunition required by the United States might be fabricated among ourselves. It is possible the expence may be greater than if the articles were imported, but this circumstance is not of such moment as to be compared with the solid advantages which would result from extending and perfecting the means upon which our safety may ultimately depend. I have the honor to be with the highest respect Sir, your Obedient Servant.

H: Knox.
Secretary of War.

Copy, DNA: RG 233, Third Congress, 1793–95, House Records of the Office of the Clerk, Records of Reports from Executive Departments; Copy, NNGL: Knox Papers. This letter was communicated to the Senate by Knox on 16 Dec. (*ASP: Military Affairs*, 1:44).

1. For the return, see *ASP, Military Affairs*, 1:45–60.

2. New London is about 8 miles southwest of Lynchburg, Va., in Campbell County.

3. Congress passed on 2 April 1794 "An Act to provide for the erecting and repairing of Arsenals and Magazines, and for other purposes," which provided for "three or four arsenals with magazines . . . in such places as will best accommodate the different parts of the United States" (1 *Stat.* 352).

From Thomas Jefferson

Dec. 15. 1793.

Th: Jefferson has the honor to return to the President the letter of mister Rumaine praying to be relieved from duties on the wrecks of fortune with which he escaped from St Domingo.[1] Th: J. has put the letter of the same person to himself, with those of mister Genet into the hands of mister Murray, to make them the foundation of a bill of relief.[2]

AL, DNA: RG 59, Miscellaneous Letters; LB, DNA: RG 59, George Washington's Correspondence with His Secretaries of State.

1. See Jean Louis Du Rumaine to GW, 15 November.

2. Du Rumaine's letter to Jefferson, also of 15 Nov., has not been identified. For French minister Edmond Genet's letters supporting the remission of tonnage duties for the vessels of Saint Domingue refugees, and the decision to submit them informally to Congress, see Cabinet Opinion, 7 Dec., and n.3. On 19 Dec. the House of Representatives ordered "That a committee be appointed to enquire into, and report a state of facts, respecting sundry French vessels which have taken refuge in the ports of the United States, and their opinion on the propriety of remitting the foreign tonnage thereon," and on 7 March 1794 Congress passed "An Act for the remission of the duties arising on the tonnage of sundry French vessels which have taken refuge in the ports of the United States" (*Journal of the House*, 6:36; 1 *Stat.* 342).

From Henry Knox

sir   [Philadelphia] 15 Decr 1793

I beg leave respectfully to submit to Your consideration the draft of a letter, which if it meets Your approbation, I propose to prefix to the return of ordnance and military Stores, which will be transmitted to Congress tomorrow.[1] I am sir Your most obedient Servant

H. Knox

ALS, DLC:GW; LB, DLC:GW.

1. The enclosed draft has not been identified. Knox's letter of 16 Dec. to House Speaker Frederick A. Muhlenberg (LB, DNA: RG 233, Confidential Reports and Other Communications from the Secretary at War) submitted the return (for which, see *ASP, Military Affairs*, 1:45–60), asked the House to consider "whether it would not be proper at the present time to make this document public," and submitted additional papers about Indian relations on the southwest frontier (for which, see *ASP, Indian Affairs*, 1:361–468).

To Frances Bassett Washington

My dear Fanny,   Philadelphia 15th Decr 1793

Your Aunt has delivered me your letter of the 22d ulto—but as she did not arrive in this City until the 9th instt and forgot she had such an one until some days afterwards, this answr, I fear, will not reach Mount Vernon until you will have left it. I will have the furniture ready to send by the Spring Vessels to Alexandria. The frost will soon put a stop to all intercourse between the two places until that period.

I would very chearfully have complied with your request to add another Story to my house in town would the lower frame support it. But as it is a single house and not calculated to receive such an additional weight, it would endanger the whole fabrick & every thing within; especially as if I am not mistaken, it is at present a Story & half of flush Walls—Of this however I am not half as certain as I am that the frame is too weak, and in no respect calculated to receive the weight of another Story which could not, *now,* be so framed as to resist high winds & impetuous storms.

I have directed this letter in such a manner as that, if you should have left Mount Vernon; it may follow you without expence under the care of Mr Julius Dandridge[1]—I wish you a pleasant journey and a happy meeting with your friends below— My compliments to them and love to the Children concludes me Your Affecte friend

Go: Washington

ALS, NNGL.

1. Julius Burbidge Dandridge (c.1769–1828) was Martha Washington's nephew, a brother of Bartholomew Dandridge, Jr.

To Daniel Carroll

Dear Sir,   Philadelphia 16th Decr 1793

I have been favored with your letter of the 9th & sample of free stone from my Quarry, sent by Mr Hoban; for which I thank you both; and should be obliged to him for information of the spot from whence it was taken. I always knew, that the River banks from my Spring house, to the Ferry formerly kept by Captn Posey,[1] were almost an entire bed of free stone; but I had conceived before the late sample came to hand, that is was of a *very soft* nature.

As the quantity, from outward appearances, is, in a manner, inexhaustable; I should have no objection to an investigation of the Banks by skilful, & orderly people; as the public as well as myself might be benefitted by the discovery of a quarry of *good stone*, so near the Federal City.

Mr Greenleaf is, I presume, with you, he left this City for George Town on friday last.[2] He has a plan for the disposal of lots, & building thereon; to which he expressed a wish to receive the sanction of my opinion: I told him, my wish was, that all matters of that sort should come to me through the Commissioners; and when approved by them (after the consideration which I knew would be given to any proposition which seemed to have a tendency to advance the growth of the City) would certainly not be discountenanced by me.[3] A similar answer I gave to a suggestion respecting the site for the Hospital in the City; Which he seemed desirous of giving grounds *out* of the City in exchange for. My motive for hinting these things to you, in this manner, is that you may understand precisely what passed between us on these subjects. For some reasons which he assigned, he thought a Hospital in the bosom of the City improper & dangerous. I am inclined to that opinion, but realy, as I told him, did not recollect that it had been so intended. I remain in haste Your Obedt & Affe. Servt

Go: Washington

ALS, NNGL; ALS (letterpress copy), DLC:GW; LB, DNA: RG 42, Records of the Commissioners for the District of Columbia, Letters Sent, 1791–1802; LB (dated 15 Dec.), DNA: RG 42, Records of the Commissioners for the District of Columbia, Letters Sent, 1791–1802; LB, DLC:GW.

1. In the 1760s Capt. John Posey resided at Rover's Delight, near the Potomac River about a mile southwest of Mount Vernon, and operated a public ferry from the landing near his house across the Potomac to Maryland. In 1769 John West, Jr., sued Posey, claiming title to the six-acre strip of land between Dogue Creek and Little Hunting Creek that included the ferry. GW acquired title to the land in 1772 (see Robert Hanson Harrison to GW, 10 Jan. 1772, and n.1, and cash accounts, June 1772, and n.2, *Papers, Colonial Series*, 9:2–4, 52–54).

2. The previous Friday was 13 December.

3. For the commissioners' response to James Greenleaf's plans, see their letter to GW, 23 December.

From William Goddard

Sir   Johnston (near Providence) Decr 16, 1793.

Removed to the humble Vale of rural Life, it was but recently that the "Memoirs of the Life of Charles Lee, Esquire," &c. &c. fell under my observation—and as I once announced a Design of publishing a Work nearly similar in Title, though far different in Contents, I am impelled by the most unfeigned Respect to your Character, as well as Justice to myself, to address you on the Subject, presuming upon the Liberality and Candour I have formerly experienced from you, that you will give due Credit to my Assertions, when I utterly disclaim, as I now solemnly do, all Share, or Concern, in the printed "Memoirs," that have been so improperly ushered (viâ London) to the Public Eye.[1]

The Editor, while I was absent, clandestinely took the Manuscripts of General Lee from my House, and urged by his Necessities and Avarice, hath, without Judgment to discriminate, compiled, and sent abroad, a heterogeneous Collection of Letters, Essays and Fragments—even private Letters, written to and by distinguished Characters, at Periods of Friendship and Confidence, which ought, and, I am persuaded, was the Wish of the Writers, to have been buried in Oblivion.[2]

When I contemplated the Publication of the Memoirs of the late General Lee, my Design was to publish certain literary and military Papers, with such epistolary Writings, as would, I judged, by interesting the Public, at once promote my own Interest, as a Printer, and enhance the Fame of a departed Friend, who, it must be allowed, inherited, from Nature, a rare and brilliant Genius, and possessed a cultivated understanding—It was, indeed, foreign to my Design to introduce an Essay, a Letter, or a Sentiment, that would wound the Feelings, or excite the Disapprobation, of a single worthy Person—or cast the least Blemish upon the Reputation of General Lee, by sporting with his lively Sallies, and unguarded (because confidential) Communications—or even to give Currency to a single Line that, dying, he would wish to blot.

Sensible, Sir, of the great Importance (particularly at this Juncture) of your Avocations, I shall not presume longer to obtrude on your time, having, I hope, been sufficiently explicit to exculpate myself from an Imputation of Disrespect to a Character—for whom, with applauding Millions, I feelingly accord my humble, tho' sincere, Tribute of grateful Veneration.

William Goddard

ALS, DLC:GW.

1. Goddard was referring to *Memoirs of the Life of the Late Charles Lee, Esq. Lieutenant-Colonel of the Forty Fourth Regiment, Colonel in the Portuguese Service, Major General, and Aid du Camp to the King of Poland, and Second in Command in the Service of the United States of America during the Revolution: To Which Are Added His Political and Military Essays. Also, Letters to, and from Many Distinguished Characters, Both in Europe and America* (London: J. S. Jordan, 1792). By the end of 1793, editions of the *Memoirs* had also been published at Dublin and New York City. The memoir, which is only part of the volume, was written by Edward Langworthy and dated at Baltimore, 10 March 1787. In 1785 Goddard and Langworthy had issued a proposal, dated 15 July 1785, for printing by subscription a three-volume edition of "Miscellaneous Collections from the Papers of the late Major-General Charles Lee . . . to which are prefixed memoirs of his Life" (*Maryland Journal and Baltimore Advertiser*, 26 July 1785; also issued as a broadside). For Goddard's correspondence with GW about that proposal, see *Papers, Confederation Series* 3:24–26, 50, 54–55.

2. Goddard was referring to Langworthy (c.1738–1802), a former delegate to the Continental Congress from Georgia, who associated with Goddard in publishing the *Maryland Journal* in 1785. Langworthy had severed his connection with the *Journal* by 1786, when, according to the preface to the *Memoirs*, he sent the materials to England "for the purpose of publication" (p. v).

From G. Legal

Près Charleston, Caroline Du Sud, Middleton Place,[1]
Monsieur Le President   16. Xbre 1793

C'est parce que Je Suis plein de Confiance dans vos Dispositions a obliger des malheureux, que Je prends La Liberté de m'adresser directement a vous pour un objet dans le quel d'ailleurs votre intervention me sera du plus grand Secour.

Vous avez eu dans la Guerre derniere, au Service des Etats unis, Sous vos ordres, Je ne Sai dans quelle partie de ce continent, un officier nommé Jacques Lemaire, Capitaine a la Suite des Dragons en france, & au quel Les Etats unis ont accordé dans la Suite L'ordre du Cincinnatus, & un grade que Je crois être celuy de Colonel des dits Etats.

Cet officier obtint également une ou plusieurs Concessions (Je crois que c'est deux) d'une assez considerable portion de Terrein, a titre d'Indemnité ou de Récompense de Ses Services; mais Je ne Sai ni le nombre d'acres, ni le lieu ou ils Sont Situés, ni l'époque de la Concession, ni Le Bureau on peut eu avoir été fait L'enrégistrement: Je n'ai eu les titres en ma possession qu'a une époque ou il m'étoit impossible d'y porter assez d'attention, pour que ces circonstances restassent Gravées dans ma mémoire.[2]

Je suis un Pauvre Saint-Domingois, Comme tant d'autres ruiné par Les Evenements, chargé d'une femme & d'un enfant également malheureux, & finalement Sans moyen quelconque.

Mr Jacques Lemaire est décédé a St Domingue; Je Suis celui qui le represente dans Sa Succession; ma Position cruelle me met dans la necessité de rechercher tous les moyens de la rendre plus Supportable, & elle le Servit en effet Si J'étois mis en possession des Terres accordées au deffunt Lemaire.

Mais dans un Paÿs ou Je ne connois que peu de Personnes & ou Je Suis Très peu Connu, il me Seroit bien difficile de Savoir Comment & a qui m'adresser pour obtenir ce que je demande. Les Bonnes Dispositions des chefs peuvent donc Seules me tirer d'embarras, & Je vous prie d'Etre infiniment Convaincu Monsieur, qu'il m'a falu une grande Confiance dans vos bontés, & L'ignorance de tout autre moyen de Réussite, Pour oser occuper une Seule minute de vos moments précieux.

J'ai perdu par le Concours des Evenements, tous les titres relatifs a ma réclamation, mais Je vais faire L'impossible pour me procurer des Expeditions de ceux qui me donnent des Droits Sur la Succession Lemaire: Le Service essentiel que Je Reclame donc de vous Monsieur, & qui Excitera a Jamais toute ma Reconnoissance, C'est de vous employer assez pour moi, pour me procurer des Expéditions des Concessions accordées a celui que Je represente. J'ai L'Espoir que la Connoissance de toutes les affaires de ce tems, des Bureaux qui ont pu en Connoitre, & peut être quelque Souvenir de cet officier, vous rendront vos obligeantes démarches moins difficiles.[3]

Recevez de Rechef mes Excuses, & L'assurance du Profond respect avec le quel Je Suis Monsieur Le President Votre Très humble & très obéissant Serviteur

G. Legal

P. S. Mad[am]e Middleton chez la quelle Je passe L'hiver, ayant Su que J'avois L'honneur de vous écrire, me charge de vous offrir, Monsieur, Ses Compliments & L'assurance de Son Respect.[4]

ALS, DNA: RG 59, Miscellaneous Letters.

1. Middleton Place is a plantation on Ashley River Road about fourteen miles northwest of Charleston.

2. Jacques Le Maire de Gimel (b. 1749) came to America in 1776 and returned to France in March 1778 as a purchasing agent for Virginia. When he returned to America in late 1779, he was paid for his purchases in severely depreciated currency but also given a grant of 2,000 arpents of land and a brevet commission as lieutenant colonel of dragoons by the state of Virginia (see Thomas Jefferson to Benjamin Harrison, 29 Oct. 1779, *Jefferson Papers*, 3:124; *Pennsylvania Packet or the General Advertiser* [Philadelphia], 9 Dec. 1779). Le Maire was working with artillery at Boston in 1780 (*American Journal and General Advertiser* [Providence, R.I.], 17 May 1780), and apparently he later claimed to have been captured three times and imprisoned in Canada (Bodinier, *Dictionnaire des officiers de l'armée royale*, 305). For Le Maire's subsequent efforts to collect from the Virginia legislature, see Le Maire to Jefferson, 12 May 1781, and Jefferson to Benjamin Harrison, c. September 1784, *Jefferson Papers*, 5:639; 7:430–31.

3. No reply from GW and no subsequent evidence of Legal's attempt to obtain the land awarded to Le Maire has been found.

4. Legal was referring to Mary Izard Middleton (1747–1814), widow of the former Continental Congress delegate Arthur Middleton (1742–1787).

To the United States Senate and House of Representatives

United States December 16th 1793.
Gentlemen of the Senate and of the House of Representatives.

The situation of affairs in Europe, in the course of the Year 1790. having rendered it possible that a moment might arrive favorable for the arrangement of our unsettled matters with Spain, it was thought proper to prepare our representative at that Court to avail us of it. A confidential person was therefore dispatched to be the bearer of instructions to him, and to supply by verbal communications any additional information of which he might find himself in need. The Government of France was at the same time applied to for it's aid and influence in this negociation.[1] Events however took a turn which did not present the occasion hoped for.

About the close of the ensuing Year, I was informed through the representatives of Spain here, that their Government would be willing to renew at Madrid the former conferences on these subjects,[2] though the transfer of scene was not what would have been desired, yet I did not think it important enough to reject the proposition; and therefore, with advice and consent of the Senate, I appointed Commissioners plenipotentiary for negociating and concluding a treaty with that Country on the several subjects of boundary, navigation and Commerce, and gave them the instructions now communicated.[3] Before these negociations however could be got into train, the new troubles which had arisen in Europe had produced new combinations among the powers there, the effects of which are but too visible in the proceedings now laid before you.

In the mean time, some other points of discussion had arisen with that country, to wit, the restitution of property escaping into the territories of each other, the mutual exchange of fugitives from Justice, and above all the mutual interferences with the Indians lying between us. I had the best reason to believe that the hostilities threatened and exercised by the Southern Indians on our border were excited by the agents of that government. Representations were thereon directed to be made, by our Com-

missioners, to the Spanish Government, and a proposal to cultivate with good faith the peace of each other with those people.[4]
In the mean time, corresponding suspicions were entertained,
or pretended to be entertained on their part, of like hostile ex-
citements by our agents to disturb their peace with the same
nations. These were brought forward by the representatives of
Spain here, in a stile which could not fail to produce attention. A
claim of patronage and protection of those Indians was asserted,
a mediation between them and us, by that Sovereign assumed,
their boundaries with us made a subject of his interference, and
at length, at the very moment when these savages were committing daily inroads on our frontier, we were informed by them
that "the continuation of the peace, good harmony, and perfect
friendship of the two nations was very problematical for the future unless the U.S. should take more convenient measures and
of greater energy than those adopted for a long time past."[5]

If their previous correspondence had worn the appearance of
a desire to urge on a disagreement, this last declaration left no
room to evade it, since it could not be conceived we would submit to the scalping knife and tomahawk of the Savage, without
any resistance. I thought it time therefore to know if these were
the views of their sovereign, and dispatched a special messenger
with instructions to our Commissioners which are among the
papers now communicated. Their last letter gives us reason to
expect very shortly to know the result.[6] I must add that the Spanish representatives here, percieving that their last communication had made considerable impression, endeavored to abate
this by some subsequent professions which being also among
the communications to the legislature, they will be able to form
their own conclusions.[7]

Go: Washington

LS, DNA: RG 46, Third Congress, 1793–95, Senate Records of Executive
Proceedings, President's Messages—Foreign Relations; LB, DLC:GW; Df in
Thomas Jefferson's writing, DLC: Jefferson Papers.

This message and its enclosures are printed in *ASP, Foreign Relations,*
1:247–88. The enclosures included, in addition to the items discussed in
notes below, some documents about the negotiations between John Jay and
Diego de Gardoqui from 1785 to 1787; reports from William Carmichael and
William Short to Jefferson about the progress of negotiations with Spain,
18 April, 5 May, 6 June, 1 July, 15 Aug., and 20 Aug.; a few of Jefferson's letters

to Spanish representatives José de Jaudenes and José Ignacio de Viar; and various documents about Spanish relations with the Indians.

1. For the instructions carried by David Humphreys to the American chargé d'affaires at Madrid, William Carmichael, in 1790, see Thomas Jefferson to GW, 8 Aug. 1790, source note and n.7 to that document. A copy of Jefferson's letter to Carmichael of 2 Aug. 1790 about those instructions (*Jefferson Papers*, 17:111–12) was included among the enclosures with this message. For the approach to France, see Jefferson to William Short, 10 Aug. 1790 (*Jefferson Papers*, 17:121–25).

2. Jaudenes informed Jefferson in December 1791 of Spain's willingness to enter negotiations (see Jefferson's memorandums of conversation, 6 and 27 Dec. 1791, *Jefferson Papers*, 22:381, 459). Jefferson reported the approach in a letter to GW of 22 Dec., a copy of which was included as one of the enclosures with this message.

3. For GW's appointment of Carmichael and William Short as commissioners plenipotentiary for negotiating with Spain "a convention or treaty concerning the navigation of the River Mississippi by the Citizens of the United States," see GW to the United States Senate, 11 Jan. 1792. To communicate their instructions with this message, GW enclosed a copy of Jefferson's report on negotiations with Spain, 18 March 1792 (*Jefferson Papers*, 23:296–317).

4. For the instructions to Carmichael and Short on negotiating the mutual exchange of fugitives, see Jefferson to GW, 22 March 1792, n.1. Jefferson's letter to Carmichael and Short of 24 April 1792 transmitted those instructions and directed them to open negotiations (*Jefferson Papers*, 23:453–54). Copies of both documents were enclosed with this message. Jefferson, in letters of 14 Oct. and 3 Nov. 1792 (*Jefferson Papers*, 24:479–81, 565–67), instructed Carmichael and Short to protest the activities of Spanish agents among the Indians. A copy of the 3 Nov. letter was enclosed with this message.

5. GW was quoting from Jaudenes and Viar to Jefferson, 18 June 1793 (*Jefferson Papers*, 26:313–17). GW also enclosed translations of Jaudenes and Viar's letters to Jefferson of 25 May 1793 (misdated 1792) and 12 June 1793 (*Jefferson Papers*, 26:118–20, 263–66). The strongest Spanish claim of their protection of the Indians came in Jaudenes and Viar's letter to Jefferson of 7 May 1793, which was not enclosed with this message (*Jefferson Papers*, 25:677–78).

6. On the dispatch of James Blake with instructions for Carmichael and Short, see Thomas Jefferson's first memorandum to GW of c.11 July, n.1. Copies of Jefferson's letter to Blake of 12 July and Jefferson's letter to Carmichael and Short of 30 June (the main instructions carried by Blake) were enclosed with this. In Carmichael and Short's letter to Jefferson of 29 Sept., they promised to raise the issue with Spanish Ministro de Hacienda Diego de Gardoqui immediately and endeavor to get his answer by mid-October (*Jefferson Papers*, 27:161–63). A copy of that letter was also enclosed with this message.

7. GW enclosed translations of Jaudenes and Viar to Jefferson, 13 July, professing their "true esteem and indubitable attachment to the US," and 30 Nov., "Corroborating the good disposition of our Governors in Louisiana

and Saint Augustine towards preserving peace with the United States and the indians of the Frontiers" (*Jefferson Papers*, 26:497–98, 27:462–64).

To the United States Senate and House of Representatives

United States Decemr 16th 1793.
Gentlemen of the Senate, and of the House of Representatives.

I lay before you a Report of the Secretary of State on the measures which have been taken on behalf of the United States for the purpose of obtaining a recognition of our Treaty with Morocco,[1] and for the ransom of our Citizens and establishment of peace with Algiers.

While it is proper our Citizens should know that Subjects which so much concern their interests and their feelings have duly engaged the attention of their Legislature and Executive, it would still be improper that some particulars of this communication should be made known. The confidential conversation stated in one of the last Letters sent herewith, is one of these—both justice and policy require that the source of that information should remain secret.[2] So a knowledge of the sums meant to have been given for peace and ransom might have a disadvantageous influence on future proceedings for the same objects.

Go: Washington

LS, DNA: RG 46, Third Congress, 1793–95, Senate Records of Executive Proceedings, President's Messages—Foreign Relations; LB, DLC:GW; Df, in Thomas Jefferson's writing, DLC: Jefferson Papers.

1. For the treaty with Morocco of 28 June and 15 July 1786, ratified 18 July 1787, see Miller, *Treaties*, 185–227.

2. GW probably was referring to the conversation with Luis Pinto de Sousa Coutinho, the Portuguese minister and secretary of state for foreign affairs, reported in Edward Church's letter to Thomas Jefferson of 12 October. According to Church, the secretary stated that the truce between Portugal and Algiers had been engineered by British consul Charles Logie and was "by no means agreeable" to the Portuguese, who were "far from being disposed" to pay the required tribute to Algiers. He "intimated that the Algerines would probably ere long be less at liberty to cruise than at present" (*Jefferson Papers*, 27:230–35).

Enclosure
Thomas Jefferson's Report on Morocco and Algiers

[Philadelphia] Dec. 14. 1793.[1]

The Secretary of State having duly examined into the Papers and documents of his Office relative to the negotiations proposed to be undertaken with the Governments of Morocco and Algiers, makes thereupon to the President of the United States, the following

Report.

The Reports which he made on the 28th of Decemr 1790, on the trade of the United States in the Mediterranean to the House of Representatives, and on the situation of their Citizens in captivity at Algiers to the President, having detailed the transactions of the United States with the Governments of Morocco & Algiers from the close of the late war to that date, he begs leave to refer to them for the state of things existing at that time.

On the 3d of March 1791, the Legislature passed an Act appropriating the sum of 20,000 Dollars, to the purpose of effecting a recognition of the Treaty of the United States with the new Emperor of Morocco,[2] in consequence whereof Thomas Barclay, formerly Consul General for the United States in France was appointed to proceed to Morocco in the character of Consul for the United States, to obtain a recognition of the Treaty; and on the 13th of May in the same year the following Letter was written to him.

To Thomas Barclay Esqr.

Sir   Philadelphia May 13t. 1791.

You are appointed by the President of the United States to go to the Court of Morocco for the purpose of obtaining from the new Emperor a recognition of our Treaty with his father. As it is thought best that you should go in some definite character, that of Consul has been adopted, and you consequently receive a Commission as Consul for the United States, in the dominions of the Emperor of Morocco, which having been issued during the recess of the Senate, will of course expire at the end of their next session. It has been thought best however not to insert this limitation in the Commission as being unnecessary, and it might perhaps embarrass. Before the end of the next session of the Senate it is expected the objects of your mission will be accomplished.

Lisbon being the most convenient port of correspondence between us and Morocco, sufficient authority will be given to Col. Humphreys, Resident for the United States at that place, over funds in Amsterdam for the objects of your mission. On him therefore you will draw for the sums herein allowed, or such parts of them as shall be necessary. To that port too, you had better proceed in the first vessel which shall be going there, as it is expected you will get a ready passage from thence to Morocco.

On your arrival in Morocco, sound your ground, and know how things stand at present. Your former voyage there[3] having put you in possession of the characters through whom this may be done, who may best be used for approaching the Emperor and effecting your purpose, you are left to use your own knowledge to the best advantage.

The object being merely to obtain an acknowledgment of the Treaty, we rely that you will be able to do this, giving very moderate presents. As the amount of these will be drawn into precedent on future similar repetitions of them, it becomes important. Our distance, our seclusion from the ancient world, its politics and usages, our agricultural occupations and habits, our poverty, and lastly our determination to prefer war in all cases to tribute under any form and to any people whatever, will furnish you with topics for opposing and refusing high or dishonoring pretensions, to which may be added the advantages their people will derive from our commerce, and their Sovereign from the duties laid on whatever we extract from that country

Keep us regularly informed of your proceedings and progress, by writing by every possible occasion, detailing to us particularly your conferences either private or public, and the persons with whom they are held—

We think that Francisco Chiappe has merited well of the United States, by his care of their peace & interests. He has sent an account of disbursements for us amounting to 394 Dollars. Do not recognize the account, because we are unwilling, by doing that, to give him a color for presenting larger ones hereafter, for expenses which it is impossible for us to scrutinize or controul. Let him understand that our Laws oppose the application of public money so informally; but in your presents, treat *him* handsomely, so as not only to cover this demand, but go beyond it with a liberality which may fix him deeply in our interests. The place he holds near the Emperor renders his friendship peculiarly important: Let us have nothing further to do with his brothers, or any other person. The money which would make one good friend, divided among several will produce no attachment.

The Emperor has intimated that he expects an Ambassador from us. Let him understand that this may be a custom of the old world, but it is not ours: that we never sent an Ambassador to any Nation.

You are to be allowed from the day of your departure till your return 166._ dollars a month for your time and expenses, adding thereto your passage money and Sea stores going and coming.

Remain in your post till the 1st of April next, and as much longer as shall be necessary to accomplish the objects of your mission, unless you should receive instructions from hence to the contrary.

With your Commission you will receive a letter to the Emperor of Morocco, a Cypher & a letter to Col. Humphreys.[4] I have the honor to be with great esteem &c:

Th: Jefferson—

A private instruction which Mr Barclay is to carry in his memory, and not on paper, lest it should come into improper hands—

We rely that you will obtain the friendship of the new Emperor, and his assurances that the treaty shall be faithfully observed, with as little expense as possible. But the sum of Ten thousand Dollars is fixed as the limit which all your donations together are not to exceed.

May 13th 1791   Th: Jefferson.

A Letter was at the same time written to Francisco Chiappe a person employed confidentially near the Emperor, who had been named Consul there for the United States by Mr Barclay on his former mission, and appeared to have acted with zeal for our interest. It was in these words.

To Francisco Chiappe.

Sir   Philadelphia, May 13th 1791.

Since my entrance into the Office of Secretary of State I have been honored with several of your letters, and should sooner have acknowledged the receipt of them, but that I have from time to time expected the present occasion would occur sooner than it has done.

I am authorized to express to you the satisfaction of the President at the zeal and attention you have shewn to our interests, and to hope a continuance of them.

Mr Barclay is sent in the character of Consul of the United States to present our respects to his Imperial Majesty, for whom he has a letter from the President. We have no doubt he will receive your aid as usual to impress the mind of the Emperor with a sense of our high respect and friendship for his person and character, and to dispose him to a cordial continuance of that good understanding so happily established with his father.

Our manner of thinking on all these subjects is so perfectly known to Mr Barclay, that nothing better can be done than to refer you to him for information on every subject which you might wish to enquire into. I am with great esteem, Sir &c:

Th: Jefferson—

To this was added a Letter to Col. Humphreys our Resident at Lisbon, through whom it was thought proper to require that the draughts of money should pass. It was in the following words.

To Col. David Humphreys.

Dear Sir   Philadelphia, May 13th 1791.

Mr Thomas Barclay is appointed by the President of the United States to go to Morocco in the character of Consul for the purpose of obtaining from the new Emperor a recognition of our treaty with his father.

Ten thousand dollars are appropriated for presents in such form and to such persons as Mr Barclay in his discretion shall think best; and he is to receive for himself at the rate of Two thousand dollars a year and his sea expenses.

It is thought best that the money for these purposes should be placed under your controul, and that Mr Barclay should draw on you for it. Thirty-two thousand one hundred and seventy-five Guilders current are accordingly lodged in the hands of our Bankers in Amsterdam, and they are instructed to answer your draughts to that amount, you notifying them that they are to be paid out of the fund of *March 3d 1791*, that this account may be kept clear of all others. You will arrange with Mr Barclay the manner of making his draughts so as to give yourself time for raising the money by the sale of your Bills.

A confidence in your discretion has induced me to avail the public of that, in the transaction of this business, and to recommend Mr Barclay to your counsel and assistance through the whole of it. I inclose you one Set of the Bills for 13,000 dollars before mentioned and a copy of my Letter to the Bankers.[5] Duplicates will be sent to them directly. I have the honor to be, with great & sincere esteem Dear Sir, &c:

Th: Jefferson.

On Mr Barclay's arrival in Europe he learned that the dominions of Morocco were involved in a general Civil war, the subject of which was the succession to the Throne, then in dispute between several of the Sons of the late Emperor: nor had any one of them such a preponderance as to ground a presumption that a recognition of the Treaty by him would ultimately be effectual. Mr Barclay therefore took measures for obtaining constant intelligence from that country, and in the mean time remained at Lisbon, Cadiz or Gibraltar, that he might be in readiness to take advantage of the first moments of the undisputed establishment of any one of the brothers on the Throne, to effect the objects of his mission.[6]

Tho' not enabled at that time to proceed to the redemption of our captive Citizens at Algiers, yet we endeavoured to alleviate their distresses by confiding to Col. Humphreys the care of furnishing them a comfortable sustenance, as was done in the following letter to him.

To Col. David Humphreys.

Dear Sir   Philadelphia, July 13th 1791.

Mr Barclay having been detained longer than was expected, you will receive this, as well as my letter of May 13. from him. Since the date of that, I have received your No. 15. March 31. no. 16. April 8. no. 17. April 30. no. 18. May 3. and no. 20. May 21.[7]

You are not unacquainted with the situation of our captives at Algiers. Measures were taken and were long depending, for their redemption: during the time of their dependance we thought it would forward our success to take no notice of the captives; they were maintained by the Spanish Consul, from whom applications for reimbursement through Mr Carmichael often came; no answer of any kind was ever given. A certainty now that our measures for their redemption will not succeed renders it unnecessary for us to be so reserved on the subject and to continue to wear the appearance of neglecting them. Though the Government might have agreed to ransom at the lowest price admitted with any nation (as for instance, that of the French Order of Merci) they will not give any thing like the price which has been lately declared to be the lowest by the Captors. It remains then for us to see what other means are practicable for their recovery: in the mean time it is our desire, that the disbursements hitherto made for their subsistence by the Spanish Consul, or others be paid off, and that their future comfortable subsistence be provided for. As to past disbursements, I must beg the favor of you to write to Mr Carmichael, that you are authorized to pay them off, and pray him to let you know their amount, and to whom payments are due. With respect to future provision for the captives, I must put it into your hands. The impossibility of getting letters to or from Mr Carmichael, renders it improper for us to use that channel. As to the footing on which they are to be subsisted, the ration and cloathing of a soldier would have been a good measure, were it possible to apply it to articles of food and cloathing, so extremely different as those used at Algiers. The allowance heretofore made by the Spanish Consul, might perhaps furnish a better rule, as we have it from themselves that they were then comfortably subsisted. Should you be led to correspond with them at all, it had better be with Captain Obrian, who is a sensible man, and whose conduct since he has been there, has been particularly meritorious. It will be better for you to avoid saying any thing which may either increase or lessen their hopes of ransom. I write to our Bankers to answer your draughts for these purposes, and enclose you a duplicate to be forwarded with your first draught.[8] The prisoners are fourteen in number—their names and qualities as follows—Richard Obrian, and Isaac Stephens Captains-Andrew Montgomery and Alexander Forsyth Mates-Jacob Tessanier a french passenger, William Paterson, Philip Sloan, Peleg Lorin, John Robertson, James Hall, James Cathcart, George Smith, John Gregory, & James Hermet, seamen. They have been twenty one or twenty two. I have the honor to be with great esteem, Dear Sir &c:

Th: Jefferson—

On the 8th of May 1792, the President proposed to the Senate the following questions.

If the President of the United States should conclude a Convention or Treaty with the Government of Algiers for the ransom of the thirteen Americans in captivity there, for a sum not exceeding forty thousand dollars, all expenses included, will the Senate approve the same? Or is there any, and what greater or lesser sum, which they would fix on as the limit beyond which they would not approve the ransom?

If the President of the Unites States should conclude a Treaty with the Government of Algiers for the establishment of peace with them at an expense not exceeding twenty five thousand dollars paid at the signature, and a like sum to be paid annually afterwards during the continuance of the Treaty, would the Senate approve the same? Or are there any greater or lesser sums which they would fix on as the limits beyond which they would not approve of such Treaty?

Go: Washington

These questions were answered by the following resolution of the Senate, of May 8th 1792.

In Senate. May 8th 1792
Resolved, That if the President of the United States shall conclude a Treaty with the Government of Algiers, for the establishment of a peace with them, at an expense not exceeding forty thousand dollars paid at the signature, and a sum not exceeding twenty five thousand dollars, to be paid annually afterwards, during the continuance of the treaty, the Senate will approve the same. And in case such treaty be concluded, and the President of the United States shall also conclude a Convention or Treaty with the Government of Algiers for the ransom of the thirteen American prisoners in captivity there, for a sum not exceeding forty thousand dollars, all expenses included, the Senate will also approve such Convention or Treaty.

Attest
Sam. A. Otis. Secy

In order to enable the President to effect the objects of this Resolution, the Legislature by their Act of May 8th 1792 C. 41 §. 3. appropriated a sum of fifty thousand dollars to defray any expence which might be incurred in relation to the intercourse between the United States and foreign Nations.[9]

Commissions were hereupon made out to Admiral Paul Jones for the objects of peace and ransom, and a third to be Consul for the United States at Algiers. And his instructions were conveyed in the following Letter.

To Admiral John Paul Jones
Sir   Philadela June 1. 1792.
The President of the United States having thought proper to appoint you Commissioner for treating with the Dey and Government of Algiers on the subjects of peace and ransom of our captives, I have the honor to inclose you the Commissions, of which Mr Thomas Pinckney now on his way to London as our minister plenipotentiary there, will be the bearer. Supposing that there exists a disposition to thwart our negotiations with

the Algerines, and that this would be very practicable, we have thought it adviseable that the knowledge of this appointment should rest with the President, Mr Pinckney and myself: for which reason you will perceive that the Commissions are all in my own hand writing—for the same reason, entire secrecy is recommended to you, and that you so cover from the public your departure & destination as that they may not be conjectured or noticed; and at the same time that you set out after as short delay as your affairs will possibly permit.

In order to enable you to enter on this business with full information, it will be necessary to give you a history of what has passed.

On the 25 July 1785, the Schooner Maria, Capt. Stevens, belonging to a Mr Foster of Boston, was taken off Cape St. Vincents by an Algerine Cruiser; and five days afterwards, the Ship Dauphin, Capt. Obrian, belonging to Messrs Irvins of Philadelphia was taken by another about 50 leagues westward of Lisbon. These vessels with their Cargoes and Crews, twenty-one persons in number, were carried into Algiers. Mr John Lamb appointed Agent for treating of peace between the United States and the Government of Algiers, was ready to set out from France on that business, when Mr Adams and myself heard of these two captures. The ransom of prisoners, being a case not existing when our powers were prepared, no provision had been made for it. We thought however we ought to endeavor to ransom our countrymen, without waiting for orders; but at the same time, that, acting without authority, we should keep within the lowest price which had been given by any other nation. We therefore gave a supplementary instruction to Mr Lamb to ransom our Captives, if it could be done for 200 dollars a man, as we knew that three hundred French captives had been just ransomed by the Mathurins, at a price very little above this sum. He proceeded to Algiers: but his mission proved fruitless. He wrote us word from thence, that the Dey asked 59,496 dollars for the 21 Captives, and that it was not probable he would abate much from that price: but he never intimated an idea of agreeing to give it.[10] As he has never settled the accounts of his mission, no further information has been received. It has been said that he entered into a positive stipulation with the Dey to pay for the prisoners the price above mentioned, or something near it; and that he came away with an assurance to return with the money.[11] We cannot believe the fact true; and if it were, we disavow it totally, as far beyond his powers. We have never disavowed it formally, because it has never come to our knowledge with any degree of certainty.

In February 1787, I wrote to Congress to ask leave to employ the Mathurins of France in ransoming our captives, and on the 19th of Septemr I received their orders to do so, and to call for the money from our Bankers at Amsterdam as soon as it could be furnished. It was long before they could furnish the money, and, as soon as they notified that they could, the business was put into train by the General of the Mathurins, not with the appearance of acting for the United States or with their knowledge, but merely on the usual ground of charity. This expedient was rendered abortive by the Revolution of France, the derangement of ecclesiastical orders there, and the revocation of Church property, before any proposition perhaps had been made in form by the Mathurins to the Dey of Algiers.[12]

I have some reason to believe that Mr Eustace while in Spain endeavored to engage the Court of Spain to employ their Mathurins in this same business, but whether they actually moved in it or not, I have never learned—[13]

We have also been told that a Mr Simpson of Gibralter; by the direction of the Mres. Bulkleys of Lisbon, contracted for the ransom of our prisoners (then reduced by death and ransom to 14) at 34,792 28/38 dollars. By whose orders they did it we could never learn. I have suspected it was some association in London, which finding the prices far above their conception, did not go through with their purpose, which probably had been merely a philanthropic one: be this as it may, it was without our authority or knowledge.[14]

Again, Mr Cathalan, our Consul at Marseilles, without any instruction from the Government, and actuated merely, as we presume, by a willingness to do something agreeable, set on foot another negotiation for their redemption, which ended in nothing.[15]

These several volunteer interferences, though undertaken with good intentions, run directly counter to our plan; which was to avoid the appearance of any purpose on our part ever to ransom our Captives, and by that semblance of neglect, to reduce the demands of the Algerines to such a price as might make it hereafter less their interest to pursue our Citizens than any others. On the contrary they have supposed all these propositions, directly or indirectly, came from us: they inferred from thence the greatest anxiety on our part, where we had been endeavoring to make them suppose there was none; kept up their demands for our captives at the highest prices ever paid by any nation; and thus these charitable, though unauthorized interpositions, have had the double effect of lengthening the chains they were meant to break, and of making us at last set a much higher rate of ransom, for our Citizens present and future, than we probably should have obtained, if we had been left alone to do our own work, in our own way. Thus stands this business then at present. A formal bargain, as I am informed, being registered in the books of the former Dey, on the part of the Bulkeleys of Lisbon, which they suppose to be obligatory on us, but which is to be utterly disavowed, as having never been authorized by us, nor its source ever known to us—

In 1790 this subject was laid before Congress fully, and at the late session monies have been provided, and authority given to proceed to the ransom of our captive Citizens at Algiers, provided it shall not exceed a given sum, and provided also a peace shall be previously negociated within certain limits of expense. And in consequence of these proceedings your mission has been decided on by the President.

Since then no *ransom* is to take place without a *peace* you will of course first take up the negotiation of peace, or if you find it better that peace and ransom should be treated of together, you will take care that no agreement for the latter be concluded, unless the former be established before, or in the same instant.

As to the conditions, it is understood that no peace can be made with that Government but for a larger sum of money to be paid at once for the whole time of its duration, or for a smaller one to be annually paid. The former plan we entirely refuse, and adopt the latter. We have also understood that peace might be bought cheaper with naval Stores than with money: but we will not furnish them naval Stores, because we think it not right to furnish them means which we know they will employ to do wrong, and because there might be no economy in it, as to ourselves in the end, as it would increase the expense of that coercion which we may in future be obliged to practice towards them. The only question then is, what sum of *money* will we agree to pay them *annually* for peace?

By a Letter from Captain Obrian, a copy of which you receive herewith, we have his opinion that a peace could be purchased with *money* for £60,000 sterling, or with *naval Stores* for 100,000 Dollars. An *annual* payment equivalent to the first, would be £3,000 sterling, or 13,500 dollars, the interest of the sum in gross. If we could obtain it for as small a sum as the second in *money,* the annual payment equivalent to it would be 5,000 dollars. In another part of the same letter Capt. Obrian says "if maritime Stores, and two light cruisers given and a tribute paid in maritime stores every two years, amounting to 12,000 dollars in America," a peace can be had.[16] The gift of Stores and Cruizers here supposed, converted into an annual equivalent, may be stated at 9,000 dollars, and adding to it half the biennial sum, would make 15,000 dollars to be annually paid. You will of course use your best endeavours to get it at the lowest sum practicable, whereupon I shall only say, that we should be pleased with 10,000 dollars, contented with 15,000, think 20,000 a very hard bargain, yet go as far as 25,000. if it be impossible to get it for less; but not at a copper further, this being fixed by law as the utmost limit: these are meant as annual sums. If you can put off the first annual payment to the end of the first year, you may employ any sum not exceeding that in presents to be paid down: but if the first payment is to be made in hand, that and the presents cannot by law exceed 25,000 dollars.

And here we meet a difficulty, arising from the small degree of information we have respecting the Barbary States. Tunis is said to be tributary to Algiers; but whether the effect of this be that peace being made with Algiers, is of course with the Tunisians without separate treaty, or separate price, is what we know not. If it be possible to have it placed on this footing so much the better. At any event it will be necessary to stipulate with Algiers that her influence be interposed as strongly as possible with Tunis, whenever we shall proceed to treat with the latter; which cannot be till information of the event of your negociation, and another Session of Congress.

As to the articles and form of the Treaty in general, our treaty with Morocco was so well digested that I inclose you a copy of that to be the model with Algiers, as nearly as it can be obtained, only inserting the clause with respect to Tunis.

The ransom of the Captives is next to be considered. they are now thirteen in number, to wit Richard Obrian, and Isaac Stevens, Captains—Andrew Montgomery and Alexander Forsyth, Mates—Jacob Tessanier, a French passenger, William Patterson, Phillip Sloan, Peleg Lorin, James Hull, James Cathcart, George Smith, John Gregory, James Hermit, seamen. It has been a fixed principle with Congress to establish the rate of ransom of American captives with the Barbary States at as low a point as possible, that it may not be the interest of those States to go in quest of our Citizens in preference to those of other countries. Had it not been for the danger it would have brought on the residue of our Seamen, by exciting the cupidity of those rovers against them, our Citizens now in Algiers, would have been long ago redeemed without regard to price. The mere money for this particular redemption neither has been, nor is an object with any body here. It is from the same regard to the safety of our Seamen at large that they have now restrained us from any ransom unaccompanied with peace: this being secured, we are led to consent to terms of ransom, to which otherwise our Government would never have consented; that is to say, to the terms stated by Capt. Obrian in the following passage of the same Letter- "by giving the minister of the marine (the present Dey's favorite) the sum of 1,000 Sequins. I would stake my life that we would be ransomed for 13,000 Sequins, and all expences included." Extravagant as this sum is, we will, under the security of peace in future, go so far; not doubting at the same time that you will obtain it as much lower as possible, and not indeed without a hope that a lower ransom will be practicable from the assurances given us in other letters from Capt. Obrian, that prices are likely to be abated by the present Dey, and particularly with us, towards whom he has been represented as well disposed. You will consider this sum therefore, say 27,000 dollars, as your ultimate limit, including ransom, duties, and gratifications of every kind.

As soon as the ransom is completed, you will be pleased to have the Captives well cloathed, and sent home at the expense of the United States, with as much economy as will consist with their reasonable comfort.

It is thought best that Mr Pinckney, our minister at London should be the confidential channel of communication between us. He is enabled to answer your draughts for money within the limits before expressed: and as this will be by redrawing on Amsterdam, you must settle with him the number of days *after sight;* at which your Bills shall be payable in London so as to give him time, in the mean while, to draw the money from Amsterdam.

We shall be anxious to know as soon and as often as possible, your prospects in these negociations. You will receive herewith a cypher which will enable you to make them with safety. London and Lisbon (where

Col. Humphreys will forward my letters) will be the safest and best ports of communication. I also inclose two separate Commissions for the objects of peace and ransom. To these is added a Commission to you as Consul for the United States at Algiers, on the possibility that it might be useful for you to remain there till the ratification of the treaties shall be returned from hence; though you are not to delay till their return, the sending the Captives home, nor the necessary payments of money within the limits before prescribed. Should you be willing to remain there, even after the completion of the business, as Consul for the United States, you will be free to do so, giving me notice, that no other nomination may be made. These Commissions, being issued during the recess of the Senate, are in force, by the Constitution, only till the next session of the Senate; but their renewal then is so much a matter of course, and of necessity, that you may consider that as certain, and proceed without interruption. I have not mentioned this in the Commissions, because it is in all cases surplusage, and because it might be difficult of explanation to those to whom you are addressed.

The allowance for all your expenses and time (exclusive of the ransom, price of peace, duties, presents, maintenance and transportation of the Captives) is at the rate of 2,000 dollars a year, to commence from the day on which you shall set out for Algiers, from whatever place you may take your departure. The particular objects of peace and ransom once out of the way, the 2000 dollars annually are to go in satisfaction of time, services, and expenses of every kind, whether you act as Consul or Commissioner.

As the duration of this peace cannot be counted on with certainty, and we look forward to the necessity of coercion by cruises on their coast, to be kept up during the whole of their cruising season, you will be pleased to inform yourself, as minutely as possible, of every circumstance which may influence or guide us in undertaking and conducting such an operation, making your communications by safe opportunities.

I must recommend to your particular notice Capt. Obrian, one of the Captives, from whom we have received a great deal of useful information. The zeal which he has displayed under the trying circumstances of his present situation has been very distinguished, you will find him intimately acquainted with the manner in which and characters with whom business is to be done there, and perhaps he may be an useful instrument to you, especially in the outset of your undertaking, which will require the utmost caution, and the best information. He will be able to give you the characters of the European Consuls there, tho' you will probably not think it prudent to repose confidence in any of them.

Should you be able successfully to accomplish the objects of your mission in time to convey notice of it to us as early as possible during the next session of Congress, which meets in the beginning of November and rises the 4th of March, it would have a very pleasing effect. I am with great esteem &c:

Th: Jefferson—

Rough estimate not contained in the letter.

Peace	. . . .	25,000 dollars.
Ransom	. . . .	27,000.
Cloathg & Passge	. . . .	1,000.
Negociator	. . . .	2,000.
		55,000.
Sum allowed	. . . .	50,000.

Mr Pinckney then going out as our Minister plenipo. to the Court of London, it was thought best to confide the Letter to him—to make him the channel of communication, and also to authorize him, if any circumstance should deprive us of the services of Admiral J. P. Jones, to commit the business to Mr Barclay, who it was hoped would by this time be completing the object of his mission to Morocco. The letter was therefore delivered to him, and the following one addressed to himself.

To Thomas Pinckney.

Dear Sir   Philadelphia June 11th 1792

The Letter I have addressed to Admiral Jones, of which you have had the perusal, has informed you of the mission with which the President has thought proper to charge him at Algiers, and how far your Agency is desired for conveying to him the several papers, for receiving and paying his draughts to the amount therein permitted, by redrawing yourself on our Bankers in Amsterdam, who are instructed to honor your Bills, and by acting as a channel of correspondence between us. It is some time however since we have heard of Admiral Jones. Should any accident have happened to his life, or should you be unable to learn where he is, or should distance, refusal to act or any other circumstance deprive us of his services on this occasion, or be likely to produce too great a delay, of which you are to be the judge, you will then be pleased to send all the papers confided to you for him, to Mr Thomas Barclay our Consul at Morocco, with the letter addressed to him, which is delivered you open, and by which you will perceive that he is, in that event, substituted to every intent and purpose in the place of Admiral Jones. You will be pleased not to pass any of the papers confided to you on this business through any post Office. I have the honor to be &c:

Th: Jefferson.

The Letter mentioned as addressed to Mr Barclay was in these words.

From the President of the United States to Thomas Barclay Esq.

Sir   Philadelphia, June 11th 1792.

Congress having furnished me with means for procuring peace, and ransoming our captive Citizens from the Government of Algiers, I have thought it best, while you are engaged at Morocco, to appoint Admiral

Jones to proceed to Algiers, and therefore have sent him a Commission for establishing peace, another for the ransom of our Captives, and a third to act there as Consul for the United States, and full instructions are given in a Letter from the Secretary of State to him, of all which papers, Mr Pinckney, now proceeding to London as our Minister plenipotentiary there, is the bearer, as he is also of this Letter. It is some time however since we have heard of Admiral Jones, and as, in the event of any accident to him, it might occasion an injurious delay, were the business to await new Commissions from hence, I have thought it best, in such an event, that Mr Pinckney should forward to you all the papers addressed to Admiral Jones, with this Letter, signed by myself, giving you authority on receipt of those papers to consider them as addressed to you, and to proceed under them in every respect as if your name stood in each of them in the place of that of John Paul Jones. You will of course finish the business of your mission to Morocco with all the dispatch practicable, and then proceed to Algiers on that hereby confided to you, where this Letter with the Commissions addressed to Admiral Jones, and an explanation of circumstances, will doubtless procure you credit as acting in the name and on the behalf of the United States, and more especially when you shall efficaciously prove your authority by the fact of making, on the spot, the payments you shall stipulate. With full confidence in the prudence and integrity with which you will fulfil the objects of the present mission, I give to this Letter the effect of a Commission and full powers, by hereto subscribing my name this Eleventh day of June, One thousand seven hundred and ninety two.

Go. Was'hington

By a Letter of July 3d the following arrangements for the payment of the monies was communicated to Mr Pinckney, to wit.

To Thomas Pinckney Esqr.

Dear Sir   Philadelphia, July 3d 1792.

Enclosed is a letter to our Bankers in Amsterdam, covering a Bill of Exchange drawn on them by the Treasurer for one hundred and twenty-three thousand seven hundred and fifty current Guilders which I have endorsed thus—"Philadelphia, July 3d 1792. enter this to the credit of the Secretary of State for the United States of America. Th: Jefferson"[17]—to prevent the danger of interception: my letter to them makes the whole, subject to your order. I have the honor &c:

Th. Jefferson.

On Mr Pinckney's arrival in England he learned the death of Admiral J. P. Jones. The delays which were incurred in conveying the papers to Mr Barclay on this event will be best explained in Mr Pinckney's own words extracted from his letter of December 13th 1792, to the Secretary of State. They are as follows:

As soon after my arrival here as the death of Admiral J. P. Jones was ascertained I endeavored to obtain information whether Mr Barclay was still at Gibralter, or had returned to Morocco; but not knowing his correspondent here, and Mr Johnson our Consul not being able to clear up the uncertainty it was some time before I learnt that he was still at Gibralter—the particular injunctions of caution in the conveyance which I received with Mr Barclay's dispatches, and the secrecy which I knew to be so essential to the success of his operations determined me to intrust them to none but a confidential person—I accordingly endeavored to find some one of our countrymen (who are frequently here without much business) who might be induced to undertake the conveyance; but tho' in addition to my own enquiries, I requested our Consul and several American Gentlemen to endeavor to procure a confidential person to undertake a journey for me without naming the direction, it was a considerable time before I met with success—the rage for quitting the City which emptied all the western parts of this town during the summer months seemed to have swept away all our unemployed Countrymen, and the failure of Mr Short's dispatches for which I could not account, the miscarriage of some of my private letters, added to the extraordinary jealousy and watchfulness of correspondences here, made me unwilling to employ any but an American in this business. At length however I prevailed on a Mr Lemuel Cravath a native and Citizen of Massachusetts to undertake the delivery of the dispatches into Mr Barclay's hand, whether at Gibralter or Morocco, and to remain a few weeks with Mr Barclay if he should require it to reconvey his answer; for which service I agreed to pay him One hundred Guineas, besides defraying his expenses.[18] No vessel for Gibralter or any neighboring port offered immediately, but Mr Cravath availed himself of the first which occurred, and embarked about a month ago in an English vessel bound to Cales, from whence he may readily get to Gibralter: so that if the wind has proved favorable Mr B. may by this time have set out on his mission. I fear the terms of Mr Cravath's journey will be considered as expensive, but when I reflected on the importance of the object & the delay which had already occasioned me so much uneasiness I would undoubtedly have given much more had he insisted on it. I trust however that Mr Barclay could not have arrived at a better time at his place of destination to avoid interruption in his negotiations from the European powers as their attention is now wholly engrossed by the more interesting theatre of politics in Europe.

In the mean time Mr Barclay had been urged to use expedition by the following letter, from hence.

To Thomas Barclay.

Sir   Philadelphia, Novr 14th 1792.

Your Letters to the 10th of September are received. Before this reaches you, some papers will have been sent to you, which on the supposition that you were engaged in your original mission were directed to Admiral J. P. Jones, but in the event of his death were to be delivered to you. That event happened. The papers will have so fully possessed you of every thing relating to the subject, that I have nothing now to add, but the most pressing instances to lose no time in effecting the object. In the mean while the scene of your original mission will perhaps be cleared, so that you may then return and accomplish that. I am, &c:

Th: Jefferson.

Mr Barclay had received the papers, had made preparations for his departure for Algiers, but was taken ill on the 15th and died on the l9th of January 1793, at Lisbon. This unfortunate event was known here on the 18th of March, and on the 20th and 21st the following letters were written to Mr Pinckney & Col. Humphreys.

To Thomas Pinckney Esq.

Dear Sir   Philadelphia, March 20th 1793.

The death of Mr Barclay having rendered it necessary to appoint some other person to proceed to Algiers on the business of peace and ransom, the President has thought proper to appoint Col. Humphreys, and to send on Captain Nathaniel Cutting to him in the character of Secretary, and to be the bearer of the papers to him. I am to ask the favor of you to communicate to Col. Humphreys whatever information you may be able to give him in this business, in consequence of the Agency you have had in it. I have given him authority to draw in his own name on our Bankers in Amsterdam for the money deposited in their hands for this purpose according to the Letter I had the honor of writing to you July 3d. 1792. I have now that of assuring you of the sincere sentiments of esteem and respect, with which I am &c:

Th: Jefferson.

To Col. David Humphreys.

Sir   Philadelphia, March 21st 1793.

The deaths of Admiral Paul Jones first, and afterwards of Mr Barclay, to whom the mission to Algiers explained in the inclosed papers was successively confided, have led the President to desire you to undertake the execution of it in person. These papers, being copies of what had been delivered to them will serve as your guide. But Mr Barclay having also been charged with a mission to Morocco, it will be necessary to give you some trouble with respect to that also.

Mr Nathaniel Cutting the bearer hereof, is dispatched specially, first to receive from Mr Pinckney in London any papers or information, which his Agency in the Algerine business may have enabled him to communicate to you. He will then proceed to deliver the whole to you, and accompany and aid you in the character of Secretary.

It is thought necessary that you should, in the first instance settle Mr Barclay's accounts respecting the Morocco mission, which will probably render it necessary that you should go to Gibralter. The communications you have had with Mr Barclay in this mission will assist you in your endeavors at a settlement. You know the sum received by Mr Barclay on that account and we wish as exact a statement as can be made of the manner in which it has been laid out, and what part of it's proceeds are now on hand. You will be pleased to make an Inventory of these proceeds now existing. If they or any part of them can be used for the Algerine mission, we would have you by all means apply them to that use, debiting the Algerine fund, and crediting that of Morocco with the amount of such application. If they cannot be so used, then dispose of the perishable articles to the best advantage, and if you can sell those not perishable for what they cost, do so, and what you cannot so sell, deposite in any safe place under your own power. In this last stage of the business return us an exact account 1st of the specific articles remaining on hand for that mission, and their value. 2d of its cash on hand. 3d of any money which may be due to or from Mr Barclay or any other person on account of this mission, and take measures for replacing the clear balance of Cash in the hands of Messrs W. & T. Willinks and Nichs & Jacob van Staphorsts and Hubbard.

This matter being settled, you will be pleased to proceed on the mission to Algiers. This you will do by the way of Madrid, if you think any information you can get from Mr Carmichael, or any other may be an equivalent for the trouble, expense and delay of the journey. If not, proceed in whatever other way you please to Algiers.

Proper powers and Credentials for you addressed to that Government are herewith enclosed—The instructions first given to Admiral Paul Jones are so full that no others need be added, except a qualification in one single article, to wit: Should that Government finally reject peace on the terms in *money*, to which you are authorized to go, you may offer to make the first payments for peace and that for ransom in *naval Stores*, reserving the right to make the subsequent annual payments in money.

You are to be allowed your travelling expenses, your Salary as minister Resident in Portugal going on. Those expenses must be debited to the Algerine mission, and not carried into your ordinary account as Resident. Mr Cutting is allowed one hundred dollars a month, and his expenses, which as soon as he joins you, will of course be consolidated with yours. We have made choice of him as particularly qualified to aid under your direction in the matters of account, with which he is well acquainted. He receives here an advance of one thousand dollars by a draught on our Bankers in Holland in whose hands the fund is deposited. This and all other sums furnished him to be debited to the Algerine fund. I inclose you a Letter to our Bankers giving you complete authority over these funds, which you had better send with your first draught, though I send a copy of it from hence by another opportunity.[19]

This business being done, you will be pleased to return to Lisbon, and to keep yourself and us thereafter well informed of the transactions in Morocco, and as soon as you shall find that the succession to that Government is settled and stable so that we may know to whom a Commissioner may be addressed, be so good as to give us the information that we may take measures in consequence. I am &c:

Th: Jefferson

Captain Nathaniel Cutting was appointed to be the Bearer of these Letters and to accompany and assist Col. Humphreys as Secretary in this mission. It was therefore delivered to him, and his own Instructions were given in the following Letter.

To Captain Nathaniel Cutting.

Sir   Philadelphia, March 31st 1793.

The Department of State with the approbation of the President of the United States, having confidential communications for Mr Pinckney, our Minister plenipoy at London, and Col. Humphreys, our Minister Resident at Lisbon, and further services to be preformed with the latter—you are desired to take charge of those communications, to proceed with them in the first American vessel bound to London, and from thence without delay, to Lisbon in such way as you shall find best. After your arrival there, you are appointed to assist Col. Humphreys in the character of Secretary, in the business now specially confided to him, and that being accomplished, you will return directly to the United States, or receive your discharge from Col. Humphreys, at your own option.

You are to receive, in consideration of these services, one hundred dollars a month, besides the reasonable expences of travelling by land and sea (apparel not included) of yourself and a servant: of which expenses you are to render an account and receive payment from Col. Humphreys, if you take your discharge from him, or otherwise from the Secretary of State if you return to this place: and in either case Col. Humphreys is authorized to furnish you monies on account within the limits of your allowances: which allowances are understood to have begun on the 20th day of the present month, when you were engaged on this service, and to continue until your discharge or return. You receive here One thousand dollars on account, to enable you to proceed.

Th: Jefferson, Secretary of State.

But by a vessel which sailed on the day before from this port to Lisbon directly, and whose departure was not known till an hour before, the following Letter was hastily written and sent.

To Col. David Humphreys.

Dear Sir   Philadelphia, March 30th 1793.

Having very short notice of a vessel just sailing from this port for Lisbon, direct, I think it proper to inform you summarily that powers are made out for you to proceed and execute the Algerine business committed to Mr Barclay. Capt. Cutting who is to assist you in this special business as Secretary, leaves this place three days hence, and will proceed in the British packet by the way of London, and thence to Lisbon where he will deliver you the papers. The instructions to you are in general to settle Mr B's Morocco account and take care of the effects provided for that business, applying such of them as are proper to the Algerine mission, and as to the residue converting the perishable part of it into cash, and having the other part safely kept. You will be pleased therefore to be preparing and doing in this what can be done before the arrival of Mr Cutting, that there may be as little delay as possible. I am &c:

Th: Jefferson.

Captain Cutting took his passage in a vessel bound for London which sailed about the 13th or 14th of April, but he did not leave England till the 3d of September, and on the 17th of that month Col. Humphreys embarked from Lisbon for Gibraltar, from whence he wrote the Letter herewith communicated, of October the 8th last past informing us of the truce of a year concluded between Algiers and Portugal, and from whence he was to proceed to Algiers.[20]

These are the circumstances which have taken place since the date of the former reports of December 28th 1790. and on consideration of them it cannot but be obvious that whatever expectations might have been formed of the issue of the mission to Algiers at it's first projection, or the subsequent renewals to which unfortunate events gave occasion, they must now be greatly diminished, if not entirely abandoned. While the truce with two such commercial Nations as Portugal and Holland has so much lessened the number of vessels exposed to the capture of these Corsairs, it has opened the door which lets them out upon our commerce and ours alone; as with the other nations navigating the Atlantic they are at peace. Their first successes will probably give them high expectations of future advantage, and leave them little disposed to relinquish them on any terms.

A circumstance to be mentioned here is that our Resident and Consul at Lisbon have thought instantaneous warning to our commerce to be on it's guard, of sufficient importance to justify the hiring a Swedish vessel to come here express with the intelligence; and there is no fund out of which that hire can be paid.[21]

To these details relative to Algiers it is to be added as to Morocco, that their internal war continues, that the succession is not likely soon to be settled, and that in the mean time their vessels have gone into such a state of decay as to leave our commerce in no present danger for want of the recognition of our treaty: but that still it will be important to be in readiness to obtain it the first moment that any person shall be so established in that Government as to give a hope that his recognition will be valid.

Th: Jefferson

DS, DNA: RG 46, Third Congress, 1793–95, Senate Records of Executive Proceedings, President's Messages—Foreign Relations; ADf, DLC: Jefferson Papers; Copy, DNA: RG 233, Third Congress, 1793–95, House Records of the Office of the Clerk, Records of Reports from Executive Departments.

For the genesis of this report, see Bartholomew Dandridge, Jr., to Jefferson, 11 December. Despite the date on the report, Jefferson evidently sent it to GW on 15 Dec. (see Jefferson to GW, 14 Dec.). On 22 Dec. Jefferson received additional letters regarding Algiers and Morocco, which he submitted to GW the next day (see Dandridge to Jefferson, 23 Dec.). GW sent those letters to the U.S. Senate and House of Representatives on 23 December.

1. The date is with the signature on the document and in Jefferson's writing.

2. The first three lines of this paragraph are indented and a citation is placed in the space created: "1791 Mar. 3 Act C. 17." The correct citation would have been to chapter 16 (1 *Stat.* 214). For the treaty with Morocco of 28 June and 15 July 1786, see Miller, *Treaties,* 185–227. On the death of Sultan Sidi Muhammed and succession of his son Yazid Ibn Muhammed (1748–1792), see Giuseppe Chiappe to GW, 13 May 1790, and n.1 to that document.

3. Barclay negotiated the 1786 Moroccan treaty.

4. See GW to the Emperor of Morocco, 31 March 1791. A copy of Jefferson's letter to David Humphreys of 13 May 1791 is part of this report.

5. See Jefferson to Willink, Van Staphorst, & Hubbard, 13 May 1791 (*Jefferson Papers,* 20:407).

6. Barclay's dispatches to Jefferson of 18, 26, and 31 Dec. 1791; 16 and 30 Jan.; 23 and 24 Feb.; 1, 16, and 31 March; 10 and 15 April; 7, 10, and 17 May; 12 June; 13 and 31 July; 22 Aug.; 8 Sept.; 1 and 26 Oct.; 20 Nov.; and 17 and 19 Dec. 1792 describe the chaotic situation in Morocco that prevented his entering that country to undertake his mission (DNA: RG 59, Consular Despatches, Gibraltar; DNA: RG 59, Consular Despatches, Cadiz; abstracts in *Jefferson Papers,* 22:416–18, 447–48, 471; 23:46–47, 88–89, 144–45, 174, 285–86, 356–57, 391–92, 426–27, 485–86, 490, 519–20; 24:67–68, 224–25, 269–70, 312–13, 345–46, 430, 534, 643, 749, 756. Barclay was writing from Cadiz beginning with his letter of 26 Oct. 1792).

Sultan Yazid's rule was challenged actively by his brother "Muley Ischem" (Hisham Ibn Muhammed; d. 1799) and more passively by his brother "Muley Slema" (Maslama Ibn Muhammed). After Yazid's death in February 1792, a third brother, "Muley Suliman" (Mawlay Sulayman Ibn Muhammed, 1766–1822), emerged as another strong contestant. Meanwhile other brothers were mentioned as possible rulers, some regions asserted autonomy, and consideration was given to selecting an emperor from outside the ruling family. By 1795 Mawlay Sulayman had emerged as the new sultan, and his letter to GW of 18 Aug. 1795 was transmitted to the Senate on 21 Dec. 1795 as a recognition of the treaty.

7. These letters are abstracted in *Jefferson Papers,* 19:643–44; 20:168–69, 327, 361–62, 474–76.

8. See Jefferson to Willink, Van Staphorst & Hubbard, 13 July (*Jefferson Papers,* 20:626–27).

9. See "An Act making certain appropriations therein specified," 8 May 1792 (1 *Stat.* 284–85).

10. See Supplementary Instructions to John Lamb, 1–11 Oct. 1785, and Lamb to the American Commissioners, 20 May 1786, (*Jefferson Papers,* 8:616–17; 9:549–54). For more on the capture of the two ships and the fate of their crews, see Mathew Irwin to GW, 9 July 1789, and enclosure. John Lamb, a ship's captain and merchant from Norwich, Conn., was appointed by Congress in February 1785 to negotiate with the Barbary powers. He arrived at Paris in September 1785, but did not reach Algiers until March 1786.

11. For this claim, see Jonathan Trumbull, Jr., to GW, 27 July 1792, n.1.

12. Jefferson requested authority in his letter to John Jay of 1 Feb. 1787, and Congress resolved on 18 July to grant it, which resolution was enclosed in Jay's letter to Jefferson of 24 July (*Jefferson Papers,* 11:99–103, 618–20; *JCC,* 32:364–65). Jefferson evidently had received the authority by 18 Sept. 1787 (see Jefferson to the Commissioners of the Treasury, that date, *Jefferson Papers,* 12:149).

13. In July 1789 John Skey Eustace wrote the Rev. Jacques Audibert, de la Merci, Procureur général des Captifs, à Bordeaux, to ask about the role of his order in redeeming and giving aid to captives at Algiers and about the relationship between the French and Spanish branches of the Order of Mercy. Upon receiving Audibert's response, Eustace wrote Congress to suggest that the Spanish order be employed to negotiate for the captives (see Eustace to Jay, 15 July 1789, and enclosures, DNA: RG 59, Miscellaneous Letters, filed at 1 Jan. 1791).

14. On this effort, see James Simpson to GW, 25 Aug. 1790.

15. Stephen Cathalan, Jr. (d. 1819), was appointed as vice-consul for Marseilles in June 1790 and served until his death. He described his negotiation in an enclosure to his letter to Jefferson of 22 Jan. 1791 (*Jefferson Papers,* 18:585–91).

16. See Richard O'Bryen to Cathalan, 27 Sept. 1791, DLC: Jefferson Papers.

17. See Jefferson to Willink, Van Staphorst & Hubbard, 3 July 1792 (*Jefferson Papers,* 24:157).

18. Lemuel Cravath (c.1746–1815) was a merchant at Boston and, for a time, Baltimore.

19. See Jefferson to Willink, Van Staphorst & Hubbard, 20 March (*Jefferson Papers,* 25:413–14).

20. A copy of Humphreys's letter to Jefferson of 8 Oct. is filed with this report, along with copies of Humphreys to Jefferson, 26 Sept., and Edward Church to Jefferson, 12 Oct., on the latter of which is Jefferson's undated note that the "preceding letters are true copies from those remaining in the

office of this department." For the original texts of these letters, see *Jefferson Papers*, 27:152–53, 222–23, 230–35.

21. See Humphreys to Jefferson, 6 and 7 Oct., and Church to Jefferson, 12 Oct., *Jefferson Papers*, 27:196–200, 230–35. About payment of the *Maria*, the snow that Church had chartered for £800 sterling, see Jefferson to Alexander Hamilton, 12 Dec., and Hamilton to John Lamb, 16 Dec., *Hamilton Papers*, 15:456–57, 460.

From Burgess Ball

Dear sir,   Leesburg [Va.]—17th Decr—93.

I recd yours of the 24th Ult: with a Bank note of 200 dollars, and ought e'er this to have acknowledged the rect thereof, but have thus long delay'd writing, that I might be able to give you some satisfactory Accot respecting Buck wheat. I am now satis-fyed that I shall be able to procure the quantity you want, as I have got about 300 Bushells, and the Ball: I may be sure of ob-taining. I cou'd not have conciev'd this Grain wou'd have been so difficult to procure, but, the scarcity of Corn, and the quantity which had been consumed (of Buck wheat) in fattening Hoggs, has been the Cause of much difficulty. 'Tho I had circulated Advertizements, and sent my overseer about, little or no Suc-cess cou'd I obtain 'till I went about myself. I can't get it for less than 2/6 ⅌ Bush:, and, the Expence of Waggonage will be (at least) one shilling more—The Buck wheat is this Year very heavy, weighing from 50 to 54 lbs. which is nearly equal to the other wheat in general—For some time past and (I expect) to come, it has been, and will be impracticable to have the B: wheat haul'd down, but, as soon as the Roads will permit, it shall, as fast as possible, be carryed to Mt Vernon. You may rely on my best Ex-ertions for your Interest, and that nothg but extraordinary Ac-cident shall cause a disappointment. The Situation of Fanny for some time past, (expectg to be laid up) and the Small Pox being all around us, has kept me close at Home; but, she being a few days ago happily deliver'd of a fine Boy,[1] I shall now be able to go about more, & to attend particularly to getting the Buck wheat, in which I take great pleasure, as I shou'd be sorry your System of Husbandry shoud be deranged thro unsuccessfull attempts of mine, and (more especially) as I had led you to think this Grain cou'd so easily have been obtain'd here.[2]

When you've an Opporty you'll oblige me exceedingly by forwarding the Clover Seed (of wch I gave Mr Dandridge a Memdm) to Mt Vernon, or Alexandria, as I wish to sow it on the last Snows in February or March.[3] The friends to Governmt here, are much pleas'd to find the Proclamation approved of by Congress—Those of the other Stamp (of which in this County I fear there are many) are on the other hand much disappointed.[4] That Philada shou'd be sufficiently cleansed, of the dreadful malady under which it had labour'd, for the reception of Congress, was a filicity little expected indeed, and an Event which probably may prevent an accumulation of Parties. We hear very frequently from Colo. Washingtons—They are well, and as usual.[5] The Ladies join in wishing you & Mrs Washington every filicity, and I am Dear sir with the highest Esteem Yr Affect. Hbe servt

B: Ball

ALS, DLC:GW.

1. Charles Burgess Ball (1793–1823) was born on 14 December.

2. See Ball to GW, 16 November.

3. The memorandum has not been identified. In GW's letter to Ball of 3 Feb. 1794, he reported that he had procured and would soon send to Alexandria three bushels of clover seed.

4. Ball was referring to GW's Neutrality Proclamation of 22 April. For the congressional approval, see the United States House of Representatives to GW, 7 Dec., and the United States Senate to GW, 9 December.

5. Charles Washington and his wife, Mildred Thornton Washington, were Ball's father- and mother-in-law.

Letter not found: to Robert Taylor, 17 Dec. 1793. On 30 Jan. 1794, Taylor thanked GW for "two letters from you under date of the 10th and 17th December."

To William Aylett Booth

Sir,   Philada 18. Decemr 1793.

The attachment, expressed by the resolutions of Shenandoah County, to the Constitution of the U. States; the importance of cultivating peace & harmony with all the world, by just & honorable means; and the grateful acknowledgment of the services rendered by the French nation, meet my full assent.[1] For the favorable sentiments towards myself, I must entreat you, Sir, to communicate my thanks to my Fellow Citizens of Shenandoah.

Go. Washington

LB, DLC:GW.

1. See Resolutions from Shenandoah County, Va., Citizens, 13 November.

Letter not found: from George Clinton, 18 Dec. 1793. On 25 Dec., GW wrote Clinton: "Your favor of the 18th instt enclosing a statement of sales of lots in Coxburgh, belonging to us, has been duly received."

From Thomas Jefferson

[Philadelphia] Dec. 18. 1793.

Th: Jefferson has the honor to submit to the President's approbation the draught of letters to mister Genet and the Attorney Genl on the subject of the prosecution desired by the former to be instituted against Messrs Jay & King.[1]

He also incloses the form of a warrant for Đ2544.37 for the Director of the Mint for the purchase of copper.[2]

AL, DNA: RG 59, Miscellaneous Letters; AL (letterpress copy), DLC: Jefferson Papers; LB, DNA: RG 59, George Washington's Correspondence with His Secretaries of State.

1. Jefferson's letter of this date to Attorney General Edmund Randolph informed him that a copy of Edmond Genet's letter to Randolph of 16 Dec., requesting the prosecution of John Jay and Rufus King for their "libellous publications" about Genet, had been laid before GW, who, "never doubting your readiness on all occasions to perform the functions of your office, yet thinks it incumbent on him to recommend it specially on the present occasion, as it concerns a public character peculiarly entitled to the protection of the laws. On the other hand, as our citizens ought not to be vexed with groundless prosecutions . . . if you judge the prosecution in question to be of that nature . . . consider this recommendation as not extending to it." Jefferson's letter to Genet of this date enclosed to him a copy of the letter to Randolph (*Jefferson Papers,* 27: 583, 587–88). GW approved the drafts and returned them to Jefferson on this date (*JPP,* 269).

For the initial publication by John Jay and Rufus King asserting that Genet "had said he would Appeal to the People from certain decisions of the President," see *Diary; or Loudon's Register* (New York), 12 August. On 14 Nov. Genet sent through Jefferson a request that the attorney general prosecute the two men for libel, and he had his request and Randolph's response published (*Diary; or Loudon's Register,* 22 Nov.; see also *Jefferson Papers,* 27:367–68). Jay and King responded in early December by publishing a more detailed statement of their information, dated 26 Nov. and supported by a certificate from Alexander Hamilton and Henry Knox dated 29 Nov. (*Daily Advertiser* [New York], 2 Dec.). On 16 Dec. Genet sent through Jefferson another letter to Randolph that was the immediate impetus for the drafts enclosed here. In that letter, Genet cited the new publication and the involvement of Hamilton and Knox, and asked again that Randolph bring before the Supreme Court an "accusation . . . against Messrs. Jay and King, as also against all those who have participated in the calumnies which have been perfidiously disseminated solely with a view of injuring the interests of France under a republican government" (translation published with the responses of Jefferson and Randolph and additional correspondence in the *Federal Gazette and Philadelphia Daily Advertiser,* 24 Dec.; see also *Jefferson Papers,* 27:527–29).

This controversy continued into March 1794, with Jay and King writing GW on 27 Jan. 1794 (letter not found) complaining about the actions of Randolph and Jefferson and requesting a document that would support their position (see GW to Knox, 15 Feb. 1794; GW to Jay and King, 3 March 1794; and King's endorsement on Jay to King, 25 Feb. 1794, NHi).

2. A letterpress copy of the warrant for $2,544.37 is in DLC: Jefferson Papers, and a letter-book copy is in DLC:GW. GW signed the warrant and returned it to Jefferson (*JPP,* 269).

To William Pearce

Mr Pearce,   Philadelphia 18th Decemr 1793.

The paper enclosed with this letter will give you my ideas, generally, of the course of Crops I wish to pursue.[1] I am sensible more might be made from the farms for a year or two—but my object is to recover the fields from the exhausted state into which they have fallen, by oppressive crops, and to restore them (if possible by any means in my power) to health & vigour. But two ways will enable me to accomplish this. The first is to cover them with as much manure as possible (winter & summer). The 2d a judicious succession of Crops.

Manure cannot be had in the abundance the fields require; for this reason, and to open the land which is hard bound by frequent cultivation and want of proper dressings, I have introduced Buck Wheat in the plentiful manner you will perceive by the Table, both as a manure, and as a substitute for Indian Corn for horses &ca; it being a great ameliorater of the Soil. How far the insufferable conduct of my Overseers, or the difficulty of getting Buck Wheat & Oats for Seed, will enable me to carry my plan into effect, I am unable at this moment to decide. You, possibly, will be better able to inform me sometime hence. Colo. Ball of Leesburgh has promised to use his endeavours to procure & send the first to Mount Vernon;[2] but where to get as much of the latter as will answer my purposes (unless I send them from this City) I know not; but before I can decide on the quantity it may be necessary for me to purchase, it is essential I should know the quantity grown on my own estate; and which after I went to Virginia in September last I directed should no longer be fed away. The common Oats which are brought from the Eastern shore to Alexandria for sale, I would not sow—first, because they are not of a good quality—and 2dly because they are rarely, if ever, free from Garlick & wild Onions; with which, unfortunately, many of my fields are already but too plentifully stocked from the source already mentioned; and that too before I was aware of the evil.

I have already said that the insufferable conduct of my Overseers may be one mean of frustrating my plan for the next year—I will now explain myself. You will readily perceive by the rotation of Crops I have adopted, that a great deal of Fall plowing is indispensible. Of this I informed every one of them, and pointed out the fields which were to be plowed at this season. So anxious was I, that this work should be set about early, that I made an attempt soon after you were at Mount Vernon in September, to begin it; and at several times afterwards repeated the operation in different fields at Dogue run farm; but the ground being excessively hard & dry, I found that to persevere would only destroy my horses without effecting the object, in the manner it ought to be, & therefore I quit it; but left positive directions that it should recommence at every farm as soon as ever there should come rain to moysten the earth—& to stick constantly at it, except when the horses were employed in treading out Wheat (which was a work I also desired might be accomplished as soon as possible). Instead of doing either of these, as I ordered, I find by the reports, that McKoy has, now & then, plowed a few days only as if it were for amusement. That Stuart has but just begun to do it. and that neither Crow, nor Davy at Muddy hole, had put a plow into the ground so late as the 7th of this month. Can it be expected then, that frosts, Snow & Rain will permit me to do much of this kind of work before March or April? When Corn planting, Oats sowing, and Buck Wht for manure, ought to be going into the grd, in a well prepared state, instead of having it to flush up at that Season—and when a good deal of Wheat is to be got out with the same horses. Crow having got out none of his that was stacked in the field, nor Stuart & McKoy much of theirs, which is in the same predicament; the excuse being, as far as it is communicated to me, that their whole time & force since the month of October has been employed in securing their Corn— When God knows little enough of that article will be made.

I am the more particular on this head for two reasons—first to let you see how little dependence there is on such men when left to themselves (for under Mr Lewis it was very little better)—and 2dly to shew you the necessity of keeping these Overseers strictly to their duty—that is—to keep them from running about, and to oblige them to remain constantly with their people; and moreover, to see at what time they turn out of a morning—for I have strong suspicions that this, with some of them, is at a late hour, the consequence of which to the negroes is not difficult to foretell. All these Overseers as you will perceive by their agreements, which I herewith send are on standing wages;[3] and this with men who are not actuated by the principles of honor or honesty, and not very regardful of their characters, leads naturally to endulgences—as *their* profits, whatever may be *mine,* are the same whether they are at a horse race or on the farm—whether they are entertaining company (which I believe is too much the case) in their own houses, or are in the field with the Negroes.

Having given you these ideas, I shall now add, that if you find any one of them inattentive to the duties which by the articles of agreement they are bound to perform, or such others as may reasonably be enjoined, Admonish them in a calm, but firm manner of the consequences. If this proves ineffectual, discharge them, at any season of the year without scruple or hesitation, & do not pay them a copper; putting the non-compliance with their agreemt in bar.

To treat them civilly is no more than what all men are entitled to, but my advice to you is, to keep them at a proper distance; for they will grow upon familiarity, in proportion as you will sink in authority, if you do not. Pass by no faults or neglects (especially at first)—for overlooking one only serves to generate another, and it is more than probable that some of them (one in particular) will try, at first, what lengths he may go. A steady & firm conduct, with an inquisitive inspection into and a proper arrangement of every thing on your part, will, though it may give more trouble at first, save a great deal in the end—and you may rest assured that in every thing which is just, and proper to be done on your part, shall meet with the fullest support on mine. Nothing will contribute more to effect these desirable purposes than a good example—unhappily this was not set (from what I have learnt lately) by Mr Whiting, who, it is said, drank freely—kept bad company at my house and in Alexandria—& was a very debauched person—where ever this is the case it is not easy for a man to throw the first stone for fear of having it returned to him: and this I take to be the true cause why Mr Whiting did not look more scrupulously into the conduct of the Overseers, & more minutely into the smaller matters belonging to the Farms—which, though individually may be trifling, are not found so in the agregate, for there is no addage more true than an old Scotch one, that "many mickles make a muckle."

I have had but little opportunity of forming a correct opinion of my white Overseers, but such observations as I have made I will give.

Stuart appears to me to understand the business of a farm very well, and seems attentive to it. He is I believe a sober man, & according to his own account a very honest one. As I never found him (at the hours I usually visited the farm) absent from some part or another of his people I presume he is industrious, & seldom from home. He is talkative, has a high opinion of his own skill & management—and seems to live in peace & harmony with the Negroes who are confided to his care. He speaks extremely well of them, and I have never heard any complaint of him—His work however, has been behind hand all the year, owing, he says, and as I believe, to his having too much plowing to do—and the last omission, of not plowing when he knew my motives for wishing it, has been extremely reprehensible—But upon the whole, if he stirs early, & works late, I have no other fault to find than the one I have just mentioned—His talkativeness & vanity may be humoured.

Crow is an active man, & not deficient in judgment. If kept strictly to his duty would, in many respects, make a good Overseer. But I am much mistaken in his character if he is not fond of visiting, & receiving visits. This, of course, withdraws his attention from his business, and leaves his people too much to themselves; which produces idleness, or slight work on one side, & flogging on the other—the last of which besides the dissatisfaction which it creates, has, in one or two instances been productive of serious consequences—I am not clear either, that he gives that due attention to his Plow horses & other stock which is necessary, although he is very fond of riding the former—not only to Alexandria &ca but about the farm, which I did not forbid as his house was very inconvenient to the scene of his business.

McKoy appears to me to be a sickly, slothful and stupid fellow. He had many more hands than were necessary merely for his Crop, & though not 70 acres of Corn to cultivate, did nothing else. In short to level a little dirt that was taken out of the Meadow ditch below his house seems to have composed the principal part of his Fall work; altho' no finer season could have happened for preparing the Second lot of the Mill Swamp for the purpose of laying it to grass. If more exertion does not appear in him when he gets into better health he will be found an unfit person to overlook so important a farm, especially as I have my doubts also of his care & attention to the horses &ca.

As to Butler, you will soon be a judge whether he will be of use to you or not. He may mean well, and for ought I know to the contrary may, in something have judgment; but I am persuaded he has no more authority over the Negroes he is placed, than an old woman would have; and is as unable to get a proper days Work done by them as she would, unless led to it by their own inclination wch I know is not the case.

Davy at Muddy hole carries on his business as well as the white Overseers, and with more quietness than any of them. With proper directions he will do very well, & probably give you less trouble than any of them, except in attending to his care of the stock, of which I fear he is negligent; as there are deaths too frequent among them.

Thomas Green (Overlooker of the Carpenters) will, I am persuaded, require your closest attention, without which I believe it will be impossible to get any work done by my Negro Carpenters—in the first place, because, it has not been in my power, when I am away from home, to keep either him, or them to any settled work; but they will be flying from one trifling thing to another, with no other design, I believe, than to have the better opportunity to be idle, or to be employed on their own business—and in the next place, because—although authority is given to him—he is too much upon a level with the Negroes to exert it; from which cause, if no other every one works, or not, as they please, & carve out such jobs as they like. I had no doubt when I left home the 28th of Oct. but that the house intended for Crow wd have been nearly finished by this time, as in order to facilitate the execution I bought Scantling, Plank & Shingles for the building, instead of this I do not perceive by his weekly report that a tool has yet been employed in it—nor can I find out by the said report that the Barn at Dogue run is in much greater forwardness than when I left it.

To correct the abuses which have crept into all parts of my business—to arrange it properly, & to reduce things to system; will require, I am sensible, a good deal of time and your utmost exertions; of the last, from the character you bear, I entertain no doubt; The other, I am willing to allow, because I had rather you should probe things to the bottom, whatever time it may require to do it, than to decide hastily upon the first view of them; as to establish good rules, and a regular system, is the life, and the Soul of every kind of business.

These ⟨are general thoughts—In my next letter (which, if possible shall be by the next Post) I will go more into detail upon some particular matters. In the mean while I remain Your friend & Servant

Go: Washington⟩

AL[S] (fragment), ViMtvL; ALS (letterpress copy), DLC:GW. The last page is missing from the AL[S]. The text in angle brackets is taken from the letterpress copy.

1. The enclosure may have been a version of the document below.

2. See Burgess Ball to GW, 16 November.

3. The enclosed copies of overseer agreements have not been identified. An undated DS fragment of an agreement with Hiland Crow, probably that sent here, is at ViHi: Mary Custis Lee Papers. The surviving pieces suggest that the agreement was similar to that made with Crow by George Augustine Washington on 15 Sept. 1790 and renewed in 1791 (DLC:GW). Henry McCoy was working under an agreement made with Anthony Whitting, 17 Dec. 1792 (DLC:GW).

Fig. 3. Washington's drawing of his farms at Mount Vernon, 1793.
(Henry E. Huntington Library, San Marino, Calif.)

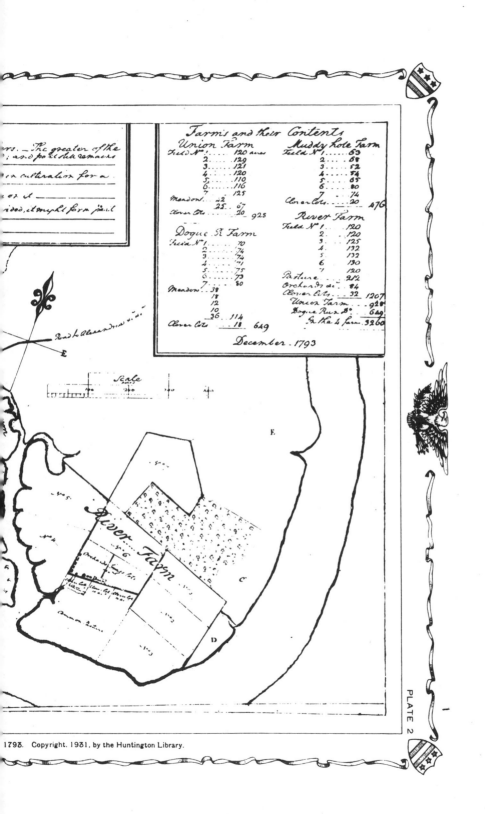

PLATE 2

Enclosure
Crop Rotations for Mount Vernon Farms

[1793]

Rotation of Crops for Dogue Run Farm

Fields distingd by Nos.	Crops wch will be in each of those fields, in the years at the head of each column							
	1793	1794	1795	1796	1797	1798	1799	1800
1	B: Wheat for Manure	Wheat	Manurg	Oats	Manurg	Corn & Potats.	Wheat & Clover	Clover
2	Wheat	Oats	Pasture	Wheat & B. Wheat	Oats	Manurg	Corn & Potats.	Wheat & Clover
3	Corn	Wheat & Clover	Clover	Clover	Wheat & B. Wheat	Oats	Manurg	Corn & Potats.
4	Pasture	Corn & Potats.	Wheat & Clover	Clover	Clover	Wheat & B. Wheat	Oats	Manurg
5	Pasture	Manurg	Corn & Potats.	Wheat & Clover	Clover	Clover	Wheat & B. Wht	Oats
6	Pasture	B. Wheat for Manure	Wheat	Corn & Potats.	Wheat & Clover	Clover	Clover	Wheat & B.Wht
7	Wheat	Pasture	Oats	Manurg	Corn & Potats.	Wheat & Clover	Clover	Clover

The above fields are not exactly of the same size, but the average of them is 70 Acres—and when cultivated in regular succession, agreeably to the above course, the annual plowing in each will be, both as it respects seasons, and the number of days required for each working, nearly as follow.

acres in the Fields	Crops annually growing	Kind of Plowing necessary for these Crops	Seasons at wch these plowings shd be given									
			Fall	Winter	Mar:	Apr	May	June	July	Augt	Sepr	Total
70	of Corn &	Flushing	70									70
		Listing 2 furrows			15							15
	Potatoes	Crossing to Plant				9						9
		Plowing balks[1]				25						25

Acres	Field	Operation / Note				Total
		Harrowing				9
		Roundg with Plow				15
		Plowg out same way			30	30
		Crosg last Plowing		36	36	36
		Levellg with Harrow for seeding			15	15
		Sowing Wheat		30	30	60
70			15 · 34 · 24 · 30 · 36 · 45 · 30 · 30			**284**
70	of Wheat & Clover	The above work in quantity, & seasons, does for this Crop				
70	of Clover for Wht on	nothing being sown on the Wheat in February				
		Clover lay plowed for Wheat in Sepr			70	70
		Harrowg in Do			12	12
70	of Wheat	nothing being put in as above				
70	B. Wheat	Plowing as soon as the Wht comes off			70	70
		Harrowing before sowg to level the grd			12	12
		Harrowing in the Seed			12	12
70	Oats	Flushing			70	70
		Crossing			70	70
		Harrowg before sowg			12	12
		Harrowg in the Seed			12	12
70	Pasture	to Manure on for the Crop of Corn—nothing				
490		**140 · 109 · 34 · 24 · 300 · 130 · 45 · 112**				**624**

The annual yield of the foregoing fields—cultivated in the manner, and for the purposes there mentioned—may reasonably be calculated as follow—and it is hoped they will become more and more productive every year, from the mode of cropping them—and from the advantage this Farm will have in an abundance of Mowing ground—and the increase of stock consequent thereof.

70 Acres in Corn	a 12½ bushls	875 Bushls	a 2/6	£109.7.6[2]
same in Potatoes	Do Do	875 Do	1/	43.15
70 Wheat	10 Do	700 Do	5/	175
Clover	fed the yr the Wheat comes off			
70 Ditto	Mowed or fed accordg to cir[cumstance]s.			
70 Ditto	Mowed—½ a Ton pr acre			
	amountg to 35 Tons		a £3	105
70 Wheat	10	700	5/	175
70 Buck Wht	10	700	2/	70
70 Oats	12½	875	2/	87.10
70 Pasture	to Manure on			

Total 490 Acs. in 7 fields producing[3]

£765.12.6.

The probable consumptn of Corn on this Farm will be—for

Negros	600 Bushls
Overseer	30
Hogs	250
Total	880[4]

The horses[5] will be fed with Oats & Buck Wheat; the latter chopped at the Mill. Other animals will be supported on Hay, Indian Corn fodder, and Straw.

Besides the produce of the above fields, there will be three lots adjoining the Barn as may be seen by the plan of about 5 acres each—one of which will be in Potatoes, succeeded the Spring following by Oats; with clover sown thereon for the purpose of soiling the work horses &ca the year following[6] & affording good pasturage in the mean while. The 3d year this field will be in prime order for cutting, either for Hay, or for the purpose of feeding green as above, to the horses. The other two fields follow the same course in Rotation.

When No. 5 is cultivated in Corn & Potatoes in 1795, as may be seen by the foregoing table, the woodland part of it (about 15 acres) must be cleared and tilled in these articles along with the rest of the Inclosure, to replace the difficiency therein, occasioned by taking from it the ground for the Barn, the Barn yard, and two of the three lots abovementioned for Clover amounting altogether to 12½ acres. 2½ being for the Yard.

Rotation of Crops for Union Farm.

Fields distingd by Nos.	Crops which will be in each of those fields in the years mentiond at the head of each column							
	1793	1794	1795	1796	1797	1798	1799	1800
1	Past[ur]e	Mang	Corn	Wheat	Buck Wht for Manure	Wheat	½ B. Wht & ½ Oats	Paste
2	Corn	Wheat	Manug	Corn	Wheat	Buck Wh. for Manure	Wheat	½ B. Wh. & ½ Oats
3	Half Wheat	½ B. Wht & ½ Oats	Paste	Manug	Corn	Wheat	Buck Wh. for Manure	Wheat
4	Paste	Paste	½ B. Wht & ½ Oats	Paste	Manurg	Corn	Wheat	Buck Wh. for Manure
5	Wheat	Buck Wht for Manure	Wheat	½ B. Wht & ½ Oats	Paste	Manug	Corn	Wheat
6	Corn	Wheat	Buck Wh. for Manure	Wheat	½ B. Wh. & ½ Oats	Paste	Manurg	Corn
7	Paste	Corn	Wheat	Buck Wht for Manure	Wheat	½ B. Wh. & ½ Oats	Paste	Mang

The above fields like those of the preceeding Farm at Dogue run are not exactly of a size, but the average of them is 118 acres and when cultivated in regular succession agreeably to the above course the annual ploughing will be nearly as follow.

Acres in the Fields	Crops actualy thereon annually	Kind of Plowg necessary for these Crops	Seasons at wch these plowings shd be given									
			Fall	Wintr	Mar.	Aprl	May	June	July	Augt	Sep	Total
118	Corn	Flushing	118									118
		Listing 2 furrws			25							25
		Crossg to Plant				15						15
		Plowg balks				42						42
		Harrowing					15					15
		Roundg with the Plow					25					25
		Plowg out the same way						50				50
		Crossg the last plowing							60			60
		Levellg with the Harrow for Seeding								25		25
		Plowg in Wheat								50	50	100
			118		25	57	40	50	60	75	50	475
118	Wheat	The above work in qty, & Seasons, does for this Crop										118
118	Buck Wht for Manure	Flushing	118									118
		Crossing for sowg				118						118
		Harrowg to level				15						15
		Harrowg in the Seed				15						15
		Plowing in B. Wheat						118				118
		Harrowg to level the grd							15			15
		Plowed in on B. Wht man[ur]e								118		118
118	Wheat	Flushing	118									118
118	Oats & B. Wheat[7]	Crossing for Oats		59								59
		Harrowg for the same		7								7
		Harrowg to cover them		8								8
		Crossing for B. Wheat					59					59
		Harrowg to level						8				8
		Harrowing in Seed							8			8

236   In Pasture—& for Manuring

| 826 | 354 | 99 | 205 | 99 | 176 | 83 | 193 | 50 | 1259 |

When the fields at this Farm (Union) come to be cropped in the order mentioned in the preceeding Table, it is presumed the yield of them may be estimated as follow

118 acrs in Corn	a 12½ bushls	1475 B.	a 2/6	£184.7.6
118	Wheat	Corn ground[8]	1180	5/	295
118	Buck Wheat for Manure			
118	Wheat	1180	5/	295
59	Oats	12½	737½	2/	73.15.0
59	Buck Wht	10	590	2/	59
118	Pasturage			
118	Manuring by Penning &ca			
Total 826	amount of the fields—& produce[9]			£907.2.6

The probable consumption of Corn on this Farm will be

For Negros	800 Bushls
Overseer	30
Hogs	300
	1130
Surplus	345
Made as above	1475

Rotation of Crops for River Farm

Fields distingd by Nos.	Crops which will be in each field in the years at the head of each column							
	1793	1794	1795	1796	1797	1798	1799	1800
1	Paste	Buck Wh. for Manure	Wheat	½ B. Wht & ½ Oats	Paste	Manurg	Corn	Wheat
2	Corn	Wheat	Buck Wh. for Manure	Wheat	½ B. Wht & ½ Oats	Paste	Manurg	Corn
3	Paste	Corn	Wheat	Buck Wht for Manure	Wheat	½ B: Wht & ½ Oats	Paste	Manurg
4 now 9	Paste	Manurg	Corn	Wheat	Buck Wh. for Manure	Wheat	½ B. Wht & ½ Oats	Paste
5 now 8	Past.	Paste	Manug	Corn	Wheat	Buck Wh. for Manure	Wheat	½ B. Wht & ½ Oats
6	Wheat	Paste	Paste	Manug	Corn	Wheat	Buck Wh. for Manure	Wheat
7	Wheat	Paste	½ B. Wh. & ½ Oats	Paste	Manug	Corn	Wheat	Buck Wh. for Manure

The above fields, like those of Dogue run and Union Farm are a little varient in point of size—but not essentially so—The average of them is 125 acres. The annual ploughings, when brought into regular succession will be as follow.[10]

Acres in the Fields	Crops annualy growg thereon	Kind of Plowgs required for these Crops	Seasons at wch these Plowgs shd be given									
			Fall	Wintr	Mar.	Aprl	May	June	July	Aug.	Sep.	Total
125	Corn	Flushing	125									125
		Listing–2 furrows			27							27
		Crossing to Plant				17						17
		Plowing balks				45						45
		Harrowing					17					17
		Roundg with Plows					27					27

	Acres	Operations									Total
Wheat	125	Plowg out—same way									53
		Crossing the last Plowg									64
		Levellg with Harrow for sowing Wheat									27
		Plowing in Wheat					53			54	107
		The above work sows this Crop	125	27	62	44	53	64	80	54	509
B: Wheat for Mane	125	Flushing	125								125
		Crossg for Sowing	125								125
		Harrowg to level			16						16
		Harrowg in the Seed			16						16
		Plowg in B: Wheat			125						125
		Harrowg to levl grd		16							16
Wheat	125	Plowed in, on B: Wheat Manure							125		125
		Flushing					125				125
Oats & B. Wheat	125	Crossg for Oats				63					63
		Harrowg for the same						8			8
		Harrowg them in						8			8
		Crossg for B. Wheat		63							63
		Harrowg to level						8			8
		Harrowg in Seed					8				8
In Past[ur]e and for Manuring	250										
	875		375	106	219	107	186	88	205	54	1340

The rotation of Crops at the River farm being precisely the same (when the fields are brought into a regular course) as that of Union farm, it is unnecessary to repeat the observations, and to suggest the same things over again as are there mentioned; because they apply without the least variation equally to this Farm. And the lands differing but little in quality the yield—to the Acre—must be nearly the same—as follow. viz.

		a 12½ bushls	1562½ B.	a 2/6	£195.6.3
125 acs.	in Corn				
125	Wheat in Corn gd		1250	5/	312.10.0
125	Buck Wheat—for Manure				
125	Wheat		1250	5/	312.10
62½ 125	Oats	12½	781	2/	78.2.0
62½ 125	B: Wheat	10	620	2/	62
125	Pasturage				
125	Manuring by Penning &ca				

Total 875 acs. in 7 fields producing[11] £960.8.3

The quantity of Corn required at this Farm may be estimated as follow

	Bushls	
For Negros	800	
Overseer	30	
Hogs	300	
	1130	
Surplus	432½	Mansn He 400
Made as above	1562½	

Rotation of Crops for Muddy hole Farm

Fields distingd by Nos.	Crops which will be in each field in the years mentioned at the head of each column							
	1793	1794	1795	1796	1797	1798	1799	1800
1	Corn	Wheat	Buck Wh. for Manure	Wheat	½ Oats & ½ B. Wht	Paste	Manug	Corn
2	Paste	B. Wheat for Manure	Wheat	B: Wheat for Manure	Wheat	½ Oats & ½ B. Wht	Paste	Mang
3	Paste	Mang	Corn	Wheat	B. Wht for Manure	Wheat	½ Oats & ½ B. Wht	Paste
4	Wheat	Paste	Mang	Corn	Wheat	B. Wht for Manure	Wheat	½ Oats & ½ B. Wht
5	Paste	½ B. Wh. & ½ Oats	Paste	Mang	Corn	Wheat	B. Wheat for Manure	Wheat
6	Paste	Paste	½ B. Wh. & ½ Oats	Paste	Mang	Corn	Wheat	B. Wht for Manure
7	Paste	Corn	Wheat	½ B. Wh. & ½ Oats	Paste	Mang	Corn	Wheat

The above fields like those of the other Farms, differ a little in size, but the average number of acs. in each is 64—The annual Plowings in each when the fields are in regular rotine will be as follow[12]

Acres in the Fields	Crops growg thereon annually	Kind of Plowgs necessary for these Crops	Fall	Wintr	Mar.	Apl	May	June	July	Aug.	Sep.	Total
							Seasons at wch these plowings shd be given					
64	Corn	Flushing	64									64
		Listing—2 furrows			14							14
		Crossing to plant				8						8
		Plowing balks				23						23
		Harrowing					8					8
		Roundg with Plows					14					14
		Plowg out—same way						28				28
		Crossing the last Plowg							33			33
		Levellg with the harrow to sow wheat								14		14
		Plowing in wheat								28	28	56
			64		14	31	22	28	33	42	28	262
		The above work puts in this Crop of Wheat										
64	Wheat	Flushing	64									64
64	B. Wht for Mane	Crossing for sowg				64						64
		Harrowg to level				8						8
		Harrowg in the Seed				8						8
		Plowg in B. Wheat						64				64
		Harrg to level grd							8			8
		Ploughed in, on B. Wheat Manure										
64	Wheat	Flushing	64									64
64	Oats & B. Wt	Crossg for Oats			32							32
		Harrowg for the same			4							4
		Harrowg them in			4							4
		Crossg for B. Wht					32					32
		Harrowg to level						4				4
		Harrowg in Seed							4			4

In Pasture—& for Manuring

448	192	—	54	111	54	96	45	106	28	686

The rotation at this Farm being the same as at the last two, in all respects; and the suggestions and observations applying equally to it nothing further is necessary than to refer to them.

Corn for Negros   450 Bushls
Overseer   20
Hogs   230
700[13]

Yield of the foregoing fields may be computed—& the land being indifferent & much exhausted as below[14]

64	acs. in Corn	a 10 Bushls	640	a 2/6	£80.0.4
64	Wht in Corn grd		384	5/	96
64	B. Wht for Man[ur]e				
64	Wheat or B. Wht		384	5/	96
32	Oats	10	320	2/	32
32	B. Wh.	8	256	2/	26.12.0
64	Pasturage				
64	Mang by Penng &ca				
Total	448 acs. in 7 fields—producing				£330.12.4

Toll Corn received by the Mill will contribute in a degree towards the supply of my demands for this article; but as there are contingent expenditures & waste that cannot be accurately calculated this resource may be placed against them upon a supposition that they will be adequate thereto.

AD, DLC:GW; AD (fragment), DLC:GW. The fragment apparently is missing one page, which includes most of the text in note 13 as well as the last paragraph of the document.

1. A balk is a ridge or strip of ground left unplowed as a boundary between two furrows.

2. The second AD omits the price and value estimations from the yield tables of the four farms.

3. On the second AD, this sentence continues, "of Hay & Grain 4725."

4. An asterisk at this point references the following note: "This being a larger quantity than the field (which is in this article) is calculated to yield— and as the Mantion house will have a call upon the different Farms for 1200 Bushls and the proportion thereof for this Farm to furnish, amounts to 222 bushels it becomes necesy to give more land to Corn at this place. For this reason, & because the Mill swamp will not only yield it abundantly, if properly ditched & the se⟨ason⟩ should not prove wet, but by raising Corn therein it will be sooner reclaimed, & laid to grass; the 2d lot or Inclosure from the Mill road may be applied to this purpose, provided it cannot be got in order for grass next year without such tillage. But if it can, then to prepare it for this purpose and take the lot next above it for Corn & so proceed until the whole swamp is in good Meadow. from the Mill road up to the tumbling dam."

5. The second AD adds "& mules" at this point.

6. The remainder of this sentence is not present on the second AD.

7. An asterisk at this point references the following note: "The article thus marked, is stated as if Oats & Buck Wheat *only* were to be raised in that field; but this is done that the Ploughings, and the yield thereof, might with more ease & certainty be calculated than if the articles were more varient & numerous. But in Case the field which is designed entirely for Corn is though⟨t⟩ insufficient to raise enough of that grain for the var⟨ious⟩ uses to which it will be applied—viz.—Negros & Hogs on the Farm—and a due proportion towards the calls of the Mansion, which requires 1200 bushels (the proportion of the farm amountg to 375 bushels.)—part of this field may be thus applied; though it is not desir⟨able⟩ if it can well be avoided. Parts of it may also be applied (according to the nature of the soil and the advantages expected to result from it) to the growth of Potatoes—Turnips—Pumpkins—Pease—Beans or any thing else that requires one season only for sowing & gathering. the principle if not the sole design being to raise things which will supply the place of Indian Corn for Horses, Oxen, and Stock of every kind. and whereas Buck Wheat when designed for a crop is not usually sown until the beginning of July; and the ground for it according to the foregoing system is broke up the preceeding Autumn; if there be any Crops, for instance Spring Barley (if it would answer in that climate)—Flax—& more especially such as would require working, as Beans, &ca that would come off in time; these might serve to fill, in part that part of the Field which is allotted to Buck Wheat; but not less than half the whole field must be appropriated to Oats, as the consumption of this article at the Mansion house, over & above what is required for the use of the Farm, will always be great.

"The uncultivated fields in the foregoing course are left for common pasturage—that is—pasturage not sown with grass Seeds. The reasons are, th⟨at⟩ until they are brought into better condition they would not produce clover worth cultivating; and the Seed ⟨set⟩ out, would be too expensive for a thin Crop, which remains only two or three years on the ground; and because they do not lay long enough uncultivated for Timothy, and such like grasses, admitting they would yield them in sufficient quantities. Clover lots therfore at each farm (not less than three, four would be better) of proportionate sizes to the number of P. horses thereon, must be substituted for the purpose of soiling—that is feeding the horses with it—when cut green—And these lots ought to be contiguous to the Stables.

"Whenever the fields shall be so improved by such dressings as circumstances will admit, and by judicious cultivation, they may be laid to grass; and the rotation which is directed for D. Run Farm may be adopted at this, and all the rest, as the most productive with the least labour, and greatest advantage to the ground.

"It will be perceived that the greatest quantity of plowing in the preceeding estimate, for this Farm, is in the Autumn, and months of April and August; but the Fall plowing may be extended into Winter: March & May, may participate in that allotted for April; and September more than probable will share what is given to August."

8. The second AD lacks the words "Corn ground" and indicates 10 bushels at this point.

9. The second AD states a total of 5162½ bushels.

10. The second AD omits the chart and explains: "the course of Crops being precisely the same as that of Union farm, the plowgs will be the same; differing only in quantity, proportioned to the different sizes of the fields—that is as 118 to 125. It is unnecessary therefore to calculate in this place the number of days plowing wch are required at this farm."

11. The second AD continues this sentence with "5463½ Bushels."

12. The second AD omits the chart and explains: "The course of Crops being the same as the last mentioned farms (Union & River) the kinds of plowings will be exactly the same: the difference in the quantity on it will only be as 64 is to 118 or 125 these being the average of the Fields at the three farms which pursue the same rotatn. It is unnecessary therefore to give the detail of them."

13. An asterisk at this point references the following note: "This quantity exceeding by 60 bushls the estimated Crop of Corn on the Farm—as does that at Dogue Run 5 bushls more than the calculation for that place reduces the surplussage of Union & River Farms—(viz.—345 at the first & 432 at the latter making together 777 bushls) to 712 bushls and this being short of the demand from the Mansion house (which requires 1200 bushls) 488 bushels—shews more clearly the necessity of cultivating some part of those fields which are designed for Oats & Buck Wheat, in Corn—or substituting some other grounds (not taken into the regular course) for this purpose: for instance the Mill swamp—until the fields become more productive by judicious courses & proper dressings. The doing of which, as has been observed in another place, answers a most valuable purpose besides that of increasing

the quantity of Corn; to wit—reclaiming and getting in order this valuable Land for Grass; with which it is my earnest desire to lay it as soon as possible; being firmly persuaded that whensoever the whole of this swamp is improved into meadow and properly divided into lots, that the quantity of Hay which might be annually sold; the Meats that might be fatted thereon, if thought more eligable; the additional stock which they would afford means for raising; and the quantity of Butter which might be made, would go near to double the profits of my Estate.

"Buck Wheat & Potatoes, in lieu of Corn for Hogs, might also be made to contribute something towards the reduction & demand for this article; of which it is not my wish to raise more than necessity requires as it is an exhausting Crop and destructive to land, from the manner of its cultivation.

"The proportion of Corn required from this Farm for the use of the Mansion would, if each gave according to the size of their fields, amount to 203 Bushels—& the whole would stand thus

Dogue Run Farm	222 Bushls
Union. . . . . Ditto . . . . ,	375
River. . . . . . Ditto	400
Muddy Hole Do.	203
Total	1200"

14. The second AD elaborates this sentence: "But as this farm in its original state was more indifferent than the others, and has been as hardly used I do not conceive that the Crops will bear a greater proportion to those of the other farms than the following."

From George Clinton

Sir,   New York 19th December 1793

Although Mr Williamson mentions in his Letter to me of the 26th of November that he has transmitted to the secretary of state the affidavit of George Rankin yet I have thought proper to enclose a duplicate of it together with a Copy of his said Letter[1] It is my duty at the same time not only to solicit redress from the Union of the Injury this State sustains from a foreign power's continuing to hold military posts within our territory but also to express to you my apprehensions that the repeated insults which our Citizens experience from those garrisons may at length provoke a retaliation which it will not be in my power to prevent and which may involve consequences of the highest national concern.

Permit me sir to remind you of the exposed condition of our Frontiers—To the Westward we are accessible to the depredations of the Indians now in actual hostility against the United states—and perhaps our only immediate security against their incursions arises from the friendly disposition of the six nations, which ought not to be too much confided in.

The Caughnawagas of lower Canada (a settlement of whom, has, as I am informed since the peace been established under the patronage of the British Government at Oswegotchie[2] on our side of the River st Lawrance) have joined the confederacy of Hostile Indians—which places our Northern Frontiers in a critical situation—and what increases the danger is that our Militia in those exterior settlements are generally destitute of fire arms and many are without the means of procuring them.

There is reason to believe that considerable inattention has taken place in this respect from an expectation that Congress would have made some efficient provision for arming the Militia.

Nor is our sea-board in a more eligible condition—This Port which is so easy of access and on which the public revenues so mu⟨ch⟩ depend, has no fortifications to defend it from the insults even of a single Pirate. I am with the highest respec⟨t⟩ Your most humble and most Obedt serv⟨t⟩

Geo: Clinton

ALS, DNA: RG 59, Miscellaneous Letters; LB, N-Ar: Papers of George Clinton.

1. Charles Williamson (1757–1808), a native of Scotland, was general agent for the Pulteney Association, a London investment group developing lands in the present-day New York counties of Steuben, Allegany, Livingston, Yates, Monroe, Schuyler, and Wayne. Williamson was appointed as a judge for Ontario County in 1793 and 1795, and he represented Ontario and Steuben counties in the New York general assembly from 1796 to 1800. Williamson's letter to Thomas Jefferson of 26 Nov., with the enclosed deposition by Rankin of the same date, are in DNA: RG 59, Miscellaneous Letters (see also *Jefferson Papers*, 27:447–49). For the documents that Clinton enclosed here, see below.

Jefferson replied to this letter on 30 Dec., writing Clinton: "The President has received your letter on the seisure of goods in the county of Ontario by certain officers of the British government, and measures having been taken to procure a full and certain statement of the case, whenever that shall be received, he will proceed to have done in it whatever the facts shall render proper" (*Jefferson Papers*, 27:636).

2. Oswegatchie was an Iroquois village located at the current site of Ogdensburg, N.Y.

Enclosure I
Charles Williamson to George Clinton

Sir   Bath Ontario County 26 Novr 1793

I have the Honor to inclose you an Affidavit taken before me as a Magestrate of this County—as the outrage complained of has been attended with the most distressing consequences to some of the sufferers, and a most dangerous Precident to the safety of the Settlers on this Frontier—I thought it my duty to lay it before your Excellency.

As I consider this unwarantable stretch of Local power on the part of the British goverment—as a gross insult to the goverment of the United States—I took the liberty of transmitting to Mr Jefferson a Copy of the Affidavit enclosed to your Excellency—requesting of him to lay it before the President of the United States.

That spirited Exertion which has ever marked your Excellencys goverment will I hope on this Occasion lead you to recommend to the Executive of the United States such measures as will at once put an end to such Authorised Insults and show to the goverment of Upper Canada that however insignificant they may suppose the County of Ontario—that its Inhabitants have the Honor of living under a free goverment that will protect its Citizens from Insult—I have the Honor to be with great esteem Sir your most Obet and humble Sert

                                                Chas Williamson

(Copy[)]

Copy, DNA: RG 59, Miscellaneous Letters.

Enclosure II
Affidavit of George Rankin

[26 November 1793]

Personally appeared before me Chas Williamson one of the judges of the Court of Common Pleas for the County Ontario in the State of New York. Geo. Rankin of Newtonpoint[1] in the County and State aforesaid who being duly sworn, deposeth and saith that he this deponent with three other Men in Two boats passed the British Garrison at oswego within the jurisdiction of the State of New York, About 20th August last, that said Boat had on board Cargoes consisting of Castings, Tar, Iron, and one

Barrel Gin; valued at about 500 Dollars, that he this Deponent with said Boats proceeded to a place called the 18 Mile Creek,[2] where about one half of said Cargoes were landed—and from there proceeded with the remaining part of said Cargoe to a distance of about 12 Miles from the Garrison at Niagara both of which said places, where the Cargoes were landed is within the jurisdiction of the County of Ontario in the State of New York.

And he this deponent further saith that he went to Tarento now in the possession of the British with a view to obtain permits for Entering said cargoes in the British lines—that permits were Granted, and now in possession of this Deponent—but that in the Intermediate time a Seizure was made of said Cargoes at the several places, where they had been landed by Men (as this Deponent was informed) under the direction and orders of a Revenue Officer of Upper Canada.

And he the Deponent further saith that in Consiquence of said Seizures he personally applyed to a Sheriff of one of the Counties in said Upper Canada for a writ of Replevin—that said Sheriff replyed that he could not grant a writ of Replevin as the seizure had been made within the jurisdiction of the Goverment of the United States.

And further this Deponent saith that the Cargoes mentioned as Aforesaid had not to his knowledge while as his property been out of the jurisdiction of the United States and that he saw an advertisement at Niagara exposing to sale said Cargoes as Contraband property and as such he believes was actually sold—which said advertisement was signed by a Mr McKnab whome this Deponent believes to be a revenue Officer under the Goverment of Upper Canada.[3]

And this Deponent further saith that a Mr Lafferty and James McDonald were Chief Owners in the property together with this Deponent—that said permits were granted in their Several Names that he this deponent veryly believes that said Men will be materially affected by loss of said property—as being men in low Circumstances in Life.

And further this Deponent saith not.

George Rankin

Sworn before me Chas Williamson this Twenty sixth Day of Novr 1793 at Bath in the County of Ontario and the State of New York.

Chas Williamson

Copy, DNA: RG 59, Miscellaneous Letters.

1. Newtown Point was officially renamed Elmira in 1808.

2. Eighteenmile Creek, which flows into Lake Ontario, is located in Niagara County immediately north of Lockport.

3. Colin McNabb (c.1764–1810) was appointed superintendent of inland navigation at Niagara in 1788 and collector of customs at that place in 1801.

From Thomas Jefferson

Dec. 19. 93.

Th: Jefferson has the honor to inclose to the President translations of papers received from Mr Jaudenes.[1] he submits whether it will not be proper to communicate them to Congress, as being nearly similar to those which closed the great communication on Spanish affairs. if the President thinks they should be sent in, Th: J. will have copies prepared.[2]

AL, DNA: RG 59, Miscellaneous Letters; AL (letterpress copy), DLC: Jefferson Papers; LB, DNA: RG 59, George Washington's Correspondence with His Secretaries of State.

1. Jefferson sent translations of José de Jaudenes to Jefferson, 18 Dec., and the two documents enclosed with that letter, which discussed American and Spanish relations with Cherokee, Creek, and Chickasaw Indians on the southern border, stressing American provocations and Spanish restraint. Jaudenes, who also signed on behalf of the absent José Ignacio de Viar, requested that the information be given to GW, "to the end that these may determine what they shall judge convenient, seeing how much good may be produced by the friendly convention proposed, and how much evil by the omission of it" (*Jefferson Papers*, 27:584–85).

2. These documents were submitted with GW's message to Congress of 23 December.

From George Meade

Decr 19th 1793

Mr Meades most respectful Compliments to the President, & takes the liberty, of Informing him, that his Seed arrived, in the Mohawk, from London, & on enquiry of the Capt. for it, he informd him, it was sent to the Custom house.[1] Mr Meade sent the Original order a Year ago, & the Vessell never arrived, he repeated it some time since, to his Correspondent George Barclay Esqr., who writes him 28 Sepr from London "I have bought the Presidents Seed here, it is the best French, & from Ireland, it goes by the Mohawk, when I get Gordons Acct of the Cost, I will send it to You, there is about 40 lb. of it, 1/ ℔ lb. You may depend on its being the very best, they have it from Ireland on Purpose."[2]

When Mr Meade receives the Acct he will send it to the President, Mr Lear was so particular that he accompanied the order with a Ten Dollar Bank Note.[3]

AL, DLC:GW.

1. The *Mohawk* arrived at Philadelphia on 25 November.

2. George Barclay was a merchant located at 84 Hatton Street in London. James Gordon (d. 1794) was a partner in Gordon, Dermer and Co., seedsmen located at 25 Fenchurch Street in London.

3. Meade is referring to Tobias Lear's letter to him of 1 Jan. 1793, which requested that Meade procure furze seed for GW.

From Richard Dobbs Spaight

Sir   North Carolina Fayetteville Dec: 19th 1793.

By the last post I received the Secretary of wars letter of the 12th Novem: in answer to my letter to you of the 21st of October last respecting the trunk of money which was taken from Captain Hervieux by the revenue officers and lodged in the hands of the deputy Marshal at Wilmington, and which I had given him in order to detain on a presumtion, it had been taken from on board the Spanish brig a prize to L'Amee Margueritte.[1]

From the depositions which I sent you in novem: I have no doubt but that the money was the property of the Spaniards and taken from them by Captain Hervieux, but in order to get every information that can be obtained to prove the fact, I have directed the Marshal (which I did not think myself authorized to do before I knew whether any part of the prize was to be secured, that was within the jurisdiction of the State.) to have the invoices and such other of the shipping papers as are in the trunk fait[h]fully translated and authenticated and sent on to me: and if they cannot be translated there to send the original papers that I may have it done.[2]

Should those papers make it fully appear that the property was taken from on board the Spanish brig, which I am confident will be the case, I shall be glad to know to whom I shall cause the trunk money and papers to be delivered: as the brig her Captain and crew, have been carried into Charleston So. Carolina where they at present remain and there is no Spanish Consul in this State.[3]

I should further wish to be informed whether the expence and trouble of the deputy Marshall, in detaining and Securing the property (he having as I understand employed some persons to assist him to guard it) is to be paid by the persons to whom the property is restored or by the United States.[4]

The Secretary of War in his letter of the 12th of Novem: and that of the 16 August last makes a difference of two months, between the time, after which prizes brought or sent into the ports of the United States by proscribed vessels shall be secured for the purpose of restoring them to their former owners. In his letter of the 16th August, the 5th of that month was the time specified in that of the 12th of Novem: he goes back to the fifth of June last.[5]

As the instructions are contradictory I shall not take any steps to secure the L'Amee Margueritte formerly the Sloop providence untill I shall receive further instructions from you on that head: the more so, because in my letter to you of the 24th June last I particularly mentioned that the Vanqueur de la Bastille, sailed from the port of Charleston on the 7th day of June last, and afterwards captured the Sloop providence of Montego bay, and brought her into the port of Wilmington.

The Secretary of wars letter of the 7th August which conveyed to me the general instructions respecting the conduct I should persue, in regard to Vessels arm'd and equipped in the United States as privateers on behalf of any of the parties at War, did not contain any instructions to secure the Sloop providence for her former owners: nor did I receive any instructions to secure any prize whatever 'till it was communicated to me by the Secretary's letter of the 16th Augt.[6] I am therefore induced to conclude that he has made a mistake in his letter of the 12th Novem: by inserting the 5th June instead of the 5th Augt.[7]

The Sloop L'Amee Margueritte remains still in the port of Wilmington but near the mouth of Cape Fear river, where the Militia without the assistance of an armd Vessel cannot readily take her. The revenue cutter I have reason to beleive is neither armed or well manned—As Capt: He[r]vieux will wait the decision respecting the money and his commission being likewise in the hands of the marshal, it is probable he will not leave the port before I have an answer from you.[8] I have the honor to be wt. respect Sr yrs &c.

Rd D. Spaight

LB, Nc-Ar: Governors' Letterbooks. Secretary of War Henry Knox replied to this letter, and to Spaight's letter to GW of 26 Nov., in a letter to Spaight of 13 Jan. 1794 (Nc-Ar: Governors' Letterbooks).

1. Secretary of War Henry Knox's letter to Spaight of 12 Nov. acknowledged Spaight's letter to GW of 21 Oct., gave Spaight directions for obtaining repayment of expenses incurred "in the prosecution of any of the requests made in behalf of the United States," and instructed him: "From your representation of the circumstances attending the L'Amee Margueritte it is concluded, that she as well as the Vanqueur de la Bastille, was originally constituted a privateer within the jurisdiction of the United States, and is therefore a proscribed vessel. If this has been the case, of which your Excellency will please to obtain accurate information, it will follow that her prize, if within your ports, together with all the property which was taken from her is to be restored to her former master or owner.

"If there are circumstances which render it questionable whether the L'amee Margueritte is of the foregoing description, it will be necessary that the same should be stated for the information of the president of the United States and in the mean time to detain her for an ultimate decision.

"If the said Vanqueur de Bastille, being a proscribed vessel made prize of the Sloop providence and brought her into our ports after the fifth day of June, it would also follow that the said Sloop providence now supposed to be the L'Amee Margueritte should also be restored to her master, or the consul of the nation to whom she belonged at the time of her capture.

"As to the Vanqueur de Bastille neither she nor any other proscribed privateer can be permitted to make any sort of repairs in our ports unless she or they divest themselves of all warlike equipments and reduce themselves to the situation of a mere commercial vessel—This is to be considered as a standing rule" (Nc-Ar: Governors' Letterbooks).

2. The depositions were sent with Spaight's letter to GW of 26 Nov., which has not been found. Spaight's letter directing the deputy marshal at Wilmington, John Blakeley, to translate and send the papers was dated 9 Dec. (Nc-Ar: Governors' Letterbooks). Blakeley responded on 22 Dec. (Nc-Ar: Governors' Correspondence).

3. Secretary of War Knox instructed Spaight in a letter of 18 Jan. 1794 to deliver the money "to the agent who has been appointed by the Spanish commissioners for that purpose" (Nc-Ar: Governors' Letterbooks).

4. In his letter to Spaight of 13 Jan., Knox replied that the expenses "incurred in the prosecution of this business" were to "be defrayed by the general Government" upon accounts authenticated by Spaight.

5. For Knox's circular letter to the governors of 16 Aug., see Knox to Tobias Lear, 17 Aug., n.1.

6. For Knox's circular letter to the governors of 7 Aug., see Cabinet Opinion on French Privateers and Prizes, 5 Aug., n.3.

7. In Knox's letter to Spaight of 13 Jan. 1794, he confirmed that this conclusion was correct.

8. When Spaight wrote GW on 31 Jan. 1794 to announce the seizure of *L'Aimée Marguerite,* he had not yet received Knox's reply, which arrived on 6 Feb. 1794.

Letter not found: to John Hyde, 20 Dec. 1793. In a letter to GW of 23 Dec., Hyde mentioned receiving "your Letter of the 20."

From Frederick Augustus Conrad Muhlenberg

Sir   Philada Dec. 20th 1793.

Permit me to lay before You a Recomendation of Jno. Witman of the Borough of Reading for the Office of Inspector of the Revenue of that District[1] & to assure You that I am with the highest Respect Sir Your most obdt humble Servt

Fredk A. Muhlenberg

ALS, DLC:GW.

1. This recommendation has not been identified with certainty. Muhlenberg may be referring to the recommendation dated (but possibly misdated) 17 Dec. 1792 and signed by Muhlenberg and eleven other citizens, which is the only other document in the application file for John Witman, Jr. For that recommendation, see *Papers, Presidential Series,* 11:524–25. Witman did not receive this appointment; he remained the state government's collector of excise for Berks County at least until the end of 1797.

From Thomas Jefferson

Dec. 21. 93.

Th: Jefferson with his respects to the President incloses a letter from the Governor of Pensylvania in answer to one from mister Genet praying him to deliver the French sailors (whom he calls *deserters*) on board a vessel to be transported to New York, there to be put on board a man of war.[1] The Convention having directed the proceeding to be observed in this case, and the laws having directed the District judge to attend to it, Th: J. has prepared an answer to the Governor informing him that the Federal Executive has nothing to do in it, but to leave the law to take it's course.[2]

AL, DNA: RG 59, Miscellaneous Letters; LB, DNA: RG 59, George Washington's Correspondence with His Secretaries of State.

1. For the impetus behind Genet's letter to Thomas Mifflin of 16 Dec., see Sundry Frenchmen in a Philadelphia Jail to GW, 3 Dec., and source note to that document. Genet advised Mifflin that he would have recourse to Mifflin's good offices to have the prisoners brought under guard to a ship that would transport them to New York, where they would be kept aboard the French ship *Normande* (DNA: RG 59, Miscellaneous Letters). Mifflin's letter to Jefferson of 20 Dec. enclosed the copy of Genet's letter, in order "to know the sentiments of the General Government" on Genet's "request, which I do not, at this time, think myself authorised to grant" (*Jefferson Papers*, 27:597).

2. For the "Convention Defining and Establishing the Functions and Privileges of Consuls and Vice Consuls" (1788), see Miller, *Treaties*, 228–44. Jefferson's response to Mifflin of this date, which GW approved on 23 Dec., stated that as the prisoners were in the custody of the judicial authority, "the Federal Executive does not think itself authorized to interfere either as to their enlargement or detention" (*Jefferson Papers*, 27:605; *JPP*, 272).

From Thomas Jefferson

Dec. 22. 1793.

Th: Jefferson has the honor to return to the President Govr Clinton's letter.[1] also to send him a statement of mister Genet's conversation with him in which he mentioned Gouvernr Morris. this paper Th: J. prepared several days ago, but it got mislaid which prevented it's being sent to the President.[2]

AL, DNA: RG 59, Miscellaneous Letters; LB, DNA: RG 59, George Washington's Correspondence with His Secretaries of State.

1. See George Clinton to GW, 19 December.

2. Jefferson's statement, dated 11 Dec., reads: "The President doubtless recollects the communications of mister Ternant expressing the dissatisfaction of the Executive council of France with mister Morris our minister there, which however mister Ternant desired might be considered as informal: that Colo. Smith also mentioned that dissatisfaction, & that mister LeBrun told him he would charge mister Genet expressly with their representations on this subject; & that all further consideration thereon lay over therefore for mister Genet's representations.

"Mr Genet, some time after his arrival (I cannot now recollect how long, but I think it was a month or more) coming to my house in the country one evening, joined me in a walk near the river. our conversation was on various topics, & not at all of an official complexion. as we were returning to the house, being then I suppose on some subject relative to his country (tho' I really do not recall to mind what it was) he turned about to me, just in the passage of the gate, & said 'but I must tell you we all depend on you to send us a good minister there, with whom we may do business confidentially, in the place of mister Morris.' these are perhaps not the identical words, yet I believe they are nearly so; I am sure they are the substance, & he scarcely employed more in the expression. it was unexpected; &, to avoid the necessity of an extempore answer, I instantly said something resuming the preceding thread of conversation, which went on, & no more was said about mister Morris. from this I took it for granted he meant now to come forward formally with complaints against mister Morris, as we had been given to expect, & therefore I mentioned nothing of this little expression to the President. time slipped along, I expecting his complaints & he not making them. it was undoubtedly his office to bring forward his own business himself, & not at all mine to hasten or call for it; & if it was not my duty, I could not be without reasons for not taking it on myself officiously. he at length went to New York, to wit, about the [   ] of [   ] without having done anything formally on this subject. I now became uneasy lest he should consider the little sentence he had uttered to me as effectively, tho' not regularly, a complaint. but the more I reflected on the subject the more impossible it seemed that he could have viewed it as such; & the rather because if he had, he would naturally have asked from time to time 'Well, what are you doing with my complaint against mister Morris?' or some question equivalent. but he never did. it is possible I may at other times have heard him speak unfavorably of mister Morris, tho' I do not recollect any particular occasion: but I am sure he never made to me any proposition to have him recalled. I believe I mentioned this matter to mister Randolph before I left Philadelphia: I know I did after my return: but I did not to the President, till the reciept of mister Genet's letter of Sep. 30. which from some unaccountable delay of the post never came to me in Virginia, tho I remained there till Oct. 25. (and received there three subsequent mails) and it never reached me in Philadelphia till Dec. 2.

"The preceding is the state of this matter, as nearly as I can recollect it at this time, & I am sure it is not materially inaccurate in any point" (ADS, DNA: RG 59, Miscellaneous Letters).

From the Commissioners for the District of Columbia

Sir,   Washington 23d December 1793.

You will receive inclosed a copy of an Agreement we have entered into with Messrs Morris and Greenleaf for the Sale of three thousand Lots farther, at 35£ a Lot, somewhat modifying the old and stating the whole in this new Contract[1]—A consideration of the uncertainty of Settled Times, and an unembarrassed Commerce, weighed much with us: as well as Mr Morris's Capital, Influence, and Activity—the Statement of Funds inclosed,[2] may enable the prosecution of the work even in a War; in which Event we should without this Contract have been almost still—Under this Contract as the rest we have entered into, the purchasers cannot claim a Deed or legal Title, till the

Terms and Conditions of the Sale are complied with—It may be desireable to Messrs Greenleaf and Morris, to have the legal Title for the purpose of taking up Money on a part of this property, and that they may dispose of parcels to purchasers—we have had some conversation with Mr Greenleaf, especially as to the last; but do not feel ourselves at Liberty to depart from the common mode of our Business in this Instance, without your approbation—Mr Greenleaf has expressed a willingness, that himself Mr Morris and Mr Nicholson should join in a Bond for the payment of the Money, and[3] performing the other parts of the Contract; we have intimated that there would be a propriety in joining another such Security as Mr Nicholson, and it appears to us, that in this Business which will be a good while in winding up, if it rests on personal Security, there ought to be a strong probability of having at least two monied Securities to apply to, for the Payment of such large Sums, and the Discharge of such heavy burthens. Should you advise or approve the transferring the Security to personal as mentioned, the inclosed Copy of a Bond may we think answer the purpose.[4]

Mr Greenleaf had also a conversation with us on the exchange of the ground reserved for a Hospital as he had with you. We have always thought the place reserved improper on several Accounts; and Should advise a Change to a better Site, but we believe, a preliminary step must be, to purchase the Interest of the proprietors in that spot; for on releasing it from the present reserve we are apprehensive it will fall under the general Rule of dividing it into Squares and Lots.[5]

The Assembly has indulged this place with a Corporation Bank. we wish to bring it into such Credit as to perform the operation, of which a Sketch is inclosed, and by being the Holders of the Shares allowed to be subscribed by the Commissioners they will have not only that power, but a right to discount occasionally which may prevent Embarrassment from Money not being punctually paid.[6]

We have been Surprized and concerned that Mr Blodget should have proceeded in a new Lottery, not only without our Consent but after a contrary Explanation which took place with him a little before he left this place: he has drove us to tell him frankly that unless he withdraws it we shall disavow it to the public.[7]

Major Ellicott after his absence great part of the Summer, and all the fall, as we hear in other Service, has returned to us in the Winter: we do not accept his farther Services—the business we believe was going on full as Well without him.[8]

There has been a discovery of Foundation Stone from the Key of all Keys for a considerable distance this way, which we expect will be valuable[9]—the price was rising on us, nor could we lately form a new Contract or get an old one executed to our Satisfaction: we have promised Mr Greenleaf to let him have the use of part of it—We wish to act in concert with him and his friends, in aiding eventually and keeping Materials at a reasonable price—with these views we intend to interest him in the quarries at Aquia,[10] he benefiting us in the use of the Brick Machine—Messrs Greenleaf and Morris do not bound themselves to the City; they have embraced the Great falls and seem desirous of acquiring on other parts of Potomac.[11]

Our Attention has been very much taken up and so has Mr Greenleafs in first settling the Outlines of Mr Morris's Contract and afterwards—Particulars of that and his combined—We had no Information of the building Scheme or a sight of it 'till today after the signing the Contract and therefore have not formed any Opinion of it farther than that which is obvious to every Body that is that every Addition of Capital in Building must add to the Improvement and population of the City. We are Sir most respectfully & truly Your very affectionate Servants

Th: Johnson
Dd Stuart
Danl Carroll

LS, DLC:GW; LB, DNA: RG 42, Records of the Commissioners for the District of Columbia, Letters Sent, 1791–1802.

Edmund Randolph replied to this letter on 19 Jan. 1794 (DNA: RG 42, Records of the Commissioners for the District of Columbia, Letters Received, 1791–1802).

1. A copy of the contract with James Greenleaf and Robert Morris, dated 24 Dec., was entered into the commissioners' book of proceedings, DNA: RG 42, Records of the Commissioners for the District of Columbia, Proceedings, 1791–1802. The previous contract, for the purchase of 3,000 lots at £25 (Maryland money) per lot, was with Greenleaf and dated 23 September. The payments were to be made in seven annual installments beginning in May 1794.

2. This enclosure may have been the undated document in Thomas Johnson's writing titled "City Funds" (DLC: Records of the U.S. Commissioners of

the City of Washington, 1790–1816). That document listed assets of £465,000 (£15,000 from the "last Virginia Donation," £180,000 from the sale of 6,000 lots to Greenleaf and Morris, and the remainder from two other sales totaling 6,000 lots). Noting that the lots sold "are supposed to make good the Appropriations at £25 ℔ Acre," and that the land near the bridge and causeway "is expected to return the Money laid out on that Work," the document listed for 1794 £15,000 from the Virginia donation and £25,714 as one-seventh of the £180,000; and for 1795, "taking in Mr Greenleafs Loan of 12,000 if necessary 37,714 besides Sales."

3. The text from this point through the word "intimated" was omitted from the letter-book copy.

4. The enclosed copy of the bond has not been identified. Randolph replied for GW that while GW did not doubt that Morris and Greenleaf could fulfill the contract, "he does not conceive himself authorized, to approve a departure from the common mode of retaining the legal title, until payment." He did, however, "wish, that every facility, short of abandoning your hold, should be afforded to the objects, which those gentlemen have in view" (Randolph to Commissioners, 19 Jan. 1794).

5. For Greenleaf's ideas about the hospital site, see GW to Daniel Carroll, 16 December. Randolph replied that GW believed the hospital site marked on the plan was not "irrevocably appropriated to that use," so that there was no necessity to exchange land with Greenleaf. GW would, however, "make no decision on this head, until he shall hear again from you" (Randolph to Commissioners, 19 Jan. 1794).

6. The enclosure has not been identified. Article IV of the "ACT to establish a bank in the district of Columbia," passed by the Maryland legislature, allowed the District of Columbia commissioners to subscribe, in their capacity as commissioners, for up to 2,000 shares in the bank (*Md. Laws 1793*, ch. 30). Randolph responded that it was "somewhat difficult to discover how to authorize" such a subscription and that it was "very questionable, whether the style of execution, in the event of a possible delinquency on your part, will comport with the interest of the city." He requested the commissioners' "sentiments upon these topics" for submission to GW (Randolph to Commissioners, 19 Jan. 1794).

7. Samuel Blodget advertised in November his plan to hold a second lottery after the conclusion of the much-delayed first lottery: "By this Lottery the Commissioners will be enabled to give an elegant Spicimen of the private Buildings to be erected in the City of Washington.—Two Beautiful Designs are already selected for the entire Fronts on two of the Public Squares; from these Drawings it is proposed to erect two Centre and four corner Buildings, as soon as possible after this Lottery is sold, and to convey them, when complete, to the fortunate Adventures" (*Virginia Chronicle And, Norfolk & Portsmouth General Advertiser,* 23 Nov.).

The commissioners wrote Blodget on 16 Dec. asking him to "stop this Business as soon as possible and not drive us to the necessity of a public disavowal of it" (DNA: RG 42, Records of the Commissioners for the District of Columbia, Letters Sent, 1791–1802). Despite the commissioners' disapproval, Blodget continued his plans for a second lottery, issuing a broadside on the subject dated 1 Jan. 1794, which stated that the money raised would go to the planned national university (DNA: RG 42, Records of the Commissioners for the District of Columbia, Letters Received, 1791–1802). When Blodget visited Philadelphia in January, GW had Randolph give him "explicit" instructions to "instantly suspend all further proceeding therein until the sanction of the Commissioners should be unequivocally obtained" (GW to Thomas Johnson, 23 Jan. 1794). With Blodget returning to the Federal City "in order to settle with" the commissioners "what he calls a mistake," GW directed the commissioners to "prevent the progress of this second scheme, unless you can obtain the most complete security, that there will be a perfect punctuality in furnishing Satisfaction for the prizes" (Randolph to Commissioners, 19 Jan. 1794).

On 18 May 1794 the commissioners approved a letter, dated 17 May, declaring "that we have given no Countenance to the publishing or carrying on this Lottery nor will have anything to do with the conduct of it" (DNA: RG 42, Records of the Commissioners for the District of Columbia, Proceedings, 1791–1802; printed in the *Maryland Journal and Baltimore Advertiser,* 23 May 1794). Nonetheless, on 30 Aug. 1794 Blodget published a formal announcement of the lottery, to "commence as soon as the Tickets are sold, or at all events on Monday, the 22nd of December next" (*Gazette of the United States and Daily Evening Advertiser* [Philadelphia], 3 Sept. 1794). The lottery drawing was never completed.

8. For some of the commissioners' disagreements with the surveyor Andrew Ellicott, see their letters to GW of 5 Jan., 11–12 March, and 13 March; and Andrew Ellicott, Benjamin Ellicott, and Isaac Briggs to GW, 29 June. The commissioners wrote Ellicott on 17 Dec. telling him that his resumption of duties "we expected would depend on our request," and adding that, not having had his services when "they might have been most useful," the commissioners would "not add to an establishment in Winter" (DNA: RG 42, Records of the Commissioners for the District of Columbia, Letters Sent, 1791–1802). After a further exchange, Ellicott responded on 21 Dec. with a long resignation letter defending his conduct, which, he informed the commissioners in his cover letter of the same date, "is for the Public" (DNA: RG 42, Records of the Commissioners for the District of Columbia, Letters Received, 1791–1802). Randolph responded, "The subject of Mr Ellicott, the President leaves to your own judgment" (Randolph to Commissioners, 19 Jan. 1794).

9. The Key of All Keys, also known as Braddock's Rock, was a large rock formation jutting into the Potomac River. It was located to the left of what is now 23rd Street at the Theodore Roosevelt Memorial Bridge ramp.

10. Sandstone quarried from along Aquia Creek in Stafford County, Va., was used in the construction of the White House and Capitol, among other buildings.

11. The remainder of the LS is in the writing of Thomas Johnson.

To Hiland Crow

Mr Crow,   Philadelphia 23d Decr 1793

I really am at a loss for words to express my vexation and displeasure at your neglect in plowing, after I told you how anxious I was that this business should be carried on with all the dispatch in your power, the moment the ground was softened by Rains; when I had pointed out to you the quantity you had to flush up during the fall, to prepare for the Crops I named to you; and when you know that I had, during my stay at home, made several attempts to begin this work at D: Run, but was obliged to desist because the earth was so dry & hard as not to be broke without killing the horses. And this neglect is the more extraordinary as it does not appear that you have tread a single bed of Wheat from the Stacks in No. 3. By this unaccountable management I have now all that Wheat to get out, amidsts the frosts, Snows, and rains of Winter; and shall have 350 Acres of ground, (from the same causes) to flush up at a season of the year when the fields ought to be in a state of high preparation for the reception of Oats; for sowing Buck Wheat for Manure; and planting of Corn.

How am I to account for this? Mr Lewis has said for you, that you we⟨re⟩ ordered to gather Corn; but were you no⟨t⟩ ordered also to Plow; and told where: could not both have been carried on at the same? Was not this always my practice? Has your Crop of Corn turn⟨d⟩ out so large as to have employed you⟨r⟩ whole time ever since I left home? I wish ⟨I⟩ may find it so.

In a word I have been so mu⟨ch⟩ disturbed at your insufferable negle⟨ct⟩ that it is with difficulty I have been restrained from ordering you instantl⟨y⟩ off the Plantation. My whole plan for next year is ruined by your conduct: And look ye, Mr Crow, I have too good reasons to believe that your running about, & entertaining company at home, contrary to your agreement (by which my business is untended) is the cause of this, now, irremediable evil in the progress of my business; and I do hereby give you notice, that I have now (I hope and believe) got a Person of property, character, and judgment to Manage my business, & that he is not only authorised, but expressly ordered if those practices are not departed from; if you are not constantly with you people; or if you do not comply with your agreement (which is sent to him)

most strictly (as I will do with mine) to turn you off the plantation at any season of the year, and not to pay you one shilling:
you may sue, if you please, and your agreement shall be given
in bar.[1]

I sent a horse to you for the Plow, because I never intended
(as he had got stiff & unfit for the road) that he should ever go
out of a walk; instead of which I learn you were figuring away at
the races with him, & have converted him into the very thing, I
parted with because of his unfitness for. I am very willing and
desirous to be your friend—but if your conduc⟨t⟩ does not merit
it—you must abide the ⟨co⟩nsequences from Yrs

Go: Washington

ALS (letterpress copy), DLC:GW.

1. Crow's contract of 15 Sept. 1790 (renewed to 1 Jan. 1793) had specified "that he will not absent himself from said Farms without permission,"
that "the entertainment of Travelers" was "particularly restricted," and that
"he will (when not necessarily called off for other purposes) be constantly
with some part or other of his people at their work," and it provided that "in
case of departure from this agreement the said president or his Agent may
discharge him at any season of the Year" (DLC:GW). The first of these provisions appears in the surviving fragment of Crow's new contract (DS, ViHi:
Mary Custis Lee Papers), and presumably the other provisions were repeated
as well. GW had enclosed copies of his agreements with his overseers in his
letter to William Pearce of 18 December.

To John Christian Ehlers

Mr Ehler,   Philadelphia Decr 23d 1793.

By a Vessel which left this City ten or twelve days ago I sent
you Grafts of several kinds of fruit, according to a list which was
enclosed to Mr Lewis, & which I presume he gave you.[1]

I now give you a letter to a Gentleman living about 12 miles
from you, where there used to be, and I dare say still is, a great
variety of choice apples and other fruits[2]—Go then when you
find it convenient, for them, & it may be done by land or water,
as you like best. Do not omit grafting a good many of the Golden
Pippin which grows in my own Orchard.

I expect Mr Pearce who is to superintend my business will be
at Mount Vernon by the time this letter will get to your hands,
and I expect you will observe his directions, & pay the same
attention to any regulations he may establish, as if they were

given, and made by myself; the same will be expectd from your wife, and from John—The last of whom, that is John, you may inform, has displeased me, by giving himself impudent airs, in saying he would not have this thing, nor he would not have that thing, because they were either not good enough, or not made to his liking.[3] You may tell him from me, that this is neither the way to make me his friend, or to get better things. The way to obtain them is to ask for what he wants modestly; without wch he will not get them at all—or at least nothing more than what is absolutely necessary.

I hope, and do expect, that you will use your best exertions in planting out trees—making good the hedges—Keeping the Gardens—the Lawns—and the Vineya⟨rd⟩ in order, with such other things as was to have been done last winter but was not then accomplished. And as I have desired Mr Pearce to have cuttings of the Lombardy Poplar, & the Willows planted along the ditches at the Plantations, for hedges do not trim those along the Walks, or elsewhere until they are wanted for this purpose.

I shall not close this letter without exhorting you to refrain from spiritous liquors—they will prove your ruin if you do not. Consider how little a drunken Man differs from a beast; the latter is not endowed with reason—the former deprives himself of it; and when that is the case acts like a brute; annoying, and disturbing every one around him—But this is not all—nor as it respects himself the worst of it; By degrees it renders a person feeble & not only unable to serve others but to help himself—and being an act of his own he fall from a state of usefulness into contempt and at length suffers, if not perishes in penury & want.

Don't let this be your case. Shew yourself more of a man, and a Christian, than to yield to so intolerable a vice; which cannot, I am certain (to the greatest lover of liquor) give more pleasure to sip in the poison (for it is no better) than the consequences of it in bad behaviour at the moment, & the more serious evils produced by it afterwards, must give pain. I am—Your friend

Go: Washington

ALS (letterpress copy), DLC:GW.

1. An entry for 11 Dec. in GW's household accounts records the payment of $2 "for grafts of trees to send to Mt Vernon" (Household Accounts; see also Account Book, 2 Sept. 1793–4 April 1794, DLC:GW). The list has not been identified.

2. This letter has not been identified.

3. John Gottleib Richler, an indentured servant, had been brought to Mount Vernon in July as another gardener.

To Thomas Green

Thomas,   Philadelphia 23d Decembr 1793

It is eight weeks this day since I left Mount Vernon—and what have you done? Not a stroke to Crows House so late as the 15th of this month (the date of the last report)—Not a stroke to the sheds at Dogue run Barn. Very little that I can discover to the Barn itself; and scarcely any thing else, except running to Alexandria and repairing your own house. In doing which (by your own reports) you have employed Tom Davis & Muclus [   ] days: at a time too, when, on account of the season of the year, not one man out of their labour ought to have been withdrawn from the out doors work on Crows house, and the Walls of the Barn sheds.

Is it possible for any misconduct, or impudence to exceed this transaction? when you knew how extremely anxious I was to get the Brick work of these buildings done before the frosts set in; & when I had told you in the most explicit language I was able, that my Carpenters should stick close to those works until they were compleated; and that this was the case while I remained at home you know—yet, notwithstanding my anxiety on this head; notwithstanding my express orders on the occasion: No soone⟨r⟩ was my back turned than every man set about what pleased him best; and, as usual, I have got little or nothing done.

I know full well, that to speak to you is of no more avail, than to speak to a bird that is flying over one's head; first, because you are lost to all sense of shame, & to every feeling that ought to govern an honest man, who sets any store by his character; and secondly, because you have no more command of th⟨e⟩ people over whom you are placed, than I have over the beasts of the forists: for if they chuse to work, they may; if they do not you have not influence enough to make them; or if they incline to do one sort work (only for an excuse to be idle or, to be after their own pranks) you can not compel them to do another: why else has Is⟨aac⟩ been the Lord knows how long getting ⟨*illegible*⟩ when I expressly ordered that Nothing should take them from the work I left you engaged in, until it was compleated? And how durst you, take Tom Davis from the Brick work I directed him to execute, before it was done in order to execute your own projects.

Although you pay so little regard to my orders at a distance, and your time, and those of my Carpenters are so miserably mispent, it may be well for you to know that, I have got a person now, who is not only a man of character, but is also a good judge of Work; and, that he has not only the authority, but he has my express orders, if he finds you inattentive to your duty, in any respect whatsoever, unable to govern the people who are placed under you, or to regulate their work to the best advantage; or finds you departing from the articles of your agreement, to discharge you that momt; and to disposses your family of the house they are in;[1] for I cannot, nor will not submit to such infamous treatment as I meet with from you, how ever well disposed I may be to befriend them—or wish to be your friend, if you would let me.

Go: Washington

ALS (letterpress copy), DLC:GW.
    1. See GW to William Pearce, 18 December.

From Alexander Hamilton

Treasury Depmt Decr 23d 1793.
    The Secretary of the Treasury has the honor to submit to the consideration of the President a communication from the Commissioner of the revenue, dated the 18h of December respecting Mr James Collins, Inspector of the Revenue for Survey No: 2 of the District of Pennsylvania.[1] It has at length become certain (what has been for some time feared) that Mr Collins is incapable of executing the duties of the office and that the good of the public service requires his removal.

Alexandr Hamilton
Secy of the Treay

LB, DLC:GW.
    1. Tench Coxe's letter about James Collins has not been identified. On 29 Jan. 1794 GW nominated John Boyd to replace Collins (*Senate Executive Journal,* 147).

From Alexander Hamilton

Treasury Depart. Decr 23d 1793.

The Secretary of the Treasury has the honor respectfully to submit to the President of the U. States a communication from the Commissioner of the revenue of the 18 inst: enclosing a provisional Contract for the Stakage of Neus River in North Carolina; the ratification whereof appears to be for the interest of the Ud States.[1]

Alexandr Hamilton
Secy of the Treasy

LB, DLC:GW.

1. For Tench Coxe's letter to Hamilton of 18 Dec., enclosing a contract with John Bragg and Richard Wade for 1794, see *Hamilton Papers*, 15:471. For a letter-book copy of the contract, dated 20 Nov. and approved by GW on 24 Dec., see DNA: RG 26, Lighthouse Deeds and Contracts, 1790–1812.

From John Hyde

Honor'ed Sir   New York Decer 23. 1793

your Letter of the 20 I am favour'd with,[1] I have communed with Mr Baur on the Several parts of it he Excepts the fortytwo Guineas a year, I have taken the Liberty to send him to philadelphia, he will deliver this Letter to your Excellence, and I hope he will be a good and faithfull Sart.[2] I am your Excellence's most obliged most Humble Sart to Command

John Hyde

ALS, DLC:GW.

1. This letter has not been found.

2. Jacob Baur joined GW's household on Christmas 1793 and remained employed as a valet and butler until November 1794 (GW's testimonial for Baur, 4 Nov. 1794, DLC:GW, series 9).

Bartholomew Dandridge, Jr.,
to Thomas Jefferson

23d Decemr 1793.

By the President's direction Bw Dandridge has the honor to return to the Secretary of State the papers herewith enclosed[1]—& to inform the Secretary that the President agrees in opinion with him that they ought to be communicated to Congress, & wishes copies may be prepared for that purpose.

AL, DLC: Jefferson Papers; ADf, DNA: RG 59, Miscellaneous Letters; LB, DNA: RG 59, George Washington's Correspondence with His Secretaries of State. Jefferson docketed the AL as received on 23 December.

1. The enclosed documents included correspondence of Edward Church with Jacob Dohrman & Company, 15 Oct., regarding the charter of a vessel to carry dispatches; a letter from Dominick Browne to Church of the same date, about warning American vessels of the danger resulting from the truce between Algiers and Portugal and about the seizure of the American ship *Birmingham* by a British vessel; a letter from Church to Portuguese minister Luís Pinto de Sousa Coutinho, 21 Oct., requesting him to procure protection for American vessels against the Algerine corsairs; Coutinho's reply to Church, 22 Oct., granting protection provided the American vessels would assemble in numbers deserving of a convoy; and two letters from Church to Jefferson, 22 Oct., covering the preceding letters, discussing reaction to the treaty between Portugal and Algiers, and sending news of the European war. A letter from David Humphreys to Jefferson, 7 Oct., discussing the Portugal and Algiers truce, ship and troop movements, and war news, was probably also enclosed (see *JPP*, 271–73, and *Jefferson Papers*, 27:199–200, 262–67; see also *ASP, Foreign Relations*, 1:297–300).

From Thomas Johnson

sir.   Washington 23d Decemr 1793.

We are just about finishing the Business of this Meeting. it has been very important, much influenced by the Considerations hinted in our general Letter and I hope will meet your Approbation[1]—Funds are now secured, I think, to carry on the public Buildings to a considerable Length under the most disagreeable Events and if our public Affairs should brighten a powerful Influence is secured to do what is right and proper and which ought to have been done in the Outset.

Mr Blodget has involved us in unpleasant Circumstances Doctr Stuart and I cannot quit our Post to our own Satisfaction till we see the present Lottery in a Way of being settled and we had all determined that another should not be offered in the present Temper of the public or at all 'till without a farther Security than mere Honor—I will deal frankly with you, Sir, tho' I dare say your own Observation renders mine unnecessary Mr Blodget will not be useful in the Affairs of the City he wants Judgment and Steadiness I cannot think of leaving him to a Successor we all wish to part from him and that quietly.[2]

As soon as the Lottery Business is smoothed, and I hope it will be so by the first of March, I wish to be relieved: my Affairs are pretty extensive and require much of my Attention: I wish too to avail myself of the Moment which I saw and has almost past away to benefit myself by the rise of the City to which a long Friendship for Potomack and every Exertion in my power in it's favor fairly intitle me. I am sir. with the most perfect Esteem and Respect. Your very affectionate Servant.

Th. Johnson

ALS, DLC:GW.

1. See Commissioners for the District of Columbia to GW, this date.

2. Not long after taking his position as superintendent for the District of Columbia in January 1793, Samuel Blodget, Jr., obtained the commissioners' approval and began to advertise "A Lottery for the Improvement of the Federal City," offering ownership of a hotel to be built in the District and many lesser cash prizes. The drawing was to begin on 9 Sept., and while the hotel would be delivered when completed, Blodget's advertisement promised that the other prizes would be paid "*in one month after the drawing*" (*Gazette of the United States* [Philadelphia], 23 Jan. 1793). Initially the drawing was delayed because too many tickets remained unsold, but after a company of "gentlemen" took on all the remaining tickets, the drawing was commenced on 23 Sept. (*Gazette of the United States,* 14 Sept.). By mid-December, however, few of the highest prizes had been drawn, and it was alleged that "The drawing at present is carried on slowly, in order to enable the company to dispose of their tickets at a liberal advance" (*General Advertiser* [Philadelphia], 20 Dec.).

In June 1794 Blodget announced that all inquiries should be directed to him or to William Deakins, Jr., "The commissioners never having contemplated any further concern in this business, than in their assent to receive the bonds and approve the names of the managers" (*Gazette of the United States and Evening Advertiser* [Philadelphia], 7 June 1794). For the proposed second lottery, see Commissioners to GW, this date, and n.7.

From Henry Knox

Sir,　　　　　　　　　　　　War department December 23d 1793

I submit to your Consideration a proposed message to the Six Nations in answer to theirs by General Chapin.[1] I have the honor to be with the greatest respect Your obedient Servant

H. Knox

LS, DLC:GW; LB, DLC:GW.

1. The enclosed draft has not been identified. On 24 Dec. Henry Knox sent to Israel Chapin two addresses "To the Sachems, Chiefs and Warriors of

the Six Nations," both dated 24 Dec. (PHi: Wayne Papers). The second told them that "Your father George Washington has directed, as an evidence of his affection, and a reward for your Services the last Summer that you and your families should be well supplied with good warm clothing." The draft evidently was a version of the other address, which reads: "Brothers! A Copy of your proceedings at Buffaloe Creek on the eighth day of October last hath been received by General Chapin.

"These proceedings contain the sentiments of several Chiefs of the various Tribes who were assembled at the great council Fire which was kindled at the rapids of the Miami the last Summer.

"And in addition to this information you add in your meeting of the tenth of the same month, your desires of a boundary which you say will be further explained by General Chapin.

"All these communications have been submitted to your father, General Washington, the President of the United States, who desires the Six Nations to receive his sincere and hearty thanks for their assurances and acts of friendship to the United States.

"While your father, the President has observed with great pleasure, the pains you have taken to effect a peace between the United States, and the hostile Indians; he is at the same time very sorry that any circumstances should have prevented the accomplishment of a measure affecting the happiness of both parties. Peace is best for the whites as well as for the red People, and it is always the cause of sorrow among good Men when misunderstandings arise which create wars.

"The United States consider that they have taken all the requisite means to obtain a Peace, which their duty or their humanity required. They appointed respectable and wise characters as Commissioners, who were accompanied by a deputation of friends, the known advocates for Peace. Those Commissioners under discouraging circumstances persevered for a long time to obtain an interview with the great council of Indians. This being ineffectual they made, in good faith, such liberal Offers in writing to ensure the future comfort and prosperity of the Indians as were never before given to the Indians of North America.

"These circumstances being known, for ever acquit the character of the United States from all imputations of desiring a continuance of the War.

"The same principles of moderation and humanity, which before dictated the offers to the Indians, and a sincere friendship for the Six Nations have induced your father, the President to consider attentively your proposition or a new boundary. Altho' the lines you mention are considered as liable to considerable objections, yet it is hoped when all difficulties shall be discussed at a treaty or conference by moderate Men with upright views, that some agreement may be made which would lead to a general Peace.

"On this ground, the President consents that a conference should be held at Venango, on the fifteenth or middle of May next.

"It is expected that the chiefs of the Six Nations and Chippewas will attend, and the chiefs of all such of the western tribes, as the said Six Nations and Chippewas may invite. And if the hostile Tribes should think proper to attend, they will be well received and treated as people ought to be who are holding friendly Treaties.

"But it cannot be unknown to you, that by the late abortive efforts to negotiate, the American Army was restrained from offensive operations against those Tribes, who appear deaf to the voice of reason and peace. Such a conduct will not be observed by the United States again. This must clearly be understood: Let it be remembered therefore there is no deception on our parts. Our army must be left entirely at liberty to act as circumstances may require. The scene of operations however will be far distant from Venango, the proposed place of meeting.

"It is to be observed that in case any of the western Indians attend at Venango it would be proper that they should proceed by water at least as far east as Presque Isle, and thence to french Creek by land. It would be dangerous for them to proceed from the westward by land for the same reason they gave the last year, namely, that the said paths are bloody paths.

"Brothers, If you agree to the time and place of meeting, it will be proper that you should immediately signify the same to General Chapin that due preparations may be made at said place."

For the proceedings of the council held at Buffalo Creek, 8 and 10 Oct., see *ASP: Indian Affairs*, 1:477–78.

To Henry Knox

Dear Sir,   Philadelphia 23d Decr 1793

I have read the proposed message to the "Sachems, Chiefs and Warriors of the Six Nations" and approve of it, except that I question whether the 8th and the 11th paragraphs are expressed *quite* strong enough. The 8th gives too much ground, in my opinion, to expect a compliance with their request in its full extent; and the 11th although the sense is plain, seems hardly decisive enough for Indian comprehension & there shd be no misconception.[1] Yrs always

Go: Washington

ADfS, DLC:GW; LB, DLC:GW.

1. For the message as finally sent, see Knox to GW, this date, n.1.

To Henry McCoy

Mr McKoy   Philadelphia Decr 23d 1793.

You may well conceive how di⟨s⟩appointed and vexed I have been at the manner in which your plowing has been carried on since the rains, which set in the latter end of October, put the ground in order to be flushed. Had you forgot the repeated charges I gave you on this head, and the early attempts that were made, but discontinued, on account of the drought, and the hardness of the ground? Did you forget that I told you there were three fields to flush up this fall; and that all of them, but one in particular was so wet that it was almost impos⟨sib⟩le to work it after the rains set in, ⟨unti⟩ll late in the Spring? And did you forget moreover that I charged you to have your ⟨*illegible*⟩ in order, that not a moment might be lost when the ground was in such a state as to admit plowing to advantage? How durst you ⟨*illegible*⟩ disobey this order, and instead of bringing the whole force of your plows to ⟨*illegible*⟩ employ them now & then only— or one or two a week, as if it were for amusement? thereby doing everything which was in your power to derange my whole plan for the next year; the probability now being, that the frosts—the Snows and the Rains of the Winter, which makes the ground at Dogue Run extremely wet & heavy, will prevent your plowing till the spring months; when the Oats, & Buck Wheat for Manure, ought to be sown; & Corn planting will be coming on.

What excuse can you have fo⟨r⟩ this neglect? Was it the great quantity of Corn you made? God knows there will be little enough of that I fear; Was it the great quantity of Meadow you prepared in the Mill swamp? Of this you did nothing—In short, since the month of October, the principal part of your work seems to ha⟨ve⟩ been to level a little dirt that was thro⟨wn⟩ out of the Ditch below your House. I bore more of this when I was at home ⟨than⟩ I should have done, on account of the ⟨ill⟩ness with which you were afflicted. but I now desire you to be impressed with this belief; that the person who has now undertaken the superintendency of my Estate is a man of property, of good character, and well skilled in the business he is employed in; and that he is not only vested with authority, but has it in positive orders, that if you are not attentive to your business in all its parts. If you are not constantly at home, & with your people; and executing with fidility & strictness, the articles to which you are bound by the agreement you have entered into (and which he is in possession of) to turn you of[f] the Plantation at any season of the year without paying you a shilling.[1] My money is to be paid, and the allowances are to be made, for services which are expressed, & stipulated on your part—If these are rendered with industry and good faith, the obligations on mine shall be fulfilled with great punctuality. But If I suffer by your neglect, you shall not benefit by the money of one, who wishes to be your friend, if your conduct will entitle you to it from Yours

Go: Washington

ALS (letterpress copy), DLC:GW.

1. See GW to William Pearce, 18 December. McCoy's agreement, made with Anthony Whitting, is dated 17 Dec. 1792 (DLC:GW).

To William Pearce

Mr Pearce,   Philadelphia [23d] Decr 1793[1]

The letter which I wrote to you on the 18th and the papers therein enclosed with the Plans of the several farms (which Mr Lewis was directed to leave with you) were designed to give you a general view of the business entrusted to your care. I shall now, as intimated in that letter, give you my sentiments on many other matters of a more particular nature.

Among the first things to be done after you are well fixed yourself, will be, I presume, that of taking an exact account of the Stock of every species—Tools—and implements on each of the farms: charging them therewith; that a regular account thereof may be rendered whenever called for. Buy in Alexandria a proper (bound) book for this purpose, and another to enter the weekly reports in. The latter is required not only for my present satisfaction, but that it may also, at any time hereafter shew in what manner the hands have been employed; and the state of the Stock and other things at any past period; and it is my wish, as this is intended as a register of the proceedings on the farms, that they may be made with correctness; always comparing the last with the preceeding weeks report and all differences satisfactorily accounted for. The Overseers are allowed paper for these Reports. Suffer no excuse therefore for their not coming into you[2] every Saturday night, that you may be enabled to forward a copy of them to me by the wednesday's Post following. And as it is not only satisfactory, but may be of real utility, to know the state of the weather as to heat & cold, but drought or moisture; prefix, as usual, at the head of every weeks report a meteorological account of these; The Thermometer which is at Mount Vernon will enable you to do the first.

The work essentially necessary to be done by my Carpenters, & which presses most—is—compleating the New Barn at Dogue Run, & the sheds there for horses &ca—building the house for Crow—Repairing my house in Alexandria for Mrs Fanny Washington—which must be done before the first[3] of May—Inclosing the lot on which it stands for a Garden or Yard. Repairing the Millers house. Removing the larger kind of the Negro quarters (the smaller ones or cabbins, I presume the people with a little assistance of Carts can do themselves) to the ground marked out for them opposite to Crows New house. Repairing at a proper time those he will remove from. Lending aid in drawing the houses at River farm into some uniform shape, in a convenient place. Repairing the Barn & Stables at Muddy hole. Compleating the Dormant Windows in the back of the Stables at Mansion house and putting two in the front of it agreeably to directions already given to Thomas Green—after which, and perhaps doing some other things which do not occur to me at this moment, my intention is to build a large Barn, and sheds for Stables upon the plan of that at Dogue run (if, on trial it should be found to answer the expectation wch is formed of it) at River Farm.

I give you this detail of Carpenters work, that by having the subject before you in a collected view, you may be the better able to direct the execution; and to prevent Green from flying from one thing to another without order or system; and thereby judging whether he carries it on with that dispatch & judgment which is necessary.

As you know my anxiety with respect to thc Substitution of live fences in place of dead ones (as soon, & as fast as the nature of things will admit) I should not again mention it, were it not that this is the Season for saving the Haws of the thorn—Berries from the Cedar trees—and such things as are fit for the purpose of hedging; and to prevent trimming the Lombardy Poplar and Willows, that the cuttings may be applied to this use—for as these two last are of very quick growth, I am of opinion fences[4] might soon be raised by means of them, that will be competent against every thing but Hogs, whilst those of slower growth may be coming on to supply their places; and whether it is not better to raise Porke in Styes, is a matter worthy of serious consider-

ation—for I believe by the common mode I never get the half
of what is raised by the Sows; especially if they are kept in good
order; to do which is attended with no small expence,[5] & to have
them stolen afterwds is vexatious.

When I left home, Davy at Muddy hole had finished getting
out his wheat, and had nothing but the security of his Corn &
some fencing, to employ his people about, during the fall and
Winter—I was induced from this consideration, and the anxious
desire I have to reclaim, and lay to grass my Mill Swamp, to order
him to give all the aid he could to McKoy in the accomplishment
of this work but it really appears to me that the fall, fine as it has
proved, has actually been spent About I know not what. What
can be done with those swamps, must now be left to you—&
the state the weather will put them in. My hope, & expectation
once, was, that the second lot might have been laid to grass next
spring if not this Fall, and that the one above it, would have been
ditched—grubbed—& planted in Corn—but as the matter now
stands, you must be governed by circumstances and your own
view of the case; with this caution, not to undertake in this, or
any thing else, more than you can accomplish well: recollecting
always, that a thing but half done is never done; and well done,
is, in a manner done for ever.

At McKoys, I staked out two Clover lots adjoining the Barn
yard, and gave him & Tom Davis (who was present) my ideas
respecting them. The sooner these can be inclosed—especially
that on the West side, next the Wood—the better; as it is my
wish to plough it this fall, & plant Potatoes therein in the Spring.
Serving that on the East side of the Barn in like manner next
year—and the Spot which was in oats, adjoining thereto the year
following. It is my intention also to run a lane from the first
Gate you enter going into this Farm up to the Barn yard—and
another lane from the Wood to No. 4[6] across the Meadow, and
between fields No. 3 & 5. I do not expect that all these things
can be accomplished in a moment—but having them in your
view at the sametime you will know better how to proceed—As
the Wood in No. 5 will be to be cleared when that field comes
into Corn, it will be proper that all the Timber, Rails and wood
that is wanted on the farm, should be taken from hence as far as
it will go—and cut with an eye to this event.

One of the Grass lots at Muddy hole, the South western one

(pointed out to Davy) ought to be plowed up this fall, & planted with Potatoes in the Spring. And at Union farm it is intended to take of four five acre lots from field No. 2 directly in front of the Barn as will appear more clearly by the Sketch herewith enclosed—The lots marked No. 1 & 2 in which, should be sowed in Feby or beginning of March with clover seed on the Wheat. At the Rive[r] farm I propose three lots for Grass, South of the lane in front of the Barn, as you will perceive by another Sketch also enclosed.[7] What will be done with the ground between the Barn at that place & No. 6 when the fence comes to be run there, is left to yourself to decide, after taking a full view of things & seeing what the force is competent to in fencing (of which much is wanting) &ca—Stuart wished much for another fellow at this place, and as that boy Cyrus, at Mansion house, is now nearly a Man,[8] and very unfit I believe to be entrusted with horses, whose feed there is strong suspicions he steals,[9] I have no objection to your sending there. nor indeed have I any to your disposing of any of the others, differently from what they are, after you have taken time to consider what arrangements can be made for the best, & most advantageous purposes. Thomas Davis & Muclus must however be considered as among the tradesmen; & when not employed in making & laying of Bricks & other jobs in that way, may be aiding the Carpenters. and the fellow called Muddy hole Will, as he has for many years been a kind of Overseer, had better remain in his present Station; with respect to the rest, I have no choice about them.

There is nothing which stands in greater need of regulation than the Waggons & Carts at the Mansion House which always whilst I was at home appeared to me to be most wretchedly employed—first in never carrying half a load; 2dly in flying from one thing to another; and thirdly in no person seeming to know what they really did; and oftentimes under pretence of doing this, that, and the other thing, did nothing at all; or what was tantamount to it. that is—instead of bringing in, or carrying to any place, full loads, and so many of them in a day; the Waggon, or a Cart, under pretence of drawing wood, or carrying Staves to the Mill wd go the places from whence they were to be taken, and go to sleep perhaps; and return with not more than half a load. Frequently have I seen a Cart go from the Mansion house, or from the river side to the new Barn with little or no more lime or sand in it, than a man would carry on his back—the consequence of this was that the Brick layers were half their time idle; for it required no more time to make the trip with a full load than it did with half a load—of course, double the qty would be transported under good regulation.

You will perceive by my agreemt with Ehler, the Gardener, that he & his wife were to eat of the Victuals that went from my Table (in the Cellar) instead of having it Cooked by his wife as had been the custom with them.[10] At the time that agreement was made I kept a Table for Mrs Fanny Washington, but as she has resolved to live in Alexandria, this will no longer be kept up; and therefore it would be best I should conceive, to let them return to their old mode, & for the young Gardener to eat with them[11]—but as the agreement is otherwise I would not force this upon them, unless it was their own choice—especially if Butler remains there, for in that case as Lucy (the Cook) must get Victuals for him, it will make but little difference whether she gets for one or more; you will therefore do what seems best, & most agreeable in this matter taking care that they have a sufficiency without waste, or misapplication—I am very willing to allow them enough, and of such provisions, day by day, as is wholesome & good, but no more—they have, each of them been allowed a bottle of Beer a day—and this must be continued to them—that is a quart each, for when I am from home the Beer will not be bottled though it may be brewed as the occasion requires—The Gardener has too great a propensity to drink, and behaves improperly when in liquor; admonish him against it as much as you can, as he behaves well when sober—understands his business—and I believe is not naturally idle—but only so when occasioned by drink—His wife has been put in charge of the spinners—that is, to deliver out the Wool & flax, & receive the thread yarn &ca; she seems well disposed, but how far she is worthy of trust, or is capable of having the work done properly, you will be better able to judge after a while, than I am now. Method, in all these things, is desirable, and after it is once adopted, and got into a proper train things will work easy.

Do not suffer the Quarter Negro Children to be in the Kitchen, or in the yards unless brought there on business—As besides the bad habit—they too frequently are breaking limbs, or twigs from, or doing other injury to my shrubs—some of which at a considerable expence, have been propagated.

From some complaints made by my Negroes, that they had not a sufficent allowance of meal, and from a willingness that they should have enough, the quantity was increased by Mr Whiting so as to amount (by what I have learnt from Mr Stuart) to profusion. This is an error again on the other side—My wish & desire is that they should have as much as they can eat without waste and no more. Under these Ideas I request you would examine into this matter & regulate their allowance upon just principles. I always used to lay in a great quantity of Fish for them—and when we were at home Meat, fat, & other things were now and then given to them besides; But it would seem (from their accts at least) that the Fish which were laid in for them last Spring have disappeared without their deriving much benefit from them.

By this time I expect the Hogs that were put up for Porke, either are killed—or are fit to kill. I request, after every person has had their allowance given to them, that the residue may be made into Bacon, and due attention given to it; for allmost every year, since we left home, half of it or more, has been spoilt—either for want of salt, or want of proper attention in smoking it; if not spoiled in the pickle. Davy at Muddy hole, has always had two or three hundd weight of Porke given to him at killing time, & I believe the Insides of the Hogs—that is—the Hastlets, Guts (after the fat is stripped of) &ca is given among the other Negroes at the different places.

After the drilled Wheat at Union farm is taken off, let particular care be used to prevent its being mixed with any other; as, if it answers the character given of it, it will be a great acquision. that, & the drilled Wheat at Stuarts are of the same kind, and were sown in drills that the ground might be worked whilst it was growing, and the most made of it that can be. Whether to sow the ground which is at Union farm (in this Wheat) with Buck Wheat and grass Seeds immediately after harvest or with Buck Wheat alone to be plowed in for manure & grass seeds afterwards I shall leave to you to decide. I shall want all the ground within that Inclosure laid down with grass & leave the manner of doing it to you. And as the other parts within the same Inclosure—as also in that of McKoys, was sown very late in the fall with grass-seeds pray examine them attentively, from time to time, and if you shall be of opinion that the Seed is not come well, or is too thin, sprinkle as much more over it as you shall deem necessary, as I am very anxious to have them well taken, & without delay with grass. The Wheat fields at Dogue run are to be sown in the Month of February or March with grass Seeds—No. 3 with Clover alone—The other with Clover & Timothy or Clover & Orchard grass mixed, as it is intended to be laid to Grass.

It is indispensably necessary that the alteration marked out in the Mill Race should be accomplished as soon as possible— 1st because the waste of Water in the old part (which it avoids) is more than can be afforded except at times of the greatest plenty[12]—and 2dly because I am at more expence and trouble in repairing (after every heavy rain) the breaches, in the part that will be thrown out, than in digging the new.[13] There is another job that is essential; and that is, to make the Post & Rail fence from the Millers house up to the trunnel fence which runs across the meadow, or to the next cross fence, if that lot is cultivated next year of such stout & strong materials and of such a height as to bid defiance to trespassers of every kind, among wch the worthless people who live near it are the worst as I am satisfied they give every aid in their power which can be done without discovery to let in their Hogs—The whole of this outer fence, will be, I am sure, to be done anew; but it can only be accomplished by degrees—but let that which is done, be compleated effectually as well by a good and sufficient ditch as by a stout[14] Post & rail fence—along which if a hedge of Honey locust could be got to grow entirely round it would form a sufficient barrier against bad neighbours as they would hardly attempt to cut them down to let their stock in upon me which, I am sure is the case at present as without the aids some of them derive from my Inclosures and their connexion with my Negroes they would be unable to live upon the miserable land they occupy.

Whenever the field No. 3 at Union farm is prepared for a Crop, which was intended to be the case next year—if the piece of Wood within, is touched at all, let there be a handsome clup of trees left at the further end of it—or more than one—according to the shape & growth of the Wood.

I have, for years past, been urging the Superintendant of my business at Mount Vernon to break a number of Steers to the yoke, that no set of Oxen may be worked low[15]—but do not believe it is yet done to the extent I wish. My reasons for this measure are, that the Oxen may never be worked after they are eight years of age, but then fatted for marked; that by having a number of them, they may, by frequent shifting, always be in good order; and because, when they are only fed, when they do work—and at other times only partake of the fare which is allowed to the other Cattle, twenty yoke is not more expensive than five yoke.

The Potatoes which were made last year, except such as you may require for your own eating, which you are welcome to, must all be preserved for Seed; & will be short enough, I fear, for the purposes they are intended. It has been intimated that several of the large stone Jugs which were sent to the different farms with spirits in them at Harvest has never yet been returned. Call upon the several Overseers to give them in immediately, or they will have to pay for them. Enclosed is an Inventory of the several articles which are in the Store house at Mansion house which I send for your information—Take an account of what is delivered from thence—to whom—and for what purpose—that it may be known how things go.[16]

There is one thing I wish to impress you pretty strongly with, that you may use every precaution in your power to guard against—and that is—suffering my horses to be rode at unseasonable hours in the night without your knowledge or that of the Overseers—No doubt rests upon my mind that this is too much practiced and is one, if not the primary cause of my loosing a number of horses—the poverty of others—and the slinking of foals which happens so frequently that I make a miserable hand of breeding Mules. It must be remembered in time, that the Jacks and Stud horse are advertised for covering the ensuing Season—February or beginning of March; however, will be in time.

I am told that the Well by the Quarter is rendered useless for want of a proper rope. It is sometime since I wrote to Mr Lewis to get a hair one (for none other answers well) from the rope maker in Alexandria—but what he has done in it I know not.[17] He will be able to inform you; and he, and the Gardeners wife, will let you know what Negroes have been cloathed & who are yet to Cloath, with the means of doing it.

My Superfine, & fine flour always waits for directions from me, to be sold; but the midlings & Ship stuff you will dispose of whenever you can get a suitable price, and your want of money may require. And this also may be done with Beeves, Mutton &ca; after supplying the several demands upon the former, where it has not already been done. The Miller and Thomas Green, I understand, have each had a Beef the weights of which will, I presum⟨e⟩ be given to you by Mr Lewis; and as it will exceed their allowance of this article they must account for it by lessening the quantity of Porke, or be charged the (Alexandria) market price for it. And as Thomas Green has drawn in the course of last year more Meal from my Mill than his allowance let him be charged with the Overplus and It is necessary you should know that he is always craving money and other things but let him no more than his dues—for he is in debt I believe to every body and what ever is advanced beyond would probably be lost.

I have directed Mr Lewis to leave with you an Acct of all the money he has paid, & what (if any) may remain in his hands. And it is my request that you will pay no Accts (not of your own contracting) without learning from him that they are due, or first sending them on to me; for Mr Whiting always paid as he went, & what was left unpaid either by him, or contracted after his death, was paid to the utmost farthing whilst I was at home. So that I know of nothing remaining unpaid except the Overseers wages, and to the Weaver, but what has fallen under Mr Lewis's management since I left home & of course can be explained by him.

Send me an exact account of the quantity of Corn made at each farm and the yield of each field. I directed Mr Lewis to have a certain quantity, at each farm put into seperate Corn houses for the use thereof; and the residue in other houses for the Mansion house, and other purposes[18]—& I hope it has been done, but wish to be informed. The keys of the last mentioned houses I did not intend should be left in the care of the Overseers, but the doors well secured and, the keys remain in your own custody.

As your family may be the better accomodated by it, I wrote Mr Lewis sometime ago that you might lodge, yourself, in the room which he now occupies;[19] and I repeat it to you, as I am willing to make your situation as comfortable as may be.

It would be well to have the Seins overhauled immediately, that if new ones are wanting, or the old ones requiring much repair, they may be set about without loss of time; for if this work is delayed until the Spring the Sein Netters will be so much employed, as to disappoint you altogether & of course my people of

Fish. If twine is not to be had in Alexandria let me know it, and I will, by the first vessel afterwards send it from hence.

If I recollect rightly, Thomas Green is allowed a certain quantity of Wood, by the agreement which has been entered into between us (by the old one I know it was so) it would be well therefore to have the quantity carried to his house and corded up at once, otherwise he will be always complaining, and denying that the quantity (Six cord I think it is) has been recd by him.[20]

I shall write to you if nothing extraordinary prevents it, by every Mondays Post, and shall expect a copy of the weekly reports by the Mail which leaves Alexandria on Thursday if no change has taken place—by which means I shall write to you, & receive a letter from you every week when the occurrences (not contained in the reports) may be mentioned. And now, having given you my sentiments upon all those points with which my recollection has furnished me I have only to add that the enclosed letters (which are sent open for you to peruse & then to put wafers in) will shew the person to whom they are directed what it is they have to expect, & the ground they stand upon.[21] Wishing you well I remain Your friend &ca

Go: Washington

ALS, ViMtvL; ALS (letterpress copy), DLC:GW. The letterpress copy has been over-written and in many places altered by GW, and GW also added some phrases to the ALS after using the letterpress. The most significant differences between the two documents are noted below.

1. The ALS at ViMtvL reads only "Philadelphia [   ] Decr 1793." GW added "22d" to the letterpress copy, but in his letter to Pearce of 12 Jan. 1794 he referred to this letter as "my letter of the 23d of December." As the five letters to overseers enclosed with this letter are all dated 23 Dec., that probably is the correct date.

2. On the letterpress copy, GW substituted "non-compliance" for the preceding four words.

3. The letterpress copy has "month" instead of "first."

4. The letterpress copy uses the word "hedges" here instead of "fences."

5. The rest of this sentence is not on the letterpress copy.

6. The letterpress copy has "&" in place of "No. 4."

7. The enclosed sketches have not been identified. However, the features here described appear on GW's 1793 map of Mount Vernon (Fig. 3).

8. Cyrus was a dower slave, the son of Sall, a housemaid at the mansion house. In February 1786, when GW recorded a list of slaves in his diary, Cyrus was listed as 11 years of age (DLC:GW). In 1799, when GW made another list, Cyrus was employed as a postilion and married to Lucy, a slave at River farm (*Papers, Retirement Series*, 4:529, 533).

9. In the letterpress copy the word here is "misapplies."

10. The agreement under which John Christian Ehlers had come to Mount Vernon in 1789 expired earlier this year, and he had sought and obtained improved terms from GW before agreeing to stay (see GW to Anthony Whitting, 26 May and 9 June). His new contract has not been found.

11. The young gardener was John Gottleib Richler (see GW to Frances Bassett Washington, 28–29 July, n.8).

12. On the letterpress copy the text from "possible" to this point reads: "to prevent the waste of water in the old part (of which it is very scarce except at times of the greatest plenty)."

13. At GW's request, George Gilpin in September had marked out with stakes "a piece of digging" to alter the mill race (see Gilpin to Howell Lewis, 12 Sept., DLC:GW).

14. This word appears as "strong" on the letterpress copy.

15. On the letterpress copy, the remainder of this sentence reads: "By this means they would grow larger, and become more gentle." The next sentence then begins with the words "The advantages of," rather than "My reasons for."

16. The enclosed inventory has not been identified.

17. See GW to Lewis, 3 November.

18. See GW to Lewis, 3 November.

19. This letter has not been found.

20. Green's articles of agreement with GW of 25 Oct. included in his compensation "six cords of wood delivered at his house—& if more is wanting he is to supply himself by collecting drift wood as not a *living* tree in the enclosures is to be disturbed" (ViMtvL). Similar language appeared in Green's agreement of 9 Nov. 1790, extended on 14 Dec. 1791 until January 1793 (DLC:GW).

21. See GW's letters of this date to Hiland Crow, John Christian Ehlers, Thomas Green, Henry McCoy, and William Stuart.

To William Stuart

Mr Stuart,   Philadelphia Decr 23d 1793

I am extremely dissatisfied at your not commencing your fall Plowing the moment the Rains, which began the latter end of October, and continued all through the Month of Novr, put the ground in a proper state for it. This neglect, and having your Wheat yet to tread out, will, with the frosts, snows, & Rains of Winter, inevitably defeat all my plans for the next year; for instead of having the ground which was intended for Oats and Buck wheat, ready to receive the first early in March, & the other shortly after: & the Corn Ground ready for listing;[1] all will be to be broke up at that time. This is an extremely mortifying circumstance to me, as I did not intend that any thing should, any longer, prevent me from adopting my system of rotation, which I have been preparing to carry into affect for some years past.

I have given Mr Pearce full power & authority to manage my business the same as if I was present myself; you will therefore apply to him for what is wanting on the farm, and follow his directions in the same manner as if they came from my own mouth.

You will shew him the places ⟨we⟩ had viewed as the best for the reception of the Negro quarters, that when the time shall arrive at which they can be moved conveniently, they may be placed to the best advantage. Shew him the place on which the fence between No. 6 and the Orchard Inclosure used to run, and where it ought still to go, to keep the said No. 6 to the size it originally was. What use he will put the ground to, which lye between that fence (whenever it is run) an⟨d⟩ the lane, must be determined by circumstances. He may be shewn too, in wh⟨at⟩ manner it was proposed to enlarge the lot just before your door. I am—Your friend &ca

Go: Washington

ALS (letterpress copy), DLC:GW.

1. "Listing" is the preparation of land for a crop by creating ridges and furrows with a plow.

To the United States Senate and House of Representatives

United States 23d December 1793.

Gentlemen of the Senate, and of the House of Representatives.

Since the communications which were made to you on the affairs of the United States with Spain and on the Truce between Portugal and Algiers, some other papers have been received which making a part of the same subjects are now communicated for your information.[1]

Go: Washington

LS, DNA: RG 46, Third Congress, 1793–95, Senate Records of Legislative Proceedings, President's Messages; Copy, DNA: RG 233, Third Congress, 1793–95, House Records of Legislative Proceedings, Journals; LB, DLC:GW. The letter-book copy at the DLC contains the note, "Copies of the above mentioned papers may be found on file." This message was received by Congress on 24 Dec. (*Journal of the House,* 6:41–42; *Journal of the Senate,* 6:19).

1. For the previous communications, see GW's two letters to Congress of 16 December. The documents enclosed with this message included José de Jaudenes to Thomas Jefferson, 18 Dec., with enclosures, and Jefferson's reply to Jaudenes and José Ignacio de Viar, 21 Dec., about Indian relations on the southern border (*ASP, Foreign Relations,* 1:304–6; see also *Jefferson Papers,* 27:584–85, 603–4). Also submitted were Edward Church's two letters to Jefferson of 22 Oct., with enclosures, and David Humphreys's letter to Jefferson of 7 Oct., about dangers to U.S. shipping arising out of the truce between Algiers and Portugal (see Bartholomew Dandridge, Jr., to Jefferson, 23 Dec., and *Jefferson Papers,* 27:199–200, 262–67).

From Elizabeth Foote Washington

Dear Sir   Hay-Feild [Va.] Dec. 23d 1793.
Your letter of the 9th covering Doctor Tates opinion came duly to hand[1]—Mr Washington acknowledges himself very much oblig'd to you for the part *you* have taken in this business, & highly approves of your sending him forword immediately—he has anxiously look'd for him on every Stage day Since, but as yet has seen nothing of him, he begs if he has not yet left Philadelphia for the purpose of coming to Virginia you will urge him to as speedy departure for that purpose as is possible—Mr Washington is much in the same situation as he has been for some length of time past, except we think he sees less & less every day almost, indeed it may be said he cannot see any thing more than the light, mr Washington joins in most respectful compliments to Mrs Washington & her children, & believe us dear Sir to be yours most affectionately

Eliza. Washington

ALS, ViMtvL.
1. See GW to Lund Washington, 9 December.

Letter not found: from William Pearce, 24 Dec. 1793. On 28 Dec. GW wrote Pearce, "Your letter of the 24th instant . . . came to hand yesterday."

To Edmund Randolph

(Private)

⟨My⟩ dear Sir,   Philadelphia Decr 24th 1793.

It was my wish, for many reasons (needless to enumerate) to have retained Mr Jefferson in the Administration to the end of the present Session of Congress, but he is so decidedly opposed to it that I can no longer hint this desire to him.

I now wish for your permission to nominate you to it the Office of Secy of State and will add that your compliance would give me pleasure. Mr Jefferson will quit it[1] the last day of this month and proposes to set out for Virginia a few days afterwards—I am always & sincerely Your Affecte friend & Servt

Go: Washington

ADfS, DNA: RG 59, Miscellaneous Letters; LB, DLC:GW.

1. GW originally wrote "resign his Commission," but struck those words and wrote "quit it" above the line.

From Edmund Randolph

My dear sir   German Town [Pa.] Decr 24. 1793.

Permit me either to have a personal interview with you on thursday,[1] if the eruption on my hand will permit, or to write to you a candid opinion upon your kind, and always too friendly conduct towards me. I hope, that this delay will not be too long. I have the honor to be, Dear sir, with sincere and affectionate attachment and respect yr obliged humble serv.

Edm: Randolph

ALS, DLC:GW.

1. The next Thursday was 26 December.

To George Clinton

Dear Sir,   Philadelphia Decr 25th 1793.

Your favor of the 18th instt enclosing a statement of sales of lots in Coxburgh, belonging to us, has been duly received; and I thank you for the particular manner in which they are rendered. I did not mean to give you so much trouble. To know summarily what had been sold, and what remained on hand, was all I had in view.[1]

I hereby acknowledge the receipt of a Bank note (New York) for Sixteen hundred and fifty nine 50/100 Dollrs being the bal[anc]e pr acct stated on the sales abovementioned.

Mrs Washington joins me in offering you, Mrs Clinton & your family the compliments of the season, & the happy return of many, many of them. With great & sincere friendship,[2] I am— Dear Sir Your most Obedt & Affecte Ser.

Go: Washington

ALS (photocopy), ViMtvL; ADfS, DLC:GW; LB, DLC:GW.

1. Clinton's letter to GW of 18 Dec. and its enclosure have not been found. However, GW entered the information on his account with Clinton in Ledger C: "To my moiety of 6053 Acres of Land purchased in Partnership with him on the Mohawk River, in Coxburgh. Which said land he was empowerd to sell as a joint concern, & part thereof actually hath been sold as will appear by his letter of the 18th of Decr 1793—accompanied by an acct, of which the following is an exact copy—viz." The accompanying account includes a list of seventeen "Lotts in Coxburgh which belonged to G.W. & G.C. and have been sold," from 1 May 1788 to 9 Oct 1793, comprising 4,034 acres for £3400.2. in "York Currency"; a list of "Cash recd by G.C. on the difft Sales"; and a list of nine "Lots unsold," comprising 2,019 acres (Ledger C, 2). GW had requested the statement in his letter to Clinton of 27 November. Coxeborough township (Coxe's Patent) was in Montgomery County, N.Y., at the time of purchase in 1784, but by 1793 the land was in Herkimer County, and after 1798 it was in Oneida County.

2. On the draft, GW initially wrote "sincere regard," but struck "regard" and added "friendship" above the line.

From Tobias Lear

My dear Sir,   Glasgow [Scotland] December 25th 1793

I have the vanity to think you will not be displeased to hear of my safe arrival at this place. We had a passage of 28 days from New York, and in the course of it experienced much stormy weather.

I have been here a fortnight, during which time I have been busily engaged in viewing the several large manufactories in the City and its neighbourhood, in some of which they exceed any other part of Great Britain, particularly in the fabric of muslins, which branch they have, 'till within this year past, carried on to a vast extent, not less than two hundred thousand persons having been employed in the several parts of this manufacture in this place & its vicinity: But the war and its concomitants have thrown more than 5/6ths of the above number out of employment. Notwithstanding which, and the similar effect which I am told is produced in other large manufacturing places in the Kingdom, there seems to be no prospect of a peace.

As the muslin is made here in greater perfection than perhaps in any other part of Europe, and knowing that you & Mrs Washington have sometimes occasion to purchase goods of this kind I have ventured to send you a few articles agreeably to the enclosed Invoice, as they are of a quality not often met with in America—and much cheaper than I know such things are with you.[1] The Cotton Cambrick is a new attempt at a substitute for that usually worn, and it bids fair to become a great object, as this sent is afforded at less than one half of what cambrick of equal quality generally costs. I have also added 3 dozen of glass tumblers for punch from a manufactory here which is an excellent one lately established, and with great improvements in its operation, all the cut & cypher work in the glass being performed by a steam engine, which has lessened the cost of cut glass more than 20 pr Cent. I gave to the manufacturer the crest of your arms which I had on the seal of a letter, which he has engraved on the front of each glass.

I trust to that goodness which I have so often experienced to pardon the liberty which I have taken to send these articles without being desired to do it. Whenever it is convenient Mr Dandridge may pay the amount to my friend Mr James Greenleaf.[2]

Our Country is here pronounced emphatically the happy land—and the wisdom of keeping out of the bloody contest in which the nations of Europe are engaged has given a respectability to the American Government in the opinion here, which it would have been long in obtaining without the intervention of such a crisis to bring it to the test; and it seems to be as much the ardent prayer of many here that we may continue to preserve our enviable situation, as it would be of those who felt more immediately the blessings of it. Curses seem to be imprecated everywhere hereabouts upon those Barbarians, the Algeriens, who have again committed depredations on some of our unfortunate Countrymen, and an astonishment is expressed at their being permitted by the maritime powers to pass thus with impunity: But interest in a national question will generally prevail over humanity.[3]

I shall tomorrow set out for Edinburgh, where I shall continue for a few days, and then proceed to London, visiting such manufacturing places as Leeds—Manchester, Sheffield &c. which lay almost in my route.

A Report of the taking of Toulon by the French is all we have new of a public nature; and as the vessel which takes this letter may not sail for two or three weeks, you will undoubtedly know whether this is a fact or not before this reaches you.[4]

In riding about to the manufactories in this neighbourhood I observed the hedges were mostly of furze, and that it formed an excellent hedge, and finding on enquiry that it grew readily, I got a pound of the seed, which is in the box with the other things, and likewise a pound of the Scotch Kail seed, which is said to be hereabouts of a superiour quality—it stands the winters here without injury—and at this time there are fields of it round the City that have all the verdure of a fresh clover field; but this is not to be wondered at, for there has been not the smallest symptom of frost in this County yet; the weather since I have been here corresponds very well with ours in Philada in April I have forwarded your letter to Mr Young[5]—and when I get to London I shall remember the thorn bushes which I am to send out for you.[6]

I have taken up more of your valuable time with this letter than I intended when I began; but will trespass no further than to beg the favour of having my best & grateful respects made acceptable to your good Mrs Washington & my love to Mr Dandridge & my young friends. With the purest respect & truest affection I have the honor to be, my dear Sir, Your grateful friend & faithful servant

Tobias Lear.

ALS, DLC:GW.

1. The invoice has not been identified. However, a duplicate invoice sent with Lear's letter to GW of 26–30 Jan. 1794 listed 25 yards of cotton shirting, 8 yards of cotton cambric, 6 handkerchiefs, 10 yards of sewed muslin, kale and furze seed, and three dozen tumblers, at a total cost of £17.8.11. sterling (DLC:GW). The entry dated 24 Dec. 1793 in GW's account with Lear, recording "Cash pd for the following articles sent us from Glasgow," includes only one dozen tumblers and has a different cost for the seed, resulting in a total cost of £15.18.5 sterling (Ledger C, 4).

2. For the arrival of these articles and arrangements to pay for them, see James Greenleaf to GW, 19 May 1794, and Bartholomew Dandridge, Jr., to Greenleaf, 21 May 1794.

3. For the recent seizures of American vessels by Algerine corsairs, see Richard O'Bryen to GW, 5 Nov., and n.1 to that document.

4. Toulon was retaken by the French forces on 19 December.

5. See GW to Arthur Young, 1 September.

6. Lear sent GW 5,000 white thorn plants in February 1794 (Lear to GW, 4 Feb. 1794; Ledger C, 4).

From John George Gibson

South Hiendly near Pomfret Yorks.[1]
[England] Decr 26th 1793

Having often heard it mentioned in our family that we were in some distant manner connected to your Excellency, I have anxiously wished to ascertain the truth of the report, feeling a great ambition to rank amongst my relatives, a man, whose public and private virtues have so eminently exalted him in the hearts and opinion of mankind. Being on a visit last summer at a distant relations (a Mrs White's, whose Maiden name was Gibson) I was making some inquiry respecting the family, when she likewise mentioned the circumstance of our being distantly related, and as a proof, said she had a Letter, which she gave me, wrote in the year 1699, by Your Excellency's Grand Father in Virginia to his Sister in England, who married my Great Grand Father, of which the following is a Copy.[2]

Virginia June the 22d 1699

Dear & Loving Sister,

"I had the happiness to see a Letter which you sent to my Aunt Howard, who died about a year and a half ago;[3] I had heard of you by her before, but could not tell whether you were alive or not. It was truly great joy to hear that I had such a relation alive as yourself; not having any such a one by my Father's side as yourself. My Father had one Daughter by my Mother, who died when she was very young, before my remembrance.[4] My Mother had three Daughters when my Father married her, one died last winter, and left four or five Children, the other two are alive & married and have had several children. My Mother married another man after my Father, who spent all, so that I had not the value of twenty shillings of my Fathers Estate, I being the youngest & therefore the weakest, which generally comes off short.[5] But I thank God my Fortune has been pretty good since, as I have got a kind and loving Wife, by whom I have had three Sons and a daughter, of which I have buried my daughter and one Son.[6] I am afraid I shall never have the happiness of seeing you, since it has pleased God to set us at such a distance: But hoping to hear from you by all opportunities, which you shall assuredly do from him that is, Your ever loving Brother till death

Jno. Washington

If you write to me direct yours to me in Stafford County on Portomack River in Virginia, Vale. J.W.

To Mrs Mary Gibson, Living at Hawnes in Bedf's., These sent with care.["]

From this Letter it appears that your Excellency's Grandfather, and my Fathers Grand Mother were Brother and Sister. And as a proof that it must be the same family of the Gibson's (there being a great number of that name) There is a small Estate at Hawnes of about 40£ a year, half of which at the death of the above mentioned Mrs White, devolves to me, as Heir at law to my Father who is lately dead, and which was left him and his heirs by his Uncle, (Mrs White's Father who purchased it of his Brother, to whom it had descended) at Mrs Ws. decease without heirs. This Ancestor of mine whom yours married was the Vicar of Hawnes and purchased this Estate, who as well as his Wife lie buried there.

Understanding from report that Your Excellency had not many relations living, I thought it might not be considered by you as too great a liberty, if I informed you, that there were some in this Country who consider themselves honoured in being allied to you tho in a distant manner.

Having (as I before observed) lately lost my Father, the Family now, consist only of my self, a Sister and Brother. I married 4 years ago—a daughter of Mr Charles Payne Sharpe's of the Island of St Vincents, by whom I have had three Children, the eldest I lost. The little fortune I obtain by my Wife, added to my income as Curate, amounts to £140 a year, with which tho small, being happily possessed of domestic felicity, I should feel contented did I not look forward, to the claims of an increasing family, as the whole of our income (my Wife's being an Annuity) dies with us. Had the man, whom I was proud, and honoured in being permitted to call friend, lived a few years longer, I should have been provided for, but by the death of Sr Geo. Savile, I was deprived of one, who possessed both the ability and inclination to serve me:[7] I have however a prospect, tho distant, of possessing a small Living in South Wales in the gift of a relation of my Wife's. My Sister married a son of the Revd Mr Rawstorne, Rector of Badsworth, an uncle of Sr Thomas Pilkington's, and is connected with his Brothers in a Cotton Manufactory.[8] My Brother is nearly the eldest Lieut. in His majesty's 54th Regt[9]—I will not trespass further on your time than to observe, that Mr Naylor, the Gentleman in this Country who transmits this to Mr Bond to be forwarded to your Excellency, will answer any question you may think proper to ask relative to me, through the medium of Mr Bond, or his Brother the Agent to Mr Naylor, in America; and should you wish to see the original Letter, of which the inclosed is a copy, I will transmit it with pleasure. With the greatest respect I remain Your Excellency's Most Obedt Hle Sevt

John George Gibson

ALS, DNA: RG 59, Miscellaneous Letters.

John George Gibson (1758–1833) was appointed rector at Llanthewy Skirrid, Wales, in 1799 and remained at that post until his death.

1. The town of South Hiendly was about six or seven miles south-southwest of Pontefract (Pomfret) in the West Riding of Yorkshire.

2. The following letter evidently was written by John Washington (c.1671–c.1720), a cousin of GW's grandfather Lawrence Washington (1659–1697/98), to his half sister Mary Washington Gibson (c.1663–1721), wife of Edward Gibson (1661–1732), vicar of Hawne (see Worthington C. Ford, "The Washington Connection," *The Nation*, 53 [15 Oct. 1891]: 293; and, about the Washington lineage more generally, *Burke's Genealogical and Heraldic History of the Landed Gentry*, 2 vols. [London, 1939], 2:2959–63).

3. John Washington's aunt Martha Washington Hayward (d. 1697) was the wife of Samuel Hayward (died c.1695) of Stafford County, Virginia.

4. John Washington's father, Lawrence Washington (c.1635–c.1675), and mother, Joyce Washington (d. 1685), had a daughter, Ann Washington (c.1669–c.1675).

5. Lawrence Washington was the third of Joyce Washington's four husbands. When they married, she was the widow of Alexander Fleming (c.1612–1668), and after his death she married James Yates (d. 1685). The three daughters were Elizabeth and Anne Hoskins, by her first marriage to Anthony Hoskins (c.1613–1665), and Elizabeth Fleming (see Lenora Higginbotham Sweeny, "Captain Alexander Fleming and Joyce, His Wife, of 'Westfalia,' Rappahannock County, Virginia," *Americana*, 33 [1939]: 326–48).

6. John Washington's wife was Mary Townshend Washington (c.1669–1729). Their surviving sons born before 1699 were Lawrence (born c.1693) and John (c.1697–1741/42) Washington.

7. Sir George Savile (1726–1784) represented Yorkshire in the House of Commons from 1759 to 1783.

8. William Rawstorne (d. 1790) was rector of Badsworth, Yorkshire, from about 1738 to his death. His daughter Isabella (d. 1823) was the mother of Sir Thomas Pilkington (1773–1811), seventh baronet.

9. Godfrey Gibson (d. 1801), who was a lieutenant in the 54th Regiment of Foot, was promoted to captain in 1795 and was killed while serving with the regiment at the battle of Alexandria in March 1801.

Bartholomew Dandridge, Jr., to Thomas Jefferson

26. Decemr 1793

By the President's direction Bw Dandridge has the honor to transmit to the Secretary of State a resolution of the House of representatives, just received[1]—& to request the Secretary to furnish the several papers therein required.[2]

AL, DLC: Jefferson Papers; ADf, DNA: RG 59, Miscellaneous Letters; LB, DNA: RG 59, George Washington's Correspondence with His Secretaries of State. The AL is docketed as "recd Dec. 26."

1. This resolution of 24 Dec. reads: "Resolved, that the President of the United States be requested to cause to be laid before this House, the substance of all such laws, decrees or ordinances respecting commerce, in any of the kingdoms or countries with which the United States have commercial intercourse, and which have been received by the Secretary of State, and not already stated to this House in his report of the sixteenth instant" (LB, DLC:GW).

2. Jefferson responded with a supplementary report on commerce of 30 Dec. (see *Jefferson Papers*, 27:639–43), which GW submitted to the House of Representatives on that same date.

From Thomas Mifflin

Sir.   Phil: 26 Dec. 1793.

Inclosed I have the honor to communicate to you, copies of a letter, which I have received from Mr Cassan, the Vice-Consul of the French Republic, and of the answer which I have transmitted to him, relatively to the intended departure of the Brigantine Peggy for the Mole and Jeremie.[1]

The sentiments, which I have expressed on this occasion, are in conformity to those that were lately communicated to me as yours, in the letter of the Secretary at War, dated the [   ] instant.[2] I am, with perfect respect, Sir, Your most obed. & most Hble Serv.

Df, PHarH: Executive Correspondence, 1790–99; LB, PHarH: Executive Letterbooks. The draft is in Alexander J. Dallas's writing.

On 27 Dec. Bartholomew Dandridge, Jr., sent this letter to Secretary of State Thomas Jefferson and informed him "that the President wishes if any thing is necessary to be done in consequence thereof, the Secretary will take such steps as he may conceive to be proper" (AL, DLC: Jefferson Papers; see *JPP*, 274). No record of any subsequent action by Jefferson has been identified.

Secretary of War Henry Knox acknowledged this letter in his letter to Mifflin of 10 Jan. 1794 (see Mifflin to GW, 31 Dec., source note).

1. The enclosed copies have not been found, but an LS of Jean-Baptiste Cassan to Mifflin, 24 Dec., and a draft of Alexander J. Dallas to Cassan, 26 Dec., are in PHarH: Executive Correspondence, 1790–99 (see also PHarH: Executive Letterbooks). Cassan's letter protested the proposed departure of the *Peggy* to "Places occupées par des rébelles." He warned that the laws of nations, which recognized as legal the seizure of all aid given to rebels and the arrest of ships bound to besieged or blockaded ports, would allow French vessels to seize any ships bound to the rebellious ports of Saint Domingue. Cassan explained that "les traîtres, qui habitent les places" were no friends of the United States and claimed that the Americans could have no connection with the rebels without compromising "leur alliance avec la République française."

The reply informed Cassan "that, although the General Government will not permit a military enterprize against any of the belligerent powers to be formed within the territory of the U.S., it is not thought just or expedient to deter the Hispaniola emigrants from returning to their homes, or peaceably going to any other place. I shall, however, communicate your letter to the President for his instructions; and at the same time intimate to the owners of the Peggy, the risques to which, according to your statement, they will be exposed on this occasion."

2. Mifflin probably was referring to Henry Knox's letter to him of 29 Nov. (see Mifflin to GW, 2 Dec., n.1).

To George Read

Dear Sir, Philadelphia 26th Decr 1793.

Two of the unhappy female fugitives from St Domingo have (as you will see by the enclosed letters) laid their distresses before me; which, if true in the degree they have stated, merits much commiseration. But I have received so many applications of a similar nature, and some of them from Imposters, that

I find it necessary to guard what little relief I am able to afford, against impos⟨i⟩tion. For this reason—and because I am not well acquainted with any other Gentleman in Newcastle (from whence the letters come) I have taken the liberty of putting my answer to them, under cover to you, open, that if upon enquiry the authors are found to merit relief it may be sealed and handed to them—if on the other hand it should prove a fictitious tale it may be returned to me.[1]

I will make no apology for giving you this trouble because, to be employed in acts of humanity cannot, I am sure, be disagreeable to such a mind as yours. With very great esteem & regard I am—Dear Sir Yr Most Obedt Serv.

Go: Washington

ALS, DeHi; ALS (letterpress copy), DLC:GW; LB, DLC:GW.
1. GW enclosed two letters written to him by Laurent De Saxÿ and Laurent De Verneüil, dated 6 and 10 Dec., and his reply to the two ladies, dated 26 December. Read wrote him on 4 Jan. 1794 that after "making every inquiry within my reach then of their charecter situation and circumstances," he was "induced to believe they are such persons as they represent themselves in their enclosed Letters and further that their family Connections have been among the most respectable of that Island. Under this Impression I delivered your Letter addressed to them with it's particular contents and they expressed much satisfaction at receiving it" (PHi: Sprague Collection). Read returned the letters that the ladies had written to GW.

To Laurent De Saxÿ & Laurent De Verneüil

Madames,   Philadelphia 26th Decr 1793.
I have been favored with your letters of the 6th & 10th of the present month, but not in due time.

I wish my resources were equal to the relief of the distresses which you, and many others under like circumstances have described. But the truth is, my private purse is inadequate, & there is no public money at my disposal.

Such as the first was competent to, I placed early in the hands of a Committee in this City, to be disposed of for the benefit of the unfortunate Sufferers from St Domingo whose necessities ⟨were⟩ greatest & means least.[1]

I prefered this mode of contributing my mite, 1st because it was not in my power to enquire into the degree of individual wants—2dly because I did not possess the means of Administering to them in the extent which might be required. and 3dly to guard against impositions, several of which had been attempted with Success.

In almost every City and large Town in the United States, Committees similar to the one I have already mentioned, are established. To the one nearest you, I should conceive it might be well to make your case known. In the meanwhile to supply your momentary wants I send you Twenty five dollars in Bank notes.[2]

With very poignant feelings for the distress you describe yourselves to be in I am—Madames Your Most Obedt and Very Hble Servant

Go: Washington

ALS (letterpress copy), DLC:GW; LB, DLC:GW.

1. At a meeting held in Philadelphia on 9 July "to consult on measures for the relief of the distressed citizens of Cape Francois," a committee was created to "ascertain the number of the persons to be relieved" and "to afford temporary relief" (*Dunlap's American Daily Advertiser* [Philadelphia], 12 and 15 July). GW's accounts, under the date of 18 July, debit $250, "gave by the President's order into the hands of Israel Israel, one of the Committee, towards the Relief of the French from St. Domingo" (Household Accounts).

2. The $25 is debited under the date 27 Dec. in GW's accounts: "Contingt Exps. delivd the President to send to two distressed French women at New Castle" (Household Accounts).

Certificate

United States to wit   [Philadelphia 27 December 1793]

I hereby certify that the sum of two thousand Dollars was allowed to Gouverneur Morris esq. for his expences and services on a special mission to London, previous to his appointment as Minister Plenipotentiary for the U.S. to France. Given under my hand this 27.[1] day of Dec. 1793.

Go. W.

L, in Thomas Jefferson's writing, DNA: RG 59, Miscellaneous Letters; LB, DNA: RG 59, George Washington's Correspondence with His Secretaries of State.

1. This number and GW's initials were added by Bartholomew Dandridge, Jr. GW's journal of proceedings indicates that he gave the certificate

to Thomas Jefferson on 26 Dec. (*JPP*, 274). For Morris's appointment as a "private Agent" to discuss at London fulfillment of the terms of the treaty of peace and the possibility of a new treaty of commerce, see GW's second and third letters to Morris of 13 Oct. 1789. Jefferson apparently wanted the document in preparation for the settlement of his accounts upon leaving the Department of State.

From Thomas Jefferson

Dec. 27. 93.

Th: Jefferson has the honor to inclose to the President the translation of a letter he received last night from Messrs Viar & Jaudenes and which he supposes should be communicated to the legislature as being in answer to one communicated to them.[1]

AL, DNA: RG 59, Miscellaneous Letters; LB, DNA: RG 59, George Washington's Correspondence with His Secretaries of State.

1. The enclosed letter of 26 Dec. from José de Jaudenes and José Ignacio de Viar rebutted American complaints about the behavior of the governor of Louisiana, particularly in regard to Indian relations on the southwest frontier (*Jefferson Papers*, 27:622–25). Bartholomew Dandridge, Jr., replied to Jefferson on this date, returning the letter and informing him "that the President thinks it should be communicated to Congress—& wishes copies to be prepared for that purpose" (DLC: Jefferson Papers). GW submitted a copy with his first message to the United States Senate and House of Representatives of 30 December.

To the United States Senate

United States
Gentlemen of the Senate,   27th Decemr 1793.
I nominate the following persons to fill the offices annexed to
    their names respectively, to which, having fallen vacant dur-
    ing the recess of the Senate, they have been appointed.
John Fitzgerald, of Virginia, to be Collector for the District of
    Alexandria; vice Charles Lee, resigned.
John Hobby, of Maine District, to be Marshal of and for the said
    District; vice Henry Dearbourne, resigned.
Nicholas Fish, of New York, to be Supervisor for the District of
    New York; vice John Armstrong, who declined accepting.
Hardy Murfree, of North Carolina, to be Inspector of the Rev-

enue for Survey No. 2. in the District of North Carolina; vice Samuel Tredwell, resigned.[1]

Joseph Tucker, of Massachusetts, to be Collector for the District of York; and Inspector of the revenue for the port of York; vice Richard Trivett, deceased.

Daniel Delozier, of Maryland, to be Surveyor for the District of Baltimore, and Inspector of the revenue for the port of Baltimore; vice Robert Ballard, deceased.

Samuel Hitchcock, of Vermont, to be Judge of the District Court in and for Vermont district; vice Nathaniel Chipman, resigned.

Robert Forsyth, of Georgia, to be Marshal of and for the Georgia District; continued: the legal term of his former appointment having expired.[2]

Samuel McDowell, of Kentuckey, to be Marshal of and for the Kentuckey District; continued, the legal term of his former appointment having expired.

Thomas Lowry, of New Jersey, to be Marshal of and for the New Jersey District; continued: the legal term of his former appointment having expired.

Allan McLean, of Delaware, to be Marshal of and for the Delaware District; continued, the legal term of his former appointment having expired.[3]

Nathaniel Ramsay, of Maryland, to be Marshal of and for the Maryland District; continued, the legal term of his former appointment having expired.

Philip Bradley, of Connecticut, to be Marshal of and for the Connecticut District; continued; the legal term of his former appointment having expired.

David Lenox, of Pennsylvania, to be marshal of and for the Pennsylvania District; vice Clement Biddle, resigned.

Vincent Gray, of Virginia, to be Surveyor for the District of Alexandria, and Inspector of the revenue for the port of Alexandria; vice Samuel Hanson, resigned.

David Austin, of Connecticut, to be Collector for the District of Newhaven; vice Jonathan Fitch, deceased.

John Brakenridge, of Kentuckey, to be Attorney for the United States in & for the District of Kentuckey; vice George Nicholas resigned.[4]

Robert Scott, of Pennsylvania, to be Engraver for the Mint.

William McPherson, of Pennsylvania, to be Naval Officer for the District of Philadelphia; vice Frederick Phile, deceased.

I also nominate

John Randall, to be Collector for the District of Annapolis, and Inspector of the revenue for the port of Annapolis; vice Robert Denny who declined accepting.[5]

Go: Washington

LS, DNA: RG 46, Third Congress, 1793–95, Senate Records of Executive Proceedings, President's Messages—Executive Nominations; LB, DLC:GW. On 30 Dec. the Senate approved all of these nominations except that of Philip Bradley, "postponed on supposition of a mistake in the Christian name Philip, for Philip Burr" (*Senate Executive Journal*, 143–44). GW resubmitted that nomination with the full name on 2 Jan. 1794.

1. Hardee Murfree (1752–1809), a Revolutionary War officer, had been a member of the North Carolina convention that ratified the federal Constitution in 1789. In February 1790 GW appointed him to be surveyor of the port of Murfreesboro. Samuel Tredwell (1763–1826) was a nephew of North Carolina governor and senator Samuel Johnston. GW appointed Tredwell to be collector and inspector of the revenue for the port of Edenton and inspector of Survey No. 2 on 19 February 1793 (DS, Nc-Ar). In 1821 he was appointed collector of the customs for the district, and inspector of the revenue for the port of Edenton, and he served in that post until his death.

2. Robert Forsyth (c.1754–1794), a Revolutionary War officer and commissary of purchases, was first appointed to be marshal for Georgia in September 1789, and he was killed while serving court papers in January 1794.

3. Allen McLane (1746–1829), a Revolutionary War officer, was appointed marshal for Delaware in September 1789 and served until 1797, when he became collector at Wilmington, a post he retained until his death.

4. John Breckinridge (1760–1806), who had just moved to Kentucky from Virginia, declined this post. Breckinridge served as attorney general of Kentucky, 1795–97, United States senator, 1801–5, and attorney general of the United States from 1805 until his death.

5. John Randall (1752–1826) was an Annapolis merchant who had served as commissary of stores and clothing for Maryland troops during the Revolutionary War. He remained collector and inspector of the revenue at Annapolis until his death, adding after 1810 the post of navy agent. Randall also served three terms as mayor of Annapolis between 1813 and 1818. GW had written a commission for Robert Denny as collector at Annapolis on 23 Nov. (*JPP*, 257).

From Auguste de Grasse

Duplicata

Mon Général   charleston[1] [S.C.] le 28 Xbre 1793

á mon arrivée ici dans les premiers jours d'aoust, j'ai Eu L'honneur de Vous Ecrire par la Voie de la poste Et par celle de la mer En même tems.[2]

je n'ai reçu de Vous aucune reponse, j'ai Soupçonnés que Les Calamités de philadelphie avoient detou[r]nées mes Lettres de leur destination. Et je vous En ait adressé de nouvelles par Le Commodore Guillon qui se disposoit a partir pour philadelphie immediatement aprés L'issüe de L'assemblée de la Caroline du Sud, mais dans L'incertitude ou je suis sur la Realité de son départ Et Consequemment sur Le sort des Lettres que je lui ait Confié, je profites Encor de la voye de la poste persuadé que Les premiers inconveniens qui ont pû detourner mes Premieres Lettres, ne subsistent plus Et que je serai plus heureux.[3]

je ne vous Jetois aucuns details Générale, des malheurs de St domingue Et des Evénémens qui m'avoient forcé de fuir Et de venir, Comme presque tous Les habitans de cette Colonie, me refugier ici, j'Etois passé a St domingue dans Le Cours de 1788, relativement aux biens Considerables que mon Pere m'y avoit Laissé, je comptois y Rester peu de tems Parce que L'Etat militaire au quel j'Etois attaché me rapelloit à mes devoirs mais la Revolution française m'y Surprit En 1789. Les troubles de la france, la desorganisation de tous les Etats, la degradation de la noblesse, Les dangers aux quels Elle y Etoit Exposée, Les Entraves que Les assemblées de St domingue mirent au depart des Colons Pour L'Europe Et plus que tous cela, Encore L'insurection Générale des Esclaves dans cette Colonie,[4] me determina à me consacrer avec mes Concitoyens a la Guerre Cruelle Et infructueuse qui nous á accablée, tous nos Efforts n'ont pû faire rentrer nos Esclaves dans L'ordre, un demon invisible rendoit nos Succès innutiles, Et je n'ai pû Comme bien d'autres Evitter L'incendie Et La destruction de mes Biens, Enfin Les derniers Excés du 20 juin dernier ont mis Le Comble à nos infortunes, Et ne nous ont Laissé que Le Choix de la fuitte ou d'une mort Cruelle,[5] Et je Suis arrivés ici avec ma femme nouvellement accouchée au milieu des flames Et des poignards. Mr de la hogue Conseillier au Conseil Superieur du Cap mon beau pere Et son Epouse, après avoir Eté depouillés En mer sur un Corsaire de la providence,[6] nous avons trouvés ici tous Les secours que L'humanité peut offrire En pareille Circonstence, Et avec une Générosité Et des temoignages de sensibilité bienfait pour demeurer Gravés Eternellement dans nos Cœurs, mais ces Bienfaits doivent avoir un terme, Et Les Circonstences ne nous Permettent pas Encor de ne pas En abuser trop Longtems, D'ailleurs ils sont Bornés à une Existence mediocre Et Génante pour nos Bienfaiteurs Et pour nous, C'Est pour cela mon Général, que dans ma premiere Lettre je vous demendois au nom de la mémoire de mon pere au quel Vous avés Donnés des temoignages d'Estime, Les Conseils necessaires pour Sortir de Cet Etat precaire Et pour n'Etre plus journellement à charge, ainsi que la famille de ma femme à des personnes aux quelles nous avons trop d'obligations pour ne pas desirer de les delivrer de la Surcharge que nous Leurs occasionnons, Et En même tems S'il ne seroit pas Possible d'obtenir des Etats unis un Emprunt d'ont L'Employ put Subvenir à notre Existence[7] je n'aurois cependant á offrir pour gage de Cet Emprunt que mes Biens de france Et Ceux de St domingue dont j'ignore Le Sort present Et avenir, je ne puis Guere Songer à retourner En france tant que Les troubles Et L'anarchie y Subsisteront, mon nom y Est peut Etre un Crime, quand a St domingue C'Est aussi un problĕme dont la Resolution Est Ensevelie dans Les Evenements avenir. je dois avoir dans un des Etats de L'amerique des proprietés En terre qui ont Eté concedés par Le Congrés à mon pere, mais je n'ai pas Encor⟨e⟩ malgrés mes demarches me procurer aucune connoissances sur Leurs consistences[8] Et sur Leurs situation, je vous prie Mon Général de me donner S'il Est Possible quelques renseignements à Cet Egard Et Sur Les moyens d'En prendre possession, j'ai Encor une autre Grace Particuliere a Vous demander, des L'instant de la naissance de ma fille, je lui ait donnée Le nom de Caroline, Et je me suis promis de Vous inviter à Etre Son parein, j'Espere que vous ne me refuserés pas cette faveur, Et En ce Cas je vous Prieois d'Envoyer à cet Effet votre pouvoir pour vous representer Et de faire choix de la mareine, Et des noms que vous voudr⟨ez⟩ ajouter à celui de Caroline que je lui ait déja donné En mémoire de L'acceuil fraternel que nous avons reçu des habitans de cet Etat,[9] je me flattes mon Général que j'aurois Enfin la satisfaction de recevoir une Reponse de Vous, Et je ne Cesserai de la Solliciter tant que j'aurai lieu de Croire que vous n'aurés Pas reçu mes Lettres.

Mon Epouse, mon beau pere Et ma belle mere Vous Prie Mon Général d'agreer Leurs respects Et Civilités. j'ai L'honneur D'Etre avec Respect Et Consideration Mon Général Votre très humble Et très obeissent Serviteur

Auguste De Grasse

ALS (duplicate), DNA: RG 59, Miscellaneous Letters.

1. At the end of this letter, De Grasse indicated his location as "chez Mr jonh Bee Holmes Esqr. a charleston." Holmes resided at what is now 15 Meeting Street.

2. See de Grasse to GW, 24 August. No other letter from de Grasse in August has been found.

3. Alexander Gillon (1741–1794), a Charleston merchant, was appointed a commodore in the South Carolina navy in February 1778. Gillon, who served several terms in the South Carolina general assembly, was not a member during the 1793 session, but his conduct as a commissioner for settling public accounts in the 1780s was under investigation. The legislature adjourned on 21 Dec., but the general assembly had voted on 20 Dec., after Gillon had testified, to "recommend . . . that he remain in this State until the final adjustment of his Accounts with the Public" ("Journals of the House of Representatives of the State of South Carolina, 1793," pp. 537–42, Microfilm Collection of Early State Records).

4. A slave rebellion commenced in the northern part of Saint Domingue in August 1791, and sporadic rebellions in the other two regions added to the general unrest on the island.

5. On 20 June, Governor General Thomas François Galbaud, dismissed by the French commissioners Etienne Polverel and Léger Félicité Sonthonax and encouraged to resist by colonists hostile to the commissioners' rule, commenced an attack on Cap Français using sailors from the fleet in the harbor. By 21 June the town was in flames and the commissioners had issued a proclamation giving freedom to the blacks who fought on their side in the struggle. When Galbaud withdrew two days later, many of the colonists fled the island.

6. The ship *Thomas* was stopped on 30 July by the British sloop *Susannah*, out of New Providence, and property was seized from the passengers (see de Grasse to GW, 24 Aug., n.3).

7. On 29 Jan. 1794 Bartholomew Dandridge, Jr., replied to de Grasse's request for a loan from the United States, informing him that GW had no public funds to disburse for relief but that the subject of relief for the refugees from Saint Domingue had been laid before Congress (DLC:GW).

8. No evidence that Congress gave land to De Grasse's father, François-Joseph-Paul, comte de Grasse, has been identified.

9. No reply from GW has been found to the request that he allow himself to be named godfather of de Grasse's infant daughter Caroline.

From Thomas Jefferson

Dec. 28. 93.

Th: Jefferson has the honor to inclose to the President a copy of mister Genet's instructions which he has just recieved from him with a desire that they may be communicated to the legislature.[1]

AL, DNA: RG 59, Miscellaneous Letters; LB, DNA: RG 59, George Washington's Correspondence with His Secretaries of State.

1. In a letter to Jefferson of 20 Dec., Genet enclosed the printed translations of "Instructions to Citizen Genet, Minister Plenipotentiary from the French Republic to the United States, from the Executive Council, and Minister of Marine" which were to appear in his *Correspondence between Citizen Genet, Minister of the French Republic, to the United States of North America, and the Officers of the Federal Government; to Which Are Prefixed the Instructions from the Constituted Authorities of France to the Said Minister. All from Authentic Documents* (Philadelphia, 1793), 1–9.

Genet requested that Jefferson ask GW to lay the translations before Congress so that they might judge whether Genet's actions had been conformable to his instructions. This done, Genet continued, "nothing will remain for me to do but to prosecute in your courts of Judicature, the authors and abettors of the odious and vile machinations that have been plotted against me by means of a series of impostures which for a while have fascinated the minds of the public, and misled even your first magistrate, with a view to shake at least, if not to break off entirely, the alliance between two nations which every consideration calls upon to unite and rivet still faster the bonds which tie them to each other, at a period when the most imminent danger equally threatens them both" (Genet's translation from *Correspondence*, [ii–iii]; for the original French, see *Jefferson Papers*, 27:593–95).

The "Instructions" included a "memorial" from the executive council to Genet of 4 Jan. 1793, an "Extract from a supplement to the instructions" of 17 Jan., two letters from Minister of the Marine Gaspard Monge and Minister of the Navy Jean Dalbarade to Genet of 8 Feb. and 28 May, and Genet's credentials of 30 Dec. 1792. The instructions in essence directed Genet to negotiate a new commercial treaty, but added various rhetorical flourishes.

The council prescribed that Genet "exert himself to strengthen the Americans in the principles which led them to unite themselves to France; to make them perceive that they have no ally more natural or more disposed to treat them as brethren." They criticized the "machiavelian principle" and "duplicity" that guided the former French regime and suggested that the new commercial treaty "admits a latitude still more extensive in becoming a national agreement, in which two *great* people shall suspend their commercial and political interests and establish a mutual understanding, to befriend the empire of liberty, wherever it can be embraced, to guarantee the sovereignty of the people, and punish those powers who still keep up an exclusive colonial and commercial system, by declaring that their vessels shall not be received in the ports of the contracting parties." Such a pact would "quickly contribute to the general emancipation of the new world." The council claimed that America's "safety still depends on ours, and if we fail they will sooner or later fall under the iron rod of great Britain." However, in case "false representations" should make America's ministers "adopt a timid and wavering conduct" in the negotiations, Genet was charged "to take such steps as will appear to him exigencies may require, to serve the cause of liberty and the freedom of the people." In addition Genet was told that he should "avoid as much as he can those ridiculous disputes about etiquette which so much occupied the old diplomacy," but "insist on all the prerogatives the French power has at any time enjoyed."

The supplement discussed the negotiation of the new treaty, if not impeded "by secret manœuvres of the English minister and his partizans at Philadelphia, by the timidity of certain members of the federal government, who notwithstanding their known patriotism have always shewn the strongest aversion to every measure which might be unpleasing to England." In the meantime, they instructed Genet to "employ all the means in his power to procure a religious observance of the 17th, 21st, and 22d articles of the treaty of commerce" (giving prote ction to prizes seized by either party when brought to the other's ports, while denying shelter to prizes seized from either party; forbidding either nation from issuing letters of marque against the other; and forbidding the fitting out of enemy privateers in the ports of either party). The letters from the naval ministers enclosed 300 letters of marque and commissions for the conductors of prizes, to be issued to Americans who wished to fit out as privateers against the enemies of France. For the original instructions, see Turner, *Correspondence of the French Ministers,* 2:201–11.

From the instructions, Genet omitted specifics included in the "emancipation of the new world"—opening the navigation of the Mississippi to Kentuckians, freeing Louisianans from Spanish tyranny, and, perhaps, adding Canada to the United States—and he suppressed under the phrase "such steps" his authority to germinate the principles of liberty in Louisiana and other provinces near the United States by using agents in Kentucky and Louisiana to support free navigation of the Mississippi. From the supplement, he omitted passages explaining the importance of insisting on a reciprocal exemption from the duty on tonnage, discussing the use of French sympathizers in the American government, and indicating that the enclosed army commissions were for Indians who might take arms against France's enemies.

To Thomas Jefferson

Dear Sir,   Saturday Afternoon [28 December 1793]
I have received with vexation the enclosure you have just sent me from the French Minister: and pray you to take the opinion of the Gentlemen upon the measure proper to be taken in this business.[1] Every day, more & more discovers the intention of this Agent to perplex this Government, and to scatter thick & wide the Seeds of dissention. Yours always—

Go: Washington

ALS, DLC: Jefferson Papers. Jefferson endorsed this letter as "recd Dec. 28."
1. A note signed by Alexander Hamilton, Henry Knox, and Edmund Randolph on Jefferson's retained draft of his letter to French Minister Edmond Genet on this subject, 31 Dec., states that the letter was "submitted to the correction of the Secretaries of the Treasury & war & the Atty Genl" and "approved" (*Jefferson Papers*, 27:649). For that letter, see GW to Jefferson, 31 Dec., n.1.

To William Pearce

Mr Pearce,   Philadelphia Decr 28th 1793
Your letter of the 24th instant from Kent County in Maryland came to hand yesterday.[1] I am sorry to find you had not then removed to Mount Vernon, and am concerned for the cause of your detention. Acts of Providence no human foresight can guard against, and it is our duty to submit to them. In the situation you describe your daughter to be, I certainly should not have desired you to leave her;[2] however inconvenient, & injurious your not doing it, is to me: the last of which has been, & will continue to be very injurious, among other things, on Account of the Hogs which were up for Porke—and with which no body at Mount Vernon will know what to do, especially as your arrival at that place has been expected ever since the 20th of this month, agreeably to the advice I had communicated to my Nephew Mr Lewis;[3] who is young & entirely unacquainted with every thing of this sort; and is only left there merely to keep things together until you were present to take charge of them.
By the Post, several days ago, I wrote very fully to you in two letters, giving you my sentiments on every thing which had occurred to me that I conceived it might be necessary for you to

be informed in, respecting my business—these letters were sent under cover to Mr Lewis, & you will find them at Mt Vernon. You will perceive by them, & others enclosed in them, to my Overseers how much I have been dissatisfied with the conduct of the latter since I left home in October.[4] I shall not repeat it here. How far it may be in your power, by considerable exertions, to recover the business from their neglects will depend very much upon the nature of the Winter and Spring.

I had, in order to make your situation at Mount Vernon more comfortable (even if you had removed wi⟨th⟩ your whole family, as you will percei⟨ve⟩ by one of the letters which you will find there) offered you the room in the house which Mr Lewis usually lodges in—& you may, as your own furniture can not now be got round until the Winter frosts are passed, make use of any of mine which you shall find necessary to your comfort & convenience 'till this happens; and you are very welcome to such provisions from my Meat house &ca as you shall find occasion for.

I shall only add my best wishes for the restoration of health to your afflicted daughter—and that I am Your friend &ca

Go: Washington

ALS (letterpress copy), DLC:GW. The ALS was offered for sale in the American Art Association catalog of 5–6 Feb. 1936, item 317.

1. Pearce's letter has not been found.

2. Pearce's eldest daughter remained sickly even after the family came to Mount Vernon, and she died in late October 1794.

3. GW wrote Howell Lewis on 10 Nov. that Pearce could be expected at Mount Vernon "by the middle of next month."

4. See GW to Pearce, 18 and 23 Dec., and GW's letters of 23 Dec. to Hiland Crow, John Christian Ehlers, Thomas Green, Henry McCoy, and William Stuart. The cover letters from Bartholomew Dandridge, Jr., to Howell Lewis of 18 and 23 Dec. have not been found.

From Thomas Jefferson

Sir, Philadelphia Dec. 30. 1793.

I am informed, by the Director of the Mint, that an impediment has arisen to the coinage of the precious Metals, which it is my Duty to lay before you.

It will be recollected, that, in pursuance of the Authority, vested in the President, by Congress, to procure Artists from abroad, if necessary, Mr Drotz, at Paris, so well known by the superior style of his coinage, was engaged for our mint; but that, after occasioning to us a considerable delay, he declined coming: That thereupon, our minister at London, according to the instructions he had received, endeavored to procure, there, a Chief Coiner and Assayer; That, as to the latter, he succeeded, sending over a Mr Albion Coxe, for that Office, but that he could procure no person, there, more qualified to discharge the duties of chief Coiner, than might be had here; and therefore did not engage one.[1] The Duties of this last Office, have consequently been hitherto performed, and well performed by Henry Voight, an Artist of the United States: but the law requiring these Officers to give a security in the sum of 10,000 dollars each, neither is able to do it.[2] The coinage of the precious metals, has, therefore, been prevented, for sometime past, though, in order that the mint might not be entirely idle, the coinage of copper has been going on; the trust in that, at any one point of time, being of but small amount.

It now remains to determine how this difficulty is to be got over. If, by discharging these Officers, and seeking others, it may well be doubted if any can be found in the United States, equally capable of fulfilling their duties; and to seek them from abroad, would still add to the delay; and if found either at home or abroad, they must still be of the description of Artists, whose circumstances & connections rarely enable them to give security in so large a sum. The other alternative would be to lessen the Securityship in money, and to confide that it will be supplied by the vigilance of the Director, who, leaving as small masses of metal in the hands of the Officers, at any one time, as the course of their process will admit, may reduce the risk to what would not be considerable.[3]

To give an idea of the extent of the trust to the several Officers, both as to sum, and time, it may be proper to state the course of the Business, according to what the Director is of Opinion it should be.[4] The Treasurer, he observes, should receive the Bullion; the Assayer, by an operation on a few Grains of it, is to ascertain it's fineness. The Treasurer is then to deliver it to the Refiner to be melted and mixed to the standard fineness[5]—the Assayer, here again, examining a few grains of the melted mass, and certifying when it is of due fineness; the Refiner then delivers it to the Chief Coiner to be rolled and coined, and he returns it when coined, to the Treasurer. By this it appears, that a few grains only, at a time, are in the hands of the Assayer, the mass being confided, for operation, to the Refiner and Chief Coiner. It is to be observed that the law has not taken notice of the Office of Refiner, though so important an officer ought, it should seem, to be of the President's nomination, and ought to give a Security nearly equal to that required from the Chief Coiner.

I have thought it my duty to give this information, under an impression that it is proper to be communicated to the Legislature,[6] who will decide in their Wisdom, whether it will be expedient to make it the Duty of the Treasurer to receive and keep the Bullion before coinage.

To lessen the pecuniary Security required from the Chief Coiner & Assayer; And

To place the office of the Refiner under the same nomination with that of the other Chief Officers, to fix his Salary, & require due Security.[7]

I have the honor to be with the most perfect respect & attachment Sir, your most obedient & most humble servant,

Th: Jefferson

LS, DNA: RG 46, Third Congress, 1793–95, Senate Records of Legislative Proceedings, President's Messages; L (letterpress copy), DLC: Jefferson Papers; ADf, DLC: Jefferson Papers; LB, DNA: RG 59, Domestic Letters; LB, DNA: RG 46, Third Congress, 1793–95, Senate Records of Legislative Proceedings, President's Messages; LB, DNA: RG 46, Transcribed Reports and Communications Transmitted by the Executive Branch to the U.S. Senate, 1789–1819; LB, DNA: RG 233, Third Congress, 1793–95, House Records of the Office of the Clerk, Records for Reports from Executive Departments. Jefferson's draft contains numerous emendations, the most important of which are indicated in the notes below.

1. The authority for GW to employ artists was conferred by a resolution of 3 March 1791 (*Journal of the House*, 3:95). Jefferson instructed Thomas Pinckney to engage an assayer and coiner and engraver in his letter to Pinckney of 14 June 1792. For Pinckney's engagement of Albion Cox (d. 1795), a native of England who had been involved in minting coins for New Jersey in 1786, to be assayer of the U.S. Mint, see Pinckney's first letter to Jefferson of 12 March 1793 (*Jefferson Papers*, 24:74–76, 25:370–71).

2. Jefferson was referring to the fifth section of "An Act establishing a Mint, and regulating the Coins of the United States," 2 April 1792 (1 *Stat.* 246–51).

3. At this point in his draft, Jefferson wrote several paragraphs of text, which he then struck and replaced with an insertion in the margin that

corresponds to the paragraph following. The deleted text reads: "Another obstacle to the coinage arises from the following source. the laws have not enabled or authorized the mint to take in any bullion on public account. the only coinage of gold or silver therefore which can be carried on is that for individuals bringing bullion to be coined. but it is rarely convenient for them to await the operation of coining. they therefore carry away their bullion to those who will give them ready money. a deposit of a few thousand dollars of public property in the mint, ready coined, to serve merely as a basis of prompt exchange, would very greatly increase the quantities to be coined on private account: and seems to have been contemplated tho not provided by the law where it allows an half per cent to be retained for prompt paiment.

"Without such a deposit too a separate coinage for each individual as directed by the law, is from the nature of the operation impracticable. the bullion is to be rolled into plates, the round peices to be cut from these plates, & consequently there remains a considerable portion of corners & scraps, supposed one fifth of the whole. these may be melted over again rolled, & cut; but a like proportion will always remain & a great multiplication of work take place. this would be avoided were the mint enabled to give to the individual his whole sum at once, and to carry on the process of coinage in such masses as should be found most advantageous.

"the law too authorizes the individual to receive a quantity of pure metal in coin, equal to that he gave in. as no degree of skill & care can prevent a small waste in the operation, the giving back the exact quantity is impossible unless there be some deposit from which this waste can be made up. such a deposit once made it's loss by waste would probably be more than supplied by the half percent retained from those who prefer prompt paiment at that price. it should therefore be provided that whenever a replenishment of the deposit shall be applied for, satisfactory statements shall be furnished of the quantity of coined metal whereon that waste has arisen to shew that it has not been greater than it ought to be from the nature of the operation.

"As the legislature alone is competent to decide whether these difficulties are such as ought to be obviated by any change in the existing laws, I think it my duty to propose that they be submitted to their consideration."

4. On the draft, Jefferson began his insertion with the following text, which he revised and then struck out, substituting the preceding sentence: "indeed as to the Assayer the course of the business places but few grains of metal in his hands at a time, his duty being to ascertain the quantity of pure metal in any mass whatever, which he does by an operation on a few grains, taken from it. it is the refiner who is necessarily entrusted with the mass while under the operation of ⟨*illegible*⟩, as the Treasurer ought to be for this is what the director thinks should be the course of the business."

5. The previous text of this sentence is missing from the letter-book copy in House Records.

6. GW enclosed this letter in his second letter to the United States Senate and House of Representatives of this date. Congress received the letter on 31 Dec., and in the House it was referred to a committee of three members for report (*Journal of the House,* 6:51–52). On 3 March 1794 Congress passed

"An Act in alteration of the act establishing a Mint and regulating the Coins of the United States," which incorporated the first two of the three proposals following (1 *Stat.* 341).

7. In his draft, Jefferson completed this sentence with additional text that he then struck: "and to authorize some determinate sum to be deposited in the Mint on public account, to be the basis of prompt exchange, always subject to the disposal of the legislature."

From Thomas Jefferson

Sir,   Philadelphia, Decr 30.[1] 1793.

Certain proceedings of the ministers of the United States abroad, on Behalf of M. de la Fayette rendering it necessary that I should do myself the honor of addressing you on that subject in order that the proper sanction may be obtained for what is done, I shall be justified by the interest which yourself and our fellow citizens generally feel in the fortunes and sufferings of that Gentleman in suggesting something more for his future aid.

Soon after his captivity and imprisonment, and before the ministers had received our instructions to endeavor to obtain his liberation, they were apprised that his personal restraint, and the peculiar situation of his fortune disabled him from drawing resources from that, and would leave him liable to suffer for subsistence, and the common necessaries of life. After a consultation by letter, therefore, between our ministers at Paris, London, and the Hague, they concurred in opinion that they ought not in such a case to wait for instructions from hence, but that his necessities should be provided for until they could receive such instructions. Different sums have been therefore either placed at his disposal, or answered on his draughts, amounting, as far as we hitherto know to about twelve or thirteen hundred Guineas. This has been taken from a fund not applicable by law to this purpose nor able to spare it: and the question is whether, and how it is to be made good? To do this, nothing more is requisite than that the United States should not avail themselves of the Liberalities of M. de la Fayette, yielded at a moment when neither he nor we could foresee the time when they would become his only resource for subsistence. It appears by a statement from the war office, hereto annexed, that his pay and commutation as a major General in the service of the United States to the 3rd of nov. 1783 amounted to 24,100 dollrs thirteen Cents exclusive of ten years interest elapsed since that time, to the payment of which the following obstacle has occurred. at the foot of the original engagement by Mr Deane, a copy of which is hereto annexed, that a certain roll of officers there named, and of which M. de la Fayette was one, should be taken into the american service in the grades there specified, M. de la Fayette alone has subjoined for himself a declaration that he would serve without any *particular allowance or pension.*[2] It may be doubted whether the words in the original French do strictly include the general allowance of pay and commutation.[3] and if they do, there is no evidence of any act of acceptance by Congress. Yet, under all the circumstances of the case, it is thought that the legislature alone is competent to decide it. If they decline availing the United States of the declaration of M. de la Fayette, it leaves a fund which not only covers the advances which have been made, but will enable you take measures for his future relief. It does it too, in a way which can give offence to nobody, since none have a right to complain of the payment of a debt, that being a moral duty, from which we cannot be discharged by any relation in which the creditor may be placed as to them. I therefore take the liberty of proposing that this matter may be submitted to the consideration of the Legislature, who will determine in their wisdom whether the supplies already furnished, or any others in future, shall be sanctioned by them, and made good in the way here suggested, or in any other which they shall deem more proper. I have the honor to be, with the most perfect respect & attachment, Sir, Your most obedient and Most humble servant

Th: Jefferson

LS, DNA: RG 46, Third Congress, 1793–95, Senate Records of Legislative Proceedings, President's Messages; ADf, DLC: Jefferson Papers; LB, DNA: RG 233, Third Congress, 1793–95, House Records of the Office of the Clerk, Records for Reports of Executive Departments; LB, DNA: RG 46, Transcribed Reports and Communications Transmitted by the Executive Branch to the U.S. Senate, 1789–1819.

GW transmitted this letter and its enclosures with his second letter to the United States Senate and House of Representatives of this date, and Congress passed on 27 March 1794 "An Act allowing to Major General La Fayette his pay and emoluments while in the service of the United States," which allowed Lafayette $24,424 to "be paid out of any moneys which may be in the treasury and not otherwise appropriated" (6 *Stat.* 14).

1. On the LS the date was changed from "31" to "30"; the draft is dated "Dec. 31."

2. This enclosure consists of a list of thirteen foreign officers engaged between 7 Nov. and 7 Dec. 1776, with their agreed ranks, signed on 7 Dec. by Silas Deane, Lafayette, and Johann Kalb, to which is appended statements of the same date by Deane and Lafayette, given first in French and then in English translation. The translation of Deane's statement reads: "The desire which Mr the Marquis de la Fayette shews, of serving among the Troops of the United States of north America, and the interest which he takes in the justice of their cause making him wish to distinguish himself in this war and to render himself as useful as he possibly can: but not thinking that he can obtain leave of his family to pass the seas and serve in a foreign country till he can go as a General Officer; I have thought I could not better serve my Country and those who have entrusted me than by granting to him in the name of the very honorable Congress the rank of Major General which I beg the States to confirm to him, to ratify and deliver to him the Commission to hold and take rank, to count from this day, with the General Officers of the same degree. His high birth, his alliances, the great dignities which his family holds at this Court, his considerable estates in this Realm, his personal merit, his reputation, his disinterestedness, and above all his zeal for the liberty of our provinces, have only been able to engage me to promise him the rank of Major General in the name of the United States."

The translation of Lafayette's statement reads: "On the conditions here explained I offer myself, and promise to depart when and how Mr Deane shall judge proper, to serve the United States with all possible zeal, without any pension or particular allowance, reserving to myself the liberty of returning to Europe when my Family or my King shall recall me." In French the significant phrase reads, "sans aucune Pension ny traittement particulier" (copy, DNA: RG 46, Third Congress, 1793–95, Senate Records of Legislative Proceedings, President's Messages).

Deane (1737–1789), formerly a Connecticut delegate to the Continental Congress, was sent to France in April 1776 to buy supplies. Later that year he was designated one of three American commissioners at Paris, a post he continued to hold until recalled in 1778.

3. In his draft, Jefferson began the next sentence with the following clause, which he then struck: "however it may be well conceived that the officers of the government would not undertake in a case of doubtful construction."

Enclosure
Lafayette's Revolutionary War Account

[24 December 1793]

Marquis de la Fayette

Dollars

Received of Mr Trumbull[1] the 31st March 1778 on his
  private account . . . . .1700.

He paid in May 1778, to Capn Celeron[2] .... <u>80.</u>
Leaving this sum to be accounted for, to be reduced at 5 for one, 1620.
will equal specie .... Dollars <u>324.</u>
His pay as Major General from the 31st July 1777 to the 31st
December 1780, 41 months & 1 day a[t] 166 dollars p. Month. ... 6811.48
Deduct as above stated .... <u>324.</u>
Balance on interest from the 1st Jany 1781 .... 6487.48/90
His pay for the year 1781 on interest 1st Jany 1782 .... <u>1992.</u>
His pay for the year 1782 interest 1st Jany 1783 .... <u>1992.</u>
His pay from the 1st Jany to the 3d Nov: 1783 .... 1676.54
Commutation of 5 years full pay in lieu of half during life...... <u>9960.</u>
.... Dollars   11,636.54/90

Summary

Balance to the 1st Jany 1781 .... 6487.48
Pay of the year 1781 .... 1992.
Pay of .... 1782 .... 1992.
Ditto .... 1783 & commutn 11,636.54
To extra pay, while on separate command, suppose one year
the precise time to be ascertained a future period ...:.... <u>1992.</u>
                              Dollars   24100.12/90

War Department Accountants office December 24th <u>1793</u>
Signed Joseph Howell Accountant.

Copy, DNA: RG 46, Third Congress, 1793–95, Senate Records of Legislative
Proceedings, President's Messages; copy, DNA: RG 46, Transcribed Reports
and Communications Transmitted by the Executive Branch to the U.S. Senate, 1789–1819. War Department Chief Clerk John Stagg, Jr., certified that
the account was a "Copy—Original on file in the war office."

1. Jonathan Trumbull, Jr. (1740–1809), served as Continental paymaster
general for the northern department from 1775 to 1778. In 1793 he was a
congressman from Connecticut, and he later became a senator and governor
of that state.

2. Paul-Louis Céleron de Blainville (b. 1753) became a lieutenant in the
Continental army in 1777 and was promoted to captain in 1778. He was captured at Charleston in 1780 and resigned his commission in 1782.

From William Vans Murray

Sir,   30. Dec. 1793.

Among the candidates for the office of Collector of the port
of Annapolis is Mr Pinckney[1]—a young gentleman in high estimation among his acquaintances—He is a store Keeper but not
an importer. He is a steady, competent & worthy man to whom
the office might be an object & of whose capacity as well as in-

tegrity I have a very good opinion. I am Sir with great deference Yr most obt ser.

W. V. Murray.

ALS, DLC:GW.

1. Murray was almost certainly recommending one of the sons of Annapolis storekeeper Jonathan Pinkney, most likely Jonathan Pinkney, Jr. (1768–1828), later cashier of the Farmers Bank of Maryland, or possibly Ninian Pinkney (1771–1824), clerk of the Maryland Executive Council from about 1794 until his death. By the time GW received this letter, he had nominated John Randall to the post (GW to U.S. Senate, 27 Dec.).

To the United States House of Representatives

United States
December 30th 1793.

Gentlemen of the House of Representatives,

I now transmit you a report by the Secretary of State, of such laws, decrees and ordinances, or their substance respecting commerce in the countries, with which the United States have commercial intercourse, as he has received, and had not stated in his report of the sixteenth instant.[1]

Go: Washington

Copy, DNA: RG 233, Third Congress, 1793–95, House Records of Legislative Proceedings, Journals; LB, DLC:GW. This letter was received by the House on 31 Dec. (*Journal of the House*, 6:50).

1. Thomas Jefferson's supplementary report on commerce, issued this date, was a response to the request made to GW by a House resolution of 24 Dec. (see Bartholomew Dandridge, Jr., to Jefferson, 26 Dec., and n.1). The report provided a translation of the French decree of 26 March exempting U.S. vessels from various duties and restrictions; mentioned a French decree of 27 July allowing U.S. vessels "to be carried against their will into the ports of France" and to have enemy goods on board seized as prizes, although it had not been "received officially"; gave the substance of a Spanish decree of 9 June regulating the commerce of Louisiana and the Floridas; and took note of a 1788 British act about commerce with the West Indies that previously "had escaped his researches" (*Jefferson Papers*, 27:639–43). For Jefferson's report on commerce of 16 Dec., see *Jefferson Papers*, 27:567–79.

To the United States Senate and House of Representatives

United States 30th December 1793.
Gentlemen of the Senate, and of the House of Representatives,

I communicate to you the translation of a letter received from the Representatives of Spain here, in reply to that of the Secretary of State to them of the 21st inst: which had before been communicated to you.[1]

Go: Washington

LS, DNA: RG 46, Third Congress, 1793–95, Senate Records of Legislative Proceedings, President's Messages; Df, in Thomas Jefferson's writing, DLC: Jefferson Papers; Copy, DNA: RG 233, Third Congress, 1793–95, House Records of Legislative Proceedings, Journals; LB, DLC:GW. This letter was received by the House of Representatives on 30 Dec. and by the Senate on 31 Dec. (*Journal of the House,* 6:48; *Journal of the Senate,* 6:22).

1. GW enclosed a translation of José de Jaudenes and José Ignacio de Viar to Thomas Jefferson, 26 December. Viar and Jaudenes defended the governor of Louisiana from Jefferson's criticisms, writing in part: "having produced incontestable documents that the Georgians and some of the agents of the United States have fomented them—it appears that the said Governor does not calumniate, in repeating on proof, the hostile acts which are committed on those frontiers by the said agents & individuals. The opposition which the said Governor has hitherto made and intends to make to the passage along the Missisippi by the citizens of the United States above the 31st degree of latitude, is neither unjust nor extraordinary, since you well know that we have been, are and will remain in possession of it, until by agreement or force, we yield our right.

"That the Governor administers arms & war stores to the Nations of Indians, who inhabit the Territory in question, is as little extraordinary, and it would be unjust were he not to do it since he would fail in good faith under the treaties executed between Spain and the different Nations of Indians in the year 1784." The two ministers continued by giving assurances of their desire "to preserve good faith and friendship," mentioning "the plan which to the Governor of Louisiana and to ourselves appeared very proper to conciliate the minds of the subjects of the King our master, on that frontier— The citizens of the United States, and the intermediate nations of Indians to which we have not received an answer," and closed by asking that GW be informed of the contents of their letter (DNA: RG 46, Third Congress, 1793–95, Senate Records of Legislative Proceedings, President's Messages; see also *Jefferson Papers,* 27:622–25). For Jefferson's letter to Jaudenes and Viar of 21 Dec., which was transmitted with GW's letter to Congress of 23 Dec., see *Jefferson Papers,* 27:603–4.

To the United States Senate and House of Representatives

United States Decr 30. 1793.
Gentlemen of the Senate and of the House of Representatives
I lay before you for your consideration a letter from the Secretary of State, informing me of certain impediments, which have arisen to the coinage of the precious metals at the mint.[1]

As also a letter from the same Officer relative to certain advances of money, which have been made on public account. Should you think proper to sanction what has been done, or be of opinion that any thing more shall be done in the same way, you will judge whether there are not circumstances which would render secrecy expedient.[2]

Go: Washington

LS, DNA: RG 46, Third Congress, 1793–95, Senate Records of Legislative Proceedings, President's Messages; LB, DNA: RG 46, Transcribed Reports and Communications Transmitted by the Executive Branch to the U.S. Senate, 1789–1819; Copy, DNA: RG 233, Third Congress, 1793–95, House Records of Legislative Proceedings, Journals; LB, DLC:GW. The LS is in the writing of the State Department chief clerk, George Taylor, Jr. This letter was received by Congress on 31 Dec. (*Journal of the House,* 6:51; *Journal of the Senate,* 6:21–22).

1. See Thomas Jefferson to GW, this date (first letter).
2. See Jefferson to GW, this date (second letter).

To Thomas Jefferson

Dear Sir   31st Decr 1793.
It is my wish that the result of the determination on Mr G—ts request may go to him with your Signature, and of this date.[1] It was for this reason I aimed at a decision on it Sunday or yesterday.[2] Yours always

Go: Washington

ALS, owned (1984) by Edward N. Bomsey, Springfield, Virginia.
1. GW was referring to Edmond Genet's letter to Jefferson of 20 Dec., in which he asked that GW transmit to Congress translations of Genet's instructions from the French government (see Jefferson to GW, 28 Dec., and n.1). In Jefferson's letter to Genet of 31 Dec., he returned the instructions and

informed Genet "that your functions as the missionary of a foreign nation here, are confined to the transaction of the affairs of your nation with the Executive of the United States, that the communications, which are to pass between the Executive and Legislative branches, cannot be a subject for your interference" (*Jefferson Papers,* 27:649).

2. The previous Sunday was 29 December.

From Thomas Jefferson

Sir,   Philadelphia Decr 31. 1793.

I have the honor to enclose you a statement of the expenditure of the monies appropriated to our intercourse with foreign nations to be laid before the legislature according to the requisitions of the law.[1]

The account of the Secretary of State commences July 1. 1792, where that rendered at the last session, ended; and is brought down to this time. In the two preceding Years of this appropriation, Bills of Exchange were given me from the Treasurer on our Bankers at Amsterdam: so that the remittance of these Bills to the Bankers, for the credit of the Department of State, constituted a separate Deposite in their hands, on which the public Agents abroad, might draw for their salaries & other authorized expenditures. For the last year an order was given me by the Treasurer on the Bank of the United States, Bills of Exchange were purchased by an Agent employed for that purpose, and the money was paid to the Drawers by the Bank, on my Orders. As Amsterdam was at one time in danger of an attack, and the seat of war continued not very distant from it, it was thought safer to make the Bills payable to Mr Pinckney, our Minister in London, to be remitted by him to our Bankers in Amsterdam, if the place were safe.

The Deposite being thus transferred to the Bankers of the United States in Amsterdam, the monies pass from them into the hands of the public agents abroad, with whom the expenditures are final, being for their salaries and other authorized disbursements. The account of the Bankers now rendered, from July 1. 1792 to July 1. 1793, shews the sums paid to each of these.[2]

With these payments the ministers are debited, and are required annually on the 1st day of July to state and forward their separate accounts to be settled by the proper officers of the Treasury. This, with the payments to occasional Agents (generally a very small Article) completes the system of accounts for the foreign fund confided to the Department of State.

I enclose herewith Statements from the accounting Officers of the Treasury vouching my own account, begging leave only to observe that the 4,786 dollars, 67 Cents therein stated to be due from me, are the same which are stated in my account to be remaining on hand in the Bank, and which never have been taken out of it, as is vouched by the Bank book.[3] I have the honor to be, with the most perfect respect and attachment, Sir, Your most obedient & most humble servant

Th: Jefferson

LS, DNA: RG 46, Third Congress, 1793–95, Senate Records of Legislative Proceedings, President's Messages; LS (letterpress copy, signature added by Jefferson after use of letterpress), DLC: Jefferson Papers; LS (letterpress copy of different version), DLC: Jefferson Papers; ADf (letterpress copy; first page only), DLC: Jefferson Papers; LB, DLC:GW; LB, DNA: RG 59, Domestic Letters; LB, DNA: RG 233, Third Congress, 1793–95, House Records of the Office of the Clerk, Records of Reports from Executive Departments; LB, DNA: RG 46, Transcribed Reports and Communications Transmitted by the Executive Branch to the U.S. Senate, 1789–1819.

1. The relevant law was "An Act to continue in force for a limited time, and to amend the act intituled 'An act providing the means of intercourse between the United States and foreign nations,'" 9 Feb. 1793. The earlier law, of 1 July 1790, had required the president to "cause a regular statement and account" of the expenditures "to be laid before Congress annually," and the continuing act did not alter that requirement (1 *Stat.* 128–29, 299–300). The enclosed statement of "The Department of State (for the foreign fund) in account with the United States" shows the expenditure of most of $39,500 from 11 April to 30 Sept. 1793, leaving $4,786.67 cash on hand in the Bank of the United States (DNA: RG 46, Third Congress, 1793–95, Senate Records of Legislative Proceedings, President's Messages; see also *Jefferson Papers*, 27:654). Jefferson also submitted a draft for GW's message of this date sending the statement to Congress. GW's LS followed that draft.

2. The account of Willink, Van Staphorst & Hubbard exhibits the expenditure of 83,144.9 florins between 1 Aug. 1792 and 2 April 1793, and an additional 23,540.11 florins between 2 April and 1 July 1793. This, after the subtraction of the balance on hand as of 30 June 1792, left 36,795.17 florins due to the bankers (DNA: RG 46, Third Congress, 1793–95, Senate Records of Legislative Proceedings, President's Messages).

3. The two reports of Jefferson's accounts, certified by Treasurer Joseph Nourse, 30 Dec., as true copies of originals on file in his office, show Jefferson charged with $183,000 in warrants and credited with various remittances, most to the Amsterdam bankers Willink, Van Staphorst & Hubbard, leaving the balance stated here (DNA: RG 46, Third Congress, 1793–95, Senate Records of Legislative Proceedings, President's Messages; see also *Jefferson Papers*, 27:658–61).

From Thomas Jefferson

Dear Sir   Philadelphia Dec. 31. 1793.

Having had the honor of communicating to you in my letter of the last of July, my purpose of retiring from the office of Secretary of state at the end of the month of September, you were pleased, for particular reasons, to wish it's postponement to the close of the year.[1] that term being now arrived, & my propensities to retirement daily more & more irresistible, I now take the liberty of resigning the office into your hands. be pleased to accept with it my sincere thanks for all the indulgencies which you have been so good as to exercise towards me in the discharge of it's duties. conscious that my need of them has been great, I have still ever found them greater, without any other claim on my part than a firm pursuit of what has appeared to me to be right, and a thorough disdain of all means which were not as open & honorable, as their object was pure. I carry into my retirement a lively sense of your goodness, & shall continue gratefully to remember it. with very sincere prayers for your life, health and tranquility, I pray you to accept the homage of the great & constant respect & attachment with which I have the honor to be Dear Sir Your most obedient & most humble servt

Th: Jefferson

ALS, DNA: RG 59, Miscellaneous Letters; ALS (letterpress copy), DLC: Jefferson Papers; LB, DNA: RG 59, George Washington's Correspondence with His Secretaries of State.

1. See Jefferson's second letter to GW of 31 July, and n.3.

From Thomas Mifflin

Sir.   Phil: 31 Dec. 1793

I have the honor, by the inclosed copies, to communicate to you, a second letter, dated the 30 instant, which M. Cassan the Vice-Consul of the French Republic has addressed to me, relatively to the intended departure of the Brigantine Peggy, as he supposes, for the Mole and St Jeremie; and ⟨my⟩ answer to him on the subject.[1]

This opportunity is, likewise, taken, to lay before you, a copy of the report of the Master Warden of the port of Phila., on the real destination of the vessel in question.[2] I am, with perfect respect, Sr, Yr most obed. serv.

Df, in Alexander James Dallas's writing, PHarH: Executive Correspondence, 1790–99; LB, PHarH: Executive Letterbooks.

Secretary of War Henry Knox replied for GW in a letter to Mifflin of 10 Jan. 1794, observing that "the report of the Master Warden appears entirely to preclude all grounds of future complaint" and that the "general subject stated by the Vice Consul Cassan is placed upon its proper footing by the late Secretary of State in his letter to the French Minister of the 30th of November last" (PHarH: Executive Correspondence, 1790–99; for Thomas Jefferson's letter to Edmond Genet, see *Jefferson Papers*, 27:458–60).

1. The letter from Jean-Baptiste Cassan to Mifflin of 30 Dec. has not been identified. Mifflin replied on 31 Dec., "I must refer to the answer, which has been already communicated to you, as the only one that my official situation permits me to give. Your second letter, however, will likewise be submitted to the consideration of the President; but, independent of any misapprehension of the principles that ought to regulate the conduct of the American Government on this occasion, it will appear from the report of the Master Warden of the Port of Phila. (a copy of wh. is enclosed for your satisfaction) that you have probably, been misinf[ormed] even as to the destination of the vessel in question" (PHarH: Executive Correspondence, 1790–99). For Cassan's earlier letter and Mifflin's earlier reply, see Mifflin to GW, 26 Dec., n.1.

2. Master Warden Nathaniel Falconer wrote Mifflin on this date: "I apprehend the Consul of the French Republic, must have been misinformed, The Brig Peggey Cleared out at this Office on the 23d Inst. and at the Custom House the same day for Savannah in Georgia: She is owned by Mr James Gailbreath [Calbraith] of this City, & he informes me that there was no passengers on Board, but a Poor Family from Ireland, and a negro wench going to her Mistress there. This Vessel is now ashore in the Ice below Chester; and the Passengers are come up to the City" (PHarH: Executive Correspondence, 1790–99).

To the United States Senate and House of Representatives

United States December 31. 1793.
Gentlemen of the Senate and of the House of Representatives
I now lay before you a letter from the Secretary of State with his account of the expenditure of the monies appropriated for our intercourse with foreign nations from the 1st of July 1792. to the 1st of July 1793. and other papers relating thereto.[1]

Go: Washington

LS, DNA: RG 46, Third Congress, 1793–95, Senate Records of Legislative Proceedings, President's Messages; Df (letterpress copy), in the writing of George Taylor, Jr., DLC: Jefferson Papers; Copy, DNA: RG 233, Third Congress, 1793–95, House Records of Legislative Proceedings, Journals; LB, DLC:GW.

1. See Jefferson to GW, this date (first letter), and notes.

To William White

(Private)
Dear Sir,   Philadelphia 31st Decembr 1793

It has been my intention ever since my return to the City, to contribute my mite towards the relief of the *most* needy inhabitants of it. The pressure of public business hitherto, has suspended, but not altered my resolution. I am at a loss, however, for whose benefit to apply the little I can give; & into whose hands to place it; whether for the use of the fatherless children & widows (made so by the late calamity) who may find it difficult, whilst Provisions, Wood & other necessaries are so dear, to support themselves; or to other, and better purposes (if any) I know not; and therefore have taken the liberty of asking your advice.[1]

I persuade myself, justice will be done my motives for giving you this trouble. To obtain information, & to render the little I can afford without ostentation or mention of my name are the sole objects of these enquiries—With great & sincere esteem and regard I am—Dear Sir Your Most Obedt & Affecte Servt

Go: Washington

ALS, RPJCB; ADfS, DLC:GW; LB, DLC:GW.

1. For the arrangements for this gift, see White to GW, 1 Jan. 1794 (three letters), and GW to White, 1 Jan. and 2 Jan. 1794. GW's accounts for 28 Jan. 1794 record: "Contgt Exps delivd the President to put into the hands of Dr White to be distributed among the poor of Philada [$]250" (Household Accounts; see also Account Book, 2 Sept. 1793–4 April 1794, DLC:GW).

From Adhemar de Brethoux

Mon general   [December 1793]

de grands malheurs qui vous sont déja Connus M'ont obligé de venir reclammer un asile de la generosité du peuple que vous presides, et contre toute attente, aulieû d'arriver á philadelphie pour oû je M'étois embarqué d'autres malheurs qu'on risque à la mer, ont apparemment Contraints le Capitaine de faire voile á la providance oû je suis arrivé de mon depart de lisle de saint domaingue.

les Sollicitudes, les chagrins, que me casent ma famille passe dans des terres etrangeres, et des persecutions personnelles dans le pays francais, ont tellement alteré ma santé que je nai cessé d'etre malade dans cétte ville oû ma situation me fait luire un jour que je n'avais jamais vû, même, au milieu, des revolutions oû je me suis trouvé. Je ne parle point la langue, j'ai tout perdu dans l'incendie du Cap francais, argent bijoux habits et presque la vie. mon sort, et les grands actions dont mes parents qui etoient à la tete de l'armée dans le francaise puis et qui ont servi avec vous, m'ont parlé sancesse a votre sujet, Mon general, m'ont encouragé dans mes peines actuelles et me font esperer que vous prandrai part aux infortunes d'un gentilhomme qui a projetté depuis plusieurs annees de venir vous pries d'accuillir ces civilités respectueuses, et admirer un grand homme, C'est une Continuation de contrarieté qui casent que je ne suis pas deja a philadelphie. Vuilles Bien je vous prie mon general ecrire au gouverneur de cétte ville l'intérét que vous voudres prandre a moi, et de me secourir dans des Besoins que je n'avois jamais prevû.[1] je lui remettres votre lettre; on m'a assuré qu'il etoit on ne peut pas plus digne d'un emploi de Bienfaisance.

j'aurai mille fois mieux aimé vous conter de vive voix Ce qui est dans ma lettre, mais j'espere Bien M'en dedommager des que je le pourrai en vous presentent Ces Sentiments respectueux avec les quels j'ai l'honneur d'etre Mon general Votre tres humble et tres obeissant Serviteur

le chevalier adhemar de Brethoux
Chevalier honnaraire de l'ordre des Malthe

ALS, DNA: RG 59, Miscellaneous Letters. The date is taken from the docket, "Decr 93."

1. No indication has been found that GW wrote any letters on Brethoux's behalf.

From Citizens West of the Allegheny Mountains

[December 1793]
The remonstrance of the Citizens West of the aligany Mountains Respectfully shewith That your remonstrants are Entitled

by Nature and by stipulation to the undisturbed Navigation of the river Mississippi; and consider it a right Inseperable from their prosperity. That in colonizing this distant and dangerous desart, they always contemplated the free Enjoyment of this right, and considered it as an inseperable Appendage to the country they had sought out, had fought for, and acquired. That for a series of years during their Early settlement, their petitions to government to Secure this right, were answered by its alledged weakness, and your remonstrants taught to Expect, that the time was approaching fast, when both power and Inclination would both unite, to establish it on the firmest grounds. In this anxious expectation they waited, and to the insolence of those who arrogated its exclusive Exercise they patiently submitted, till the government of america had so Strengthened itself, as to hold out an assurance of future protection to all its citizens, and of redress for all their wrongs.

That protection has not been extended to us, we need only refer to our present situation, and that that situation has not been concealed from, or unknown to, congress we appeal to its archives. We have without ceasing deplored to you our degraded situation, and burdened you with our humble petitions and requests but alas! we still experience, that the strong nerved government of america extends its arm of protection to all the branches of the Union, but to your remonstrants. That it is competent to every End, but that single one, by which alone it can benefit us; The protection of our territorial rights. It is competent to exact obedience, but not to make that return, which can be the only Just and natural Exchange for it. Long have your remonstrants been anxiously in Quest of the obstacles that have stood in your way, to the establishment of this our right; and as long has their persuit been fruitless. Formal and Tardy Negotiations have no doubt been often projected, and have as often Miscarried. It is true some Negotiations were once attempted, that were neither *formal* nor *tardy* and gave an early shock to our encreasing population, and to our peace of mind;[1] but your remonstrants are constrained to be of Opinion, that the neglect or local policy of american councils, has never produced one single real effort to procure this right. Could the government of america be for ten years seriously in pursuit of the establishment of a grand territorial right, which was arrogantly suspended,[2] and return to that quarter of the union to whom it was all-important, but an Equivocal answer? We think it high time that we should be thoroughly informed of the situation on which your negociations, if any, have left this right: for apathy itself has grown hopeless from long disappointed expectations.

Your remonstrants yield not in patriotism to any of their fellow citizens: but patriotism, like every other thing, has its bounds. We love those states from which we were all congregated, and no event (not even an attempt to barter away our best rights) shall alien our affections from the individual members who compose them: but attachment to governments cease to be natural, when they cease to be natural.[3] To be subjected to all the burthens, and enjoy none of the benefits arising from government, is what we will never submit to. Our situation compels us to speak plainly. If wretchedness and poverty awa[i]t us it is of no concern to us how they are produced. We are gratified in the prosperity of the atlantic States, but would not speak the language of Truth and Sincerity, were we not to declare our unwillingness to make any sacrifices to it, when their importance and those sacrafices result from our Distress. If the Interest of eastern america requires, that we should be kept in poverty, it is unreasonable from such poverty to exact contributions. The first, if we cannot emerge from, We must Learn to bear; but the latter, We never can be taught to submit to.

From the general government of america, therefore, your remonstrants now ask protection, in the free enjoyment of the navigation of the river mississippi, which is withheld from them by the spaniards. We demand it as a right which you have the power to invest us With, and which not to exert, is as great a breach of our rights, as to withhold. We declare, that nothing can retribute us for the suspension or loss of this inestimable right. We declare it to be a right which must be obtained; and do also declare, that if the General Government will not procure it for us, We shall hold ourselves not answerable for any consequences that may result from our own procurement of it. The God of nature has given us both the right and means of acquiring and enjoying it; and to permit a Sacrafice of it to any earthly consideration, Would be a crime against ourselves and against our posterity.

Copy, DLC: Papers of the Breckinridge Family.

This copy bears a note, written by John Breckinridge: "A Copy of the Remonstrance which I drew, for the Committee of the Democratic Scociety.

Decr 1793. J. Bdge." The Democratic Society of Kentucky, which was formed at Lexington in August 1793 on the model of the Philadelphia Democratic Society, began considering a resolution on Mississippi River navigation at its meeting of 7 October (*Kentucky Gazette* [Lexington], 24 and 31 Aug., 12 Oct.).

When the society met at Lexington on 11 Nov., they resolved "That the free and undisturbed use and navigation of the river Mississippi is the NATURAL RIGHT of the inhabitants of the countries bordering on the waters communicating with that river" and "that the inhabitants of the Western Country had a right to expect that the present Federal Government would before this time have taken effectual measures to obtain from the King of Spain an acknowledgment of their undoubted right to the free navigation of the river Mississippi." They further resolved to "prepare in the name of the inhabitants of the western waters, a remonstrance to the President and Congress of the United States on this subject, stating (in the bold decent and determined language proper to be used by injured freemen, when they address the servants of the people) that we consider the feeble attempts which have been made by the executive under the present government, and the total silence of Congress on this important subject, as strong proofs that most of our brethren in the eastern part of America, are totally regardless whether this our just right is kept from us or not" (*Kentucky Gazette* [Lexington], 16 Nov. 1793). This address "To the President and Congress of the united States of America" evidently was prepared in response to that resolution.

By 31 Dec. the committee of correspondence was distributing printed copies of the address, with the request that each recipient "exert your influence to induce your neighbouring fellow-citizens to give their sanction to the Remonstrance." The committee continued, "The Remonstrance when signed, may be transmitted to the representative in Congress from your district, or to any other member of that body, delegated from the Western Country. It is intended that a decision upon this subject should be obtained during the present Session of Congress, and to effect this, it is necessary that the Remonstrance should be presented as soon as possible" (William Murray et al. to George Muter, 31 Dec. 1793, DLC: Papers of Harry Innes).

On 15 April 1794 "remonstrances from citizens of the United States, west of the Allegany mountains, whose names are thereunto subscribed, were presented to the House and read, stating their right to a free enjoyment of the navigation of the river Mississippi, and praying that the general government will adopt such measures, as shall be most expedient and effectual to secure the same from encroachment by the citizens or subjects of foreign countries." The remonstrances were referred to a committee, which reported on 23 April 1794. The report "was read, and ordered to lie on the table." On 5 June the House took up the report and resolved that as "the right of the United States, to the free navigation of the Mississippi, is now the subject of negociation with the court of Spain . . . no farther proceeding should be had on the said remonstrance" (*Journal of the House*, 6:257, 271, 412).

1. This was a reference to the negotiations between United States secretary for foreign affairs John Jay and Spanish negotiator Diego de Gardoqui from 1785 to 1787 (see James Madison to GW, 26 Sept. 1788, n.1).

2. Until the conclusion of the Revolutionary War, western settlers had enjoyed the right to navigate the Mississippi River under concessions granted by Spain to England in 1763 and Spanish instructions extending the privilege for the war's duration. In 1784, however, Spanish agents in America were instructed, "Until the limits of Louisiana and the two Floridas shall be settled and determined with the United States of America, his Majesty commands that you should give the states and Congress to understand that they are not to expose to process and confiscation the vessels which they destine to carry on commerce on the River Mississippi, inasmuch as a treaty concluded between the United States and England, on which the former ground their pretensions to the navigation of that river, could not fix limits in a territory which that power did not possess" (Josef de Galvez to Francisco Rendon, 26 June 1784, *JCC*, 27:690).

3. The printed copies of the remonstrance use the word "mutual" here.

Letter not found: to Charles Lee, 1793. An ADfS of this letter was offered for sale on 5 Dec. 1889 as item 334 in Bangs & Co., *Catalogue of a Valuable Collection of Autographs.* The catalog entry reads: "Written at Mt. Vernon. This is the first draft of the letter and is interesting, showing how careful Washington was to make corrections before sending off the clean copy."

Rotations of Crops for Dogue Run

Rotations of Crops for Dogue Run

Rotation No. 1

No. of the Fields	1793	1794	1795	1796	1797	1798	1799
3	Corn & Potatoes	Wheat	B. Wheat for Manure	Wheat	Clover or Grass	Clover or Grass	Clover or Grass
4	Clover or Grass	Corn & Potatoes	Wheat	B. Wheat for Manure	Wheat	Clover or Grass	Clover or Grass
5	Clover or Grass	Clover or Grass	Corn & Potatoes	Wheat	B. Wheat for Manure	Wheat	Clover or Grass
6	Clover or Grass	Clover or Grass	Clover or Grass	Corn or Potatoes	Wheat	B. Wheat for Manure	Wheat
7	Wheat	Clover or Grass	Clover or Grass	Clover or Grass	Corn or Potatoes	Wheat	B. Wheat for Manure
1	B. Wheat for Manure	Wheat	Clover or Grass	Clover or Grass	Clover or Grass	Corn & Potatoes	Wheat
2	Wheat	B. Wheat for Manure	Wheat	Clover or Grass	Clover or Grass	Clover or Grass	Corn & Potatoes

Number of Plowings—the times at which they must be given—and the days it will take

	acres			Fall	Wintr	Mar.	Aprl	May	June	July	Augt	Sep.	Total
No. 3	75	Corn & Pots.	Breaking up	100									100
			layg off, & listing			60							60
			crossing for Plantg				10						10
			Plowing Balks					70					70
			Crossing them						70				70
			Re-crossing							70			70
			Sowing Wheat								75		75
4 5 6	225	Clovr or Grass											
1	75	B. Wheat for Man[ur]e	Breaking up	100									100
			Crossing for Sowg				100						100
			Plowing in						100				100
2	75	Wheat	Corn grd										
7	75	Ditto	on B: Wheat								100		100
	525			200		60	110	70	170	70	175		855

Probable Yield.

No. 3						
75	in Corn & Potatoes	a 12½ bushls	937½ bushls	a 2/6	£117.3.9
2 } 7		12½	937½	1/	46.17.6
7 } 1	150 Wheat	10	1500	5/	375
	75 B. Wht for Mane				
4 } 5 } 6	255 Clover or Grass				
	525		3375		£539.1.3

Remarks

The above Rotation favors the land very much; inasmuch as there are but three Corn Crops taken in Seven years from any field, & the first Wheat Crop is followed by a Buck Wheat manure for the second Wheat Crop, wch is to succeed it; & which by being laid to Clover or Grass & continued therein three years will aford much Mowing or Graising, according as the Seasons happen to be, besides being a restorative to the Soil. But then, the produce of the Saleable Crops is small, unless encreased by the improving State of the fields. Nor will the Grain for the use of the Farm be adequate to the consumpti<con> of it in this Course, and this is an essential object to attend to--& quere--whether the Clover does not remain too long.

Rotation No. 2 Same place.

No. of the Fields	1793	1794	1795	1796	1797	1798	1799
3	Corn & Potatoes	B: Wheat	B. Wheat for Manure	Wheat	Clover	Wheat	Clover
4	Clover	Corn & Potatoes	B: Wheat	B. Wheat for Manure	Wheat	Clover	Wheat
5	Pasture	Pasture	Corn & Potatoes	B: Wheat	B: Wheat for Manure	Wheat	Clover
6	Pasture	Wheat	Clover	Corn & Potatoes	B: Wheat	B. Wheat for Manure	Wheat
7	Wheat	Clover	Wheat	Clover	Corn & Potatoes	B. Wheat	B: Wheat for Manure
1	B: Wheat for Manure	Wheat	Clover	Wheat	Clover	Corn & Potatoes	B. Wheat
2	Wheat	B. Wheat for Manure	Wheat	Clover	Wheat	Clover	Corn & Potatoes

Plowings &ca &ca for the above Crops

	Acrs.			Fall	Wintr	Mar.	Aprl	May	June	July	Aug.	Sep.	Total
No. 3	75	in Corn & Potatoes	same as N. 1	100		60	10	70	70	70	75		455
4} 6}	150	Clover											
1	75	B: Wheat Crop	breaking up			100							100
			2d Plowing						100				100
2	75	Wheat Corn grd	breaking up	100									100
7	75	Ditto on B: W.	crossg & Sowing				100						100
			Plowing in B: W.						100				100
			Sowing Wheat								100		100
	75	Buck Wht for M. as above.											
	525			200		160	110	70	270	70	175		1055

Probable Yield

			Bushls		
No. 3	75 in Corn & Potatoes	12½ bushls	937½	a 2/6	£117.3.9
		12½ Do	937½	1/	40.17.6
4 5 6	225 Clover & Grass				
2 7	150 Wheat	10	1500	5/	375
	75 suppd in B. Wheat	12	900	1/8	75
	525		4,275		£614.1.3

Remarks.

By the above Rotation, 900 bushls of B. Wheat, amounting to £75, is added to the proceeds of No. 1 at the expence of 200 days more plowing—And no two Corn Crops follow in immediate succession. Wheat, in one instance, follows a Clover lay on a single Plowing; the success of this, tho' well ascertained in England, may not answer so well in this Country, where our lands from the exhausted State of them require more manure than the Farm can afford & our Seasons are very precarious.

Rotation No. 3 same place

No. of the Fields	1793	1794	1795	1796	1797	1798	1799
3	Corn & Potatoes	Wheat	B: Wheat for Manure	Wheat	B: Wheat	Clover or othr Grass	Clover or other Grasses
4	Clover or othr Grasses	Corn & Potatoes	Wheat	B. Wheat for Manure	Wheat	B: Wheat	Clover or other Grasses
5	Clover or other Grasses	Clover or other Grasses	Corn & Potatoes	Wheat	B: Wheat for Manure	Wheat	B: Wheat
6	B: Wheat	Clover or other Grasses	Clover or other Grasses	Corn & Potatoes	Wheat	B: Wheat for Manure	Wheat
7	Wheat	B. Wheat	Clover or other Grasses	Clover or other Grasses	Corn & Potatoes	Wheat	B: Wheat for Manure
1	B: Wheat for Manure	Wheat	B: Wheat	Clover or other Grasses	Clover or other Grasses	Corn & Potatoes	Wheat
2	Wheat for Manure	B: Wheat or other	Wheat or other	B. Wheat	Clover or other Grasses	Clover or other Grasses	Corn & Potatoes

Plowings &ca &ca for the above Crops

No.	acrs.		Fall	Winr	Mar.	Apl	May	June	July	Aug.	Sepr	Total
No. 3	75	in Corn as before &P.	100		60	10 ·	70	70	70	75		455
4, 5	150	Clover or &ca										
6	75	B: Wheat				100						100
		2d Plowing						100				100
1	75	B: Wht Mane										
		1st Plowing			100							100
		2. do & sowg					100					100
		3 do plowg in							100			100
		4 do Sowg Wht								100		100
7	75	Wheat sown as above										
2	75	Wht with Corn										
			100		160	110	110	170	170	170	175	955[1]

Probable Yield

	acrs.		Bushls		
No. 3	75 in Corn	a 12½ bushls	937½	2/6	£117. 3.9
	& Potatoes	12½ Do	937½	1/	40.17.6
4, 5	150 Clovr or Grass				
6	75 B. Wheat	12	900	1/8	75
1	75 B. Wht Mane				
2, 7	150 Wheat	10	1500	5/	375
	525		4275		£614.1.3

The above Rotation in point of produce & profit is precisely the same as No. 2 but differs in the succession of Crops. It requires about the same Plowings; and these plowings are pretty regularly distributed through the Spring & Summer Months. The Wheat field which follows the B: Wheat manure, might have the Stubble turned in immediately after harvest for manure and for Green food (proceeding from the shattered grain) for Sheep, Calves &ca in the Winter & Spring.

Rotation No. 4 same Place

No. of the Fields	1793	1794	1795	1796	1797	1798	1799
3	Corn & Potatoes	Wheat	B. Wht	Clover	Wheat	B: Wheat	Clover
4	Clover	Corn & Potatoes	Wheat	B. Wht	Clover	Wheat	B. Wheat
5	B. Wht	Clover	Corn & Potatoes	Wheat	B. Wht	Clover	Wheat
6	Clover	B. Wht	Clover	Corn & Potatoes	Wheat	B. Wht	Clover
7	Wheat	Clover	B. Wht	Clover	Corn & Potatoes	Wheat	B. Wheat
1	B. Wht	Wheat	Clover	B. Wht	Clover	Corn & Potatoes	Wheat
2	Wheat	B. Wht	Wheat	Clover	B. Wht	Clover	Corn & Potatoes

Plowings &ca &ca for the above Crops

	acs.		Fall	Win	Mar.	Aprl	May	June	July	Aug.	Sep.	Total
No. 3	75	for Corn & Potatoes	100		60	10	70	70	70	75		455
4 6	150	Clover										
5 1	150	B. Wheat breakg				100	100					200
		Sowing						100	100			200
7 2	150	Wheat—one field follows. Corn. The other Clover. 1 plowing								100		100
			100		60	110	170	170	170	175		955

Probable Yield

No. 3		Acrs.	Bushls	Bushls	
4 6 }	75 in Corn	a 12½	937½	a 2/6	£117.3.9
	same in Potatoes	12½	937½	1/	46.17.6
5 1 }	150 Clover				
	150 B. Wheat	12	1800	1/8	150
7 2 }	150 Wheat	10	1500	5/	375
	525		5175		£689.1.3

Remarks.

This Rotation, for quantity of Grain & the profit arising from it, is more productive than either of the preceeding; and with no more plowing, excepting No. 1—No field gives more than three Corn Crops in 7. years, except the Crop of B: Wht. The last of wch with the Indian Corn, will be more than adequate for all the demands of the Farm. The Clover is to be Sown with the B. W. in July; and by being only one year in the grd may be too expensive on acct of the Seed—nor will the fields in this Course receive any green manure. and the advantages of sowing Wheat on a Clover lay in this Country is not well ascertained—again, preparg 2 fields for B. Wht may in practi<ce> be found difficult—Wheat Stubble might be plowed in here for Spring food.

Rotation No. 5 Same Place.

No. of the fields	1793	1794	1795	1796	1797	1798	1799
3	Corn & Potato's B. Wheat	Wheat	Clover	Wheat	Clover	Whea	B. Wheat
4	Corn & Potatoes	B: Wht	Wheat	Clover	Wheat	Clover	Wheat
5	Wheat	B: Wht	Corn & Potatoes	Wheat	Clover	Wheat	Clover
6	Clover	Wheat	B: Wht	Corn & Potatoes	Wheat	Clover	Wheat
7	Wheat	Clover	Wheat	B: Wht	Corn & Potatoes	Wheat	Clover
1	Clover	Wheat	Clover	Wheat	B: Wht	Corn & Potatoes	Wheat
2	Wheat	Clover	Wheat	Clover	Wheat	B. Wht	Corn & Potatoe

Plowings &ca &ca for the above Crops

	Acs.		Fall	Winr	Mar.	Apl	May	June	July	Augt	Sep.	Total
No. 3	75	for Corn & Potatoes	100		60	10	70	70	70	75		455
4	75	B: Wht breakg up		100								100
		2d Plowing						100				100
6 ⎫ 1 ⎬	150	Clover										
2	75	Wheat corn grd										
5 ⎫ 7 ⎬	150	Ditto on Clovr 1 Plowing								105	105	210
			100	100	60	10	70	170	70	180	105	865

Probable Yield.

	Acrs.		Bushls		
No. 3	75 in Corn	12½ Bushls	937½	2/6	£117. 3.9
	same in Potatoes	12½	937½	1/	46.17.3
4 6 {	75 B. Wheat	12	900	1/8	75.0.0
1 2 {	150 Clover				
5 7 {	225 Wheat	10	2250	5/	562.10.0
	525		5025		£801.11.0

Remarks

By the above Rotations, the quantity of Grain is nearly equal to that of No. 4, and the value of it greater; occasioned by the encrease of Wheat. This rotation is effected with as little plowing as No. 1. and with less than in either of the other three Numbers, 2, 3 & 4. But in this course no Green manure is introduced, except plowing in Clover is so considered; and the quality of the Clover on much reduced Land is to be questioned—& the practice of sowing on it as has been observed in some of the other numbers not much used, nor the advantages of it well ascertained—Besides there is the expence of Clover Seed for 150 Acres every year to be encountered.

Rotation No. 6 same Farm.

No. of the Fields	1793	1794	1795	1796	1797	1798	1799
3	Corn & Potatoes	Wheat	B: Wheat for Manure	Wheat & the Stubble Plowed in	B. Wh. ½Crop & ½ Mane	Wheat	B. Wheat for Manure
4	B. Wheat for Manure	Corn & Potatoes	Wheat	B. Wheat for Manure	Wheat & the Stubble Plowed in	B. Wh. ½ Crop & ½ Mane	Wheat
5	Wheat	B. Wheat for Manure	Corn & Potatoes	Wheat	B. Wheat for Manure	Wheat & the Stubble Plowed in	B. Wh. ½ Crop ½ Mane
6	B. Wh. ½ Crop ½ Mane	Wheat	B. Wheat for Manure	Corn & Potatoes	Wheat	B. Wheat for Manure	Wheat & the Stubble Plowed in
7	Wheat & the Stubble Plowed in	B. Wh. ½ Crop ½ Mane	Wheat	B. Wheat for Manure	Corn &	Wheat	B. Wheat for Manure
1	B. Wheat for Manure	Wheat & the stubble Plowed in	B. Wh. ½ Crop ½ Mane	Wheat	B. Wheat for Manure	Corn & Potatoes	Wheat
2	Wheat	B. Wheat for Manure	Wheat & the stubble Plowed in	B. Wh. ½ Crop ½ Mane	Wheat	B. Wheat for Manure	Corn & Potatoes

Plowings &ca &ca for the above Crops

No.	Acrs.		Fall	Winr	Mar.	Aprl	May	June	July	Aug.	Sep.	Total
No. 3	75	of Corn & Potatoes	100		60	10	70	70	70	75		455
4	75	B: Wheat for Mane		100								100
		breaking up										
		2d Plowing				100						100
5	75	Wheat single Plowg									100	100
6	75	B. Wheat for Mane &ca			100							100
		breaking up										
2		plowing					50		50			100
1	75	B. Wht for Mane	100									100
		breaking up										
		2d Plowing 1st of June						100				100
2	75	Wheat Corn grd							100			100
7	75	Ditto on B. Wht										
		1st plowg in B. Wh.										
		2 Plowing in Wht								100		100
			200	100	160	110	120	170	220	175	100	1355

Probable Yield

	Acrs.		a 12½	937½ Bushls	a 2/6	£117.3.9
No. 3	75	in Corn	a 12½	937½ Bushls	a 2/6	£117.3.9
		Same in Potatoes	12½	937½	1/	46.17.6
5 7 2	225	Wheat	10	2250	5/	562.10.
4 1 6	150	B. Wheat Man.				
	75	½ Mane 37½ Crop	12	450	1/8	37.10.0
	525			4575		764.1.3

The above is the 2d most productive Rotation; but the fields receive no rest, being every year under the Plow, nor in this course is there any field in grass or pasture: and besides, the qty of Plowing exceeds any of the other Rotations by 280 days & most of them considerably more. The advantage it has over any of the others is, the frequent dressings with Green manure. Plowing one of the Wheat fields immediately after Harvest will by means of the Wheat Stubble also help the Land, and afford Green food for Ewes & Lambs, Calves & Mules during the Winter & Spring.

Note,

No mention is made of Harrowing in any of the foregoing Rotations; because, except in the Indian Corn, it may be done principally, if not wholly by Oxen.

The plowing is calculated at ¾ of an Acre pr day.2 If then, one Plow will go over a 75 Acre field in 100 days—five plows will do it in 20 days. In some ground, in the State of it—and according to the Seasons, an Acre at least ought to be plowed pr day by each Team; but ¾ of an Acre is calculated upon in order to reduce it to more certainty.

The fields are all estimated at 75 Acs. each (although they run a little more or less) for the sake of more easy calculation of the Crops & to shew their comparative yield.

AD, DLC:GW. Since this document discusses alternative future crop rotations, it probably was written before the spring planting season of 1793. For an earlier example of GW's consideration of alternative rotations, see the comparison of GW's and Anthony Whitting's rotations for an unspecified farm for the years 1790 to 1796 (DLC:GW, filed at the end of 1794).

1. GW apparently added the "Total" column, which omits 100 days for the first plowing of buckwheat manure. Had he added the total row, which included that plowing, he would have reached the correct number of 1,055.

2. At this point GW wrote and struck out, "with allowance for Sundays but none for bad weather."

From Anonymous

permettez moi, mr le président qu'après avoir lu un voyage fait dans votre heureuse république en 1788[1] je vous fasse part de l'effusion de mon Coeur et des réfléxions quil m'a fait faire.

Je Suis ravi, enchanté de la beauté, de la bonté de votre gouvernement et Ce qui me Comble C'est que je vois dans l'avenir, Si vous Continuez t'jours de meme Ce que j'espere, réaliser Ce réve enchanteur de l'age d'or, reve du jour fait par toutes les ames Sensibles, caressés par tous les coeurs aimants, tourné et retourné en tous Sens par tous les esprits ornés, décrit dans toutes les langues, raconté dans tous les idiomes, à la veillée au Coin du feu, un grand genie a dit—

un jour, pcut-etre un jour Ces flatteuses images
Seront la vérité pour des hommes plus Sages
déja n'a-on pas vu l'intrépide Boston
dirigé par Franklin Conduit pa⟨r⟩ Washington
rompre les fers honteux d'un indigne esclavage
et S'elever au rang que donne le Courage . . .

Braves, genereux, inconcevables Américains restez unis vous Serez, Sinon invulnérables, du moins indomptables, vous Serez heureux, vous améliorerez l'espece humaine, vous Serez les Sauveurs de la terre entiere, et la découverte de l'amérique Si fatale à Ses anciens habitans Sera le refuge de tous les infortunés ou proscrits des autres Continens. les Européens informés de vos ressources vont Se Cacher et chercher leur Salut dans la playe horrible quils ont faite à Cette belle partie de la terre; C'est Ce qui doit resoudre le probleme—Si la decouverte de l'Amérique a eté avantageuse ou non à l'humanité. pauvre Europe combien l'amérique va te laisser en arriere! Sa destinée future est, non de tout envahir, mais de tout eclairer. quels rapides progrets vous faites déja dans tous les genres! que vous etes estimables, que votre hystoire devient interessante! quelle différence, d'avec l'hystoire ancienne de tous les peuples! vos Commencemens Sont aussi brillans que leurs beaux Siecles. vous faites Sur la terre la meme Sensation qu'un astre eclatant ⟨et⟩ nouveau ferait au Ciel. Comme vous etes Créateurs aspirez à la gloire de donner des noms propres, nouveaux, beaux, Sonores, expressifs à tout ce que vous trouvez, à tout Ce que vous inventez. les noms d'europe que vous donnez à vos villes naissantes, un jour Si florissantes! ne doivent pas vous rappeller des idées bien flatteuses, et leur hystoire, pour la plupart, des traits bien honorables. Européenisés, Anglisés Francisés les noms anciens des lieux, des arbres, des plantes, des rivieres, des montagnes &c. ohio ramasse toutes mes idées Sur le Cours majestueux de Cette riviere dont les bords rians et fertiles enchantent le voyageur.—la belle riviere—ne fait pas le meme effet et puis pourquoi trois mots pour un Seul qui est encor plus indicatif. Comme à st Domingue où il ni a pas un Seul quartier qui n'ayt Sa grande riviere &c. il fallait Conserver les noms propres dont les anciens habitans Se Servaient, ou du moins en donner d'analogues. l'arbre à pain avait Sûrement un nom propre, Cet arbre nourissier est l'arbre véritable de la liberté, il faut le planter, le naturaliser par tout où il Sera possible dc l'aclimater et prodiguer, Sil le faut les dépenses nécessaires, les Soins ⟨les⟩ peines Constans et Suivis pour le faire reussir. le chene, l'orme, le Cerisier &c. de st domingue nous rappellent des arbres d'europe qui ne Sont pas les memes, ils avaient S.d. leurs noms Comme l'acajou; l'acouma, le Sapoticr &c. pourquoi ne leur avoir pas Conservé? l'erable à sucre qui va donner une nouvelle branche de Commerce n'est pas le meme que l'erable qui n'en donne point; il merite donc bien l'honneur d'avoir un nom propre. la reconnaissance vous y invite. un genie versé dans cette nomenclature qui S'appliquerait à classer, Spécifier et nommer chaqu'objet important rendrait un plus grand Service à l'hystoire qu'on ne pense, il Serait Sur d'aller à l'immortalité. quelle Confusion S'accumule pour la Suite des Siecles! la nouvelle Angleterre, la nouvelle France, la nouvelle hollande &c. Seront vielles alors, et l'on S'implifierait les noms de toutes especes en leur otant le Surnom d'europe ou d'amérique.

Vous réunissez aux productions de l'amérique Celles des trois autres Continens avec leurs varietés; vous améliorerez le regne végétal en croisant les especes, peut-etre en produirez vous de nouvelles: la nature qui n'a que la force productive est Si féconde lorsque l'art la Seconde! avec de l'adresse, du travail et de la patience vous vous aproprirez les grains, les fruits les legumes de tous les Continens en les mariant aux votres. il en Sera de meme des animaux utiles et domestiques: ah! Si les hommes en eussent toujours agi ainsi nous Serions tous dans le jardin d'Eden.

ô bons Amériquains, terre régénératrice, terre hospitaliere qui avez ouvert votre Sein paternel à la foule innombrable de malheureux que la tirannie royale, ministérielle, feodale, Sacerdotale... Sacerdotale! la pire de toutes a forcé de fuir de tous les Coins de l'europe avilie. que je regrette avec une infinité d'autres de ne pouvoir aller jouir de vos bienfaits! il ni a que mon Corps en europe, mon esprit et mon Coeur Sont chez vous; mes yeux mourans Se fixeront Sur vous, mon dernier Souhait, mon dernier Soupir Seront pour vous. Courage, Courage, nation intrépide allez en avant ne vous rebutez d'aucun obstacle: eh! il ni en a point pour vous, vous les franchissez tous de plein Saut. C'est de vous S.d. qu'Horace a voulu parler lorsqu'il a dit audacieuse race de Japet.[2] profitez des 1ies marches que l'europe a posées pour monter plus haut. les hommes de toutes les nations, de toutes les couleurs, de toutes les langues, de toutes les religions fondus en un ont produit Ce genie unique qui vous distingue Spècialement, qui vous fera tout entreprendre et reussir en tout et partout: Comme aussi de tous les idiomes reunis melés Sortira la langue americaine, langue mere, langue universelle qui Sera Celle de la nature que parleront dans un heureux avenir tous les hommes reunis en une Seule famille. tous les gouts, toutes les habitudes, toutes les modes prendront aussi un ton, une tournure, une forme particulieres dans la fonte génèralle qui S'en fera en Amérique. heureux Ceux qui, peut etre dans moins d'un Siecle naitront pour jouir de vos bonnes in[s]titutions, de vos utiles ou agréables découvertes! Combien ils béniront les auteurs de tant de biens!

Si un concert unanime vous fait Constamment tendre tous au meme but, vos destinées Seront plus brillantes et plus Solides que Celles des Grecs et des Romains parce quelles Seront assises Sur la base de la nature Cimentée par les Siences. aussi voyez quels progrès rapides vous avez fait dans environ l'espace d'un Siecle, et la france après 14 ou 15 Siecles Se voit aujourdhui forcée de renverser Son gouvernement rapetassés pour l'établir Sur des bases plus naturelles.

vous travaillez avec la vigueur de la jeunesse et la maturité de la viellesse, avec la force des instrumens neufs et la perfection des anciens, Comment ne reussiréz vo⟨us⟩ pas! l'imprimerie, don du Ciel! qui met partout où elle est etablie la bibioteque d'alexandrie à l'abri de la fureur des tyrans, vous met Sous les yeux les découvertes, les usages, les Coutumes, les Costumes de tous les ages; de tous les peuples; les lois de tous les gouvernemens; les Secrets de la nature et des arts: tout vous est dévoilé, et votre genie familier, Comme Celui de Socrate vous poussera tjours au meilleur choix. les autres ont Couru pour vous les risques et le hazard des essais. aussi votre gouvernement passe-il pour le plus parfait de tous ceux qu'on Connaisse. le déluge a noyé les hommes Sans les changer, vous les changez Sans les noyer. vous enchainez les ames, et les Corps Sont à vous. C'est vous nouveaux Américains race chéri de Dieu et des hommes qui devez relever les ruines eparses que les européens les papistes et les Musulmans ont laissé partout ou ils ont pu penetrer.

L'imprimerie est le jardin de la liberté où Se trouvent réunis toutes les productions propres à la faire désirer, chercher, cherir et Conserver après l'avoir trouvée. les auteurs fournissent les plantes, les imprimeurs les Cultivent. C'est de Ce jardin dont on ne peut plus detruire les plantes parce quelles Sont heureusement multipliées à l'infini que Sont Sortis des fruits de toutes les especes pour Satisfaire tous les gouts et nourrir jusqu'a une utile et agréable Satieté tous les Commensaux de Cette table universelle. le Genie du Mexique et du perou profondément endormi depuis plusieurs Siecles a Soulevé Sa tete au 1er bruit de votre Ste insurrection, il S'est retourné et après un long Soupir il est retombé dans un Sommeil leger, Semblable à Celui du matin, embelli par le Songe flatteur et prophetique de la liberté qui lui annonce la délivrance prochaine de Ces beaux empires trop longtems courbés Sous un indigne joug. C'est vous encor, vous les 1ers qui en Susciterez le réveil enchanteur en réalisant Son heureux Songe. Ces beaux empires remontront au rang et à la dignité des nations. il Se trouvera quelque rejetton du bon Ataliba[3] qui, Sortant tout à Coup de Son abaissement profitera des Connaissances européennes pour relever le trone de Ses ancetres Sur une base plus Solide que l'or; il prendra le nom Sacré et cheri d'Incas, il tirera Ses Sujets de l'esclavage, les gouvernera en pere de famille, leur rendra la religion naturelle avec le culte Sublime du Soleil qui réunit tous les hommes.

la politique des hommes la plus profonde, la plus réfléchie et la mieux Suivie ne peut rien Contre le Cours lent mais inévitable de la nature et du tems. qui aurait pu prévoir que Ce Serait l'angleterre qui, la 1ere, Couperait le fil qui aretait le mouvement du nouveau monde, elle qui avait tant d'interet à le Conserver, le jumeler et le renouer?

le duc de Montezuma que l'espagne nourrit bonnement dans Son Sein Se rappellera un jour que Ses ancetres y ont regné et qu'un interregne quoique long n'ote pas le droit au trone.[4] heureux Ceux qui verront et jouiront de Ces Salutaires et inévitables révolutions. Cest ainsi que la découverte de l'amérique qui, Contre toute attente, n'avait encor rien produit de grand prépare une epoque qui Surpassera toutes Celles dont les fastes de l'univers nous ont Conservé la memoire. C'est ainsi que la liberté a fait eclorre aux Seins des arts votre république qui, dès Son aurore parait avec tant d'eclat: les Sciences la Soutiendront, l'expérience de toutes les nations qui la Composent formera les loix les plus Sages, une tolérance eclairée les consolidera. ô bons pèruviens, habitans de quito, habitans de Cusco, et vous Méxicains ecrasés Sous le double joug de la politique et de la Superstition prenez Courage, relevez vous tous, vos lâches tirans vont disparaitre voycz venir les Américains nouveaux, tendez leur les bras, Ce Sont Ceux quil faut recevoir Comme des Dieux tutelaires qui viennent rompre vos chaines et vous rendre avec la liberté le beau gouvernement et les Stes loix de vos Sages Incas qu'a juste titre vous avez tant de raison de regretter.

On a établi une chapelle catholique à Boston, dit Ce meme voyageur,[5] je Suis Surpris et faché que les Amériquains Si Sages, Si prévoyans, idolatres de leur liberté ayent laissé prendre racine dans leur république à une plante aussi dangereuse, aussi vorace: il n'i a qu'avec les intolérants quil faut etre intolerans et les papistes le Sont par principes, par orgeuil et par gout; il ne faut pas les persécuter, mais leur deffendre absolument tout Culte extérieur et public. j'aimerais mieux y voir établir le Culte grossier et lascif du Dieu des jardins,[6] les bonnes moeurs, la pudeur naturelle, le ridicule le feraient tomber bien vite; au lieu que l'exterieur eclatant et fastueux que les pretres Catholiq⟨ues⟩

Romains étaleront à l'envie dans leurs Cérémonies religieuses en imposera à la longue au peuple qui Se laisse prendre par les Sens, il Suivra machinalement Son penchant à l'erreur et ne S'apercevra du piege que lorsquil ne pourra plus S'en tirer. il est tems heureux Américains, pensez que le mal est plus facile à prévoir qu'a détruire; pensez que partout où le mal a pris on n'a pu l'extirper qu'avec le fer et le feu. voyez les ravages qu'il fait en france, tandis que Ses partisans auraient pu et du en faire le bonheur en aretant ou Calmant les maux inévitables d'une révolution quelconque.

vous avez eu le Courage et l'adresse de vous délivrer des betes feroces et vénimeuses qui infestaient le beau pays que vous habitez, après avoir appris à vous guérir de leurs morsures et de leur venin. vous avez vaincu, eloigné de vos fertiles habitations les Sauvages de la mauvaise espece après vous etre liés de Commerce et d'amitié avec Ceux de la bonne. vous avez forcé à demander la paix Ces orgueilleux anglais vos freres qui, dans une guerre de famille vous ont fait tous les maux qu'une animosité aveugle, une vengeance réfléchie ont pu inventer. eh bien tous les maux réunis Seront Surpassés chez vos neveux infortunés Si vous aidez ce germe fatal à Se développer parmi vous dans toute Sa plénitude: et ne pensez pas quil y ait à Composer avec lui, partout où vous le laisserez croitre il etouffera les plantes indigenes. ne vous laissez pas endormir vous ou les votres, vous vous exposeriez à un réveil plus épouventable et plus réel que Celui quils nous ont peint après le grand Sommeil. n'oubliez jamais et gravez le en Caracteres ineffacables dans le Coeur de vos enfans qui en feront de meme aux leurs pour détruire absolument enfin la peste religieuse de dessus la terre, n'oubliez pas, dis-je Ce qu'a dit l'autheur universel et Sublime qui a travaillé toute Sa vie à ramener l'homme à la raison—que S'il etait possible de ramasser dans un lac immense tout le Sang humain que la religion crétienne a fait répandre l'on pourrait y faire voguer un navire à pleines voiles. et puis réfléchissez pourquoi et Comment Cette enorme quantité de Sang a été répandu vous verrez que Celui qui a dit—homo lupus est homini[7]—n'as pas dit assès pour les fanatiques il fallait mettre—tigris—encor Ces especes ne Se dev⟨orent⟩ et ne Se mangent pas elles memes, leurs besoins Satisfaits elles ne détruisent pas inutilement et par plaisir, elles reposent jusqu'aux nouveaux besoins; au lieu que parmi les

hommes les plus civilisés, dans des tems de despotismes, de révolutions, de fanatisme, de fléau quelconque on a vu des atrocités
réfléchies, des barbaries Si grandes qu'on les a cru jusqu'alors
inouies, et Tjours et partout la rage Sacerdotale S'est distinguée.
les beaux empires de l'asie qui Semblent posés Sur des bases
eternelles n'ont évité leur ruine assurée qu'en expulsant absolument de leurs vastes etats Cette Secte crétienne qui Si etait
glissée furtivement et qui déja, Se croyant assès forte, voulait
donner des loix.

La reconnaissance envers l'etre Supreme dans les biens; la ré-
signation à Ses décrets dans les maux. ne pas faire à autrui Ce
que l'on ne voudrait pas que l'on nous fit à nous memes—et Si
l'on a le Courage d'aller plus loin—faire à autrui Ce que l'on
voudrait qu'on nous fit à nous memes. voila la Seule religion utile
et nécessaire, la Seule qui puisse Soutenir l'examen Severe de
la philosophie. toutes les autres Servent d'amulettes aux vielles
femmes, de joujoux aux enfans, d'egide aux lâches et d'armes
aux fourbes.

admettre pour vertus Cardinales, la tolérance fille ainée de
la philosophie, la bienfaisance Sa fille favorite, la temperance
et la propreté: n'admettre que des Cultes Simples qui donnent à
l'ame la Consolation, la gayeté et l'instruction. le Culte riant de
Bacchus chez les anciens, en lui Sacrifiant un bouc qu'on faisait
rotir avec des broches de Coudrier, disait au peuple. ne laissez
pas entrer les chevres dans les vignes et ne faites point d'échalas
de bois de Coudrier il mange la graisse de la terre &c.—Celui de
Venus Uranie temperait celui de Venus aux—belles fesses—&c.
aussi voyons nous par les armures et les travaux des anciens quils
etaient plus fort que nous malgré les débauches que nous leur
prètons. jettés une digue Sur un torrent il S'arrete quelque tems,
Se gonfle et finit par déborder de tous Cotés: il faut en laissant
à la nature un Cours aisé et libre le diriger et Conduire adroite-
ment à une heureuse fin.

Ceux qui viendront longtems après nous liront, je crois notre
hystoire presente Comme nous lisons l'hystoire fabuleuse des
anciens; ils Seront Surpris entrautres faits Singuliers qu'un peuple qui Se croyait assés eclairé pour Se dire le precepteur du
genre humain ayt, en fait de religion fait Complettement la Sot-
tise dont Ciceron a parlé lorsquil a dit—il ne reste qu'une Sot-
tise à faire aux hommes—C'est de manger leur Dieu. et ce dieu
conserve la memoire des abominables Sacrifices hum[ains]. J'ai

lu avec peine que les amèricains libres ont dressé des chiens de race anglaise pour la chasse des Sauvages, le Seul moyen quils ont trouvé pour les découvrir dans leurs embuscades. eh bien ne les voila-il pas assimilés en Ce Cas à Ces espagnols à jamais exécrables qui ont détruit les paisibles habitans de St Domingue? on reproche aux Sauvages des défauts qu'on ne peut nier quils tiennent tous ou presque tous de leur Communication avec les européens. le portrait que le Celebre pen en a fait est encor ressemblant—forts, bien taillés, adroits; leur langage est elevé, Concis; aimant leurs enfans, généreux, braves, pleins de bonne foy, hospitaliers.[8] ô dieu que de vertus Sublimes reunies! vous les tenez de votre bonne mere, enfans de la nature, que vous avez eu le Courage de ne pas abandonner. ils Sont fins, rusés, méfians, irascibles, vindicatifs, cruels à l'excés quand ils sont offensés, dit-on, mais Ce Sont les européens qui les ont forcé à devenir tels: ils Sont chez eux, nous les en chassons, Ce sont leurs terres que nous envahissons tout d'un Coup ou à la longue. que dirions nous, que ferions nous Si un peuple quelconque venait tenir parmi nous en europe une pareille Conduite? il aurait pourtant les memes droits. les espagnols n'ont-ils pas exterminés, chassés les Maures jusqu'au dernier de toutes les espagnes quand ils l'ont pu? les portugais, les français &c. n'ont-ils pas fait le meme chose à plusieurs reprises à l'egard des juifs après les avoir dépouillés; Comme les anglais ont fait pour les loups dans leur isle? et dans Ces derniers tems les jesuites dont l'europe a craint l'ambition démesurée n'ont-ils pas ete anéantis? l'espagne n'a-elle pas ren-chéri Sur les autres nations? elle a proscrit le Corps et chassé Sans miséricorde de toutes Ses possessions tous les individus.

Jai beaucoup lu, j'ai un peu voyagé, j'ai ecouté les discours des hommes de toutes les classes, etudié leur maniere de faire et d'agir, aprécié leurs actions publiques et Secrettes j'ai vu que partout, à quelques nuances près assés légeres, notre espece est tjours la meme: dans l'asie, dans l'europe, dans l'afrique, dans l'amerique, Cest l'espece humaine que l'on y trouve avec Ses habitudes Caractheristiques; Comme toutes les autres especes ont aussi partout les leurs: et Si lon decouvre un 5e Continent Ce Sera de meme S.d.—mais un point essentiel qui distingue la notre dans tous les Coins où elle Se trouve C'est Sa réunion Constante et uniforme dans l'adoration dun Seul Dieu. C'est—l'interet—Ce vil dieu des mortels, on lui a trouvé partout des autels. quelques Sages pourtant Conduits par l'instinc, la raison, ou la philosophie dans tous les ages et parmi toutes les nations n'ont pas fléchi le genou devant le veau d'or Cest le Seul et doux espoir qui nos avive qu'en ramassant leurs preceptes Sublime⟨s⟩ epars dans les écrits précieux qui nous en restent, l'homme pourra atteindre enfin au gouvernement le plus parfait dont Sa Condition est Susceptible.

C'est dans un pays neuf où l'aire est nette, c'est chez vous que doit S'operer Ce prodige, C'est chez vous que la pauvre humanité partout ecrasée a osé lever Sa tete quelle tenait courbée depuis tant de Siecles: elle a Souris à vos 1er élans, un doux espoir l'anime, elle vous hâte, elle vous tend les bras, Soutenez les, de grace Soutenez les, n'abandonnez pas une Cause Si généralle, jamais, non jamais il n'en fut portée une plus majestueuse, aussi interessante au tribunal des nations: elles ont toutes les yeux Sur vous, la terre attentive attend de vous Son Salut. oubliez, laissez de Coté les richesses, les honneurs particuliers, meme publics pour ne tendre qu'au but unique qui doit procurer un bonheur incalculable aux peuples, et à vous une gloire immortelle. rappellez vous Sans Cesse, n'oubliez pas un instant que le denouement de la pièce doit faire de vous le 1er de tous les peuples. C'est vous qui devez donner au monde entier le bonheur Constant et général qui ne S'est trouvé que passager dans quelque république ou Sous quelques bons princes.

Mais je ne le vois, je ne le Sens que trop. C'est avec la plus vive douleur que je laisse Coulcr Cette affreuse vérité de ma plume. la guerre a ete de tous tems parmi les hommes occasionnée par la diversité d'opinions, d'interets, de religions, elle y Sera toujours Seulement plus ou moins Selon les Circonstances. le bonheur général ou la paix universelle ne Sera, je crois que dans le Coeur des hommes bons Sera Tjours le voeu chéri des ames Sensibles; mais l'un ou l'autre n'en restera pas moins un reve charmant, une belle chimere qui pourra etre quelquefois partielle, temporaire, mais jamais universelle. heureux Ceux qui Se trouveront dans un de Ces éclaircis.

la position de notre planete ne peut l'admettre. le nord est le foyer non le plus ardent mais le plus vigoureux de l'espece humaine. je Suppose éteintes dans le Coeur de l'homme l'ambition, la fureur des Conquetes, le fanatisme, la Soif de l'or, toutes les passions destructives: la nature et la raison lui prescrivent d'eviter la douleur et de chercher le plaisir. les peuples du nord hardis et forts las d'etre Sous la neige et Sur la glace S'empareront quand ils le pourront, Comme ils l'ont fait de tous tems des beaux pays fertilisés par des climats plus heureux. les Russes aguerris aujourdhui veulent enlever aux terres Ces belles et vastes provinces dont Ces derniers S'emparerent jadis lorsqu'ennuyés de vivre dans les déserts de l'arabie ils epouvanterent Successivement l'asie, l'afrique et l'europe du bruit de leurs rapides conquetes. Ces fiers Conquerants ne donnerent point d'autres—manifestes—que la loi du plus fort La meme loi peut donc leur oter une possession usurpée malgré une jouissance de trois Siecles qui, Selon—les droits de l'homme—ne la justifie pas. tous les peuples qui ont abandonné tant de fois la zone glaciale pour chercher les douceurs d⟨'une⟩ région temperée Sont persuadés que la terre est un domaine où tous les hommes ont le droit de choisir un espace qui fournisse à leurs besoins, où ils puissent trouver l'aisance et le bonheur. il en a presque tjours eté de meme malgré les Conventio⟨ns⟩, pourtant il y reste un espoir, C'est de vous qu'on l'attend et, Comme je lai dit plus haut vous reussirez en tout; C'est vous qui, Sil est possible devez établir parmi les hommes une autre loi géneralle que Celle du plus fort, C'est l'unique moyen de remettre tout à Sa place. Comme aussi, Si vous n'avez point de noms, propres aux choses que vous trouvez, que vous inventez, forgez en d'analogues, avec des epitetes et les Verbes Signifiants, vous enrichirez votre langue d'autant.

Je prévois deux découvertes bien intéressantes pour les Societes nombreuses, elles Sont dignes de vos recherches, vous etes à meme, et je ne doute pas que vous n'ajoutiez ⟨*illegible*⟩ un jour Ces deux inestimables bienfaits à Ceux dont vous Comblez l'humanité—préparer le Cuivre—dessecher les morts—il est dit dans l'hystoire des Incas que les anciens américains avaient trouvé la façon de préparer ou de tremper le C⟨uivre⟩ de Sorte que leurs vases de Ce metal ne donnaient pas plus de ver de gris que ⟨Ceux⟩ d'or: Cette précieuse découverte Serait bien préferable aux mines d'or qu'on a trouve dans Ces riches Contrées, quelqu'ami de lhumanité pourrait proposer un prix, pour tacher de retrouver l'usage Salubre d'un métal Si avantageux à la Societé populeuse les indigenes, est-il dit, outrés des atrocités des espagnols leur Cacherent ce Secret ⟨*illegible*⟩ beaucoup d'or quils enfouirent; la reconnaissance pourrait faire trouver ce que la haine a fait Cacher; vous etes Sur les lieux. voici l'indice pour l'autre decouverte.

Dans la guerre de 1744 l'escadre espagnolle aux ordres de

dom Navarro etait bloquée à Toulon par Matheus amiral anglais[9]; dans un Combat à la Sortie du port, le royal philippe que montait le général blessé descendit à la Calle et ne reparut plus; Mr de Gérardin, officier français 1er Capitaine du royal philippe fut blessé à mort. Mr de Lage deffendit avec une bravoure rare le vaisseau espagnol. les Anglais qui avaient résolu de le détruire envoierent un brulot pour le réduire en Cendres. voici ce quil raconte de l'intrépidité des officiers du brulot anglais—"avant l'embrasement du brulot j'i avais vu deux jeunes officiers habillés de bleu et un 3e plus agé en veste rouge: je les entendis ordonner de mettre le feu aux artifices, ils regardaient la mort avec un mépris infini, ils pouvaient Se Sauver Sils n'avaient pas eté déterminés à acrocher le royal ph. je les vis donc Sauter en lair, je les Conduisis des yeux jusqu'a la hauteur de leur hune de misaine Sans que leurs habits changeassent de Couleur. à Cette élevation ils furent enveloppés de flammes et réduits en charbons. ils tomberent à Coté du royal phi. legers Comme du liège nayant pas plus de deux pieds de long" dans l'honneur français par Saci, tome onzieme p. 109e à paris chez noyon en 1784.[10]

  chercher à dessecher ainsi les morts avec de la poudre en les enfermant dans quelques machines propres à recevoir l'explosion et à en procurer l'effet désiré et Sans danger; lopération est Subite. Cette méthode ne doit pas tant répugner que l'idée Seule de pourriture qui attend nos Corps après la mort. on dépense tant de poudres inutilement, en fetes ou à détruire les hommes, Celle ci du moins leur Serait utile. peut-etre parviendrait-on ainsi à peu de frais à remettre en vigueur l'usage des anciens et Conserver dans des urnes propres et Commodes les Cendres cheries de nos parens et de nos amis. on pourrait inventer une machine, peut etre bien Simple et peu dispendieuse où l'on enfermerait le, ou les Corps morts pour operer l'explosion Sans danger. proposer un prix ou une Souscription en faveur de l'inventeur d'une machine Si utile, Si nécessaire. Cette opération Serait bien Salutaire dans les épidémies et Surtout en tems de peste, en Cas de grandes mortalités pour éviter l'infection et l'embarras des morts qui dans de pareilles Circonstances Sont traités d'une maniere atroce et désesperante pour les vivans que le meme Sort attend; Comme il arriva à la peste de Marseille où les Cadavres pestiférés pourissaient Sans Sepulture dans les rues, à la Campagne, et dont un grand nombre flottait dans le port pèle-mêle avec dix mille chiens morts attaqués des memes mal. Mr Lavoisier, quel Souvenir! quel Soupir amer il tire du fond du Coeur des am⟨is⟩ des arts! dans l'appareil pour faire des expériences Sur l'air avait inventé une machine pour bruler de l'air inflammable et de l'air vital qui réunis brule⟨nt⟩ par un procédé qui pourrait aussi Conduire à la meme découverte par un autre moyen tiré de la chymie qui renferme encor bien des Secrets.[11]

quel Service l'on rendrait aux hommes Si l'on pouvait trouver et mettre en usage Ces deux objets! que je m'estimerais heureux d'en avoir donné le 1er éveil! dumoins je ne Serais pas né en vain, j'aurais rempli ma tâche Sur la terre que je quitterais Sans regret, Satisfait de laisser aux générations à venir une aisance de plus.

je Suis avec un entier et admirable devouement votre trés obeissant Serviteur

⟨5pé.⟩

p.S. le ministre thayer de Boston dit—que la vie et les miracles du bienheureux labre lui ont ouvert les yeux à la lumiere et quil va la repandre dans le nouveau Continent.[12] thayer est un fourbe qui veut Se faire remarquer, ou un pauvre docteur S'il n'a pas apprécié dans Son voyage d'italie Ce que C'est que le papisme. il choisit un plaisant heros pour modele, un gueux dont toute la vie passée dans la plus honteuse mendicité repugne à tout homme qui pense, et à qui rome moderne n'a pas rougi d'avoir donné l'apothéose à la fin du 18e Siecle!

eloignez, chassez de vos possessions nouvelles qui demandent des bras cette vermine dont labre est le patron, elle S'engendre et Se nourrit dans le Sein de la religion romaine. il y ramenerait plutot les tenebres que vous avez Si heureusement dissipé. un autre protestant qui avait bien examiné Cette indigne Cour a frappé au but, il dit qu'il etait Surpris que tous les hommes Sensés ne Se réunissaient pas pour aller exterminer Cette vermine insolente, ce repaire de brigans amphibis qui depuis tant de Siecles Souillaient la terre et foulaient les Cendres des anciens Romains, ce Serait votre tâche judicieux Américains Si Cette Cour ridicule etait chez vous; ce Sera S.d. Celle des français: puissent-ils parvenir enfin un jour à nétoyer Cette écurie d'augias! amen—amen—Echos répétés ce doux refrein.

un homme instruit et digne de foi qui a passé l'hyver de 179⟨3⟩
à Baltimore m'a dit avoir assisté à la messe d'un eveque qui y ré-
side, que le peuple faisait foule à Cette messe pour le voir habiller
par d'autres pretres, et voir les autres Cérémonies ridicules aux
yeux de l'homme Sensé qui ne voit, dans Cet homme qu'un pre-
tre Comme un autre. il me dit aussi que quelques chanoines de
paris Si etaient réfugiés avec les vases Sacrés quils avaient enlevés
de leur Cathedrale, quils avaient preté le Soleil pour donner la
bénédiction, que les assistans en avaient beaucoup admiré la
beauté.[13] le magnifique disque du Soleil de Cusco embleme Sublime de Celui dont il avait emprunté le nom annoncait aux hommes un point de fraternité de réunion: Celui Ci renferme un tal-
isman fatal qui a porté la désolation partout où il S'est fourré.

celui qui a dit—le tems présent est gros de l'avenir—n'a pas
prévu S.d. toutes ces Suites facheuses de Cette grossesse, il aurait indiqué quelque moyen pour nous procurer un acouche-
ment moins laborieux.

vous etes hors de dangers, fortunés mortels, et Semblables a
une mere heur⟨eusemt⟩ delivrée, vous oubliez vos maux passés
pour jouir des fruits de votre heureux révolution. ô Washington! votre nom est gravé en Caractheres inéffaçables dans le
Coeur de tous les amis de l'humanité, et nos derniers neveux,
heureux encor par vous, vous rendront des hommages bien plus
merités que Ces demi dieux dont l'antiquité nous a tant vanté
les prouesses. labrc a des autels . . . et Pen le divin Pen n'en a
point![14] les Si⟨ens⟩ Sont placés dans le Coeur de tous les hommes Sensibles, les autres Seraient trop grossiers pour une ame
Si Sublime.

AD, DLC:GW. This letter is docketed on the last page as "Anonymous French."
The unknown author celebrates the possibilities of the American republic
and the New World, while warning Americans to avoid the flaws of the Old
World, especially Catholicism.

1. The writer may have read Jacques Pierre Brissot de Warville, *Nouveau
voyage dans les États-Unis de l'Amérique septentrionale, fait en 1788* (3 vols., Paris,
1791).

2. The writer was referring to Horace's *Odes*, book 1, ode 3, verse 27, where
Horace uses the phrase "Audax Japeti genus" to refer to Prometheus in his
theft of celestial fire. Iapetos (Japetos) was the Titan father of Prometheus.

3. Atahualpa (c.1500–1533) was the Incan emperor at the time of Pizarro's
conquest.

4. This is evidently a reference to the Aztecs, Montezuma being the name
of the emperor of that nation at the time of the Spanish conquest.

5. A Roman Catholic chapel on School Street in Boston was opened and consecrated on 2 Nov. 1788 (*Independent Chronicle: And the Universal Advertiser* [Boston], 6 Nov. 1788).

6. The god of the gardens is most likely a reference to Aristaios (Aristaeus), an ancient Greek pastoral deity.

7. The proverb "Man is a wolf to man" was used by the Roman Titus Maccius Plautus in his *Asinaria* and by Thomas Hobbes (1588–1679) in the dedication to his *De Cive.*

8. The writer evidently is summarizing the description of the natives of America in *A letter from William Penn, proprietary and governour of Pennsylvania in America, to the Committee of the Free Society of Traders of that province, residing in London* ([London], 1683), 5–7.

9. The battle between a combined French and Spanish fleet at Toulon and a British fleet led by Admiral Thomas Mathews (1676–1751) occurred in February 1744. The Spanish commander was Don Juan José Navarro (1687–1772). His flagship, the *Real Felipe,* of 114 guns, was commanded by Nicolás Geraldino (Gerardin). The exploits in that battle of Gil-Fernando de Lage de Cueilly, a captain in the Spanish navy, were described in his memoir, published at Amsterdam in 1746 (see Thomas G. Carter, trans., "The Journal of M. de Lage de Cueilly, Captain in the Spanish Navy during the Campaign of 1744," *The Navy Miscellany,* 2:207–88 [Publications of the Naval Records Society, vol. 40]).

10. Claude Louis Michel de Sacy (1746–1790) published *L'honneur françois, ou Histoire des vertus et des exploits de notre nation, depuis l'établissement de la monarchie jusqu'à nos jours* in 12 volumes between 1769 and 1784. The citation is to the revised and corrected edition, issued at Paris in 1783–84 by Jean Luc Nyon, l'aîné (d. 1799). The quoted passage, which continues onto page 110, has been somewhat cropped in this letter.

11. Antoine-Laurent Lavoisier (1743–1794) was a pioneer of chemistry especially noted for his work identifying oxygen.

12. John Thayer (1758–1815) arrived as a Catholic missionary at Boston on 4 Jan. 1790 and headed the church at Boston in 1791 and 1792. For his reference to Benedict Joseph Labre (1748–1783), an impoverished religious wanderer who was canonized in 1881 by Pope Leo XIII, see *An account of the conversion of the Reverend Mr. John Thayer, lately a Protestant minister, at Boston in North-America, who embraced the Roman Catholic religion at Rome, on the 25th of May, 1783; written by himself. To which are annexed several extracts from a letter written to his brother, in answer to some objections. Also, a letter from a young lady lately received by him into the church, written after making her first communion* (Baltimore, 1788), 3, 10–11, 13.

13. The bishop of Baltimore was John Carroll (1735–1815). The refugee canons from Paris probably were members of the Sulpician Order, who began arriving at Baltimore in 1791 for the purpose of founding a seminary there.

14. The author apparently is contrasting principles of religious freedom espoused by William Penn (1644–1718), founder of Pennsylvania, with Labre's Catholicism.

Index

704 *Index*

Ebeling, Christoph Daniel: id., 193;
letters from: to GW, 192
Eccleston, John (see 11:509): letters to:
from GW, 22, 36
Edenton (N.C.): customs officers at,
632; refugees at, 373–74
Edinburgh (Scotland): Tobias Lear
visits, 622
Edmondson, Peter: letters from: to
William Vans Murray, 365
Edmundsbury (Va. plantation):
id., 70
Education: medical, 283–84; music
teachers, 287; in North Caro-
lina, 497; proposed military
academy, 385, 389, 404, 468;
public schools, 340–41; teachers, 433
Edwards coffeehouse (Petersburg,
Va.), 16
Ehlers, Catherine, 597; and clothing
for slaves, 613; duties of, 610
Ehlers, John Christian (see 3:65):
agreement with, 610, 616; GW's
opinion of, 610; letters to: from
GW, 596–98
Eighteenmile Creek (N.Y.), 583; id.,
584
Eld, George, 20–21
Elizabeth (Elizabeth Town; N.J.), 73,
179; and yellow fever, 129
Ellery, William (1727–1820; see
5:519), 176
Ellicott, Andrew: conflict with D.C.
commissioners, 592; letters
from: to commissioners for
the District of Columbia, 594;
letters to: from commissioners
for the District of Columbia,
594
Ellicott, Benjamin: and plan of Federal City, 29
Elliott, Matthew, 144, 146, 380; id.,
221
Ellsworth, Oliver (see 1:59), 495
Embuscade (frigate; privateer),
48–49, 131, 156; at New York
City, 155, 179
Emerson, Ann (see 8:148), 53;
health, 261
England, Richard G. (see 11:316),
150

England. See Great Britain
Engle, Archibald: id., 258; letters
from: to GW, 257–58
Erskine, David Steuart. See Buchan,
eleventh earl of
Eustace, John Skey (see 3:67): and
Algerine captives, 542, 554

Fairfax, Ferdinando (see 1:98, 5:317),
310
Fairfax, George William (see 1:87):
estate of, 310
Fairfax County (Va.): address from
citizens of, 242–44, 272–73;
plantations, 110
Fair Hill (Pa.), 265; id., 313
Falconer, Nathaniel (see 3:147–48):
letters from: to Thomas Mifflin,
457–58, 653; letters to: from
Thomas Mifflin, 457
Fanny (brig), 165, 167, 467
Fanny (ship), 314
Farrar, Thomas: id., 487
Fauchet, Jean Antoine Joseph: ap-
pointed minister to the United
States, 363, 375–76; id., 364
Favorite (French sloop), 95
Fayette County (Pa.): militia, 33
Federal City. See United States:
Federal City
*Federal Gazette and Philadelphia Daily
Advertiser*, 199, 287, 427; list of
burials, 267; prints GW letters,
342; publications on yellow
fever, 102, 115, 248–49
Felicity (schooner), 150
Fendall, Philip Richard (see 1:62):
letters from: to GW, 295
Fenner, Arthur (see 5:410): letters
from: to GW, 175–77
Ferree, Joseph: id., 297; letters from:
to GW, 340–41
Ferries: at Mount Vernon, 526–27;
on Schuylkill River, 259
Fierer, Charles (see 13:197): letters
from: to GW, 87; letters to: from
Tobias Lear, 87
Filicchi, Anthony: letters from: to governor of Leghorn, 298–99
Filicchi, Philip: id., 298; letters
from: to governor of Leghorn,

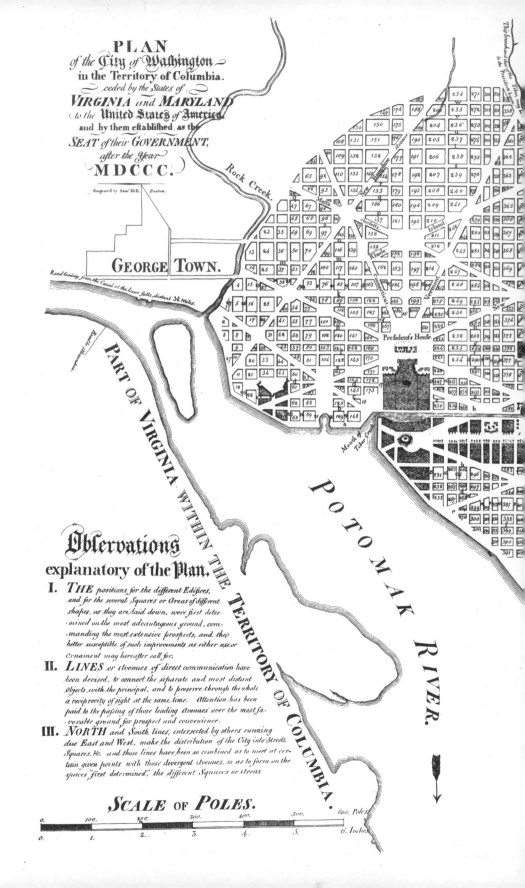

PLAN
of the City of Washington
in the Territory of Columbia.
ceded by the States of
VIRGINIA and MARYLAND
to the United States of America
and by them established, as the
SEAT of their GOVERNMENT,
after the Year
MDCCC.

Engrav'd by Sam'l Hill, Boston.

GEORGE TOWN.

Rock Creek.

Road leading from the Canal at the lower falls, distant 3½ Miles.

PART OF VIRGINIA WITHIN THE TERRITORY OF COLUMBIA.

Mouth of Tiber Creek

President's House.

POTOMAK RIVER.

Observations
explanatory of the Plan.

I. THE positions for the different Edifices, and for the several Squares or Areas of different shapes, as they are laid down, were first determined on the most advantageous ground, commanding the most extensive prospects, and the better susceptible of such improvements as either use or Ornament may hereafter call for.

II. LINES or avenues of direct communication have been devised, to connect the separate and most distant Objects with the principal, and to preserve through the whole a reciprocity of sight at the same time. Attention has been paid to the passing of those leading Avenues over the most favorable ground for prospect and convenience.

III. NORTH and South lines, intersected by others running due East and West, make the distribution of the City into Streets, Squares, &c. and those lines have been so combined as to meet at certain given points with those divergent Avenues, so as to form on the spaces first determined, the different Squares or Areas.

SCALE OF POLES.

0.   100.   200.   300.   400.   500.   600. Poles

0.   1.   2.   3.   4.   5.   6. Inches